65B

The sources of social power

VOLUME I

A history of power from the beginning to A.D. 1760

This is the first part of a three-volume work on the nature of power in human societies. In it, Michael Mann identifies the four principal "sources" of power as being control over economic, ideological, military, and political resources. He examines the interrelations between these in a narrative history of power from Neolithic times, through ancient Near Eastern civilizations, the classical Mediterranean age, and medieval Europe, up to just before the Industrial Revolution in England. Rejecting the conventional monolithic concept of a "society," Dr. Mann's model is instead that of a series of overlapping, intersecting power networks. He makes this model operational by focusing on the logistics of power – how the flow of information, manpower, and goods is controlled over social and geographical space – thereby clarifying many of the "great debates" in sociological theory.

The present volume offers explanations of the emergence of the state and social stratification; of city-states, militaristic empires, and the persistent interaction between them; of the world salvation religions; and of the peculiar dynamism of medieval and early modern Europe. It ends by generalizing about the nature of overall social development, the varying forms of social cohesion, and the role of classes and class struggle in history. Volume II will continue the history of power up to the present, centering on the interrelations of nation-states and social classes. Volume III will present the theoretical conclusions of the whole work.

This ambitious and provocative attempt to provide a new theoretical frame for the interpretation of the history of societies will be challenging and stimulating reading for a wide range of social scientists, historians, and other readers concerned with understanding large-scale social and historical processes.

The sources of social power

VOLUME I

A history of power from the beginning to A.D. 1760

MICHAEL MANN

London School of Economics and Political Science

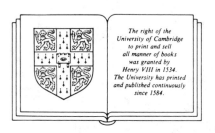

The right of the
University of Cambridge
to print and sell
all manner of books
was granted by
Henry VIII in 1534.
The University has printed
and published continuously
since 1584.

CAMBRIDGE UNIVERSITY PRESS

Cambridge

New York   New Rochelle   Melbourne   Sydney

Published by the Press Syndicate of the University of Cambridge
The Pitt Building, Trumpington Street, Cambridge CB2 1RP
32 East 57th Street, New York, NY 10022, USA
10 Stamford Road, Oakleigh, Melbourne 3166, Australia

First published 1986
Reprinted 1987, 1988

Printed in the United States of America

Library of Congress Cataloging in Publication Data
Mann, Michael, 1942–
The sources of social power.
Includes index.
Contents: v. 1. A history of power from the
beginning to A.D. 1760.
1. Social history.   2. Power (Social sciences)
I. Title.
HN8.M33   1986   303.3   85–14962

British Library Cataloguing in Publication Data
Mann, Michael, 1942–
The sources of social power.
Vol. 1: A history of power from the beginning
to A.D. 1760
1. Power (Social sciences)
I. Title
303.3   HM141

ISBN 0 521 30851 8 hard covers
ISBN 0 521 31349 X paperback

Contents

Preface		*page*	vii
1	Societies as organized power networks		1
2	The end of general social evolution: how prehistoric peoples evaded power		34
3	The emergence of stratification, states, and multi-power-actor civilization in Mesopotamia		73
4	A comparative analysis of the emergence of stratification, states, and multi-power-actor civilizations		105
5	The first empires of domination: the dialectics of compulsory cooperation		130
6	"Indo-Europeans" and iron: expanding, diversified power networks		179
7	Phoenicians and Greeks: decentralized multi-power-actor civilizations		190
8	Revitalized empires of domination: Assyria and Persia		231
9	The Roman territorial empire		250
10	Ideology transcendent: the Christian *ecumene*		301
11	A comparative excursus into the world religions: Confucianism, Islam, and (especially) Hindu caste		341
12	The European dynamic: I. The intensive phase, A.D. 800–1155		373
13	The European dynamic: II. The rise of coordinating states, 1155–1477		416
14	The European dynamic: III. International capitalism and organic national states, 1477–1760		450
15	European conclusions: explaining European dynamism – capitalism, Christendom, and states		500
16	Patterns of world-historical development in agrarian societies		518
Index			543

Preface

In 1972, I wrote a paper called "Economic Determinism and Structural Change," which purported not only to refute Karl Marx and reorganize Max Weber but also to offer the outlines of a better general theory of social stratification and social change. The paper began to develop into a short book. It would contain a general theory supported by a few case studies, including historical ones. Later I decided that the book would set forth a sweeping theory of the world history of power.

But while developing these delusions, I rediscovered the pleasure of devouring history. A ten-year immersion in that subject reinforced the practical empiricism of my background to restore a little respect for the complexity and obduracy of facts. It did not entirely sober me. For I have written this large history of power in agrarian societies, and I will follow it shortly with Volume II, *A History of Power in Industrial Societies,* and Volume III, *A Theory of Power* – even if their central thrust is now modest. But it gave me a sense of the mutual disciplining that sociology and history can exercise on each other.

Sociological theory cannot develop without knowledge of history. Most of the key questions of sociology concern processes occurring through time; social structure is inherited from particular pasts; and a large proportion of our "sample" of complex societies is only available in history. But the study of history is also impoverished without sociology. If historians eschew theory of how societies operate, they imprison themselves in the commonsense notions of their own society. In this volume, I repeatedly question the application of essentially modern notions – such as nation, class, private property, and the centralized state – to earlier historical periods. In most cases, some scholars have anticipated my skepticism. But they could have generally done so earlier and more rigorously had they converted implicit contemporary common sense into explicit, testable theory. Sociological theory can also discipline historians in their selection of facts. We can never be "sufficiently scholarly": There are more social and historical data than we can digest. A strong sense of theory enables us to decide what might be the key facts, what might be central and what marginal to an understanding of how a particular society works. We select our data, see whether they confirm or reject our theoretical hunches, refine the latter, collect more data, and continue zigzagging across between theory and data until we have established a plausible account of how this society, in this time and place, "works."

Comte was right in his claim that sociology is the queen of the social and human sciences. But no queen ever worked as hard as the sociologist with pretensions needs to! Nor is the creation of historically supported theory nearly as streamlined a process as Comte believed. Zigzagging between theoretical and historical scholarship has unsettling effects. The real world (historical or contemporary) is messy and imperfectly documented; yet theory claims pattern and perfection. The match can never be exact. Too much scholarly attention to the facts makes one blind; too much listening to the rhythms of theory and world history makes one deaf.

So, to preserve my health during this venture, I have depended more than usually on the stimulus and encouragement of sympathetic specialists and fellow zigzaggers. My greatest debt is to Ernest Gellner and John Hall. In our "Patterns of History" seminar, held since 1980 at the London School of Economics and Political Science (LSE), we have argued over much of the ground covered by this volume. My thanks go especially to John, who has read virtually all my drafts, commented copiously on them, argued with me all the way, and yet been invariably warm and supportive toward my enterprise. I have also shamelessly exploited the seminar's distinguished visiting speakers, in discussion turning their excellent papers toward my own obsessions, pumping them for ideas and specialist knowledge.

Many scholars commented generously on individual chapters, correcting my howlers, putting me in touch with up-to-date research and controversies in their field, demonstrating that I was wrong, even hoping that I would stay longer in their field and dig deeper. In rough order of their interests as organized by my sequence of chapters, I thank James Woodburn, Stephen Shennan, Colin Renfrew, Nicholas Postgate, Gary Runciman, Keith Hopkins, John Peel, John Parry, Peter Burke, Geoffrey Elton, and Gian Poggi. Anthony Giddens and William H. McNeill read the whole of my penultimate draft and made many sensible criticisms. Over the years, colleagues commented helpfully on my drafts, seminars, and arguments. I would like particularly to thank Keith Hart, David Lockwood, Nicos Mouzelis, Anthony Smith, and Sandy Stewart.

Essex University and LSE students were sympathetic audiences for trying out my general ideas in sociological-theory courses. Both institutions were generous in giving me leave to research and lecture on the material in this book. Seminar series at Yale University, New York University, the Academy of Sciences at Warsaw, and Oslo University gave me extended opportunities to develop my arguments. The Social Science Research Council awarded me a personal research grant for the academic year 1980–1 and was most supportive toward me. In that year I was able to complete most of the historical research necessary for the earlier chapters, which I would not have been able to do easily while carrying a normal teaching load.

Library staff at Essex, the LSE, the British Museum, and the University Library, Cambridge, coped well with my eclectic demands. My secretaries at

Essex and the LSE – Linda Peachey, Elizabeth O'Leary, and Yvonne Brown – were unfailingly efficient and helpful through all the drafts thrust at them.

Nicky Hart made the breakthrough that reorganized this work into three volumes. Her own work and her presence – together with Louise, Gareth, and Laura – prevented me from being blinded, deafened, or even too obsessed, by this project.

Obviously, the mistakes are mine.

1 Societies as organized power networks

The three projected volumes of this book provide a history and theory of power relations in human societies. That is difficult enough. But a moment's reflection makes it seem even more daunting: For are not a history and theory of power relations likely to be virtually synonymous with a history and theory of human society itself? Indeed they are. To write a general account, however voluminous, of some of the principal patterns to be found in the history of human societies is unfashionable in the late twentieth century. Such grandly generalizing, Victorian ventures – based on imperial pillaging of secondary sources – have been crushed under the twentieth-century weight of massed volumes of scholarship and serried ranks of academic specialists.

My basic justification is that I have arrived at a distinctive, general way of looking at human societies that is at odds with models of society dominant within sociology and historical writing. This chapter explains my approach. Those uninitiated into social-science theory may find parts of it heavy going. If so, *there is an alternative way of reading this volume.* Skip this chapter, go straight to Chapter 2, or indeed to any of the narrative chapters, and continue until you get confused or critical about the terms used or the underlying theoretical drift. Then turn back to this introduction for guidance.

My approach can be summed up in two statements, from which a distinctive methodology flows. The first is: *Societies are constituted of multiple overlapping and intersecting sociospatial networks of power.* The distinctiveness of my approach will be perceived swiftly if I spend three. paragraphs saying what societies are *not.*

Societies are not unitary. They are not social systems (closed or open); they are not totalities. We can never find a single bounded society in geographical or social space. Because there is no system, no totality, there cannot be "subsystems," "dimensions," or "levels" of such a totality. Because there is no whole, social relations cannot be reduced "ultimately," "in the last instance," to some systemic property of it – like the "mode of material production," or the "cultural" or "normative system," or the "form of military organization." Because there is no bounded totality, it is not helpful to divide social change or conflict into "endogenous" and "exogenous" varieties. Because there is no social system, there is no "evolutionary" process within it. Because humanity is not divided into a series of bounded totalities, "diffusion" of social organization does not occur between them. Because there is no totality, individuals are not constrained in their behavior by "social structure as a

1

whole," and so it is not helpful to make a distinction between "social action" and "social structure."

I overstated my point in the preceding paragraph for the sake of effect. I will not dispense altogether with these ways of looking at societies. Yet most sociological orthodoxies – such as systems theory, Marxism, structuralism, structural functionalism, normative functionalism, multidimensional theory, evolutionism, diffusionism, and action theory – mar their insights by conceiving of "society" as an unproblematic, unitary totality.

In practice, most accounts influenced by these theories take polities, or *states*, as their "society," their total unit for analysis. Yet states are only one of the four major types of power network with which I will be dealing. The enormous covert influence of the nation-state of the late nineteenth and early twentieth centuries on the human sciences means that a nation-state model dominates sociology and history alike. Where it does not, pride of place is sometimes given among archaeologists and anthropologists to "culture," but even this is usually conceived of as a single, bounded culture, a kind of "national culture." True, some modern sociologists and historians reject nation-state models. They equate "society" with transnational economic relations, using either capitalism or industrialism as their master concept. This goes too far in the other direction. State, culture, and economy are all important structuring networks; but they almost never coincide. There is no one master concept or basic unit of "society." It may seem an odd position for a sociologist to adopt; but if I could, I would abolish the concept of "society" altogether.

The second statement flows from the first. Conceiving of societies as multiple overlapping and intersecting power networks gives us the best available entry into the issue of what is ultimately "primary" or "determining" in societies. *A general account of societies, their structure, and their history can best be given in terms of the interrelations of what I will call the four sources of social power: ideological, economic, military, and political* (IEMP) *relationships.* These are (1) *overlapping networks of social interaction,* not dimensions, levels, or factors of a single social totality. This follows from my first statement. (2) They are also *organizations, institutional means of attaining human goals.* Their primacy comes not from the strength of human desires for ideological, economic, military, or political satisfaction but from the particular *organizational means* each possesses to attain human goals, whatever these may be. In this chapter I work gradually toward specifying the four organizational means and my IEMP model of organized power.

From this a distinctive methodology will emerge. It is conventional to write of power relations in terms of a rather abstract language, concerning the interrelation of economic, ideological, and political "factors" or "levels" or "dimensions" of social life. I operate at a more concrete, *sociospatial* and *organizational* level of analysis. The central problems concern *organization, control, logistics, communication* – the capacity to organize and control people, materials, and territories, and the development of this capacity throughout history. The four sources of social power offer alternative organizational means of social control. In various times and places each has offered enhanced capacity for organization that has enabled the form of its organization to dictate for a time the form of societies at large. My history of power rests on measuring sociospatial capacity for organization and explaining its development.

That task is made slightly easier by the discontinuous nature of power development. We shall encounter various spurts, attributable to the invention of new organizational techniques that greatly enhanced the capacity to control peoples and territories. A list of some of the more important techniques is given in Chapter 16. When I come across a spurt, I stop the narrative, attempt to measure the enhanced power capacity, and then seek to explain it. Such a view of social development is what Ernest Gellner (1964) calls "neo-episodic." Fundamental social change occurs, and human capacities are enhanced, through a number of "episodes" of major structural transformation. The episodes are not part of a single immanent process (as in nineteenth-century "World Growth Stories"), but they may have a cumulative impact on society. Thus we can venture toward the issue of ultimate primacy.

Ultimate primacy

Of all the issues raised by sociological theory over the last two centuries, the most basic yet elusive is that of ultimate primacy or determinacy. Are there one or more core, decisive, ultimately determining elements, or keystones, of society? Or are human societies seamless webs spun of endless multicausal interactions in which there are no overall patterns? What are the major dimensions of social stratification? What are the most important determinants of social change? These are the most traditional and taxing of all sociological questions. Even in the loose way in which I have formulated them, they are not the same question. Yet they all raise the same central issue: How can one isolate the "most important" element or elements in human societies?

Many consider no answer possible. They claim that sociology cannot find general laws, or even abstract concepts, applicable in the same way to societies in all times and places. This skeptical empiricism suggests we start more modestly, analyzing specific situations with the intuitive and empathic understanding given by our own social experience, building up to a multicausal explanation.

However, this is not a secure epistemological position. Analysis cannot merely reflect the "facts"; our perception of the facts is ordered by mental concepts and theories. The average empirical historical study contains many implicit assumptions about human nature and society, and commonsense concepts derived from our own social experience – such as "the nation," "social class," "status," "political power," "the economy." Historians get along without examining these assumptions if they are all using the same ones; but as soon as distinctive styles of history emerge – Whig, nationalist, materialist, neoclassical, and so forth – they are in the realm of competing general theories of "how societies work." But even in the absence of competing assumptions, difficulties arise. Multicausality states that social events or trends have multiple causes. Thus we distort social complexity if we abstract one, or even several, major structural determinants. But we cannot *avoid* doing this. Every analysis selects some but not all prior events as having an effect on subsequent ones. Therefore, everyone operates with some criterion of importance, even if this is rarely made explicit. It can help if we make such criteria explicit from time to time and engage in theory building.

Nevertheless, I take skeptical empiricism seriously. Its principal objection is well founded: Societies are much *messier* than our theories of them. In their more candid moments, systematizers such as Marx and Durkheim admitted this; whereas the greatest sociologist, Weber, devised a methodology (of "ideal-types") to cope with messiness. I follow Weber's example. We *can* emerge with a proximate methodology – and perhaps even eventually with a proximate answer – for the issue of ultimate primacy, but only by devising concepts suited to dealing with a mess. This, I claim, is the virtue of a sociospatial and organizational model of the sources of social power.

Human nature and social power

Let us start with human nature. Human beings are restless, purposive, and rational, striving to increase their enjoyment of the good things of life and capable of choosing and pursuing appropriate means for doing so. Or, at least, enough of them do this to provide the dynamism that is characteristic of human life and gives it a history lacking for other species. These human characteristics are the source of everything described in this book. They are the original source of power.

Because of this, social theorists have always been tempted to proceed a little farther with a *motivational model* of human society, attempting to ground a theory of social structure in the "importance" of the various human motivational drives. This was more popular around the turn of the century than it is now. Writers like Sumner and Ward would first construct lists of basic human drives –such as those for sexual fulfillment, affection, health, physical exercise and creativity, intellectual creativity and meaning, wealth, prestige, "power for its own sake," and many more. Then they would attempt to establish their relative importance as drives, and from that they would deduce the ranks in social importance of family, economy, government, and so forth. And though this particular practice may be obsolete, a general motivational model of society underpins a number of modern theories, including versions of materialist and idealist theories. For example, many Marxists claim to derive the importance of modes of economic production in society from the supposed strength of the human drive for material subsistence.

Motivational theories will be discussed more fully in Volume III. My conclusion will be that though motivational issues are important and interesting, they are not strictly relevant to the issue of ultimate primacy. Let me briefly summarize that argument.

The pursuit of almost all our motivational drives, our needs and goals, involves human beings in external relations with nature and other human beings. Human goals require both intervention in nature – a material life in the widest sense – and social cooperation. It is difficult to imagine any of our pursuits or satisfactions occurring without these. Thus, the characteristics of nature and the characteristics of social relations become relevant to, and may indeed structure, motivations. They have *emergent* properties of their own.

This is obvious in nature. For example, the first civilizations usually emerged where there was alluvial agriculture. We can take for granted the motivational drive of humans to seek to increase their means of subsistence. That is a constant. What rather explains the origin of civilization is the opportunity presented to a few human groups by flooding, which provided ready-fertilized alluvial soil (see Chapters 3 and 4). No one has argued seriously that the dwellers in the Euphrates and Nile valleys had stronger economic drives than, say, the prehistoric inhabitants of the European landmass who did not pioneer civilization. Rather, the drives that all shared received greater environmental help from the river valleys (and their regional settings), which led them to a particular social response. Human motivation is irrelevant except that it provided the forward drive that enough humans possess to give them a dynamism wherever they dwell.

The emergence of *social* power relations has always been recognized in social theory. From Aristotle to Marx the claim has been made that "man" (unfortunately, rarely woman as well) is a social animal, able to achieve goals, including mastery over nature, only by cooperation. As there are many human goals, there are many forms of social relations and large and small networks of interacting persons, ranging from love to those involving the family, the economy, and the state. "Symbolic interactionist" theorists such as Shibutani (1955) have noted that we all dwell in a bewildering variety of "social worlds," participating in many cultures – of occupation, class, neighborhood, gender, generation, hobbies, and many more. Sociological theory heroically simplifies, by selecting out relations that are more "powerful" than others, influencing the shape and the nature of other relations and, therefore, the shape and nature of social structures in general. This is not because the particular needs they satisfy are motivationally more "powerful" than others but because they are more effective as means to achieve goals. Not ends but means give us our point of entry into the question of primacy. In any society characterized by a division of labor, specialized social relations satisfying different clusterings of human needs will arise. These differ in their organizing capacities.

Thus we leave the area of goals and needs altogether. For a form of power may not be an original human goal at all. If it is a powerful *means* to other goals, it will be sought for itself. It is an *emergent* need. It emerges in the course of need satisfaction. The most obvious example may be military force. This is probably not an original human drive or need (I shall discuss this in Volume III), but it is an efficient organizational means of fulfilling other drives. Power is, to use Talcott Parsons's expression, a "generalized means" for attaining whatever goals one wants to achieve (1968: I, 263). Therefore, I ignore original motivations and goals and concentrate on emergent *organizational power sources*. If I talk sometimes of "human beings pursuing their goals," this should be taken not as a voluntaristic or psychological statement but as a given, a constant into which I will inquire no further because it has no further social force. I also bypass the large conceptual literature on "power itself," making virtually no reference to the "two (or three) faces of power," "power versus authority" (except in Chapter 2), "decisions versus nondecisions," and similar controversies (well discussed in the early chapters of Wrong 1979). These are important issues, but here I take a different tack. Like Giddens (1979: 91) I do not treat "power *itself* as a resource. Resources are the media through which power is exercised." I have two limited conceptual tasks: (1) to identify the major alternative "media," "generalized means," or, as I prefer, power sources and (2) to devise a methodology for studying organizational power.

Organizational power

Collective and distributive power

In its most general sense, power is the ability to pursue and attain goals through mastery of one's environment. *Social* power carries two more specific senses. The first restricts its meaning to mastery exercised over other people. An example is: Power is the probability that one actor within a social relationship will be in a position to carry out his own will despite resistance (Weber 1968: I, 53). But as Parsons noted, such definitions restrict power to its *distributive* aspect, power by A *over* B. For B to gain power, A must lose some – their relationship is a "zero-sum game" where a fixed amount of power can be distributed among participants. Parsons noted correctly a second *collective* aspect of power, whereby persons in cooperation can enhance their joint power over third parties or over nature (Parsons 1960: 199–225). In most social relations both aspects of power, distributive and collective, exploitative and functional, operate simultaneously and are intertwined.

Indeed, the relationship between the two is dialectical. In pursuit of their goals, humans enter into cooperative, collective power relations with one another. But in implementing collective goals, social organization and a division of labor are set up. Organization and division of function carry an inherent tendency to distributive power, deriving from supervision and coordination. For the division of labor is deceptive: Although it involves specialization of function at all levels, the top overlooks and directs the whole. Those who occupy supervisory and coordinating positions have an immense organizational superiority over the others. The interaction and communication networks actually center on their function, as can be seen easily enough in the organization chart possessed by every modern firm. The chart allows superiors to control the entire organization, and it prevents those at the bottom from sharing in this control. It enables those at the top to set in motion machinery for implementing collective goals. Though anyone can refuse to obey, opportunities are probably lacking for establishing alternative machinery for implementing their goals. As Mosca noted, "The power of any minority is irresistible as against each single individual in the majority, who stands alone before the totality of the organized minority" (1939: 53). The few at the top can keep the masses at the bottom compliant, provided their control is *institutionalized* in the laws and the norms of the social group in which both operate. Institutionalization is necessary to achieve routine collective goals; and thus distributive power, that is, social stratification, also becomes an institutionalized feature of social life.

There is, thus, a simple answer to the question of why the masses do not revolt – a perennial problem for social stratification – and it does not concern value consensus, or force, or exchange in the usual sense of those conventional sociological explanations. The masses comply because they lack collective organization to do otherwise, because they are embedded within collective and distributive power organizations controlled by others. They are *organizationally outflanked* – a point I develop in relation to various historical and contemporary societies in later chapters (5, 7, 9, 13, 14, and 16). This means that one conceptual distinction between power and authority (i.e., power considered legitimate by all affected by it) will not figure much in this book. It is rare to find power that is either largely legitimate or largely illegitimate because its exercise is normally so double-edged.

Extensive and intensive and authoritative and diffused power
Extensive power refers to the ability to organize large numbers of people over far-flung territories in order to engage in minimally stable cooperation. *Intensive power* refers to the ability to organize tightly and command a high level of mobilization or commitment from the participants, whether the area and numbers covered are great or small. The primary structures of society combine extensive and intensive power, and so aid human beings in extensive and intensive cooperation to fulfill their goals – whatever the latter may be.

But to talk of power as organization may convey a misleading impression, as if societies were merely collections of large, authoritative power organizations. Many users of power are much less "organized"; for example, market exchange embodies collective power, for through exchange people achieve their separate goals. And it embodies distributive power, whereby only some persons possess ownership rights over goods and services. Yet it may possess little authoritative organization to assist and enforce this power. To use Adam Smith's famous metaphor, the principal instrument of power in a market is an "Invisible Hand," constraining all, yet not controlled by any single human agency. It *is* a form of human power, but it is not authoritatively organized.

Hence, I distinguish two more types of power, authoritative and diffused. *Authoritative power* is actually willed by groups and institutions. It comprises definite commands and conscious obedience. *Diffused power,* however, spreads in a more spontaneous, unconscious, decentered way throughout a population, resulting in similar social practices that embody power relations but are not explicitly commanded. It typically comprises, not command and obedience, but an understanding that these practices are natural or moral or result from self-evident common interest. Diffused power on the whole embodies a larger ratio of collective to distributive power, but this is not invariably so. It, too, can result in the "outflanking" of subordinate classes such that they consider resistance pointless. This is, for example, how the diffuse power of the contemporary world capitalist market outflanks authoritative, organized working-class movements in individual nation-states today – a point I elaborate in Volume II. Other examples of diffused power are the spread of solidarities such as those of class or nation – an important part of the development of social power.

Putting these two distinctions together gives four ideal-typical forms of organizational reach, specified with relatively extreme examples in Figure 1.1. Military power offers examples of authoritative organization. The power of the high command over its own troops is concentrated, coercive, and highly mobilized. It is intensive rather than extensive – the opposite of a militaristic empire, which can cover a large territory with its commands but has difficulty mobilizing positive commitments from its population or penetrating their everyday lives. A general strike is the example of relatively diffuse but intensive power. Workers sacrifice individual well-being in a cause, to a degree "spontaneously." Finally, as already mentioned, market exchange may involve voluntary, instrumental, and strictly limited transactions over an enormous area – hence it is diffuse and extensive. The most effective organization would encompass all four forms of reach.

Intensivity has been much studied by sociologists and political scientists, and I have nothing new to add. Power is intensive if much of the subject's life is controlled or if he or she can be pushed far without loss of compliance (ultimately to death). This is well understood, though not easily quantifiable

	Authoritative	*Diffused*
Intensive	Army command structure	A general strike
Extensive	Militaristic empire	Market exchange

Figure 1.1. *Forms of organizational reach*

in the societies covered in this volume. Extensivity has not figured greatly in previous theories. This is a pity, for it is easier to measure. Most theorists prefer abstract notions of social structure, so they ignore geographical and sociospatial aspects of societies. If we keep in mind that "societies" are *networks*, with definite spatial contours, we can remedy this.

Owen Lattimore can start us on our way. After a lifetime studying the relations between China and the Mongol tribes, he distinguished three radii of extensive social integration, which he argued remained relatively invariant in world history until the fifteenth century in Europe. The most geographically extensive is *military action*. This is itself divisible into two, inner and outer. The inner reaches over territories that, after conquest, could be added to the state; the outer is extended beyond such frontiers in punitive or tribute raids. Hence the second radius, *civil administration* (i.e., the state) is less extensive, being at maximum the inner radius of military action and often far less extensive than this. In turn this radius is more extensive than *economic integration*, which extends at the maximum to the region and at the minimum to the cell of the local village market, because of the feeble development of interaction between units of production. Trade was not altogether lacking, and the influence of Chinese traders was felt outside the effective range of the empire's armies. But communications technology meant that only goods with a high value-to-weight ratio – true luxury items and "self-propelled" animals and human slaves – were exchanged over long distances. The integrating effects of this were negligible. Thus, for a considerable stretch of human history, extensive integration was dependent on military and not economic factors (Lattimore 1962: 480–91, 542–51).

Lattimore tends to equate integration with extensive reach alone; and he also separates too clearly the various "factors" – military, economic, political – necessary for social life. Nevertheless, his argument leads us to analyze the "infrastructure" of power – how geographical and social spaces can be actually conquered and controlled by power organizations.

I measure the reach of authoritative power by borrowing from *logistics*, the military science of moving men and supplies while campaigning. How are commands actually and physically moved and implemented? What control by what power group of what type is erratically or routinely possible given existing logistical infrastructures? Several chapters quantify by asking questions like how many days it takes to pass messages, supplies, and personnel across given land, sea, and river spaces, and how much control can be thus exercised. I borrow heavily from the most advanced area of such research, military logistics proper. Military logistics provides relatively clear guidelines to the outer reaches of power networks, leading to important conclusions regarding the essentially *federal* nature of extensive preindustrial societies. The unitary, highly centralized imperial society of writers like Wittfogel or Eisenstadt is mythical, as is Lattimore's own claim that military integration was historically decisive. When routine military control along a route march greater than about ninety kilometers is logistically impossible (as throughout much of history) control over a larger area cannot be centralized in practice, nor can it penetrate intensively the everyday lives of the population.

Diffused power tends to vary together with authoritative power and is affected by its logistics. But it also spreads relatively slowly, spontaneously, and "universally" throughout populations, without going through particular authoritative organizations. Such *universalism* also has a measurable technological development. It depends on enabling facilities like markets, literacy, coinage, or the development of class and national (instead of locality or lineage) culture. Markets, and class and national consciousness, emerged slowly throughout history, dependent on their own diffused infrastructures.

General historical sociology can thus focus on the development of collective and distributive power, measured by the development of infrastructure. Authoritative power requires a logistical infrastructure; diffused power requires a universal infrastructure. Both enable us to concentrate on an organizational analysis of power and society and to examine their sociospatial contours.

Current stratification theory

What, then, are the main power organizations? The two main approaches in current stratification theory are Marxian and neo-Weberian. I am happy to accept their initial joint premise: *Social stratification is the overall creation and distribution of power in society.* It is *the* central structure of societies because in its dual collective and distributive aspects it is the means whereby human beings achieve their goals in society. In fact agreement between them generally goes further, for they tend to see the same three types of power organization as predominant. Among Marxists (e.g., Wesolowski 1967; Anderson 1974a and b; Althusser and Balibar 1970; Poulantzas 1972; Hindess and Hirst 1975), among Weberians (e.g., Bendix and Lipset 1966; Barber 1968; Heller 1970; Runciman 1968, 1982, 1983a, b, and c), they are *class, status,* and *party.* The two sets of terms have roughly equivalent coverage, so in contemporary sociology the three have become the dominant descriptive orthodoxy.

I am largely happy with the first two, with economic/class and ideology/status. My first deviation from orthodoxy is to suggest *four*, not three, fundamental types of power. The "political/party" type actually contains two separate forms of power, *political* and *military* power: on the one hand, the central polity, including the state apparatus and (where they exist) political parties; on the other hand, physical or military force. Marx, Weber, and their followers do not distinguish between the two, because they generally view the state as the repository of physical force in society.

To equate physical force with the state often seems to make sense in the case of modern states that monopolize military force. However, conceptually they should be regarded as distinct, to prepare for four eventualities:

1. Most historic states have not possessed a monopoly of organized military force and many have not even claimed it. The feudal state in some European countries in the Middle Ages depended on the feudal military levy controlled by decentralized lords. Islamic states generally lacked monopoly powers – for example, they did not see themselves as having power to intervene in tribal feuding. We can distinguish the political from the military powers of both states and other groups. *Political powers are those of centralized, institutionalized, territorial regulation; military powers are of organized physical force wherever they are organized.*

2. Conquest is undertaken by military groups that may be independent of their home states. In many feudal cases, any freeborn or noble warrior could collect an armed band for raiding and conquering. If this military group did conquer, this increased its power against its own state. In the case of barbarians attacking civilizations, such a military organization often led to the first emergence of a state among the barbarians.

3. Internally, military organization is usually institutionally separate from other state agencies even when under state control. As the military often overthrows the state political elite in a coup d'état, we need to distinguish them.

4. If international relations between states are peaceful but stratified, we will wish to talk of a "political power structuring," of the wider international society that is not determined by military power. This is so today, for example, with respect to the powerful but largely demilitarized Japanese or West German states.

We shall thus treat separately *four* power sources, economic, ideological, military, and political.[1]

"Levels, dimensions" of "society"

The four power sources will be enumerated in detail later in the chapter. But, first, what exactly are they? Orthodox stratification theory is clear. In Marxian theory they are generally referred to as "levels of a social formation"; in neo-

---

[1]Giddens (1981) also distinguishes four types of power institution: symbolic orders/modes of discourse, economic institutions, law/modes of sanction/repression, and political institutions.

Weberian theory they are "dimensions of society." Both presuppose an abstract, almost geometric, view of a unitary society. The levels or dimensions are elements of a larger whole, which is indeed composed of them. Many authors represent this diagrammatically. Society becomes a large box or circle of an *n*-dimensional space, subdivided into smaller boxes, sectors, levels, vectors, or dimensions.

This is clearest in the term *dimension*. It derives from mathematics and has two special meanings: (1) Dimensions are analogous and independent, being related in the same way to some underlying structural property. (2) Dimensions inhabit the same overall space, in this case a "society." The Marxian scheme differs in details. Its "levels" are not independent of each other, for the economy has ultimate primacy over the others. Actually, it is more complicated and ambiguous because the Marxian economy plays a double role, as an autonomous "level" of the "social formation" (society) and as the ultimately determining totality itself, given the title of "mode of production." Modes of production give overall character to social formations and, therefore, to the individual levels. Thus the two theories differ: Weberians develop a multifactor theory where the social totality is determined by the complex interplay of the dimensions; Marxists see the totality as "ultimately" determined by economic production. Yet they share a symmetrical vision of society as a single, unitary whole.

This impression of symmetry is reinforced if we look within each dimension/level. Each combines symmetrically three characteristics. They are, first, *institutions*, organizations, stable subsystems of interaction visible in most societies as "churches," "modes of production," "markets," "armies," "states," and so forth. But they are also *functions*. Sometimes these are, secondly *functional ends* pursued by humans. For example, Marxists justify economic primacy on the grounds that humans must first pursue economic subsistence; Weberians justify the importance of ideological power in terms of the human need to find meaning in the world. More often they are viewed, thirdly, as *functional means*. Marxists view political and ideological levels as necessary means to extract surplus labor from the direct producers; Weberians argue that they are all means of power. But organizations, functions as ends, and functions as means are homologous. They are analogous and inhabit the same space. Each level or dimension has the same internal content. It is organization, function as end, and function as means, wrapped up in a single package.

If we carry on down to empirical analysis, the symmetry continues. Each dimension/level can be unpacked into a number of "factors." Arguments weigh the importance of, say, a number of "economic factors" against a number of "ideological factors." The dominant debate has been between a "multifactor" approach, drawing its most important factors from different dimensions/levels, and a "single-factor" approach, drawing its most important factor from a single one. On the multifactor side there must now be literally hundreds of books and articles that contain the assertion that ideas, or cultural, or ideological, or symbolic factors are autonomous, have a life of their own, cannot be reduced to material or economic factors (e.g., Sahlins 1976; Bendix 1978: 271–2, 630; Geertz 1980: 13, 135–6). On the single-factor side has run a traditional Marxian polemic against this position. In 1908 Labriola published his *Essays on the Materialist Conception of History*. There he argued that the multifactor approach neglected the *totality* of society, given character by man's praxis, his activity as a material producer. This has been repeated many times since by Marxists (e.g., Petrovic 1967: 67–114).

Despite the polemics, they are two sides of the same assumption: "Factors" are part of functional, organizational dimensions or levels that are analogous, independent subsystems of an overall social whole. Weberians emphasize the lower, more empirical aspects of this; Marxians emphasize the upper aspect of wholeness. But it is the same underlying symmetrical, unitary vision.

The rival theories have virtually the same master concept, "society" (or "social formation" in some Marxian theory). The most frequent usage of the term "society" is loose and flexible, indicating any stable human group, adding nothing to words like the social group or social aggregate or association. This is how I will use the term. But in more rigorous or more ambitious usage, "society" adds a notion of a unitary social system. This is what Comte himself (the coiner of the word "sociology") meant by the term. So, too, did Spencer, Marx, Durkheim, the classical anthropologists, and most of their disciples and critics. Of major theorists, only Weber showed a wariness of this approach and only Parsons has confronted it explicitly. This is his definition: "A society is a type of social system, in any universe of social systems which attains the highest level of self-sufficiency as a system in relation to its environment" (1966: 9). By dropping the excessive use of the word "systems" while preserving Parsons's essential meaning, we can arrive at a better definition: *A society is a network of social interaction at the boundaries of which is a certain level of interaction cleavage between it and its environment.* A society is a unit with boundaries, and it contains interaction that is relatively dense and stable; that is, it is internally patterned when compared to interaction that crosses its boundaries. Few historians, sociologists, or anthropologists would contest this definition (see, e.g., Giddens 1981: 45–6).

Parsons's definition is admirable. But it concerns only degree of unity and patterning. Too often this is forgotten, and unity and patterning are assumed to be present and invariable. This is what I call the *systemic* or *unitary* conception of society. Society and system appeared interchangeable in Comte and his successors, who believed them to be requirements for a science of society: To make general sociological statements requires that we isolate a society and observe regularities in the relationships between its parts. Societies in the system sense, bounded and internally patterned, exist in virtually every work of sociology and anthropology, and in most theoretically informed works of political science, economics, archaeology, geography, and history. They also exist implicitly in less theoretical works in these disciplines.

Let us examine the etymology of "society." It derives from the Latin *societas*. This elaborated *socius,* meaning a non-Roman ally, a group willing to follow Rome in war. Such a term is common in Indo-European languages, deriving from the root *sekw,* meaning "follow." It denotes an asymmetrical alliance, society as a loose confederation of stratified allies. We will see that this, not the unitary conception, is correct. Let us use the term "society" in its Latin, not its Romance, sense.

But I continue with two broader arguments against the unitary conception of society.

Criticisms

Human beings are social, not societal

A theoretical assumption lies at the base of the unitary conception: Because people are social animals, they have a need to create a society, a bounded and patterned social totality. But this is false. Human beings need to enter into social power relations, but they do not need social totalities. They are social, but not societal, animals.

Let us consider some of their needs again. As they desire sexual fulfillment, they seek sexual relations, usually with only a few members of the opposite sex; as they desire to reproduce themselves, these sexual relations usually combine with relations between adults and children. For these (and other purposes) a family emerges, enjoying patterned interaction with other family units from which sexual partners might be found. As humans need material subsistence they develop economic relationships, cooperating in production and exchange with others. There is no necessity that these economic networks be identical to family or sexual networks, and in most cases they are not. As humans explore the ultimate meaning of the universe, they discuss beliefs and perhaps participate with others similarly inclined in rituals and worship in a church. As humans defend whatever they have obtained, and as they pillage others, they form armed bands, probably of younger men, and they require relations with nonfighters who feed and equip them. As humans settle disputes without constant recourse to force, they set up judicial organizations with a specified area of competence. Where is the necessity for all these social requirements to generate identical sociospatial interaction networks and form a unitary society?

Tendencies toward forming a singular network derive from the emergent need to *institutionalize* social relations. Questions of economic production, of meaning, of armed defense, and of judicial settlement are not fully independent of one another. The character of each is likely to be influenced by the character of all, and all are necessary for each. A given set of production relations will require common ideological and normative understandings, and it will require defense and judicial regulation. The more institutionalized these interrelations, the more the various power networks converge toward one unitary society.

But we must recall the original dynamic. The driving force of human society is not institutionalization. History derives from restless drives that generate various networks of extensive and intensive power relations. These networks have a more direct relation to goal attainment than institutionalization has. In pursuit of their goals humans further develop these networks, outrunning the existing level of institutionalization. This may happen as a direct challenge to existing institutions, or it may happen unintentionally and "interstitially" – between their interstices and around their edges – creating new relations and institutions that have unanticipated consequences for the old.

This is reinforced by the most permanent feature of institutionalization, the division of labor. Those involved in economic subsistence, ideology, military defense and aggression, and political regulation possess a degree of autonomous control over their means of power that then further develops relatively autonomously. Marx saw that the forces of economic production continuously outdistance institutionalized class relations and throw up emergent social classes. The model was extended by writers like Pareto and Mosca: The power of "elites" could also rest on noneconomic power resources. Mosca summarized the result:

If a new source of wealth develops in a society, if the practical importance of knowledge grows, if an old religion declines or a new one is born, if a new current of ideas spreads, then, simultaneously, far-reaching dislocations occur in the ruling class. One might say, indeed, that the whole history of civilised mankind comes down to a conflict between the tendency of dominant elements to monopolise political power and transmit possession of it by inheritance and the tendency toward a dislocation of old forces and an insurgence of new forces; and this conflict produces an unending ferment of endosmosis and exosmosis between the upper classes and certain portions of the lower. [1939: 65]

Mosca's model, like Marx's, ostensibly shares the unitary view of society: Elites rise and fall within the same social space. But when Marx actually described the rise of the bourgeoisie (his paradigm case of a revolution in the forces of production), it was not like that. The bourgeoisie rose "interstitially"; it emerged between the "pores" of feudal society, he said. The bourgeoisie, centered on the towns, linked up with landowners, tenant farmers, and rich peasants, treating their economic resources as commodities to create *new* networks of economic interaction, capitalist ones. Actually, as we see in Chapters 14 and 15, it helped create two different overlapping networks – one bounded by the territory of the medium-sized state and one much more extensive, labeled by Wallerstein (1974) the "world system." The bourgeois revolution did not change the character of an existing society; it created new societies.

I term such processes *interstitial emergence*. They are the outcome of the translation of human goals into organizational means. Societies have never been sufficiently institutionalized to prevent interstitial emergence. Human beings do not create unitary societies but a diversity of intersecting networks of social interaction. The most important of these networks form relatively stably around the four power sources in any given social space. But underneath, human beings are tunneling ahead to achieve their goals, forming new networks, extending old ones, and emerging most clearly into our view with rival configurations of one or more of the principal power networks.

In which society do you live?

Empirical proof can be seen in the answer to a simple question: In which society do *you* live?

Answers are likely to start at two levels. One refers to national states: My society is "the United Kingdom," "the United States," "France," or the like. The other is broader: I am a citizen of "industrial society" or "capitalist society" or possibly "the West" or "the Western alliance." We have a basic dilemma – a national state society versus a wider "economic society." For some important purposes, the national state represents a real interaction network with a degree of cleavage at its boundaries. For other important purposes, capitalism unites all three into a wider interaction network, with cleavage at its edge. They are both "societies." Complexities proliferate the more we probe. Military alliances, churches, common language, and so forth, all add powerful, sociospatially different networks of interaction. We could only answer after developing a sophisticated understanding of the complex interconnections and powers of these various crosscutting interaction networks. The answer would certainly imply a *confederal* rather than a unitary society.

The contemporary world is not exceptional. Overlapping interaction networks are the historical norm. In prehistory, trading and cultural interaction was of enormously greater extent than could be controlled by any "state" or other authoritative network (see Chapter 2). The rise of civilization is explicable in terms of the insertion of alluvial agriculture into various overlapping regional networks (Chapters 3 and 4). In most ancient empires, the mass of the people participated overwhelmingly in small-scale local interaction networks yet were also involved in two other networks, provided by the erratic powers of a distant state, and the rather more consistent, but still shallow, power of semiautonomous local notables (Chapters 5, 8, and 9). Increasingly there arose within, outside, and across the boundaries of such empires more extensive, cosmopolitan, trading-and-cultural networks, which spawned various "world religions" (Chapters 6, 7, 10, and 11). Eberhard (1965: 16) has described such empires as "multilayered," containing both many layers existing one on top of another, and many small "societies" existing side by side. They are not social systems, he concludes. Social relationships have rarely aggregated into unitary societies – although states sometimes had unitary pretensions. "In which society do you live?" would have been an equally difficult question for the peasant in Roman North Africa or twelfth-century England. (I examine these two cases in Chapters 10 and 12.) Or again, there have been many "culturally federal" civilizations, like ancient Mesopotamia (Chapter 3), classical Greece (Chapter 7), or medieval and early modern Europe (Chapters 12 and 13), where small states have coexisted in a wider, loosely "cultural," network. The forms of overlap and intersection have varied considerably, but they have been always there.

The promiscuity of organizations and functions

To conceive of societies as confederal, overlapping, intersecting networks rather than as simple totalities complicates theory. But we must introduce further complexity. Real institutionalized networks of interaction do not have a simple one-to-one relationship to the ideal-typical sources of social power from which I started. This will lead us to break down the equation of functions and organizations and to recognize their "promiscuity."

Let us consider an example, the relation between the capitalist mode of production and the state. Weberians argue that Marx and his followers neglect the structural power of states and concentrate exclusively on the power of capitalism. They also argue that this is the *same* criticism as saying that Marxists neglect the autonomous power of political factors in society as compared to economic. Marxists reply with a similar packaged answer, denying both charges, or, alternatively, justifying their neglect of both states and politics on the grounds that capitalism and economic power are ultimately primary. But the arguments on both sides must be unpacked. Advanced capitalist states are not political *rather than* economic phenomena: They are both, simultaneously. How could they be otherwise when they redistribute about half of gross national product (GNP) accruing on their territories, and when their currencies, tariffs, educational and health systems, and so forth, are important economic power resources? It is not that Marxists neglect political factors. It is that they neglect that states are economic actors as well as political ones. They are "functionally promiscuous." Thus the advanced capitalist mode of production contains at least two organized actors: classes and nation-states. Disentangling them will be a principal theme of Volume II.

But not all states have been so promiscuous. Medieval European states, for example, redistributed very little of contemporary GNP. Their roles were overwhelmingly, narrowly political. The separation between economic and political functions/organizations was clear and symmetrical – states were political, classes were economic. But the asymmetry between medieval and modern situations worsens our theoretical problem. Organizations and functions weave across each other in the historical process, now separating clearly, now merging in varying forms. Economic roles can be (and normally are) performed by states, by armies, and by churches, as well as by specialized organizations we generally call "economic." Ideologies are brandished by economic classes, by states, and by military elites, as well as by churches and the like. There are no one-to-one relations between functions and organizations.

It remains true that a broad division of function between ideological, economic, military, and political organizations is ubiquitous, popping up again and again through the interstices of more merged power organizations. We must hang onto this as a simplifying tool of analysis in terms either of the interrelations of a number of autonomous dimensional functions/organizations *or* of the ultimate primacy of one of them. In this sense both Marxian and neo-Weberian orthodoxies are false. Social life does not consist of a number of realms – each composed of a bundle of organizations and functions, ends and means – whose relations with one another are those of external objects.

Organizations of power

If the problem is so difficult, what is the solution? In this section I give two empirical examples of relative predominance by a particular power source. These point to a solution in terms of power *organization*. The first example is of military power. It is often easy to see the emergence of a new military power because the fortunes of war can have such a sudden and clear-cut issue. One such was the rise of the European pike phalanx.

Example 1: the rise of the European pike phalanx
Important social changes were precipitated by military events just after A.D. 1300 in Europe. In a series of battles the old feudal levy, whose core was semiindependent groups of armored mounted knights surrounded by their retainers, was defeated by armies (mainly Swiss and Flemish) that placed greater reliance on dense masses of infantry pikemen (see Verbruggen 1977). This sudden shift in the fortunes of war led to important changes in social power. It hastened the demise of Powers that did not adjust to the lessons of war – for example, the great duchy of Burgundy. But in the long run it strengthened the power of centralized states. They could more easily provide resources to maintain the mixed infantry-cavalry-artillery armies that proved the answer to the pike phalanx. This hastened the demise of classic feudalism in general because it strengthened the central state and weakened the autonomous lord.

Let us consider this first in the light of "factors." Considered narrowly, it seems a simple causal pattern – changes in the technology of military power relations lead to changes in political and economic power relations. With this model we have an apparent case of military determinism. But this takes no account of the many other factors contributing to the military victory. Most crucial was probably the form of morale possessed by the victors – confidence in the pikeman to the right and to the left and at one's back. In turn, this probably derived from the relatively egalitarian, communal life of Flemish burghers, Swiss burghers, and yeoman farmers. We could continue elaborating until we had a multifactor explanation; or perhaps we could argue that the decisive point was the mode of economic production of the two groups. The stage is set for the kind of argument between economic, military, ideological, and other factors that looms in virtually every area of historical and sociological research. It is a ritual without hope and an end. For military power, like all the power sources, is itself promiscuous. It requires morale and economic surpluses – that is, ideological and economic supports – as well as drawing upon more narrowly military traditions and development. *All* are necessary factors to the exercise of military power, so how can we rank their importance?

But let us try to look at the military innovations in a different, *organizational* light. Of course, they had economic, ideological, and other preconditions. But they also had an intrinsically military, emergent, interstitial power of reorganization – a capacity through particular battlefield superiority to restructure general social networks distinct from those provided by existing dominant institutions. Let us call the latter "feudalism," – comprising a mode of production (extraction of surplus from a dependent peasantry, interrelation of peasant plots of land and lords' manors, delivery of surplus as commodities to the towns, etc.); political institutions (the hierarchy of courts from the vassal to lord to monarch); military institutions (the feudal levy); and a European-wide ideology, Christianity. "Feudalism" is a loose way of describing the dominant way in which the myriad factors of social life, and, at the core, the four sources of social power, were organized and institutionalized across medieval western Europe. But other areas of social life were less central to, and less controlled by, feudalism. Social life is always more complex than its dominant institutions because, as I have emphasized, the dynamic of society comes from the myriad social networks that humans set up to pursue their goals. Among social networks that were not at the core of feudalism were towns and free peasant communities. Their further development was relatively interstitial to feudalism. And in a crucial respect two of them, in Flanders and Switzerland, found that their social organization contributed a particularly effective form of "concentrated coercion" (as I shall define military organization later) to the battlefield. This was unsuspected by anyone, even themselves. It is sometimes argued that the first victory was accidental. At the battle of Courtrai the Flemish burghers were penned against the river by the French knights. They were unable to engage in their usual tactic against charging knights – flight! Not desirous of being slaughtered, they dug their pikes into the ground, gritted their teeth, and unhorsed the first knightly rank. It is a good example of interstitial surprise – for everyone concerned.

But it is *not* an example of "military" versus "economic" factors. Instead it is an example of a competition between two ways of life, one dominant and feudal, the other hitherto less important and burgher or free peasant, which took a decisive turn on the battlefield. One way of life generated the feudal levy, the other the pike phalanx. Both forms required the myriad "factors" and the functions of all four major power sources necessary for social existence. Hitherto one dominant organizational configuration, the feudal, had predominated and partially incorporated the other into its networks. Now, however, the interstitial development of aspects of Flemish and Swiss life found a rival military organization capable of unhorsing this predominance. Military power *reorganized* existing social life, through the effectiveness of a particular form of "concentrated coercion" on the battlefield.

Indeed the reorganization continued. The pike phalanx sold itself (literally) to rich states whose power over feudal, and town, and independent peasant networks was enhanced (as it was also over religion). An area of social life – undoubtedly a part of European feudalism, but not at its core and so only weakly institutionalized – unexpectedly and interstitially developed a highly concentrated and coercive military organization that first threatened, but then induced a restructuring of, the core. The emergence of an autonomous military organization was in this case short-lived. Both its origins and its destiny were promiscuous – not accidentally so, but in its very nature. Military power enabled a reorganizing spurt, a regrouping both of the myriad networks of society and of its dominant power configurations.

Example 2: The emergence of civilizational cultures and religions

In many times and places, ideologies have spread over a more extensive social space than that covered by states, armies, or modes of economic production. For example, the six best-known pristine civilizations – Mesopotamia, Egypt, the Indus Valley, Yellow River China, Mesoamerica, and Andean America – (with the possible exception of Egypt) arose as a series of small states situated within a larger cultural/civilizational unit, sharing common monumental and artistic styles, forms of symbolic representation, and religious pantheons. In later history, federations of states within a broader cultural unit are also found in many cases (e.g., classical Greece or medieval Europe). The world-salvation religions spread over much of the globe more extensively than any other power organization. Since then, secular ideologies like liberalism and socialism have also spread extensively across the boundaries of other power networks.

So religions and other ideologies are extremely important historical phenomena. Scholars drawing our attention to this argue in factorial terms: It shows, they claim, the autonomy of "ideal" factors from "material" ones (e.g., Coe 1982, and Keatinge 1982 in relation to ancient American civilizations; and Bendix 1978, in relation to the spread of liberalism across the early modern world). Again the materialist counterblast comes: These ideologies are not "free floating" but the product of real social circumstances. True, the ideology does not "float above" social life. Unless ideology stems from divine intervention in social life, then it must explain and reflect real-life experience. But – and in this lies its autonomy – it explains and reflects aspects of social life that existing dominant power institutions (modes of economic production, states, armed forces, and other ideologies) do not explain and organize effectively. An ideology will emerge as a powerful, autonomous movement when it can put together in a single explanation and organization a number of aspects of existence that have hitherto been marginal, interstitial to the dominant institutions of power. This is always a potential development in societies because there are many interstitial aspects of experience and many sources of contact between human beings other than those that form the core networks of dominant institutions.

Let me take up the example of the cultural unity of pristine civilizations (elaborated in Chapters 3 and 4). We observe a common pantheon of gods, festivals, calendars, styles of writing, decoration, and monumental building. We see the broader "material" roles religious institutions performed – predominantly the economic role of storing and redistributing produce and regulating trade, and the political/military role of devising rules of war and diplomacy. And we examine the content of the ideology: the concern with genealogy and the origins of society, with life-cycle transitions, with influencing the fertility of nature and controlling human reproduction, with justifying yet regulating violence, with establishing sources of legitimate authority beyond one's own kin group, village, or state. Thus a religiously centered culture provided to people who lived in similar conditions over a broad region with a sense of collective normative identity and an ability to cooperate that was not intense in its powers of mobilization but that was more extensive and diffuse than state, army, or mode of production provided. A religiously centered culture offered a particular way of organizing social relations. It fused in a coherent organizational form a number of social needs, hitherto interstitial to the dominant institutions of the small familial/village/state societies of the region. Then the power organization of temples, priests, scribes, and so forth, acted back and reorganized those institutions, in particular establishing forms of long-distance economic and political regulation.

Was this the result of its ideological content? Not if we mean by this its ideological answers. After all, the answers that ideologies give to the "meaning of life" questions are not all that varied. Nor are they particularly impressive, both in the sense that they can never be tested and found true, and in the sense that the contradictions they are supposed to resolve (e.g., the question of theodicy: Why do apparent order and meaning coexist with chaos and evil?) still remain after the answer has been given. Why then do a few ideological movements conquer their region, even much of the world, whereas most do not? The explanation for the difference may reside less in the answers ideologies provide than in the way they set about answering. Ideological movements argue that human problems can be overcome with the aid of *transcendent, sacred authority,* authority that cuts through and across the "secular" reach of economic, military, and political power institutions. Ideological power converts into a distinctive form of social organization, pursuing a diversity of ends, "secular" and "material" (e.g., the legitimation of particular forms of authority) as well as those conventionally considered as religious or ideal (e.g., the search for meaning). If ideological movements are distinct as *organizations,* we can then analyze the situations in which their form seems to answer human needs. There should be determinate conditions of the capacity of transcendent social authority, reaching through, "above," and beyond the reach of established power authorities to solve human problems. It is one of the conclusions of my historical analysis to argue that this is so.

Therefore, the power sources are not composed internally of a number of stable "factors" all showing the same coloration. When an independent source of power emerges, it is promiscuous in relation to "factors," gathering them from all crannies of social life, giving them only a distinctive organizational configuration. We can now turn to the four sources and the distinctive organizational means they imply.

The four sources and organizations of power

Ideological power derives from three interrelated arguments in the sociological tradition. First, we cannot understand (and so act upon) the world merely by direct sense perception. We require concepts and categories of *meaning* imposed upon sense perceptions. The social organization of ultimate knowledge and meaning is necessary to social life, as Weber argued. Thus collective and distributive power can be wielded by those who monopolize a claim to meaning. Second, *norms,* shared understandings of how people should act morally in their relations with each other, are necessary for sustained social cooperation. Durkheim demonstrated that shared normative understandings are required for stable, efficient social cooperation, and that ideological movements like religions are often the bearers of these. An ideological movement that increases the mutual trust and collective morale of a group may enhance their collective powers and be rewarded with more zealous adherence. To monopolize norms is thus a route to power. The third source of ideological power is *aesthetic/ritual practices.* These are not reducible to rational science. As Bloch (1974) has expressed it, in dealing with the power of religious myth, "You cannot argue with a song." A distinctive power is conveyed through song, dance, visual art forms, and rituals. As all but the most fervent materialists recognize, where meaning, norms, and aesthetic and ritual practices are monopolized by a distinctive group, it may possess considerable extensive and intensive power. It can exploit its functionality and build distributive on top of collective power. In later chapters I analyze the conditions under which an ideological movement can attain such power, as well as its overall extent. Religious movements provide the most obvious examples of ideological power, but more secular examples in this volume are the cultures of early Mesopotamia and classical Greece. Predominantly secular ideologies are characteristic of our own era – for example, Marxism.

In some formulations the terms "ideology" and "ideological power" contain two additional elements, that the knowledge purveyed is false and/or that it is a mere mask for material domination. I imply neither. Knowledge purveyed by an ideological power movement necessarily "surpasses experience" (as Parsons puts it). It cannot be totally tested by experience, and therein lies its distinctive power to persuade and dominate. But it need not be false; if it is, it is less likely to spread. People are not manipulated fools. And though ideologies always do contain legitimations of private interests and material domination, they are unlikely to attain a hold over people if they are merely this. Powerful ideologies are at least highly plausible in the conditions of the time, and they are genuinely adhered to.

These are the functions of ideological power, but to what distinct organizational contours do they give rise?

Ideological organization comes in two main types. In the first, more autonomous form it is sociospatially *transcendent*. It transcends the existing institutions of ideological, economic, military, and political power and generates a "sacred" form of authority (in Durkheim's sense), set apart from and above more secular authority structures. It develops a powerful autonomous role when emergent properties of social life create the possibility of greater cooperation or exploitation that transcend the organizational reach of secular authorities. Technically, therefore, ideological organizations may be unusually dependent on what I called *diffused* power techniques, and therefore boosted by the extension of such "universal infrastructures" as literacy, coinage, and markets.

As Durkheim argued, religion arises out of the usefulness of normative integration (and of meaning and aesthetics and ritual), and it is "sacred," set apart from secular power relations. But it does not merely integrate and reflect an already established "society"; indeed it may actually create a society-like network, a religious or cultural community, out of emergent, interstitial social needs and relations. Such is the model I apply in Chapters 3 and 4 to the first extensive civilizations, and in Chapters 10 and 11 to the world-salvation religions. Ideological power offers a distinctive sociospatial method of dealing with emergent social problems.

The second configuration is ideology as immanent *morale,* as intensifying the cohesion, the confidence, and, therefore, the power of an already-established social group. Immanent ideology is less dramatically autonomous in its impact, for it largely strengthens whatever is there. Nevertheless, ideologies of class or nation (the main examples) with their distinctive infrastructures, usually extensive and diffuse, contributed importantly to the exercise of power from the times of the ancient Assyrian and Persian empires onward.

Economic power derives from the satisfaction of subsistence needs through the social organization of the extraction, transformation, distribution, and consumption of the objects of nature. A grouping formed around these tasks is called a *class* – which in this work, therefore, is purely an *economic* concept. Economic production, distribution, exchange, and consumption relations normally combine a high level of intensive and extensive power, and have been a large part of social development. Thus classes form a large part of overall social-stratification relations. Those able to monopolize control over production, distribution, exchange, and consumption, that is, a dominant class, can obtain general collective and distributive power in societies. Again I shall analyze the conditions under which such power arises.

I will not enter here into the many debates concerning the role of classes in history. I prefer the context of actual historical problems, beginning in Chapter 7 with class struggle in ancient Greece (the first historical era for which we have good evidence). There I distinguish four phases in the development of class relations and class struggle – *latent, extensive, symmetrical,* and *political* class structures. I use these in succeeding chapters. My conclusions are stated in the last chapter. We will see that classes, though important, are not "the motor of history" as Marx, for one, believed.

On one important issue the two main traditions of theory differ. Marxists stress control over labor as the source of economic power, and so they concentrate on "modes of *production.*" Neo-Weberians (and others, like the substantivist school of Karl Polanyi) stress the organization of economic *exchange.* We cannot elevate one above the other on a priori theoretical grounds; historical evidence must decide the issue. To assert, as many Marxists do, that production relations must be decisive because "production comes first" (i.e., it precedes distribution, exchange, and consumption) is to miss the point of "emergence." Once a form of exchange emerges, it is a social fact, potentially powerful. Traders can react to opportunity at their end of the economic chain and then act back upon the organization of production that originally spawned them. A trading empire like the Phoenician is an example of a trading group whose actions decisively altered the lives of the producing groups whose needs originally created their power (e.g., developing the alphabet – see Chapter 7). Relations between production and exchange are complex and often attenuated: Whereas production is high on intensive power, mobilizing intense local social cooperation to exploit nature, exchange may occur extremely extensively. At its fringes, exchange may encounter influences and opportunities that are far removed from the production relations that originally generated selling activities. Economic power is generally diffuse, not controllable from a center. This means that class structure may not be unitary, a single hierarchy of economic power. Production and exchange relations may, if attenuated, fragment class structure.

Thus classes are groups with differential power over the social organization of the extraction, transformation, distribution, and consumption of the objects of nature. I repeat that I use the term *class* to denote a purely economic power grouping, and the term *social stratification* to denote any type of distribution of power. The term *ruling class* will denote an economic class that has successfully monopolized other power sources to dominate a state-centered society at large. I leave open for historical analysis questions concerning the interrelations of classes to other stratification groupings.

Economic organization comprises circuits of production, distribution, exchange, and consumption. Its main sociospatial peculiarity is that although those circuits are extensive, they also involve the intensive practical, everyday labor – what Marx called the praxis – of the mass of the population. Economic organization thus offers a distinctively stable, sociospatial blend of extensive and intensive power, and of diffused and authoritative power. Therefore, I shall call economic organization *circuits of praxis*. This perhaps rather pompous term is intended to build upon two of Marx's insights. First, at one "end" of a reasonably developed mode of production are a mass of workers laboring and expressing themselves through the conquest of nature. Second, at the other "end" of the mode are complex, extensive circuits of exchange into which millions may be locked by impersonal, seemingly "natural," forces. The contrast is extreme in the case of capitalism, but nonetheless present in all types of economic-power organization. Groups defined in relation to the circuits of praxis are classes. The degree to which they are "extensive," "symmetrical," and "political" across the whole circuit of praxis of a mode of production[2] will determine the organizing power of class and class struggle. And this will turn on the tightness of linkage between intensive local production and extensive circuits of exchange.

Military power was partly defined earlier. It derives from the necessity of organized physical defense and its usefulness for aggression. It has both intensive and extensive aspects, for it concerns questions of life and death, as well as the organization of defense and offense in large geographical and social

---

[2]From now on I will use the term *mode of production* as shorthand for "mode of production, distribution, exchange and consumption." I do not thereby imply the primacy of production over the other spheres.

spaces. Those who monopolize it, as military elites, can obtain collective and distributive power. Such power has been neglected of late in social theory, and I return to nineteenth- and early-twentieth-century writers like Spencer, Gumplowicz, and Oppenheimer (although they usually exaggerated its capacities).

Military organization is essentially *concentrated-coercive*. It mobilizes violence, the most concentrated, if bluntest, instrument of human power. This is obvious in wartime. Concentration of force forms the keystone of most classic discussions of military tactics. But as we shall see in various historical chapters (especially 5–9), it may endure beyond the battlefield and the campaign. Militaristic forms of social control attempted in peacetime are also highly concentrated. For example, directly coerced labor, whether slave or corvée, often built city fortifications, monumental buildings, or main communication roads or channels. Coerced labor appears also in mines, on plantations, and on other large estates, and in the households of the powerful. But it is less suited to normal dispersed agriculture, to industry where discretion and skill are required, or to the dispersed activities of commerce and trade. The costs of effectively enforcing direct coercion in these areas have been beyond the resources of any known historical regime. Militarism has thus proved useful where concentrated, intensive, authoritative power has yielded disproportionate results.

Second, military power also has a more extensive reach, of a negative, terroristic form. As Lattimore pointed out, throughout most of history military striking range was greater than the range of either state control or economic-production relations. But this is minimal control. The logistics are daunting. In Chapter 5, I calculate that throughout ancient history the maximum unsupported march practicable for an army was about 90 kilometers – scant basis for intensive military control over large areas. Faced with a powerful military force located, let us say, 300 kilometers away, locals might be concerned to comply externally with its dictates – supply annual tribute, recognize the suzerainty of its leader, send young men and women to be "educated" at its court – but everyday behavior could be otherwise unconstrained.

Thus military power is sociospatially dual: a concentrated core in which positive, coerced controls can be exercised, surrounded by an extensive penumbra in which terrorized populations will not normally step beyond certain niceties of compliance but whose behavior cannot be positively controlled.

Political power (also partly defined earlier) derives from the usefulness of centralized, institutionalized, territorialized regulation of many aspects of social relations. I am not defining it in purely "functional" terms, in terms of judicial regulation backed by coercion. Such functions can be possessed by any power organization – ideological, economic, military, as well as states. I restrict it to regulations and coercion centrally administered and territorially bounded – that is, to *state* power. By concentrating on the state, we can analyze its distinctive contribution to social life. As here defined, political power heightens boundaries, whereas the other power sources may transcend them. Second, military, economic, and ideological power can be involved in *any* social relationships, wherever located. Any A or group of As can exercise these forms of power against any B or group of Bs. By contrast, political relations concern one particular area, the "center." Political power is located in that center and exercised outward. Political power is necessarily centralized and territorial, and in these respects differs from the other power sources (see Mann 1984, for fuller discussions; a formal definition of the state is also given in my next chapter). Those who control the state, the state elite, can obtain both collective and distributive power and trap others within their distinctive "organization chart."

Political organization is also sociospatially dual, though in a different sense. Here we must distinguish domestic from "international" organization. Domestically, the state is *territorially centralized* and territorially-bounded. States can thus attain greater autonomous power when social life generates emergent possibilities for enhanced cooperation and exploitation of a central-ized form over a confined territorial area (elaborated in Mann 1984). It depends predominantly upon techniques of authoritative power, because centralized, though not as much so as military organization. When discussing the actual powers of state elites, we will find it useful to distinguish formal "despotic" powers from real "infrastructural" powers. This is explained in Chapter 5 in the section titled "The Comparative Study of Ancient Empires."

But states' territorial boundaries – in a world never yet dominated by a single state – also give rise to an area of regulated interstate relations. *Geo-political diplomacy* is a second important form of political-power organiza-tion. Two geopolitical types – the hegemonic empire dominating marcher and neighboring clients, and varying forms of multistate civilization – will play a considerable role in this volume. Clearly, geopolitical organization is very different in form from the other power organizations mentioned so far. It is indeed normally ignored by sociological theory. But it is an essential part of social life and it is not reducible to the "internal" power configurations of its component states. For example, the successive hegemonic and despotic pre-tensions of the German emperor Henry IV, Philip II of Spain, and Bonaparte of France were only in a superficial sense humbled by the strength of the states and others who opposed them – they were really humbled by the deep-rooted, multistate diplomatic civilization of Europe. Geopolitical power organization is thus an essential part of overall social stratification.

To summarize so far: Human beings pursuing many goals set up many net-works of social interaction. The boundaries and capacities of these networks do not coincide. Some networks have greater capacity for organizing inten-sive and extensive, authoritative and diffused, social cooperation than others.

The greatest are the networks of ideological, economic, military, and political power – the four sources of social power. Each then implies distinctive forms of sociospatial organization by which humans can attain a very broad, but not exhaustive, package of their myriad goals. The importance of these four lies in their combination of intensive and extensive power. But this is translated into historical determinacy through the various organizational means that impose their general shape onto a large part of general social life. The main shapes I identified were *transcendent* or *immanent* (from ideological power), *circuits of praxis* (economic), *concentrated-coercive* (military), and *centralized-territorial* and *geopolitical diplomatic* (political) organization. Such configurations become what I called "promiscuous," drawing in and structuring elements from many areas of social life. In example 2 above, the transcendent organization of the culture of early civilizations drew in aspects of economic redistribution, of rules of warfare, and of political and geopolitical regulation. Thus we are dealing not with the external relations between different sources, dimensions, or levels of social power but rather with (1) the sources as ideal types that (2) attain intermittent existence as distinct organizations within the division of labor and that (3) may exert more general, promiscuous shaping of social life. In (3) one or more of these organizational means will emerge interstitially as the primary reorganizing force in either the short term, as in the military example, or the long term, as in the ideological example. This is the IEMP model of organized power.

Max Weber once used a metaphor drawn from the railways of his time when trying to explain the importance of ideology – he was discussing the power of salvation religions. He wrote that such ideas were like "switchmen" (i.e., "pointsmen" in British railways) determining down which of several tracks social development would proceed. Perhaps the metaphor should be amended. The sources of social power are "tracklaying vehicles" – for the tracks do not exist before the direction is chosen – laying different gauges of track across the social and historical terrain. *The "moments" of tracklaying, and of converting to a new gauge, are the closest that we can approach the issue of primacy.* In these moments we find an autonomy of social concentration, organization, and direction that is lacking in more institutionalized times.

That is the key to the importance of the power sources. They give collective organization and unity to the infinite variety of social existence. They provide such significant patterning as there is in large-scale social structure (which may or may not be very great) because they are capable of generating collective action. They are "the generalized means" through which human beings make their own history.

The overall IEMP model, its scope and omissions

The overall model is presented in summary diagrammatic form in Figure 1.2. The predominance of broken lines in the diagram indicates the messiness of

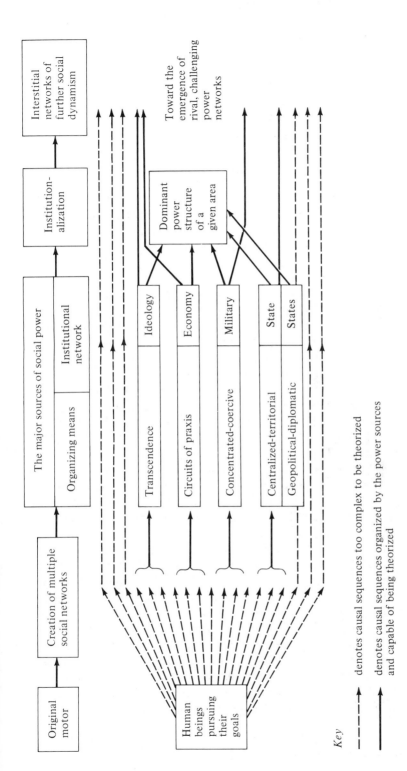

Key

- - - - - → denotes causal sequences too complex to be theorized

————→ denotes causal sequences organized by the power sources
and capable of being theorized

Figure 1.2. *Causal IEMP model of organized power*

human societies: Our theories can only encompass some of their broadest contours.

We start with humans pursuing goals. I don't mean by this that their goals are "presocial" – rather that what the goals are, and how they are created, is not relevant for what follows. Goal-oriented people form a multiplicity of social relationships too complex for any general theory. However, relationships around the most powerful organizational means coalesce to form broad institutional networks of determinate, stable shape, combining both intensive and extensive power and authoritative and diffused power. There are, I suggest, four such major sources of social power, each centered on a different means of organization. Pressures toward institutionalization tend to partially merge them in turn into one or more dominant power networks. These provide the highest degree of boundedness that we find in social life, though this is far from total. Many networks remain interstitial both to the four power sources and to the dominant configurations; similarly, important aspects of the four power sources also remain poorly institutionalized into the dominant configurations. These two sources of interstitial interaction eventually produce a more powerful emergent network, centered on one or more of the four power sources, and induce a reorganization of social life and a new dominant configuration. And so the historical process continues.

This is an approach to the issue of ultimate primacy, but it is not an answer. I have not even commented at all on what is the major point of contention between Marxian and Weberian theory: whether we can single out economic power as ultimately decisive in determining the shape of societies. This is an empirical question, and so I first review the evidence before attempting a provisional answer in Chapter 16 and a fuller answer in Volume III.

There are three reasons why the empirical test must be historical. First, the model is essentially concerned with processes of social change. Second, my rejection of a conception of society as unitary makes one alternative mode of inquiry, that of "comparative sociology," more difficult. Societies are not self-contained units to be simply compared across time and space. They exist in particular settings of regional interaction that are unique even in some of their central characteristics. The chances for comparative sociology are very limited when there are so *few* comparable cases. Third, my methodology is to "quantify" power, to trace out its exact infrastructures, and it is immediately obvious that quantities of power have developed enormously throughout history. The power capacities of prehistoric societies (over nature and over human beings) were considerably less than those of, say, ancient Mesopotamia, which were less than those of the later Roman Republic, which again were greatly exceeded by sixteenth-century Spain, then nineteenth-century Britain, and so forth. It is more important to capture this history than to make comparisons across the globe. This is a study of "world time," to use Eberhard's expression (1965: 16), in which each process of power development affects the world around it.

The most appropriate history is that of the most powerful human society, modern Western civilization (including the Soviet Union), whose history has been just about continuous from the origins of Near Eastern civilization around 3000 B.C. to the present day. It is a developmental, though not an evolutionary or a teleological, history. There has been nothing "necessary" about it – it just happened that way (and it nearly ended on several occasions). It is not a history of any single social or geographical space. As such enterprises generally do, mine starts with the general conditions of neolithic societies, then centers on the ancient Near East, then gradually moves west and north through Anatolia, Asia Minor, and the Levant to the eastern Mediterranean. Then it moves into Europe, ending in the eighteenth century in Europe's westernmost state, Great Britain. Each chapter concerns itself with the "leading edge" of power, where the capacity to integrate peoples and spaces into dominant configurations is most infrastructurally developed. Such a method is in a sense unhistorical, but its jumpiness is also a strength. Power capacities have developed unevenly, in jumps. So studying those jumps and trying to explain them gives us the best empirical entry into the issue of primacy.

What have I left out of this history? An enormous amount of detail and complexity, of course, but beyond that every model puts some phenomena at center stage and relegates others to the wings. If the latter ever manage to occupy center stage, then the model will not deal effectively with them. There is one conspicuous absence from this volume: gender relations. In Volume II, I seek to justify my uneven treatment in terms of their actual unevenness in history. I will argue that gender relations remained broadly constant, in the general form of *patriarchy,* throughout much of recorded history until the eighteenth and nineteenth centuries in Europe, when rapid changes began to occur. But that discussion awaits Volume II. In the present volume power relations discussed are normally those in the "public sphere" between male household heads.

From the specialist historian, I plead for generosity and breadth of spirit. Having covered a large slice of recorded history, I have doubtless committed errors of fact, and probably a few howlers. I ask whether correcting them would invalidate the overall arguments. I also ask more aggressively whether the study of history, especially in the Anglo-American tradition, would not benefit from more explicit consideration of the nature of societies. To the sociologist I also speak with some acerbity. Much contemporary sociology is ahistorical, but even much historical sociology is concerned exclusively with the development of "modern" societies and the emergence of industrial capitalism. This is so decisive in the sociological tradition that, as Nisbet (1967) has shown, it produced the pivotal dichotomies of modern theory. From status to contract, from gemeinschaft to gesellschaft, from mechanical to organic solidarity, from sacred to secular – these and other dichotomies locate the watershed of history at the end of the eighteenth century. Eighteenth-century theorists like Vico, Montesquieu, or Ferguson did not thus regard history.

Unlike modern sociologists who know only the recent history of their own national state, plus some anthropology, they knew that complex, differentiated, and stratified societies – secular, contractual, organic, gesellschaft, but *not* industrial – had existed for at least two thousand years. Throughout the nineteenth and early twentieth centuries, that knowledge declined among sociologists. Paradoxically, its decline has continued through the very time when historians, archaeologists, and anthropologists have been using new techniques, many from sociology, to make striking discoveries about the social structure of these complex societies. But their analysis is weakened by their relative ignorance of sociological theory.

Weber is an outstanding exception to this narrowing. My debt to him is enormous – not so much in terms of adopting his specific theories, but rather, in adhering to his general vision of the relationship between society, history, and social action.

My demand for sociological theory based on historical depth and breadth is not based merely on the intrinsic desirability of realizing the rich diversity of human experience – though that would be valuable enough. More than this, I claim that some of the most important characteristics of our world today can be appreciated more clearly by historical comparison. It is not that history repeats itself. Precisely the opposite: World history develops. Through historical comparison we can see that the most significant problems of our own time are novel. That is why they are difficult to solve: They are interstitial to institutions that deal effectively with the more traditional problems for which they were first set up. But, as I shall suggest, all societies have faced sudden and interstitial crises, and in some cases humanity has emerged enhanced. At the end of a long historical detour, I hope to demonstrate the relevance of this model for today in Volume II.

Bibliography

Althusser, L., and E. Balibar. 1970. *Reading Capital*. London: New Left Books.
Anderson, P. 1974a. *Passages from Antiquity to Feudalism*. London: New Left Books.
  1974b. *Lineages of the Absolutist State*. London: New Left Books.
Barber, L. B. 1968. Introduction in "stratification, social." In *International Encyclopedia of the Social Sciences*, ed. D. Sills. New York: Macmillan and Free Press.
Bendix, R. 1978. *Kings or People*. Berkeley: University of California Press.
Bendix, R., and S. M. Lipset. 1996. *Class, Status and Power*. 2d rev. ed. (orig. pub. 1953). New York: Free Press.
Bloch, M. 1974. Symbols, song, dance and features of articulation. *Archives Européenes de Sociologie*, 15.
Coe, M. D. 1982. Religion and the rise of Mesoamerican states. In *The Transition to Statehood in the New World*, ed. G. D. Jones and R. R. Kautz. Cambridge: Cambridge University Press.
Eberhard, W. 1965. *Conquerors and Rulers: Social Forces in Modern China*. Leiden: Brill.

Geertz, C. 1980. *Negara: The Theatre State in Nineteenth Century Bali*. Princeton, N. J.: Princeton University Press.

Gellner, E. 1964. *Thought and Change*. London: Weidenfeld & Nicolson.

Giddens, A. 1979. *Central Problems in Social Theory*. London: Macmillan.

1981. *A Contemporary Critique of Historical Materialism*. London: Macmillan.

Heller, C. S. 1970. *Structured Social Inequality*. London: Collier-Macmillan.

Hindess, B., and P. Hirst. 1975. *Pre-Capitalist Modes of Production*. London: Routledge.

Keatinge, R. 1982. The nature and role of religious diffusion in the early stages of state formation. In *The Transition to Statehood in the New World*, ed. G. D. Jones and R. R. Kautz. Cambridge: Cambridge University Press.

Labriola, E. 1908. *Essays on the Materialist Conception of History*. New York: Monthly Review Press.

Lattimore, O. 1962. *Studies in Frontier History*. London: Oxford University Press.

Mann, M. 1984. The Autonomous Power of the State. In *Archives Européennes de Sociologie*, 25.

Mosca, G. 1939. *The Ruling Class*. New York: McGraw-Hill.

Nisbet, R. 1967. *The Sociological Tradition*. London: Heinemann.

Parsons, T. 1960. The distribution of power in American society. In *Structure and Process in Modern Societies*. New York: Free Press.

1966. *Societies: Evolutionary and Comparative Perspectives*. Englewood Cliffs, N.J.: Prentice-Hall.

1968. *The Structure of Social Action*. New York: Free Press.

Petrovic, G. 1967. *Marx in the Mid-Twentieth Century*. New York: Doubleday (Anchor Press).

Poulantzas, N. 1972. *Pouvoir politique et classes sociales*. Paris: Maspero.

Runciman, W. G. 1968. Class, status, and Power? In *Social Stratification*, ed. J. A. Jackson. Cambridge: Cambridge University Press.

1982. Origins of states: the case of archaic Greece. *Comparative Studies in Society and History*, 24.

1983a. Capitalism without classes: the case of classical Rome. *British Journal of Sociology*. 24.

1983b. Unnecessary revolution: the case of France. *Archives Européenes de Sociologie*, 24.

1983c. *A Treatise on Social Theory, Volume I: The Methodology of Social Theory*. Cambridge: Cambridge University Press.

Sahlins, M. 1976. *Culture and Practical Reason*. Chicago: University of Chicago Press.

Shibutani, T. 1955. Reference groups as perspectives. *American Journal of Sociology*, 40.

Verbruggen, J. F. 1977. *The Art of Warfare in Western Europe During the Middle Ages*. Amsterdam: North-Holland.

Wallerstein, I. 1974. *The Modern World System*. New York: Academic Press.

Weber, M. 1968. *Economy and Society*. New York: Bedminster Press.

Wesolowski, 1967. Marx's theory of class domination. In *Polish Round Table Yearbook, 1967*, ed. Polish Association of Political Science, Warsaw: Ossolineum.

Wrong, D. 1979. *Power: Its Forms, Bases and Uses*. New York: Harper & Row.

2 The end of general social evolution: how prehistoric peoples evaded power

Introduction: the conventional evolutionary tale

A history of power should begin at the beginning. But where are we to place that? As a species, humans appeared millions of years ago. For most of those millions they lived principally as wandering gatherers of wild fruit, berries, nuts, and grasses and as scavengers around the hunting activities of larger creatures. Then they developed their own hunting repertoire. But from what we can guess about these gatherer-scavengers and gatherer-hunters, their social structure was extremely loose, ad hoc, and variable. They did not stably institutionalize power relations; they did not know classes, states, or even elites; even their distinctions between gender and age-sets (within adulthood) may not indicate permanent power differentials (this is much debated today). And, of course, they were not literate and did not have a "history" in our terms. So in the true beginnings there was neither power nor history. The concepts developed in Chapter 1 have virtually no relevance to 99 percent of humanity's life span to date. So I will not start at the beginning!

Then – seemingly all over the world – occurred a series of transitions, to agriculture, to the domestication of animals, and to permanent settlement, which brought humanity much closer to power relations. Stable, bounded, supposedly "complex" societies developed, embodying a division of labor, social inequality, and political centrality. Here perhaps we can begin to talk of power, though our account would contain many qualifications. But this second phase, accounting for about 0.6 percent of human experience to date, was not one of literacy. Its "history" is virtually unknown, and our account must be extremely tentative.

Finally, around 3000 B.C. began a series of associated transformations that led a part of humanity to the remaining 0.4 percent of its life span to date: the era of civilization; of permanent power relations embodied in states, stratification systems, and patriarchy; and of literate history. This era became general to the world, but it began in only a small number of places. This minute third phase is the subject matter of this book. But in telling its story, how much earlier should we begin in deciding its origins?

Two obvious questions arise: Given such marked discontinuity, is the whole of human social experience a single story? And given our almost total ignorance of 99 or 99.6 percent of it, how could we possibly know whether it

34

was? There is, however, one firm anchor to a whole story. From the Pleistocene period (about a million years ago) onward, there is no evidence of any "speciation," biological differentiation, within human populations. In fact, there is only one known earlier case of speciation over the whole 10-million–year life span of hominids: the coexistence of two hominid types in the early Pleistocene in Africa (one of which became extinct). This might seem curious, for other mammals originating at the same time as humanity, like elephants or cattle, have shown considerable subsequent speciation. Think of the difference between Indian and African elephants, for example, and contrast that to the minor phenotypical differences in skin pigmentation and the like among humans. Over the whole range of humanity, therefore, some unity of experience has existed (the argument is made forcefully by Sherratt 1980: 405). What kind of unified story can we tell?

Most stories are evolutionary ones. They tell first how human beings developed their innate capacities into social cooperation; then how each successive form of social cooperation emerged immanently from the potentialities of its predecessor toward "higher," or at least to more complex and powerful, social organization. Such theories predominated in the nineteenth century. Stripped of the notions of progress from lower to higher forms, but retaining the notion of evolution in power capacity and complexity, they still do dominate.

There is, however, one peculiarity about this story that its proponents recognize. Human evolution has differed from the evolution of other species by the very fact that it has retained its unity. Speciation has not occurred. When a local population has evolved a particular form of activity, very frequently this has been diffused among virtually the whole of humanity throughout the globe. Fire, clothing, and shelter, together with a more variable collection of social structures have spread, sometimes from a single epicenter, sometimes several, from the equator to the poles. Axehead and pottery styles, states and commodity production have spread very widely over history and the prehistory of which we have knowledge. So this story has been one of *cultural* evolution. Its presupposes continuous cultural contact between groups, based on an awareness that, despite local differences, human beings are all one species, face certain common problems, and can learn solutions from each other. A local group evolves a new form, perhaps stimulated by its own environmental needs, but the form proves to have general utility for groups in quite different environs, and they adopt it, perhaps in modified form.

Within the overall story, different themes may be emphasized. We may stress the number of cases of independent invention – for if all humans are culturally similar, they may be similarly capable of the next evolutionary step. This is the school that believes in "local evolution." Or we may stress the diffusion process and argue for very few epicenters of evolution. This is the "diffusionist" school. The two are often contrasted, often locked in bitter controversy. But they are essentially similar, telling the same overall story of continuous cultural evolution.

So almost all current accounts answer my initial question – "Is the whole a single story?" – with a clear "Yes." This shows through the accounts of most historians, fortified by their current predilection (especially in the Anglo-American historical traditions) for the "what happened next" style of continuous narrative. Discontinuities get bypassed by this method. For example, Roberts in his *Pelican History of the World* (1980: 45–55) describes the discontinuities between the three stages as merely a "quickening of the pace of change" and a geographical shifting of the focus in an essentially "cumulative" development of human and social powers, "rooted in ages dominated by the slow rhythm of genetic evolution." In the more theoretical, scientistic traditions of American archaeology and anthropology, the evolutionary story has been told in the language of cybernetics, with flowchart diagrams of the rise of civilization through various stages from hunter-gatherers, complete with positive and negative feedbacks, alternative "steplike" and "ramplike" models of incremental development, and so forth (e.g., Redman 1978: 8–11; cf. Sahlins and Service 1960). Evolutionism dominates, sometimes explicit, sometimes covert, as an explanation of the origins of civilization, stratification, and the state.

All the rival theories of the rise of stratification and the state presuppose an essentially natural process of general social development: They are viewed as the outgrowth of the dialectical development of the core structures of prehistoric societies. This particular story originates in normative political theory: We should comply with the state and stratification (Hobbes, Locke), or we should overthrow it (Rousseau, Marx) because of reconstructed or hypothetical prehistorical events. Recent anthropologists allied with archaeologists tell a story of the continuity of all known forms of human society (and, therefore, also of the relevance of their own academic disciplines to the world today!). Their central orthodoxy continues to be a story of stages: from relatively egalitarian, stateless societies; to rank societies with political authority; and eventually to stratified, civilized societies with states (admirably summarized by Fried 1967; see Redman 1978: 201–5 for alternative sequences of stages; and see Steward 1963 for the most influential of the modern archaeological/anthropological sequence of stages).

The logic of this approach has been expanded by Friedman and Rowlands (1978), who point out a defect in evolutionary tales. Although a sequence of stages is identified, transitions between them are precipitated by the somewhat random forces of population pressure and technological change. Friedman and Rowlands close this gap by developing a detailed, complex, "epigenetic" model of a "transformational process" of social organization. "In this way," they conclude, "we expect to be able to predict the dominant forms of social reproduction in the next stage in terms of the properties of the current stage.

This is possible because the reproductive process is itself directional and transformational'' (1978: 267–8).

The method of these models is identical. First the characteristics of gathering-hunting societies in general are discussed. Then a theory of a general transition to agricultural settlement and pastoralism is presented. The general characteristics of these societies then lead on to the emergence of a few particular societies: Mesopotamia, Egypt, and North China, sometimes with the Indus Valley, Mesoamerica, Peru, and Minoan Crete added.

Let us consider the usual stages and define their crucial terms.

1. *An egalitarian society* is self-explanatory. Hierarchical differences between persons and between age- and (perhaps) between gender-related roles are not institutionalized. Those in higher positions cannot lay their hands upon collective power resources.

2. *Rank societies* are not egalitarian. Those in higher ranks can use general collective power resources. This may be institutionalized and even transmitted hereditarily into an aristocratic lineage. But rank depends almost entirely upon *collective power*, or authority, that is, legitimate power used only for collective purposes, freely conferred and freely withdrawn by the participants. Thus high rankholders have status, make decisions, and use material resources on behalf of the whole group, but they do not possess coercive power over recalcitrant members and cannot divert the material resources of the group to their own private use and so make it their "private property."

But there are two subsets of rank societies that may be also arraigned on an evolutionary scale.

2a. In *relative rank societies,* persons and lineage groups can be ranked relative to each other, but there is no absolute highest point of the scale. In most groups, moreover, sufficient uncertainty and argument exist for relativities to be ultimately inconsistent with one another. Rank will be contested.

2b. In *absolute rank societies,* an absolute, highest point emerges. A chief or paramount chief is accredited uncontested highest rank, and all other ranks' lineages are measured in terms of their distance from his. This is usually expressed ideologically in terms of his descent from the ultimate ancestors, perhaps even the gods, of the group. So one characteristic institution appears: a ceremonial center, devoted to religion, controlled by the chief's lineage. From this centralized institution onward to the state is only a step.

3. Definitions of *the state* will be discussed at greater length in Volume III of this work. My provisional working definition is derived from Weber: *The state is a differentiated set of institutions and personnel embodying centrality, in the sense that political relations radiate outward to cover a territorially demarcated area, over which it claims a monopoly of binding and permanent rule-making, backed up by physical violence.* In prehistory, the introduction of the state converts temporary political authority and a permanent ceremonial

center into permanent political power, institutionalized and routinized in its ability to use coercion over recalcitrant social members as necessary.

4. *Stratification* involves the permanent, institutionalized power of some over the material life chances of others. Its power may be physical force or the ability to deprive others of the necessities of life. In the literature on origins it is usually a synonym for private property differentials and for economic classes, and so I treat it as a decentralized form of power, separate from the centralized state.

5. *Civilization* is the most problematic term, because so value-laden. No single definition suffices for all purposes. I discuss the issue further at the beginning of the next chapter. Again a provisional definition suffices. Following Renfrew (1972: 13), civilization combines three social institutions, the ceremonial center, writing, and the city. Where combined they inaugurate a jump in human collective power over nature and over other humans that, whatever the variability and unevenness of the prehistoric and historic record, is the onset of something new. Renfrew calls this a jump in "insulation," the containment of human beings behind clear, fixed, confined social and territorial boundaries. I use the metaphor of a *social cage*.

With these terms we can see close connections between the parts of the evolutionary tale. Rank, the state, stratification, and civilization were closely interconnected because their rise slowly but generally ended a primitive kind of freedom, the beginning of the constraints and the opportunities represented by permanent, institutionalized, bounded collective and distributive power.

I wish to dissent from this story, although for the most part I draw together the doubts of others. One theme of dissent has been to remark an oddity: Whereas the Neolithic Revolution and the emergence of rank societies occurred independently in many places (on all continents, usually in several seemingly unrelated places), the transition to civilization, stratification, and the state was comparatively rare. The European prehistorian Piggott declared; "All my study of the past persuades me that the emergence of what we call civilization is a most abnormal and unpredictable event, perhaps in all its Old World manifestations ultimately due to a single set of circumstances in a restricted area of western Asia some 5,000 years ago" (1965: 20). I argue in this chapter and the next that Piggott is only slightly overstating the case: Perhaps in Eurasia up to four peculiar sets of circumstances generated civilization. Elsewhere in the world we should add at least two more. Although we can never be precise as to an absolute total, it is probably under ten.

Other dissent focuses on the sequence of stages, noting the occurrence of backward or cyclical movement rather than a simple developmental sequence. Gathering confidence from dissent within biology, the citadel of evolutionism, some anthropologists suggest that social development is rare, sudden, and unpredictable, resulting from "bifurcations" and "catastrophes" rather than from cumulative, evolutionary growth. Friedman and Rowlands (1982) have been voicing doubts about their earlier evolutionism. I use their doubts, though departing from their model. Civilization, in the few cases of its independent evolution, was indeed a long, gradual, cumulative process, not a sudden response to catastrophe. Over the world as a whole, however, patterned change was cyclical – as they argue – rather than cumulative and evolutionary.

In this chapter I build on such dissent in two main ways, both of which will be developed further over the next chapters. First, general evolutionary theory may be applied to the Neolithic Revolution, but its relevance then diminishes. True, beyond that, we can discern further general evolution as far as "rank societies" and then, in some cases, to temporary state and stratification structures. But then general social evolution ceased. So much has also been argued by Webb (1975). But I go further and suggest that the further general processes were *"devolutions"* – movement back toward rank and egalitarian societies – and a *cyclical* process of movement around these structures, failing to reach permanent stratification and state structures. In fact, human beings devoted a considerable part of their cultural and organizational capacities to ensure that further evolution did *not* occur. They seem not to have wanted to increase their collective powers, because of the distributive powers involved. As stratification and the state were essential components of civilization, general social evolution ceased before the emergence of civilization. In the next chapter we see what did cause civilization; in later chapters we see that relations between civilizations and their noncivilized neighbors differed according to the point of the cycle reached by the latter when they encountered the influence of the former.

This argument is reinforced by a second. It returns us to the notion, discussed in Chapter 1, of "society" itself. This emphasizes boundedness, tightness, and constraint: Members of a society interact with one another but not, to anything like the same extent, with outsiders. Societies are limited and exclusive in their social and territorial coverage. Yet we find a discontinuity between civilized and noncivilized social groupings. Virtually no noncivilized groupings discussed in this chapter had or have such exclusivity. Few families belonged for more than a few generations to the same "society," or if they did, this was constituted by such looseness of boundaries as to be quite unlike historic societies. Most had choices available to them in their allegiances. The looseness of social bonds, and the ability to be free of any particular power network, was the mechanism by which the devolution mentioned above was triggered. In noncivilized societies escape from the social cage was possible. Authority was freely conferred, but recoverable; power, permanent and coercive, was unattainable.

This had a particular consequence when civilized cages did emerge. They were small – the city-state being typical – but they existed in the midst of looser, broader, but nonetheless identifiable, social networks that it is customary to call a "culture." We shall only understand these cultures – "Summer," "Egypt," "China," and so forth – if we remember that they combined earlier, looser relationships and the new, caged societies. That, too, is a task for later chapters.

So, in this chapter I set the scene for a later *history* of power. It will always be a history of particular places, for that has been the nature of the development of power. The general capacities of human beings faced with their earthly environment gave rise to the first societies – to agriculture, the village, the clan, the lineage, and the chiefdom – but not to civilization, stratification, or the state. Our thanks, or curses, for that are due to more particular historical circumstances. As these are the principal subject of this volume, I will skip quickly over the processes of general social evolution that preceded history. That is indeed a different story. All I do is recount the broad outline of the last stages of evolution and then demonstrate in more detail that it did come to an end. I adopt a distinctive methodology. In a spirit of generosity toward evolutionism, I first assume that it is correct, that the evolutionary story can be continued. We will then see most clearly the exact point in the narrative when it falters.

The evolution of the first settled societies

In the Neolithic and early Bronze ages, more extensive, settled, and complex forms of society gradually emerged out of the initial gatherer-hunting base. It was long drawn out, lasting in world-historical terms from about or before 10,000 B.C. to just before 3000 B.C. when we can discern civilized societies. Our knowledge is subject to the chance probing of the archaeologist's spade and the variable error ranges of carbon dating and other modern scientific techniques. The events span at least seven thousand years, longer than the whole of recorded history. So the narrative of the next three paragraphs is, perforce, breathless.

At quite unknown dates, a few confined and semipermanent settlements arose right across the world. Enough probable independent cases exist for us in interpret it as a general evolutionary trend. Many of the first settlements may have been communities of fishing people and flint miners, for whom settlement was not after all an extraordinary invention. It could then have been copied by others if they saw advantages in it.

The next stage occurred around 10,000 B.C. perhaps first in Turkestan or Southeast Asia, probably independently of one another. Labor was invested in cultivating and reaping plants from sown seeds and planted cuttings. In the Middle East this developed from harvesting wild barley and wheat. Modern writers have reconstructed the stages of this "discovery" of cultivation (Farb 1978: 108–22; Moore 1982). Whether it really happened this way is another matter. But the step seems the product of a slow association of intelligence, a drive toward increased rewards, opportunity, and trial and error – the normal components of evolution. Almost everywhere that agriculture emerged, hand-held wooden hoes tilled small, intensively cultivated gardens, grouped into settled villages. Most were not permanent. When the soil was exhausted, the village would move elsewhere. Perhaps at the same time animal husbandry appeared. Sheep and goats were domesticated in Iraq and Jordan around 9000 B.C., followed by other animals. There developed across Eurasia both specialized and mixed agricultural and herding groups, exchanging produce along long-distance trading tracks. Where trade routes, proximity to sources of flint and obsidian, and fertile land coincided, permanent settlement could result. By 8000 B.C. at Jericho, an older agricultural village had become a ten-acre settlement of mud-brick houses surrounded by fortifications. By 6000 B.C. these fortifications were stone. Giant water tanks, suggesting artificial irrigation, also existed – another step in an evolutionary tale. It could develop from observation and gradual improvement of nature's examples: Natural reservoirs after rains and floods can be artificially enhanced before water tanks and dams are developed; and the advantages of silt (as fertilized soil) provided by flooding can be adapted long before we arrive at the great silting achievements of the river-valley civilizations. The remains at Jericho and Catal Hayuk, in Anatolia, suggest fairly extensive and permanent social organization, with indications of ceremonial centers and extensive trading networks. But writing was not present, whereas population density (which might indicate whether they were what archaeologists mean by a "city") remains uncertain. We know nothing of any "state," but grave remains suggest little inequality among the inhabitants.

The wooden plow appeared, perhaps soon after 5000 B.C., followed by the cart and the potter's wheel. The extent and permanence of cultivated fields grew with the animal-drawn traction plow. Deeper soil nutrients could be turned over. Fields could be left fallow, turned over perhaps twice a year. Copper, gold, and silver were being exploited as luxuries by the fifth millennium. We find them in elaborate burial chambers and we deduce social differentiation and long-distance trade. The astonishing "megalithic" remains of Britain, Brittany, Spain, and Malta indicate complex social organization, large-scale management of labor, a knowledge of astronomy, and probably religious ritual during the period 3000–2000 B.C., probably developing independently of Near Eastern trends. But in this period, Near Eastern developments became crucial. Probably as a result of irrigation techniques, denser permanent settlements appeared in Mesopotamia, emerging into history around 3000 B.C. with writing, city-states, temples, stratification systems – in short, civilization.

This is the broad terrain I now examine in more detail. Evolutionary theory is plausible in the beginning of the story because the developments were widespread, seemingly independent, and, in enough cases, cumulative. When agriculture appeared, it continued to pioneer new techniques and organizational forms. Some areas may have returned to gathering-hunting, but enough did not to give the impression of irreversible development. Through it all was a drift toward greater *fixity* of settlement and organization, the core of the evolutionary story. Fixed settlement traps people into living with each other, cooperating, and devising more complex forms of social organization. The metaphor of a *cage* is appropriate.

So let us consider the least caged of human beasts, the gatherer-hunter. His or her freedom had two main aspects. First, shockingly to modern eyes, anthropologists have argued that contemporary gatherer-hunters live a life of ease. Sahlins (1974) has described the gatherer-hunter stage as the "original affluent society." Gatherer-hunters satisfy their economic wants and calorific requirements by working intermittently, on average three to five hours daily. Contrary to our image of "man the hunter," their diet may derive about only 35 percent from hunting, with 65 percent coming from gathering – though the former percentage probably increased in colder climates. This is still controversial, especially since in the 1970s feminists seized delightedly upon the findings to devise an alternative prehistoric label, woman the gatherer! I compromise with "gatherer-hunter." But the combination of hunting and gathering may produce a more balanced, nutritious diet than that found among either specialist agriculturalists or herders. Thus the transition to agriculture and herding may not have resulted in greater prosperity. And some archaeologists (e.g., Flannery 1974; Clarke 1979) broadly support the anthropological picture of affluence.

Second, their social structure was, and is, loose and flexible, permitting freedom of choice in social attachments. They are not dependent on specific other people for their subsistence. They cooperate in small bands and in larger units but, broadly, they can choose which ones. And they can disengage when they wish. Lineages, clans, and other kinship groupings may give a sense of identity but not substantial duties or rights. Nor is there much territorial constraint. Despite earlier anthropological accounts based on some Australian aborigines, most gatherer-hunters do not possess fixed territories. Given their social flexibility, it would be difficult for such collective property rights to develop anyway (Woodburn, 1980).

Within this overall flexibility, we can discern three or perhaps four social units. The first is the nuclear family of parents and dependent children. In a normal life span, persons will be members of two families, once as children, once as parents. It is tight, but impermanent. The second unit is the band, sometimes called the "minimum band," a group moving in close association, fulfilling subsistence needs through gathering and hunting in cooperation. This is a more or less permanent unit involving persons of all ages, although its tightness is seasonally variable. Its normal size range is 20–70 persons.[1] But

---

[1] For discussion of numbers, see Steward 1963: 122–50; Fried 1967: 154–74; Lee and DeVore 1968; and Wobst, 1974.

the band is not self-sufficient. Most particularly, its reproductive needs are not secured by such a small potential pool for finding fertile young adults as sexual partners. It requires regulated forms of marriage with other adjacent groups. The band is not a closed group but a loose congeries of nuclear families, occasionally attaining an overall collective life. Its size fluctuates. Outsiders often join a group with spare capacity. There may also be exchange of goods as gifts (or as a simple form of social regulation) if there is ecological diversity in an area.

The population within which such contacts occur is the third unit, variously called the "tribe," the "dialectical (in the linguistic, not the Hegelian sense!) tribe," or the "maximum band." This is a loose confederation, of 175–475 people, comprising a number of bands. Wobst (1974) puts the central range of this number at 7–19 bands. A favorable environment may push population above these levels, but the "tribe" then splits into two units that go their own way. Direct face-to-face communication among human beings may have practical upper limits. Above about 500 persons and we lose our ability to communicate! Gatherer-hunters are not literate and are dependent on face-to-face communication. They cannot use roles as shorthand communication, for they have virtually no means of specialization beyond sex and age. They relate as whole human beings differentiated only by age, sex, physical characteristics, and band membership. Their extensive powers would remain negligible until this was abandoned.

Was there a fourth wider "cultural" unit beyond that, as there was later after agricultural settlement? We suspect it because we are dealing with one human process. Exchange of goods, persons, ideas occurred, not intensively but extensively, linking together tenuously gatherer-hunters over large landmasses. There was an openness and flexibility about early social structure. Wobst (1978) claims that models of gatherer-hunters remain parochial. Despite evidence that gatherer-hunters were tied into continent-wide cultural matrices, there has been little study of regional and interregional processes. The "parish" of the ethnographer is an artifact of academic specialization and anthropological influence, he says, yet it becomes in research reports an actual "society," a bounded social unit, with its own "culture." The kinds of "society" that existed in prehistory were like nothing that any anthropologist today has seen. They had not yet filled out landmasses; they were not constrained by more advanced societies. Such peculiarities ensured that prehistoric groups were largely uncaged. "Mankind" has *not* "everywhere wandered in troops," despite Ferguson's famous assertion. The etymology of "ethnography" gives the game away. It is the study of *ethne,* peoples. Yet peoples, bounded kin groups, did not originally exist – they were created by history.

How the transitions to agriculture and to herding occurred is too controversial to be discussed here. Some writers emphasize pull factors of increased agricultural yields, others push factors of population pressure (e.g., Boserup

1965; Binford 1968). I will not attempt to adjudicate. I note only that the contending arguments are variants of a single evolutionary story. The general capacities of human beings, engaged in minimal forms of social cooperation and faced with widespread environmental similarities, led all over the world toward the agricultural and pastoral transformations we call the Neolithic Revolution. Greater settlement of larger socially and territorially trapped populations began. The scale and density of groupings increased. The small band disappeared. The larger, looser "tribe" was affected in two alternative ways. Either the rather weak unit of up to 500 now hardened into a permanently settled village, swallowing up the smaller 20–70-band unit, or the exchange process developed extensive but looser role specialization based on the extended kinship network – clans, lineage groups, and tribes. Locality or kin – or a combination of both – could offer organizational frameworks for denser, role-specialized social networks.

In prehistoric Europe, the egalitarian and largely nonspecialized village settlements comprised about 50–500 persons, usually living in nuclear family huts, working a maximum of about 200 hectares (Piggott 1965: 43–7). In the Near East, the upper limits may have been more normal. There is also ample evidence of large, looser tribal units in prehistory. Among Neolithic peoples in New Guinea today, according to Forge (1972), once the limit of 400–500 is reached, either settlements split or role and status specialization occurs. This is consistent with Steward's evolutionary theory of how growing groups found "socio-cultural integration" at a higher and more mixed level through the development of multilineage villages and loose clans (1963: 151–72). Horizontal and vertical cleavages allowed social groups to enlarge themselves in numbers.

Intensive exploitation of nature enabled permanent settlement and dense primary interaction of 500 persons instead of 50; role specialization and emerging authority permitted secondary interaction among numbers that were in principle limitless. Extensive societies, the division of labor, and social authority now began their human prehistory.

The emergence of stabilized relations of collective economic power

How salient were these first societies? That depends on how fixed they were, how trapped were the people inside them. Woodburn (1980, 1981) has argued that permanence in primitive societies is guaranteed if they are "delayed return," rather than "immediate return," "labour investment systems." Where a group invests labor in creating tools, stores, fields, dams, and so forth, whose economic returns are delayed, a long-term and in some respects a centralized organization is necessary to manage the labor, protect the investment, and apportion its yields. Let us consider the implication of three different types of delayed return labor investment.

The first is in nature, that is, in land and livestock – planted crops, irrigation ditches, domesticated animals, and the like. All imply territorial fixity. Animals' grazing grounds may vary, and crops, while seeds, are moveable, but with these exceptions, the greater the delayed return investment in nature, the greater the territorial fixity of production. Fixed plant horticulture commits a group, or at least its core members. "Slash-and-burn" commits a group for several years if they fertilize the soil by periodically burning tree stumps, and if they graze animals on the stubble. Then soil fertility declines. Some move elsewhere, to either repeat the process by deforestation or to find land with lighter soils. A whole group rarely moves as a unit, for its organization is attuned to the old ecology, not to either movement or the new one. Smaller family or neighbor groups, probably with younger people overrepresented, tend to split off. Permanent social organization does not result, as we will see later in this chapter.

Herders who move around, especially on steppe-type terrains, are less fixed. Yet herders acquire goods, equipment, and a variety of animals that are not easily portable; and they develop relations with agriculturists for cattle fodder, grazing on stubble, exchange of produce, and so forth. As Lattimore remarked, the only pure nomad is a poor nomad. Yet commitment to territory is not as great as in the case of agriculturists.

Both agriculturalists and pastoralists may be territorially bound for other reasons too. Proximity to raw materials like water, wood, or other groups' animals, or strategic location in exchange networks between different ecological niches, also bind people. Most binding of all is land that is naturally fertilized and can support permanent agriculture or herding – in river valleys, lakesides, and deltas subject to flooding and silting. Populations there are unusually committed to territory. Elsewhere the patterns vary more, but with some tendencies toward greater fixity than among gatherer-hunters.

Second, investment can be in the social relations of production and exchange, in the form of labor gangs, the division of labor, markets, and so forth. These tend to be socially rather than territorially fixed. Regular labor relations (without military force) require normative trust, found between people who are members of the same group – family, neighborhood, clan, lineage, village, class, nation, state, or whatever. This is truer for production than exchange relations because its cooperation is more intense. Normative solidarity is necessary to cooperation, and it tends to fix interaction networks and to foster a common ideological identity. Investment over a long period means a tighter shared culture among the generations, even among the living and the yet-to-be-born. It tightens the bonds of villages and of kin groups like clans into societies with temporal continuity.

But to what extent? Compared to gatherer-hunters, agriculturalists and pastoralists are more fixed. But again there is variability between ecologies and throughout time. Variations through the seasons, through the cycle of slash-and-burn (more cooperation in the tree-felling stage than later), and through other agricultural cycles support rather flexible cooperation. Again the caging extreme is the river-valley floodplain, provided that irrigation is possible. This requires cooperative labor effort far in excess of the agricultural norm, a point to which I return in the next chapter.

The third investment is in the instruments of labor, tools or machinery that are not part of nature and that in principle can be moved. For several millennia, tools tended to be small and portable. They fixed people socially and territorially not to large societies, but to the household or to the group of households rotating tools. In the Iron Age, discussed in Chapter 6, a revolution in tool making tended to reduce the size of existing societies.

Thus the effects of social investment were varied, but the overall trend was toward greater social and territorial fixity because of increasing exploitation of the land. Agricultural success was inseparable from constraint.

Yet if we add two other important trends, population pressure and a degree of ecological specialization, the picture becomes more complex. Few agriculturalists or herders have developed the full panoply of drastic steady-state birth-control measures seen among gatherer-hunters. Their subsistence surpluses have been periodically threatened by population surplus and soil erosion/disease "Malthusian cycles." Responses were fissions within groups, migrations of whole peoples, and perhaps more organized violence. These have contrary effects on social cohesion: The first weakens it, the second and third may strengthen it.

The effects of ecological specialization amid a developing agriculture are even more complex. Some believe that specialization encouraged greater division of labor within a society (exemplified by the theory of the "redistributive chiefdom" we will encounter later). If products are exchanged within a village or a kinship structure, commitment to a fixed organization of markets, storehouses, and so forth, is increased. Specialized roles and hierarchical statuses proliferate, and the division of labor and rank hierarchies intensify. But as size, specialization, diffusion, and exchange grew, the contactable world was always larger than could be organized practicably into one group. As the group stabilized, so too did intergroup relations. The difficulty of integrating plowed land with land used for herding encouraged the emergence of relatively specialized agricultural and herding groups. Thus the growth of *two* networks of social interaction, the "group" or "society" and the broader exchanging, diffusing network.

The emergence of collective ideological, military, and political power

This same duality appears in the emergence of ideological power – of more stabilized and extensive religions, and what archaeologists and some anthropologists call culture. Of religion we know very little from archaeology and more, though of uncertain historical relevance, from anthropology.

The evolutionary-caging approach is exemplified by Bellah (1970: 2–52). He delineates the main phases of religious evolution. The first two are relevant here. In his earliest phase, the primitive human ability to control life and environment, to do more than passively suffer, depends on the development of symbolic thought. This separates subject and object and leads to the ability to manipulate the environment. Primitive religion did this in rudimentary fashion. The mythical symbolic world was not clearly separated from either the natural world or human beings. Some religions merged a human clan, natural phenomena like rocks and birds, and mythical, ancestral persons in one totem classification, distinguishing it from similar configurations. Hence religious action was participation in this world, not action upon it. However, as the bounded social group emerged, a second phase appeared. Emergent regularities of economic, military, and political cooperation were conceived of as a *nomos,* a sense of the ultimate order and meaning of the cosmos. The gods were now located *within,* in a privileged relationship to the clan, lineage, village, or tribe. The divine was domesticated by the society. Durkheim's theory of religion, to be considered in later chapters, could now be applied: Religion was merely society "stretched ideally to the stars." As society became caged, so did religion.

But there are two defects of this argument. First, the anthropological record indicates that the divine may indeed become more social, but not more unitary. The gods of group A are not sharply separate from those of neighboring group B. There is overlap and often a loose and changing pantheon in which spirits, gods, and ancestors of adjacent villages and kin groups coexist in a competitive status hierarchy. In West Africa, for example, if a particular village or kin group increases its authority over its neighbors, its ancestors may become rapidly adopted as important personages within the latters' pantheon. This smacks of greater ideological flexibility and a dialectic between the small group and the larger "culture." Second, the archaeological record reveals that common artistic styles were usually much more extensive than any village or kin group. That surviving pottery, stone, or metal decorations were similar over large areas is of no great significance. But the same style of representing divine figures or figures representing humankind, life or death, points to a common culture over an area much bigger than that of authoritative social organizations. The spread of the "Beaker" style across most of Europe, of "Dong-son" in southeast Asia, or "Hopewell" in North America indicate extensive links of – what? Trade, probably; exchange of population in cross-migrations and wandering specialist artisans, perhaps; similarity of religion and ideology, perhaps; but it cannot have involved any substantial, formal, constraining *authoritative* organization. It was one of the earliest expressions of *diffused power.* In the next chapter, we shall see that the first civilizations comprised two levels: a small political authority, normally a city-state; and the larger "cultural" unit, for example, of Sumer or Egypt. The same dialectic emerges between two networks of social interaction, one small and authoritative, the other large and diffuse. Both were an important part of what we would wish to call "the society" of the time.

Thus ideological power patterns were less unitary, less caged than evolutionary theory implies. However, caging was increased by our third source of power, military power, also emerging in this period. The greater the surplus generated, the more desirable it was to preying outsiders. And the greater the fixity of investment, the greater the tendency to defend rather than to flee from attack. Gilman (1981) argues that in Bronze Age Europe capital-intensive subsistence techniques (the plow, Mediterranean polyculture of olives and grain, irrigation, and offshore fishing) preceded and caused the emergence of a "hereditary elite class." Their assets needed permanent defense and leadership.

This is not the moment to attempt to explain war. I merely note two points. First, war is ubiquitous to organized social life, even if not universal. We *can* find apparently peaceful social groups – and so a theory relating warfare to invariant human nature cannot be supported – but they are usually isolated, obsessed with a battle against nature at its harshest (like the Eskimo) or refugees from warfare elsewhere. In a quantitative study, only four out of fifty primitive peoples did not routinely engage in warfare. Second, comparative anthropology shows that its frequency, organization, and its intensity in lives killed, increase substantially with permanent settlement and, then again, with civilization. Quantitative studies reveal that half the warfare of primitive peoples is relatively sporadic, unorganized, ritualistic, and bloodless (Brock and Galtung 1966; Otterbein 1970: 20–1; Divale and Harris 1976: 532; Moore 1972: 14–19; Harris 1978: 33). But all civilizations of recorded history have engaged routinely in highly organized and bloody warfare.

Armed hostility between groups reinforces their sense of "in group" and "out group." It also intensifies objective distinctions: Economically specialized groups develop specialized forms of warfare. The weaponry and organization of early fighters derived from their economic techniques – hunters threw projectiles and shot arrows; agriculturalists wielded sharpened, modified hoes; herders eventually rode horses and camels. All used tactics consonant with their forms of economic organization. In turn these military differences increased their sense of general cultural distinctiveness.

The different forms of investment into military activities had broadly similar implications for the economy. Military investment in nature, for example, in fortifications, increased territoriality. One difference was that military investment in livestock (cavalry) generally increased mobility rather than fixity. Military investment in social relations, that is, in organization of supplies and coordination of movement and tactics, greatly intensified social solidarity. It also required normative morale. Military investment in the tools of war, weapons, tended at first to encourage individualistic combat and decentralize military authority.

Overall, the growth of military power reinforced the caging of social life. Thus the evolutionary story tends to center on certain economic power relations and on military power in general. These culminate in the emergence of the state, the fourth source of social power. As I have defined it, as centralized, territorialized, permanent, and coercive, the state was not original. It is not found among gatherer-hunters. The state's component elements are encouraged by social and territorial fixed investment, economic and military. This would complete the evolutionary story, linking together prehistory and history in one sequence of development. From gathering-hunting to the permanent, civilized state a continuous series of stages embody greater social and territorial fixity as the "price" of an increase in human powers over nature. Let us examine the rival evolutionary theories of the origins of stratification and the state.

Evolutionary theories of the origins of stratification and the state

Neither stratification nor the state was an original social form. Gatherer-hunters were egalitarian and stateless. Evolutionists argue that the transition to settled agriculture and herding heralded a slow, prolonged, connected growth in stratification and the state. Four types of evolutionary theory are considered here – *liberal, functionalist, Marxist,* and *militarist.* Rightly, they see as connected the two most important and baffling questions: (1) How did some acquire permanent power over the material life chances of others, giving them the capacity to acquire property that potentially denied subsistence to others? (2) How did social authority become permanently lodged in centralized, monopolistic, coercive powers in territorially defined states?

The nub of these issues is the distinction between authority and power. The evolutionary theories offer plausible theories of the growth of authority. But they cannot explain satisfactorily how authority was converted into power that could be used *either* coercively against the people who granted authority in the first place *or* to deprive people of the rights of material subsistence. Indeed, we shall see that these conversions did not happen in prehistory. There were *no* general origins of the state and stratification. It is a false issue.

Liberal and functional theories argue that stratification and states embody rational social cooperation, and so were originally instituted in a kind of "social contract." Liberal theory sees these interest groups as individuals with livelihoods and private-property rights. Thus private property preceded and determined state formation. Functional theories are more varied. I consider only the functionalism of economic anthropologists, with their emphasis on the "redistributive chiefdom." Marxists argue that states strengthen class exploitation and thus were instituted by the first property classes. Like liberalism, Marxist theory argues that private-property power preceded and determined state formation, but orthodox Marxism goes farther back and claims that in turn private property emerged out of originally communistic property. Finally, militarist theory argues that states and pronounced social stratification originated in conquest and the requirements of military attack and defense. All four schools argue with force, not to say dogmatism.

There are three puzzling aspects of their confidence. First, why should theorists who wish to make some point about the state today support it with a lightning raid into the wooded slopes of prehistory? Why should Marxism care anything about the origins of states in justifying a particular stance toward capitalism and socialism? It is not necessary to a theory of later states to demonstrate that the first states originated in this or that way. Second, the theories are reductionist, reducing the state to preexistent aspects of civil society. By maintaining continuity between origins and development, they deny that the state possesses *emergent* properties of its own. And yet "civil society" interest groups like social classes and armies are joined in the pages of history by states – chiefs, monarchs, oligarchs, demagogues, and their household staffs and bureaucracies. Can we deny autonomy to them? Third, anyone who examines empirical evidence concerning the earliest of states realizes that single-factor explanations belong to the kindergarten stage of state theory because origins are extremely diverse.

Of course, the theories were originally advanced when writers had little empirical evidence. Nowadays we have a wealth of archaeological and anthropological studies of early and primitive states, ancient and modern, all over the world. They force us to deal harshly with the theories' confident assertions, especially with those of liberalism and Marxism. This is especially so in the case of their reliance on the supposed importance of individual property in early societies.

I start with the weakest part of liberal theory – its tendency to locate social inequality in differences between individuals. Whatever the precise origins of stratification, they are *social* processes. Original stratification had little to do with the genetic endowment of individuals. Nor had any subsequent social stratification. The range of difference in the genetic attributes of individuals is not great, and it is not cumulatively inherited. If societies were ruled by human reasoning powers, they would be almost egalitarian in structure.

Far greater inequalities are found in nature, for example, between fertile and barren land. Possession of these differential resources will lead to greater power differences. If we combine chance occupation of land of varying qualities with different capacities for hard and skillful work, we arrive at the traditional liberal theory of the origins of stratification, found especially in the work of Locke. In the next chapter we see that in Mesopotamia chance occupancy of relatively fertile land may have been relevant. Also, perhaps a little support for Locke's emphasis on differences in diligence, industriousness, and thrift could be inferred from the evidence on gatherer-hunters. After all, if some of them did work eight hours instead of four they would have been rich in surplus (or double in population!). But things are not that simple. As studies of gatherer-hunters show, everyone in the group is entitled to share in unexpected surpluses, however produced. Thrift does not bring its bourgeois reward! That is one reason why entrepreneurial development projects among today's hunter-gatherers generally fail – no incentives exist for individual effort.

To keep a surplus, even one individually produced, requires social organization. It requires norms of possession. As these are adhered to imperfectly, it also requires armed defense. Also production is normally not individual but social. Thus the possession, use, and defense of natural resources are greatly affected by even the simplest practices of social organization: Three men (or three women) fighting or working as a team can normally kill or greatly outproduce three men acting as individuals, however strong the latter may be as individuals. Whatever the power in question – economic, military, political, or ideological – it is conferred overwhelmingly by social organization. Social, not natural, inequality is what matters – as Rousseau observed.

But Rousseau still concluded that stratification resulted from private property held by individuals. This is his famous statement: "The first man who fenced in an area and said, 'This is mine' and who found people simple enough to believe him, was the real founder of civil society." This does not dispose of the objections I have just mounted. Yet oddly enough, it has been adopted by what is supposed to be the main opposition to liberalism, socialism. Marx and Engels enshrined an antithesis between private and communal property. Stratification emerged as private-property relations grew out of an original primitive communism. Nowadays most anthropologists deny this (e.g., Malinowski 1926: 18–21, 28–32; Herskovits 1960). Studies of property, like that of Firth on the Tikopia (1965), show a myriad different ownership rights – individual; familial; age-, village-, and clan-banded. In what circumstances will private ownership develop far?

Groups vary in their property rights according to their forms of delayed return labor investment. The emergence of private unequal property is speedier if the investment is portable. The individual can possess it physically without having to exclude others by force. If the delayed-return investment is in portable tools (used perhaps to cultivate small plots intensively), then narrow property forms based on individual, or perhaps household, ownership may develop. At the other extreme is extensive labor cooperation. Here it is inherently difficult for individuals or households within the cooperating group to achieve exclusionary rights against others within the group. Land is variable in its implications. If worked in small plots, perhaps with great investment in tools, it may lead to individual or household ownership – although it is not easy to see how enormous inequalities develop rather than a group of roughly equal peasant properietors. If extensively worked through social cooperation, exclusionary ownership is not likely to occur.

But ecological specialization may take herders closer to private ownership. Their investment in nature is primarily in portable animals, penned into a particular terrain, surrounded with boundaries, normally not territorially fixed but guarded. Exclusionary rights are the norm among nomad herdsmen. These are reinforced by patterns of population pressure. If agriculturalists are threatened by pressure, then simple Malthusian controls will suffice. Some will starve and the death rate will rise until a new balance between resources and population is struck. This does not cause permanent damage to the main forms of investment, in land, buildings, tools, and social cooperation. But as Barth has demonstrated, herders must be sensitive to ecological imbalances between flocks and pastures. Their productive investment is in animals that must not be used up as food in difficult times. If they are eaten, virtually the whole group will perish later. Effective population controls must operate before the Malthusian cycle can occur. Barth argues that private ownership of herds is the best survival mechanism: Ecological pressures strike differentially, eliminating some families without affecting others. This would be impossible if collective equality prevailed and if authority were centralized (1961: 124).

Thus among herders, unlike other groups, an antithesis between private property and communal control exists. Differential population pressures may further inequalities and labor expropriation. A family surviving in prosperity amid the difficulties of others may take on free labor or serfs from the harder-hit families. Even this is not usually individual but family property arranged in a multilevel structure, "the genealogical clan." The clan and the family own property – the powers of individuals depend on their power within these collectivities.

Nowhere, therefore, do we find either individual or total-community property. Power in social groups is not a simple product of the sum of individuals multiplied by their different powers. *Societies are actually federations of organizations.* In stateless groups powerful individuals invariably represent some quasi-autonomous collectivity in a wider field of action – a household, an extended family, a lineage, a genealogical clan, a village, a tribe. Their powers derive from their ability to mobilize the resources of that collectivity. This is well-expressed by Firth:

There is an institution of property in Tikopia, supported by definite social conventions. It is expressed largely in terms of ownership of goods by kinship groups, but allows for some individual holding of smaller items, as well as for the rights of chiefs over certain types of goods such as land and canoes, and rights also over them by other members of the community as a whole. Decisions about the use of these goods in further production are taken in practice by the heads of the kinship groups – chiefs, elders, heads of families, senior members of a "house" – in consultation with other members of the group, so that in the case of the more important goods such as land and canoes "individual ownership" can only be expressed in degrees of responsibility for and enjoyment of the group property. [1965: 277–8]

The source of all hierarchy lies in representative authority that is not unitary.
But we still have some way to the end of the evolutionary path along which we are customarily guided. For this type of authority is extremely weak. The chiefs – for there are usually several of them ranged under the nominal headship of one – usually enjoyed negligible powers. The term *rank society* covers a whole phase of general social evolution (in fact, the last one!) in which power was almost totally confined to the use of "authority" on behalf of the collectivity. All this conferred was status, prestige. Elders, "bigmen," or chiefs could only with difficulty deprive others of scarce, valued resources, and they could never arbitrarily deprive others of subsistence resources. Nor did they possess great wealth. They might distribute wealth around the group, but they could not retain it. As Fried comments, "such persons were rich for what they dispensed and not for what they hoarded" (1967: 118). Clastres, reviewing Amerindians, denies the chief authoritative decision-making powers: He possesses only prestige and eloquence to resolve conflicts – "the chief's word carries no force of law." The chief is held "prisoner" in that confined role (1977: 175). Collective, not distributive, power is being exercised. The chief is its mouthpiece. This is a *functionalist* argument.

This overcomes one potential obstacle to the eventual emergence of pronounced inequalities – that of *permanence* of authority. If it is merely collective power, there is no problem as to who exercises it. The authority role will simply reflect the characteristics of the social structure beneath it. If age and experience are valued in decision making, then an elder may assume the role; if there is material acquisition by the nuclear family, a "bigman," defined by acquisitive abilities; if lineages are dominant, a hereditary chief.

Collective power antedated distributive power. Rank societies preceded stratified societies – and lasted for an enormous period of time. However, this merely puts forward in time our difficulty in explaining how egalitarian societies became inegalitarian in the distribution of scarce and valued resources, especially material resources. In later rank societies, according to the theories, how was consent to equality turned into consent to inequality, or, alternatively, how was consent overridden?

There is, as Clastres notes (1977: 172) one answer that *seems* simple and plausible: Inequality is imposed from outside by physical violence. This is the *militarist* argument. Group A subjugates group B and expropriates its property. It hands back to group B a return to labor, perhaps leasehold or serfdom rights, perhaps only slavery. At the turn of the century such a theory of the origins of stratification was popular. Gumplowicz and Oppenheimer were among those who argued that conquest by one ethnic group of another was the only way to economic betterment involving elaborate labor cooperation. Intensive production methods entailed expropriating the property rights of labor, which could be imposed only upon strangers, not upon one's "fellow-men" (the word having for Gumplowicz a kin-base; 1899 116–24; see also Oppenheimer 1975).

Nowadays we would modify this nineteenth-century racist theory to see ethnicity as much a *result* of such processes as a cause: Forcible conquest and enslavement produced ethnic sentiments. Ethnicity only offers an explanation of the dominance of one whole "people" or "society" over another whole people or society. This is only *one* type of stratification, not its totality; it is comparatively rare among primitive groups; and it may have been absent in prehistory where "peoples" did not exist. The most extreme forms of domination – total expropriation of rights to land, herds, and crops, and loss of control over one's own labor (i.e., slavery) – have generally followed conquest. Significant improvements in surplus acquisition have often come in *historical* societies from increasing the intensity of labor – usually requiring increased physical force. But this has not been universal. For example, the irrigation breakthroughs discussed in the next chapter seem not to have been based on increasing coercion through conquest, but on more "voluntary" means. We need an explanation of how military power might have "voluntary" effects.

Militaristic theory provides this in two ways. Both explain the origins of the state, the first its powers of organizing the conquered, the second the conquerors. Militarist theories start from one bold proposition: The state invariably *originated* in warfare. This was expressed by Oppenheimer:

The state, completely in its genesis essentially and almost completely during the first stages of its existence, is a social institution, forced by a victorious group of men on a defeated group, with the sole purpose of regulating the dominion of the victorious group over the vanquished, and securing itself against revolt from within and attacks from abroad. [1975: 8]

A loose association of raiders transformed itself into a permanent, centralized "state" with a monopoly of physical coercion, "when first the conqueror spared his victim in order permanently to exploit him in productive work" (1975: 27). The early stages, Oppenheimer believed, were dominated by one type of conquest, of sedentary agriculturalists by pastoral nomads. Various stages in the history of the state can be distinguished: from robbing and raiding to conquest and the foundation of the state, thence to a permanent means of collecting the surplus of the conquered, thence to the gradual merging of conquerors and conquered into one "people" under one set of state laws. This people and state is continually enlarged or reduced by victory or defeat in war throughout history. This process will only cease when one people and state will control the world. But then it will dissolve into an anarchist "Freemen's Citizenship." Without war, there is no need of the state.

Some of these ideas show the distinctive concerns of the late nineteenth century. Others reflect Oppenheimer's own anarchism. But the general theory has been periodically resurrected. Here, for example, is the sociologist Nisbet, confidently asserting that "there is no known historical instance of a political state not founded in circumstances of war, not rooted in the distinctive disciplines of war. The state is indeed hardly more than the institutionalization of the war-making apparatus" (1976: 101). Nisbet, like Oppenheimer, sees the state subsequently diversifying its activities, acquiring peaceful functions previously resident in other institutions like the family or religious organization. But in origin the state is violence against outsiders. Similar views are held by the German historian Ritter:

Wherever the state makes its appearance in history it is first of all in the form of a concentration of fighting power. National policy revolves around the struggle for power: the supreme political virtue is a ceaseless readiness to wage war with all its consequences of irreconcilable enmity, culminating in the foe's destruction, if necessary. In this view, political and military virtue are synonymous. . . .

Yet fighting power is not the whole of the state . . . it is essential to the idea of the state to be the guardian of peace, law and order. Indeed, this is the highest, the proper end of policy – to harmonize conflicting interests peaceably, to conciliate national and social differences. [1969: 7–8]

All these writers are expressing variants of the same view: The state originated in warfare, but human evolution carried it onward to other pacific functions.

In this refined model, military conquest settles down into a centralized state. Military force is disguised as monopolistic laws and norms administered by a state. Though the origins of the state lie merely in military force, it subsequently develops its own powers.

The second refinement concerns power among the conquerors. The great weakness so far concerns the organization of the conquering force: Doesn't this *already* presuppose inequality of power and a state? Spencer addressed this issue directly, arguing that *both* significant material inequality and a centralized state originated in the necessity for military organization. On the origins of the state, he is clear:

Centralized control is the primary trait acquired by every body of fighting men. . . . And this centralized control, necessitated during war, characterizes the government during peace. Among the uncivilized there is a marked tendency for the military chief to become also the political head (the medicine man being his only competitor); and in a conquering race of savages his political headship becomes fixed. In semi-civilized societies the conquering commander and the despotic king are the same, and they remain the same in civilized societies down to late times . . . few, if any, cases occur in which societies . . . have evolved into larger societies without passing into the militant type. [1969: 117, 125]

Centralization is a functional necessity of war, among *all* the combatants – conquerors, conquered, and those involved in inconclusive struggles. This is exaggerated. Not all types of military struggle require centralized command – for example, guerrilla warfare does not. But if the goal is either systematic conquest or the defense of whole territories, centralization is useful. Such armies' command structure *is* more centralized and authoritarian than is generally found in other forms of organization. And this helps achieve victory. Where victory or defeat may ensue in a matter of hours, speedy unfettered decision making and the unquestioned downward transmission of orders is essential (Andreski 1971: 29, 92–101).

As a true evolutionist, Spencer is inferring an empirical tendency, not a universal law. In a competitive struggle between societies, those that adopt the "militant" state have higher survival value. At times he takes this further, arguing that stratification itself owes its origin to warfare. At any rate, in such societies stratification and the mode of production are subordinate to the military: "The industrial part of the society continues to be essentially a permanent commissariat existing solely to supply the needs of the governmental-military structures, and having left over for itself only enough for bare maintenance" (1969: 121). This *militant society* is governed by "compulsory co-operation." Centrally, despotically regulated, it dominated complex societies until the emergence of industrial society.

Spencer's views are valuable even if his ethnography seems distinctly Victorian and his argument overgeneralized. There was no overall "militant" unity to historic societies, though in Chapters 5 and 9 I use the notion of compulsory cooperation in analyzing particular ancient societies.

But as an explanation of the origins of the state, Spencer's argument cannot go unchallenged. One particular aspect is rather glib, how military power becomes permanent. Granted his argument that battlefield and campaign coordination require central power, how does the military leadership keep its power afterward? Anthropologists tell us that primitive societies are actually well aware of what might follow and they take deliberate steps to avoid it. They are "assertively egalitarian," as Woodburn (1982) says. The powers of war chiefs are limited in time and scope, precisely so that military authority will not become institutionalized. Clastres (1977: 177–80) describes the tragedies of two war chiefs, one the famous Apache Geronimo, the other the Amazonian Fousive. Neither warrior, brave, resourceful, and daring as he was, could maintain his wartime preeminence during peacetime. He could have exercised permanent authority by leading perpetual war parties, but his people soon tired of war and abandoned him – Fousive to death in battle, Geronimo to write his memoirs. Spencer's model can only work for an extraordinarily successful military group.

Further, it is best suited to conquest, for then the conquered land, its inhabitants, and their surplus can be appropriated by the military leadership and distributed to the troops as rewards. In this case, the vital carryover of autonomy from the conqueror's society has been attained. The division of the spoils requires cooperation among the soldiery, but the home-base society can be disregarded. The spoils of war have supplanted its surplus as the infrastructure of military power. Here military power stems from occupying the power space between two societies, conquering and conquered, and playing off one against the other. This is also the opportunity in certain types of military defense. Where the outside threat persists, and where social fixity requires defense of a whole territory, then a specialized soldiery may be required. Their power is permanent, and their autonomy comes from playing off the attackers against the home-base society.

But conquest and specialized territorial defense are not generally found among primitive peoples. They presuppose considerable social organization, on the part of the conquerors, and also usually among the conquered. Conquest involves exploiting a stable, settled community using either its, or the conquerors', own organizational structures. Thus Spencer's model seems appropriate *after* the initial emergence of the state and social stratification, with far more organizational resources than those available to war leaders like Geronimo or Fousive.

Let us review the empirical evidence. I begin with a compendium of twenty-one case-studies of "early" states, some based on anthropology, others on archaeology, edited by Claessen and Skalnik (1978). No quantitative study of the origins of states can be properly statistical. There is no known overall population of original or "pristine" states – those that emerged autonomously from all other states. Thus one cannot sample from that population. However, such a population would be very small, probably well under ten and hardly a figure capable of statistical analysis. Therefore any larger sample of "early states," such as that of Claessen and Skalnik, is a sample of a heterogeneous and interacting population – a few "pristine" states and a large assortment of others involved in power relations with them and with each other. They are not independent cases. Any properly statistical analysis should include the nature of their interactions as a variable, which neither these authors nor any others have done.

With these considerable limitations in mind, let us turn to the data. Out of Claessen and Skalnik's twenty-one cases, only two (Scythia and Mongolia) took the form specified by Oppenheimer, the conquest of agriculturalists by pastoralists. In three others, state formation was caused by specialized military coordination against foreign attack. In another eight, other types of conquest were an important factor in state formation. And voluntary association for warlike purposes reinforced state formation in five of the abovementioned "conquest" cases. The general direction of these results is confirmed by another quantitative study (rather less detailed in vital respects, though more statistical in its methods) undertaken by Otterbein (1970) of fifty anthropological cases.

Thus by qualifying militarist theory to cover effects on *relatively organized* conquerors and/or defenders, we arrive at a largely single-factor account of a minority of cases (around a quarter) and an important contributory factor in a majority of cases. But this route presupposes a high degree of "almost-statelike" collective powers, with conquest or long-term defense adding only a final touch. How did they get that far?

It is difficult to penetrate far merely from the evidence of a number of cases that are presented as being independent when we knew that they involved long-term processes of power interaction. More promising is the regional study of East African governmental institutions undertaken by Mair (1977). Examining relatively centralized and relatively decentralized groups existing close to one another, she is better able to trace the transition. A single regional study is not a sample of all types of transition, of course. None of these were "pristine" states – all were influenced by the Islamic states of the Mediterranean as well as by the Europeans. In East Africa the characteristics of relatively prosperous herding peoples were also to the fore. Also *all* the transitions here involved a great deal of warfare. Indeed, the only improvement offered by the centralized over the noncentralized groups appears to have been better defense and attack prospects. But the form of the warfare takes us away from the simple conquerors-versus-conquered dichotomy (implying the conflict of two unitary societies) offered by militarist theory. Mair shows how relatively centralized authorities emerged out of a welter of federal crosscutting relationships between villages, lineages, clans, and tribes, characteristic of prestate human groups. As the surplus of the herders grew and their investment became more concentrated in herds, so did their vulnerability to loose federations of raiders. Thus, those who could best offer protection were often submitted to more or less voluntarily. This was not submission to a foreign conqueror or to a specialized group of warriors from one's own society, but to the authority figure of some collectivity to which the submissive group already had kin or territorial connections. It was a gigantic protection racket, embodying the same peculiar combination of coercion and community offered, for example, by the feudal lords of the European Middle Ages or by the New York Mafia. It did not usually lead to slavery or other extreme expropriation, but to the exaction of just enough tribute to give the military protector, an emerging king, resources to reward armed retainers, set up a court, improve communications, and (only in the most developed cases) engage in rudimentary public-works projects. This was, perhaps, the normal early militaristic route *toward* the state. Both organized conquest and systematic territorial defense were probably a much later route, presupposing this consolidating phase. We still need an explanation of the "middle phase," and actual emergence of pristine states.

Let us turn to economic power relations, and return to liberal and Marxist theory. Liberalism reduces the state to its function of maintaining order within a civil society that is essentially economic in nature. Hobbes and Locke provided a conjectual history of the state in which loose associations of people voluntarily constituted a state for their mutual protection. The main functions of their state were judicial and repressive, the maintenance of domestic order; but they saw this in rather economic terms. The chief aims of the state were the protection of life and individual private property. The chief threat to life and property came from within society. In the case of Hobbes, the danger was potential anarchy, the war of all against all; whereas for Locke a dual threat was posed by potential despotism and the resentment of the property-less.

As Wolin (1961: chap. 9) has observed, the tendency to reduce the state to its functions for a preexisting civil society permeated even the sternest critics of liberalism – writers like Rousseau or Marx. Thus liberal and Marxist theory of the origins of the state are both unitary and internalist, neglecting federal and international aspects of state formation. Both stress economic factors and private property. The difference is that one talks in the language of functionality, the other exploitation.

Engels in his *The Origins of the Family, Private Property and the State* argues that the original production and reproduction of real life contains two types of relationships, economic and familial. As the productivity of labor grows, so too do "private property and exchange, differences in wealth, the possibility of utilising the labour power of others, and thereby the basis of class antagonisms." This "bursts asunder" the old familial structure, and "a new society appears, constituted in a state, the lower units of which are no longer groups based on ties of sex, but territorial groups." He concludes, "The cohesive force of civilised society is the state, which in all typical periods is exclusively the state of the ruling class and in all cases remains essentially a machine for keeping down the oppressed, exploited class" (1968: 449–50, 581).

Liberal and Marxian views greatly overstate the salience of private property in early societies. But both can be modified to take account of this. Marxism's essence is not private property but *decentralized* property: The state emerges to institutionalize ways of extracting surplus labor already present in civil society. This can be easily transferred to clan- and lineage-based forms of appropriation, whereby one clan or lineage, or the elders or aristocracy in it, appropriates the labor of others. Fried (1967), Terray (1972), and Friedman and Rowlands (1978) have argued along these lines. This model dates significant differences in economic power (what it calls "stratification" or "classes") well before the emergence of the state, and it explains the latter in terms of the needs of the former.

Now it is true that a time lag exists between the emergence of authority differentials and the territorial, centralized state. States emerged out of associations of clans and lineages, in which an authority division between the clan, lineage, and village elite and the rest was evident. I called them rank, not stratified, societies, however, because they did not embody clear coercive rights or the ability to expropriate. In particular, their higher ranks were productive. Even chiefs produced or herded, combining manual and managerial economic functions. They had particular difficulty in persuading or coercing others to work for them. At this point the Marxian evolutionary tale has to give prominence to slavery, either from debt bondage or conquest. Friedman and Rowlands seem to accept Gumplowicz's militarist argument that the labor of kin cannot be expropriated, and they depend upon conquest factors – with all the defects I have commented on – for their explanation of the emergence of material exploitation.

Liberalism gives a functional explanation in terms of common economic benefits introduced by the state. If we drop the notion of private property, but retain the functional and the economistic principles, we arrive at the dominant explanation offered by contemporary anthropology, the *redistributive chiefdom,* a clearly *functional* theory. Here is Malinowski:

> Throughout the world we would find that the relations between economics and politics are of the same type. The chief, everywhere, acts as a tribal banker, collecting food, storing it, and protecting it, and then using it for the benefit of the whole community. His functions are the prototype of the public finance system and the organization of state treasuries of today. Deprive the chief of his privileges and financial benefits and who suffers most but the whole tribe? [1926: 232–3]

Perhaps we should not connect this with liberalism at all. For the principal developer of Malinowski's notion of the redistributive state was Polanyi, who argued long and polemically against the dominance of liberal market theory in our understanding of precapitalist economies. Liberal ideology has bequeathed to us the notion of the universality of market exchange. Yet Polanyi argued that markets (like private property) are recent. Exchange in primitive societies mainly takes the form of *reciprocity* "giving like for like," "vice versa" movements of goods, between two groups or persons. If that simple exchange were to develop into the generalized exchange characteristic of markets, then a measure of "value" would have to emerge. Goods could then be traded for their "value," which could be realized in the form of any other type of goods or in the form of credit (see several of the essays published posthumously in Polanyi 1977 – especially Chapter 3). But, characteristically – so argues Polanyi's "substantivist school" – in primitive societies this transitional point is approached, not by the development of "spontaneous" trading mechanisms but by the *authority* of kinship rank. Either the powerful kin leader lays down rules governing exchange or he makes gifts that create reciprocal obligations, brings in a following, and creates a large storehouse out of his dwelling. That storehouse is the location of the redistributive chiefdom and the state. Redistribution, Sahlins observes, is merely a highly organized version of kinship-rank reciprocity (1974: 209).

As this discussion has revealed, one liberal assumption permeates most versions of the redistributive state – the dominance of exchange over production, which is relatively neglected. However, it is simple to put this right – for in redistributive chiefdoms the chief is as involved in coordinating production as exchange. Thus, the chief emerges as the organizer of production and exchange where there is a high level of investment in collective labor, a factor whose importance I have repeatedly emphasized.

Let us add ecological specialization. It benefits adjacent specialists not only to exchange but also to coordinate their production levels. If there are at least three such groups coordination can center on an authoritative allocation of value to their products. Service (1975) pushes this to an explanation of early states. He argues that they coordinated territories containing different ''ecological niches.'' The chief organized redistribution of the various foodstuffs produced in each. The state was a warehouse, though the redistributive center also acted back along the chain of distribution to affect production relations. The route to generalized exchange and therefore to extensive ''property'' went through an incipient state. As redistribution increased the surplus, so too it heightened the power of the centralized state. This is an economistic, internalist, and functional theory of the state.

Clan, village, tribe, and lineage elites gradually enforced measures of value onto economic transactions. Authority became necessarily centralized. If it involved ecologically rooted peoples, it was territorially fixed. If it was to be accepted as a fair measure of value, it had to become autonomous of particular interest groups, to be ''above'' society.

Service offers numerous but unsystematic case-study materials to support his argument. In archaeology Renfrew (1972, 1973) has argued for the relevance of the redistributive chiefdom in prehistoric Europe in early Mycenaean Greece and megalithic Malta. In Malta, he argues from the size and distribution of the monumental temples, combined with the known capacities of the agricultural land, for the existence of many neighboring redistributive chiefdoms each coordinating the activities of between 500 and 2,000 people. He also finds such cases in anthropological reports of many Polynesian islands. Finally, he argues that civilization emerged through a growth in the powers of the chief toward the redistributive palace-temple complex, as in Mycenae and Minoan Crete.

This might seem impressive documentation, but in reality it is not. The main problem is that the notion of redistribution is highly colored by experience of our own modern economy. This is ironic, as Polanyi's principal mission was to liberate us from the modern market mentality! But whereas the modern economy involves systematic exchange of specialized subsistence goods, most primitive economies did not. If the United Kingdom or the United States today did not import and export a range of foodstuffs, raw materials, and manufactured goods, their economy and living standards would break down immediately and catastrophically. In Polynesia or prehistoric Europe exchanges were between groups who were not highly specialized. Generally they produced similar goods. The exchange was not fundamental to their economy. Sometimes they were exchanging similar goods for ritual purposes. Where they exchanged different, specialized goods these were not usually essential to subsistence, nor were they redistributed for individual consumption among the exchanging chiefs' peoples. More frequently they were used for personal adornment by the chiefs or they were stored and consumed collectively at festive, ritual occasions. They were "prestige," rather than subsistence, goods: Their display brought prestige to their distributor. Chiefs, elders, and bigmen vied in personal display and public feasts, "spending" their resources rather than investing them to produce further power resources and power concentration. It is difficult to see how long-term concentration of power would develop from this rather than short cyclical bursts of concentration, followed by overreaching and dispersal of power among rivals, before another cycle was started. After all, the people had an escape route. If one chief became overweening, they could switch allegiance to another. And this is true even in the few cases where we find genuine, specialized ecological niches and exchanges of subsistence produce. If the form of "society" that precedes the state is not unitary, why should the people develop only *one* storehouse rather than several competing ones? *How do the people lose control?*

These doubts are reinforced by the archaeological evidence. Archaeologists also find ecological niches to be the exception rather than the rule (Renfrew's Aegean examples are some of the principal exceptions). Over the landmass of prehistoric Europe, for example, we find few traces of storehouses. We find many burial chambers indicating a chiefly rank, because strewn with costly prestige goods – for example, amber, copper, and battle axes from the mid fourth millennium. In the same societies we dig up indications of great feasts, for example, the bones of a great number of pigs seemingly slaughtered at once. This evidence parallels the anthropological. The redistributive chiefdom was feebler than suggested by its first proponents, a characteristic of rank, not stratified societies.

None of the four evolutionary theories bridges the gap I set up at the beginning of this section. Between rank and stratified societies, and between political authority and the coercive state, is an unexplained void. This is also true of mixed theories. Those of Fried (1967), Friedman and Rowlands (1978) and Haas (1982) are probably the best eclectic evolutionary theories. They bring together all factors discussed so far to construct a complex and highly plausible story. They introduce the distinction between "relative rank" and "absolute rank." Absolute rank can be measured in terms of distance (usually genealogical distance) from absolute, fixed points, the central chief and through him, the gods. When ceremonial centers appear, absolute rank has also appeared, they say. But they produce no good arguments as to how ceremonial centers become permanent, how relative rank can be *permanently* converted into absolute rank, and thence *permanently, against resistance,* into stratification and the state. The unexplained void still exists.

Let us turn to archaeology, to see that the void existed in prehistory. All the theories are wrong because they presuppose a general social evolution that had, in fact, stopped. Local history now took over. We will see, however, that, after a pause that moves us into the realm of history, all those theories began to have local and specific applicability. We shall find them useful in later chapters, though not in their most ambitious guise.

From evolution to devolution: Avoiding the state and stratification

What we have puzzled over is how the people were constrained to submit to coercive state power. They would freely give collective, representative authority, to chiefs, elders, and bigmen for purposes ranging from judicial regulation to warfare to feast organization. Chiefs could thence derive considerable rank prestige. But they could not convert that into permanent, coercive power. Archaeology enables us to see that this was, indeed, the case. There was no swift or steady evolution from rank authority to state power. Such a transition was rare, confined to a very few, unusual cases. The crucial archaeological evidence is *time*.

Consider, for example, the prehistory of Northwest Europe. Archaeologists can delineate a vague outline of social structures from just after 4000 B.C. to just before 500 B.C. (when the Iron Age introduced massive changes). This is an extremely long passage of time, longer than the whole of the subsequent history of Europe. During this period, with one or two exceptions, western European peoples lived in relatively egalitarian or rank societies, not stratified ones. Their "states" have left no evidence of permanent, coercive powers. In Europe we can discern the dynamics of their development. I will discuss two aspects of the dynamic, one in southern England, one in Denmark. I have chosen western cases because they were relatively insulated from Near Eastern influence. I am well aware that had I chosen, say, the Balkans, I would be describing more powerful, near-permanent chiefdoms and aristocracies. But these cases were much influenced by the first civilizations of the Near East (see Clarke 1979b).

Wessex was one of the main centers of a regionally varied tradition of collective tomb building spreading after 4000 B.C. to include much of the British Isles, the Atlantic coast of Europe, and the western Mediterranean. We know of this tradition because some of its astonishing later achievements still survive. We still boggle at Stonehenge. It involved dragging – for there was no wheel – enormous 50-ton stones over land for at least 30 kilometers, and 5-ton stones over land and sea for 240 kilometers. To lift the largest stones must have required a labor force of 600. Whether the purpose of the monument was equally complex – in religious or calendrical terms – will be forever debated. But the labor coordination and surplus distribution to feed the laborforce *must* have involved considerable centralized authority – a "quasi-state" of some size and complexity. Though Stonehenge was the most monumental achievement of the tradition, it does not stand isolated, even today. Avebury, Silbury Hill (the largest earthwork in Europe), and a host of other monuments stretching from Ireland to Malta testify to powers of social organization.

But it was an evolutionary "dead-end." Monuments did not develop further, they stopped. We have no evidence of later comparable feats of centralized social organization in any of the main areas – Wessex, Brittany, Spain, Malta – until the arrival of the Romans, three millennia later. The dead end may have been paralleled elsewhere among neolithic peoples all over the world. The monuments of Easter Island are similar to those of Malta. Massive earthworks comparable to Silbury Hill dot North America. Renfrew speculates that they resulted from paramount chiefdoms similar to those found among the Cherokee Indians, where 11,000 people spread through about 60 village units, each with a chief, could be mobilized for short-term cooperation (1973: 147–66, 214–47). But something within this structure prevented its stabilization.

In the case of Stonehenge we know a little prehistory. I am gratefully dependent upon the recent work of Shennan (1982, 1983) and Thorpe and Richards (1983). They reveal a cyclical process. Stonehenge was occupied before 3000 B.C., but its greatest monumental period began around 2400. This stabilized and began again about 2000. Once again it stabilized, to be renewed, though less vigorously, before 1800 B.C. After that date the monuments were progressively abandoned, apparently playing no significant social role by 1500 B.C. But the monumental-based organization was not the only one in the area. The "Bell Beaker" culture spread from the continent just before 2000 B.C. (see Clarke 1979c for details). Its remains reveal a less centralized social structure and "aristocratic" burials containing "prestige goods" such as fine-quality ceramic ware, copper daggers, and stone wrist guards. These affected monumental activity but ultimately undermined and outlived it. Few now suggest that there were two different peoples involved – rather two principles of social organization coexisted among the same loose grouping. Archaeologists see monumental organization as absolute rank dominance by a centralized, lineage elite monopolizing religious ritual; and Beaker organization as relative rank dominance by decentered, overlapping lineage and bigmen elites with lesser authority based on the distribution of prestige goods. Of course, talk of lineages and bigmen is guesswork, based on analogical reasoning from modern Neolithic peoples. It may be that the monumental culture was not lineage-centered at all. It is equally plausible to regard it as a centralized form of primitive democracy in which ritual authority was held by village elders.

But such quibbles cannot obscure the central point. In competition between relatively centralized and decentralized authority, the latter won out, despite the astonishing powers of collective organization of the former. Authority never did consolidate into a coercive state. Instead it fragmented into lineage and village groups whose elites' own authority was precarious. This was not accompanied by social decay. The people mildly prospered. Shennan (1982) suggests that decentralization among the European peoples as a whole was a response to increasing long-distance trade and the circulation of prestige goods. Their distribution enhanced inequality and authority, but not of a permanent, coercive, centralized type.

In other regions prehistoric cycles can be found even in the absence of great monuments. But, curiously, the most illuminating discussions occur in the work of writers who are divided in their attitude toward evolutionism. On the one hand, they are concerned to attack unilinear notions of evolution. On the other, they are influenced by Marxian evolutionary accounts centered on "modes of production." I present their model before criticizing it. Friedman and Rowlands in various articles have outlined prehistorical development in general, whereas Kristiansen (1982) has applied it to one part of the European archaeological record, northwestern Zealand (in modern Denmark).

Friedman starts from current orthodoxy: Social structures among settled peoples were at first egalitarian, with elders and bigmen exercising only weak consensual authority. As agricultural production intensified, they acquired distributive rights over more surplus. They institutionalized this through feasting, personal display, and ritual contact with the supernatural, into chiefly ranked authority. They now organized the consumption of much of the surplus. Marriage alliances extended the authority of some chiefs over a greater space. Then Friedman adds a Malthusian element: When territorial expansion was blocked by natural boundaries or other chiefs, population grew faster than production. This increased population density and settlement hierarchies. This increased the centralized authority of the major chiefs. But in the long run this was undermined, by both economic success and economic failure. The development of interregional trade could break the Malthusian cycle. But the chief could not control this. Secondary settlements became more autonomous, their aristocracies becoming rivals to the old paramount chief. Economic failure, for example, through soil erosion also fragmented authority. Failure led to cycles, success to development. Competing settlements become more urbanized and monetarized: City-states and civilizations emerged and, with them, private-property relations. In their 1978 article, Friedman and Rowlands emphasized the developmental process. Subsequently they have seen that as rarer than the cycle. But their solution is that "in the last instance" (to quote Engels) development breaks through cyclical processes, perhaps suddenly and unexpectedly, but nevertheless as an epigenetic process (Friedman 1975, 1979; Rowlands 1982).

The bogs of Zealand offer fertile soil for the archaeologist. Kristiansen analyzes their results in terms of the above model. From about 4100–3800 B.C. slash-and-burn agriculturalists cleared the forests, grew cereals, and fenced in cattle. They engaged in little trade, and their graves reveal only limited differences of rank. But success led to population growth and to large-scale forest clearings. Between 3800 and 3400 B.C. more permanent and extensive settlements appeared, dependent on agricultural improvements and more complex social and territorial organization. The familiar remains of rank societies now appear – ritual feasting and elite burials of prestige goods. Up to 3200 B.C. this intensified. Megaliths and causewayed camps were built, centered upon chiefly authority. The productivity of cleared forest land was high and wheat strains relatively pure. Amber, flint, copper, and battle axes (prestige goods) circulated more widely. Stable chiefdoms were appearing for the first time in northern Europe. The state seemed on its way.

But between 3200 and 2300 B.C., the territorial chiefdoms disintegrated. Megaliths, communal rituals, fine pottery, and prestige goods declined, and interregional exchange ceased. Graves are single burials of men and women in small local lineage or family mounds. Battle axes predominate, their widespread dispersal indicating the end of chiefly control over violence. A segmentary clan structure probably predominated. Kristiansen explains this decline in material terms. The ex-forest soils were exhausted, and many people shifted from settled agriculture to pastoralism, fishing, and hunting. They developed a more mobile, less controllable way of life. Greater competition for the remaining fertile land broke up larger territorial chiefdoms. Many families migrated to lighter virgin soils on heathland in central Jutland and elsewhere, opening up extensive but sparsely settled forms of life. The wheel and the wagon were introduced, enabling basic communication and some degree of trade, but chiefly powers were inadequate to control such areas. Up to about 1900 B.C. economic recovery took place within this egalitarian structure. A mixed economy of light and heavy soils, and of agriculture, pastoralism, and fishing, increased the surplus and stimulated interregional trade. Yet no one could monopolize this trade, and prestige goods circulated widely.

Around 1900 B.C. a second chiefly ascent began, revealed again in remains of feastings, chiefly graves, and craftsmanship in prestige goods. Up to about 1200 B.C. hierarchies widened. Central chiefly settlements of considerable size controlled craft production, local exchange, and ritual. Kristiansen attributes this to the introduction of metal artifacts: Bronze, relatively rare, high in value, could be monopolized by chiefs. This was rather like the chiefly monopoly of prestige goods in Polynesia, he says. But around 1000 B.C., there occurred a check, due perhaps to a shortage of metal. Agricultural production was still intensifying, but the display of wealth in burials now reduced, as did settlement hierarchy.

Then, in the transition to the Iron Age, rank chiefly society collapsed, more fully than the first time. Settlement extended into the heaviest, hitherto virgin soils, and chiefly authority could not follow. A more egalitarian structure developed, organized in autonomous local settlements. The village, not the tribe, predominated. In this area (unlike, e.g., Mesopotamia) the village broke through the cyclical processes, transforming the whole system toward the sustained social development of the Iron Age. We shall rejoin these people, at that point, in Chapter 6.

Such a brief summary of bold historical generalizations doubtless contains errors and oversimplifications. Two and a half millennia have just been summarized! Nevertheless, this constructed history is *not* one of the evolution of social stratification or the state. Development was not from egalitarian to rank to stratified societies or from equality to political authority to coercive state power. Movement "back" from the second "stage" to the first was as frequent as from first to second, and indeed the third stage, if reached at all, was not long stabilized and institutionalized before collapsing. A second more tentative conclusion throws doubt even on Kristiansen's residual economic evolutionism. His own estimates of the economic productivity of each period, in terms of hectares per barrel of hard corn, must obviously be crude and approximate. But they reveal an increase throughout the whole period of about 10 percent, hardly impressive. Obviously the Iron Age did then lead to sustained development. But it was not largely indigenous to Europe. I argue in Chapter 6 that iron developed mainly in response to the influence of Near Eastern civilizations. For Europe it was as much a deus ex machina as part of an epigenesis. Europe saw more of the cycle than the dialectic.

And, to be fair, this is the general direction in which Friedman and others have taken their arguments. Friedman (1982) noted that Oceania cannot have passed through the traditional egalitarian–rank-stratification stages. Within Oceania, Melanesia is the older, more productive region, yet it "regressed" from chiefs to bigmen. East Polynesia is economically the poorest, most starved of long-distance trade, yet came closest to coercive states. Friedman formulates essentially cyclical models of the various regions of Oceania, centering on "bifurcations," thresholds that produce a rapid transformation of the whole system when confronted by the unanticipated consequences of its own developmental tendencies. Examples would be those changes of direction already described in prehistoric Europe. He concludes that evolution is essentially blind and "catastrophic" – it results from sudden, unanticipated bifurcations. Perhaps it was only in a few accidental bifurcations that the state, stratification, and civilization developed.

Indeed, we have found much to support this. Most of the prehistory of society saw no sustained movement toward stratification or the state. Movement toward rank and political authority seems endemic but reversible. Beyond that, nothing sustained.

But we can go farther to identify the cause of the blockage. If most societies have been cages, the doors have been left unlocked for two main actors. First, the people have possessed freedoms. They have rarely given away powers to elites that they could not recover; and when they have, they have had opportunity, or been pressured, to move away physically from that sphere of power. Second, elites have rarely been unitary: Elders, lineage heads, bigmen, and chiefs have possessed overlapping, competitive authorities, viewed one another suspiciously, and exercised those same two freedoms.

Hence there have been two cycles. Egalitarian peoples can increase intensity of interaction and population density to form large villages with centralized, permanent authority. But they stay broadly democratic. If the authority figures become overmighty, they are deposed. If they have acquired resources such that they cannot be deposed, the people turn their backs on them, find other authorities, or decentralize into smaller familial settlements. Later, centralization may begin again, with the same outcomes. The second pattern involves more extensive, but less intensive, cooperation in extended lineage structures, typically producing the chiefdom rather than the village. But here, too, allegiance is voluntary, and if the chief abuses this, he is resisted by the people and rival chiefs.

Both patterns presuppose a less unitary form of social life than theorists have generally assumed. It is important to liberate ourselves from modern notions of society. Though it is true that prehistory did show a trend toward *more* territorially and socially fixed social units, the prehistoric terrain did not consist of a number of discrete, bounded societies. Social units overlapped, and in the areas of overlap authority figures and others could *choose* membership in alternative social units. The cage was not yet closed.

Thus stabilized, permanent, coercive states and stratification systems did not generally emerge. Let me explain this a little more fully, for it might seem contradicted by, for example, Mair's East African regimes, which she calls states. True, village heads and chiefs perform useful centralized roles. If efficient, they can acquire considerable authority. This occurred all over Africa, as Cohen, a contributor to the Claessen and Skalnik (1978) volume, demonstrates. Cohen notes the minimal coercive powers they possessed and argues that they were merely more centralized versions of prestate lineage authorities. Compliance was largely voluntary, based on a desire for greater efficiency in dispute regulation, marriage arrangements, collective labor organization, the distribution and redistribution of goods, and common defense. Dispute and marriage regulation may be more important chiefly activities than redistributive economies or coordinated military functions, normally requiring a higher level of social organization. The chief can exploit his functionality. The most successful can make despotic claims. They can even acquire surplus to pay armed retainers. This happened in East Africa, and it must have happened countless times in the prehistory of society in all continents.

But what is *not* general is the despot's ability to institutionalize coercive power, to make it permanent, routine, and independent of his personality. The weak link is that between the king together with his retainers and kinsmen on the one hand and the rest of society on the other. The link is dependent on the personal strength of the monarch. There are no stabilized institutions routinely transferring it to a successor. Such succession rarely occurs, and almost never beyond a couple of generations.

We have good information on the Zulu kingship (though there was influence from more advanced European states). A remarkable man of the Mtetwa branch of the Ngoni people, Dingiswayo, was elected its chief, having learned of more advanced European military techniques. He created disciplined regiments and acquired chiefly paramountcy throughout northeastern Natal. His military commander was Shaka, from the Zulu clan. On Dingiswayo's death, Shaka had himself elected paramount chief, inflicted repeated defeats on surrounding peoples, and received the submission of those who stayed. Then he met the British Empire and was crushed. But his empire could not have endured. It remained a federal structure in which the center lacked autonomous power resources over its clients.

In areas where the modern colonial empires found great chiefs like Shaka, they found *two* levels of authority. Beneath the Shakas were minor chiefs. In East Africa these "client" chiefs have been documented extensively by Fallers (1956) and Mair (1977: 141–60). Each client chief was a replica of his superiors. When the British entered Uganda they delegated administrative authority to at first 783 and then 1,000 chiefs. Now, on the one hand, this amounts to power space for the forceful would-be monarch: Locality can be played off against locality, client against client, clan against village, chiefs, elders, bigmen, and so forth, against people. It is in this multilayered, decentralized struggle that the chief can exploit his centrality. But on the other hand, the client chiefs can play the same game. The monarch must bring them to court, to exercise personal control over them. But now they, too, acquire the advantage of centralization. It is not a way forward to the institutions of the state, but to an endless cycle of intriguing aspirant rulers, the rise of a formidable despot, and the collapse of his or his son's "empire" in the face of a rebellion of intriguing chiefs. Choice of authority network undermined the emergence of the social cage represented by civilization, stratification, and the state.

This cycle is an example of the extended kin variant form of rank society. A second cycle would be characteristic of the village variant form: toward greater central authority with the capacity to manage, at its peak, Stonehenge-type structures, then overextension and fragmentation toward more decentralized households. Perhaps most common would be a mixed type where village and kin intermingled, the dynamic of their intermingling added to the hierarchical dynamic. A good example would be the political systems of Burma, described by Leach (1954), in which hierarchical and egalitarian local political systems coexist and oscillate, the presence and influence of both preventing any single type of stratification from becoming thoroughly institutionalized.

Perhaps the Shakas and the Geronimos were the dominant personalities of prehistory. But they did not found states or stratification systems. They lacked sufficient caging resources. In the next chapter we will see that where those resources developed this was the result of local sets of circumstances. *No general social evolution occurred beyond the rank societies of early, settled neolithic societies.* We must now move to local history.

Bibliography

Andreski, S. 1971. *Military Organization and Society.* Berkeley: University of California Press.

Barth, F. 1961. *Nomads of South Persia.* Oslo: University Press.

Bellah, R. 1970. Religious evolution. In his book *Beyond Belief.* New York: Harper & Row.

Binford, L. 1968. Post-Pleistocene adaptations. In S. Binford and L. Binford, *New Perspectives in Archeology,* Chicago: Aldine.

Bloch, M. 1977. The disconnections between power and rank as a process: an outline of the development of kingdoms in central Madagascar. *Archives Européennes de Sociologie,* 18.

Boserup, E. 1965. *The Conditions of Agricultural Growth.* Chicago: Aldine.

Brock, T., and J. Galtung. 1966. Belligerence among the primitives: a reanalysis of Quincy Wright's data. *Journal of Peace Research,* 3.

Claessen H., and P. Skalnik. 1978. *The Early State.* The Hague: Mouton.

Clarke, D. L. 1979a. Mesolithic Europe: the economic basis. In *Analytical Archaeologist: Collected Papers of David L. Clarke.* London: Academic Press.

1979b. The economic context of trade and industry in Barbarian Europe till Roman times. In ibid.

1979c. The Beaker network – social and economic models. In ibid.

Clastres, P. 1977. *Society against the State.* Oxford: Blackwell.

Divale, W. T., and M.Harris. 1976. Population, warfare and the male supremacist complex. *American Anthropologist,* 78.

Engels, F. 1968. The origins of the family, private property and the state. In K. Marx and F. Engels, *Selected Works.* London: Lawrence and Wishart.

Fallers, L. A. 1956. *Bantu Bureaucracy.* Cambridge: Heffer.

Farb, F. 1978. *Humankind.* London: Triad/Panther.

Firth, R. 1965. *Primitive Polynesian Economy,* 2d ed. London: Routledge.

Flannery, K. V. 1974. Origins and ecological effects of early domestication in Iran and the Near East. In *The Rise and Fall of Civilizations,* ed. C. C. Lamberg-Karlovsky and J. A. Sabloff. Menlo Park, Calif.: Cummings.

Forge, A. 1972. Normative factors in the settlement size of Neolithic cultivators (New Guinea). In *Man, Settlement and Urbanism,* P. Ucko et al. London: Duckworth.

Fried, M. 1967. *The Evolution of Political Society.* New York: Random House.

Friedman, J. 1975. Tribes, states and transformations. In *Marxist Analyses and Social Anthropology,* ed. M. Bloch. London: Malaby Press.

1979. *System, Structure and Contradiction in the Evolution of "Asiatic" Social Formations.* Copenhagen: National Museum of Denmark.

1982. Catastrophe and continuity in social evolution. In C. Renfrew et al., eds., *Theory and Explanation in Archaeology.* New York: Academic Press.

Friedman, J., and M. Rowlands. 1978. *The Evolution of Social Systems.* London: Duckworth.

Gilman, A. 1981. The development of social stratification in Bronze Age Europe. *Current Anthropology,* 22.

Gumplowicz, L. 1899. *The Outlines of Sociology.* Philadelphia: American Academy of Political and Social Sciences.

Haas, J. 1982. *The Evolution of the Prehistoric State*. New York: Columbia University Press.

Herskovits, M. J. 1960. *Economic Anthropology*. New York: Knopf.

Kristiansen, K. 1982. The formation of tribal systems in later European pre-history: northern Europe 4000 B.C.–500 B.C. In Renfrew et al., eds., *Theory and Explanation in Archaeology*. New York: Academic Press.

Leach, E. 1954. *Political Systems of Highland Burma*. London: Athlone Press.

Lee, R., and J. DeVore. 1968. *Man the Hunter*. Chicago: Aldine.

Mair, L. 1977. *Primitive Government*. Rev. ed. London: Scolar Press.

Malinowski, B. 1926. *Crime and Custom in Savage Society*. London: Kegan Paul.

Moore, A. M. T. 1982. Agricultural origins in the Near East: model for the 1980s. *World Archaeology*.

Nisbet, R. 1976. *The Social Philosophers*. St. Albans: Granada.

Oppenheimer, F. 1975. *The State*. New York: Free Life Editions.

Otterbein, K. 1970. *The Evolution of War. A Cross-Cultural Study*. N.p.: Human Relations Area Files Press.

Piggott, S. 1965. *Ancient Europe: From the Beginning of Agriculture to Classical Antiquity*. Edinburgh: Edinburgh University Press.

Polanyi, K. 1977. *The Livelihood of Man,* essays ed. H. W. Pearson. New York: Academic Press.

Redman, C. L. 1978. *The Rise of Civilization*. San Francisco: Freeman.

Renfrew, C. 1972. *The Emergence of Civilisation: The Cyclades and the Aegean in the Third Millennium B.C.* London: Methuen.

    1973. *Before Civilization: The Radiocarbon Revolution and Prehistoric Europe*. London: Cape.

Ritter, G. 1969. *The Sword and the Sceptre. Volume I: The Prussian Tradition 1740– 1890*. Coral Gables, Fla.: University of Miami Press.

Roberts, J. 1980. *The Pelican History of the World*. Harmondsworth, England: Penguin Books.

Sahlins, M. 1974. *Stone Age Economics*. London: Tavistock.

Sahlins, M., and E. Service. 1960. *Evolution and Culture*. Ann Arbor: University of Michigan Press.

Service, E. 1975. *Origins of the State and Civilization*. New York: Norton.

Shennan, S. 1982. Ideology and social change in Bronze Age Europe. Paper given to Patterns of History Seminar, London School of Economics, 1982.

    1983. Wessex in the Third Millennium B.C. Paper given to Royal Anthropological Institute Symposium, Feb. 19, 1983.

Sherratt, A. 1980. Interpretation and synthesis – a personal view. In *The Cambridge Encyclopedia of Archaeology*, ed. A. Sherratt. Cambridge: Cambridge University Press.

Spencer, H. 1969. *Principles of Sociology*. One-volume abridgement. London: Macmillan.

Steward, J. 1963. *Theory of Culture Change*. Urbana: University of Illinois Press.

Terray, E. 1972. *Marxism and "Primitive Societies": Two Studies*. New York: Monthly Review Press.

Thorpe, I. J., and C. Richards. 1983. The decline of ritual authority and the introduction of Beakers into Britain. Unpublished paper.

Webb, M. C. 1975. The flag follows trade: an essay on the necessary interaction of military and commercial factors in state formation. In *Ancient Civilisation and Trade*, ed. J. Sabloff and C. C. Lamberg-Karlovsky. Albuquerque: University of New Mexico Press.

Wobst, H. M. 1974. Boundary conditions for paleolithic social systems: a simulation approach. *American Antiquity*, 39.

1978. The archaeo-ethnology of hunter-gatherers: the tyranny of the ethnographic record in archaeology. *American Antiquity*, 43.

Wolin S. 1961. *Politics and Vision*. London: Allen & Unwin.

Woodburn, J. 1980. Hunters and gatherers today and reconstruction of the past. In *Soviet and Western Anthropology*, ed. E. Gellner. London: Duckworth.

1981. The transition to settled agriculture. Paper given to the Patterns of History Seminar, London School of Economics, Nov. 17, 1981.

1982. Egalitarian Societies. *Man*, new series 17.

3 The emergence of stratification, states, and multi-power-actor civilization in Mesopotamia

Introduction: civilization and alluvial agriculture

The argument of the last chapter was somewhat negative: The emergence of civilization was not an outgrowth of the general properties of prehistoric societies. This appears to be immediately supported by the fact that it happened independently only a few times – probably on six occasions, perhaps as rarely as three or as frequently as ten. Yet it has long been believed that there was something of a common pattern among these cases, centering on the presence of alluvial agriculture. So was the emergence of civilization, together with its concomitant features of social stratification and the state, more than a historical accident? Even if the cases were few, were they patterned? I will argue that they were. Identifying the pattern, and its limitations, is the purpose of this chapter and the next.

We can never exactly define what we mean by "civilization." The word has too much resonance, and the prehistoric and historic record is too varied. If we focus on a single supposed characteristic of civilization, we get into difficulties. Writing, for example, is characteristic of peoples we intuitively regard as civilized. It is a perfect indicator of "history" rather than "prehistory." But it is also found, in rudimentary form, in prehistoric southeastern Europe, unaccompanied by the other usual appurtenances of civilization. The Incas of Peru, generally thought of as "civilized," did not have writing. Urbanization, also general to "civilization," does not give us a perfect indicator. The early cities of Mesopotamia may have been rivaled in population size, if not quite in density, by prehistoric village settlements. No single factor is a perfect indicator of what we mean. This is the first reason why civilization is usually defined in terms of extensive lists of characteristics. The most famous is Childe's (1950) list of ten: cities (i.e., greatly enlarged size and density of settlement); full-time specialization of labor; social concentration of surplus management into "capital"; unequal distribution of the surplus and the emergence of a "ruling class"; state organization based on residence rather than kinship; growth of long-distance trade in luxuries and necessities; monumental buildings; a standardized, naturalistic artistic style; writing; and mathematics and science. This is often criticized (e.g., Adams 1966) because it is just a list of disconnected items, useful only as a description of stages, not as an explanation of processes. Nevertheless, these characteristics do clus-

73

ter together in "civilizational complexes." If there was a "civilized whole," what was its essential character?

Here I follow Renfrew. He notes that Childe's list consists of *artifacts.* They interpose human-made objects between human beings and nature. Most attempts to define civilization center on the artifact. Thus Renfrew defines civilization as *insulation from nature:* "It seems logical to select as criteria the three most powerful insulators, namely ceremonial centres (insulators against the unknown), writing (an insulation against time), and the city (the great container, spatially defined, the insulator against the outside)" (1972: 13). Note the similarity of the metaphor to the social-cage metaphor. Civilization was a complex whole of insulating and caging factors emerging fairly suddenly together.

Taking Renfrew's three characteristics as our proxy indicator, only a few cases of the emergence of civilization were autonomous. So far as we know, there were four literate, urban, and ceremonially centered groups that seem to have arisen independently of each other in Eurasia: the Sumerians of Mesopotamia; the Egyptians of the Nile Valley; the Indus Valley civilization in present-day Pakistan; and the people of several North China river valleys, beginning with the Yellow River. Only the earliest, Sumer, is *certainly* independent, and so there has been periodic interest in diffusion and conquest theories of the other cases. However, the present consensus among specialists is to accord all four probable independent status. To these some add a fifth, the Minoans of Crete, though this is disputed. If we turn to other continents we can, perhaps, add two further cases, the pre-Columbian civilizations of Mesoamerica and Peru,[1] probably not in contact with one another, and independent of Eurasia. This makes a probable total of six independent cases. However, no two authors agree on exact numbers. For example, Webb (1975) also adds Elam (adjacent to Mesopotamia; discussed later in this chapter) and the lake region of East Africa, not included here. Other civilizations probably interacted with these established civilizations or their successors. Thus civilization is not a matter for statistical analysis. Given the uniqueness of societies, we might be unable to establish *any* generalizations on the basis of such a small number!

However, one feature of almost all the cases stands out: They arose in river valleys and practiced *alluvial agriculture.* In fact, most went farther, artificially *irrigating* their valley land with flood water. In contrast to prehistory, in which development occurred in all manner of ecological and economic situations, history and civilization might seem a product of one particular situation: alluvial and perhaps also irrigation agriculture.

Even after most of the cases mentioned spread out further, their core long

[1]Assuming that the ancient Peruvians possessed a functional equivalent to writing in their unique quiypu system (see Chapter 4).

remained in the irrigated river valleys. The Indus Valley civilization spread around the western coasts of Pakistan and India but remained centered on its single river until its collapse. Egypt remained confined to the Nile for far longer, from 3200 to 1500 B.C., when it developed an expansionist policy. During this period only its length along the river varied. Even thereafter its power base still lay on the banks of the Nile. China developed ramified territories, but its economic and strategic core lay on the loess soil of the irrigated North China plain. The Sumerian, the Akkadian, the old Assyrian, and the Babylonian empires centered on the Tigris and (mainly) the Euphrates from 3200 to 1500 B.C. All these cases sparked off imitation in similar ecologies throughout the river valleys, and even the desert oases, of Eurasia. In America, although the agricultural origins of the pre-Columbian peoples varied, some (though not all) of the crucial breakthroughs toward urbanization and writing appear connected with irrigation, which remained the core of the empires until the arrival of the Spaniards.

Now the relationship is not invariant. If Minos is counted, it is deviant, for alluvial and irrigation agriculture were largely absent. In Mesoamerica, the Mayan contribution is deviant. And later, in all cases, the role of the alluvium and irrigation diminished. We could not explain the Hittite, Persian, Macedonian, or Roman empire in this way. Nevertheless, in earliest history in Eurasia and America something was happening, predominantly in river valley alluvia, that was of profound consequence for civilization. Why?

My answer adapts and combines existing explanations. But I emphasize two points. First, whereas most local evolutionary tales are *functional,* told in terms of opportunity and incentive for social advancement, I will tell of the inseparability of functionality and exploitation. The cage metaphor will continue: The decisive feature of these ecologies and of human reactions to them was *the closing of the escape route.* Their local inhabitants, unlike those in the rest of the globe, were constrained to accept civilization, social stratification, and the state. They were trapped into particular social and territorial relationships, forcing them to intensify those relationships rather than evade them. This led to opportunities to develop both *collective* and *distributive* power. Civilization, social stratification, and the state resulted. The argument is similar to Carneiro's (1970, 1981) theory of "environmental circumscription," repeated by Webb (1975) (discussed later in the chapter), though without that theory's emphasis on population pressure and militarism. Therefore, the key to the role of irrigation may be found in considerable intensification of the insulating or caging forces present in prehistory. These caging forces must occupy the causal role in our explanation, not the alluvium or irrigation itself, which was merely their usual form or indicator in this historical epoch.

Second, at various stages of the narrative in this and the next two chapters, I play down the importance of the alluvium and irrigation itself in the first civilizations. We must consider also their relationship to, and stimulation of, other adjacent ecologies and populations. I do not pretend to originality in this respect either – see the recent work of scholars like Adams (1981) and Rowton (1973, 1976) on Mesopotamia, or Flannery and Rathje on Mesoamerica (discussed in the next chapter). All I do is to formalize the emphasis with *the model of overlapping power networks* explained in Chapter 1: The extraordinary development of civilization in Mesopotamia and elsewhere can be understood by examining the overlapping power networks stimulated by alluvial and irrigation agriculture. To a degree, these networks can be understood with the aid of another conventional model, "core" and "periphery," although this model has limitations. In particular, a power-network model enables us to understand better that these were *multi-power-actor civilizations:* They were not unitary societies. They were normally composed of two levels of power, a number of small political units, often city-states, and a broader civilizational "cultural/religious" complex. Again, this observation is not original (e.g., Renfrew 1975).

Yet both approaches can be pushed farther. The archaeologists, in confronting the new vistas they open up, sometimes embrace rather tired sociological theory. It is thus possible for a sociologist to point this out and to take the general argument a little farther. I will illustrate this through sympathetic criticism of a collection of essays on the transition to statehood seen from an ancient New World viewpoint, Jones and Kautz (1981). Among the essays, the arguments of Cohen and of MacNeish are generally similar to my own in a descriptive sense. They are suspicious of evolutionary accounts and are concerned to analyze particular local triggering mechanisms toward statehood based on caging processes amid regional diversity. But the more theoretical essays in the volume fail to take this further. They become bogged down in two disputes long familiar to sociologists.

The first occurs in the essay by Haas. He is understandably irritated with functionalist theories of the state. He feels compelled to develop what he calls a "conflict" model, centered on class struggle rather than on processes of social integration. No sociologist needs yet another dose of "conflict" versus "integration" models, familiar throughout the late 1950s and the 1960s! Modern sociology sees the two as closely, dialectically entwined: Function generates exploitation and vice versa. Only in exceptional circumstances (on the one hand a community of equals, on the other a war of simple expropriation and extermination) can we distinguish either integration- or conflict-dominated societies. We will not find examples in this or the next chapter, dealing with early states.

Second, two other contributors, Coe and Keatinge, draw attention, correctly, to the importance of religion to state formation in the New World, particularly its capacity to integrate culturally a wider territory than a state could rule. This means, they say, that religious, cultural, and ideological factors must have a considerable "autonomy" in social life. This argument is taken up at length in the editors' introduction. They suggest various ways in which ideological factors might be combined in an explanation with more material ones. I should add that fondness for "independent ideological factors" is entering other areas of archaeological-anthropological collaboration (e.g., Shennan's 1983 account of Stonehenge). Here I can hardly claim that mainstream sociology offers a solution. All it provides is half a century of disputes between advocates of "independent ideological factors" and materialists. But I attempt a solution in Volume III of this work. Its beginnings were sketched in Chapter 1.

The mistake is to conceive of ideology, economy, and so forth, as analytic ideal types that are actualized in societies as autonomous structures, or "dimensions," or "levels" of a single overall "society." According to this model, it should then prove possible to rank their relative contributions to determining the overall structure of society. But this is not the situation that Coe and Keatinge are describing in the ancient New World. Instead they show that the various social relations that people enter into – production, trade, and exchanging views, spouses, artifacts, and so forth – generated two sociospatial networks of interaction. One was relatively small, the state; the other was relatively broad, the religion or culture. It would be ridiculous to suggest that the state did not contain "ideal" factors, or that the religion did not contain "material" ones. They are instead, different potential bases for constituting "real" as well as "ideal" societies. One of these, the state, corresponds to social needs, which require *territorially centralized,* authoritative organization and which could be organized as yet only over restricted areas. The other, the culture or religion, corresponds to social needs based on a broader, diffused similarity of experience and mutual interdependence. I called this *transcendent* organization in Chapter 1 (I complete this argument in the conclusion to Chapter 4). Thus the relations between ideological, economic, military, and political aspects of social life are to be seen most usefully in sociospatial terms. Societies are series of overlapping and intersecting power networks.

The model used in this chapter combines two principal elements. It suggests that civilization, stratification, and the state emerged as the result of the impetus given by alluvial agriculture to diverse, overlapping networks of social interaction present in the region surrounding it. This encouraged further caging interaction between alluvium and hinterlands, leading to intensification of civilization, stratification, and the state – now, however, intensified as overlapping *power* networks, embodying permanent, coercive power.

Such a model will lead to methodological difficulties, however. Although we might expect to find some degree of similarity between the alluvial agricultures of the "pristine civilizations," the regional contexts into which these were inserted varied greatly. This reduces, both initially and then further throughout time, overall similarity between cases. As the cases also differed in other ways, we are unlikely to be able to apply this (or any other) model mechanically to them all.

Because of these differences, I first concentrate on one case, Mesopotamia.

This is the best documented, combining richness of records with breadth of archaeological excavation. Special reference should be made to the topographical survey techniques of Adams (1981 and, with Nissen, 1972), who has given us an immensely improved base for generalizing about the history of the settlements that became the first civilization. On this Mesopotamian data base, I examine the model in detail. Then in the next chapter I briefly review the other cases to see their principal similarities and differences, concluding with an overall model of the origins of civilization.

Mesopotamia: irrigation and its regional power interactions

The earliest evidence for irrigation in Mesopotamia is from about 5500–5000 B.C., well after urban settlements like Catal Hayuk and Jericho had emerged elsewhere in the Near East. Before then we can find traces of largish fixed settlement above the floodplain, which probably indicate a broadly egalitarian, mixed village/clan system typical (as we saw in the last chapter) of all continents over many millennia. Until irrigation was developed, moreover, this area remained relatively backward even in its development toward "rank society," probably because of the paucity of its raw materials, particularly stone and wood. This was also true to a lesser extent of the other Eurasian river valleys. Thus irrigation was probably entered into from a broadly egalitarian social base in all of them.

In the river valleys, the ecology is of obvious importance. I discuss the details of the ecologies later when discussing Wittfogel's thesis. But, in general, the decisive point is that the river in flood bears mud and silt, which when deposited is fertilized soil. This is called the *alluvium*. If it can be diverted onto a broad area of existing land, then much higher crop yields can be expected. This is the significance of *irrigation* in the ancient world: the spreading of water and silt over the land. Rain-watered soils gave lower yields. In Europe soils are generally heavy and were then often forested. Their fertility depended on deforestation, on turning over the soil and on breaking it up. Even after the forest is removed, as any gardener in the temperate zone knows, the work of regenerating the topsoil is heavy. Before the iron ax, plow, hoe, and spade, it was barely possible to remove large trees or turn the soil to any depth. In the Near East there was little forest, and so lighter soils, but much less rain. Considerable potential advantage lay with those who could use the river flood for water and topsoil.

The inhabitants of these plains lived originally above the flood level. Whether they themselves learned to irrigate or borrowed it from others is not known. But, eventually, enough stumbled on more activist intervention in nature. Between 5500 and 5000 B.C. we have evidence of artificial canals, of which the major ones required about five thousand hours of labor time to construct. Therefore, we find them adjacent to distinctly larger settlements.

Then, at some point between about 3900 and 3400 B.C. – in what archaeologists refer to as the Early to Middle Uruk period (after the major city of Uruk) – came a shift in population patterns, unparalleled anywhere else in the world up to that time. According to Adams (1981: 75) about half the people in southern Mesopotamia now lived in settlements of at least 10 hectares with populations of about a thousand or more. The urban revolution had occurred, and with it some (though not all) of the features we associate with civilization. Writing appeared about 3100 B.C., and from then we are in the realm of history and civilization. In what did the breakthrough consist? And why did it happen?

But before we are tempted to rush into a familiar story of local evolution, let us pause and look at the time scale involved. It was not a continuous, steady evolutionary pattern. The growth seems, at first, extraordinarily slow. It took almost two millennia to go from irrigation to urbanization: Before the early Uruk period settlement patterns changed little, and irrigation, though known, was not predominant. And we find traces of ancient irrigation, without social complexity or subsequent local evolution, in various places in the world. Histories of irrigation systems in places like Ceylon and Madagascar stress long cyclical struggles between villages, their chiefs/elders, and the hilltop kingdoms of their neighbors in which eventual further development occurred only because of interaction with more powerful established states (Leach 1954; Bloch 1977). Presumably Mesopotamia had its own, relatively egalitarian, version of the cycles of prehistory described in the last chapter.

The slowness of the emergence means that irrigation cannot be the whole explanation, for that was present by 5000 B.C. It seems more probable that when the breakthrough came it was also dependent on the slow development and diffusion of agricultural and pastoral techniques and organization across the Near East. We have evidence, for example, of gradual increase of long-distance trade throughout the region during the fifth and fourth millennia. Various groups were slowly increasing the surplus available for exchange and for supporting specialized crafts and trading people. Scholarly orthodoxy is now that "trade preceded the flag," that is, that well-developed networks of exchange preceded the formation of states in the area (see, e.g., the essays in Sabloff and Lamberg-Karlovsky 1976; and in Hawkins 1977). If this slow advance was of the order of the European one, reported in the previous chapter by Kristiansen (1982), we might expect a 10 percent increase in the surplus in two millennia. This figure is notional, but it does indicate what was probably an almost glacial pace of development. Perhaps it passed some threshold in the early fourth millennium that gave the boost to a few irrigators on which to base their 500-year drive through to civilization. Thus, the opportunities and constraints of the local ecology, now to be discussed, fed into a much broader set of social networks and were partially oriented toward them.

That said, we must turn to the opportunities represented by the alluvium and by irrigation. Everything that follows has, as a necessary precondition, the increase in the agricultural surplus generated first by natural flooding and silting and then by artificial irrigation, increasing soil fertility by distributing water and silt to a wider area of land. In Mesopotamia this took the form first of small-scale irrigation along the back slopes of natural levees. A local network of such ditches and dykes would generate a surplus far greater than that known to populations on rain-watered soil.

This led to an increase in population and density, perhaps beyond that supported by rain-watered agriculture. The latter was attaining densities of 10 to 20 persons per square kilometer. In Mesopotamia it was around 10 by 3500 B.C., 20 by 3200 B.C., and 30 by 3000 B.C. (Hole and Flannery 1967; Renfrew 1972: 252; Adams 1981: 90). But the surplus also grew faster than population, for numbers were released from agricultural production into artisanal manufacture, into trading, and (part time) into the managerial and luxurious activities of the first part-leisure class in human experience.

But irrigation meant constraint as well as opportunity. As soon as improvements began, the inhabitants were territorially caged. Fixed pieces of land provided the fertile soil; no other would do outside the river valley. This was unlike the dominant slash-and-burn agriculture of the prehistorical period, where far greater necessity and possibility for movement existed. But this cage was less pronounced in Mesopotamia than in Egypt. In the former, irrigated land in ancient times was always a smaller area than that potentially usable. In the earlier phases irrigation covered only a narrow strip immediately surrounding the main river channels. This was probably also the early Chinese and Indus pattern.[2] In contrast, the Nile fertilized only a narrow trench of land and was probably early populated in its entirety.

Territory also caged people because it coincided with substantial labor investment to secure a surplus – a *social cage*. To irrigate was to invest in cooperative labor with others, to build artifices fixed for many years. It produced a large surplus, shared among the participants, tied to this particular investment and artifice. The use of large labor forces (of hundreds rather than thousands) was occasional but regular and seasonal. Centralized authority would also be useful to manage such irrigation schemes. Territory, community, and hierarchy were coinciding in irrigation more than they did in either rain-watered agriculture or herding.

But let us not become too obsessed with floodplains or irrigation. Alluvial agriculture implies a regional environment: adjacent, upstream mountains receiving substantial rainfall or winter snows; the concentration of water flow in valleys with desert, mountains, or semiarid land between them; and swamps

---

[2]This is why ''population pressure'' seems less important as a factor in the growth of civilization than is often assumed. It emerges particularly to flaw the otherwise powerful models of ''environmental circumscription'' offered by Carneiro (1970, 1981) and Webb (1975).

and marshes in the plain. The alluvium is situated amid great ecological *contrasts*. That was decisive, producing both boundedness and interaction distinct from, say, that of the relatively even terrain of Europe. Such contrasts seem the recipe for the emergence of civilization.

Let us consider the successive economic spinoffs of irrigation in these contrasting ecologies. First, in the river valleys were large marshes, grass, and reed thickets, unused areas of river, and one extremely useful tree, the date palm. Irrigation fertilized the palm, provided investment for its extension, and exchanged produce with "peripheral" environments. Wildfowling, hunting of pigs, fishing, and reed collecting interacted with agriculture, providing a division of labor between loosely kin-structured gatherer-hunters and the sedentary village-dwelling, caged irrigators. The latter were the dominant partner, for their's was the initial impetus to development. Then, slightly farther out on the periphery, was abundant land, occasionally fertilized by river inundation or watered by whatever rain fell. This supported some agriculture and pastoralism, providing meat, skins, wool, and dairy produce. Sumer's peripheries were varied. To the west and southwest lay deserts and pastoral nomads; to the southeast, swamps and the Persian Gulf; to the east, the perhaps-dependent irrigated valleys of Khuzistan; to the northwest, the unusable middle reaches of the Tigris and the Euphrates, and between them desert; to the northeast, a fertile corridor up the Diyala River to the rain-watered plains of northern Mesopotamia (later to become Assyria), yielding winter cereals, and the well-watered Taurus and Zagros mountains. Social contacts were thus also varied and included desert nomads and their sheikhs, primitive and loosely structured swamp villages, rival irrigators, developed and relatively egalitarian agricultural villages, and mountain pastoral tribes.

Irrigation released specialists to manufacture products, especially woolen textiles, and to reexchange with all these neighbors. Products were used in long-distance trade, in exchange for stone, wood, and precious metals. The rivers were navigable downstream, especially after irrigation channels regularized their flow. The rivers were thus as important as communications channels as irrigators. From the beginning, long-distance trade preceded state consolidation. Foreign goods were of three main types: (1) raw materials shipped by river over long distances – from the woods of Lebanon and the mines of the mountains of Asia Minor, for example; (2) medium-distance trade from adjacent nomads and pastoralists, mainly in animals and cloths; and (3) long-distance trade by river, sea, and even land caravan in luxury items, that is, manufactured goods high in value-to-weight ratio, mainly precious ores from mountain regions but also goods from other centers of emerging civilization – river and seaport settlements and desert oases scattered over the Near East from Egypt to Asia (Levine and Young 1977).

Such interactions enhanced not only the power of irrigation itself but also the varied social activities overlapping it. And as well as enhancing the irrigation cage, they had an impact on the more diffuse social networks of the periphery. Most of these are more shadowy, but their territorial and social fixity would be less than that of the irrigators. Contact and interdependence would push them somewhat in the direction of fixity, often under the loose hegemony of the irrigators. Marfoe (1982) suggests that initial Mesopotamian colonies in the raw-material supply areas in Anatolia and Syria gave way to autonomous local politics. These were joined by other local agricultural and pastoral polities, all of whose power was enhanced by trade with Mesopotamia.

Trade gave advantages of "unequal exchange" to Mesopotamia. Exchanged for precious metals, its products of manufacturing and artisanal trades and high-investment agriculture brought "prestige goods," useful tools and weapons, and relatively generalized means of exchange. But the logistics of control were daunting, and no sustained direct control could be exercised from Mesopotamia. We will not see in this chapter any substantial innovation in either the *logistics* or the *diffusion* (see Chapter 1 for an explanation of these terms) of power. When the state first emerged, it was a tiny city-state. Its power resources were concentrated upon its center rather than under extensive control. Thus the Mesopotamian stimulus enhanced rivals rather than dependents. Urbanization and autonomous state formation grew all over the Fertile Crescent, from the Mediterranean coast, through Syria and Anatolia, to Iran in the east.

One may call these relationships "core" and "periphery," as many scholars do. But the periphery could not be controlled from the core, and its development was necessary to that of the core and vice versa. The growth of civilization involved all these loosely connected, part-autonomous power networks. Similarly, Rowton's (1973, 1976) metaphor of the diomorphic growth of civilization – though usefully pointing to the central relationship between urban irrigators and manufacturers and successive waves of nomads and seminomads – is also open to misinterpretation. As Adams (1981: 135–6) points out, the two ways of life were not sharply bounded. They overlapped in a "structural and ethnic continuum," exchanging material and cultural products, energizing and transforming both ways of life and providing potentially powerful "marcher" groups that could mobilize elements of both.

The emergence of stratification and the state to about 3100 B.C.

The interaction of irrigation and its region led to two associated caging tendencies, the rise of quasi-private property and the rise of the state.

Private property was encouraged by territorial and social fixity. As it emerged from a broadly egalitarian village and clan mixture, it took the form of extended-family, or even clan, property rights rather than individual rights. The key economic resources were fixed, in the permanent possession of a settled family group. Such land was the main source of Sumerian wealth. It was both the major surplus-producing resource and the place where exchanges with all other ecologies focused. Resources were concentrated on this land but dispersed throughout the other authority networks. The *contrast* is important, for it enabled those who controlled this land to mobilize a disproportionate amount of collective social power and to turn it into distributive power used against others.

Let us recall two of the theories of the origins of stratification discussed in Chapter 2, the liberal and the revisionist Marxian theories. Liberalism located the original stimulus in interpersonal differences of ability, hard work, and luck. As a general theory, it is absurd. But it has great relevance where adjacent occupied plots of land vary considerably in their productivity. In ancient irrigation accidental proximity to fertilized soil produced large differences in productivity (emphasized by Flannery 1974 as the heart of subsequent stratification). But we must also abandon the individual, so beloved of liberalism. This was family, village, and small-clan property. From revisionist Marxian theory we draw the notion of effective possession of such property by village and lineage elites. For irrigation also reinforces the cooperation of units larger than individual households.

When so much of the preparation and protection of the land is collectively organized, it is difficult for individual or household ownership of the land by peasants to be maintained. Sumerian records after 3000 B.C. divided irrigated land into tracts much larger than could be worked by individual families, unlike the situation in most prehistoric villages. One of their forms was private ownership by an extended-family group. Kin and local tribal relations generated rank-authority irrigation management, and this seems to have eventuated in private-property concentrations.

One further basis for permanent inequalities, arising out of lucky or schemed possession of land, was possession of a strategic position at the point of contact with more diffuse networks. River junctions, water-channel fords, plus crossroads and wells, offered the chance of controls exercised through marketplace and storage organization, as well as "protection rent," to adjacent settlers. Some scholars attribute much Sumerian social organization to strategic factors (e.g., Gibson 1976). As the rivers were so important to communications, most strategic positions were located on the core irrigated land.

Thus such lucky inequalities do not derive merely from differential access to water or soil fertility. They also presuppose a *juxtaposition* of fixed property rights induced by irrigation, on the one hand, and more fluid, dispersed, nonterritorial rights over surpluses that were also growing in different ecologies, on the other. Concentration of population, of wealth and power, occurred in the former faster than in the latter. The differential between them grew exponentially (Flannery 1972). Major power actors in the former exercised hegemony over both sectors. Stratification did eventually intensify along this axis. As the surplus grew, some of the core, propertied, irrigating families or villages withdrew either wholly or partially from direct production into crafts, trade, and official positions, being replaced predominantly by "dependent laborers" receiving prebendary land and rations, probably recruited from the peoples of the adjacent areas, and secondly, but much less importantly, by slaves (normally war captives from outlying areas). Our detailed knowledge of this process derives from later, after about 3000 B.C., but it probably dates from the very beginnings of urbanization (Jankowska 1970). It is a lateral stratification, across the floodplain, between the core and parts of the periphery. A second stratification, within the core, whereby the rank authority of the kin and village leader was converted into a quasi-class position over his own kin or village members, may have accompanied it.

This does offer a solution to the labor problem posed in the last chapter by writers in the militarist school (e.g., by Gumplowicz). They argued that a distinction between landowners and landless laborers could not emerge spontaneously within a kin or village group because kin are not allowed to exploit kin. Thus, they argued, the distinction must originate in the conquest by one kin group of another. Yet the origins of property in Mesopotamia do not seem to have been accompanied by much organized violence. Not slavery but a semifree labor status predominated (Gelb 1967). Late Uruk art does on occasion depict soldiers and prisoners, but such motifs are not as common as in later periods. Fortifications appear rare – although archaeologists are reluctant to argue from absence of remains. And, in general, as Diakonoff (1972) observes, early Mesopotamia is characterized by a virtual absence of militaristic (or, indeed, of any noneconomic) status differences. In any case, the militarist argument assumes that clearly demarcated societies existed, yet social boundaries were still somewhat fuzzy. Dominance by a core over a periphery, with attendant patron–client relations – if the core has exclusive possession of fertile land – may lead to more-or-less voluntary forms of labor subordination. The periphery may experience more population growth than it can support; alternatively, the rations available as wages to landless labor in the core may have provided a more secure standard of living than the periphery. Subordination may be abetted by the chiefs or elders of the periphery – the principal providers of slaves and bonded laborers to more developed societies throughout history. Thus, the origins of stratification become more comprehensible if we abandon an "internal" explanation based on unitary societies.[3]

Such stratification emerged throughout the late fourth millennium. The grave remains and the architecture reveal widening wealth differentials. After 3000 B.C., inequalities entailed legally recognized differentials in access to property in land. Four groups confront us: leading families with access to the

---

[3] I might add that although both bastardy and debt-bondage can provide "internal" exploited labor, they do not provide sufficient numbers or stability of institutionalized exploitation in primitive societies to account for the origins of stratification.

resources of temples and palaces; ordinary free persons; semifree dependent laborers; and a few slaves. But to understand this more fully, we must turn to the second great social process generated by social and territorial caging, the rise of the state.

The same factors that encouraged property differentials also intensified a territorially centralized authority, that is, a state. Irrigation management played a part. Exchange of produce where the more powerful party's territory was fixed and strategic for transport meant that the redistributive storehouse or the exchanging marketplace would be centralized. The more resources are centralized, the more they require defense, hence also military centralization. The imbalance between the parties created another centralized political function; for the irrigators would seek more ordered routines of exchange than pastoralists and gatherer-hunters' own existing social organization could provide. In later history this is called "tribute," authoritatively regulated exchange, whereby the obligations of both parties are expressed formally and accompanied by rituals of diplomacy. This had fixing consequences for the pastoralists and gatherer-hunters, too: It civilized them. Once contacts become regularized, diffusion of practices occurs. Although settled irrigating agriculturalists like to picture themselves as "civilized" and the others as "barbarians," there is growing similarity and interdependence. This probably happened laterally across the floodplains as irrigators, wildfowlers, fishers, and even some pastoralists drew closer together.

One principal form of their interdependence in the period around 3000 B.C. may have been the emergence of a redistributive state. There was elaborate central storage of goods, and it is often suggested that this amounted to exchange not through a market but through the authoritative allocation of value by a central bureaucracy. But writers who emphasize this (e.g., Wright and Johnson 1975; Wright 1977) do not see it in quite the functional terms of "redistributive-chiefdom theory" (discussed in the previous chapter). They emphasize redistribution, not as a rational solution to exchange between different ecological niches in the absence of advanced marketing techniques, but rather as the irrigated core imposing a part-arbitrary power over the periphery. Other writers (e.g., Adams 1981: 76–81) also think that such a core-periphery model is too rigid. We should visualize a looser hegemony of the patron over the client. Thus the state emerged out of loose patron-client relations, just as social stratification did.

Centralization was also encouraged by vertical linkages along the rivers. The inner core of the floodplain began to fill up, and village or kin groups began to rub up against one another. They required relatively fixed, regulated relationships. Authority, long present within the lineage group and the village, was required also in intervillage relations. This resulted in a second tier of larger quasi-political entities. In Sumer, a particular type of ceremonial center (the second of Renfrew's three indicators of civilization), the *temple*, seems to have been associated with this process, often as arbitrator between villages. The importance of the temple was fairly general among the earliest civilizations – an issue to which I shall return in the conclusion to Chapter 4. Steward (1963: 201–2) notes that extensive social cooperation in irrigation agriculture was virtually everywhere associated with a strong priesthood in the New World cases as well as the Old World ones. He argues that a relatively egalitarian group engaged in cooperation had unusually strong needs for normative solidarity. Modern scholars resist the religious connotations of the word "priesthood" in Mesopotamia. They regard priests as more secular, more administrative and political, as a diplomatic corps, irrigation managers, and redistributors. Through a process whose details are not known to us, the temple emerges as the first state of history. As irrigation proceeded, more extensive labor cooperation was required. Exactly *what* territorial area was collectively interdependent in hydraulic agriculture is disputed, as we shall see. But flood prevention and control, the building of dams, dikes, and irrigation channels, required, both regularly and during occasional natural crises, *some* degree of delayed-return investment in labor cooperation between villages – say, for example, across a lateral area of floodplain, and along a river length, of a few miles. This was a powerful impetus toward larger political units than the kin group or village. A principal function of the Sumerian temple soon became irrigation management, and it remained so for a thousand years.[4]

These temple states do not seem particularly coercive. It is difficult to be sure, but Jacobsen's (1943, 1957) view is widely accepted: The first permanent political form was a primitive democracy in which assemblies composed of a large proportion of the free adult males of the town made major decisions. Jacobsen suggested a two-house legislature, an upper house of elders and a lower one of freemen. If this may be a little idealized – for the principal source is later myths – the likely alternative is a loose and rather large oligarchy consisting of the heads of the more important families and, perhaps also, of the territorial wards of the town.

We may tentatively conclude that just before 3000 B.C. these were transitional polities, making that elusive move from rank authority toward stratified state. But the transition occurred first less in the realm of coercion of the ruled by the rulers than in the realm of coercion in the sense of *caging*, the growth of focused, inescapably intense, centralized social relations. The transition to coercion and exploitation was slower. Differences between the leading families and the rest and between freemen and dependent or slave laborers were

---

[4]Gibson (1976) has argued that an accidental factor heightened this role in Sumer. Around 3300 B.C. the eastern branch of the Euphrates dried up quite suddenly as the waters suddenly opened up new channels further west. Thus mass emigration to the western branch resulted, organized of necessity on an extensive basis (probably by the temples). The cities of Kish and Nippur were founded because of this, he believes.

"absolute-rank" differences. But rank within the leading families seems to have been "relative" and changeable. Rank largely depended on proximity to economic resources, which were themselves changeable. There seems no evidence of ranking in relation to "absolute" genealogical criteria, like supposed proximity to the gods or ancestors. In these ways, the emergence of stratification and the state was slow and uneven.

Nevertheless, the two processes of state and private property growth were connected to, and in the end mutually supportive of, one another. In modern capitalism, with its highly institutionalized private-property rights and nonintervening states, we characteristically view the two as antithetical. Yet in most historical periods this would be mistaken, as we shall see repeatedly. Private, familial property and the state emerged together, encouraged by the same processes. When our records begin – the excavated tablets of the early city of Lagash – we find a complicated mixture of three property forms in land administered by the temple. There were fields owned by the city's gods and administered by the temple officials, fields rented out by the temple to individual families on an annual basis, and fields granted to individual families in perpetuity without rent. The first and third forms were often sizable, denoting large-scale collective and private property, both employing dependent labor and a few slaves. The records indicate that collective and private property steadily merged, as stratification and the state developed more extensively. Access to land came to be monopolized by a unified but still representative elite, which controlled the temples and large estates and held priestly, civil, and military office.

The integrated nature of agriculture in irrigation conditions and of exchange and diffusion between it and the surrounding ecologies generated *merged* authority structures in kin groups, villages, and emerging states. As we can find no trace of political conflict between supposedly private and collective aspects, it is sensible to treat them as a single process. Thus, the organization of the emerging redistributive state revealed in the temple sector by the Lagash tablets was probably also paralleled in the ill-documented private-estate sector. The temples budgeted and organized production and redistribution in a detailed, sophisticated way – so much for the costs of production, so much in temple consumption, so much in tax, so much as reinvestment in seed, and so forth. It is a redistributive state in Polanyi's sense (referred to in the previous chapter). But it is likely that the same principles applied in the private sector. The state was a household writ large, coexisting amicably with kin-based households.[5]

[5]Sumerian evidence on property forms can be found in Kramer 1963; Gelb 1969; Lamberg-Karlovsky 1976; and Oates 1978. Unfortunately, the researches of the Soviet scholar Diakonoff, which emphasize the early role of private-property concentrations, remain largely untranslated, apart from Diakonoff 1969. On temple budgeting, see Jones 1976.

The merging and caging of authority relations had one further consequence: the appearance of the third of Renfrew's indicators of civilization, writing. If we examine closely the origins of literacy, we get a good sense of the initial civilizing process. Sumer becomes crucial here, because its records are relatively good and because it is the one *certain* case of the spontaneous development of writing in Eurasia. The other possibly independent cases of literacy in Eurasia may have received their stimulus from Sumer. In any case, two scripts, the Indus Valley and Minoan Crete (linear A), are still undeciphered, whereas in the remaining two only biased selections of scripts have been preserved. For Shang China we have records only of the early rulers' consultations with oracles, preserved because they were inscribed on tortoiseshell or similar bony surfaces. These indicate that the gods' main role is to give guidance on political and military problems. For Egypt we have funerary inscriptions on metal and stone, that is, religious inscriptions, although most writing was on papyrus or leather that has perished. We see in them a mixture of religious and political concerns. In all other cases writing was imported. And that is important. Writing is technically useful. It can further the goals and stabilize the meaning system of *any* dominant group – priests, warriors, merchants, rulers. Later cases thus show a great variety of power relations implicated in the development of writing. So for precision as to the origins of literacy, we depend on the Sumerians.

In Sumer, the first records were cylinder seals on which pictures were incised so that they could be rolled on clay. This is fortunate for us because clay survives the millennia. They seem to record goods being exchanged, stored, and redistributed, and often appear to denote who owned them. These developed into pictograms, simplified stylized pictures of objects inscribed with a reed stalk on clay tablets. These were gradually simplified into ideograms, more abstract representations capable of standing for classes of objects and then for sounds. Increasingly they took their form from the technical variations possible from making marks with a wedge-shaped chopped reed rather than from the form of the object being represented. Thus we call it *cuneiform,* meaning wedge-shaped.

In all this development, from about 3500 to 2000 B.C., the overwhelming mass of the more than 100,000 surviving inscriptions are *lists* of goods. Indeed, the list became a general theme of the culture: Soon we find also lists of conceptual classifications of all kinds of objects and names. Let me quote one relatively short list to give the flavor of Sumerian literacy. It comes from the third millennium, from the Third Dynasty of Ur, from the Drehem archive:

> 2 lambs (and) 1 young gazelle
> (from) the governor of Nippur;
> 1 lamb (from) Girini-isa the overseer
> 2 young gazelles (from) Larabum the overseer
> 5 young gazelles (from) Hallia
> 5 young gazelles (from) Asani-u;
> 1 lamb

(from) the governor of Marada;
delivered.
The month of the eating of the gazelle
The year when the cities Simurum (and) Lulubu were
destroyed for the 9th time
On the 12th day [reproduced, with many others, in Kang 1972]

This is mostly how we learn of the existence of overseers and governors, produce and herds, of the Sumerian calendar, even of the repeated destruction of cities – from clerks and accountants. They are primarily interested in preserving a proper accounting system for gazelles and lambs, not the epic history of their era. From this evidence, their temples were merely decorated stores; the inscribers less priests than clerks. But these were important stores, being at the center of the production-redistribution cycle. The lists record relations of production and redistribution and of social rights and obligations especially over property. The more complicated lists also record the exchange values of different goods. In the absence of coinage, they coexisted with precious metals as generally recognized means of value. The stores appear to have been at the center of Sumerian power organization. Perhaps the gods were fundamentally guardians of the stores. In the stores private-property rights and central political authority merged into one, expressed as a set of seals and eventually as writing and civilization itself. Writing was later turned to the telling of myth and religion. But its first and always its major purpose was to stabilize and institutionalize the two emerging, merging sets of authority relations, private property and the state. It was a technical matter, involving a particular specialist position, the scribe. It did not diffuse literacy even to the ruling stratum as a whole. Indeed, the increasingly abstract nature of the script may have rendered it less intelligible to anyone other than a scribe.

The techniques were also bound to particular, centralized locations. Most tablets were heavy and not suitable for movement. They required deciphering by temple scribes. So the messages could not be diffused throughout the social territory. The people affected by them upheld their rights and duties in the center of the small city-state. Although to write down authority rights is to objectify them, to "universalize" them (in the language of Chapter 1), the degree of universalism was still extremely limited, especially in territory. Few means of *diffusing* power, beyond those of prehistory, had been discovered: It is still to be enforced authoritatively at one central place and over a small area. Nevertheless, the writing did code in permanent form the rights of property and of political authority. It reveals a new era by 3100 B.C.: that of civilized caged societies. The jump has been made.

Civilization as federation

So far, it might also seem that the merging of property and political authority was creating a new realm of unitary societies, caged and bounded. But this is misleading because of my neglect of wider repercussions of the expansion and merging of territorial and kin groups. Remember that a number of such groups were expanding across the floodplain. As trade increased, so did their common dependence on the rivers as a communications system. All had an interest in freedom of trade, in keeping the river channel free of piracy and silt, and therefore in diplomatic regulation. At the same time conflicts arose over water rights and boundaries. In certain ecologies upstreamers had advantages over downstreamers. It is uncertain whether this resulted from an ability to divert water channels, from the more important trade routes being northerly ones, or from soil salinization in the south. Conflict often occurred on a north-south axis, often to the advantage of the northerners.

But despite their differences, the major participants had quite similar life experiences: Artistic forms and ideologies diffused quickly among them because, broadly, they sought solutions to the same problems. The cycle of the seasons; the importance of silt; the unpredictable beneficence of the river; relations with herders, gatherer-hunters, and foreign merchants; emerging social and territorial fixity – all led to broad similarity of culture, science, morality, and metaphysics. In prehistory, pottery and architectural styles were already strikingly similar over the whole area. By the time they enter the historical record, perhaps half a million inhabitants of southern Mesopotamia were part of a single civilization, though it contained multiple power actors. They may have spoken the same language. Their few professional scribes wrote in a common script, learned their trade with the help of identical word lists, and asserted that they were indeed one people, the Sumerians.

The exact nature of their unity, collective identity, and ideology, however, is far from clear. Our evidence from literacy is not without ambiguity. As Diakonoff has reminded us: "None of these ancient writing systems was designed to render utterances of speech directly as expressed in the language; they were only systems of aid to memory, used mainly for administrative purposes (and later, to a certain degree, in the cult)" (1975: 103). It is possible that the people whose goods, rights, and duties were registered by the scribes did not at first even speak the same language. Such skepticism might be considered too radical by most scholars, for a common core language and culture did develop at some point. But, first, it always coexisted with the language and culture of other groups, and, second, its core was not a unitary but a "federal" or "segmentary" culture.

The Sumerians were not the only "people" in the area. Some writers speculate about an original indigenous people with whom Sumerian immigrants intermingled. More certain is the existence of at least two other "peoples" who also became civilized. The first was in the area known as Elam, 300 kilometers to the east in present-day Khuzistan. Its origins lie in alluvial land along three rivers, although the evidence for irrigation is less certain (Wright and Johnson 1975). Its later prehistory and early history seem uneven, with alternating periods of autonomous development and heavy influence by Sumer. Whether it was a "pristine state" is unclear. But its language remained distinct, and it was not politically part of Mesopotamia.

The second "people" were Semitic speakers. These are generally presumed to have been a large, widely diffused group of Arabian origin. From among them, at least two subgroups, the Akkadians and the Eblaites, developed literate civilizations to the north of Sumer. They were seemingly stimulated by Sumerian commercial, even colonial, activities. But they developed complex autonomous city-states around the mid third millennium B.C. Ebla, being farther away, retained autonomy longer. The adjacent Akkadians penetrated Sumer in large numbers, first as dependent laborers, then as military lieutenants, and finally, around 2350 B.C., as conquerors (described at the beginning of Chapter 5). Before 2350 B.C., we do not have evidence of struggles between Sumerians and Akkadians. There are two plausible interpretations of the absence. *Either* the Sumerians exercised hegemony over the Akkadians and secured their allegiance and dependence without undue recourse to organized violence, *or* neither the Sumerians nor the Akkadians were a fully distinct ethnic group and areas of overlap existed between the two social identities. It is probable that the development of Sumer also civilized Akkad and that the latter's (originally tribal?) leaders used cuneiform and became involved in the power politics and the identity of Sumer. Many later parallels present themselves. For example, in Chapter 9 we will see that the identity "Roman" was successively embraced by the elites of a large conglomeration of originally distinct "peoples." For these reasons, we may doubt whether the identity "Sumerian" was clear-cut, or whether it was coterminous with a bounded civilized territory.

Second, Sumerian culture was not unitary. By the time Sumerian religion and mythology had been written down – perhaps for the Akkadian conquerors in the mid third millennium B.C. – it was federal, or segmental, with two distinct levels. Each city-state had its own tutelary deity, resident in its temple, "owning" the city and providing its focus of loyalty. Yet each deity had a recognized home in a common Sumerian pantheon. Anu, later the king of heaven, buttressing royalty, resided at Uruk, as did his consort Inanna. Enlil, the king of earth, resided in Nippur. Enki, the king of water and a god with great human sympathies, resided in Eridu. Nanna, the moon god, resided in Ur. Each of the important city-states possessed its place, and many possessed a distinctive claim to preeminence, in this pantheon. Whatever the conflicts between the cities, they were regulated, both ideologically and perhaps in diplomatic practice, by the pantheon. Thus Nippur, the home of the council of the gods, headed by Enlil, played some early role in dispute mediation. As in modern relations between nation-states, some degree of normative regulation between the individual states existed. There was warfare, but there were rules of war. There were boundary disputes, but procedures for settling them.

A singular civilization, fuzzy at the edges, contained multi-power actors within a geopolitical, diplomatically regulated power organization.

Let me stress that up to half a million persons may have thought of themselves as Sumerian, a number far in excess of the 10,000 or so coordinated by the first city-states, the first *authoritatively* regulated societies. How did this *diffused* "nation" or "people" arise? "Peoples" are striding continuously across the pages of history books about the ancient world. But because in our own era we take extensive peoples for granted, we do not boggle sufficiently at the mystery of this. It is emphatically *not* correct to adopt nineteenth-century ethnography and to claim that the Sumerians were united by ethnicity, by membership in a common gene pool. Again there is a parallel with modern nationalism. Although in intermarriage patterns the boundaries of modern nation-states erect a degree of cleavage, it is not of sufficient size or duration to produce the genetic pool or "race" beloved of modern ideologists. This is even less conceivable in prehistory. In any case, if there were restrictions on intermarriage in prehistory, our problem is to explain how they arose, given that no extensive authority for the restriction could have existed (unlike the modern nation-state).

Peoples, races, and tribes are socially created. They did not exist in the first place. They are the product of confined power interactions over a long period between persons who are caged within boundaries. In the case of the first civilizations, the principal boundary was given by the social exploitation of contrasting adjacent ecologies. Irrigation is a social activity that then emphasizes ecological barriers. In ancient Egypt, where virtually no one could live outside the Nile Valley, the barrier became almost absolute, and so did the identity of "Egyptian" (as I argue in Chapter 4). In Mesopotamia, and other Eurasian river-valley civilizations, caging was more partial. Over a number of centuries, the various cores and parts of the periphery probably developed an overall cultural identity. Not a "nation" in the modern sense, but perhaps what Anthony Smith (1983) has called an "ethnic community," a weak but nonetheless real sense of collective identity, buttressed by language, foundation myths, and invented genealogies. The archaeological record cannot fully confirm (or deny) this. The origins of the Sumerians are still a matter of speculation (Jones 1969 reviews the controversies). But I add my own speculation: "They" did not exist as a collectivity before the urban revolution but became one as two sets of interdependencies grew: first, lateral dependencies, across the floodplain, of irrigators, wildfowlers, fishers, and some herders; second, vertical dependencies, as each of these cities spread out along the river.

This is congruent with the segmental, two-level nature of the culture and its lack of clear-cut external boundaries. It derives from one of the central arguments of this chapter: The drive to civilization was not merely a product of tendencies within the irrigated core. The impetus from the core led outward, laterally and vertically, across and along the river system. As it occurred amid originally loose, overlapping social networks, the impetus could not be confined within a narrow territorial core. Though some of its consequences caged peoples into small city-states, others strengthened the interaction networks of a much more extensive area. The latter were not as fixed territorially and socially as the former. At the outer edges, where floodplain met desert or upland, cultural identity was probably quite unclear.

I suggest further that this was the dominant ecological and cultural pattern of the ancient Near East. Scattered across the region grew various segmental concentrations of populations of tens of thousands in irrigated river valleys and oases, separated by inhabited but marginal steppes, mountains, and plains. This contrasted with Europe, where more even ecology encouraged continuous distribution of population, a looser social structure, and an absence of moderately caged, segmental cultural identities. It is why civilization arose in the Near East, not Europe.

We have reached a period between about 3100 and 2700 B.C. Across southern Mesopotamia there stretched a predominantly settled, urban form of life. In a number of towns a caged population, exerting loose hegemony over the inhabitants of the inner periphery, was developing closely connected family–private-property and central-political relations. Their leaders were exercising coercive powers over the inner periphery and, perhaps, beginning to do so over the lesser families of the core. Writing, and presumably other artifacts less visible to us, were increasing the permanence of these relations. Their culture and their religion were stabilizing these tendencies, yet also giving some wider, competing sense of civilized identity as an ethnic community. This was the first stage of civilization – two-level, segmental, semicaged.

All these processes intensified throughout the next millennium. We know with hindsight that a fully fledged, stratified, multistate civilization emerged from this area – and we owe much subsequent civilization, including our own, to it. Increasingly the state and stratification hardened. The original democracy/oligarchy turned into monarchy. Then one monarchy conquered the rest. This led to an imperial form of regime dominant throughout much of ancient history. Simultaneously, property relations hardened. By the time we get to imperial regimes, we find them ruling through aristocracies with monopolistic rights over most land. It looks like a single, local evolutionary process in which Mesopotamia in 3000 B.C. was a transitional phase. But was it? Can we deduce the later characteristics of state, stratification, and civilization from the forces we have already seen in motion?

Let us start with the simplest affirmative answer to this question. It was the orthodoxy of the late nineteenth century and has been most powerfully expressed in the twentieth by Wittfogel. We will find its failures instructive. It is the thesis of "hydraulic agriculture and despotism." As it has been expressed in general comparative terms, I widen my focus to deal with more cases.

Irrigation agriculture and despotism: a spurious correlation

The strands of the hydraulic agriculture thesis, common among nineteenth-century writers, were drawn together by Wittfogel in his *Oriental Despotism* (1957). Some of the chapter titles of his book speak for themselves: "A State Stronger than Society," "Despotic Power – Total and Not Benevolent," "Total Terror." Wittfogel's argument rested on his conception of a "hydraulic economy," that is, large-scale canal and irrigation works that he thought necessitated a centralized, imperial, "agro-managerial despotism." His is the only systematic, consistent attempt to account for the political structure of the first civilizations in terms of their economies. Unfortunately, Wittfogel considerably overextended his model, applying it to all large-scale societies in the ancient world. Many of those he mentions – like Rome – barely knew irrigation agriculture. In these cases his argument has no validity. It is only plausible to apply it to the four great river-valley civilizations, or to the three that can be studied in any detail, Mesopotamia, China, and Egypt.

Wittfogel's theory combines a functional with an exploitative, a collective with a distributive, view of power. He argues that hydraulic agriculture requires for its efficient functioning a centralized, managerial role. It extends the "redistributive state" to the sphere of production. This gives the state a functional role that it can exploit to its private advantage. The agro-managerial state spread across the entire river system, conferring organizational superiority on the despot and his bureaucracy. The sociological mechanism of power usurpation is elegant and plausible.

Let us start with China, where Wittfogel's scholarship developed. One thing is undeniable: China has long been unusually dependent on irrigated land. But there are a number of different water-control systems. Wittfogel, in earlier work, had distinguished them according to several variables – the rain's quantity, temporal distribution, and reliability; the precise function and degree of necessity of the control system; the physical nature of the works themselves. As he saw at that time these varied in their implications for social organization. Others have expanded the number of variable factors (e.g., Elvin 1975). Indeed only one common feature of water-control systems can be discerned: They intensified social organization per se. For they were inherently cooperative enterprises in their initiation and maintenance.

But the *form* of the organization varied considerably. The vast majority of Chinese irrigation schemes – and indeed those of every country yet investigated – were relatively small, confined to a village or a group of villages. They were usually organized by locals, sometimes villagers and more often local lords. This variation was not technologically or ecologically determined. Fei (1939) describes a Yangtze Valley scheme in which control over a small system rotated annually between the heads of fifteen smallholder families. Other identical projects were run by local gentry.

But state interest was greater in three particular types of project. First, the few large-scale entire-valley irrigation schemes were under the control of a state official from later Han times. Second, the canal network, especially the Grand Canal linking the Yangtze and Huang Ho rivers, was built and administered by the state. Third, flood-defense systems, especially in coastal regions, were often extensive, beyond local resources, and built and maintained by the state. Only the first concerns hydraulic agriculture as the term has been customarily understood. It was also the weakest of the three in terms of effective control. The official in charge relied on locals, and his main role was to arbitrate local disputes, especially over rights to water. The canal system was controlled more effectively because it brought in a bureaucracy concerned with tolls and taxes and because it was useful for the movement of troops. The basic fiscal strategy of the agrarian imperial state was "If it moves, tax it." In China the waterways were crucial to fiscal and military power. Flood defenses did boost state control in these areas. But these were not the heartland of the Chinese Empire and could not have determined its initial imperial-despotic structure. Indeed, all three cases *postdate* the emergence of the imperial-despotic state.

In some respects, Wittfogel's characterization of China as an "Oriental Despotism" is accurate – even if it considerably exaggerates the *actual* infrastructural powers of the state, as we shall see. But the cause of its development was not hydraulic agriculture.[6]

The two remaining cases, Egypt and Sumer, differ for they center on the irrigation of one or two rivers. The characteristics of these rivers are crucial.

Sometime about 3000 B.C., Egypt was unified. Between then and the present day it has resembled a long, narrow trench, between five and twenty kilometers wide, broken only by the single side trench of the Fayum depression and by widening at the Delta into multiple channels. Its length alone has varied. The Old Kingdom (2850–2190 B.C.) possessed a trench a thousand kilometers in length, from the First Cataract (the modern Aswan Dam) to the Delta. Only in a long, narrow trench and its two offshoots was (is) irrigation possible. Even pastoralism was (is) largely impossible outside it. Between July and October each year the Nile floods, leaving mud and silt over much of the trench. Channeling and spreading this flood and then running off the water once the soil is soaked are the main purposes of coordinated irrigation. Egypt developed perhaps the clearest and certainly the earliest example of "oriental despotism" in Wittfogel's terms. Was this due to hydraulic agriculture?

---

[6] Apart from works cited, sources for Chinese hydraulic agriculture are Chi 1936; Eberhard 1965: 42–6, 56–83; Perkins 1968; Needham 1971: IV,3; and Elvin 1975. I acknowledge also the stimulus of two excellent talks in the London School of Economics "Patterns of History" seminar, 1980–1, given by Mark Elvin and Edmund Leach.

The simple answer is no. The Nile is largely unstoppable. The flood is so strong that it cannot be diverted, only watched. Before and after it floods, its lateral movement across the trench can be altered by social organization. This means that each lateral flood basin and its social organization is technically independent of the others. *Local* control is all that is required. Butzer (1976) shows that in imperial Egypt water legislation was rudimentary and locally administered; there was no centralized irrigation bureaucracy. The only major coordinated irrigation work of which we have evidence was the opening up of the Fayum depression in the nineteenth century B.C., well into the Middle Kingdom, and much too late to explain Egypt's imperial structure. The Nile was crucial for state power (as we see in the next chapter), but not by virtue of hydraulic agriculture.

Sumer was founded on two rivers, the Tigris and the Euphrates.[7] The Euphrates was the crucial river in the early stages. Like the Nile, these rivers were annually inundated. But the inundation took different forms. The main channel was equally unstoppable, but the broad, flat plain of Mesopotamia, "the land between the streams," created many subsidiary channels whose waters could be diverted onto fields (but then, unlike the Nile, not run off – so producing soil salinization). It also flooded later in the season than the Nile. After the Nile floods there was plenty of time for planting. But planting in Mesopotamia was required *before* the flood. Dikes and levees protected the seeds and water tanks stored flood water. This necessitated tighter, more regular social cooperation, vertical as well as lateral organization, given that channel flows could be controlled. But whether an extensive length of river could be controlled, and why it should be considered desirable to control it, are different matters. The main irrigating interest was in lateral flow. The main vertical effects were on the adjacent downstream area, introducing a strategic and military element: Upstreamers could control the water supply of downstreamers, leading perhaps to coercive blackmail backed by military force. Upstreamers' despotism would rest not on control of downstreamers' labor, as in the Wittfogel model, but on control of their vital natural resources.

But both the Euphrates and the Tigris were in the final analysis uncontrollable. The Tigris flowed too fast and deep, the Euphrates' channels changed too unpredictably, to be fully managed by any hydraulic managerial system known to the ancient world. Variability destabilized existing balances of power, as did soil salinization. After the first irrigation breakthrough, existing social organization was used to further irrigation management, rather than vice versa. Cities, literacy, and temples developed five centuries before either the introduction of technical terms for irrigation – found at the end of the Early Dynastic period (Nissen 1976: 23) and even longer before the building of large dams

---

[7]My sources on the characteristics of the rivers are Adams (1965, 1966, and especially 1981: 1–26, 243–8); Jacobsen and Adams (1974); Oppenheim (1977: 40–2).

and canals (Adams 1981: 144, 163). And irrigation was precarious enough to break existing social organization as often as extend it. The social form that emerged was the city-state, exerting control over only a limited length and lateral flow of the river. It may have embodied a degree of stratification, centralized political authority, and coercive labor control, and these – especially the last – owed something to the necessities of irrigation. But it did not embody a despotic state, not even kingship at first. When larger territorial states with kings and emperors later emerged, control over irrigation was a *part* of their power, especially the strategic upstreamers' power, but we shall see that this was only a subsidiary factor.

In short, there was no necessary connection in the ancient world between hydraulic agriculture and despotism, even in the three apparently favorable areas of China, Egypt, and Sumer. Hydraulic agriculture played a large part in the emergence of literate civilizations and in their intensification of territorially and socially fixed organization. The extent of hydraulic agriculture probably did have a substantial influence on the extent of social organization, but not in the direction assumed by Wittfogel. Hydraulic agriculture encouraged dense but small social groups and protostates, controlling a limited length and breadth of a floodplain or river valley – say, city-states as in Sumer, or the domains of local lords or *nomarchs* as in China and Egypt, or self-governing village communities as elsewhere in China, or, indeed, virtually *any* form of local government. In numbers the early Sumerian towns may have been typical of capacities generated by irrigation. They usually varied from about 1,000–20,000 in population, with an unknown number of clients in their hinterlands. As I stressed, much of even this size and concentration was due to the more diffuse effects of irrigation on its environs, not to irrigation management alone. At most in the Early Dynastic I period a town would exercise loose hegemony over its neighbors, a political control over perhaps 20,000 persons. The radius of such a zone would vary from about five to fifteen kilometers. These were tiny societies. In Mesopotamia it is especially striking that of the most important cities, Eridu and Ur, and Uruk and Larsa, were within sight of one another!

Irrigation carried a substantial increase in the organizing capacities of human groups – but on *nowhere near* the scale of the world empires, containing millions of inhabitants over hundreds or thousands of kilometers, as envisaged by Wittfogel.

Wittfogel's thesis has four principal failings. (1) It cannot explain the *form* of even the early city-state, not despotic but democratic/oligarchic. (2) It cannot explain the growth of larger and later empires and states. (3) It cannot explain the larger elements of social organization that were already present in the early city-states, the segmental, federal culture – thus some of the forces making for more extensive power were not within the control of the individual state, whether it be despotic or not, an irrigating state or not. (4) It cannot explain the fact that even the growth of the city-state core was not unitary, but *dual*. What emerged was both centralized state *and* decentralized stratification relations based on private property. The latter are neglected by Wittfogel. His model of all ancient states is quite fanciful in the real infrastructural power it attributes to them. We will see continuously that the *same* forces that increased state power then also decentralized and destabilized (see especially Chapter 5). Along with the state grew a stratum of leading families with private landholdings: Along with monarchy and despotism grew aristocracy.

This formidable catalogue of failure rests on an underlying model of a unitary society. Wittfogel's failings are attributable mainly to this model. All but the first turn upon the federal, segmental nature of social development in those times. This gives us a basis for arriving at a better explanation of the forms of early social development.

But the intensification of civilization, the state, and social stratification was a long-drawn-out business. I cannot in this chapter arrive at an alternative explanation of imperial despotic regimes to Wittfogel, because they didn't emerge in early Mesopotamia. That is principally a task for Chapter 5, which discusses the Akkadian dynasty (the first real "empire" of history) and its successors. However, we can anticipate to a degree that explanation. An old force, *militarism*, became of greater significance as Mesopotamian society matured.

Militarism, diffusion, despotism, and aristocracy: true correlations

To explain the growth of states and social stratification in Mesopotamia, we must acknowledge a slight gearshift around the twenty-seventh century B.C. in the transition from what is called Early Dynastic I to Early Dynastic II. According to Adams (1981: 81–94), settlement patterns shifted around then. Although most of the population was already living in towns, the towns were roughly the same size. With the exception of Uruk, little "settlement hierarchy" had appeared. Uruk then greatly increased its size, as did several other cities. At the same time, many of the smaller settlements were abandoned, which means – deduces Adams – that tens of thousands of persons must have been persuaded or compelled to move. Uruk now covered two square kilometers with a population of up to 40,000–50,000. To support this population required organized control over a large hinterland. Adams suggests a radius of fourteen kilometers of controlled, fairly regularly cultivated land, plus looser hegemony over a broader area. In both areas, the logistics of commuting and transporting produce suggests that fields were tilled and herds grazed by local dependent labor, not by the free central city dwellers. In turn, this suggests further division of labor and stratification between the urban core and rural periphery. The interaction processes evident earlier intensified throughout the early third millennium.

But with intensification came changes. The cities were now surrounded by massive fortified walls. Personages appear who are named *lugal* and reside in large building complexes called *é-gal* – translated as "king" and "palace." They appear in texts alongside new terms for military activities. If we engage in the risky business of giving dates to the first rulers mentioned in the king list (written down in about 1800 B.C.), we get to about the twenty-seventh century for the first great kings, Enmerkar of Uruk and Gilgamesh, his famous successor. Jacobsen conjectured on this basis that kings originated as war leaders, elected for a temporary period by the democratic oligarchic assembly of the city. In a period of conflict and instability, they gained long-term authority because war and fortifications required military organization over a number of years. For a period the *lugal* sometimes existed alongside other figures like the *sanga,* and the *en* or *ensi,* temple officials who combined ritual with administrative roles. Gradually, the king monopolized authority and, though the temple retained some autonomy vis-à-vis the palace, he eventually became also the main initiator of religious ritual.

The Gilgamesh epic, written down about 1800 B.C., gives a full account of this, although whether it is fact or later ideology is another matter. Gilgamesh, who starts as the *en* of Uruk, leads resistance to an attack mounted by the city of Kish. At first he needs the permission of both a council of elders and an assembly of the entire male population before he can make major decisions. But his victory boosts his authority. The distribution of the spoils and subsequent near-permanent fortification building give him private resources with which he gradually turns his representative authority into coercive power. One part of this has turned out to be fact: The town walls of Warka, attributed to Gilgamesh in the legend, have been dated to the correct period.

By 2500 B.C., the dozen or so city-states of which we have evidence seem to have been led by a king with despotic pretensions. In their military struggles, several seem to have attained a temporary hegemony. The militarism culminated in the first major empire, of Sargon of Akkad, described in Chapter 5. In short, we enter a distinctive militarist phase. We can reintroduce militarist theories of the origins of the state, discussed in the last chapter, not to explain origins but to assist in the explanation of *further* state development. As applied to origins, the theories had two major weaknesses in Chapter 2: Military organization of the type that boosted the power of its commanders actually presupposed the power capacity of states; and societies took steps to ensure that their military commanders were not able to convert temporary authority into permanent, coercive power. But with states, stratification, and civilization already developing, these objections lose force. Managerial techniques that had been applied already to irrigation, to redistribution and exchange, and to patron-client relations between core and periphery could develop military offshoots. High-investment defense at first predominated, both in fortifications and in the dense, slow-moving phalanxes of infantry and animal carts that constituted the early armies. Such formations boost centralized command, coordination, and supply.

The conversion of temporary authority into permanent, coercive power is slightly more problematic. However, one boost was the caging of the population into these particular city-states. This point has been made by Carneiro (1961, 1970; cf. Webb 1975) in his militarist theory of "environmental circumscription." He notes, as I have done, the importance of circumscribed agricultural land in the origins of civilization. He argues that when agriculture is intensified, the population becomes even more trapped. Population pressure worsens the situation. War is the only solution. As there is nowhere for the defeated to flee, they are expropriated and become a lower class in an enlarged society. This is used by Carneiro as an explanation of state origins, and so it has defects. Agriculture did not exhaust usable river-valley land; there is a disturbing absence of military artifacts in the earliest remains; and there can be no direct evidence either way about population pressure. But Carneiro is essentially correct on another key issue. He has perceived the problem normally posed to early regimes by authority freely given, and thus freely recoverable. Hence the importance of "circumscription," the social cage, which eliminates part of the freedom. In societies that were already being territorially and socially caged by other pressures, circumscription intensified. The city-walls symbolized and actualized the cage of authoritative power. Adherence to diffused authority crossing its boundaries weakened – one accepted *this* state and its military commander. The gigantic protection racket of political history began: Accept my power, for I will protect you from worse violence – of which I can give you a sample, if you don't believe me.

Yet two problems remain. *Why* did warfare become more important in this period? And how did military authority become permanent coercion?

Answers to the first question tend to depend less on any relevant evidence than on general assumptions about the role of war in human experience. There is little evidence, unfortunately. But if we put our stress not on the frequency of violence but on its organization, we are a little less dependent on general assumptions about human nature. War may be endemic, but centralized military command and conquest are not. They presuppose considerable social organization. It seems plausible that an organizational threshold was passed in Mesopotamia some time after 3000 B.C. The raiding party now had the resources to stay in possession of the enemy's storehouse temple, and stably extract surplus and labor services from them. A response was possible: Invest in defense. An arms race may have been under way, concerned less with weaponry than with developing military organizations whose contours derived from more general social organization. Whether there was also an increase in the frequency of violence is unknown. But the social ecology of Mesopotamia probably led to its persistence through higher levels of social organization. Probably many boundary disputes concerned areas hitherto at the periphery of the territory of the city-states, suddenly rendered more fertile by the variable flow of the river. Many of the prowar party within the city-state were strategically placed to take advantage or – conversely – were the sufferers from the river's change of direction. This is conjecture, however, because of the lack of information concerning the combatants.

We are also uncertain about the extent of the new military authority/power and, therefore, strictly unable to answer the second question posed above. It is difficult, however, to see how a military despotic state could be elevated above society in the continued absence of one crucial resource, a standing army. There was no warrior elite (Landsberger 1955). The army mixed two elements, a "citizen army" of all free, adult males and a "feudal levy" of members of the leading families and their retainers (though these are not terms with Mesopotamian resonance). The *lugal* was probably in origin the primus inter pares of the latter element. He was a rather superior head of a household (as, indeed, was the city god). Kingship legitimated itself in terms of "absolute rank." It introduced a fixed highest point into rank and genealogical measurement out from it. A few later kings did found short-lived dynasties. In these cases, absolute rank was institutionalized. But none claimed divinity or special relationship to past generations, and most were merely strongmen, drawn out of the leading families and dependent upon them. The king could not keep the state's resources to himself. Militarism enhanced not only the *lugal* but also the private-property resources of the leading families. Toward the end of the Early Dynastic period, there were signs of tension between monarchy and aristocracy, with new peripheral elements playing a key role. The last kings were employing lieutenants with Semitic names, indications perhaps that they were attempting to build up their own mercenary force, independent of the leading Sumerian families. We know with hindsight that the mercenaries took over (but they were far more than mere mercenaries). They considerably intensified state and stratification. But to explain that (in Chapter 5) will involve further widening the argument.

So even the intensification of state and stratification at the end of the Early Dynastic period did not proceed far. The population was more clearly caged – what irrigation had started, militarism continued – but neither class nor the state had attained the permanent coercive force normal to the next four and a half millennia of history. Exploitation there was, but only part time. As Gelb (1967) noted, everybody still worked. To take the state and stratification further, to imperial dynasties and to landowning classes, requires that we bring in the Akkadians, the first marcher lords of history. That will widen our focus even farther away from irrigation, in Chapter 5.

Conclusion: Mesopotamian civilization as a product of overlapping power networks

I have tried in these sections on Mesopotamia to demonstrate the utility of a model of societies as overlapping power networks. Mesopotamian social development was based on the caging brought by two main networks of interactions: (1) lateral relations between alluvial agriculture and rain-watered agriculture, herding, mining, and foresting – often called core and periphery; and (2) vertical relations along rivers between different alluvial areas and their hinterlands. These intensified both private-property concentrations and a territorial centralization of local social units, so encouraging the development of social stratification and the state. But relations between these principal social networks were loose and overlapping, reducing the force of the cage. Their sum total was Sumerian civilization, a multistate cultural and diplomatic geopolitical power organization. This was the largest organized network with which we were dealing, but itself diffuse, segmental, of uncertain boundaries, and prone to fragment into smaller authoritative city-state units. In later years militarism began to overcome segmentalism and reconsolidate the civilization (more fully described in Chapter 5). The dynamic development depended on these overlaps, not to have been a product of some endogenous dynamic analogous to that outlined by Wittfogel. Mesopotamia was not unitary but a multi-power-actor civilization. It resulted from various interaction networks created by ecological diversity, opportunity, and constraint. Let us see in the next chapter whether such patterns were specific to Mesopotamia or general to the earliest civilization. On that basis we can arrive at general conclusions regarding the origins of civilization, stratification, and states, which we shall do at the end of Chapter 4.

Bibliography

Adams, R. McC. 1965. *Land Behind Baghdad*. Chicago: University of Chicago Press.
1966. *The Evolution of Urban Society*. London: Weidenfeld & Nicolson.
1981. *Heartland of Cities*. Chicago: University of Chicago Press.
Adams, R. McC., and H. J. Nissen. 1972. *The Uruk Countryside*. Chicago: University of Chicago Press.
Bloch, M. 1977. The disconnections between power and rank as a process: an outline of the development of kingdoms in central Madagascar. *Archives Européennes de Sociologie*, 18.
Butzer, K. 1976. *Early Hydraulic Civilization in Egypt*. Chicago: University of Chicago Press.
Carneiro, R. L. 1970. A theory of the origins of the state. *Science*, 169.
1981. The chiefdom: precursor of the state. In *The Transition to Statehood in the New World*, ed. G. D. Jones and R. R. Kautz. Cambridge: Cambridge University Press.
Chi, T.-T. 1936. *Key Economic Areas in Chinese History*. London: Allen & Unwin.

Childe, G. 1950. The Urban Revolution. *Town Planning Review*, 21.

Diakonoff, I. M. 1969. Main features of the economy in the monarchies of ancient western Asia. *Third International Conference of Economic History*, Munich, 1965. Paris: Mouton.

1972. Socio-economic classes in Babylonia and the Babylonian concept of social stratification. In *XVIII Rencontre assyriologique international*, ed. O. Edzard. Munich: Bayer, Ak-abh, phil, hist kl. Abh.

1975. Ancient writing and ancient written language: pitfalls and peculiarities in the study of Sumerian. *Assyriological Studies*, 20.

Eberhard, W. 1965. *Conquerors and Rulers: Social Forces in Modern China*. Leiden: Brill.

Elvin, M. 1975. On water control and management during the Ming and Ch'ing periods. In *Ching-Shih wen Li*, 3.

Fei, H. T. 1939. *Peasant Life in China*. London: Routledge.

Flannery, K. 1968. The Olmec and the valley of Oaxaca. *Dumbarton Oaks Conference on the Olmec*. Washington: Dumbarton Oaks.

1972. The cultural evolution of civilizations. *Annual Review of Ecology and Systematics*, 3.

1974. Origins and ecological effects of early domestication in Iran and the Near East. In *The Rise and Fall of Civilisations*, ed. C. C. Lamberg-Karlovsky and J. A. Sabloff. Menlo Park, Calif.: Cummings.

Gelb, I. 1967. Approaches to the study of ancient society. *Journal of the American Oriental Society*, 87.

1969. On the alleged temple and state economics in ancient Mesopotamia. *Studi in Onore di Eduardo Volterra*, 6.

Gibson, M. 1976. By state and cycle to Sumer. In *The Legacy of Sumer*, ed. D. Schmandt-Besserat. Malibu, Calif.: Undena.

Hawkins, J. 1977. *Trade in the Ancient Near East*. London: British School of Archaeology in Iraq.

Hole, F., and K. Flannery. 1967. The prehistory of southwestern Iran. *Proceedings of the Prehistoric Society*, 33.

Jacobsen, T. 1943. Primitive democracy in ancient Mesopotamia. *Journal of Near Eastern Studies*, 2. (Also chap. 9 in Jacobsen, 1970.)

1957. Early political developments in Mesopotamia. *Zeitschrift Fur Assyriologies*, N.F., 18. (Also chap. 8 in Jacobsen 1970.)

1970. *Towards the Image of Tammuz and other Essays in Mesopotamian History and Culture*. Cambridge, Mass.: Harvard University Press.

Jacobsen T., and R. McC. Adams. 1974. Salt and Silt in Ancient Mesopotamian Agriculture. In C. C. Lamberg-Karlovsky and J. Sabloff, *Ancient Civilization and Trade*. Albuquerque: University of New Mexico Press.

Jankowska, N. B. 1970. Private credit in the commerce of ancient western Asia. In *Fifth International Conference of Economic History*, Leningrad, 1970. Paris: Mouton.

Jones, G. D., and Kautz, R. C. 1981. *The Transition to Statehood in the New World*. Cambridge: Cambridge University Press.

Jones, T. B. 1969. *The Sumerian Problem*. New York: Wiley.

1976. Sumerian administrative documents: an essay. *Assyriological Studies*, 20.

Kang, S. T. 1972. *Sumerian Economic Texts from the Drehem Archive*, vol. 1. Urbana: University of Illinois Press.

Kramer, S. N. 1963. *The Sumerians*. Chicago: University of Chicago Press.

Kristiansen, K. 1982. The formations of tribal systems in later European pre-history:

northern Europe 4000 B.C. – 500 B.C. In *Theory and Explanation in Archaeology*, ed. C. Renfrew et al. New York: Academic Press.

Lamberg-Karlovsky, C. C. 1976. The economic world of Sumer. In *The Legacy of Sumer*, ed. D. Schmandt-Baesserat. Malibu, Calif.: Undena.

Landsberger, G. 1955. Remarks on the archive of the soldier Ubarum. *Journal of Cuneiform Studies*, 9.

Leach, E. 1954. *The Political Systems of Highland Burma*. London: Athlone Press.

Levine, L. P., and T. C. Young. 1977. *Mountains and Lowlands: Essays in the Archeology of Greater Mesopotamia*. Malibua, Calif.: Undena.

Marfoe, L. 1982. Cedar Forest to silver mountain: on metaphors of growth in early Syrian society. Paper given to a Conference on Relations between the Near East, the Mediterranean World and Europe: 4th–1st Millennia B.C., Aarhus, Aug. 1982.

Needham, J. 1971. *Science and Civilisation in China*, vol. IV, pt. 3 (pub. separately). Cambridge: Cambridge University Press.

Nissen, H. J. 1976. Geographie. In *Sumerological Studies in Honor of Thorkild Jacobsen*, ed. S. J. Lieberman. Chicago: University of Chicago Press.

Oates, J. 1978. Mesopotamian social organisation: archaeological and philological evidence. In *The Evolution of Social Systems*, ed. J. Friedman and M. J. Rowlands. London: Duckworth.

Oppenheim, A. L. 1977. *Ancient Mesopotamia*. Chicago: University of Chicago Press.

Perkins, D. 1968. *Agricultural Development in China 1368–1968*. Chicago: University of Chicago Press.

Renfrew, C. 1972. *The Emergence of Civilisation: The Cyclades and the Aegean in the Third Millennium B.C.* London: Methuen.

  1975. Trade as action at a distance. In *Ancient Civilization and Trade*, ed. J. Sabloff and C. C. Lamberg-Karlovsky. Albuquerque: University of New Mexico Press.

Rowton, M. B. 1973. Autonomy and Nomadism in western Asia. *Orientalia*, 4.

  1976. Dimorphic structure and the problem of the 'Apiro-Ibrim'. *Journal of Near Eastern Studies*, 35.

Sabloff, J., and C. C. Lamberg-Karlovsky. 1976. *Ancient Civilization and Trade*. Albuquerque: University of New Mexico Press.

Shennan, S. 1983. Wessex in the third millennium B.C.: a case study as a basis for discussion. Paper given to a symposium "Time and History in Archaeology and Anthropology," Royal Anthropological Institute, London.

Smith, A. 1983. Are nations modern? Paper given to the London School of Economics "Pattern of History" seminar, Nov. 28, 1983.

Steward, J. 1963. *Theory of Culture Change*. Urbana: University of Illinois Press.

Webb, M. C. 1975. The flag follows trade. In *Ancient Civilization and Trade*, ed. J. Sabloff and C. C. Lamberg-Karlovsky. Albuquerque: University of New Mexico Press.

Wittfogel, K. 1957. *Oriental Despotism*. New Haven, Conn.: Yale University Press.

Wright, H. 1977. Recent research on the origin of the state. *Annual Review of Anthropology*, 3.

Wright, H., and G. Johnson. 1975. Population, exchange and early state formation in southwestern Iran. *American Anthropologist*, 73.

4 A comparative analysis of the emergence of stratification, states, and multi-power-actor civilizations

Does my model of the caging impact of alluvium and irrigation on overlapping regional power networks apply to other cases as well as to Mesopotamia? Were they also essentially dual, combining small, intense city-states within a segmental, multistate civilization? I consider this in the briefest possible terms, examining only whether the other cases would seem to fit broadly into, or deviate from, the general model. I will spend more time on deviations, suggesting, where I can, their possible causes. Let me add that I respect the unique and the ideographic in local histories. All these cases were different. I expect the model to be of suggestive, not mechanical, application.

I start with the cases that seem most similar, those of the Indus Valley and China. Then I move to a case whose origins may be broadly similar but whose later development is quite different – that of Egypt. Then I discuss the final, possibly independent, and, if so, distinctly deviant, Eurasian case – that of Minoan Crete. Finally, I shift continents to the two American cases, which offer generally greater difficulties to the model. In conclusion, I delineate the dominant path taken to civilization, stratification, and states.

The Indus Valley civilization

Sometime around 2300 to 2000 B.C. (exact dating is not possible), there existed a literate, urban, ceremonially centered civilization in the Indus Valley in present-day Pakistan.[1] We do not know much about this civilization, and we will not until its script is deciphered. Scholars believe its origin to be largely indigenous, its civilization and state "pristine." But its end is unknown. It collapsed (this accounts for our failure to read its script, for no later bilingual texts survive). The usual explanations of collapse are destruction by Aryan invaders who later dominated the Indian subcontinent, and ecological disasters such as climatic or river change, but there is no evidence for either. If it collapsed under internal strain, this would make it different from my Mesopotamian model.

Thus similarities should not be pressed too far. This is especially true for

---

[1] Sources used in this section were Allchin and Allchin 1968; various essays in Lamberg-Karlovsky and Sabloff 1974; Sankalia 1974: 339–91; Chakrabarti 1980; and Agrawal 1982: 124–97.

irrigation, a centerpiece of my Mesopotamian explanation. There are agricultural parallels. The Indus settlements, like the Mesopotamian, follow almost exactly the line of alluvial floodplain. The agricultural boost to civilization was, almost certainly, nature's artificial fertilizer, silt. Settlement resulted once again in a population caged socially and territorially between floodplain and, in this case, surrounding jungle mixed with waste scrub. Scholars generally assume that the inhabitants did practice irrigation, but the rivers have obliterated almost all the evidence. The towns did use water channels for domestic use, and they were well protected from floods.

In other respects, too, there is a complex mixture of differences and similarities. The importance of rather secular temples linked to massive storehouses recalls Mesopotamia, as does the "federal" structure of the civilization with at least two major cities, each of about 30,000–40,000 population, surrounded by hundreds of other small settlements. Trade, both local and regional, both "lateral" and "vertical," and reaching even to Mesopotamia, was also extensive. This may indicate the same lateral and vertical overlapping networks of social interaction as in Mesopotamia. But in this case the development of internal hierarchy seems not so pronounced. Burials do not reveal many differences of wealth or social stratification. Yet the regularity of the town planning, the wealth of standardized weights and measures, and the dominance by a few central temples or palaces indicate a stronger city political authority, though not necessarily a state that could coerce its people. In fact, warlike remains are few. The state might have been a "primitive democracy," as Jacobsen suggested for early Mesopotamia.

It is tempting to view this civilization as a cross between the Early Dynastic I phase of Mesopotamian development and a more developed version of the monument builders of prehistory – an alluvial, literate Stonehenge, perhaps. Because caged and able to produce a large surplus, it developed a civilization, but one heavily centered on political authority, without the developmental dynamics of the interrelations between state and dominant economic class, and between core and periphery, that I shall guess to be the main motor of social development in other surviving, successful civilizations.

In short, Indus offers a degree of support to my general model: a Mesopotamian-type early civilization abruptly arrested. Given the paucity of evidence, we should not expect more.

Shang China

The first Chinese civilization flourished around the Huang Ho (the Yellow) River from about 1850 to 1100 B.C.[2] Scholarly consensus is now that in most

[2]Main sources for this section were Cheng 1959, 1960; Creel 1970; Wheatley 1971; Ho 1976; Chang 1977; and Rawson 1980.

major respects it was an autonomous development, a pristine civilization. I find this a surprisingly firm conclusion, given that it was over a millennium later than Mesopotamia and Egypt and centuries behind the Indus Valley – did news travel that slowly in prehistory? The civilization acquired the name Shang from the dynasty of kings accredited by later Chinese to the period. From very early we have indications of a high degree of inequality, craft specialization, large "palace" buildings, and a level of development of bronze metallurgy unparalleled anywhere else in the world. By about 1500 b.c., we have the essential ingredients of civilization – writing, urbanization, and large ceremonial centers – plus monarchy with divine claims, cities with massive fortifications probably involving a labor force of over ten thousand, a high level of warfare, and large-scale human sacrifice. This represents a faster move toward a highly stratified, coercive civilization.

Again, the civilization originated along a river that carried alluvial silt. But this intersected with a second uniquely fertilized type of soil, loess. This is a thick deposit of soft soil blown from the Gobi Desert in the Pleistocene period, forming a giant irregular hollow circle through the center of which flows the Huang Ho River. Loess soil, rich in minerals, generates large cereal yields. Slash-and-burn agriculture could be practiced for unusually long periods, resulting in relatively caged settlement without irrigation. By the Shang period, two crops of millet and rice were grown on the same land per year, which may suggest the caging techniques of irrigation – although we have no direct evidence of this. The river was always the core of this civilization. Nevertheless, as in Mesopotamia we find ecological and economic diversity in and around the core. Plant fibers and silks for clothing; cattle, pigs, and chickens for food; and wild animals like boar, deer, and buffalo attest to this diversity and to the importance of core-periphery lateral relations. Again we can find evidence of regional power interactions, involving exchange and conflict with pastoralists and also exploitation of copper and tin ores, to make bronze, found about 300 kilometers from An-yang (the capital from about 1400 b.c.).

"Temple"-centered redistributive institutions emerged. As Wheatley has emphasized, temples were the first centers of the civilization. Sooner, however, than in Mesopotamia militarism became pronounced. Later, horse breeding becomes evident, one of a number of developments that suggest that Chinese civilization was more expansive and less bounded. The religious pantheon was looser and more open to outside influence. Urbanization was not so pronounced, and settlement more dispersed. The river system was itself less confining: Agriculture, trade, and culture spread along and around the Yellow River system and then to virtually all the rivers of north and central China. In these areas, indigenous inhabitants acquired Shang civilization yet were politically autonomous. Their states may have acknowledged Shang hegemony. One group, the Chou, living in the western marches, became unusually developed (as we guess from its discursive texts). Eventually the Chou conquered the Shang and founded their own dynasty, the first continuously recorded in Chinese historical sources.

I conjecture, therefore, that the origins of the civilization may not have been dissimilar to those of Mesopotamia. But once the basic organizations of power were in place, the greater openness of the terrain and the greater similarity of the activities of the inhabitants across the region gave an earlier role to militaristic intensification of state and social stratification, later also found in Mesopotamia. Monarchy rather than oligarchy appears rather earlier. Chinese culture was less segmental, more unitary. Diversity was expressed more through the "feudal" tendencies of monarchical disintegration than through a multistate structure. Later, in the Han period, Chinese ruling-class culture became far more homogeneous, even unitary.

Again the virtues seem demonstrated of an analysis centered on the impact of alluvial, perhaps irrigation, agriculture upon regional social networks. And again a segmental religious culture later became more militarist. But to press it further would unearth considerable local peculiarities.

Egypt

I will not waste time detailing the obvious: Irrigation agriculture was decisive in generating civilization, stratification, and the state in Egypt. No one has ever doubted it. Throughout ancient history the Nile trench supported the highest population density known to the world. Because of the ecological barrier presented by the surrounding deserts, it was also the most trapped. Once irrigation filled up the trench, no evasion was possible: As productivity grew, so too did civilization, stratification, and the state. The process was as in Mesopotamia, but squared. Early on, it is also possible to glimpse some of the same segmental regional elements as existed in Mesopotamia. The culture of the prehistoric peoples, and of those of the succeeding protodynastic period, was broader than any single political unit; and from earliest times longdistance trade was bringing cultural styles and artifacts from further afield. But if the model of irrigation stimulus to overlapping regional networks may have early application, it then rapidly loses explanatory power. For Egypt became unique, the one near-unitary society in the ancient world. I seek to explain its deviation from my model.[3]

The uniqueness of Egypt is revealed most obviously by the power and stability of rule of the Egyptian pharaoh. If we only had the New Kingdom (1570–715 B.C., though all Egyptian chronology involves some guesswork) to go on, we would be on the familiar ground of later chapters (especially Chapters 5, 8, and 9). True, the pharaoh was a god – but we find divine

[3]Main sources were Wilson 1951; Vercoutter 1967; Cottrell 1968; Edwards 1971; Smith 1971; Hawkes 1973; Butzer 1976; Murray 1977; Janssen 1978; O'Connor 1974, 1980.

emperors and kings elsewhere, and like them the rule of the pharaohs was beset by decentralizing tendencies and even revolts. Unlike their predecessors, they built fortified citadels. True, their temples of Karnak, Luxor, and Medinet Habu are extraordinary – but perhaps no more than the Great Wall or the Grand Canal in China, or than Rome's roads or aqueducts. The rule of the pharaohs in this period, as in other historical cases, was buttressed by large armies and an aggressive foreign policy. The dominant iconography – the pharaoh driving his chariot over the bodies of his enemies – could have come from any ancient empire of domination (see Chapter 5). We can also readily comprehend the two Intermediary periods between dynasties (2190–2052 and 1778–1610 B.C.), during which central power collapsed amid civil war and (in the latter case) foreign invasion.

But even if we exclude these periods, we are faced with the Old and the Middle kingdoms, two long phases of Egyptian history during which pharaonic power seems immense and relatively unchallenged. The Old Kingdom's height (2850–2190) is especially difficult to understand. For almost seven hundred years the pharaoh claimed to rule as a god – not god's vicar or representative on earth, but as Horus the life force or the son of Re, the sun god. From this period date the largest man-made constructions the earth has yet seen, the pyramids. Their construction without wheels must have involved labor of a scale, intensity, and coordination hitherto unparalleled even by the megalith builders.[4] Like the megaliths, they were constructed – indeed, pharaonic power was constructed – without a standing army. A few troops were supplied by each *nomarch* (local lord) to the pharaoh, but none were responsible to him alone, apart from a personal bodyguard. We find few traces of internal militarism, repression of popular revolts, slavery, or legally enforced statuses (such references are common in the Bible, but this relates to the New Kingdom).

Given the logistics of ancient communications (to be detailed in Chapter 5), the pharaoh's actual infrastructural control over local life must have been much more limited than his formal despotic powers. When the Old Kingdom began to collapse, it lost control over the *nomarchs,* who must have been able to exert power in their own areas much earlier. There were revolts and usurpers, but the latter conspired with the scribes to suppress their own origins. Ideological preference for stability and legitimacy is itself a social fact. No other society's scribes are quite as interested in these virtues. They tell us that there was no written law code, only pharaoh's will. Indeed, no words indicate

---

[4]Although they would have been surpassed by the construction of MX missile sites in the United States (see Volume II) – both monuments to nonproductive labor. It is conventional for modern writers to engage in a little speculative purple prose about the construction of the pyramids – ''What could have been the states of mind of those toiling laborers erecting monuments of such grandeur yet futility?'' etc. Perhaps we could go and ask the laborers and construction engineers of Utah.

consciousness of separation between state and society, only distinction between geographical terms like "the land" and terms applying to the pharaoh like "kingship" and "rule." All politics, all power, even all morality apparently resided with him. The crucial term *Macat*, denoting all the qualities of effective government, was the nearest the Egyptian came to a general conception of "the good."

I do not wish to convey the image of an unequivocally benevolent state. One of its oldest insignia – the entwined shepherd's crook and the scourge – could perhaps stand as a symbol of the dual functionality/exploitation of all ancient empires. But a difference between Egypt and other empires existed, at least until the New Kingdom. Why?

One possible explanation, based on hydraulic agriculture, does not work, as we have seen in Chapter 3. In Egypt, Nile irrigation would lead only to localized agro-managerial despotism, and that is precisely what did not occur. Nor do I find convincing an idealist explanation, that the power derived from the content of Egyptian religion. That content needs explaining.

Let us return to the Nile, not as hydraulic agriculture but as a communications network. Egypt had in the Nile the best communications of any extensive preindustrial state. The country was a long narrow trench, every part of which was reachable by the river. The river was navigable both ways, except at flood time. The current flowed north; the prevailing wind south. Natural conditions for extensive economic and cultural exchange and unification could not have been better. But why should this have led to a single state? After all, in medieval Germany the Rhine was similarly navigable but sustained many local lords, each regulating and exacting tolls from riverine exchanges. Nile traffic was probably controlled from the beginning of our records by the royal seal bearer, an official close to the pharaoh. Why? Centralized control was not merely a product of transport conditions.

The first answer probably lies in geopolitics. We know something of the original preliterate political struggles. Small prehistoric villages were consolidated into two kingdoms of Upper and Lower Egypt in the late fourth millennium. There was probably no period of warring city-states – or at least no legacies to any such entities that anyone wished later to acknowledge. About 3200 B.C., a king of Upper (i.e., south) Egypt, Narmer, conquered the downriver Lower Kingdom and founded his united capital at Memphis. From then on, unity was well-nigh continuous. A glance at ecology helps explain this. There were few overlapping social networks. The geopolitical options for any ruler or collectivity before unification were extremely limited. There were *no* marches, no pastoralists or rain-watered agriculturalists, no marcher lords used as counterweight. There were simply vertical relationships between adjacent powers nestled lengthwise along the river for a thousand kilometers. All communications ran through one's neighbors – therefore no federations or leagues of nonneighboring allies could arise based on anything more substantial than messages exchanged across the desert.

This is unique in geopolitical diplomacy. In Sumer, China, Greece, ancient Italy – any place of which we have knowledge – a city, tribe, or lord always had the option of finding allies, either from similar groups or from the marches, to sustain it or him against stronger neighbors. In balance-of-power systems it takes time for the weak to be absorbed by the strong, and there is always a chance of the strong fragmenting. In Egypt, there was no such defense. Absorption could proceed directly, frontally, with the river its center and the whole population socially and territorially trapped within the domain of the conqueror. From the eventual triumph of the upriver state, it is tempting to assume that upriver position gave strategic superiority. Thus geopolitical struggle and intrigue, and unusual ecology, can lead to a single state centered on possession of the river, its cage. A veritable unitary society resulted.

Once imposed, the single state was relatively easy to maintain, provided the river itself was held, because of its communications strengths. The state imposed a redistributive economy over the whole and thus penetrated everyday life. The pharaoh was the provider of life itself. As a Twelfth Dynasty pharaoh boasted: "I was one who cultivated grain, and worshipped the Harvest-god. The Nile greeted me in every valley. None were hungry in my time, none were thirsty then. All dwelt in content through which I did" (quoted by Murray 1977: 136). The term pharaoh means "great house," an indication of a redistributive state. The state made a biennial (later an annual) census of wealth in animals, and perhaps also in land and gold, and it assessed taxes (in kind or in labor) accordingly. A harvest tax was assessed in the New Kingdom – and probably also in the Old Kingdom – at between half (on large estates) and one-third (on smallholdings) of total yield. This supported the royal bureaucracy and provided seed for next year's crop, with a residue for long-term storage in case of dearth. We suspect also that the major exchanges of internal produce – barley, emmer (a kind of wheat), vegetables, poultry, game, fish – were conducted through the state's storehouses. The system was not actually quite so centralized. Taxes were farmed out to provincial notables, and from the Third Dynasty (ca. 2650 B.C.) on, private-property rights seem to have been held by such notables. This indicates once again that a powerful state and a ruling class with private-property rights are generally found together in the ancient world. The state required the provincial assistance of the latter. Even if this was not acknowledged in ideology – for the pharaoh alone was divine – in practice the body politic was sequestered in the usual way. But in this case the balance of power was unusually tilted toward the monarch. The geopolitical options of discontented *nomarchs* finding allies were few, faced with pharaonic control of the river. As long as the pharaoh remained competent and unthreatened from outside, his internal control was largely unchallenged.

Control was aided by a second ecological factor. Though the Egyptian trench contained agricultural abundance, and its fringes abundant building stones, very little wood and no metals can be found there. Copper and gold could be found in abundance within striking distance to the east and south (especially in Sinai), but desert prevented extension of Egyptian society in that direction. No iron could be found anywhere near Egypt, nor could high-quality wood, which came from the Lebanon. Of these, copper was most important until the beginning of the Iron Age (ca. 800 B.C.), for it was essential to agricultural and military implements alike, and useful (along with gold and silver) as a medium of generalized exchange. The Sinai mines were not controlled by another civilization, for they were even further away from either the Sumerian sphere or from Mediterranean settlements. Their precious metals were subject to casual raiding, especially during transit. The main military expeditions of the Old Kingdom from the First Dynasty on were to secure copper and gold. They were often led by the pharaoh himself, and the copper (and probably also the gold) mines were under direct pharaonic ownership from the First Dynasty on. At this time there were no expeditions aimed at territorial conquest, only commercial raids ensuring the flow of trade and tribute (the two being often indistinguishable) into Egypt. Problems of control over territorial provincial governors would hardly have arisen over this sphere of activity. Even weak states (e.g., in medieval Europe) exert a measure of control over the two functions implied here, smallish military expeditions and the distribution of precious metals and quasi-coinage. If these core "regalian rights" became critical for social development as a whole, then we would predict a rise in state power.

I suggest tentatively that pharaonic power rested on the peculiar combination of (1) geopolitical control over the Nilotic communications infrastructure and (2) disposition of essential metals acquired only through foreign military expeditions. Direct evidence for this assertion is lacking,[5] but it is plausible, and it also helps to make sense of two central Egyptian conundrums: How were the pyramids built without severe repression? And why were there so few towns? Despite a high overall population density, the Nile Valley apparently contained few towns. Even the architecture of the towns cannot be called urban, for aside from royal palaces and temples there were no public buildings or spaces and the great houses were identical to those located in the countryside. Egyptian texts contain no mention of native professional merchants up to 1000 B.C. The level of Egyptian civilization cannot be doubted – its population density and stability, the luxury of its privileged classes, the extent of economic exchange, its literacy, its capacity for social organization, its artistic achievements. But the urban contribution to this, so dominant elsewhere in ancient empires, appears negligible. Could it be that urban functions, especially economic exchange and trade, were undertaken here by the state?

The second conundrum, the relative absence of the lash, involves even

---

[5]It would be nice, for example, to know the causal relations between, and relative contribution to royal finances of, (1) trade and precious-metal monopolies, (2) taxation, and (3) the extensive royal estates.

more guesswork. Two sensible but partial explanations have often been proffered. First, Malthusian population cycles would intermittently create population surpluses available for labor but not supportable in agriculture. Second, the cycle of seasons makes surplus labor available for the months of the dry season and of the inundation by the Nile at a time when families' food resources were exhausted. Both explanations beg a further question – where did the state extract the resources to feed these laborers? Elsewhere in the ancient world, states had to step up coercion at times of population surplus and food dearth if they wished to extract resources from their subjects. Characteristically, they were *unable* to accomplish it, and disintegration, civil war, pestilence, and population decline would ensue. But if the state possesses resources necessary for survival in the first place, it need not extract them from its subjects. If the Egyptian state exchanged "its" copper, its gold, and its foreign-trade goods for foodstuffs, and if it intercepted the flow of the exchange of foodstuffs along the Nile, it might possess food surpluses with which to feed its laborers.

The Egyptian state was probably essential to the subsistence of the mass of its population. If the sources are to be believed, its two periods of disintegration brought famine, a violent death, and even cannibalism to the land. They also brought regional diversity in pottery styles, lacking in other periods. The state's physical possession of the Nile communications infrastructure, foreign trade, and precious metals gave it a monopoly of resources essential to its subjects. Unless subjects sought to organize their own trading expeditions or to control the Nile, force need not be used as directly as it was elsewhere in the ancient world. The pharaoh controlled one consolidated "organization chart," centered on the Nile, uniting economic, political, ideological, and a modicum of military power. There was no alternative power network, cross-cutting this one, in social or territorial space, no system of potential alliances to be built up by the discontented that could enjoy a different power base than the Nile itself.

A consequence of this extraordinary degree of social and territorial caging was that Egyptian culture seems virtually unitary. We have no evidence for clans or lineage groups – the usual horizontally divided groupings in an agrarian society. Although many gods had local origins, most were worshiped throughout the kingdom as part of a common pantheon. Almost uniquely in an empire of the ancient world before the era of the salvation religions, rulers and masses seem to have worshiped more or less the same gods. Naturally their religious privileges were not equal – peasants were not credited with an afterlife, and may not have been buried – but beliefs and participation in ritual became fairly similar across classes. Keith Hopkins has shown for the later period of Roman occupation that brother-sister incest, long assumed to be only a royal practice, was prevalent among all classes (1980). The degree of common cultural participation in a single (and, naturally, highly unequal) society was unique. This was as close an approximation to a unitary social system – the model of societies I am rejecting in this work – as we find throughout recorded history. I suggest that such a social system was the product of quite peculiar circumstances.

Such peculiarities of Egyptian ecology and geopolitics also account for its distinctive pattern of power development – early and rapid development, then stabilization. The greatest pyramids come almost at the beginning. The principal social forms to which I have alluded were established by the mid-third millennium B.C. This also applies to most Egyptian innovations diffused to other civilizations: navigational techniques, the art of writing on papyrus instead of stone tablets; the 365-day, and then the 365¼-day, calendar.

It is a far quicker enhancement of power techniques than we found in Mesopotamia, or in any pristine civilization. Why so rapid? From my general model I speculate that the early Egyptians were forced into a more caged, more intense pattern of social cooperation from which there was no escape. Civilization was the consequence of social caging, but here we find the process intensified. The same economic project as in other pristine civilizations – the creation of unprecedented surpluses – combined with an unusual degree of centralization and coordination of social life to provide both large, ordered, provisioned labor forces and the possibility of releasing personnel into centralized, nonproductive tasks. Communications difficulties with the outside world restricted mercantile or artisanal development or interference. Hence the surpluses and the labor cooperation were turned to monumental and religious-intellectual forms of expression and creativity. The pyramids and the priesthoods, together with their writing and their calendars, were the outcome of an irrigated, centralized, isolated social cage. All the pristine civilizations disturbed the uncaged patterns of prehistory. But Egyptian civilization turned them upside down.

Thereafter the development of power techniques decelerated almost to a standstill. True, the New Kingdom managed to respond to rival land-based empires of domination and to expand militarily into the Levant. But Egypt was protected considerably by its natural boundaries and enjoyed time to react to threats. When later empires learned to combine large-scale land and sea operations, Egyptian independence was finished, first by the Persians, then by the Macedonians and their Hellenistic successors. In any case, the New Kingdom's military adaptations – chariots, Greek mercenaries – were foreign, with little resonance in Egyptian society. As early as the end of the third millennium B.C., Egyptian society had reached a plateau. Its stability was recognized throughout the ancient world. Herodotus, for example, a sensitive observer of the virtues of other peoples, tells us that the Egyptians were credited with being the originators of many things – from the doctrine of the immortality of the soul to prohibiting intercourse in temples! He acknowledges great Egyptian influence upon Greece. He respects their ancient knowledge and admires their stability, dignity, reverence for their own traditions, and rejection of things foreign. He respects them because, as a historian, he respects the *past*.

Nevertheless, we can see an intellectual development in these qualities. In the late New Kingdom, the gods Ptah and Thoth came to represent pure Intellect and the Word by which creation occurred. Between that and Hellenistic Christianity ("In the beginning was the Word") was a probable connection. Eternal verity, life everlasting, was an Egyptian obsession that became a more general desire of humanity. But the Egyptians thought that they had come close to achieving it. The Egyptian state mastered the problems confronting it and then settled back, reasonably satisfied. The restlessness of the later quest for the Word and for Truth came from entirely different sources. Egyptian restlessness, after the first great flowering, seems muted. We see it most clearly in the illicit life of the Pyramids.

The tombs, whose entrances became more and more intricately concealed, were robbed almost invariably, almost immediately. It is the one certain indication of an underworld – not the theocracy's own ideological conception of an underworld of spirits, but the criminal conception. It shows that the records tell us a limited, ideological tale. But it also shows that the struggle over power and resources was as pervasive in Egypt as anywhere else. All that Egypt lacked was the organizational structure for the legitimate expression of *alternative* power interests, either "horizontal" (struggles between clans, towns, lords etc.) or "vertical" (class struggle). The social cage was as total as has ever been seen. In this respect it has not been the dominant model of social organization. We encounter its formidable powers of solidaristic organization once more, around 1600 B.C. But that is all. The development of social organization has, for the most part, had different sources, the interplay of overlapping power networks and, later, of organized social classes.

Minoan Crete

Minoan Crete is a deviant case, but perhaps its deviance matters less for it may not have been an independent, "pristine" civilization.[6] Towns were built in Crete around 2500 B.C., and complexes that we call palaces emerged just after 2000 B.C. Final destruction, after a century of apparently Greek domination, occurred rather suddenly around 1425 B.C. The civilization was thus long-lived. It was also literate, first in pictographs, then from around 1700 B.C. in a (linear A) script that we cannot decipher, finally in a fifteenth-century Greek script (linear B). Linear B tablets reveal again the intersection of private ownership of goods and land with the central storehouse of a redis-

---

[6]My picture is drawn from Nilsson 1950; Branigan 1970; Renfrew 1972; Chadwick 1973; Dow 1973; Matz 1973; Warren 1975; and Cadogan 1976.

tributive economy – again, the palaces and temples may be little more than decorated storehouses and accounts offices. Yet they were reinforced, perhaps later, by a single dominant religion and culture. The scale of social organization is difficult to assess because we are not sure about the extent of coordination between the various palace/temple/urban concentrations. But the biggest, that of Knossos, probably contained at least 4,600 dependents, supported by a directly controlled agricultural population of around 50,000. Minoan Crete was similar to early Sumerian civilization, being a loose cultural segmental federation of palace/temple/urban centers of economic redistribution. Its scale of social organization was comparable to that of the first river-valley breakthroughs.

But there are two major differences from elsewhere. First it seems an unusually peaceful civilization, with few traces of war or fortification. No one can give a good explanation of this, but it does mean that this case cannot be explained by militaristic theories. Second, it was not an irrigation or even an alluvial civilization. Although, as everywhere, agriculture was best rewarded in river valleys (and coastal plains), and although doubtless some diverting of the river waters was practiced, rain-watered agriculture predominated. This makes Minoan Crete unique among the first literate civilizations of Eurasia and has long prompted inquiry and controversy into its origins. It was long believed that literacy and civilization must have diffused from the Near East; nowadays the advocates of an independent local evolution for Crete are vocal (e.g., Renfrew 1972). The most probable route would combine elements from both positions.

Let us distinguish three artifacts that archaeologists find and that might have been diffused: agricultural techniques, decorated artifacts, and writing. We find in late prehistoric times in the Aegean a steady improvement in diversity and purity of grain and vegetable seed and domesticated animal stock, and an increase in the diversity of fish and seafood remains. Considerable diffusion of such improvements can be traced. It is probable that the stimulus for many of these improvements flowed from the Near East, more from imitation of one's neighbors and migrations than through formal trade. The social organization bolstered by such improvements would be essentially local. In the Aegean of the third millennium two particularly useful plants, vines and olives, both of which grew in the same terrain, reinforced this local boost to a surplus through exchange and broke through into regional trade. Areas in which vines, olives, and cereals intersected (like Crete) had key strategic significance and may have had pronounced caging effects upon the population – a "functional equivalent" to irrigation.

The second type of artifact, decorated vases and other trade artifacts, including bronze tools and weapons, now emerged to await the archaeologist. Analysis of their styles reveals that they were largely confined within the Aegean region, relatively uninfluenced by Near Eastern designs. The supposition is that trade was predominantly local. Perhaps the Aegean peoples still had little of value for the Near East. So moves toward urban concentration and pictographs may have been largely indigenous. Their trade was inspired by a combination of three factors: the initial agricultural diffusion, an unusual degree of ecological specialization in which vines and olives played a large role, and excellent communications routes where virtually every settlement was reachable by sea. These various networks intersected in the same area of the Aegean.

The intersection seems to have moved the culture on to writing. As elsewhere, the general cause of writing was the usefulness of stabilizing the point of contact between production and private property on the one hand, and economic redistribution and the state on the other. This makes improbable a purely diffusionist case for literacy. Diffusionists generally assume that writing is so useful that everyone encountering it would seek to acquire it. But in its earliest phases writing had rather precise uses. Unless an ancient society was developing a production/redistribution cycle, it is unlikely that it would have been impressed by writing. Writing answered local needs. Now it is possible that in Crete, and every other ancient case, writing was diffused in the simplest possible sense that the idea was imitated from the single foreign trader with pictograph seals on his pots and bags of goods, or by the single indigenous trader seeing the tablets of a foreign storehouse. In this case only minimal long-distance trade would be necessary for diffusion. We have evidence for trade beyond this minimal level. Trade with Egypt, the Levant, and even northern Mesopotamia flourished in the first literate period. But the details of writing were probably not borrowed, for Minoan script was unlike any other in its signs and its apparent total restriction to the realm of official administration. Indeed, "literacy" would be the wrong word – there is no evidence of general use, in literature or in public inscriptions, for this script.

The combination of the three factors mentioned above had probably carried the early Minoans to the brink. But the brink was one that countless other peoples all over the globe failed to cross. In view of the proximity of Crete to the Near Eastern civilizations and the fact of *some* trade with them, we cannot treat this as a pristine civilization or state. The case seems to show, how much less is required of the breakthrough to civilization once the techniques are already available in a region. The cage in Crete was less barred than in Mesopotamia. The intersection of vine, olive, and cereals was a point of great strategic power. But its capture by a permanent, "literate" state backed by a cohesive religion seems contingent upon wider regional-interaction networks.

Mesoamerica

The importance of the New World civilizations to theories of social development is that scholars generally, though not universally, consider them as autonomous from other civilizations. Because they were indigenous to **another** continent, with different ecology, their development was unique in all kinds of ways. For example, they did not use bronze. Their tool technology was in the Neolithic Age, unlike all the Eurasian civilizations. Nothing can be gained by fitting them into a rigid developmental model, whether based on irrigation, the social caging process, or anything else. Broad, crude similarities are the most to be expected. This may also be true if we compare Mesoamerica with Peru. They were more than a thousand kilometers apart in different environments and had few actual contacts.

In Mesoamerica[7] the appearance of settlement, then of ceremonial centers and perhaps "states," then of urbanization and writing seems to have been a more geographically varied process than elsewhere. Developmental leadership passed successively to different subareas. There were probably three main phases.

What might be termed the first breakthrough, to the appearance of ceremonial centers, to the "Long Count" calendar, and to the beginnings of a script, occurred in lowland areas of the Gulf of Mexico. Archaeological work suggests that its core was rich alluvial land along river levees. Interaction with tropical swiddening agriculture, with fishing villages, and with peripheral peoples supplying raw materials like obsidian encouraged economic and political inequalities, with a rank, chiefly elite based on the alluvial land (see the research reports of Coe and Diehl 1981; the review by Flannery 1982; and the general statement by Sanders and Price 1968). This protocivilization, the Olmec, fits into my overall model. It is similar to early premilitarist Shang China. It shared a low density of urban settlement. San Lorenzo, the most complex settlement, comprised only 1,000–2,000 people. It also shared detailed similarities of religion, calendar, and writing system (though a full script did not develop here). This encourages diffusionist theories: The Shang, or other Asian offshoots of the Shang, might have influenced Olmec culture (see, e.g., Meggers 1975). The possibility of transpacific culture contact remains to cloud any certainty we might feel about Olmec origins.

The second phase presents no major difficulties. The Olmec, following the usual civilizational pattern, also raised up the power capacities of the highland peoples with whom they traded, especially those of the Oaxaca Valley (see Flannery 1968). The Olmec also traded with and influenced the whole of Mesoamerica, as is visible in monumental architecture, hieroglyphs, and the calendar. From now on, though with regional variations, there was one diffuse segmental Mesoamerican culture, much more extensive than the power reach of any single authoritative organization.

But the Olmec did not develop to full statehood (and here the analogy with the Shang breaks down). They were, perhaps, insufficiently caged. They

[7]Apart from the sources detailed below, a good concise account of Mesoamerica is O'Shea 1980, and a longer general account is Sanders and Price 1968. See also various essays in Jones and Kautz 1981.

declined from about 600 B.C. But they had transmitted power capacities to other groups, two of whom pursued distinctive developmental paths in the third phase. One were the Maya of the northern lowlands. By about A.D. 250 they were developing full-scale literacy, the Long Count calendar, large urban centers, their distinctive architecture with the corbel arch, and a permanent state. Nevertheless, the Maya were not particularly caged. The population density of their urban sites was low, probably even lower than in the case of the Shang. Their state was also weak. Both state and aristocracy lacked stable coercive powers over the population. *Absolute rank*, rather than either stratification and state, may be the most appropriate term. There may be ecological reasons for this. The Maya did not practice irrigation. Abundant tropical rainfall gave them two crops per year, and a few alluvial areas made this permanently possible; but there is little evidence of socially and territorially fixed agriculture, and in most areas soil exhaustion would have required periodic movement. In fact, such noncaging conditions are not generally favorable to the emergence of civilization. Even if we allow a strong diffusion from the Olmec and the contemporaneous peoples of the central valleys (to be discussed in a moment) (see Coe 1971; Adams 1974), I cannot claim that my model is on strong ground here. The "regional interaction" theory of Rathje (1971) is similar to my own model, but it can only be a necessary, not a sufficient, explanation. It is easier to explain Mayan collapse (around A.D. 900) than origins. Whether, as scholars debate (see the essays in Culbert 1973), the immediate cause was soil exhaustion, external invasion, or internal civil or "class" war, there would be relatively little forced commitment to fixed social and territorial cages to see them through such crises.

The second group developing civilization were the people of the central valley basin of Mexico. This returns us to the safer ground – or rather water – of irrigation, this time of lakeside areas, within a broader region that had natural mountainous boundaries. From Parsons (1974) and Sanders et al. (1979) we discern slow growth from about 1100 B.C. for several hundred years. Then around 500 B.C. irrigation canals appeared here (and in other parts of highland Mesoamerica), associated with population expansion and nucleation. In the north of the valley around Teotihuaca, this growth was disproportionate, apparently because of unusually good irrigation conditions as well as a strategic position for mining and finishing obsidian. There was intensive exchange with the gatherer hunters and foresters of the periphery. It is a similar pattern of irrigation core and regional interaction networks to Mesopotamia – and with similar social results: growing settlement hierarchy and architectural complexity. By A.D. 100 there had emerged two regional political centers of about 50,000–60,000 people, focused on a capital city, incorporating a few thousand square kilometers of territory, and hierarchically organized. It was by now a "civilization," for it also comprised temples, marketplaces, and calendric and hieroglyphic literacy. By the fourth century A.D., Teotihuaca was a permanent coercive urban state of about 80,000–100,000 people dominating several other states, all in the Highlands. Its influence spread throughout Mesoamerica and dominated the nearer areas of Mayan culture. But it, too, collapsed, more mysteriously, between A.D. 550 and 700. After a short interregnum, it was supplanted by more militaristic, marcher lords of the north, the Toltecs, large-scale exponents of human sacrifice. They expanded an empire over a large part of Mesoamerica. From there we are on recognizably similar terrain to that of the next chapter: the cycle between imperial expansion and fragmentation, and the dialectic between empires and marcher lords. The most famous marcher conquerors were the last. The Aztecs combined a high level of militarism (and human sacrifice) with the most intense level of irrigation agriculture and urbanism seen in Mesoamerica.

Many of these processes are of the same general order as those discerned in Mesopotamia. There are also differences. The origins of the Maya stand out, as in all general models. But for the most part, civilization was built upon widely diffused prehistoric organizational developments. Then the first phase and the central valley part of the third phase introduced caging: confinement to territory, represented by proximity to alluvial river and lake areas and either local or regional raw materials. Hence the dual emergence of tight authoritative organization built around irrigation and of the diffuse networks of exchange and culture radiating outward from it. In turn, that caging process created a familiar outcome. It gave advantages to the marcher lords, and a cycle of core-periphery dominance (discussed in the next chapter) ensued.

But the analogy with Eurasian civilizations should not be pressed too far. The ecology was distinctive. It presents neither the broad regional uniformity of China nor the greatness of contrast between valley and upland of Mesopotamia. It is a region of many but not sudden or great contrasts. This probably ensured that societies were less caged, less prone to centralization and permanence. The political structures of the various civilized and semicivilized peoples were looser than those of the Near East or China.

There was probably a lesser development of collective power in the fifteen hundred years of Mesoamerican civilization than in a comparable stretch of Eurasian time. Its fragility needed the weight of only just over five hundred *conquistadores* to collapse – it is difficult to imagine the power of, let us say, the Assyrians or the Han dynasty breaking so utterly before a comparable threat. The Aztec Empire was a loose federation. Its vassals' loyalty was proven unreliable. Even in its core, Aztec society contained Mayan checks and balances against further state intensification. The religion and calendar inherited from the Maya provided for the circulation of supreme authority in a series of calendar cycles among the various city-state/tribal units of the empire. One cycle was coming to an end – indeed, some locals believed the whole calendar was ending – in the year of *our* lord 1519. The Feathered Serpent would be born and perhaps the pale ancestors would return. In 1519, the pale-bearded Spaniards arrived. The story of how the *conquistadores* were regarded as potential ruling gods even by the Aztec ruler, Montezuma, is one of the great stories of world history. It is generally told as the supreme example of the bizarre accidents of history. It is certainly that. But the calendar and the political revolutions it legitimized are also an example of the mechanisms by which early peoples sought to evade permanent states and social stratification even after we might have assumed they were fully trapped within them. Unfortunately for the Aztecs and their vassals this particular escape route led into the inescapable bondage of European colonialism.

In these respects the general model of a connection between social power and caging seems to be supported as much by the distinctiveness of Mesoamerica as by its similarity to Eurasia. Less caging resulted in less civilization, less permanent institutionalized states, and less social stratification, except when world-historical accident finally intervened.

A final note of caution, however. Many aspects of Mesoamerican history are still unclear or in contention. The creative fusion of American social science in archaeology and anthropology keeps changing the picture. Specialists will recognize that recent theoretical models – of Flannery, Rathje, and Sanders and Price – fit well into my caging/regional-interaction model. If their views are challenged by the next decade's scholarship, then my model is in trouble.

Andean America

The first semiurban settlements and ceremonial centers occurred in the narrow river valleys of the western Andes, based on the yield of simple irrigation linked to exchange with upland pastoralists and coastal fishers.[8] The next phase was of the gradual consolidation of these three components into single chiefdoms, about forty of which existed later at the time of the Inca conquest. These were loosely structured and impermanent. They were also situated within a broader similarity of regional culture, expressed from about 1000 B.C. in the Chavin art style, probably the result of extensive regional interaction networks. This is the familiar ground of later prehistory, with potentiality *either* for the further development of the normal cyclical patterns of prehistory *or* for a civilization breakthrough made possible by the irrigation-core/regional-interaction network combination. A breakthrough did occur, but by the time we know much about it, we are struck by its peculiarities. It does not fit the model.

There are three peculiarities. First, emerging political units initially expanded their influence not through territorial consolidation but through setting up a chain of colonial outposts, which existed alongside and interpenetrated the

[8]Main sources for this section were Lanning 1967; Murra 1968; Katz 1972; Schaedel 1978; Morris 1980; and various essays in Jones and Kautz 1981.

chains of other political units. This is called the "archipelago model" of Andean development. Second, therefore, trade between autonomous units was less dominant as a mechanism of economic exchange than was internal reciprocity and redistribution within each archipelago. Thus when we can begin to call these units states, around A.D. 500–700, they were more redistributive in character than those found in the other cases of pristine civilization. There was little of the overlapping-network path to development and far more of an internal, more caged, path, which is difficult to explain. Third, when one or a few became hegemonic (largely, it seems, through warfare) they incorporated these internal mechanisms. They show precocity in the logistics of power. This is evident from about A.D. 700 in the empire of the Huari, who were great builders of roads, administrative centers, and storehouses. But we know most about the astonishing imperialism of the Inca.

About A.D. 1400–30, one "tribal" grouping and chiefdom, the Inca, conquered the rest. By 1475, the Inca had used massive corvée labor gangs to build cities, roads, and large-scale irrigation projects. They had created a centralized theocratic state with their own chief as god. They had taken land into state ownership and had put economic, political, and military administration into the hands of the Inca nobility. They had either devised or extended the *quipu* system whereby bundles of knotted strings could convey messages around the empire. This was not exactly "literacy." Thus on my earlier definition, the Inca would not be fully civilized. Yet it was as advanced a form of administrative communication as any found in early empires. It was an extremely large (almost 1 million sq. km.) and populous (estimates range from 3 million persons upward) empire. Its size and rapidity of growth are astonishing, yet not wholly unprecedented – we can think of analogous conquest empires like the Zulu. But what is unparalleled is the Inca level of development of the *logistical* infrastructure of authoritative permanent states and social stratification. There were 15,000 kilometers of paved roads! Along them were dotted storehouses within a day's march of each other (the Spaniards found the first ones full of food), and relays of runners supposedly capable of transmitting a message over four thousand kilometers in twelve days (surely exaggerated, unless all the runners were accomplished middle-distance athletes!). Inca armies were well supplied and well informed. When operating abroad they were accompanied by flocks of llamas carrying supplies. Inca victories were gained by an ability to concentrate superior numbers in a given place (details of logistics can be found in Bram 1941). Inca political rule subsequent to their conquests shows the same meticulous logistical capacity. Scholars differ considerably as to the reality on the ground of the so-called decimal system of administration, which at first appears like a uniform "organization chart" imposed over the whole empire. Moore (1958: 99–125) believes it to have been only a tribute-collecting system whose local levels were staffed by conquered elites, loosely supervised by an Inca provincial governor supported by a settler-militia. Anything more developed would have been impossible in such a primitive society. But, nevertheless, such techniques show a logistical cunning only developed in other civilizational areas after a millennium or more of state development. They remind one of the Han dynasty of China, or of the Assyrians or Romans of the Near Eastern and Mediterranean world – an ideological obsession with centralization and hierarchy, pushed to the limits of the practicable.

If we focus on these logistical achievements, then the Inca (and perhaps also some of their predecessors) seem too precocious to fit easily into my model. In fact, they present difficulties for any general model. To say, for example, that they present "all the characteristics of an Oppenheimer 'Conquest state,' " as Schaedel (1978: 291) does, is to miss the essential point – they were the *only* example of a conquest pristine state, where an original state, the product of military artifice, is then stably institutionalized. Indeed, all explanations of the Inca rise that regard it as fitting into a general pattern are inadequate. If we take their achievements seriously, they are mysterious.

The alternative would be not to take Inca achievements quite so seriously. After all, they collapsed when 106 foot soldiers and 62 horsemen, led by Francisco Pizarro (and aided by European-introduced epidemics), applied pressure on the Inca himself and he gave way. Without its head, the infrastructure proved to be not a viable social organization but a series of massive artifacts – roads, stone cities – concealing a loose, weak, perhaps essentially prehistoric tribal confederacy. Were these artifacts merely the equivalent of megalithic civilizations, whose monuments also endured through their social collapse? Probably not, for their concern with the logistical infrastructure of power would be evident from their monuments alone. This places them closer in aspirations to much later empires than it does to the megalithic peoples. Their power, when tested against a far more powerful foe, proved brittle – but it seems to have been intended single-mindedly, ruthlessly, *as* power, not as that avoidance of power I argued to be typical of prehistory in Chapter 2. I admit the Inca as an exception, where logistically reinforced militarism played a greater role in the origins of civilization than elsewhere, and where civilization (viewed through the eyes of the other civilizations) seems uneven in its achievements.

Hence the other cases, with the exception of Andean America, indicate the fruitfulness of the general model. Two aspects of social ecology were decisive in the emergence of civilization, stratification, and the state. First, the ecological niche of alluvial agriculture was its core. But, second, this core also implied regional contrasts, and it was the combination of the relatively bounded, caged core and its interactions with various but overlapping regional networks of social interaction that led to further development. Egypt, once established, was exceptional for it became a quasi-unitary, bounded social system. But the rest became overlapping networks of power relations, generally with a two-level, federal core of small segmental city-state/tribal units located within a broader civilizational culture. That configuration was present in the various cases, and – it is necessary to add – generally absent in the rest of the globe.

Conclusion: a theory of the emergence of civilization

Civilization was an abnormal phenomenon. It involved the state and social stratification, both of which human beings have spent most of their existence avoiding. The conditions under which, on a very few occasions, civilization did develop, therefore, are those that made avoidance no longer possible. The ultimate significance of alluvial agriculture, present in all "pristine" civilizations, was the territorial constraint it offered in a package with a large economic surplus. When it became irrigation agriculture, as it usually did, it also increased social constraint. The population was caged into particular authority relations.

But that was not all. Alluvial and irrigation agriculture also caged surrounding populations, again inseparably from economic opportunity. Trading relations also caged (though usually to a lesser extent) pastoralists, rain-watered agriculturalists, fishermen, miners, and foresters over the whole region. Relations between the groups were also confined to particular trade routes, marketplaces, and stores. The higher the volume of trade, the more territorially and socially fixed these became. This did not add up to a *single* cage. I pointed to three sets of different sociospatial, overlapping, intersecting networks: alluvial or irrigated core, immediate periphery, and whole region. The first two settled down into small local states, the third into a broader civilization. All three fixed and made more permanent finite and bounded social and territorial spaces. It was now relatively difficult for the population caged there to turn their backs on emerging authority and inequality, as they had done on countless occasions in prehistory.

But why, within those spaces, did contractual authority then turn into coercive power, and inequality into institutionalized private property? The scholarly literature has not been particularly helpful on this point, precisely because it has rarely realized that these transformations have been abnormal in human experience. They are almost always presented in the literature as an essentially "natural" process, which they certainly were not. The most likely route to power and to property, however, was through the interrelations of several overlapping networks of social relations. To begin with, we can apply a loose "core-periphery" model to these relations.

The Mesopotamian developmental pattern contained five main elements. First, possession by one family/residential group of core land or unusual alluvial or irrigatory potential gave it a greater economic surplus than its peripheral alluvial/irrigating neighbors and offered employment to the latter's surplus population. Second, all alluvials and irrigators possessed these same advantages over pastoralists, hunters, gatherers, and rain-watered agriculturalists of the further periphery. Third, trade relations between these groups concentrated on particular communications routes, especially navigable rivers, and on marketplaces and storehouses along them. Possession of these fixed locations gave additional advantages, usually to the same core alluvial/irrigating group. Fourth, the leading economic role of the alluvial/irrigating core was seen also in the growth of manufacturing, artisanal trades, and reexport trade concentrated in the same locations. Fifth, trade further expanded into the exchange of agricultural plus manufactured goods from the core in return for precious metals from the mountains of the outer periphery. This gave the core disproportionate control over a relatively generalized means of exchange, over "prestige goods" for displaying status, and over the production of tools and weapons.

All five processes tended to reinforce one another, giving disproportionate power resources to the families/residential groups of the core. The various peripheral groups could only turn their back on this power at the cost of foregoing economic benefit. Enough chose not to do this to inaugurate states and stratification of a permanent, institutionalized, and coercive kind. Naturally the details of this development differed in every other case, primarily in response to ecological variations. Nevertheless, the same overall set of factors is everywhere visible.

Thus, when civilization appeared, its most obvious sign, literacy, was primarily used to regularize the intersection of private property and state, that is, of a defined territorial area with a center. Literacy denoted ownership rights and collective rights and duties under a small territorial, centralized, and coercive political authority. The state, its organization centered and territorial, became permanently useful to social life and to dominant groups, in a way that departed from the patterns of prehistory. Possession of the state became an exploitable power resource, as it had not been hitherto.

However, the core-periphery model can only be taken so far. The two were interdependent, and as the core developed, so too (though at different rates) did the various peripheral areas. Some became indistinguishable from the original core. The core's power infrastructure was limited. Dependent labor could be absorbed, certain terms of unequal economic exchange could be imposed, a loose patron-client dominance could be claimed, but little more. The capacity for authoritative social organization was, at first, confined to the few square kilometers of the individual city-state; while no resources for the diffusion of power outward from the authoritative center through an extensive population can yet be discerned. Hence, when peripheral areas developed surpluses, states, and literacy, they could not be controlled from the old core. Eventually the whole distinction between core and periphery evaporated. It is true that in Mesopotamia we began to see the emergence of further military power resources, and that in some of the other cases these may have been pushed further and faster, but these were less and less to the advantage of the old core (as we shall see properly in the next chapter).

In any case, militarism clearly came later, building on top of existing forms of regional organization. In all cases *ideological power* had a privileged role in solidifying regional organizations. In a comparative study of these six cases plus Nigeria (which I do not consider a pristine civilization), Wheatley (1971) concludes that the ceremonial temple complex, not the market or the fortress, was the first major urban institution. He argues that religion's boost to urbanization and civilization was its ability to provide a rational integration of diverse and new social purposes through more abstract, ethical values. This is helpful, provided we restrain the idealism of Wheatley's account and focus on the social purposes satisfied by ceremonial centers. The division between the "sacred" and the "secular" is a later one. It is not, as Wheatley argues, that economic institutions were *subordinated* to the religious and moral norms of society, or that secular institutions later emerged to share power with the already existing sacred ones. The main purposes of the Sumerian temple, on which we have good information, were essentially mundane: to serve first as an intervillage diplomatic service, and later to redistribute economic produce and encode public duties and private-property rights. What we have learned in this chapter confirms the generally mundane quality of the religious cultures of the remaining earliest civilizations. On the other hand, as I suggested in Chapter 1, the religious cultures were *socially transcendent,* providing organized solutions to problems affecting an area more extensive than any existing authoritative institutions could regulate. Regional development produced many points of contact both within and between alluvial and peripheral areas. Persistent problems and opportunities arose, especially in the areas of the regulation of trade, the diffusion and exchange of tools and techniques, marriage regulation, migration and settlement, cooperative production (especially in irrigation), exploitation of labor through property rights, and the definition of just and unjust violence. That is primarily what the ideologies of the emergent religions grappled with, and it is what was played out ritually in the temple forecourt, the temple storehouse, and the inner sanctum. Ideological institutions offered a form of collective power that was loose, diffuse, and extensive, that offered genuine diplomatic solutions to real social needs, and that was thus able to trap wider populations within its "organization chart" of distributive power.

We can thus distinguish two main phases in the development of civilization. The first contained a two-tier federal power structure: (1) Small city-states provided a merged form of economic and political authoritative power organization, that is, "circuits of (economic) praxis" with a pronounced degree of "territorial centredness" (the means of economic and political power, as defined in Chapter 1). This combination trapped relatively small populations.

But (2) these populations lived within a far more extensive, diffused, and "transcendent" ideological and geopolitical organization, generally coterminous with what we call a civilization, but loosely centered on one or more regional cult centers. In the second phase of the earliest civilizations, these two power networks tended to merge, primarily through the agency of further concentrated coercion, that is, of military organization. Although we have already glimpsed this, the story is told fully in the next chapter.

Finally, we have seen that conventional theories of the origins of the state and of social stratification are tainted with evolutionism – as was anticipated in Chapter 2. The mechanisms they claim to be "natural" are, in fact, abnormal. Nevertheless, many mechanisms have been correctly identified in those rare cases where states and stratification did develop. I endorsed a broadly economic view of first origins, mixing eclectically elements from three main theories, liberalism, a revisionist Marxism, and the functional theory of the redistributive state. For later stages of the process, the militaristic mechanisms have greater relevance. But all these attain their relevance only when allied with the model of overlapping power networks, which gives a particular role to ideological power organization, normally neglected in theories of origins. Neither state nor social stratification originated endogenously, from within the bosom of existing, systemic "societies." They originated because (1) out of the loose, overlapping social networks of prehistory emerged one network, alluvial agriculture, that was unusually caged, and (2) in its interactions with several peripheral networks, further caging mechanisms appeared that constrained them all toward greater involvement on two levels of power relations, those within the local state and those within the broader civilization. The history of power can now be carried outward from these few abnormal epicenters, as it was in reality.

Bibliography

Adams, R. E. W. 1974. *The Origins of Maya Civilization.* Albuquerque: University of New Mexico Press.
Agrawal, D. P. 1982. *The Archaeology of India.* London: Curzon Press.
Allchin, B., and R. Allchin. 1968. *The Birth of Indian Civilization.* Harmondsworth, England: Penguin Books.
Bram, J. 1941. An analysis of Inca militarism. Ph.D. dissertation, Columbia University.
Branigan, K. 1970. *The Foundations of Palatial Crete.* London: Routledge & Kegan Paul.
Butzer, K. 1976. *Early Hydraulic Civilization in Egypt.* Chicago: University of Chicago Press.
Cadogan, G. 1976. *Palaces of Minoan Crete.* London: Barrie and Jenkins.
Chadwick, J. 1973. The linear B tablets as historical documents. Chap. 13 (a) in *The Cambridge Ancient History,* ed. I. E. S. Edwards et al. 3d ed. Vol. 2, pt. I. Cambridge: Cambridge University Press.

Chakrabarti, D. 1980. Early agriculture and the development of towns in India. In *The Cambridge Encyclopedia of Archaeology*, ed. A. Sherratt. Cambridge: Cambridge University Press.

Chang, K.-C. 1977. *The Archaeology of Ancient China*. New Haven, Conn.: Yale University Press.

Cheng, T.-K. 1959. *Archaeology in China, Vol. I: Prehistoric China*. Cambridge: Cambridge University Press.

    1960. *Archaeology in China, Vol. II: Shang China*. Cambridge: Cambridge University Press.

Coe, M. D. 1971. *The Maya*. Harmondsworth, England: Pelican Books.

Coe, M. D., and R. A. Diehl. 1981. *In the Land of the Olmec*. 2 vols. Austin: University of Texas Press.

Cottrell, L. 1968. *The Warrior Pharaohs*. London: Evans Brothers.

Creel, H. 1970. *The Origins of Statecraft in China*, vol. 1. Chicago: Aldine.

Culbert, T. P. 1973. *The Classic Maya Collapse*. Albuquerque: University of New Mexico Press.

Dow, S. 1973. Literacy in Minoan and Mycenaen lands. Chap. 13 (b) in *The Cambridge Ancient History*, ed. I. E. S. Edwards et al. 3d ed. Cambridge: Cambridge University Press.

Edwards, I. E. S. 1971. The early dynastic period in Egypt. Chap. 21 in *The Cambridge Ancient History*, Edwards et al. 3rd ed. Vol. I, pt. 2. Cambridge: Cambridge University Press.

Emery, W. G. 1961. *Archaic Egypt*. Harmondsworth, England: Penguin Books.

Flannery, K. 1968. The Olmec and the valley of Oaxaca: a model for inter-regional interaction in formative times. In *Dumbarton Oaks Conference on the Olmec*, ed. E. P. Benson. Washington: Dumbarton Oaks.

    1982. Review of Coe and Diehl: *In the Land of the Olmec*. *American Anthropologist*, 84.

Hawkes, J. 1973. *The First Great Civilizations*. London: Hutchinson.

Hopkins, K. 1980. Brother–sister marriage in Roman Egypt. *Comparative Studies in Society and History*, 22.

Ho, P.-T. 1976. *The Cradle of the East*. Chicago: University of Chicago Press.

Janssen, J. J. 1978. The early state in ancient Egypt. In *The Early State*, ed. H. Claessen and P. Skalnik. The Hague: Mouton.

Jones, G. D., and P. R. Kautz. 1981. *The Transition to Statehood in the New World*. Cambridge: Cambridge University Press.

Katz, F. 1972. *The Ancient American Civilizations*. New York: Praeger.

Lamberg-Karlovsky, C. C., and J. Sabloff. 1974. *The Rise and Fall of Civilizations*. Menlo Park, Calif.: Cummings.

Lanning, E. P. 1967. *Peru Before the Incas*. Englewood Cliffs, N.J.: Prentice-Hall.

Matz, F. 1973. The maturity of Minoan civilization and the zenith of Minoan civilization. Chaps. 4 (b) and 12 in *The Cambridge Ancient History*, ed. I. E. S. Edwards et al. 3d ed. Vol. I, pt. 2. Cambridge: Cambridge University Press.

Meggers, B. 1975. The transpacific origin of Meso-American civilization. *American Anthropologist*, 77.

Moore, S. F. 1958. *Power and Property in Inca Peru*. Westport, Conn.: Greenwood Press.

Morris, C. 1980. Andean South America: from village to empire. In *The Cambridge Encyclopedia of Archaeology*, ed. A. Sherratt. Cambridge: Cambridge University Press.

Murra, J. V. 1968. An Aymara kingdom in 1567. *Ethnohistory*, 15.

Murray, M. 1977. *The Splendour That Was Egypt*. London: Sidgwick & Jackson.

Nilsson, M. P. 1950. *The Minoan-Mycenean Religion and Its Survival in Greek Religion*. Lund, Sweden: Lund University Press.

O'Connor, D. 1974. Political systems and archaeological data in Egypt: 2600–1780 B.C. *World Archaeology*, 6.

1980. Egypt and the Levant in the Bronze Age. In *The Cambridge Encyclopedia of Archaeology*, ed. A. Sherratt. Cambridge: Cambridge University Press.

O'Shea, J. 1980. Mesoamerica: from village to empire. In *The Cambridge Encyclopedia of Archaeology*, ed. A. Sherratt. Cambridge: Cambridge University Press.

Parsons, J. R. 1974. The development of a prehistoric complex society: a regional perspective from the Valley of Mexico. *Journal of Field Archaeology*, 1.

Rathje, W. 1971. The origin and development of Lowland Classic Maya Civilization. *American Antiquity*, 36.

Rawson, J. 1980. *Ancient China: Art and Archaeology*. London: British Museum Publications.

Renfrew, C. 1972. *The Emergence of Civilization: the Cyclades and the Aegean in the Third Millennium B.C.* London: Methuen.

Sanders, W. T., and B. Price. 1968. *Mesoamerica: The Evolution of a Civilization*. New York: Random House.

Sanders, W. T., et al. 1979. *The Basin of Mexico: Ecological Processes in the Evolution of a Civilization*. New York: Academic Press.

Sankalia, H. D. 1974. *Pre-History and Proto-History of India and Pakistan*. Poona, India: Deccan College.

Schaedel, R. P. 1978. Early state of the Incas. *The Early State*, ed. H. Claessen and P. Skalnik. The Hague: Mouton.

Smith, W. S. 1971. The Old Kingdom in Egypt. In *The Cambridge Ancient History*, ed. I. E. S. Edwards et al. 3d ed. Vol. I., pt. 2. Cambridge: Cambridge University Press.

Vercoutter, J. 1967. Egypt. Chaps. 6–11 in *The Near East: The Early Civilizations*, ed. J. Bottero. London: Weidenfeld & Nicolson.

Warren, P. 1975. *The Aegean Civilizations*. London: Elsevier-Phaidon.

Wheatley, P. 1971. *The Pivot of the Four Quarters*. Edinburgh: Edinburgh University Press.

Wilson, J. A. 1951. *The Burden of Egypt*. Chicago: University of Chicago Press.

5 The first empires of domination: the dialectics of compulsory cooperation

The preceding chapter contained familiar themes, some drawn from local evolutionism, some from comparative sociology. Civilization, social stratification, and states originated in the local circumstances of about six broadly similar societies scattered across the globe. Alluvial and irrigation agriculture situated amid overlapping regional networks of social interaction intensified a two-level social cage. In turn, this led to exponential growth in human collective power.

Some of these broad themes continue in this chapter, which describes a further phase of the early history of civilization. Now the social cage became more pronounced, more singular, and much more extensive as a result of another regional interaction process. This time the initial stimulus was less from economic than from military organization. And the resulting geopolitical pattern also shifted. What had been hitherto semiperipheral areas became, in a sense, the new core of civilization. "Marcher lords" were the pioneers of hegemonic empire.

As a similar broad pattern can be seen emerging across most of the cases, this again suggests a general developmental tendency. But now there are even more obvious differences between them. My response is to stick even more closely to the development of the Near Eastern civilization, the best documented and most historically significant case. As we are now firmly in the realm of history, documentation improves and I will be able to look more systematically at the infrastructure of power and at its four distinct organizational means (as promised in Chapter 1).

After discussing the development of Mesopotamian early empires, I will also turn to theories developed by comparative sociologists to explain such empires. We will see that though these theories are successful in pointing out certain broad features of imperial rule, they are static or cyclical in approach. They miss the dialectics of "compulsory cooperation," the central theme of this chapter. Through the power techniques of compulsory cooperation, the "leading edge" of power shifted away from multi-power-actor civilizations to empires of domination.

Background: the growth of militarism and the marches

For something like seven hundred years, the dominant form of Sumerian civilization was a multistate structure of at least twelve principal city-states. Thus

130

there was no swift move toward larger, more hierarchical organizations of power. In the latter half of that period, however, the city-state began to change its internal form as kingship became dominant. Then, from about 2300 B.C., the autonomy of the city-state began to weaken as regional confederations of cities emerged. Finally these were conquered by the first extensive "empire" of recorded history, that of Sargon of Akkad. The empire then remained one of the dominant social forms for three thousand years in the Near East and Europe, and even longer in East Asia. Its initial emergence was obviously a matter of some moment, requiring explanation.

As we saw in the last chapter, scholars generally attribute the first part of the process, the rise of kingship in the later Sumerian city-states, to warfare. The irrigation successes of the city-states made them more attractive as prey to poorer upland neighbors. The records also document many boundary disputes between the city-states themselves. The two types of conflict made defense more critical and led to the construction of massive city walls in the mid-third millennium. Simultaneously, we deduce that war leaders consolidated their rule into kingship. Some authorities suggest they were Akkadian, that is, northern Semites. But as I indicated, local kingship is quite compatible with the relatively centralized, local redistributive irrigation economy and would not have constituted a radical break with Sumerian traditions. Kingship, combining war leadership with direction of the economy, could continue to increase the surplus, and either population levels or living standards. But the more successful it was, the greater its impact upon the power networks of the wider region.

Thus we must look at the balance of power, not only within Sumer, but between Sumer and outside. This involved economic and military considerations, intertwined, of course, as they have been right up to the present day.

As noted in the previous chapter, Sumer was economically specialized. Though favorably placed for generating an agricultural surplus, and therefore for developing a division of labor and manufactured goods, it was relatively lacking in other raw materials, especially ores, precious stones, and wood, and it depended on foreign trade. Now, originally, this trade preceded the state – as had indeed been also true of later prehistory in general. But the more it developed, the greater it depended on the state. As the organizational capacities of all regional groupings increased, even the relatively backward became able to organize raids and to exact tribute from merchants. Trade needed protection from pillage right along its route. But even agreed peaceful exchange between state-controlled territories required a degree of diplomatic regulation, given the absence of an international "currency" denoting the commodity value of a good (see Oppenheim 1970). The growth of trade increased the vulnerability of Sumer in two ways. First it increased both the surplus and the powers of collective organization of all kinds of groups situated a long way from Sumer. Some might choose to pillage trade, others might attempt diplomatically to divert trade to themselves rather than to Sumer, and still others might simply emulate and compete peacefully with Sumer. The "comparative net advantage" in efficient production of manufactured goods lay with Sumer. But this would be irrelevant if some other group could actually prevent goods reaching them and so charge "protection rent" over trade routes. Such a group could be led by anything from a rival, organized near-literate state, to a tribal chieftain, to an adventurer and his band. Thus either organized war/diplomacy or "Mafia-type" violence could threaten the stability of Sumer's vital supplies.

Thus, in self-protection, Sumer sought to extend its political and military power along its international trade network. Its agricultural efficiency gave it a comparative advantage in the release of numbers of men and resources for military purposes over most other nearby peoples. Early on it seems to have been able to send out parties of soldiers and merchants and establish colonies along trade routes. However, it could not in the long run control these colonies. They developed autonomously and merged with local populations. Furthermore, the second source of vulnerability conferred a comparative advantage upon a rival type of group. The difficulty for Sumer was that this rival was situated on its own marches, preventing it from reaching outward at all. Here we must recall the impact of ecological specialization upon warfare, which I began to discuss in Chapter 2.

Let us, for the moment, put naval and siege warfare to one side, for they have their own peculiarities. Confining ourselves to open battlefields on land, we can note that armies throughout recorded history have been composed of three elements: infantry, cavalry (including chariots), and artillery (of which the principal type has been the bow and arrow). Each of these has many variants, and mixed forces as well as mixed types (like horse archers) have often appeared. Each tends to emerge in societies with differing economies and states, each has its strengths and weaknesses in warfare of different types, and each has effects upon economy and state. The historical advantage did not lie continuously with one form of warfare, though it is often asserted that the cavalry did have such a general advantage in the ancient world. In fact power shifted around according to the type of warfare and the development of military, political, and economic forms.[1]

The first weapons developed from agricultural and hunting implements. Horses were domesticated later, around 3000 B.C., by steppe peoples, and soon afterward in Sumer equids (perhaps onager and ass hybrids) were used as cart and chariot drawers. Sumerian armies consisted of rather unwieldy chariot carts and infantry phalanxes mobilized behind long shields. They did not have bows in numbers. These infantry armies were suited for slow,

[1]McNeill has given stimulating general accounts of early ancient warfare, both in *The Rise of the West* (1963) and more recently in *The Pursuit of Power* (1983). For the archaeological evidence, see Yadin (1963).

methodical campaigns whereby small densely settled areas could be conquered and defended. They arose from the necessity to defend the early city-state and perhaps to conquer its immediate neighbors. So far as we know, they left the hinterland well alone. Their later antithesis was the mounted steppe nomad armed with lance and bow, though as yet without much body armor, heavy weaponry, saddle, or stirrups. They would have difficulty sustaining a frontal assault on the agriculturalists, and they could not besiege their enemy, but swift raiding and treachery could make them more than an irritant.

But in the third millennium, the dominant type of warfare was not between these two antitheses. Remember that the horse was not used effectively in cavalry warfare until after 1500 B.C. (in more mobile chariotry). Before then we are comparing the supposed hardiness and mobility in getting to the battlefield of herders; the projectile-throwing capability and violence of hunters; and the greater numbers, solidity, and predominantly defensive morale of agriculturalists. None had a general advantage. Each would possess superiority in different tactical and geographical circumstances, and a *combination* of each would be the ideal. In any case, irrigated valley and steppe pasture did not generally abut. In between lay upland zones, combining argriculture and herding and growing relatively prosperous on the strategic position astride the trade routes between river valleys and steppes, woods, and mountains. Here the techniques of warfare were equally mixed, and here, presumably (for this is guesswork), were made the first attempts to combine tactics such as swift raiding and systematic marching. Furthermore, the city-states had every reason to encourage this, to use such marcher lords as a buffer against true pastoralists further out, or as a counterweight against a rival city-state. As yet the marcher lords did not possess effective cavalry, for horses were not yet bred for significant improvements in strength, and harnesses were still crude. But archery was apparently developing rapidly from hunting practices, and the use of the bow seems to have given a comparative advantage to the marchers if combined with infantry force. There is, at any rate, something to explain: the predominance for two millennia of marcher lords in warfare and their tendency to found and extend empires.

Sargon of Akkad

Sargon was the first personality of history. He conquered Sumer in 2310? B.C. and ruled it until his death in 2273? B.C. (dates involve guesswork; these are given by Westenholz 1979: 124; other useful secondary sources are King 1923: 216–51; Gadd 1971: 417–63; and Larsen 1979: 75–106; available documentary sources are detailed in Grayson 1975: 235–6). His Akkadian dynasty ruled an enlarged Mesopotamian Empire for almost two centuries, followed over the same core area (after various interregna) by several other major dynastic empires – the Third Dynasty of Ur, the Old Babylonian (whose best-known ruler was Hammurabi), and the Kassite.[2] The period covered in this chapter from Sargon to the fall of the Kassites was about a thousand years. Though such a long period contained an enormous diversity of social experience (think of the diversity of the Europeans from A.D. 1000 to 1985!), it exhibits also macrostructural similarities as well as a central direction of historical development. Both were broadly laid down by Sargon. As we do not know a great deal about Sargon himself, discussion of his empire is always a little teleological; the sources themselves, usually written down later, have this quality. My own analysis will be typical of the genre, in a sense fictionalizing Sargon into a world-historical personage, representative of his age and his dynasty.

Sargon's conquest has often been defined as a "territorial empire." I will dispute this, arguing that his power lay not in direct control over territory but, rather, in personal domination over clients. His power, however, did stretch at least several hundred kilometers in length and breadth, including the Sumerian city-states, the northerly areas of Akkad from which he himself came, the area of Elam to the east, and various other upland and plain areas. These conquests were given shape by the river system of the Tigris and the Euphrates, for obvious economic and logistical reasons. Their economic core was no longer simply lateral irrigation, but also the addition of regulated trade linkages between a large number of these lateral irrigation areas plus their hinterlands. And we can observe still another type of linkage. Conquest did not merely follow the rivers. Its backbone was military/political artifice interfering with the organizational rhythms provided by nature, just as the economic/political artifice of irrigation had earlier interfered with the rhythms of the river.

Sargon's home was Akkad, perhaps a city-state whose precise location is unknown, but in the region of northern, late-developing Mesopotamia. The "land of Akkad" included rain-watered agricultural land and upland pasture-lands as well as irrigation agriculture. Its people were probably Semites. The Akkadian language differed from the Sumerian. The Akkadian lands abutted the northerly Sumerian states and were influenced by them. Sargon's legend claims a bastard birth (the first "baby set adrift in the bulrushes" story of the Middle East). His early career was in keeping: professional warrior service as a retainer ("cupbearer") to the king of Kish, a northerly Sumerian state. This area was caught in the kinds of economic and military cross-pressures I have described. Sargon achieved hegemony (we suspect) by combining the military techniques of pastoralists with those of argriculturalists. His speed of attack was famous. He or his successor probably used a strengthened compound bow of wood and horn (see Yadin 1963). Yet his main arm was still heavy infantry.

Sargon was not a total pioneer. We have glimpses of earlier conquerors,

[2]A rough chronology of the various dynastics can be seen in Figure 5.1 later in this chapter.

usually with Semitic names, who were increasingly prominent in late predynastic Sumerian cities – for example, Lugalannemundu, an ephemeral conqueror who relied on lieutenants with apparently Semitic names and who "exercised kingship over the entire world" according to our source (Kramer 1963: 51).

From this consolidated marcher base, Sargon moved in all directions, conquering in thirty-four campaigns all the Sumerian states, reaching southeastward to the Persian Gulf, westward perhaps to the Levantine coast, and northward into northern Syria and Anatolia. He and his successors claimed to have destroyed the rival kingdom of Ebla. Most of his reported activities were in Sumer and in the Northwest, though his campaigns there differed. In Sumer his violence was selective and limited by tradition, destroying city walls but not cities, dragging the previous Sumerian king in chains to the temple of Enlil at Nippur, and assuming this role himself. Some Sumerian rulers remained in their places, though more than was felt to be traditional were replaced by Akkadians. His intent here was to *use* the power of Sumer. In the Northwest, in Syria, his behavior was more ruthless, boastful in the extent of destruction. Oddly to modern readers, these records combine destruction with the pursuit of commercial intent, such as expeditions to free the "Silver Mountains" and the "Cedar Forest" and even to protect Akkadian merchants from harassment in central Anatolia. The coupling of destruction and commercialism makes sense, however – the object was to destroy the power of states and to terrorize the peoples who were interfering with trade routes.

If we add these two areas together, we get an empire of vast extent by previous standards. Perhaps we should exclude as dubious the recorded conquests of Anatolia and the Levantine coast. Even then the northwest–southeast breadth of the empire, spread along the Tigris and Euphrates valleys, would have been well over a thousand kilometers and the breadth across and above the valley about four hundred kilometers. But the records, though boastful, are lacking in precision. We are told that Akkad extended in space 360 hours' marching, nearly two thousand kilometers by road, but we are not sure how to interpret the words "in space." Apart from that, the emphasis is on *domination* asserted over countries and peoples of uncertain extent. The language of domination is emphatic: Peoples, cities, and armies are "crushed," "knocked over" – Sargon "cast them in heaps." The Akkadian word for "king" also began to be invested with divine connotations. Naram-Sin, the grandson of Sargon, was later directly accorded divine status as well as the title "The Mighty, king of the four corners of the world."

All this may seem a comprehensive, extensive territorial and imperial form of domination. It was meant to convey that impression to contemporaries. But Sargon's was a territorial empire *not* in extent, but – if I may be permitted the pun – in *intent*. To establish this will involve detailed consideration of the logistical infrastructure and the universal diffusion of power. I assess the practical possibilities for the exercise of power in a reasonably systematic and technical way. This is not an easy task, for the records are sparse and scholars have avoided logistical matters (as Adams 1979: 397 has confessed). Speculation and hypothetical reconstruction are necessary. As some of the fundamental infrastructural problems were nearly invariant throughout the ancient civilized period, I will supplement the limited evidence for Sargon's own time with evidence from other times and places.

The fundamental infrastructure required for the exercise of all four sources of both organized and diffused power is communications. Without effective passing of messages, personnel, and resources, there can be no power. We know little of Sargon's communications. We can, however, deduce that the fundamental problems he faced were similar to those of all ancient rulers. Once three technologies had developed – the animal-powered cart, the paved road, and the sailing ship – overall constraints on communications were similar over several millennia. Fundamentally, water transport was more practicable than land transport. Two and a half millennia later, the Roman emperor Diocletian's Maximum Prices Edict set monetary figures on their relative costs. If sea costs were set at 1, the ratio of river transport was 5, and wagon transport by land was either 28 or 56.[3] That is, land transport was either 28 or 56 times more expensive than transport by sea and either more than 5 or more than 11 times more expensive than river transport. These figures indicate general orders of magnitude rather than precise ratios. Exact relative costs will vary according to distance, terrain, conditions of rivers or seas, weight of goods, precise animals used, and technologies.

There are two principal factors involved in this disparity: speed and replenishing the energy of the carriers. Speed was greater in downstream and maritime transport, and could be greater in some upstream riverine conditions. But the major contributor was the problem on land of feeding pack animals, not encountered in water transport. This did more than push up costs – it set finite limits. Animals such as oxen, mules, horses, and donkeys carrying maximum loads of fodder have to consume it within about one hundred and fifty kilometers in order to stay alive. Any further distance by land is impossible without supplies along the route. This would be possible but not cost-effective. The only land transport over eighty to one hundred fifty kilometers that would make economic sense in the ancient world was of goods high in value-to-weight ratio in relation to the ratio for animal fodder. Water transport was more cost-effective, and it could cover long distances without further food supplies. The major limitation on its range at sea was the need for fresh water, which took up a fair proportion of the weight capacity of a ship. Thus efficient ships were big, which put up capital costs of their construction. The

---

[3]There is, unfortunately, an ambiguity in the edict – see Chapter 9 for details. If camels are used by land, the edict reduces the cost by 20 percent.

seasons affected both forms of transport, the weather and river floods being major limitations on water, and harvests and the availability of food surpluses having greater effect on land.

With a little knowledge of the ecology of Mesopotamia, we can see the importance of communications in Sumerian development. The city-states were situated on, or close to, navigable rivers. They were close together and could be staging posts for longer journeys. Thus donkeys and oxcarts could make an effective contribution to intercity communications. Upstream navigation was difficult. The usual pattern was that large rafts would be sailed with their goods downstream, then disassembled and the wood used downstream. The only major obstacles were the high cost of wood, and seasonal floods, which stopped all navigation.

However, as soon as Sargon stepped outside the alluvial plain, he would encounter formidable infrastructural difficulties. These were more or less the same for all subsequent extensive empires. As he was, first and foremost, a conqueror, let us start with his military logistics.

The logistics of military power

Sargon left two boasts showing that his achievement was indeed partly logistical. On a tablet in a temple at Nippur we read that ''5,400 soldiers ate daily before him [or in his palace].'' And in the Chronicle of Early Kings we read, ''He stationed his court officials at intervals of ten hours marching time and ruled in unity the tribes of the land.'' (The tablets can be read in Pritchard 1955: 266–8; and Grayson 1975:153.) The boasts reveal a concern with organizational technique, one that was considered to be superior to his predecessors'. The number of the soldiers, the fact that they were permanently fed by a commissariat, and the fact that the commissariat was permanently and spatially organized, indicate the extent of the novelty: a large, professional army and administration. The number 5,400 may not seem great to us, but it was meant to impress then. The core unit for his conquests and rule was probably this number of armed retainers and its suppliers.

What was such a unit capable of? It could defend its leader and his court from surprise treachery. But it might not be large enough for a major battle against a city-state. In his battle against the combined forces of Ur and Lagash, it is said that Sargon killed 8,040 and took prisoner a further 5,460. We are skeptical about claims like this. The two cities could have potentially fielded a maximum of about 60,000 men of military age. I find it difficult to believe that more than a third of these peasant-farmers and artisans could be equipped, mobilized, and marched to a confined space to give battle in a minimally disciplined way. It may be that the 13,500 was the total enemy army – at any rate, the rival armies were probably of this order of magnitude. So Sargon's core unit (which in this relatively early battle might not have grown to over

5,000) would need the support of levies, recruited, as was always later practice, from his client rulers and allies. Let us imagine a total force of 10,000–20,000 in major campaigns and 5,000 or so for general purposes. What were the logistics of their use?

Here I turn to a brilliant study of logistics two millennia later, Donald W. Engel's (1978) analysis of the campaigns of Alexander the Great. I turn forward so far because there is no comparable study for the whole of the intervening period. Some of Engel's most salient findings have relevance for the whole ancient period because of the similarities of communications technology throughout the period; others are applicable to Akkad, for this is the region that Alexander himself crossed.

Let us make the worst assumption first, that there are no provisions, water, or fodder for horses along the army's route of march, in other words, that the land is barren, or it is not harvest time and the local population have fled with their food supplies. Engels calculates that, largely regardless of an army's size, the soldiers and camp followers could carry their own provisions for two and a half days. To eat for four days, they would require considerable numbers of pack animals. But they would be unable to eat for five days no matter how many pack animals were taken. The animals and soldiers would consume all the increase in food and still be consuming only half rations. Three days was the survival period of a completely self-equipped army – a conclusion that receives support from the rationing systems used in Greek and Roman armies. Three days is the limit whether the supply is carried in grain or hardtack. This is an extremely sobering base on which to rest our images of world-conquering territorial empires!

How far could they get in such a short time? That does depend on army size: The larger the army, the slower its pace. Engel calculates Alexander's average rate at about twenty-four kilometers per day (with one day's rest in seven, irrelevant to the shorter periods we are considering), for a total army, including camp followers, of about 65,000, but he reckons that a small contingent could manage double that. The Macedonian army was the swiftest of its age, of course.

Here we can add a few earlier estimates. Crown (1974: 265) cites the following rates for some ancient armies: the Egyptian army of Thutmose III (fifteenth century B.C.), twenty-four kilometers per day; that of Ramses II (thirteenth century), twenty-one kilometers; a Babylonian army of 597 B.C., twenty-nine kilometers, later Roman armies, twenty-three to thirty-two kilometers. Earlier still, and closer to Sargon, Crown (1974) estimates the progress of a smaller group of soldiers and officials in the eighteenth century B.C. in Mesopotamia at twenty-four to thirty kilometers (cf. Hallo 1964). The only greater estimate is that of Saggs (1963) for the Assyrian infantry of the eighth to seventh centuries B.C. of forty-eight kilometers a day – though in Chapter

7 I suggest that he is somewhat credulous concerning the Assyrian army. The norm before Alexander is below thirty kilometers.

There is no reason to believe that Sargon could exceed this norm. He had not dispensed with the large Sumerian carts and he only had equids, not mules or horses. His pack animals would be slower-moving, and he would gain no advantage in mobility from their use. Let us be generous and give him thirty kilometers a day. Over three days that is a maximum range of ninety kilometers, but the action must be swift and result in the capture of supplies. No competent commander would risk his troops over more than half this range. It is no solution to bring up further supplies by land along the army's route of march, for the supplies would be consumed by the commissary before they reached the army.

This is a feeble basis for conquest or domination of empire, but it is the worst possible case. Along the valley backbones of his conquests and empire, Sargon would find water, and this would ease the weight burden. Engels estimates that, carrying no water, they can triple their range, managing nine days and increasing maximum range to three hundred kilometers. A commander would risk a march of upward of a third of this if he had to fight at his destination.

Weight loads also include military equipment, and this is more complicated. Engel estimates that a maximum practicable load for a marching soldier is about thirty-six kilograms, though most army manuals today assume about thirty kilograms, and I have found that I myself cannot carry the higher amount over any distance. Landels (1980) suggests that Roman porters could manage around twenty-five kilograms over longer distances. The Macedonian infantryman carried about twenty-two kilograms of equipment, principally helmets and body armor (armor is easier to carry than a pack of the same weight, being better distributed over the body). The Akkadian equipment would be lighter than this, but I doubt if this would matter, for few troops prior to the Macedonians carried twenty-two kilograms. Alexander's father, Philip, had reduced the camp followers and carts and transferred the burden to his soldiers, to increase their mobility. Later in the Roman Republic, the general Marius did the same thing, earning for his troops the nickname "Marius's mules." Both were considered at the time remarkable innovations in the level of routinized coercion applied to troops, and they indicated highly militarized societies. In the Near East it is doubtful if soldiers could be burdened in this way. Whereas Alexander's army contained about one camp follower for every three combatants, its Persian enemy had one for one (or so our Greek sources say). Furthermore, in the many pictures of Sumerian, Akkadian, and Assyrian soldiers, we almost never see them carrying anything beyond their equipment. Carts, slaves, and camp followers are the beasts of burden in these pictures. It seems likely that Sargon's soldiers carried virtually no supplies or fodder for the animals and depended on at least an equal number of servile or slave camp followers. Their overall range could not have been greater than my first calculations, and their rate of march per day may have been less. Neither water on the route nor lighter equipment could materially increase the overall figure of a maximum practical range of ninety kilometers for an unsupported advance. Early Near Eastern monarchies may have been restricted to less than this, perhaps 80 kilometers. Let us finally assume a range of eighty to ninety kilometers. No large-scale conquest is logistically possible on this basis.

River transport could improve the situation considerably for Sargon (there are no seas relevant to his campaigns). Against Sumer, he was moving downstream and so weight problems could disappear given careful planning. On the densely populated floodplain, the inhabitants, territorially and socially trapped, could only run with their crops to the fortified city. Each city lay within striking range of the next. Sargon could raise an earth rampart to the level of the walls, receive supplies by river, storm the city, and loot the surplus and supply for the next march. Indeed, the city-states would have greater logistical problems in developing combined operations against him. We have a record of no fewer than thirty-four victorious campaigns by Sargon against the cities. He could pick them off one at a time. Conquest in the south was open to the northerner.

In the north the difficulties were greater. They were either upstream or across plains and mountains. So far, we have assumed that no land supplies were available along the route of march. If that were so, conquest would have been virtually impossible. We must relax this assumption. The terrain Sargon faced was inhabited, usually by settled agriculturalists with additional pasturelands, and this raised the possibility of "living off the land." This involved seasonal campaigning, a maximum period of a month when the harvest was there for the taking, plus a longer period of up to six months when the population would have stored surpluses to feed a small army. Army size matters here – the bigger, the worse the supply situation. The seasonal possibilities for taking young animals and finding good grazing for captured flocks and herds driven by camp followers are similar. If Sargon could descend like Byron's Assyrian, "like the wolf on the fold," then he could live off the land, for the shorter period. But most of the surplus most of the time would be in fortified stores – even the speed of the Assyrians would not carry it off without a siege.

Again we can use Alexander's experience over the same terrain. The fortified stores confronting him were scattered and varied – in villages, oases, towns, and provincial capitals of the Persian Empire. Alexander never moved forward from a supply base until he received intelligence reports on the terrain ahead, its roads, its available supplies, and the defensive capacity guarding them. He then calculated the size of force minimally capable of overawing local defenders, but maximally capable of carrying supplies supplemented by a modicum of local pillaging. He sent out this force, perhaps split between several routes. The main army stayed put until the detachment reported success, when it marched forward. The local defenders were usually in difficulty. They were made an offer of surrender which they could not refuse, unless help was at hand from their ruler. Battles were usually unnecessary: Skirmishes showed the rough balance of force, the defenders' counsels were divided, someone opened the gates.

This is so unlike modern warfare that contemporary writers often fail to understand its essential processes. Communications difficulties in ancient warfare were so great for *both* sides that their armies rarely met head-on. In such cases, both armies would head as quickly as they could in small detachments along separate routes to an arranged meeting place (with adequate water, at the height of the agricultural season, and perhaps with prearranged stores) not far from the enemy, and give battle. The generals on both sides were often keen for battle. Their methods, their sense of honor, and above all their ability to control their troops were better suited to battle, even to defeat, than to slow demoralization as they ran out of supplies (except for well-supplied defenders inside a walled city). The defending general also had an incentive to avoid the "piecemeal treachery" to be described in a moment. But apart from this, the main force was used only to overawe provincials and as the reservoir to supply fresh advance detachments. The progress of conquest was largely one of a "federally" organized advance of separate levies, followed by coercive negotiations and "piecemeal treachery." As Crown (1974) notes, the most developed part of ancient communications was the courier-cum-spy-cum-diplomat network. The courier enjoyed high status, took many initiatives, and was impressively rewarded or punished. He was critical to imperial rule.

The defenders were not being offered much of a choice. If they resisted, they might be killed or enslaved; if they surrendered, their entire visible surplus might be pillaged and their walls knocked down. But a discontented cousin or younger son and his faction could be promised more, and the city delivered up by them. This faction would be added to the army or left in charge of the city. Their presence was politically useful even if they made no significant military contribution, for they served as an example to the next provincials encountered. Hence, again surprising to modern readers, we constantly read in ancient warfare of defeated enemies being instantaneously converted into allied levies. The attackers had an incentive to negotiate quickly, so that the army could move forward to its new supplies. This is a far more *diplomatic* process than glorious imperial conquerors like Sargon have cared to acknowledge. But it fits what we know of both the beginning and the end of the Akkadian-inspired dynasties – both the number and rapidity of Sargon's campaigns, and the evidence of provincial governors at the end of the Ur Third Dynasty renouncing their loyalty and going over to the Amorites.

So Sumer was ripe for the picking, but other territories presented formidable logistical problems. Sargon probably overcame them by possessing two skills. First, his core army was professional, adapted to a prolonged routine of intelligence gathering and supply coordination, capable of cohesion either as a single unit for major battles or as foraging, besieging detachments. Second, his diplomatic acumen, or that of his principal lieutenants, must have been considerable. Their position as marcher lords probably gave them insight into the logistical-cum-diplomatic options available in a variety of terrains, dealing with a variety of defenders. Between them, these two skills provided just enough military artifice to provide organizational linkages between fertile, attackable, defensible, controllable valleys and agricultural plains.

Curiously, the constraints on military supply did not limit conquest. Sargon and his successors were limited to an area of about five hundred thousand square kilometers, but the constraints were on political control rather than conquest. Once natural boundaries were breached, military power had no obvious resting place. Given proper organization, a core army of 5,400 men plus federal levies could keep on marching, provided it could capture supplies every fifty to a hundred kilometers. Lines of communication only mattered on rivers. Land routes did not contribute supplies. Fortresses did not need to be "masked." Occasionally, an ancient army did just keep on marching. Some of Alexander's campaigns in Asia had this quality, as (from necessity) did those of Xenophon's 10,000 Greek mercenaries, suddenly cast adrift from employment fifteen hundred kilometers from home. But, generally, armies marched to institutionalize conquest, that is, to rule, and political options were restricted.

The infrastructure of political power

Sargon's power to rule was less extensive than his power to conquer. I return to the concentric rings of extensive power described by Lattimore in Chapter 1. From now on we can see the different capacities of economic, ideological, political, and military organizations to integrate extensive societies.

The political radius of practicable rule by a state was smaller than the radius of a military conquest. An army achieved success by *concentrating* its forces. It pushed through unpacified terrain, protecting continuously only its flanks and rear and keeping open intermittently its lines of communication. Those who could not run away submitted, formally. It was only because they could not run away, trapped by a millennium of caged agriculture, that the radius of conquest was so great. But ruling over those who had submitted involved *dispersing* force, which was throwing away the military advantage. No conqueror could eliminate this contradiction. An empire cannot be ruled on horseback – as Ghenghis Khan is reported to have said.

There were four principal strategies for ameliorating this and for developing genuine imperial domination. The first two – rule through clients and direct army rule – were the more readily available but the least effective. I shall deal with them briefly in a moment. The other two – "compulsory cooperation" and the development of a common ruling-class culture – eventually offered far greater resources to imperial rulers but required more complex infrastructures, which the history of power development only gradually made available. I shall deal with them at greater length. In this period we shall find only the former flourishing. By the time we reach Rome, in Chapter 9, we shall find both contributing massively to a 500-year empire. So let us start with the cruder strategies of rule.

The first of the four strategies was to rule through clients, conquered native elites. Early empires attempted this with poor and less organized neighbors, accepting formal submission and perhaps a little tribute, and allowing their rulers to continue. In case of bad behavior they launched punitive raids, replaced the ruler with perhaps his cousin, and upped the tribute level. This conquest proper could only be imposed erratically and infrequently. In any case, as we have seen already, logistical difficulties meant that even this contained political bargaining with local dissident elites. It was possible, however, to acquire more power by adding diffused power to such authoritative processes. This was to take hostages of the children of the native elite and to "educate" them and perhaps also their parents into the culture of the conquerors. As yet techniques for doing this were limited. But if the natives were backward relative to the conquerors, civilization could seduce them somewhat from their own people. The conquerors would help them maintain local control with troops whose main function in a rebellion proper was to retreat into a citadel until help arrived. In fact, until much later, supposedly "territorial empires" did not generally have clear-cut boundaries and "internal" marcher areas were usually ruled in this indirect way. Hence the pictorial representation of domination as the personal humiliation of rebels and the ritual prostration of client rulers before their masters. Rule was *through* other kings, lords, governors. This offered low-cost security, but it left an autonomous local elite, capable of mobilizing resources in revolt or in the service of a more attractive rival, internal or external. Hence we see Sargon placing Akkadians alongside local kings and appointing his daughter as high priestess of the moon god in conquered Ur.

The second strategy was to rule directly through the army – to base the state on militarism. This dispersed lieutenants and troops in strategic fortresses and towns. It presupposed greater initial slaughter of the enemy elite than the first strategy. It also required greater surpluses from the conquered agriculturalists to build up the professional troops dispersed in small units, and to build and maintain the military/governmental infrastructure of fortresses, communications routes, and supplies. It was a dominant strategy in core conquered territories and in key areas from the point of view of geopolitics. It seems Sargon's own strategy in areas ruled by Akkadians and buttressed by corvée labor; just as he used the first strategy in other areas. But this strategy faced two problems: how to maintain the loyalty and unity of the military government, and how to raise surplus extraction from the conquered?

The authority of the central commander was relatively easy to uphold in a war of conquest – it was useful for survival and victory. The fruits of conquest also boosted his authority, for he could distribute booty. This could be only maintained during pacification and institutionalization by making the rewards of administrators and troops depend on central authority. In a non-monetary economy (of which more in a moment), reward meant land and the perquisites of office through which tribute and tax (in kind and labor) flowed. Military government granted land to the troops, and land together with its tillers and state offices to the lieutenants. Unfortunately, these acts *decentralized* power, embedding the soldiers in "civil society" and giving them material resources whose enjoyment was now independent of the army or the state. The land grant might be supposedly conditional on military service and might not be transferable to heirs, but in practice such systems created an independent, hereditary, landholding aristocracy and a peasantry in conquered territories. Such were the origins of military feudalism, of "satrapy," of many marcher lordships, and of other social structures that effectively decentralized power after conquest. Eventually, imperial regimes were solidified by the development of a universal upper-class culture – as we shall see in the cases of Persia and Rome. But that was a later development. Given limited infrastructures, regimes in this period relied on far more primitive resources such as continuous fear that the conquered population might rise again. Thus, the paradox that the *more* secure the pacification, the more effective the degree of centralized regulation, the *less* centralization could derive from the military. Pacification *de*centralized the military.

These arguments can be found in the works of Weber; yet their implications have not been appreciated by scholars working on these early empires. For the "territorial" model of empire gets in the way twice, first through the metaphor of "core and periphery" territories. Core areas, it is said, were ruled directly and militaristically; peripheral areas were ruled indirectly through clients. But the logistics result, not in a stable core and stable (or unstable) periphery, but in patterns of rule that change through time as well as space. "Core" ruling elites become in time autonomous. Yoffee sees this in the Old Babylonian state of Hammurabi and his descendants. What started as direct military control of the Babylonian core disintegrated as officials held hereditary rights to their offices, intermarried with local elites, and farmed the state's taxes. He concludes, "Political and economic systems with a highly centralized bureaucracy . . . are tremendously efficient military and economic forces in their initial stages, but are seldom able to institutionalize and legitimate themselves (1977: 148)." The *whole* was politically unstable, not just a frontier "periphery." Force was regularly applied to all parts from the "center." But where was the center? For a second time, the notion of fixed territories and cores gets in the way. For the center was the army, Sargon's 5,400 men, and that was mobile. Only the ongoing campaign centralized military power. Once pacification and broader threats became uneven, the less the empire resembled an army engaged in a single campaign under its central leader. Provincial threats were responded to by mobilizing provincial armies, which put power in the hands of local commanders not the central state. To counteract fragmentation, the greatest conquerors in preindustrial communications conditions were in almost perpetual campaigning motion. Their physical presence in army headquarters centralized their power. Once they, or their successors, settled back into a court in a capital, the cracks usually showed. Indeed, many conquered empires then collapsed. We have not yet seen anything that might hold such artificial creations together except erratic fear and the energy of the ruler.

One reason for instability was that no major advances in logistics had been made toward the *political* consolidation of empires. The state apparatus, such as it was, depended upon the personal qualities and relationships of the ruler. Kinship was the most important source of permanent authority. But the greater the extent of conquest, the more kinship between ruling elites became strained and fictitious. In this period lieutenants intermarried with locals to secure themselves, but this weakened ties among the conquerors. In this period techniques of literacy were at first restricted to heavy tablets and complicated scripts. Their traditional use was to *concentrate* relations upon the central place of the city. They could not be easily adapted to the more extensive role of conveying messages and controls over distances. Some advances were made in promulgating laws. Hammurabi's splendidly preserved "code" indicates increased extensive rule-making *ambition,* but probably not an empire actually ruled by his laws.

So far, then, the military and political logistics did not greatly favor "territorial empires." *Empires of domination* would be a better description for unstable federations of rulers prostrated under the foot of Sargon and his successors, whose state was the 5,400.

When we turn, however, to what was supposedly the narrowest logistical radius, the economic, we find a third strategy available to the ruler. Here I depart from Lattimore's model, which keeps clearly separate the three logistical radii – a legacy, probably, of the "autonomous factor" approach in sociology, which I criticized in Chapter 1. The economies of early empires were not separate – they were permeated with militaristic and state structures. The linkages of compulsory cooperation provided more formidable logistical possibilities for an imperial ruler, which – together with the fourth strategy of a common ruling-class culture – became the principal power resource of empires.

The logistics of a militarized economy: the strategy of compulsory cooperation

The innermost radius in Lattimore's model was economic power. According to him, in ancient empires there were many small cell-like "economies." Such cells are indeed visible within Sargon's conquered empire, covering each of the regional economies recently brought together. The most advanced were the irrigated valleys and floodplains partially organized by redistributive central places (formerly city-states). But between each, and between these and upland areas, ran trade exchanges. These were also partially organized by the former political authorities – in the valleys, the redistributive central place; in the hills, decentralized lords. The conqueror would want to intensify production and exchange relations across his domains. Indeed, to a limited extent, this would occur spontaneously with the growing extent of pacification. The state would also wish to get its hands on any surplus increase that occurred.

Thus, conquerors found themselves driven toward a particular set of postconquest economic relationships, for which we can use the term given by Herbert Spencer, *compulsory cooperation* (see his notion of what holds together "militant society" in Spencer 1969).[4] Under these relationships, the surplus extracted from nature could be increased, the empire could be given a somewhat fragile economic unity, and the state could extract its share of the surplus and maintain its unity. But these benefits flowed *only* as a result of increasing coercion in the economy at large. The peculiarity of this is the inseparability of naked repression and exploitation from more or less common benefit.

This model, to be elaborated on in a moment, departs from recent theories that stress one side of this, the exploitation and coercion. They follow the liberal view of the state current in our own time. According to this, fundamental social dynamism, including economic growth, comes from decentralized, competitive, market organization. States hold the ring, provide basic infrastructures, but that is all. As Adam Smith remarked, "If you have peace, easy taxes and tolerable administration of justice, then the rest is brought about by 'the natural cause of things' " – which is quoted approvingly by

---

[4]Spencer overgeneralized his theory to ancient history as a whole. I regret that in my 1977 article I followed him in making overgeneral claims for compulsory cooperation. In this work I apply the notion relatively boldly to the empires discussed in this chapter and to the Roman Empire (see Chapter 9), and more tentatively to some intervening empires like the Assyrian and Persian. But it does not apply to civilizations like those of classical Greece or Phoenicia, and only marginally to most of the early "Indo-European" societies discussed in Chapter 6.

one recent theorist of economic dynamism (Jones 1981: 235). The same view
is held by many writers on comparative social development. States, especially
imperial states, coerce and expropriate to such a level that their subjects keep
goods away from the markets, restrain their investment, hoard, and generally
participate in economic and social stagnation (e.g., Wesson 1967: 206–76;
Kautsky 1982).

This negative view of empire has penetrated among the specialist scholars
of the ancient Near East, where it has often adopted the language of "core"
and "periphery." They argue that one type of empire, centered on its advanced,
urban, manufacturing, irrigated core, exploited the more backward, rural,
pastoral, rain-watered periphery in the form of taxes and tribute. The periphery, however, could strike back with its own empire in the form of conquest
by marcher lords and so exploit and loot the people and riches of the core.
Both types of empire were parasitic. This underlies polemical exchanges between
scholars, as, for example, that between two of the most distinguished Mesopotamian scholars of recent years, the Soviet Diakonoff and the American
Oppenheim. Diakonoff takes an extreme view of state parasitism, arguing that
all major dynamism in the area originated in private-property relations and in
decentralized classes (1969: 13–32). Oppenheim rightly criticizes this as
neglecting the state organization of much economic dynamism. But the relevant states are for him city-states and their trading networks. Larger imperial
states rose and fell as "superstructures" over these economic bases. When
they fell, the city-state reemerged more or less unchanged (1969: 33–40).
Both views are incorrect, as we will see in a moment.

The negative view of empire has been spelled out most rigorously by Ekholm
and Friedman. It is worth quoting them at length:

1 Empires that develop in c/p (centre/periphery) systems are political mechanisms that
  feed on already established forms of wealth production and accumulation. Where
  they do not over-tax and where they simultaneously maintain communication networks, they tend to increase the possibilities of production and trade in the system,
  i.e., the possibilities for all existing forms of wealth accumulation.
2 Empires maintain and reinforce c/p relations politically, by the extraction of tribute
  from conquered areas and peripheries. But insofar as empires do not replace other
  economic mechanisms of production and circulation, but only exploit them, they
  may create the conditions for their own demise.
3 This occurs where the revenue absorbed from the existing accumulation cycles
  increases more slowly than the total accumulation itself. In such a case an *economic
  decentralisation* sets in, resulting in a general weakening of the centre relative to
  other areas. . . . [There follow the examples of Rome – of rapid decentralization –
  and of Mesopotamia – of more gradual decentralization.]
4 Grossly stated, the balance of empire is determined by: booty + tribute (tax) +
  export revenue − (cost of empire + cost of imports) (where exports and imports
  are, respectively, from and to the centre). [1979: 52–3]

This is an exemplary statement of the balance of centralizing and decentralizing forces. A net change in balance happened, slowly but repeatedly, in the

case of Mesopotamia, and more than once (but each time suddenly) in the case of Rome. More generally, however, they locate the "original" dynamism of the whole economy in the "already established" free and decentralized forms of accumulation, the motor of social development. All the state adds is communications networks encouraging imports and exports. Apart from that, its strategic "control" over accumulation parasitically diverts surpluses but does not create them. The notion of the "parasitical centre" is also shared by Ekholm and Friedman's critics Larsen (1979) and Adams (1979).

I wish to make two contrary arguments: (1) The imperial state helped *create* accumulation processes in five specific ways. (2) Decentralization resulted from the further development of these state-assisted processes, not from the reassertion of an "original" decentralized power; the state *fragmented*, fostering the development of private, decentralized property power.

Five aspects of compulsory cooperation

Five economic processes were at the same time functional for the development of collective power yet also imposed by repression. They were military pacification, the military multiplier, the authoritative imposition of value upon economic goods, the intensification of labor through coercion, and the diffusion and exchange of techniques through conquest. Although the militarism of imperial states certainly had its negative side, when effectively and stably imposed through these five processes, it could lead to general economic development. Let us examine them in turn.

Military pacification

Trade, including long-distance trade, preceded the emergence of militaristic states (as emphasized by Friedman and Eckholm 1978). But it increasingly necessitated protection, for two reasons. As the surplus grew, it became more tempting and concentrated for pillaging or diverting; and as specialization grew, local populations became less self-sufficient and more trade-dependent. Sargon pushed northward to protect trade routes. We will see throughout recorded history up to the twentieth century A.D. many similar developments. There is little that is "spontaneous" about the development of trade throughout most of history. Human beings may have the original impulse to "truck and barter," as Adam Smith famously asserted. The events of prehistory would seem to support him. But beyond some threshold level, exchanges generate further exchanges, and so stimulate production, *if* "ownership" and "value" can be authoritatively established. This can be painfully, laboriously, and diffusely established by a large number of independent contracts embodying normative understandings between the trade partners themselves. But in many circumstances this has seemed more wasteful of social resources than a second method: monopolistic rules conferring ownership and governing exchange established and maintained internally by an authoritative state, and externally by diplomacy between several such states. Protection is established by coercion. The evidence in empires is that trade has usually flourished in times of imperial stability and decayed when empires falter. This happened in Akkadian times and repeatedly thereafter. It is true that we will see the emergence of alternative methods of trade regulation from time to time – most notably in the era of Phoenician and Greek maritime supremacy, and in Christian medieval Europe – but though these offered decentralized and sometimes more diffused forms of protection, they were not the result of "spontaneous" trade.

Diplomacy, regulated by force, was required internationally. Pacification was required in the periphery against outsiders and marcher peoples. It was needed along all trade routes, and it was needed in the core. Even close to the capital and the army pacification remained precarious in historic civilizations. This was partly because natural and unevenly distributed factors like bad harvests, soil erosion or salinization, or population growth could undermine the economy and produce desperate, hungry masses in one area liable to attack those in another. This could be dealt with by a mixture of simple repression and extending protected irrigation throughout the core and redistributive stores over the empire. In imperial phases irrigation was extended, and with it population, over a dendritic (treelike) pattern for which the older city-wall protection system was inadequate. In all areas the army was necessary for patrol and repression.

Sargon's military machine was suited to this protective role. It provided a minimum of fortresses, supported by the professional field army, whose existence depended on the success of its protective function. Its supplies depended on maintaining links between the floodplain core, the upland pastures and woods, and the mountain mines. In this sense, the 5,400 and their successors in the empires of Ur, Babylon, Assyria, and even later states were the consumption core of the economy. They were protecting themselves as well as producers and traders in general.

The military multiplier

The consumption needs of the army can be also seen as a boost to demand and, therefore, to production. Remember that these needs are for staples, not exotic luxuries – for grain, vegetables, and fruit; animals, clothing, metal, stone, and wood. Naturally, if no improvements in production, distribution, or exchange methods resulted, this would be simply parasitical. It would take vital resources from the agricultural and extractive producers and thus threaten the viability of production itself. One potential improvement, recognized by Friedman and Ekholm, was to communications. Empires built roads – in this period with corvée labor supervised by army personnel – and improved riverine and marine transport. In this we cannot distinguish economic from military elements. Staging posts where travelers and traders could be refreshed and resupplied were also markets for the exchange of goods, toll barriers where levies could be exacted from them, small garrisons for pacifying the trade and the area, and staging posts for military communications. It is impossible to separate "economic" and "military" motives, because pacification needs were similar to supply needs. The economic spinoff to most of society was considerable. Naturally we have to offset the actual cost of building and maintaining the economic infrastructure. In these early times we cannot accurately calculate the cost–benefit ratio of such techniques. Later on, however, in the case of the Roman Empire, when information became abundant, I argue that a full-fledged "military Keynesianism" was in operation. Considerable multiplier effects resulted from the consumption of the legions.

Authority and economic value

As exchange developed, so did technical measures of economic value – how much of good A was "worth" how much of good B. When both "values" can be measured against a third "value," they turn into *commodities*. From the days of the first cylinder seals it was evident that the redistributive state could often, perhaps even usually, assign exchange value more speedily, efficiently, and apparently justly than could a process based on reciprocity, that is, a market. Exchangeable objects – usually nonperishables like metals, cereals, and dates – received a kind of "money" status through the way that their quality and quantity were certified under official and semiofficial control. Once this was done, they could be lent out for interest. This seems to be the origin of usury. The tariffs we find from the third millennium onward (of which parts of Hammurabi's Babylonian law code are the most famous) may have been simple lists of maximum permissible prices. But perhaps, as Heichelheim (1958: 111) argues, they were official exchange rates – though the extent of their enforcement is unknown. The first authorities able to confer value were probably redistributive chiefdoms, as we saw in Chapter 2. In the floodplain of Mesopotamia, they were succeeded by small city-states, as we saw in Chapter 3. Hence there is no invariable fit between the militaristic empire and value creation. The fit came only when conquest expanded routine exchange to include more varied commodities over longer distances. A boost was given to quasi-coinage by military rulers, able to impose a degree of arbitrary value over large and diverse areas. But more than "coinage" was involved in the process – guaranteed weights and measures, the recording of contracts by the literate state apparatus, the honoring of contracts and rights to property through imposed law. In all respects the enlarged military state could impose economic value.

The intensification of labor

In a simple nonmonetary economy, extracting a higher level of surplus entailed, above all, extracting more labor. This could usually be done most easily by coercion. It could be used to build fortresses and communications infrastructure through corvée labor – these are tasks requiring a large volume of labor over short periods of time. Their logistical problems are similar to those of an army: extensive supplies, intensive coercion, spatially and seasonally concentrated. Sargon's military techniques were used in the civil-engineering sphere. Furthermore, coercion could be used in agricultural, mining, and crafts production, in slavery and other nonfree statuses.

As we saw in Chapter 3, the subordination of labor and its total separation from the means of production usually at first involved dependent, rather than free, labor. Large-scale military conquest extended dependency and slavery. Subsequently, slavery might be extended to members of the same people through debt bondage or through the selling by a chief of his own surplus labor to a more civilized society, but the model for both was conquest slavery. Needless to say, the benefits of such a system did not usually accrue to the slaves themselves. It could also, on occasion, undermine the economy of competing free peasants (as it did much later in the Roman Republic). But the increase in production could benefit the free population as a whole, not just slave- or serf-owners.

Slavery was not always dominant. As compulsion became institutionalized, it needed slavery less. Nonfree, servile, but nonslave groups became more visible. In the Akkadian and Ur Third Dynasty empires we can perceive large-scale military-style organization of labor, sometimes with, sometimes without, slavery. In the Drehem archive of Ur Third Dynasty times, we read of a labor gang of 21,799 listed persons, under the authority of the state, grouped into contingents, each with a captain from a large number of towns and cities whose provincial governors are also named. It appears a corvée organization, migrating around harvest fields and repairing dikes and levees, recruited disproportionately from peripheral areas of the north but did not hold slaves (Goetze 1963; Adams 1981: 144–7). On the other hand, the 9,000-person labor force of the royal wool office was based on slavery, some centralized, some scattered throughout vast grazing areas (Jacobsen 1970). When a regime was powerful and stable, its ability to increase labor productivity probably spread right across the slave/free divide. For example, when the Macedonians conquered the Near East, serfdom inherited from previous regimes was widespread, even perhaps the norm (Ste Croix 1981: 150–7).

There may have been a further stage of institutionalized labor compulsion – although it goes against the grain of modern sensibilities to suggest it. This is what we call "free" labor, although "hired labor" is a more appropriate label. Where stratification and private property are most secure and where some group de facto "owns" the means of production and others must work for it in order to subsist, laborers will "voluntarily" approach and work for owners. Hired labor did not predominate in the ancient world. In an agrarian economy it is difficult to exclude the peasant altogether from direct access to the means of production: land. Once in possession, he or she was more often coerced directly through slavery or serfdom. In Mesopotamia, hired labor does not appear in the records (though it probably existed) until the Third Dynasty of Ur (Gelb 1967). Hired labor gave a more flexible labor tap to the landowners, although it was still only a minority phenomenon. Efficient, intensive use of labor, I suggest, often, perhaps normally, went through a route of compulsion: from slavery to serfdom to "free" labor.

Coerced diffusion

The four aspects of compulsory cooperation discussed so far have involved authoritative power, a highly organized, logistical base providing a bridge between local particularisms. But much of this organization would be unnecessary if similar ways of life and similar culture could be *diffused* throughout a population, breaking down local particularisms, forcing local identities into a broader one. Early Sumerian culture, discussed in Chapter 3, diffused throughout the alluvium and its immediate periphery, resulting in more extensive collective power than that of the authoritative city-state. Though Akkadian conquest disrupted this, it presented opportunities for new types of power diffusion.

Conquest provides the most sudden, striking, and forced intermingling and readjustment of life-styles and practices. Where the process is not one-way, considerable diffusion and innovation occur. The intermingling of Akkad and Sumer, of Greece and Persia, of Rome and Greece, of Germany and Rome was strikingly innovative in its consequences for civilization. Each was cemented by the former's conquest of the latter, yet innovation did not result merely from the passive reception by the conquered of the conqueror's social practices.

The outstanding example of Akkadian-Sumerian fusion known to us was the impact on literacy. Akkadian was an inflected language, conveying part of its meaning by tone and pitch. The Akkadians conquered a literate people whose pictograms generally represented physical objects rather than sounds. But they were more interested in developing phonetic writing. The fusion of the Akkadian language and Sumerian literacy resulted in a simplified script, which helped transform pictograms into a syllabic script. The existence of fewer characters was a boon to the diffusion of literacy. Akkadian's advantage over other Middle Eastern languages was so great that in the mid-second millennium, even after papyrus was replacing the clay tablet, it became the main international language of diplomacy and trade. Even the Egyptians used it in their foreign policy. Akkadian literacy boosted not only the bureaucracy of Sargon's Empire but also the stabilizing of international trade, diplomacy, and social knowledge in general. The fusion, though beneficial, was at first enforced, for we know of resistance to it by Sumerian scribes. Thus Akkadian conquest could lead to an extension of culture, of an ideological power capable of providing further diffused power supports to empire. I will deal with this in the next section. It will modify my present emphasis on the dominance of military power and compulsory cooperation.

The most striking feature of these five items is that economic development and repression could go together. The benefits were abstract; they did not depend on the direct interdependence or exchanges of the mass of the producers or of the middlemen, but on the provision of certain uniform and repressive services by a military state. Therefore, repression was necessary to their maintenance. The material production of the major classes did not, as it were, "add up" to the overall economy, without the intervention of a militaristic elite to provide the integration of the economy as a whole. The circuits of praxis (to use the metaphor of Chapter 1) of the masses was not itself the "tracklayer" (to use my revision of Max Weber's metaphor discussed in Chapter 1) for the economy. Indeed, "class action" would probably tend to disintegrate the empire and threaten its level of development by returning to the primitive democracy of earlier times.

Because of a lack of evidence concerning the lives of the masses, such claims remain assertions for the moment. There were periods of social turbulence, perhaps involving class conflict, for rulers claimed to arbitrate them and to promote reform of debt and tenure systems, which are class-related. But there is no evidence, and it is unlikely, that class struggle played a developmental role comparable to what we will find in Chapter 7. In classical Greece different power networks gave an important development role to class struggle. In Chapter 9 Roman evidence enables us to see class struggle inherited from Greece declining in the face of horizontal power groupings characteristic of the empire of domination Rome was becoming. Perhaps the same decline of class struggle occurred in the ancient Near East as original notions of citizenship gave way before clientelist dependence on ruling elites and the imperial state.

To assert that societies that conquered by the sword lived by it runs counter to dominant assumptions of our own time. Modern social theories are profoundly antimilitarist – understandably so, given events in the twentieth century. But militarism even in modern times has often been successful in developing collective powers (as we will see in Volume II). It has not been merely parasitic but *productive*. Now I am not arguing that all militaristic empires were productive, or that any militarism is purely productive. Most militarism in all periods has been merely destructive: wasteful of lives, material resources, and culture, and not conducive to social development. My argument is more specific: There was a causal connection between some aspects of a certain type of military empire and economic and social development.

The further development of this economy of compulsory cooperation was complex. Alongside high elite consumption, and historically inseparable from it, was probably an increase in both the economic security and the population density of the masses. But the two tended to cancel each other out, a fact that Malthus noted to great effect. Empires led to greater security of existence above subsistence for the masses, and to an extension of the division of labor and communications systems so that nonbulky necessities requiring intensive production (like salt, metal, tools, pottery, and textiles) could be transported considerable distances. But they also undermined improvements by generating population growth. Higher living standards meant higher fertility, and population growth strained food resources. In some circumstances, this strain could stimulate further technological advance in food supply; usually it led to population control through abortion and infanticide. The alternative was irregular killing of adults through diseases, civil wars, and external wars, which was worse. Again, a premium was placed upon repressive order.

Economic development also increased the steepness of social stratification, due to an upsurge in the living standards of the relatively small conquering and ruling elite. Though the benefits spread widely to their direct dependents – servants, household slaves, hired artisans, administrators, and soldiers – these amounted to around 5–10 percent of the population, located usually within towns, fortresses, estates, and manorial complexes. The richer diets, conspicuous displays, and lasting monuments of this elite are regarded by moderns as parasitic, because most of the population shared only marginally in their fruits. They consumed the overwhelming majority of goods traded over long distances. Imperial civilizations were more stratified than either their primitive or city-state predecessors in terms of both the distribution of wealth and of personal and legal freedom and equality. Nevertheless, it *was* collective power development.

It also depended upon the state. The elite were not independent of the state infrastructure in a technical economic sense. The means of exchange were largely under state control. Merchants' and artisans' international dealings, prices, and (to a lesser extent) remuneration were regulated by the state. In other words, the ruling elite, created by *military* organization, but whose *political* tendency was to fragment into decentralized landowners, depended on a central state through the *economy*. Actually, as we shall see later in the chapter, the relationship became more complex and qualified with time.

All this placed a premium on centralized order, as the literate members of the empires knew. All Mesopotamian kings after Sargon who are praised in the surviving records – whether they were late Sumerian, Akkadian, Babylonian, or Assyrian – are praised for the order they provided (see, e.g., the analysis of Assyrian ideology by Liverani 1979). A late Sumerian farm manual stresses the need to discipline workers – "particular stress is laid on whips, goads, and other disciplinary instruments to keep both laborers and beasts working strenuously and continuously," writes Kramer, who comments similarly on discipline in the late Sumerian schoolroom (1963: 105–9, 236). The agricultural treatise is in this respect similar to those of another imperial society, the later Roman Republic. In empires, repression as benevolence appears to have been more than just ideology and to have pervaded actual social practices. The most extensive evidence concerning the ideological importance of compulsory cooperation is in Mesopotamian religion.

The diffusion of ideological power networks: Mesopotamian religion

I rely initially on Jacobsen's (1976) *tour de force*. It will run slightly ahead of my story.

Jacobsen traces the development of four main religious metaphors in Mesopotamian religion:

(1) *Elan vital,* a spirit indwelling in natural phenomena which are of economic importance. The dying god representing fertility problems is typical.
(2) *Rulers:* En-lil, "lord-wind," the first of the Sumerian personified gods.
(3) *Parents:* personalized god with a direct relationship to the individual.
(4) *National:* the god is identified with narrow political aspirations and with the fear of outside sorcerers and demons.

Rather neatly, each roughly corresponds to a millennium from the fourth to the first B.C. Jacobsen believes each reflects the changing balance of economic, political, and military power. The fourth-millennium situation is largely speculation. But at the beginning of the third, as we saw, kingship and the palace emerged, gradually becoming prominent over the redistributive temple. The art changes: Representations of war and victory replace ritual motifs, the epic is added to the myth, and man as ruler is the hero even to the point of challenging the gods (as in the Gilgamesh epic). The gods became active and politically organized with a worldly division of labor among them. The god Enbibulu is appointed as the divine "inspector of canals"; Utu, the god of justice, is put in charge of boundary disputes.

Here is a flavor of Sumerian religious poetry of the third-millennium "ruler" period. Enki, the god of cunning, has been appointed as a kind of chief administrator by the supreme gods An and Enlil. He says:

> My father, the king of heaven and earth,
> had me appear in the world,
> My older brother, the king of all lands,
> gathered and gathered offices,
> placed them in my hand. . . .
> I am the great god manager of the country,
> I am the irrigation officer for all the throne-daises,
> I am the father of all lands,
> I am the older brother of the gods,
> I make abundance perfect.
> [quoted in Jacobsen 1976: 110–16]

Enki, however, did not have things all his own way. The god Nimuta began as the god of the thunderstorm and spring flood, and thus of the plow. Yet in the third millennium he became the war god, in whose functions war and irrigation became merged, sometimes to the exclusion of Enki.

These changes – Jacobsen observes – reflect and grapple intellectually with political and military power development, not as crude political legitimation, but as a genuine intellectual effort to grasp the nature of life. World order (they knew of no other world) required certain talents, the priests noted: negotiation of boundaries between cities, irrigation management, above all the two roles of political fixer and warlord (which we have seen combined in a conqueror like Sargon). The tone is confident, worldly, matter-of-fact. It indicates a decline in the *transcendent* role of ideology in early Mesopotamia, discussed in Chapter 3: Religion becomes more confined within the state.

Military struggles continued. Sargon's successors were displaced by another marcher people, the Gutians. Their rule was relatively short-lived, and we then read of Sumerian successes against Semitic peoples. The political structure, imitating Sargon, moved toward a more centralized, imperial state in the Third Dynasty of Ur, under which law making, records, population, and productivity boomed. Then the state collapsed. One of its parts became Babylon and under the family of Hammurabi reestablished a single state over the area. Babylonian religion reinterpreted previous history in its creation myth. The world began as watery chaos, then the gods emerged as silt. They gradually took quasi-human form and engaged in a long struggle. First the god Ea emerged victorious but was then threatened by demon gods and monsters. His son Marduk offered to champion the gods but only if he was granted supreme authority. His spear's motto was "Safety and Obedience." He achieved victory and formed the earth in its present form from the body of his divine enemy. His motto was now significantly changed:

> When they gave Marduk the kingship
> they pronounced to him the formula
> of "Benefits and Obedience":
> "From this day forward you shall be
> the provider of our sanctuaries,
> and whatever you order let us carry out"
> [quoted in Jacobsen 1976: 178–80]

The gods then built Marduk a city, which he ruled. The city was called Babylon, and Marduk remained its father god.

The creation centered on the lifeblood of both Sumer and Babylon, river silt. Ea represents Sumer, the parent civilization. The epic struggles, containing frightening monsters and blazing images, reflected the military situation in the early second millennium. The transformation of Marduk's motto "Safety and Obedience" into "Benefits and Obedience" was the Babylonians' version of how they managed to establish order – by stabilizing militarism into

a centralized, bureaucratic, imperial regime. Again, it was not *mere* legitimation – it contained tensions, most notably the parricide theme of unease at
departing from the traditions of Sumer. But it was not transcendent. It was
immanent, grappling intellectually, morally, and aesthetically with given power
relations, and in its success strengthening them.

Then came another marcher wave, the Kassites, emerging into the area
(like the Akkadians before them) first as laborers, then as settlers, finally as
conquerors. From the sixteenth century their dynasty, having adopted local
religion and language, ruled Mesopotamia for at least four centuries (for 576
years and 9 months, according to scribal tradition). Here scholarship lets us
down, however. We have little knowledge on what seems to have been a
period of further growth and prosperity perhaps under a less centralized, more
"feudal" regime than hitherto seen in the region (see Brinkman 1968 and
Oates 1979). By now the religion seems stabilized and even conservative.
The Babylonians of the period began to use ancestral names, indicating cultural traditionalism, and the religious texts often developed a "canonical"
form.

After the fall of the Kassites, there ensued a confused period of fighting
between Elamites, Babylon, and new threats (Assyrians to the north, Chal-
deans to the south, and Arameans to the west). This was broken by brief
periods of Babylonian reassertion, notably under Nebuchadrezzar I. Finally,
Babylon fell under Assyrian dominance. Changes in military technology (of
which more in Chapter 6) gave advantage to mobile chariots and cavalry, and
city-states and even empires were under great threat. The warrior god reappeared but as death, the god of indiscriminate slaughter, to be appeased, if at
all, by abject flattery of his frightfulness. Among the conquering Assyrians,
as Liverani (1979: 301) observes, wars were always holy, because "holy"
actually meant "Assryian." Religion is now nationalized, a development discussed more fully in Chapter 8.

These changes in Mesopotamian religion probably corresponded to broad
changes in real social life. They had a high truth content. An objective
requirement for the maintenance of the successor civilizations after Sargon,
at least until the Kassites, was centrally imposed order. After the first phase
of civilizations, spontaneous elaboration of the division of labor, market
exchange of products, and a transcendent religious/diplomatic regulation of
conflict seem less effective at generating and stabilizing possession of a surplus, and of welding together disparate ecological and economic areas, than
forcible militaristic integration. In turn, this was the product of two forces.
First, the specific communications infrastructure of land, river, or canal (not
sea) made conquest and a degree of centralized control possible. Second, once
a greater surplus was generated than that possessed by its neighbors, defense
against raiding and conquest was necessary. Whether successful or unsuc-
cessful, the defense increased the militarization and centralization of the soci-

ety, though the form varied with the type of military technology and strategy employed. Imposed order was now more necessary. Order did not flow directly from the praxis of the people themselves but from "above" them, from centralized political authority. Reification of that authority appeared as objective truth; deification, the "awe-inspiring luminosity" of both king and god, was its imaginative expression. Objective knowledge and ultimate meaning were united in cosmology. The numinous was immanent in social structure. It was not opposed to, and did not transcend, the practical; it made sense of given power realities, the best sense available.

Yet for whom did it make sense? I consider separately the people and the ruling class. First, it was not apparently a popular religion from Jacobsen's second phase onward – as we might expect from low popular participation in social power in general. Priests engaged in "mysteries," somewhat removed from everyday life and confined to the privacy of certain institutions. The epics may have been enacted at court, away from public gaze. They were also read out by the king (in his own apartment) to the images of the gods. The populace saw the intermittent parade of those images, though it seems that ordinary households did make replicas of religious statues. Scholars sometimes disagree on these points. Oppenheim argues that there was no trace of the later "communion" between deity and worshipers observed in the Old Testament, in Greek and Hittite customs, and in the world religions. The Mesopotamian deity remained aloof. The Mesopotamian individual, he says, "lived in a quite tepid religious climate within a framework of socioeconomic rather than cultic co-ordinates." Oppenheim objects to the history of Mesopotamian religion being written at all: There was *no* religion of the civilization as a whole. He argues that extant records are far more particularistic than we learn from an account such as that of Jacobsen. But provided that Jacobsen's account is taken as being the state's own view of itself, this objection is answered.

We can guess at the nature of popular religions from hints in the records. Oppenheim argues that we can catch indications throughout the ancient Near East of an undercurrent that contradicts the official stress on divine order and embodies age-old, predeistic, deterministic concepts of life in which luck, demons, and the dead rule (1977: 171–227, esp. 176, 191, 200–6). More particularistic household and village gods, magical practices, and fertility rites of the prehistoric period survive through the entire archaic period.

Each empire, therefore, probably did not possess a unified cosmology or a single ideological power network. Our lack of knowledge of popular religion – unlike Egypt, for example – seems to indicate that the state lacked interest in the religion of the people. Religion was not a major source of its power over them. The rulers depended more on compulsory cooperation, integrating economic and military techniques of rule. As yet these were not ideologies that could integrate both spatially and hierarchically over such distances. The "ethnic community" of early Mesopotamia, described in Chapter 3, must have weakened, its homogeneity broken by increasing internal stratification. From now on, until the Greeks, I shall argue that "ethnic communities" were (with the exception of Egypt) small and tribal in nature, typified perhaps by the one people for whom we have good information, the Jews. Larger social units, whether imperial or tribal confederacies, were too stratified for community to cross class barriers. Ideological inventiveness, we shall see, now coped with the more restricted problem of "ruling-class" community.

The lack of ritual penetration reflected increasing stratification. Relatively "thin" interaction occurred between hierarchical levels. Where intensive coordination of irrigation was practical, this presumably led to dense, intense relations among those involved, though we find no examples where this involved the highest reaches of power. Where military service was based upon a relatively egalitarian infantry army, this would have similar consequences for social "intensity." But this was not the military norm. Furthermore, an elaborated division of labor was almost entirely urban. Interaction between rulers and masses was weakened by the low integration between city and countryside. In short, these were mostly rather nonintensive societies requiring little normative integration outside of the ruling group itself. Force could extract what little was required of the masses.

Was it then, secondly, an "aristocratic" religion, one that used the fourth and final strategy of imperial rule to weld together rulers into a coherent ruling class? This is more difficult to answer. As noted, the religion had "private" elements that might confine it to the state itself, separate from the "aristocracy." But it is doubtful if we can make such a clear distinction. In the next section dealing with the dynamics of empire, we shall see that "state" and "civil society," "monarchy" and "aristocracy" were interpenetrating. The king depended on leading families in cities and rural hinterlands alike. They were either a part of his household or they replicated such a household at the provincial level. There they would participate in the religion. Most scholars believe that religious epics were enacted, rather like medieval European mystery plays, though at court rather than, as in Europe, in streets and churches to which the public had access. The official religion also existed within a penumbra of other religious and cultural practices that were widespread among the ruling groups. Divination was particularly common. For example, a diviner normally accompanied the army and was often a general. We also find "dialogue" texts, contests involving the relative usefulness to man of rival characters – Summer and Winter, Plowman and Shepherd, and so forth – and again these imply theatrical performances for the elite and their dependents.

Part of the infrastructure of religion, literacy, was a separate craft, not wholly under the control of anyone. Kings, leading families, priests, governors, and even judges usually remained illiterate, dependent on the skills of what was in effect a craft guild with its own schools. Everyone else relied on memory, oral tradition, and oral institutions. In such circumstances it is tempting to seek analogies with the role of culture in a later, better-documented case, Rome. Although the Roman ruling class was literate, it depended on oral transmission (in the theater, rhetoric, law courts, etc.) for its "cultural cement" (see Chapter 10). Was there some such cultural cement among the Mesopotamian ruling class? The answer may be yes, although it would be far less developed than in Rome. It seems likely that the scribes at court, in the temples, following the armies, in merchant houses, and in aristocratic households were intermediaries in the diffusion of a modicum of ideological power among the ruling groups of the empires. As conquest became institutionalized, the various native elites, conquering and conquered, were provided with the language, script, culture, and religion of the Akkadian-Sumerian core. Such "education" was not direct – unlike later empires like the Roman or Persian. Early empires did not possess their cohesive ruling-class culture. Nevertheless, a beginning in such a direction had occurred. The empires did assimilate originally distinct groups. Virtually all that eventually remained of distinctive Kassite origins, for example, was their foreign-sounding names. Through scribes the elites had access to history and genealogy, science and mathematics, law, medicine, and religion. They themselves could reenact and reaffirm part of this culture, predominantly orally, through the law courts, the palace, the great households, the temples. The organized power of empire, once institutionalized, could also diffuse relatively universally among its elite groups and so make imperialism more stable.

In this respect, later Mesopotamian religion/culture did more than merely reflect a real social situation. It enhanced the collective confidence and morale, the power and the collective solidarity, of its monarchy and elite groups. They were partly a federated empire of "native" elites, partly an emerging ruling *class*. Participants in a "Great Society," they ruled the "four quarters of the world," not only because they had naked military power, the economic surplus to feed it, and the polity to institutionalize it but also because they believed themselves civilized and morally superior to the mass of the people both within and outside their domains. They were often disunited (as we shall see in a moment). But they also possessed elements of a class ideology. In this sense the role of ideological power in these empires was predominantly *immanent* to established, secular power structures, rather than transcendent of them, reinforcing not disrupting them.

On the other hand, this is only a statement of degree. Traces of transcendence are discernible. The ideology of empire was not definitely *bounded* until the appearance of late Assyrian "nationalism" (and perhaps not even then – see Chapter 8). The possibility of full entry to civilization was not denied to foreign ruling groups, nor even, in some cases, to elements of the people. The concern for enforced order, though predominant, was not all-pervasive outside the political/military realm. We also find respect for the kind of order brought into the cosmos by cultivated reason. In what is called the "wisdom literature," and in the significant development of mathematics and astronomy, we find an emphasis on rationality, varying from clear optimism through skepticism to occasional disillusionment that is not apparently confined to one class or ethnic group. The relative openness eased assimilation of foreign conquerors and conquered. Networks of ideological power were broader than those of imperial compulsory cooperation. Mesopotamia diffused its ideological practices all over the Near East, sometimes after conquest, sometimes before. It normally facilitated the diffusion of imperial power. But, as we shall see in later chapters, it could also on occasion undermine imperialism.

Thus in the ancient Near East ideological power played a dual role. First, varities of immanent ideology reinforced the moral, intellectual, and aesthetic solidarity of ruling groups, breaking down their internal particularistic divisions, solidifying them into relatively homogeneous, universal *ruling classes*. This was probably the predominant tendency in this period, though the process was hindered by a rudimentary level of communications infrastructure. Second, and subversive of the first side, ideology could also be transcendent. It opened up quasi-ruling classes to outside emulation and assimilation, especially in marcher areas, so loosening institutionalized patterns of compulsory cooperation. And it also continued to carry in unofficial and suppressed form a more popular level of ideological explanation. Later we will see explosions of these transcendent aspects. For the moment, immanent class reinforcement predominated, however.

The dialectics of empire: centralization and decentralization

The reader with some knowledge of ancient Mesopotamia or possessing a refined nose for sociological plausibility may have experienced irritation over the preceding sections. For the analysis might seem to suggest that empires were efficient, highly integrated, ordered, and stable. This was not entirely true. Dynasties usually lasted for fifty to two hundred years and then broke up into smaller warring units. Most rulers were faced by at least one serious revolt. This was true of Sargon himself, and of Naram-Sin. I discussed this tendency to disintegration already when describing political logistics. Political lieutenants and clients of the ruler escaped central control, "disappeared" into civil society, and raised the standard of revolt. These tendencies were cyclical: Empires were conquered, broke up, were reconquered, broke up, and so on. They contained no development, no true dialectic.

Yet there was a long-term developmental tendency, perceptible in ancient history right up to the fall of Rome, almost three thousand years after the death of Sargon. It will be a theme, not only of the present chapter, but of the next four as well. Even to describe its earlier phases will take me out of the strict chronological sequence of chapters to introduce important historical innovations like the diffusion of iron tools and weapons, and the spread of coinage or literacy. But these massive changes were part of a dialectic affecting the main achievements of compulsory cooperation. I will start with military technique – as Sargon started there – and then deal briefly with other power sources.

Sargon had created an organization capable of defeating foes over an area of several hundred kilometers in length and breadth. As long as a region could produce the surplus to support such an organization, it was now a continuous military possibility. It could be wielded by a power originating either from the marches or from the core, irrigated area. The next two millennia saw ubiquitous military struggles between the two types of area. Sargon was immediately confronted by a dilemma. On the one hand his distinctive military strength had come from the marches and he did not wish to see any other power emanating from there. On the other he was now dependent for his supplies on the irrigated core. He had to sit astride the two, attempting greater integration between them. But marches are never-ending: Imperial success creates further marches, and hitherto marginal peoples drawn into the imperial sphere of influence but as yet untamed.

It is conventional in world histories to stress the power of the marchers. McNeill (1963) and Collins (1977) regard conquest by marcher lords as the most frequent type of conquest in the entire ancient world. If we run a little ahead in chronology, we can see this impetus periodically reasserted. Just after 2000 B.C. innovations occurred in chariot design, increasing their flexibility and speed, and in archery. Advantage passed to charioteers wielding lance and bow. Right across Eurasia chariot-mounted peoples like the Mycenaeans, Aryans in India, Hyksos, and Kassites, all apparently originating in upland marcher areas, for a time swept aside the infantry of the agriculturalist city-states. The latter, however, could regroup with the aid of greater fortifications, armor, and the adoption of chariots themselves.

The chariot's superiority was finally ended by a metallurgical revolution occurring about 1200–1000 B.C. that developed cheap iron tools, weapons, and body armor. Massed infantrymen recruited from peasants tilling rain-watered lands with iron tools were thus enabled to stand firm against arrows and charges. Marcher tribes were the first to exploit these techniques. These two military techniques, mobile chariots and iron weapons and armor, were developed by upland pastoralists and hitherto-marginal farmers, enabling them to conquer the floodplains and valleys, unite them to their own heartlands, and thereby create larger territorial states than had hitherto existed.

Nevertheless, the process was not one-way. Throughout the period the capacity of civilized agriculturalists to respond also increased. With them lay the advantage of a greater surplus, greater methodical organization, greater discipline – and the inability to run away. The type of warfare most suited to their way of life was infantry. Once body armor developed, their means of defense increased, as did their capacity to methodically aggrandize territory. Differentiation of the forms of warfare also advantaged them, provided they could learn quickly. They reacted to new threats by diversifying, which increases the complexity of organization, discipline, and tactics. When added to the tendency of weapons and armor to develop technologically and in cost, in the long run advantage accrued to the society with more centralized, territorial coordination, in other words to the stronger state. If we add naval, fortification, and siege warfare, the tendency becomes more marked; for these required long-term construction of war implements and more elaborate provisioning than the three arms so far considered.

Yet the advantages of civilization bring their own contradictions, one beginning in a loosely defined "core," the other on the "periphery". These contradictions then tended to break down the geographical distinction between the two. The core contradiction was between the development of more complex, centrally coordinated armies and the conditions that first allowed the civilizations to withstand their foes. Infantry defenses had initially presupposed a cohesive social base, in Sumer provided by similarity of experience and membership in the community. The city-states had either been democracies or relatively benign oligarchies, and this showed in their military tactics. Cohesion and morale, faith in the man next to you, was essential for infantry. Yet an increase in costs, in professionalism, and in diversity of forces, weakened the contribution of the ordinary member of the community. Either the state turned to mercenaries or foreign auxiliaries or it turned to the rich, able to turn out heavily armored soldiers. This weakened social cohesion. The state became less embedded in the military and economic lives of the masses, more differentiated as an authoritarian center, and more associated with steep social stratification between classes. The state was more vulnerable to capture. One swift campaign to capture the capital, and kill the ruler but spare part of his staff, and the conquest was complete. The masses did not require pacification for they were not involved in this turn of events. The state was more dependent upon professional soldiers, on both central praetorian guards and on provincial lords – more vulnerable to their ambitions, and therefore to endemic civil war.

This was reinforced by the peripheral contradiction. The more successful empires were at developing economic resources in their cores, the more this raised up their peripheries. The ancient empires of this era (i.e., before Rome and the Han dynasty of China and with the exception of Egypt) did not have clearly demarcated boundaries. Their activities and their hegemony spread, sometimes loosely, sometimes along controlled lines of penetration, into the surrounding region. Trade hegemony penetrated long distances along corridors; that over herding diffused. The herds of the royal wool office, referred to earlier, spread imperial domination but also increased the power of local elites, some clients, some hostile, most varying according to the main chance.

Mesopotamian ideology did not bar these elites from civilization. Indeed, it encouraged them to emulate the imperial elite, become literate, and think of themselves as possessing cultivation, wisdom, and morality. Later they were not "barbarians" but rivals for power, often in court and capital, as well as in the marches. Their pretensions did not necessarily threaten civilization – in fact, they were as likely to boost it with their vigor as destroy it through savagery.

Royal military presence could not be routine. The more the royal activities increased, the more they invited raiding and conquest by their neighbors. After Sargon, the marches could not be left alone, for independent marches spelled danger. But the logistics of control were daunting. Some later empires incorporated marcher areas. But once the process of incorporation of borders started, there was almost no end to it, for the marches ended only when true desert was reached. And there different dangers lurked: the pastoral nomads eventually with sturdy cavalry horses peculiarly suited to raiding. They rarely stayed as pure nomads for long. Trading contact increased *their* wealth and level of civilization.

Our best evidence comes from a different case, the frontier of China. Successful invasions by "barbarian" groups like the Toba, Sha-To, Mongols, and Manchus were preceded by the emigration of Chinese advisers to their courts, and their adoption of Chinese administrative and military forms. Their military superiority lay in developing Chinese tactics to exploit the capacity of their cavalry, to concentrate its forces quickly, evade enormous infantry armies, and strike at the Chinese headquarters. The smallest known group are the Sha-To, who, numbering only ten thousand soldiers and a hundred thousand persons, conquered and ruled northern China in the tenth century A.D. (Eberhard 1965, 1977). We shall concentrate in Chapter 9 on the "barbarians" who were upgraded by, and who eventually demolished, the Roman Empire.

Such a threat could not be eliminated. A civilized agrarian society using heavy infantry/cavalry armies is unable to supply itself or to find its enemy in sparsely populated deserts or steppes. All later ancient Eurasian empires came into contact with nomadic terrains; all were similarly vulnerable (except perhaps the ancient Egyptians, whose frontiers were true, unpopulated desert). Defense constituted a considerable drain on resources – frontier fortifications and troops, bribes to barbarian chieftains, the development of mobile forces. The last of these tended to give power and autonomy to marcher lords, which made the contradiction internal as well.

I have run ahead in time in order to show the rhythm of military power networks. Conquest and compulsory cooperation bred not only economic and social development but also a plethora of marcher threats. The organization to defeat them weakened the social base of the initial success and potentially led to an excess of coercion over cooperation. I have stressed the indirect nature of rule in these early empires. Provinces were ruled *through* the power of lieutenants and provincials. They could not be easily coerced.

Parallel contradictions can be found in all areas of the militaristic state's activities. Picture, if you will, a middling prosperous province of an empire. It sits astride communications and trade routes from the capital to the periphery; its main town is garrisoned by two hundred professional soldiers aided by local levies; and its commander is charged with rendering tax or tribute to the center, supplying his own troops, and maintaining communications routes with the aid of slaves or serfs and corvée labor. If he is successful in maintaining order and a regular flow of tax or tribute, the ruler lets him alone, content to rule indirectly and unable to do anything else without a vast and unnecessary show of force. In turn, the commander rules locally with the aid of his own lieutenants and local elites. If they provide his supplies regularly, he is minimally content; if they provide more, he is more than content to also rule indirectly and appropriate the surplus himself. The more successful the state is, the wider it spreads such intermediate layers of power through the province.

So there is no contradiction between "the state" and "private property" or between the "state elite" and the "dominant class." They are aspects of the same developmental process. An older tradition of Mesopotamian scholarship used to search for phases of "state domination" and of "private wealth" and "private trading activity." As the evidence accumulates, it is becoming impossible to maintain such distinctions. In all known long-term periods, the level of state wealth and private wealth and the level of state interest in trade and private merchant trade appear positively correlated, (see, e.g., the various essays in Hawkins 1977). The attitude of the political elite/ruling class appears pragmatic, and thus dependent on broader consensual norms. Whether a state will use its own trading organization or that of a merchant, or whether a state official will be trading as agent of the state or on his own account, seems to have been largely a question of what organizational and logistical means were available. No major conflicts seem to have been involved in these choices.

The infrastructure of power, its organization and logistics, seems inherently double-edged. This is true of virtually all state contributions to the logistics of power. If it develops a quasi-coinage – stamped bars in silver, iron, or copper – this confers guaranteed wealth, "capital," on its suppliers, as well as heightening its own economic powers. In the provincial town, the garrison provisioners slowly acquire such capital, as do the local landlords whose fields produce the supplies. If the state attempts more regular control by using literate officials, their literacy becomes useful to provincial merchants and lords. For example, in the Kassite period schools fell under aristocratic dominance. The state's problem is that none of its techniques can be confined within its own body politic – they diffuse into society. Even its own body has a tendency to split off into separate provincial organisms. If the techniques of compulsory cooperation are successful, it is in everyone's interest to be a part of a larger imperial domain. But *whose* domain matters less, because all conquerors must rule in the same indirect way. If a marcher group first threatens, then infiltrates and appears to offer greater long-run protection, local calculations begin to change. If the dynastic succession is disputed, then loyalty is weighed against the importance of being on the winning side. If the present ruler reacts against such threats by seeking greater fiscal and military exactions, the provincials' eyes narrow still further as they recalculate the odds. For they have autonomous private resources, generated in part by the state's earlier successes, and they need to protect them and capitalize upon them by offering them to the winning side. A period of anarchy and devastation may endure while the warring factions fight. But it is in most groups' interest to emerge through this into a new phase of imperial consolidation – that is how private resources are generated anew.

The process suggests three departures from traditional theories. First, the very notion of clearly separated "peoples" may be the product of dynastic ideologies, not social realities. "Akkadians" and "Sumerians," "Amorites" and later "Sumerians," "Kassites" and "Babylonians" were intermixed long before a dynasty from each of the former supposedly conquered the latter. They may have *started* as core and periphery groups, but then they mingled. Can we go farther? Were these labels just legitimacy claims based on principles of genealogical succession and usurpation at which we can only guess? Everyone wanted the genealogical mantle of Sumer, successors generally wanted that of Sargon, and nobody claimed that of the Gutians, whereas the Kassites may have been less legitimate than their achievements warranted. We don't know why. We have often filled in the gap with nineteenth-century A.D. notions of ethnicity. In the twentieth century these have become sophisticated models of "core" and "periphery," with explicit conceptions of territoriality and implicit notions of ethnicity. But these conceptions are too fixed and static for the social conditions of early societies.

This is mostly speculation. The second theoretical departure, however, is better documented. It repeats an argument of previous chapters: Increases in private property resources result largely from the fragmentation of collective social organization. The dialectic between the two is not between two autonomous social spheres, "civil society" and "the state." It is between the necessity for more and more collective organization of certain power resources and the logistical impossibility of maintaining collective control over them.

This leads to the third and most important theoretical departure, the claim to discern an overall dialectic of development in compulsory cooperation, emanating less from its order than from its contradictions. The very *success* of compulsory cooperation led to its downfall, and then, in many cases, to its reconstitution at a higher level of social development. Compulsory cooperation *simultaneously* increased the power of the militaristic state (thesis) and of decentralized elites who could then overthrow the state (antithesis). But the elites continued to need imposed order. This would generally reconstitute a state, now with greater power capacities (synthesis), and the dialectic would start over again. This mechanism developed a secular tendency toward more collectively powerful forms of social organization, most taking an imperial form. The empire of Ur reconstituted the empire of Akkad in size but increased its population density, economic administration, architectural ambitions, law codes, and probably its prosperity; Babylon, though no more extensive, was in certain senses more intensively powerful; the Kassite dynasty may have brought new levels of prosperity to the region (for a good general account of all these phases of Mesopotamian political history, see Oates 1979; for the last phase, see Brinkman 1968; for a more economic analysis, see Adams 1981: 130–74). As we will see in Chapter 8, Assyria was vaster and more powerful, both intensively and extensively, than its predecessors. Then Persia and Rome were greater still (as Chapters 8 and 9 reveal). The earlier phases of this dialectic can be represented diagrammatically, as in Figure 5.1.

Of course, only in a very loose sense can we describe a ''one-dimensional'' increase in collective power in general. Over such a long time period empires changed considerably the nature of their power organizations and techniques. In the next chapters I will continue to describe the development of the two principal imperial power strategies, *compulsory cooperation* and *cohesive ruling-class culture*. The infrastructure of the former developed before that of the latter, and so I have emphasized its role in these first empires of domination. But later empires will prove to have had more variable mixtures of the two. Rome developed both to an unprecedented degree. Persia relied more on the cultural cohesion of its rulers. At what point did variability begin? In this area it perhaps began with the Kassites, about whom scholars disagree. If their rule flourished, was it looser, more feudal, dependent less on imperial compulsion than on the cohesion of its aristocracy, tolerant of diversity – a Persian-style empire? If so, the dialectic described here is already less of a simple rising crescendo of imperial strength and rigidity than an interplay between ''imperial,'' or perhaps ''patrimonial,'' and ''feudal'' regimes through which collective power, broadly conceived, nonetheless developed. This raises two of the most important concepts of comparative sociology. I will now argue that these concepts are generally used statically and so miss the developmental – and the occasional dialectical – pattern of world history.

The comparative study of ancient empires

Apart from a few stray generalizations, I have confined myself to a single millennium of Near Eastern history. Yet a body of literature within comparative sociology generalizes about historic empires located over the whole globe and throughout the five millennia of recorded history. To do so requires that

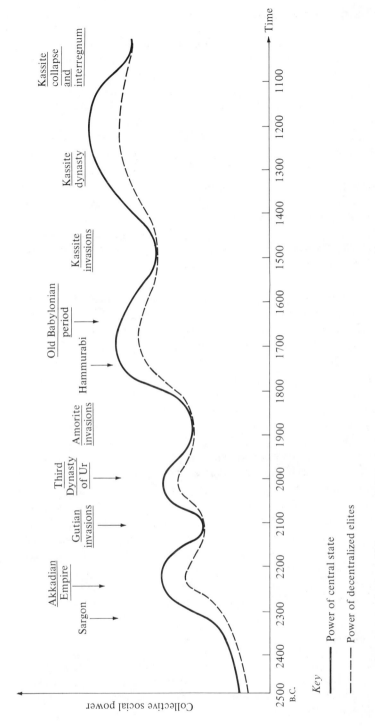

Figure 5.1. *Dialectics of Mesopotamian empires*

Key
— Power of central state
--- Power of decentralized elites

Time

Collective social power

2500 B.C. 2400 2300 2200 2100 2000 1900 1800 1700 1600 1500 1400 1300 1200 1100

Sargon

Akkadian
Empire

Gutian
invasions

Third
Dynasty
of Ur

Amorite
invasions

Hammurabi

Old Babylonian
period

Kassite
invasions

Kassite
dynasty

Kassite
collapse
and
interregnum

empires shared broad similarities that shine through the many and variegated differences of time and place. "Is it not amazing," asks John Kautsky rhetorically,

that there should be substantial similarities between Assyrians, Almoravids and Aztecs, between the empires of the Macedonians, the Mongols and the Moguls, between Ostrogothic kings, Umayyad caliphs and Ottoman sultans, between the Sassanid, Songhay and Saudi empires, between Ptolemies, Teutonic Knights and the Tutsi, between the Vandals, the Visigoths and the Vikings? [1982: 15]

Kautsky observes acutely that the basic similarity enabled conquerors like the Romans or the Spanish conquistadores to exploit politically the weak spots of their apparently "alien" opponents – for they recognized their power structure.

I do not dispute Kautsky's essential argument. This type of comparative sociology has established points of similarity between such varied regimes. I present three of these before turning to the principal defects of the model – a neglect of *history*, an inability to produce a theory of social *development*, and a failure to recognize dialectical processes.

The first point of similarity between such regimes is that, as Kautsky labels them, they were "*aristocratic* empires." They were dominated by a ruling class that monopolized landownership (sometimes in the sense of effective possession, rather than legal ownership) and so controlled the economic, military, and political power resources that land provided. And ideologically, their dominance was expressed through genealogical claims to moral and factual superiority – an aristocrat was superior because, through birth, he (or she) was connected to an endogenous kin group stretching back to an original ancestor group that founded the society, were descended from heroes or gods, or performed some other noble feats. With its hands firmly on all four sources of social power, the class was so entrenched that no ruler could dispense with its support. This is worth stating simply and forcibly because many of these regimes made a contrary ideological claim, namely, that all power flowed from it and it alone, and also because some writers have been taken in by the claim. Sargon's grandson, Naram-Sin, claimed divinity. His Akkadian or Sumerian aristocrats only claimed genealogical connections to the divine. This became a standard pattern for the more pretentious empires of history up to the modern period. It justified the personal despotism of the ruler, which in theory was exercised no less over the aristocrats than over anyone else. Some of the more credulous writers have believed that this could lead to actually "absolute" rule. This number included Wittfogel, whose theories I dismissed in Chapter 3, as well as a few other comparative sociologists (e.g., Wesson 1967: esp. 139–202). In practice, however, such regimes were feeble.

It is helpful at this point to distinguish between two types of state power. I make the distinction more fully in Mann (1984). *Despotic power* refers to the range of actions that the ruler and his staff are empowered to attempt to imple-

170   A history of power to A.D. 1760

ment without routine, institutionalized negotiation with civil society groups. A supreme despot, say a monarch whose claim to divinity is generally accepted (as in Egypt or China throughout much of their imperial histories) can thus attempt virtually any action without "principled" opposition. *Infrastructural power* refers to the capacity to actually penetrate society and to implement logistically political decisions. What should be immediately obvious about the despots of historic empires is the weakness of their infrastructural powers and their dependence upon the class of aristocrats for such infrastructure as they possessed. For many purposes, and especially in the provinces, their infrastructure *was* the aristocracy. So, in practice, empires were "territorially federal," as I expressed it – looser, more decentralized, more prone to fission, than the state's own ideology usually claimed.

All these points stemming from the first regime similarity have been made often enough, using slightly different terminology, in recent comparative sociology (see, e.g., Bendix 1978, Kautsky 1982).

The second regime similarity leads to a rather different emphasis, however. In emphasizing the power of the aristocratic class, we should not lose sight of the fact that a state still exists with power resources of its own. States exist because they are functional for social life beyond a fairly simple level. It is more relevant to the present issue that they provide something that is useful to the aristocratic class. This is *territorial centralization*. A number of activities, such as judicial rule making and enforcement, military organization, and economic redistribution, were usually more efficiently performed at this level of historical development if centralized. This central place *is* the state. Thus any autonomous power that the state can acquire derives from its ability to exploit its centrality.

This has been explored by Eisenstadt (1963). Following Weber's lead, he argued that the imperial state claims *universalism* and that this claim has some actual grounding in fact. A state cannot be *merely* aristocratic. Genealogical claims are inherently particularistic; they are the antithesis of centrality and of the state. Societies that develop permanent states have already proceeded farther than particularism. They have rationalized the symbolic sphere and begun to conceptualize the cosmos as subject to general forces with universal impact. The state, not the aristocracy, expresses this rational divinity. Materially, further argues Eisenstadt, the state's interests lie in fostering "free-floating resources," resources that are autonomous of any particularistic power actor. Eisenstadt instances many of these, and I will return repeatedly to them in the course of my historical narrative. The most striking (especially to the person concerned!) is the use of eunuchs by the state. As I have emphasized, any of the state's agents may "disappear" into civil society, escaping the control of the ruler. One way of stopping an agent from disappearing into the aristocracy is to prevent genealogical issue by castration.

Of the universalizing techniques of early states glimpsed in this and the last chapter, let me pick out three. First, in the realm of ideology, comes the attempt by the Akkadian conquerors to rationalize and systematize the pantheon and the creation myths of the Sumerian cities. Under the Akkadian Empire a "religion" is written down, codified, and given hierarchy and centrality. Second, in the realm of material infrastructure is the attempt (or at least the claim) by Sargon and his imperial successors to have improved and coordinated as a whole the communications structure of the empire. These are not just power-enhancing actions: They attempt to universalize power, and, consciously or not, their force is to reduce the power of local, particularistic elites. Third, and perhaps the best example because it combines ideology with infrastructure, is the "decimal" administrative structure imposed by the Inca conquerors on the Andean peoples (referred to in Chapter 4). In practice, of course, the Inca could only rule conquered provinces through local, indigenous elites. They might impose alongside them an Inca governor, import some loyal settler-soldiers and build roads, storehouses, and relay-posts – indeed, no conquerors were more ingenious in such respects. But they could not overcome those brute logistical problems of rule that I have outlined in this chapter. Hence the significance of the decimal rationalization. Its ideological function and perhaps, to a degree, its actual effect (though the conquistadores exposed its weaknesses), was to say to the local elites: "Yes, you may continue to rule your people. But remember that your rule is part of a wider cosmos that subordinates tribal and regional particularisms to a rational Inca order, centered on the Lord Inca himself." It reflects great credit on Eisenstadt to say that if the Lord Inca or Sargon or the Chinese or Roman emperor were to return and read his book, they would recognize his characterization of their policies and know what was meant by universalism, free-floating resources, the rationalization of the symbolic sphere, and the other pieces of Eisenstadt jargon.

I have drawn two insights from comparative sociology: on the one hand, a socially useful, despotic, universal state; on the other, a decentralized, particularistic aristocracy in actual possession of much of the power infrastructure of the society. The contrast between the two means that comparative sociology has also provided a third insight, a clear exposition of the contradictions, and sometimes of a part of the dynamics, of such regimes. For there was a continuous struggle between the two, mitigated only (but most substantially) by their mutual interdependence in order to preserve their exploitation of the mass of the population. The most famous discussion of the struggle was presented by Weber in his analysis of patrimonialism in *Economy and Society* (1968: III, 1006–69).

Weber distinguished patrimonialism and feudalism as the predominant types of political regime in preindustrial civilized societies. Patrimonialism adapts an earlier, simpler form of patriarchal authority within the household to the conditions of larger empires. Under it, government offices originate in the ruler's own household. This continues to provide the model even where the official function has little connection with the household. For example, the cavalry commander is often given a title, like "marshal," which originally denoted supervision of the ruler's stables. Similarly the patrimonial ruler shows a preference for appointing members of his own household, kinsmen or dependents, as government officers. The ensuing rule is autocratic: The ruler's authoritative commands assign rights and duties to other persons and households. Sometimes associations of persons and households are designated by the ruler as collectively responsible for rights and duties. By contrast, feudalism expresses a contract between near equals. Independent, aristocratic warriors freely agree to exchange rights and duties. The contract assigns one of the parties overall political rule, but he is restrained by the terms of the contract and he is no autocrat. Weber distinguishes these two forms of rule as ideal types and then proceeds in his characteristic fashion to elaborate the logical consequences and subdivisions of each. But he also notes that in reality ideal types become blurred and transform one into the other. In particular he acknowledges the logistical impossibility in preindustrial conditions of a "pure" patrimonialism. The extension of patrimonial rule necessarily decentralizes it and sets in motion a continuous struggle between the ruler and his agents, now become local notables with an autonomous power base. It is exactly the kind of struggle I have described in Mesopotamia. Weber details examples from ancient Egypt and Rome; ancient and modern China; and medieval Europe, Islam, and Japan. His analysis has so influenced historical understanding that it looms large in modern scholarship on all these cases and more.

Approximations to the ideal-type regimes, plus mixed cases, have dominated much of the globe. The struggle between centralized, patrimonial empires and decentralized, loosely feudal, aristocratic monarchies constitutes much of the history recorded by contemporaries. But if this were all of our history, even all of our upper-class history, it would be essentially cyclical, lacking long-term social development. In this chapter I have tried to add something else: an understanding of how such a struggle continuously revolutionizes the means of power and so constitutes a dialectic of development.

Perhaps it is open to misinterpretation to accuse Max Weber of lacking interest in historical development, since he concerned himself with this more than has any other major sociologist of the twentieth century. But his use of these ideal types was at times static. He contrasted East and West, arguing that massive social development occurred in Europe, rather than the East, because it was dominated by a contractual, decentralized feudalism, which (in contrast to Eastern patrimonialism) fostered a relatively rational spirit of acquisition and an activist orientation to the conquest of nature. In his view a relatively feudal, or at least decentralized, structure must be in place *before* dynamism can occur. This is incorrect. As we shall see repeatedly, it is the dialectic *between* the centralizing and decentralizing that provides a considerable part of social development, and this has been especially pronounced in the history of the Near Eastern/Mediterranean/Western world.

The subsequent development of neo-Weberian comparative sociology has become more static. Whatever the insights provided by Bendix, Eisenstadt, Kautsky, and others, they neglect development. To concentrate, as Kautsky does, upon the similarities of regimes such as the Inca Empire and the kingdom of Spain (both "aristocratic empires") is to forget what happened when 180 Spaniards entered an Inca Empire of millions. The Spaniards possessed power resources undreamed of by the Inca. Those resources – body armor, horses, gunpowder; the military discipline, tactics, and cohesion to use these weapons; a salvationist, literate religion; a monarch and a church able to enforce commands over six thousand kilometers; a religious/national solidarity able to overcome differences of class and lineage; even their diseases and personal immunities – were products of several millennia of world-historical development denied to the American continent. We will see the resources emerge gradually, unsteadily, but undeniably cumulatively over the next six or so chapters. Comparative sociology must be restrained by an appreciation of world-historical time.

Thus, when neo-Weberian analyses come to explain social development, they look outside of their theoretical model. Kautsky regards "commercialization" as the main dynamic process. It emerges, he says, through towns and traders who are largely outside the structure of "Aristocratic Empires," and whose emergence he cannot therefore explain. Bendix, whose aim is to explain the transition from monarchy to democracy, also turns to extraneous factors. In his case they are a number of unexplained, independent variables like population growth; technological changes; and the growth of towns, communications infrastructures, education systems, and literacy (1978: esp. 251–65). Eisenstadt has a more adequate model for understanding social development. In a few pages (1963: 349–59) he outlines how a few empires were transformed into more "modern" polities and societies. For him the decisive factor was the ability of various decentralized elites, supported by rational, salvationist religion, to appropriate the universalism and free-floating resources hitherto monopolized by the state. As we shall see in later chapters, this is indeed an important part of the answer. But after 350 pages delineating a static or cyclical model of empire, he can hardly go far in this direction in 10 pages. All these works (as with most comparative sociology) combine promiscuously material gathered from different phases in the development of social-power resources. This is their greatest weakness, for it is often the very thing they are supposedly trying to explain.

My criticism of the methodology of the comparative sociology of ancient empires is not the "typical historian's" objection that every case is unique. Though this is true, it does not preclude comparison and generalization. It is rather that comparative analysis should also be *historical*. Each case *develops* temporally, and this dynamic must itself be part of our explanation of its structure. In the present case, the dynamics of "imperial" (or "patrimonial") and "feudal" regimes have constituted a dialectic of development, ignored by comparative sociology.

Conclusion: military power reorganized social development

I have shown that the organizational capacity and the politically despotic form of the first empires in the Middle East emerged primarily from the reorganizing powers of developing military power relations. *Concentrated coercion* became unusually effective as a means of social organization. This was not because of the requirements of irrigation agriculture – as we saw Wittfogel arguing in Chapter 3. The crucial ecological background was the intersection of alluvium and hinterland in marcher areas where certain military inventions now appeared.

In the upland marches a mixed form of agriculture and herding was boosted by economic development in the floodplain involving trade with pastoralists farther out. Those who controlled the marches were able to combine the military techniques of agriculturalists and pastoralists into larger, more varied, more centralized military striking forces. Beginning with Sargon of Akkad's 5,400 men, they conquered the floodplains, ostensibly integrating them with each other and with the upland areas in a militaristic, monarchical state. The unity of such an empire was fragile. It depended overwhelmingly on a militaristic organization of both state and economy embodying "compulsory cooperation," as defined by Spencer. This led to a further burst of economic development, to a further immanent diffusion of ideological power *within* the dominant groups, and to the long-term consolidation of the empire and a ruling class.

The empire, however, was still a relatively fragile interaction network lacking intense control over its subjects. "Ethnic communities" in Smith's (1983) sense, discussed in Chapter 3, were weakened. Little was required of the masses besides regular handing over of payments in kind and in labor. Control over them, though savage, was erratic. More was routinely required of the dispersed ruling group, but it was not uncongenial to them. The empire was not territorial, nor was it unitary. It was a system of *federal domination* by a king or emperor through provincial, marcher, and even "foreign" rulers and elites. This was for fundamentally logistical reasons: I calculated that no conqueror, no matter how formidable, could organize, control and supply his troops and administrative officials on a routine basis over more than an eighty- to ninety-kilometer route march. The king or emperor used his professional army in reserve to dominate, to cow. But everyone knew that it would take a formidable logistical exercise to employ it. As long as local elites handed over tax or tribute, their own local control would not be interfered with. Their own interest was in the maintenance of the imperial system of compulsory cooperation. The imperial power continuously "spun off" into civil society, generating private power resources as well as state resources. Private property grew apace because the radius of political power was more limited than that of military conquest and because the apparatus of compulsory cooperation diffused and decentralized power, while ostensibly centralizing it. The state could not keep within its own body what it acquired either from conquest or from the successful development of techniques of compulsory cooperation. And so throughout ancient times there developed a dialectic between centralizing and decentralizing forces, powerful imperial states and private-property classes, *both* the product of the same fused sources of social power.

I have described in the main one particular phase and region of this dialectic, the Mesopotamian sphere of influence toward the end of the third millennium and the beginning of the second millennium B.C. I make no claim that the details of the dialectic can be found generally all over the globe. Let us briefly consider the other case studies of the last chapter. One had a distinctive, continuous history, to which I referred in the preceding chapter. Egypt's ecological isolation could not generate marcher lords or the subsequent imperial dialectic. Three more of the case studies also embarked on a distinctive path, that of collapse! The demise of two of them, Indus Valley and Crete, is still unclear. Both *may* have involved conquest by "marcher lords," respectively the Aryans and the Mycenaeans, but this cannot be confidently asserted. The latter is discussed briefly at the beginning of the next chapter. The third, Inca Peru, was suddenly assailed, not by marcher lords but by conquerors from as far away in world-historical time as geographical distance. The final two cases are analogous to Mesopotamia in various ways. Both China and Mesoamerica exhibit a repeated marcher-lord cycle, as well as the development of compulsory cooperation and its state–private property dialectic. But I am concerned in this book less with comparative sociology than with a specific history, one that happens to be of importance to the world in the following four millennia. Its influence was already extending during the second millennium: By 1500 B.C. two of these areas were no longer autonomous "case studies." Crete and Egypt were participating in a single, multicentered Near Eastern civilization. I will not develop comparative analogies much further.

This second phase of Near Eastern history was thus initially "switched" into a different track by military power relations, able to establish extensive empires of domination through conquest. The enduring significance of military power was not as an autonomous "factor" or "level" in society. Conquest and militarized rule both had nonmilitary preconditions into which they were embedded. Rather, military power provided two "moments of social reorganization" in which it lay down novel tracks of social development. The first was in conquest itself, in which the logic of battlefield and campaign events decided which group would predominate. In this phase the marcher lords were usually the victors. This raised the possibility that more extensive societies integrating irrigation agriculture, rain-watered agriculture, and pastoralism, and integrating town and countryside, would result. Second, this possibility became actuality, stabilized and institutionalized over a long period because military organization promiscuously penetrated political, ideological, and especially economic interaction networks through the mechanisms of compulsory cooperation. This second military reorganization made ancient empires more than superstructure. It converted their histories from the ephemeral and the cyclical to the social and developmental. *Concentrated coercion,* specified in Chapter 1 as the fundamental means of military power, proved socially useful outside the battlefield (where it is always decisive), certainly to the ruling classes, probably also to large sections of the masses. Ancient Near Eastern imperial civilization, to which our own society is connected and indebted, developed through a whole phase as a result of these two "moments" of military reorganization of social life.

Nevertheless I have also specified the limits and the dialectics of such imperialism. Empires were still not territorial or unitary, but *federal,* like their predecessors of the last chapter. They were also generating subversive, decentralizing forces within their own bodies and in their marcher regions. These forces exploded in the second millennium B.C., as the next chapter describes.

Bibliography

Adams, R. McC. 1979. "Common concerns but different standpoints: a commentary. In *Power and Propaganda: A Symposium on Ancient Empires,* ed. M. T. Larsen. Copenhagen: Akademisk Forlag.

    1981. *Heartland of Cities.* Chicago: University of Chicago Press.

Bendix, R. 1978. *Kings or People.* Berkeley: University of California Press.

Brinkman, J. A. 1968. *A Political History of post-Kassite Babylonia 1158–722* B.C. Rome: Pontificium Institum Biblicum (Analecta Orientalia No. 43).

Collins, R. 1977. Some principles of long-term social change: the territorial power of states. In *Research in Social Movements, Conflict and Change,* 1.

Crown, A. D. 1974. Tidings and instructions: how news travelled in the ancient Near East. *Journal of the Economic and Social History of the Orient,* 17.

Diakonoff, I. M. 1969. Main features of the economy in the monarchies of Ancient Western Asia. *Third International Conference of Economic History,* Munich, 1956. Paris: Mouton.

Eberhard, W. 1965. *Conquerors and Rulers: Social Forces in Modern China.* Leiden: Brill.

    1977. *A History of China,* Berkeley: University of California Press.

Eisenstadt, S. 1963. *The Political System of Empires.* Glencoe, Ill.: Free Press.

Ekholm, E., and J. Friedman. 1979. Capital, imperialism and exploitation in ancient world systems. In Larsen, *Power and Propaganda.*

Engel, D. W. 1978. *Alexander the Great and the Logistics of the Macedonian Army.* Berkeley: University of California Press.

Gadd, C. J. 1971. The cities of Babylonia, and The dynasty of Agade and the Gutian invasion. In Chaps. 13 and 19, *The Cambridge Ancient History*, ed. I. E. S. Edwards et al. 3d ed. Vol. 1, Pt. 2. Cambridge: Cambridge University Press.

Gelb, I. 1967. Approaches to the study of ancient society. *Journal of the American Oriental Society*, 87.

Goetze, A. 1963. Sakkanakkus of the Ur III Empire. *Journal of Cuneiform Studies*, 17.

Grayson, A. K. 1975. *Assyrian and Babylonian Chronicles.* Locust Valley, N.Y.: Augustin.

Hallo, W. 1964. The road to Emar. *Journal of Cuneiform Studies*, 18.

Hawkins, J. 1977. *Trade in the Ancient Near East,* London: British School of Archaeology in Iraq.

Heichelheim, F. M. 1958. *An Ancient Economic History.* Leiden: Sijthoff.

Jacobsen, T. 1970. *Towards the Image of Tammuz and other Essays in Mesopotamian History and Culture.* Cambridge, Mass.: Harvard University Press.

1976. *The Treasures of Darkness.* New Haven, Conn.: Yale University Press.

Jones, E. L. 1981. *The European Miracle.* Cambridge: Cambridge University Press.

Kautsky, J. H. 1982. *The Politics of Aristocratic Empires.* Chapel Hill: University of North Carolina Press.

King, L. W. 1923. *A History of Sumer and Akkad.* London: Chatto & Windus.

Kramer, S. N. 1963. *The Sumerians.* Chicago: University of Chicago Press.

Landels, J. G. 1980. *Engineering in the Ancient World.* London: Chatto & Windus.

Larsen, M. T. 1979. The traditions of empire in Mesopotamia. In *Power and Propaganda,* ed. M. T. Larsen. Copenhagen: Akademisk Forlag.

Levine, L. P., and T. C. Young. 1977. *Mountains and Lowlands: Essays in the Archaeology of Greater Mesopotamia.* Malibu, Calif.: Undena.

Liverani, M. 1979. The ideology of the Assyrian Empire. In *Power and Propaganda,* ed. M. T. Larsen. Copenhagen: Akademisk Forlag.

McNeill, W. 1963. *The Rise of the West.* Chicago: University of Chicago Press.

1983. *The Pursuit of Power.* Oxford: Blackwell.

Mann, M. 1977. States, ancient and modern. *Archives Européennes de Sociologie*, 18.

1984. The autonomous power of the state: its nature, causes and consequences. *Archives Européennes de Sociologie*, 25.

Oates, J. 1979. *Babylon.* London: Thames & Hudson.

Oppenheim, A. L. 1969. Comment on Diakonoff's Main Features . . . *Third International Conference of Economic History,* Munich, 1965. Paris: Mouton.

1970. Trade in the Ancient Near East. *Fifth International Conference of Economic History,* Leningrad, 1970. Paris: Mouton.

1977. *Ancient Mesopotamia.* Chicago: University of Chicago Press.

Pritchard, J. B. 1955. *Ancient Near Eastern Texts Relating to the Old Testament.* Princeton, N.J.: Princeton University Press.

Saggs, H. W. 1963. Assyrian warfare in the Sargonic period. *Iraq, 25.*

Smith, A. 1983. Are nations modern? Paper given to the London School of Economics Patterns of History seminar, Nov. 28, 1983.

Spencer, H. 1969. *Principles of Sociology,* 1-vol. abridged ed. London: Macmillan.

Weber, M. 1968. *Economy and Society.* English ed. 3 vols. Berkeley: University of California Press.

Wesson, R. G. 1967. *The Imperial Order*. Berkeley: University of California Press.
Westenholz, A. 1979. The Old Akkadian Empire in contemporary opinion. In *Power and Propaganda*, ed. M. T. Larsen. Copenhagen: Akademisk Forlag.
Yadin, Y. 1963. *The Art of Warfare in Biblical Lands in the Light of Archaeological Study*. London: Weidenfeld & Nicolson.
Yoffee, N. 1977. *The Economic Role of the Crown in the Old Babylonian Period*. Malibu, Calif.: Undena.

6   "Indo-Europeans" and iron: expanding, diversified power networks

During the second and early first millennia B.C., the Middle Eastern empires of domination were shaken by two immense challenges, which appeared external and yet which they had stimulated. Most empires did not survive – some vanished, and others were incorporated as units into others' dominions – and those that did survive were profoundly changed by the challenge into "world empires," self-styled. The two challenges were the military dominance of charioteers between about 1800 and 1400 B.C. and the spread of iron weapons and tools from about 1200 to 800 B.C. These revolutions had three similarities: They emanated from the north, from nonsettled peoples, and from nonliterate peoples. These facts create difficulties for our analysis, for we need to shift to areas whose precise location is unknown and to peoples who at first left few remains and records. In these circumstances it is difficult to avoid the mistake passed to us by the empires themselves, that these events constituted "sudden eruptions" of barbarism and catastrophe.

But the real story is not one of the clash of two separate societies. In this period the unitary model of society bears little relationship to reality. What happened is explicable in terms of (1) the initial stimulus given by the Near East to a steadily widening geographical area and to the diverse power networks contained there and (2) a subsequent growth in the extent of overlapping, intersecting power interactions within this area. At the end of the period discussed here the relevant geographical area is vastly enlarged, covering much of Europe, North Africa, and Central Asia as well as the Near East. Parts of it were divisible into societies and states with unitary pretensions, but most of it was not. All were involved in interaction that often passed right across the boundaries of supposedly unitary state societies.

The Indo-European challenge

Although the balance of power now shifted northward, it is likely that the main initial influences traveled from south to north.[1] This is not to argue for a general predominance of diffusions from the Near East, over the local evolution of the north and west. It is the interaction between the two that must be stressed: *Both* regions contained necessary factors for the interacting devel-

---

[1]Useful general sources for this section were Crossland 1971, Drower 1973, and Gurney 1973.

opment. Characteristics of northern and western prehistory are important (if largely guesswork). But by the time they erupted into history, they had been interacting for some time. They were not simply outsiders, unsullied by the influence of the irrigators.

At the beginning of the third millennium, the traders of the Middle Eastern empires had penetrated beyond Asia Minor, the Caucasus Mountains, and the Iranian plateau in their search for metal, animals, slaves, and other luxuries. They encountered "Indo-Europeans," groups that might have already belonged to a common linguistic stock. The Indo-Europeans of the eastern steppes were mounted pastoral nomads; those of the east European and Russian forests were mixed slash-and-burn agriculturalists and mounted herders. Neither possessed states or the three characteristics of civilization defined at the beginning of Chapter 3. But they were "rank" societies and some were becoming stratified. The nomads possessed a loose clan/tribal structure and probably embryonic private property centered on the household head. The slash-and-burners-cum-herders had a mixed clan/village structure.

Increased wealth and the acquisition of bronze metallurgy learned from trade heightened a decentralized form of stratification, developed aristocracies out of leading clans and village authority figures, and strengthened the private-property rights of aristocratic families. Metallurgy increased their prowess at war, made the aristocracy into a warrior elite, and sometimes evolved military leadership into weak kingship. The western Indo-Europeans took bronze battle axes westward, dominating the present European continent. Of these, the major known groups were the Celts, the Italic-speaking peoples, and the Greeks. (We will encounter them in Chapters 7 and 9.) But the wealth and the military prowess of the steppe peoples fed back into the Middle and Near East, and I discuss them first, in this chapter.

Sometime around 1800 B.C. the light chariot emerged, borne on two spoked wheels on a fixed axle, with a harness that allowed the horse to bear part of the chariot's weight. This was a swift, maneuverable, and balanced mechanism. Its battlefield prowess has impressed all subsequent historians. It carried two or three men armed with lance and compound bow. A company of chariots could wheel swiftly around the infantries and clumsy carts of the empires, shooting masses of arrows from a relatively invulnerable, armored, and moving position. When the infantry lines broke, a frontal charge could finish them off. The charioteers could not besiege cities, but they could threaten sufficient devastation on the fields and dikes of settled agriculturalists to obtain their submission. Dismounted charioteers, especially in their camps, were vulnerable to attack, and so they made their camps into simple quadrilateral earthwork fortifications to hold up an attack while they mounted. In open terrain they had a clear initial edge on the battlefield. Most of the Near East and Central Asia, but not Europe, was open terrain. They thus penetrated the first two areas but not the third.

They presumably moved first into the densely settled and irrigated oases of southeastern and central Asia, the farthest offshoots of the first two phases of Middle Eastern civilization. That movement used to be held responsible for almost simultaneous incursions into recorded history: east in China, southeast in India, and southwest in Asia Minor and the Middle East. Nowadays, however, the Shang dynasty charioteers of China, with bronze armor and rectangular fortifications, are assumed to be indigenous. Elsewhere the movement is clear. The Aryans conquered north India in successive waves sometime between about 1800 and 1200 B.C. (I discuss them in Chapter 11); the Hittites had established an identifiable kingdom in Asia Minor by 1640 B.C.; the Mitanni were established in Syria by 1450 B.C.; the Kassites overran most of Mesopotamia by about 1500 B.C.; the Hyksos conquered Egypt about 1650 B.C.; and the Mycenaeans were established in Greece by 1600 B.C. All were charioteers by the time they reached our records; all were aristocratic federations rather than single-state–centered peoples; and most knew greater private-property differentiation than had been prevalent among the indigenous peoples of the Near East.

Exactly who some of them were is rather more mysterious. The original core of the movement is generally believed to be Indo-European. But the main Hittite people (the Khattians) and the Hurrians were not, and the Hyksos (an Egyptian word meaning "chiefs of foreign lands") were probably a mixed Hurrian and Semitic group. The original Kassite language still has to be identified. It was not simply Indo-European, though their religion suggests Indo-European affinities or borrowings. It is likely that all the movements were mixed, intermarrying and picking up confederates, culture, and literacy as they moved south. The predominant mixture, known for the Hurrians and Hittites, was of a small Indo-European aristocracy initially ruling, then mixing, with a native people. It is only the merged groups of whom we have historical knowledge. But we know enough not to proceed with nineteenth-century-A.D. ethnic theories of "peoples" and "races" merely because those descendants of the groups of conquerors who were eventually literate wrote mostly in Indo-European languages. There is no evidence that any of them were genuine cross-class "ethnic communities" – they were loose military federations.

A second mysterious feature of their conquests is also worthy of note. It is not altogether clear that their dominance over the empires came merely in a wave of battlefield victories. It is unlikely that those who moved south developed the fast chariot – the basis of their military superiority – until well after they appeared in Asia Minor. It seems that they had settled for some time on the fringes of or even inside the Near Eastern civilizations. This is true of the Kassites, for example (see Oates, 1979: 83–90). There they gradually improved horse-breeding and riding techniques and gradually acquired bronze tools to fashion chariots. The war chariot probably developed, therefore, on marcher lands – as we might expect by now. Similarly, the military confrontation was probably long drawn out. Even after the appearance of the chariot, the logistical conditions were still lacking for systematic conquest. The campaign advantage of the chariot was superior mobility, especially in concentrating and dispersing forces. The logistical advantage was seasonal and conditional: Given good grazing land, the chariot force could live off the land and cover much greater distances from their supply base than could infantry. But the organizational rhythm of a chariot campaign was quite complex: to advance in small bands that had to be dispersed, extended over enemy grazing lands, but then to concentrate swiftly to attack enemy formations. It was not a task for barbarians, but for marcher lords, steadily upgrading their social organization over a long period of time.

Thus their pressure upon the civilizations to the south must have been long and sustained. It led to strains there, quite apart from the battlefield pressures. Some empires seem to have collapsed without much assistance from the latter. For example, the Aryan invaders of India may have encountered an already-declining Indus Valley civilization. Similarly, the two collapses of Minoan civilization in Crete are difficult to interpret. No theories of destruction by foreign invaders convince, not even by Mycenaeans. It is possible that Cretan civilization may have been fading over a long period, with Mycenaean traders replacing Minoans over much of the Eastern Mediterranean without a direct major war between them.

In the Middle East it also seems that the invaders hit at a time of relative weakness in most existing states. Babylon's struggles with Kassites and Hurrians were preceded by the secession of its southern territories in civil war between the descendants of Hammurabi. In any case, the whole area was contested by Babylon, the first Assyrian rulers, and the last Sumerian ones. In Egypt "the second intermediary period," conventionally begun in 1778 B.C., inaugurated a long time of dynastic strife before the Hyksos incursions.

It is tempting to look for other causes of collapse besides the battlefield. Three can be found in the mechanism of empires of domination I identified in the preceding chapter. First, and probably in evidence in the Mesopotamian region, was the lack of any safe resting place for the empire's boundaries. Its boundaries were not natural but made by armies. In Mesopotamia the various river valleys offered a core to more than one empire, for the technology of conquest and rule was still insufficient to take and keep the whole region. Thus rivalry between empires was potentially sapping the strength of each. And in all empires the loyalty of the provincials and the marches was conditional.

Second, and more general, was the delicacy of the economic, political, and ideological integration mechanisms in the system I described as one of compulsory cooperation. The integration between river valley and upland (or in the case of Crete, between coast and upland) was artificial and depended upon a high level of redistribution and coercion. Redistributive mechanisms were vulnerable to population pressures and soil erosion. Coercion required continuous energy on the part of the state. Without it, provincial revolt and dynastic strife resulted.

Third, the upgrading of the outer marches not only presented power rivals to the empires. It may have led also to economic difficulties for them: perhaps to a decline in the profits of long-distance trade, given the "protection rent" exacted by the rising power of the marcher lords. We can plausibly conclude that all the empires were under strain before the chariots delivered the coup de grace. The phenomenon was recurrent in ancient empires all over the world – it has been variously termed "oversegregation" (Rappaport 1978) and "hypercoherence" and "hyperintegration" (Flannery 1972; cf. Renfrew 1979), although such words exaggerate the unitary nature of these empires before they collapsed.

Given the nature of the conquerors, it was unlikely that they could create their own stable, extensive empires. Rule from the chariot is difficult. The chariot is an offensive, not a defensive or consolidating, weapon. Its supplies came from extensive grazing lands (and rural crafts), not intensive agriculture and urban manufacture. The chariot encouraged the development of a more decentralized aristocracy with looser boundaries. It required extensive grazing lands owned by wealthy warriors, able to maintain chariot, horses, arms, and leisure for training. It did not require systematic coordinated drilling under a centralized command, but a high degree of individual skill and a capacity to coordinate small detachments that were autonomous for much of the campaign. Feudal "caste loyalty" and honor among aristocrats seems a good social base for both qualities (see the account of Hittite warfare given by Goetze 1963). The charioteer leaders had more difficulty in creating centralized states than had the earlier Sargon-like conquerors, who had coordinated infantry, cavalry, and artillery. Indeed, their rule was at first "feudal."

The Aryans retained their decentralized aristocratic structure and did not create centralized states for centuries after their arrival in India. They resembled in the Middle East the Mitannians. The Hittites established a centralized kingdom in about 1640 B.C. that lasted until about 1200 B.C., but the nobility, a free estate of warriors, enjoyed considerable autonomy. It is conventional to describe theirs as a "feudal" state (see, e.g., Crossland 1967), indicating the prevalence of military fiefs in land: Outside their core they dominated through the "weak" strategy of rule *through* native vassals and clients. Mycenae established more centralized, redistributive palace economies, but there were several of them, and their effectiveness declined into the "Dark Ages," the period Homer described. His world was one not of states but of lords and their vassals (Greenhalgh 1973). The kingdom of Mitanni was a Hurrian confederacy. Its paramount chief ruled through clients over an area with continuously changing boundaries, as vassals joined and left the confederacy. The

Kassites established a loose feudal kingdom, making extensive land grants to their nobility and sitting loosely and flexibly over the conquered Babylonians.

The general problem all experienced was that they were initially less competent to integrate extensive territories than their predecessors. They were illiterate. They had no experience of the coercive coordination of labor, as the rulers of settled agriculturalists had. And their military strength continued to decentralize them. The more successful ones – notably the Hittites and Kassites – responded by taking over the literacy of their predecessors as well as other techniques of civilization. But this further distanced the rulers from their erstwhile followers.

The less successful of the invaders were vulnerable to counterattack. Their own techniques of rule were feeble. The settled agriculturalists could hit back either by adopting chariots themselves or by increasing the size and density of their infantry, and the extent of city fortifications. In Syria and the Levant in the seventeenth and eighteenth centuries, small city-states with large fortifications proliferated. Two old powers, Egypt and Babylon, and one recently emergent power, Assyria, managed somewhat more extensive rule. The Egyptians drove out the Hyksos and established the "New Kingdom" in 1580 B.C. Over the next century Egyptian chariots, ships, and mercenaries were used to conquer Palestine and extend Egyptian power over the southeastern Mediterranean. Egypt, for the first time, became an empire of domination. Babylonian rulers reasserted their power in the twelfth century. The major military response in Mesopotamia, however, came from the Assyrians. Deriving their culture from Sumer, they had begun to emerge as traders before the Indo-European movements. Now with chariots in the center of their line and increasing their defensive armor, they defeated their Mitanni overlords around 1370 and began their outward expansion (discussed in Chapter 8).

Thus settled agriculturalists could learn the new military techniques. Again, despite a common stereotype to the contrary, there was no general advantage to pastoral nomads or to charioteers. Moreover, the general decentralization of rule did not induce collapse in broader interaction networks. The city-states and feudal confederacies learned to combine trade with war, to exchange gods and linguistic elements. Scripts simplified toward the later "one sign, one sound" linear model (discussed in the next chapter). A broader symbiosis of *diffused power* was under way. Then came the second shock wave.

The Iron Age challenge

Around 2000 B.C., the mining and charcoal smelting of iron began, probably north of the Black Sea, again probably in response to economic stimuli proceeding from the south.[2] Iron competed with copper alloys, especially bronze.

[2]Discussion of the effects of iron is based principally upon Heichelheim 1958.

Bronze is molten copper and tin poured together, cast, and left to harden. But iron must be shaped while red hot and then carbonized by allowing the semi-molten iron to come into contact with the impure carbon contained in charcoal fuel. None of the techniques used by the ancients could produce more than a semisteel, about equal in hardness to bronze, and liable to rust badly. But by 1400 B.C. iron could be produced far more cheaply than bronze. Thus *mass* production of tools and weapons was possible. The Hittites, adjacent to the Black Sea, seem to have been the first to extensively use iron weapons. Political control of metallurgy was difficult, and the secret was sold all over Europe and Asia by 1200 B.C. Iron, unlike copper or tin, is found practically every-where on the globe, so its mining could not be practically controlled (unlike copper – remember how the Egyptian state had controlled copper mining). Iron's cheapness meant that an ax capable of uprooting trees, and a scratch-plow capable of turning over lighter rain-watered soils, was within the eco-nomic reach of the slash-and-burner who could produce a small surplus. Set-tled agriculture, rain watered and not dependent on artificial irrigation, was boosted, and the peasant farmer grew as an economic and military power.

The balance of power shifted. The shift had several aspects: from pastor-alists and irrigating agriculturalists to the peasants of rain-watered soils; from the steppes and river valleys to grassy soils; from aristocracies to peasantries; from mobile chariots to dense masses of heavily armored infantry (or even-tually to heavy cavalry), from the Middle and Near East to the West, the North, and the East; and from empires of domination and the ramified tribal confederacy to the village and the individual clan or tribe. Although some proved impermanent, they amounted to a technologically unified revolution. Iron inaugurated a social revolution centered on the "track layers" of both economic and military power.

The economic effects are comparatively easy to understand. Any agricul-turalists on rain-watered soils capable of generating a surplus could exchange produce for an ax or a plow. Any relatively prosperous peasant farmer could add oxen. In geopolitical terms economic growth shifted disproportionately toward the lighter rain-watered lands of Anatolia, Assyria, southeastern Europe, and the northern Mediterranean. This region developed an economy in which the individual peasant household related directly to elaborated economic exchange and occupational specialization. Its own labor and tools, relatively independent of any other household, had generated the surplus – a boost to private small-scale property and to the democratization and decentralization of economic power. Direct economic praxis – the relatively "intense" end of economic power (as discussed in Chapter 1) – could reassert an organizing power over history, such as it had tended to lose after the emergence of the first civilizations.

Another economic change was a strengthening of local and medium-distance trade. Remember that much long-distance trade had been in metals.

Now the dominant metal, iron, was found and traded locally. The increased demand was from peasant households, requiring semistaples – clothing, wine, and so forth – relatively bulky and still not practical to move over long distances by land. Sea transport could provide the supply. Sea transport does not move along prepared and controlled communications routes. Unless a power could control the whole of the inland seas – the Mediterranean, the Black Sea, the Arabian Gulf, and so forth – trade would decentralize and democratize economic power. The praxis of the peasant household was linked more directly to extensive trading networks. We see the strengthening of the organizational means of economic power: what in Chapter 1 I termed circuits of praxis.

The military and political consequences were more complex and varied. The peasant farmer had become a more critical and autonomous economic power actor, but local traditions would decide how this would be expressed in political and military terms. In the West, that is, in southern Europe outside Greece where no states had hitherto existed, no power existed to constrain the trader and the peasant farmer other than weakly developed tribal and village aristocracies. Thus the village and the tribe, mobilized only loosely by an aristocracy, emerged as a military and political force.

At the other extreme in the Middle East, a well-organized empire of domination like the Assyrian could maintain control over the peasantry – welding it into an infantry fighting force, supplying it with iron weapons, armor, and siege weapons. Cheap weapons and higher production on rain-watered lands increased the possibility of equipping and supplying masses. The traditional basis for coordinating such masses was the empire. In the long run this reinforced such empires.

Indeed, a third alternative was available to the traditional state that did not even possess tilling peasants: to use its surplus to pay foreign mercenaries. Running ahead of our story somewhat, this was the strategy adopted by the Egyptians. Despite being the only power never to develop its own iron smelting, it survived and prospered – by paying Greeks to undertake the whole process, from smelting to killing! In short, the political and military shifts tended to be geopolitical, changing the regional balance of power, more than the balance internal to any particular state.

In the geographical middle, such geopolitical forces came into violent conflict. But because so many of the contending forces were either illiterate or barely literate, we know only an outline chronicle of disaster. Excavations at the city-state of Troy on the Black Sea coast reveal its destruction between 1250 and 1200 B.C., probably the historical basis of Homer's Trojan War, and so perhaps the work of Mycenaean Greeks. Just before 1200 B.C., however, fortifications in the Mycenaean homeland were increased, suggesting pressure on them too. About 1200, fortified palaces at Mycenae, Pylos, and other centers were destroyed by fire. Around 1150, disaster mounted: The remnants of Mycenaean palace culture were destroyed; the Hittite kingdom collapsed, its capital and other important sites being burned; and Kassite rule in Babylon ended. Around 1200, the Egyptians repulsed with difficulty repeated attacks on the Nile Delta launched by a group it called the Peoples of the Sea. By 1165, Egypt had lost all territories beyond the Nile and the Delta under the attacks of the Sea Peoples and of Semitic peoples entering Palestine from Arabia – the Israelites, Canaanites, and other peoples of the Old Testament.

To make sense of all this, the exact dates matter a great deal. In what order did Troy, Mycenae, Bogazkoy (the Hittite capital), and Babylon fall? We do not know. With only Egyptian exact chronology and references to the Peoples of the Sea to guide us, we are left floundering.

We can add evidence from the Greek case. Subsequent Greek historians suggested that the Mycenaeans were displaced by the "Dorians," who with other Greek-speaking peoples came down from Illyria in the north. One of these, the "Ionians," then settled colonies in Asia Minor. Nobody knows how much confidence to place in this. Doric and Ionian dialects are traceable to different areas of Greece, and in certain areas like Sparta and Argos the Dorians ruled over serfs who were conquered non-Dorian Greeks. But this conquest may have occurred after the fall of Mycenae. We have no clear idea of who did destroy Mycenae. As Snodgrass has remarked, it seems "an invasion without invaders" (1971: 296–327; cf Hopper 1976: 52–66).

The inference is tempting that the Peoples of the Sea were loose confederations of the new geopolitical forces, an alliance of peasants and trader/pirates, coming from the northern Mediterranean and Black Sea coasts with iron weapons, penetrating the Hittite lands and the Mycenaean sea routes, probably learning better organization from both on the way (Barnett, 1975; Sandars 1978). The Vikings would be a later analogy – their basic unit of devastation and conquest being a band of 32–5 warrior rowers, with little organization beyond temporary union with other ships. But this is only inferential and analogical reasoning. Nevertheless, sea power was crucial to this second wave of northern conquests. The inland empires of domination were not so threatened, unlike during the first wave. This implied a break between land and sea powers – the former more traditional, the latter more novel.

More extensive territories and a greater number of peoples were brought into relations of interdependence by the two northern challenges. Yet they had also in the short run reduced the integrating capacities of the state-centered society. More smaller states and tribes were contending, trading, and entering into diffuse cultural exchanges. They were marcher peoples, lured by civilization and interested in acquiring it. They brought their own contributions to economic and military development. Scratch plowing and tree felling increased the surplus; the iron-clad warrior stimulated military power.

Thus during the first millennium B.C. three changes in power relations, inaugurated by the northern challenges, were occurring, at different rhythms and in different areas:

1. The encouragement of interstitial trading states, with their own distinctive political, military, and ideological power arrangements
2. The growth in the power of the peasant and the infantryman, a revival of *intense* mobilization of economic and military power into relatively small and democratic communities
3. The growth, slower paced over much of the area, of the extensive and intensive power of the large-scale empires of domination into something potentially able to approximate a territorial empire

This is a complex picture, composed of many overlapping networks of power. The trends, however, are well documented because the main exemplary cases of each type – Phoenicia, 1; Greece, 1 and 2; Macedonia, 3; Assyria, 2 and 3; Persia, 3; and Rome, 2 and 3 – all became literate and mostly became compulsive record keepers. Chronicling their development will take several chapters.

These societies were civilized, wielding considerable power. Yet none achieved hegemonic geopolitical power over the Near Eastern and Mediterranean world. No single mode of economic, ideological, military, or political power was dominant, although this was an area of considerable social interaction. But let us not look at this "multistate" arena with our vision colored by modern experience. The capacity of any of these states to penetrate social life was rudimentary: Their rivalry was not only "international" but also interstitial. That is, different modes of power organization, different forms of economic production and exchange, different ideologies, different military methods, different forms of political rule, all diffused right across state boundaries and through "their" populations. Hegemony was no more attainable internally than internationally.

All this makes a unique case out of the Near Eastern and Mediterranean civilization of the first millennium B.C. Even in Chapter 4, I was tentative in comparative generalizations. There were only a handful of cases of the independent emergence of civilization. Thereafter, differences between them grew. In Chapter 5, I continued with a few broad generalizations concerning ancient empires of domination. But their core (as is generally the case in comparative sociology) was the Near East–China comparison. Now these two paths diverged. By the time of the Han dynasty, China was *one* civilization. It had reached the semidesert steppes of the north and west. Although conquering nomads emerged periodically from there, China had little besides military technique to learn from them. To the south lay jungles, swamps, and less civilized and dangerous peoples. On land, China was hegemonic. To the east lay the seas and potential rivals, especially Japan. But their interrelations were fewer, and some Chinese regimes erected barriers to the outside. The civilized, cosmopolitan Near East was becoming a unique case. Thus comparative sociology now peters out (although it briefly revives in Chapter 11), not for any logical or epistemological reason but for a far more compelling reason – lack of empirical cases.

The first major peculiarity of the civilization to which the modern West is heir was that it was geopolitically multicentered, cosmopolitan, and non-hegemonic. It had three ecological roots: irrigated river valleys and confined plowlands, the core of the land empires of the Near East; more open, extensive plowlands in Europe; and the inland seas that connected them. The juxtaposition of such ecologies was unique in the world; therefore, in world-historical terms, so was the civilization to which it gave rise.

Bibliography

Barnett, R. D. 1975. The Sea Peoples. Chap. 28 in *The Cambridge Ancient History,* ed. 3d ed. Vol. II, pt. 2. Cambridge: Cambridge University Press.

Crossland, R. A. 1967. Hittite society and its economic basis. In *Bulletin of the Institute of Classical Studies,* 14.

1971. Immigrants from the North. Chap. 27 in *The Cambridge Ancient History,* ed. I. E. S. Edwards et al. 3d ed. Vol. I, pt. 2. Cambridge: Cambridge University Press.

Drower, M. S. 1973. Syria, c. 1550–1400 B.C., Chap. 10 in *The Cambridge Ancient History,* ed. I. E. S. Edwards et al. 3d ed. Vol. II, pt. 1. Cambridge: Cambridge University Press.

Flannery, K. 1972. The cultural evolution of civilizations. *Annual Review of Ecology and Systematics,* 3.

Goetze, A. 1963. Warfare in Asia Minor. *Iraq,* 25.

Greenhalgh, P. E. L. 1973. *Early Greek Warfare.* Cambridge: Cambridge University Press.

Gurney, O. R. 1973. Anatolia, c. 1750–1600 B.C.; and Anatolia, c. 1600–1380 B.C. Chaps. 6 and 15 in *The Cambridge Ancient History,* ed. I. E. S. Edwards et al. 3d ed. Vol II, pt. 1. Cambridge: Cambridge University Press.

Heichelheim, F. M. 1958. *An Ancient Economic History.* Leiden: Sijthoff.

Hopper, R. J. 1976. *The Early Greeks.* London: Weidenfeld & Nicolson.

Oates, J. 1979. *Babylon,* London: Thames & Hudson.

Rappaport, R. A. 1978. Maladaptation in social systems. In *The Evolution of Social Systems,* ed. J. Friedman and M. J. Rowlands. London: Duckworth.

Renfrew, C. 1979. Systems collapse as social transformation: catastrophe and anastrophe in early state formation. In *Transformations: Mathematical Approaches to Culture Change,* ed. C. Renfrew and K. Cooke. New York: Academic Press.

Sandars, N. F. 1978. *The Sea Peoples.* London: Thames & Hudson.

Snodgrass, A. M. 1971. *The Dark Age of Greece.* Edinburgh: Edinburgh University Press.

7 Phoenicians and Greeks: decentralized multi-power-actor civilizations

In this chapter I discuss the emergence and development of the two major decentralized civilizations of the first millennium B.C., Phoenicia and Greece. I concentrate on Greece because it is considerably better documented: We can distinguish the principal phases of its dialectic of development. I argue that the massive contributions of both peoples to the development of social power is to be attributed to the decentralized, multi-level nature of their civilizations, appropriate for taking advantage of the geopolitical, military, and economic legacy of their region, especially that bequeathed by the Near Eastern empires of domination.

I suggest that two principal dialectics can be discerned in the emergence of Phoenicia and Greece as "leading edges" of contemporary power. The first, discussed briefly and tentatively, concerns the possibility that these civilizations were part of a macrohistorical process. In this case, decentralized multi-power-actor civilizations lying on the marches of established empires of domination exploited the success plus the institutional rigidity of those empires to "emerge interstitially" and establish their own autonomous power organizations. After a long, successful process of power development, however, their own organizations became institutionalized and rigid. Now they become vulnerable in their turn to new empires of domination lying on their marches. Such a process can be traced in the first millennium B.C. The extent to which it was, indeed, part of a macrohistorical process will be left to the concluding chapter.

The second dialectic concerns that "middle period" of developmental success. It has two principal aspects. Greek social development will be interpreted, first, as the growth and interaction of three power networks, this time not so much overlapping as arranged in concentric rings – the smallest one being the city-state; the middle one, the multistate geopolitical organization and linguistic culture we know as Greece; and the outer one, a partial and hesitant conception of humanity as a whole. At the same time the participatory, democratic nature of the first two of these rings also brought another dialectic into play: popular praxis and class struggle. *Classes* became capable of a historical reorganization that has reverberated ever since. Though Greece (and Phoenicia) eventually collapsed before revitalized empires of domination, it left the imprint of these dialectics between all three interaction networks and between classes upon those empires – and probably, eventually, upon us too.

190

The emerging decentralized economy: Phoenicia – literacy and coinage

The collapse of the Hittites and the Mycenaeans, and the retreat of Egypt to the Nile, left a power vacuum along the eastern shores of the Mediterranean. The whole area became decentralized, and petty states abounded. The Phoenician states of the Levant coast were part of the ethnically diverse Canaanite peoples. They wrote Babylonian cuneiform and decorated in Mesopotamian and Syrian style, yet were strategically placed to expand westward to trade between the Middle East, Egypt, and the booming economy of Europe. In the vacuum the coastal towns began to expand, build fortifications, and extend their naval works. We learn from the Book of Kings in the Bible that Hiram of Tyre gave considerable help to King Solomon in the tenth century. Hiram brought down cedar and fir from Lebanon, in return for which Solomon gave him twenty thousand measures of wheat and twenty measures of pure oil; Hiram's workmen built the temple at Jerusalem; Hiram brought gold and jewels into Israel over the Red Sea.

The arrival of the Assyrian empire of domination (discussed in the next chapter) destroyed the Israelite state but not Phoenician sea power – the Assyrians took tribute from the ninth century but, being landlocked, could not easily organize the Mediterranean trade. The arrival of the Assryians, together with the continuous but weak presence of the Egyptians, was important because it separated land from sea. It prevented anyone in the region from combining agrarian and maritime power. Thus Phoenician power was narrowly maritime.[1]

Phoenician ships became the principal carriers from the ninth century, eventually coming into bitter rivalry with the Greeks. Many colonies and staging posts were established across the Mediterranean. The most famous, Carthage, traditionally dated from 814–813 B.C., obtained its own empire in the western Mediterranean. The Phoenician coastal towns eventually lost their naval supremacy to the Greeks and their political independence first to Nebuchadrezzar II, then to the Persians – all in the sixth century. Phoenician naval forces, however, were still valuable to the Persians, and they remained autonomous throughout the Persian war with the Greeks. Their eventual demise was at the hands of Alexander the Great in 332 B.C. Carthage and other western colonies long retained political autonomy, Carthage until destroyed by Rome in 146 B.C.

Thus Phoenicia was a major power for about five centuries – and of a novel kind. Apart from Carthage's late empire in Africa, Sardinia, and Spain from about 400 B.C., it possessed only individual ports and their direct hinterland.

---

[1]Main sources for Phoenicia were Albright 1946; Gray 1964; Warmington 1969; Harden 1971; Whittaker 1978; Frankenstein 1979; and of course the Old Testament.

Each city-state was politically independent: Even the smaller North African cities were never incorporated into Carthage. It was exclusively a naval and trading power, the "bride of the sea," united by a loose federal, geopolitical alliance of city-states.

Such naval power had preconditions. The first was that Carthage occupied a power vacuum, strategically situated between three main areas of social activity. The second was that the growth of plow agriculture all around the Mediterranean had increased the utility of sea trade. The third was that no major territorial power of the time integrated land and sea, or irrigated and plowed land. No more could Phoenicia. Its power was more narrowly naval than had been that of the previous great traders, the Minoans and the Mycenaeans.

Additionally, the nature of trade had changed. Had Phoenician ships transported merely metals, wood, stone, and luxuries between either two civilized states or a centralized state and its marches, they might have come under the hegemony of empires of domination, as had previous traders. Traders had hitherto entered city gates, gone to the central storehouse/marketplace, and there been regulated by the weighing, literacy, and solidiery of the state's bureaucracy. But the Phoenicians carried a higher proportion of staples and semistaples – cereals, wine, skins – and a higher proportion of finished goods that they themselves had manufactured. Their cities also contained workshops and factories undertaking masonry, carpentry, dyeing, and textile weaving, as well as higher-value metal crafting. Most of the finished goods were not for the royal palace but for a slightly lower-status household – the petty noble landowner, the city dweller, the relatively prosperous free peasant proprietor. They presupposed a more direct buyer-seller relationship, not mediated by the central agency of a redistributive economy but only by the merchant organization of Phoenicia. In this respect the Phoenicians organized the more diffused, decentralized economy introduced by the northern challenges. Their power rested on the mobilization of a dynamic but dispersed economy in which the direct producers were themselves incapable of territorially extensive social organization. We call that a market, and (despite Polanyi) we often do not recognize how historically rare it is.

Two features of this new diffuse, decentralized world are worthy of separate discussion, literacy and coinage. Both take us beyond the Phoenicians themselves, although their role was considerable in both.

The empires of domination had brought no major changes to cuneiform and hieroglyphic scripts. It became conventional between about 1700 and 1200 B.C. to conduct international diplomacy and trade in Akkadian cuneiform, now a "neutral" script, for no Akkadian state remained. But after the collapse of most empires there could not easily exist a lingua franca among the diverse conquerors, many of whom were not steeped in traditional, including Akkadian, civilization. A script that would merely reproduce sounds phonetically, an *alphabet* as we call it, would be useful to translate between the many languages.

Luckily we can capture this world-historical moment from excavations in the Levant. They reveal in the fourteenth to tenth centuries B.C. the simultaneous use of many scripts and dialects on the same tablets – for example, Akkadian, Sumerian, Hittite, Hurrian, Egyptian, and Cypriote at one site. One of these was Ugaritic, a Canaanite dialect written in alphabetic cuneiform. It was consonantal, each character reproducing a sound (other than vowels). Like all cuneiform, it was written on cumbersome clay tablets. Slightly later in the Levant other scripts, notably Hebrew and Phoenician (another Canaanite language), developed cursive alphabetical scripts suitable for any medium, including papyrus. Then we have examples of tenth-century B.C. Phoenician scripts of twenty-two consonants (no vowels). This was standardized by the ninth century and carried over the Mediterranean. Shortly after 800 B.C. the Greeks borrowed it, added vowels, and left the alphabet to posterity.

Let me pick out two aspects of this story. First, though the early emergence of literacy had been largely organized by the state, it now escaped the state. Its further development came through the need to translate between different peoples, especially traders. Second, although they were technical improvements – they would permit scribes to record and transmit messages quicker and at lower cost – they had power implications. The techniques were available to those with fewer resources than the state – merchants, provincial aristocrats, artisans, even village priests. It would have required a formidable craft resistance by the state's priest-scribes to prevent this diffusion (they did indeed attempt this unsuccessfully in Babylon). McNeill comments: "The democratization of learning implicit in simplified scripts must be counted as one of the major turning points in the history of civilization" (1963: 147). "Democratization" is pitching it a bit strong. Literacy was first confined to the technical advisers of a ruling elite; then it spread to the elite itself. Of Phoenician inscriptions and texts only a few survive, but they indicate a discursive, literate culture. All that can be claimed with certainty for the Phoenicians is that they were one of several groups – others were the Arameans and the Greeks – whose decentralized trading structure contributed the second breakthrough in the history of literacy.

The Phoenicians were also one of a number of groups to move slowly in the direction of coinage. They were slow to make the last move. But in some ways the story is quite similar to that of literacy.[2]

The earliest system in civilized societies by which exchange value could be conferred on an item was the weighing, measuring, and recording system controlled by the central-place irrigation state. But value was "one-off," con-

---

[2]On the origins of coinage, see Heichelheim 1958 and Grierson 1977.

ferred through a single state-guaranteed transaction, not a generalized means of exchange. This system was maintained unaltered by the empires of domination and collapsed when they did. It was retained in Egypt, Babylon, and Assyria. Other "money" systems, however, had long existed, using objects with mixed and rather more generalized use-exchange values. Cattle hides, battle axes, metal bars, and tools were among the most widely used. They could also be used repeatedly without further assigning value. The coming of iron had given impetus to some of these. Hardened iron tools could cut and stamp metal cheaply and with precision. The standardization of the tools themselves increased their own exchange value. Metal tools and stamped bars were probably the most widely used forms of money around the eastern Mediterranean between about 1100 and 600 B.C.

Tool money required no central authority. It was suited to iron plowers and was predominant in Greece in this period. Stamped bars did require some kind of authority to guarantee their validity, but they were easily checked by the recipient (more so than coinage), and once in circulation they did not have to go repeatedly through the state machinery – this was a generalized means of exchange. As we might expect, this money form emerged among trading peoples – among Arameans and Phoenicians. According to Assyrian documents of the eighth and seventh centuries, B.C. stamped bars were in general use in the Middle East. Moreover, among Phoenicians and Arameans the stamps could be those of private persons, as well as kings or city-states, indicating decentralization of authority and interpersonal trust, at least among a relatively small oligarchical group. This protocoinage could not have been used by small-scale producers. Large, clumsy, and of high value, it was appropriate for the dealings of states and large-scale middlemen.

The emergence of the first recognizable coins was at the precise geographical meeting point of the two cultures involved in exchange, the empires of domination in the Middle East and the peasant traders of the Northwest – that is, in Asia Minor. Greek tradition ascribes the invention to the half-Greek, half-Asiatic kingdom of Lydia in the seventh century B.C. Archaeology supports this, but it adds some of the Greek city-states of Asia Minor (and possibly contemporary Mesopotamia too) as coinventors. Coins were double-stamped front and back with the insignia of the kingdom or the city-state, thus making clipping and unofficial debasement difficult and guaranteeing weight and quality. The first coins were generally of high value and so were not used in exchange between ordinary producers and consumers. They were probably used to pay mercenary soldiers and receive taxes and tribute from the rich. So now we had two areas of penetration by a protomonetary economy: as a form of credit first between states and powerful trading middlemen and second between states and their soldiers. Military service was the first – and for long the only – form of wage labor.

From this area coinage spread along the mercenary/trade trail, eastward to

Persia and westward to Greece. Greece combined the two bases of the proto-monetary economy, being a trading people and the main supplier of mercenaries. Additionally Greece possessed the democratic city-state whose strong civic consciousness used coin design as a badge, a kind of "flag." Greece became the first monetary economy. About 575 B.C., Athens went over to coinage, to coins of low as well as of high value, and began the first monetary economy. This part of the story is a Greek one, to be discussed in a moment.

Coinage presupposed two independent power actors, a central state and a decentralized class of power holders capable of autonomous social and economic mobilization. Neither can be reduced to the other, for their interaction was a dialectic of development. The empire of domination interacted with the peasant proprietor and tiller to produce a two-level geopolitical structure of social organization. It had done so particularly through the organizations of trading middlemen, through mercenaries, and through the participatory city-state. We must turn to Greece if we are to understand this.

The origins of Greek power

Historical narrative on a broad scale tends toward teleology. Conceptions of what society was later to become, or what it is now, enter conceptions of what a historical society was. When that society was classical Greece, and when our narrative theme is its power achievements, this tendency becomes rampant. From then to now run direct tracks – language, political institutions, philosophy, architectural styles, and other cultural artifacts. Our history has kept alive knowledge of these tracks. It has probably suppressed knowledge of other aspects of Greek life; it has probably suppressed knowledge of the achievements of other contemporary peoples. In this chapter I struggle to situate Greece in its contemporary world, to mention what is relatively alien to us as well as what is familiar, but it is a losing battle. Three institutions have enormous significance for us: the city-state, or polis, a cult of human reason, and political class struggle. Together they constitute a power jump, a revolution in organizational capacities. If Greece did not invent them, it tried fairly successfully to suppress who did. Greece bequeathed them to a tradition that reaches to our own civilization and thence to the world at large. They are thus an important part of the history of human collective powers. How do we explain them? I start by approaching the polis and tracing several successive steps in its development.

Greece[3] was not particularly privileged in its ecology. The soil of its valleys was less fertile than many European areas, although as little initial clearing

[3] Apart from works mentioned in the text, the main sources used in this section are Snodgrass 1971, 1967; Hammond 1975; Hopper 1976; Meiggs 1972; Austin and Vidal-Naquet 1977; Davies 1978; Murray 1980; Vernant 1981; and Runciman 1982.

was needed it presented better-than-average opportunity cost to the early iron plower. Its barren hills and extensive rocky coastline made political unification unlikely, just as it made marine pursuits likely. But from ecology we would not predict the emergence of the polis, the maritime power, or the civilization of classical Greece, any more than we would in the case, say, of Brittany or Cornwall.

What distinguished Greece was its marchland position between Europe and the Near East: The closest of the European plowed lands to Near Eastern civilization, with its promontory and islands it was most likely to intercept trade and cultural exchange between the two. More than that: The original movement of the Dorians, Ionians, and others – whoever precisely they were – had actually *straddled* Europe and Asia. From its post-Mycenaean beginnings, Greece was *in* Asia, in the form of many colonies around the shores of Asia Minor. The debt of Western civilization to the Greeks should never allow us to forget that the division between East and West is a later one. Nor should we regard the Greeks' astonishing development as simply indigenous. In every respect that mattered they seem to have *fused* the practices of ancient Near Eastern civilization and of Iron Age cultivators.

There is, it is true, one indigenous aspect of Greek development of which we are ignorant: the extent of continuity from Mycenae; there was a Dark Age of four hundred years from its fall. Then, between 800 and 700 B.C., we can discern outlines. Economic and military power relations were somewhat contradictory: On the one hand, agriculture was yielding a greater surplus, as indicated by population growth in Attica between 800 and 750. We can attribute this to the growing integration of the whole Near East and Mediterranean world, in which Greece was strategically situated. Expansion increased the prosperity and power of the middling-to-large peasant householder as against the aristocracy, who were herders, especially of horses. Yet, on the other hand, in military terms the mounted, armored aristocratic warrior, dismounting for battle and surrounded by his dependents, was supreme. The dual nature of the earliest political institutions may have reflected this: An assembly of adult male members of the local community was subordinate to a council of elders composed of heads of noble families. The dual structure was common among mixed plow and herding peoples of the Iron Age, whether of this or a later period.

There were two main political variables among such peoples. One was kingship – always relatively weak – existing in some places but not others. In Greece monarchy waned during the Dark Age. Of significant states only several in the northern fringes possessed a monarchy, although Sparta had a unique two-king system. The second variable was the degree of status rigidity between aristocracy and freeborn people. In Greece this was low. Although descent was significant, and was reinforced by aristocratic norms, it never amounted to caste or estate consciousness. From the earliest times we can perceive a tension between birth and wealth. Wealth easily upset distinctions conferred by birth. In this respect the two northern waves of Chapter 6 differed. The charioteers generated rigid distinctions – the extreme being the caste-creating Aryans (discussed in Chapter 11). But iron plowers restrained aristocracies by a loose, communal, and even democratic structure of power.

The Greek polis

The polis was a self-governing, territorial state of city and agricultural hinterland, in which every male landowner, aristocrat or peasant, born in the territory possessed freedom and citizenship. The two fundamental notions were citizen equality among landowners and commitment and loyalty to the territorial city, rather than to family or lineage.

The antithesis between territory and kin was masked by the use of kin language for units that actually combined territorial and kin attributes. Thus the "tribes" *(phylai)* seem to have been originally a military band, a voluntary association of warriors. Later in Athens (as in Rome) tribes were re-created on the basis of locality. Similarly, "brotherhood" *(phratra),* as in most Indo-European languages, did not mean a blood relationship but a social group of confederates. In later Athenian history they became political factions, led by aristocratic clans and occasionally confined to them. Descent and kinship structure mattered in Greek history, which leads some classicists to elevate kinship structure above territorial unity (e.g., Davies 1978: 26).

But the importance of kinship, and its use as a symbolic model for nonkin relations, is virtually universal. Even in the nineteenth and early twentieth centuries A.D., that large-scale territorial unit the nation-state was conceptualized as being an ethnic, racial unit, which in actuality it was not. The Greeks deviated from this norm precisely to the extent that they developed local *territorial* loyalties. Aristotle tells us plainly that the first quality of the polis was that it was a community of place. The polis is also opposed to the notion of an aristocracy, an extensive blood connection that introduces hierarchical loyalties and blockages in the way of intense egalitarian territorial loyalties and blockages. So explaining the emergence of the polis becomes also a matter of explaining the drift toward local democracy, toward political participation by an adjacent mass, or at least by a substantial "class" of property holders too numerous and similar to be organized in real kin units. And this in turn implies a multistate system of small poleis. So how did the polis embedded in a multistate system emerge?

The Iron Age economy of peasant proprietors provided the first necessary condition. It generated a broadly diffused similarity of circumstance. Furthermore, as productivity and population density grew, local economic organization became necessary. Yet this is not a sufficient condition. Peasant proprietorship tends not to produce a high degree of commitment to the collectivity;

and it is rare, as we shall see (e.g., in Chapter 13), for peasants to generate permanent collective political organization. Several additional causes were involved, though in complex ways that were of different importance at different stages in the development of the polis. Their complex interrelations add to the relatively conjunctural look of Greek power. The next two to add their weight to the Iron Age economy were *trade* and *military organization*. Later we must add literacy, commercialization of agriculture, and large-scale naval warfare.

Early trade and the polis

The relationship of the polis to trade was peculiar. Trade was not central to politics. Merchant activity was not highly valued by the Greeks (although it was not looked down on). Local trade did not confer high political status. Long-distance trade was organized by professional (often foreign) merchants who had a marginal position in the community. Artists and craftsmen were initially independent, and often Phoenician. Thus political organization was not the mere outgrowth of economic organization. It could not be, because though the individual polis was unitary the economy was not. No central place containing a production-redistribution cycle, no system of compulsory cooperation, dominated the Greek world (nor had it the Phoenician). There was organizational discontinuity between production and local-market activities of the peasant farmers and the wider trading networks. Even later, when the Greeks secured control of trade, dualism remained.

On the other hand, Greeks from the earliest times moved abroad in search of commodities like metals. Exchanging them for agricultural products like olives, olive oil, and wine was the basis of their surplus, a precondition of their civilization. They founded settlements abroad that were essentially agricultural-cum-trading stations and that themselves became poleis. It was a kind of "archipelago" structure (in some ways similar to that of the earliest civilization of Andean America, referred to in Chapter 4), in which the shores of the eastern Mediterranean were gradually colonized by Greeks. It produced a distinctive orientation to trade. What we call "merchants" and the "freer" aspects of trade were left at a distance from the life of the polis. But polis– and especially inter-poleis–regulated relations entered into the economic-exchange process. In this way a multistate geopolitical system, "Greece," developed also as a collective economic organization, stimulated by the growth of trade. The two levels of city-state and multistate federal civilization were given embryonic form by an economy resulting from local ecology and regional geopolitics.

But we still have to explain the democratic element of the many poleis. This, after all, was the striking Greek innovation. Never before (and rarely subsequently) had peasant farmers ruled a civilized society, and by binding majority votes, after free discussion, in public meetings (see Finley 1983 for

The main contribution of the phalanx was thus to intensify peasant farmer commitment to the constitutional-territorial city-state. The hoplite soldier, embedded in a local economy, required political commitment to his comrades quite as much as he required his shield and sword. Tyrtaios of Sparta explained this when rejecting traditional notions of "excellence" – strength, beauty, wealth, birth, oratory. He says:

This is excellence, this is the finest possession of men, the noblest prize that a young man can win. This is a common good for the city and all the people, when a man stands firm and remains unmoved in the front rank and forgets all thought of disgraceful flight, steeling his spirit and heart to endure, and with words encourages the man standing beside him. This is the man who is good in war. [Quoted in Murray 1980: 128–9]

Excellence was social, or more precisely *political,* that is, deriving from the polis.

Such excellence was lacking in the Assyrian foot soldier and in the soldiery of other more extensive, class-divided territorial empires or aristocratic-feudal states. Their excellence was either professional competence or aristocratic honor, both removed from the experience of the mass of the people. These states could not count on such positive commitment from one-third of their adult males. The Greek hoplite army was a novel marcher army, the product of free Iron Age peasants organized into small territorial states that were adjacent to a more initially civilized and more extensive, authoritative world.

Between about 750 and 650 B.C., the communal, egalitarian, and prosperous Greek locality, organized as a territorial marketplace and receiving military diffusions from the Near East, simultaneously generated the city-state and the hoplite fighting formation. The two were interlocked and mutually generating. Like all effective military formations, the hoplite army reproduced its own form of morale. Commitment to the "common good for the city and all the people" was not merely a background normative disposition, but an integral part of the battle formation in which the soldier became trapped. If the line broke, the hoplite was exposed. He could only see frontward, his clumsy shield kept his right side exposed, and his agility (especially to run away) was negligible. The hoplite was committed, by life and the fear of death, whether he was an aristocrat or a wealthy commoner, to the city-state. It was his cage as well as his political liberation.

In hoplite warfare, bloodshed was massive but rule-governed. Vernant (in Vernant and Naquet 1980: 19–44) says that warfare *was* the polis, and so its rules expressed the life of the polis. War was publicly declared (no surprise attacks) after Assembly debates involving all citizens. War was an extension of the rhetorical struggles of the Assembly. Was was serious and bloody, because worsted hoplites ran away slowly. The Greeks economized in war in the matter of supplies and sieges. The hoplite (or his servant) carried three days' rations – as we saw in Chapter 5, this was the maximum period of effective self-supply in ancient warfare. They did not construct route camps, and they did not in general undertake siege operations on the cities. Sparta constitutes a slight exception here. Its interest in conquering adjacent territories led to a better commissariat and some sieges. But war did not endanger agricultural productivity. The hoplite formation quickly sought out its enemy, and a short, bloody, often decisive encounter resulted. It could defend a small territory, and dominate but not capture (because the city could not be easily taken) adjacent territory. The peace treaty then ratified the hegemony of one state over the other and often gave its political leadership over to the victor's local clients. Thus war also reinforced a multistate system of poleis. Considerable diplomatic regulation of warfare was already established. "Greece" was again more than the single polis. It was a broader culture, one that provided explicit regulation and legitimation of a multistate system.

Hoplites were not all-powerful, either in war or in their ability to determine social structure. In battle, limitations in mobility and in attack were obvious, and adaptations followed. Probably as a result of confrontations with looser Greek formations – the federal *ethnos* of the northern and central areas used more cavalry and light troops – the armor lightened. By the first Persian invasion (490 B.C.) the greaves had been discarded, the corselet changed from metal to leather and linen, and the helmet lightened or replaced by a leather cap. But the formation was still quite tight. The width of file was only a meter, which is very dense. It allowed greater attacking potentiality. The Persians were astonished (so say the Greeks) when heavy infantry charged them at the run. They were shattered by the concentrated force of the charge if caught in confined spaces. Before the modern saddle (invented around 200 B.C.) and to a lesser extent the stirrup,[5] the shock value of cavalry was low. If faced with infantry formations, the cavalry were used to herd the infantry close together, so that one's archers could inflict great damage upon them. The Greeks disrupted this tactic by the swiftness of their advance.

There have been dozens of comparable military innovations – Sargon's commissary, the chariot, cavalry with saddle and stirrups, the Swiss pike phalanx, gunpowder. These are parallel inventions that changed the balance of warfare. In these cases, as soon as some of the powers at the receiving end recovered their poise, they copied. But even after the Persian Wars, few in the Middle East imitated the hoplites. Three powers incorporated the phalanx: the Etruscans, the part-Greek Macedonians, and the later Romans (perhaps the minor-power, part-Greek Carians of Asia Minor did too). The probable explanation is that the masses of other powers could not lock shields together – they lacked the social solidarity. For a time only Greeks possessed this. So Greeks were employed as mercenaries throughout the Near East and the Med-

---

[5]Some military historians think the stirrup had more effect on the ability to thrust downward with a sword than it had on charging (Barker 1979).

iterranean. Greeks were Greeks even when fighting for pay for Pharaoh Psam-
metichus II or when capturing Jerusalem for Nebuchadrezzar II of Babylon.
They *still* possessed the morale to lock shields: Again, "Greece" represented
not just the individual polis, for its morale existed also in Eastern deserts,
among troops recruited from a variety of poleis.

Hoplite organization could not determine the constitution of the polis, if
only because it was not much of an organization! The phalanx did not have
much internal command structure (except among Spartan and Theban formations). Moreover, the total army comprised several phalanxes; hoplites would
each be accompanied by a servant; and lighter troops of equivalent numbers
were involved. Some form of central command structure was required from
other aspects of the polis. Military leadership was at first the responsibility of
aristocracies. Yet central command undermined the decentralized basis of the
aristocracy. Where kingship and aristocracy existed, as in Sparta, a tightening
of the links between king, nobles, and hoplites could lead to the intense,
controlled, oligarchic-yet-egalitarian form of discipline that has become known
to the whole world as simply "Spartan." Elsewhere centralization took another
form: Alliance between the hoplite class and the *tyrants,* despotical usurpers
who seized control in a number of states from the mid-seventh century B.C.
on. But the tyrant could not institutionalize his control into the peasant economy. His power rested narrowly on war leadership and on the skillful playing
off of factions. When tyranny disappeared, hoplite democracy was generally
firmly entrenched.

If military power had been preeminent in the city-state, then militaristic
Sparta would have been its dominant type. This might be argued for the earlier democratic phase – say up to about 500 B.C. All adult Spartan males were
hoplites, possessed an equal amount of land (in addition to whatever they
inherited), and were entitled to participate in assemblies – although this coexisted with a degree of oligarchy and aristocracy. The most effective hoplite
army Greece ever knew used its power in the sixth century to help expel
tyrants from other city-states and establish a Spartan-type hoplite democracy
called *eunomia.* This term, meaning "good order," combined a notion of
strong collective discipline and equality.

The combination of equality and control showed the limitations of the hoplite
fighting force as a form of collective organization. It was essentially inward-
looking. Sparta was until late relatively uninterested in overseas trade and the
founding of colonies. The importance of morale emphasized the distinction
between insiders and outsiders. Only a small army could be supported and
only local territories conquered. Sparta treated its conquered peoples as servile dependents, useful as auxiliaries but never admitted into citizenship.

The fully developed polis of the fifth century B.C. had an openness that
Sparta lacked. Its prototype was Athens, which combined in-group loyalty
with a greater openness, a wider sense of identifying both with Greece and

with "humanity at large." We can derive neither from the hoplite army, which reinforced only the small city-state. So what were these identities due to? Let us first consider the notion of "Greece."

Hellas: language, literacy, and sea power

Despite the ferocity of interpolitical struggles, the Greeks possessed a common identity. "Hellas," originally a locality, became their term for this unity. They believed they had come from a common ethnic stock. We have no means of knowing whether this was so. Their main evidence was language. By the time elite literacy developed, in the eighth and seventh centuries B.C., they had a plausible story of a single language, divided into four main dialects. From then on they were a single linguistic "people." But we should not take this as an unalterable ethnic "given." Dialect differences did not coincide with political boundaries, for example. Languages change, splinter, merge – sometimes with great rapidity. If the Greeks had a common linguistic origin, why had the uniformity endured their wider dispersal over several hundred years before literacy?

An answer is often given in terms of Greek ideology – the unity of Greek religion, especially as synthesized by Homer and such common institutions as the Delphic oracle, the Olympic Games, and the theater. Unfortunately, this only demonstrates the importance of the question. The Greek gods and rituals were established by 750 B.C.; we know that they were not "original," but we know little about their emergence and diffusion. We suspect the vital role was played by the Ionian (or Aeolic-Ionian) Greek area in Asia Minor, the probable land of origin of Homer and Hesiod. We can plausibly guess why. This area was well placed to unite the (Indo-European?) gods of the Mycenaeans, the local fertility gods of primitive religions, and the mystery cults and rites of the Near East. Such a fusion is the heart of Greek religion and ritual. But why did this fusion spread to the whole Greek world instead of splitting it apart into East and West?

Much of the answer must lie in the sea. Here I present a brief maritime equivalent to the analysis of land-transport logistics given in Chapter 5. Given the superiority of sea over land transport, the Greek world only *seems* dispersed. Let us play a little with geography, reversing the contours of the map so that the sea becomes the land. Then the Peloponnesian coast, the islands of the Aegean, the Asia Minor and Black Sea colonies, Crete, Cyprus, and the Sicilian and southern Italian colonies all appear as the coastal and lakeside areas of a large island, of which the Greeks occupied the northern part (and the Phoenicians the southern). Our modern minds, used to railways and motor vehicles, can now understand the geographical unity of the Greek world, once the Iron Age had boosted Mediterranean trade and the Phoenicians had refined the naval galley. Most trade passed seaward then. More importantly, so did the migrations. This was important in the Greek case, for population pressure could be solved by overseas migration. Supplies could be carried great distances by galleys, and the military prowess of the Greek infantry meant that they could then carve out a small colonial niche virtually anywhere on the Mediterranean and Black seas not denied to them by Phoenician naval power. They founded something near a thousand such city-states in the period 750–550 B.C.

We must not exaggerate the degree of integration of control. The logistics were still formidable. Reversing the contours of the map misleads in this respect. Modern landmasses can be politically integrated far more easily than ancient sea lanes. The colony was effectively independent from its mother state between October and April, when navigation by the stars was difficult and when storms deterred from putting to sea (and was to do so for another 2,000 years). Warship galleys managed about fifty miles a day, and merchantmen covered more variable distances according to winds. Neither usually moved directly across seas. They preferred to keep in sight of land for navigational and supply reasons, creeping around coasts and islands, calling in at a series of ports and staging posts. *Tramping* is the modern nautical expression that adequately conveys the humble, meandering gait of this potential instrument of naval control.[6] At every port supplies would be taken on, and goods exchanged. All personnel would start the voyage loaded up with as many goods as they could carry, hoping to exploit local price differences along the route to their private gain. Indeed, if aboard the swiftest galleys, they could be uniquely placed for such exploitation. The tramping pattern reveals that direct communication and control between, say, Athens and its colonial cities became attenuated by a series of other communications with ports and city-states, most of which were its colonies.

Finally, because Greece was a diplomatically stabilized multistate organization in which no polis had the resources to incorporate the others, the mother city-state lacked the resources to reconquer a rebellious colony. When centuries later Rome moved to the seas, having already established domination over the territory of Italy, it found combining land and sea imperialism possible; but this was inconceivable for the Greeks. They did not try: Each colony was self-governing; it might receive supplies and more immigrants from the mother city-state, and in return it would give favored status to the mother city-state's trade, and, on occasion, tribute. But that was all. Greek "imperialism" was *decentralized,* as was Phoenician imperialism.

There could not be an effective single set of boundaries for the Greek world, and naval and commercial expansion and migration reinforced this. The political unit could never control trade and cultural exchanges between Greeks,

---

[6]As Braudel notes in his discussion of Mediterranean shipping of A.D. 1500 – useful for the ancient period also (1975: I, 103–37, 246–52, 295–311).

and an openness was built into the Greek sphere. This was not dissimilar to Phoenician unity – an identifiable common culture combined with political decentralization. Perhaps in about 700 B.C. the two spheres of influence were similar. But later Greek cultural integration went much further, both within and between the city-states. *Literacy* provides the evidence for it.

Greece was the first known literate culture in history. The alphabet was borrowed from Phoenicia. Although the Greeks added vowels to it, they did so merely by revising Phoenician consonantal characters, for which their language had no use. The revolution was not in this technique of power but in its diffusion – to the average citizen.

Among the claims that Goody and Watt (1968) and Goody (1968) make for Greek literacy, the most powerful is that it fixed and reinforced cultural identity. This was the first shared, cross-class, stabilized culture of known history – shared by citizens and their families, about a third of the population. It penetrated also among resident foreigners, though not presumably among slaves. Why did it diffuse so widely? A two-stage diffusion process probably occurred.

At first, literacy spread from the Phoenicians along trade routes, perhaps to the southern Asia Minor colonies, then in a matter of decades to the largest traders and the wealthy in each city-state. The diffusion was thinly spread. The Olympic victor list began in 776 B.C., the record of the dates of the foundation of Sicilian colonies in 734, the list of Athenian magistrates in 683. The importance of sea trade and openness to foreign influence ensured that Sparta, the most inward-looking and land-based state, would lag behind. For reasons given in the next section, it also gave the lead in literacy to the east-central states, especially Athens.

In the second stage, in this area of Greece the democratic polis could not restrict literacy within an oligarchical elite. Written laws became prevalent in the late seventh century. Given the relatively democratic institutions of political citizenship, this indicates widespread literacy. This impression is reinforced by seventh-century survivals of alphabet instructions and exercises, as well as numerous ungrammatical and misspelled inscriptions. Perhaps the most striking survival are the graffiti scratched on the left leg of Rameses II's statue in Egypt, datable to 591 B.C. A passing group of Greek mercenaries employed by the Pharaoh Psammatichus II had written:

When king Psammatichos came to Elephantine those who sailed with Psammatichos son of Theokles wrote this. They came beyond Kerkis as far as the river allowed. Potasimto commanded the foreign-speakers [i.e., the Greeks], Amasis the Egyptians. He wrote us, Archon son of Amiobichos and Axe son of Nobody [i.e., a bastard].

Then follow six different signatures in the scripts of various Greek hometowns, mostly the smaller, less commercially active Ionian towns and those without colonies. These mercenaries were probably poor peasant proprietors (or their younger brothers). This suggests average hoplite literacy of a basic level at quite an early date (Murray 1980: 219–21).

In Athens a hundred years later, literacy in both reading and writing among the citizenry as a whole is presupposed by the institutions of ostracism (exile), and proved by the archaeological recovery of thousands of written votes for the ostracism of so-and-so. They date from the 480s. At about the same time we have casual mentions of schools where children were learning their letters. And we also have literary allusions and popular proverbs indicating normal literacy among citizen families – for example, the proverbial phrase for an ignoramus: "He can't read, he can't swim" (in a maritime state!). Athenian literacy developed further than Spartan. Harvey (1966), in a review of the evidence for literacy, suggests that literacy was encouraged by Athenian-style democracy. We can see this in literary forms that obviously bear the influence of the polis – the popularity of dialogues and rhetoric. But, as Stratton (1980) argues, unrestricted literacy actually intensified democracy by way of a "political crisis." The compliance of a literate people can only be obtained and enforced by objectified written laws. These cannot be based on traditional norms. They require a more formal democratic political organization. In other words, literacy both spread in and reinforced the relatively open, outward-looking Athenian-style polis. Its usefulness in trade, in administration, and in reinforcing citizen solidarity and democracy probably added to rising Athenian power and helped halt the rise of Sparta. But other power techniques were also involved in this shift in both the balance of power and in the dominant form of the polis.

Greek imperialism: commercialization, naval power, and slavery

The next phase of Greek democratic diffusion was the commercialization of agriculture around the second half of the sixth century B.C. Here we combine two themes: The Greeks united plowed land and sea (the most profitable agriculture and the cheapest transport), and they were geographically positioned to take advantage of the development of coinage. In Greece, unlike Phoenicia, the relatively wealthy could appropriate the agricultural surplus and deliver it to the market themselves. The circuits of praxis tightened – and, as we shall see, *classes* were strengthened. Landowners could also adopt the merchant role in international trade, or, more commonly, as a collectivity in the polis dictate the terms of trade to the foreign merchant. As a collectivity they could also provide naval power to protect, and so regulate, the merchant.

Colonial expansion increased opportunities for trade and fostered regional specialization. Mainland and island city-states intensified two particular products, wine and olive oil, exchanging them for corn from the north and Egypt and luxuries from the east. These were joined by human exchanges – Greek mercenaries going eastward, and slaves coming southward from the barbarian lands. Again the Asia Minor city-states were strategically placed for this three-way trade and, together with half-Greeks in Asia Minor, they first developed that useful technical adjunct to three-way trade, coinage. By 550 B.C. the outward colonial expansion was over. Its commercialization was well under way; unlike that of the Phoenicians, it was not based narrowly on trade, or even on trade plus manufacture, for the polis brought together (though not as one) agricultural producer, manufacturer, and trader. All kinds of social tension were introduced into the polis through the generation of enormous, unequally distributed wealth. Nevertheless the economic power of the peasant proprietor had survived through olive and grape cultivation to preserve democracy.

Commercialization also changed military requirements. Expanding trade needed naval protection – first, against pirates, Phoenicians, and Persians; second, and more subtly, to establish relatively favorable terms of trade. Sparta in 550 B.C. was still the dominant land power. But city-states facing east and northeast were better placed to expand commercially, and some (such as Corinth, Aegina, and Athens on the mainland and Chios in the Aegean off Asia Minor) began to extend their navies. Athens had particular incentive, being dependent on corn imports. Athens was also privileged because its small territory contained the richest silver mines in Greece. Naval expenses could be paid, and a currency derived, from these. This may explain why Athens, and not Corinth, Aegina, or even Chios eventually typified "classical Greece."

Navies increased their power significance. But the relationship between the Greek polis and the naval galley is not straightforward. When Athens was in its truly democratic phase and in its prime as a naval power, contemporaries argued that the two were connected. Here, for example, is the "Old Oligarch," a pamphlet writer of the 470s:

It is right that the poor and the ordinary people in Athens should have more power than the noble and the rich, because it is the ordinary people who man the fleet and bring the city her power; they provide the helmsmen, the boatswains, the junior officers, the look-outs and the ship-wrights; it is these people who make the city powerful much more than the hoplites and the noble and respectable citizens. [quoted in Davies 1978: 116]

Aristotle noticed the same connection, writing more critically of how the development of large galleys had led to rule by "a mob of oarsmen": Oarsmen "should not be an integral part of the citizen body" (Politics, V, iv, 8; vi, 6). Countless subsequent writers (including Max Weber) have elaborated the point.

However, there are problems. The naval vessels of the Athenians were the same as those of the Phoenicians, who were not democratic. The Romans acquired this galley form while abandoning what democracy they started with. The Phoenician rowers were generally free men and were usually paid, but they were not active participants in a polis, for the institution was unknown among them. The Roman rowers were at first free citizens, but later slaves. There was no necessary connection between the naval galley and democracy.

It seems, rather, that in states that already knew citizenship and were composed of a maritime people, like Athens, the naval galley reinforced a democratic ethos. In Athens Solon's reforms of 593 B.C. established who was entitled to citizenship by dividing the society into four property classes based on the numbers of bushels of corn each class could yield. The first three were the 500-, 300-, and 200-bushel men (the last corresponding to the hoplite class), and the fourth and lowest was the *thetes,* the free poor. It is probable that, unlike the other classes, the *thetes* were not entitled to hold office, but they could speak in the Assembly. *Thetes* at first formed the basis of the Athenian galleys. Their formal constitutional powers never did increase, but their influence in the Assembly seems to have grown somewhat as a result of their naval contribution.

Reinforcement of the polis also came from another characteristic of naval warfare – its decentralized command structure compared to land armies. The individual warship is autonomous because the sea offers wider unconstraining spaces. In all presteamship navies, the sea also disrupted centralized command structures, blowing ships off course during most battles. It would require a state capable of integrating armies and navies before naval warfare would operate against decentralized democracy. Rome and Carthage are the only candidates in the ancient world.

Nevertheless, as naval warfare increased in scope it generated another threat to the autonomy of the polis. Citizen manpower resources became strained. If a small city-state built up its naval power, it soon needed more oarsmen than it had citizens. Aegina contributed thirty *triremes* (galleys with three banks of oars) to the battle of Salamis in 480, requiring 6,000 men of fighting age. Yet the total population of the island of Aegina at this time was about 9,000. Thucydides reports an interesting diplomatic dialogue between Athens and Corinth in 432 B.C. Corinth announced a policy of trying to buy off Athens's oarsmen, who, it said, were mercenaries anyway. Pericles, replying for Athens, argued that the Athenians could offer more than mere wages to their oarsmen. They could provide job security and protection for the oarsmen's own home city-state (actually, he put this negatively, pointing out that Athens could deny them access to their own homeland). He admitted that the mass of oarsmen were from other Greek states, unlike the helmsmen and petty officers, who were Athenians. Thus naval expansion introduced a hierarchy. The great city-states commanded the citizens of the lesser ones: The multistate system was faltering.

Comparable changes occurred in land warfare: As mercenary forces increased in size, the citizens of the poorer states were fighting as *metic* (descendants of foreign freemen) hoplites for those of the wealthy. And as growing resources enabled larger armies to put into the field, they became more tactically varied. Thessalian cavalry, Scythian and Thracian archers – all from the northern marches – were coordinated with the hoplite force, increasing hierarchy and centralization.

All this had to be paid for. Athens exploited its hegemony by exacting tribute from client states. By 431 it received more revenue from that source than it generated internally. In 450 Athenian citizenship rules were tightened, so that the *metics* could no longer become citizens. From then on, Athens politically exploited its client states.

Thus commercial expansion and the naval galley strengthened internal democracy but heightened intercity stratification and exploitation. Within Athens, the notion of freedom itself implied imposing one's domination on other states (as it did on slaves). After a century of struggle between aristocratic and democratic factions, the triumph of democracy was secured by Kleisthenes. In 507 he confirmed the dual structures of a mass assembly of all citizens and an executive council, now 500, chosen at random by lot from the first three property classes of territorial constituencies (the "tribes"). The Athenians' own word for their system underwent similar democratization: *eunomia* ("good order") became first *isonomia* ("equal order" or "equality before the law"), then, by the 440s, *demokratia* ("people's power").

For the next hundred years, Athens saw probably world history's most genuine participatory democracy among an extensive citizenry (still, of course, a minority of the whole population – for women, slaves, and resident foreigners were excluded). Attendance at the Assembly ran regularly over 6,000. The principal executive body, the council, rotated quickly and was chosen by lot. In any decade between one-quarter and one-third of citizens over the age of thirty years would have served on it. *Isegoria* meant free speech, not in our modern negative sense of freedom from censorship, but in the active sense of right and duty to speak out in assemblies of citizens. The herald opened debates with the words "What man has good advice to give the polis and wishes to make it known?" That, said Theseus, is freedom (Finley 1983: 70–5, 139). It also implied class struggle, as we shall see later in this chapter. And it depended on Athenian imperialism.

Imperialism also carried democracy abroad. By the 420s most of the Aegean states had followed Athens's lead and developed similar constitutions, feeling the same commercial and naval pressures, plus Athenian military force. If we consider each city-state in itself, the late fifth and early fourth centuries B.C. were truly a democratic era. But this is to omit intercity relations. Athenian hegemony was based on superior commercial and military strength, based in turn on wealth and citizen mobilization. By its very success and internal democracy, Athens was leading Greece closer to the Near Eastern pattern of control by a hegemonic empire of domination.

But there were two main obstacles on this potential developmental track. The more obvious was the ultimate geopolitical resilience of the multistate system. When Athenian ambition emerged openly, it was successfully resisted by the other states in the Peloponnesian War of 431–404. The contradiction between polis democracy and "Greek" collective identity was never solved internally. It preserved the explicitly federal nature of Greek social organization and ultimately ensured its demise at the hands of marcher lords who experienced no such contradiction.

The second obstacle to Athenian imperialism was more subtle. It concerned ideology and the way in which Greek notions of culture and reason actually contained *three* notions of what "society" was – it was the polis, it was Hellas, and it was an even more outward-looking notion of humanity. Thus Greek ideology was complex and highly contradictory. The principal contradiction to modern eyes often seems that essential institution of Greek civilization: slavery. So let us discuss Greek conceptions of humanity and slavery.

The cult of human reason

The cultural difference between the Greek and the Phoenician city-state was manifest by the sixth century B.C. So far as we can tell, the Phoenicians kept close to Middle Eastern religious orthodoxy: The processes of nature depended largely on superhuman gods. Perhaps because there was no single all-powerful Phoenician state, the Phoenicians did not imitate Egyptian or Sumerian theocratic dogmas. But their main gods, among them Baal, Melqart, and Astarte (the fertility goddess), are identifiably Canaanite and of common Middle Eastern stock. Their names changed as the Phoenicians moved westward and Hellenic religious cults were incorporated, but the general character of the religion remained traditional. In the Greek Ionian states of Asia Minor, however, developments occurred that took Greek culture as a whole toward a radical break with this ideology.

In Greek religion, skepticism shows in the work of writers like Hecataeus (who said that Greek mythology was "funny") and Xenophanes (who famously said, "If the ox could paint a picture, his god would look like an ox"). But three physicists from Miletus are perhaps preeminent. In 585 Thales achieved fame by correctly predicting an eclipse of the sun. This seemed a payoff from his general scientific approach: to explain the universe in terms of natural, not supernatural principles, "laws of nature." Thales argued that the ultimate constituent of matter was water, but we really know little about how he developed this idea. In itself it is no different from, say, the Sumerian belief that silt had constituted original matter. But Thales then built up a complete "natural" explanation from this, instead of introducing gods and heroes. We know more of the theoretical structure of his follower Anaximander, who departed from an explanation in terms of the world of phenomenal objects by attributing *laws* to the interrelations of a number of abstract qualities of matter, like heat and cold, dry and wet, and so forth. Their combinations produced earth, water, air, and fire. Anaximenes continued the same speculations, postulating air rather than water as the fundamental essence. Air was changed by condensation into wind, cloud, water, earth, and rock, and by rarefaction into fire. The importance of all three men lay less in their conclusions than in their methodology: Ultimate truth could be discovered by applying human reason to nature itself. Nothing else was necessary. It is akin to what we call science today.

There has been much speculation as to why this philosophical movement arose first in Asia Minor and in Miletus. Perhaps the three most popular explanations should be combined.

First, the Greek polis encouraged the notion that the ordinary human being could control his or her world. After all, this was objectively true. It was merely to generalize from this to assert that individual human reason could understand the cosmos. It was the same *kind* of generalization as the Egyptian's granting divinity to the pharaoh, because objectively the pharaoh did guarantee order.

Second, why Miletus? Miletus, though rich, was not a conspicuously stable polis in the sixth century. It underwent severe political class conflict. This, it is sometimes argued, shows up in the theories of the physicists: The world is in equilibrium between opposed powers. These contradictions, or antinomies, are the "charge," are the breath of life in the world, are even the divine, because no person's reason can ultimately overcome them. Thus a place is left for religion by the second factor, class struggle.

Third, why Asia Minor? Asia Minor's strategic location between Asia and Europe is revealing. Greek naturalistic art, innovative and pleasing to subsequent western eyes, was probably a fusion of a Greek desire to represent human stories in art (in the early "Geometric" period) and an eastern habit of representing animals and plants in a naturalistic way (for example, the marvelously lithe lions of Assyrian hunting sculptures). The result was artistic expression of confidence in bodily power, especially in the human body. The intellectual expression of confidence in reason may have had similar stimuli. To be certain, we need more precision about times and places. Did the eastern influences of this period include Persian monotheism, that is, Zoroastrianism or its precursors, as was the case later at the accession of the Persian king Darius in 521 B.C.? Unfortunately, we do not know. The most plausible guess is that traditional polytheistic, cultic, supernatural Middle Eastern religion was beginning to disintegrate in the more advanced areas – Persia, Lydia, Phrygia – and that one of the likely settings for its replacement by a more humanistic philosophical inquiry would be a Greek city-state in Asia Minor.[7]

The Ionian School's methodology rapidly penetrated the Greek world. It splintered between those who held that experimental observation was the key to knowledge and those like Pythagoras who stressed mathematical and deductive reasoning. But confidence in human reason and dialogue, and elimination of the supernatural beings from explanation, remained characteristic

---

[7]A more positive identification of Persian origins in Greek philosophy can be found in West 1971. But see the skepticism of Momigliano 1975: 123–9.

of Greek philosophy (although, as we shall see in Chapter 10, an impersonal conception of the "divine" reentered Greek thought). Furthermore, although philosophy was an esoteric and elite practice, matter-of-fact confidence can be found in most aspects of Greek literacy – in the predominance of functional prose over poetry and myth, in careful rigorous analysis, and in the absence of distance, in the theater, for example, between the world of the gods and the human world. Greek literacy tried to represent experience rather than to preserve a "sacred tradition."

This is a controversial area. I do not want to sound like one of those Victorian classics masters who believed that the Greeks were "just like us" in their adherence to a modern scientific civilization. Their notion of science differed from ours. It gave a greater role to divinity, and it emphasized static rather than dynamic laws. Greek culture lacked what Weber called "rational restlessness," which he attributed to Christianity and especially to Puritanism. Other critics of Greek reason go further. Dodds (1951), for example, argued that commitment to rationalism only diffused widely in the fifth century B.C. and then promptly retreated in the face of a resurgence of popular magic. This seems extreme. Yet it must be admitted that the notion of reason contained contradictions. Two of the most important and illuminating contradictions were presented by class and ethnicity. Was reason shared by all classes and peoples? Or was it confined to citizens and Greeks?

Were slaves and Persians rational?

Like most conquerors, the Greeks of the Dark Age had made slaves or serfs out of conquered natives. As elsewhere, this tended to fix the slaves to particular pieces of land or types of occupation. Intermarriage and assimilation had proliferated half-free statuses (and in the Greek case "half-citizen" rights). Conquest slavery could not long sustain clear ethnic discrimination. But in the sixth century B.C., commercialization reinforced the small slave population with *chattel* slaves, who were bought and owned as commodities, not tied to fixed plots of land or occupations, and were at the free disposal of their masters. Most came from northern Thrace, Illyria, and Scythia, apparently sold by native chieftains.

I deal with the class aspects of slavery later in this chapter. Here I note how it reinforced the Greeks' notions of their own superiority over others. But we must distinguish the various groups with whom the Greeks came into contact. The peoples to the north were less civilized and were illiterate. The pejorative term *barbarian,* meaning lacking intelligible speech and reason, was applied there. But even barbarians were considered partners in social intercourse. They were enslaved, but the Greek justification of slavery was inconsistent. Two conceptions competed.

First, slavery was justified in terms of the innate lack of rationality of the enslaved peoples. This explanation was favored by Aristotle, it is the best means of reconciling the usefulness of slavery with the Greek emphasis on the dignity of human reason, and it squared with the Greeks' repugnance at the enslavement of other Greeks (which did occasionally occur, however). Perhaps only the Greeks possessed reason.

Second, slavery was also justified in a more utilitarian way: as merely the inevitable outcome of defeat in war or of similar misfortune. Actually, we are probably more interested in moral justifications for slavery than the Greeks were. We find slavery extraordinarily repugnant, and we tend to expect moralizing to legitimate it. Racism seems to fit the bill, but racism is a modern concept, not an ancient one. Slavery in the ancient world did not need much justification. It was found in small quantities everywhere conquest occurred and in large quantities when commercially produced. But it was convenient and apparently caused little trouble. Slave revolts were rare. Greek attitudes toward slavery were matter-of-fact. At the core of modern misunderstandings is our matter-of-fact attitude toward free labor, which we regard as the obvious alternative labor form. Yet "free" labor was rare in the ancient world, and in any case it was not regarded as free. Greek did not work for Greek unless he was a *metic* or in debt bondage, and neither was a free status. "The condition of the free man is that he does not live for the benefit of another," said Aristotle in his *Rhetoric* (1926: I, 9). Yet for some to be free, others must work for them in slavery, servitude, or politically regulated dependence. That seemed an inevitable fact of life.

Moreover, other peoples could not be fitted into a picture of superior and inferior peoples. Concerning the Phoenicians (and indeed the Etruscans of Italy), the Greeks said little – which is rather curious. But these peoples could hardly be regarded as lacking reason. Nor could the civilized peoples of the East. The Persians were often regarded as *the* barbarians, but what of their civilized achievements? Aristotle concedes that they did not lack skill or intelligence. They were deficient in spirit, he says in his *Politics* (1948: VII, vii, 2). Indeed the Greeks generally asserted that the peoples of the East lacked independence of spirit and did not love freedom as they did. Yet the Greeks did not rest content with such a stereotype. How could they when so many city-states acknowledged the suzerainty of Persia? They had assimilated much of value from the East, and to do that required an inquiring, skeptical, open disposition.

Nobody exemplifies this better than Herodotus, writing about 430 B.C. Herodotus relied on careful interviewing of many local priests and officials in Persia and elsewhere. Let me quote his famous anecdote about Darius of Persia:

When he was king of Persia, he summoned the Greeks who happened to be present at his court, and asked them what they would take to eat the dead bodies of their fathers. They replied that they would not do it for any money in the world. Later, in the presence of the Greeks, and through an interpreter, so they could understand what was said, he asked some Indians, of the tribe called Callatiae, who do in fact eat their parents' dead bodies, what they would take to burn them. They uttered a cry of horror and forbade him to mention such a dreadful thing. One can see by this what custom can do, and Pindar, in my opinion, was right when he called it "king of all." [1972: 219–20]

Herodotus, the cultured traveler, is here identifying with Darius against the provincial Greeks because he finds the Persian's civilized relativism congenial. Indeed, his portrayal of Darius is not only sympathetic – Darius is generous, intelligent, tolerant, honest, and honorable – it also presents his qualities are those of Persian rule in general. This sympathy had survived the epic struggle between Greece and Persia, let it be noted, in which Herodotus sided strongly with the Greeks.

It is difficult to be sure of the Greek view of the Persians during the Persian Wars, or even to know if there was, indeed, a unified view. The conflict was a clash of imperialisms. The expansion of the Persian Empire coincided exactly with the period of Athenian-led Greek commercial and naval expansion. In 545 the Persian Cyrus the Great forced the city-states of Asia Minor to capitulate; in 512 Darius conquered Thrace; in 490 Darius invaded the Greek mainland for the first time but was repelled at Marathon; in 480 the second invasion of Xerxes was repelled on land and sea, most famously at Thermopylae and Salamis. A simultaneous Carthaginian attack on Sicily was also defeated. This ended the main threat and secured the hegemony of Athens.

But how many imperialisms were there? Even at the height of the conflict, many Greeks fought on the Persian side. The nature of the Persian advance is instructive. As they marched westward, they obtained the submission of Greek states in the usual negotiated manner of ancient warfare. Greeks usually submitted through fear of Persian strength. Immediately, the Persians would levy troops and ships from them and continue their march. The ease with which they accomplished this indicates several things: that Persian rule was light and not particularly detested, that Greeks would fight for anyone who paid them, and that the imperialism of Athens and Sparta was also resented. Thrace and Thebes fought willingly on the Persian side, while dissident factions within Athens were accused – probably not without foundation – of pro-Persian sympathies. An enormous amount of intrigue was going on – one state was refusing to fight under an Athenian supreme commander, another under a Spartan; both sides were constantly persuading the other's minor Greek states to desert; the Athenians tried to make the Persians distrust their Greek allies by allowing false messages to the latter to fall into Persian hands. On the Greek side, the one constant was the unwavering solidarity of Athens and Sparta. All differences between them were sunk under the common threat – but the threat was to their own hegemony over the rest of Greece. When the Persian threat receded, they began to fight each other in the Peloponnesian War, and both then sought alliance with Persia.

The Greeks responded to the Persians in terms not of ethnic stereotypes but of geopolitical strategies learned in their own multistate system. Greek citizens wished to be self-governing. They did not wish to be ruled by Persia, and they were willing to combine to avert that danger. When the danger from Persia receded, they were more concerned to avert being ruled by other Greeks. They treated Persia as just another state whose rulers were as capable of loyalty and reason as any Greek polis. The Greeks ultimately lacked a consistent sense of their own ethnic superiority. They were too outward-looking, too interested in the characteristics of (male) humanity at large, too inclined to project outward the diplomatic rationality of their multistate system.

But what of the various categories of humanity nearer at home, the classes, which are an essential part of Greek development? So far, the story of the three networks of interaction – the polis, Greece, and humanity – has been rather too benign and functional. I turn to class struggle, an essential part of all three.

Class in classical Greece

Classical Greece is the first historical society in which we can clearly perceive class struggle as an enduring feature of social life. To understand this better, one can distinguish between the principal forms of class structure and class struggle found in human societies. (These distinctions will be explained more fully in Volume III of this work.)

Classes in the broadest sense are relations of economic domination. The sociologist of class is principally interested not in inequalities of wealth but, rather, in economic power, that is, in persons' ability to control their own and others' life chances through control of economic resources – the means of production, distribution, and exchange. Inequalities in economic power have existed in all known civilized societies. As they are never fully legitimate, *class struggle* has also been ubiquitous – that is, struggle between groups arranged hierarchically, "vertically," with different amounts of economic power. In many societies, however, this struggle has remained at a first, *latent,* level and been prevented from attaining any very pronounced organizational form by the coexistence alongside "vertical" classes of "horizontal" economic organizations – constituted by familial, clientelist, tribal, local, and other relations. We saw these to be characteristic of later prehistory and, to a lesser extent, of the earliest civilizations, which thus generally remained at a rudimentary level of class formation. Although nonclass horizontal organizations have continued to exist to the present day, history has seen a strengthening of classes at their expense.

This brings us to the second level of class organization, *extensive classes.* They exist where vertical class relations predominate in the social space in question as against horizontal organizations. The growth of extensive classes has itself been uneven, and so at this second level we may make two further

subdivisions. Extensive classes may be *unidimensional,* if there is one predominant mode of production, distribution, and exchange, or *multidimensional,* if there is more than one (and they are not fully articulated with each
other). And extensive classes may by *symmetrical,* if they possess similar
organization, or *asymmetrical,* if one does or only some do (normally the
dominant class or classes).

Finally, a third level of class emerges, *political classes,* where the class is
organized for political transformation of the state or political defense of the
status quo. This is less likely in a thoroughly multidimensional structure, but
again the political organization may be symmetrical or asymmetrical. In the
latter case only one class, usually the ruling class, may be politically organized. This began to be the pattern in the empires of domination discussed in
Chapter 5, as dominant groups began to unify into an extensive, organized
ruling class while subordinates were predominantly organized into horizontal
groupings controlled by the rulers.

These distinctions are especially useful in the case of classical Greece. It is
the first known society to have moved fully into the third level of class organization, exhibiting to us *symmetrical, political class struggle* (though only
on one of what we shall see to be two principal dimensions of its extensive
class structure).[8]

Classes did not totally dominate relations of economic power in Greece.
Two principal horizontal groupings remained that effectively excluded large
numbers of persons from the class struggles I shall shortly detail. The first
was the patriarchal household. This continued to enclose women (even more
than boy children in some city-states) and perhaps some other male dependents in the case of larger, more powerful households. This prevented any
significant independent participation by them in public life. Women were represented there by a male head of household. Women were not citizens, of
course, though if they were in a citizen household (or even more, if in a
powerful citizen household) they participated in a relatively privileged life in
other ways. Dependent males could be mobilized by more powerful citizens
as clients against lower-class citizen movements. The second horizontal grouping
was the local city-state itself, which privileged its own inhabitants at the expense
of all resident "foreigners." As the city-state was small and interaction between
states was great, there were many resident foreigners. These were mostly
other Greeks but included many other "nationalities." They were called, again,
metics, and they had definite political rights somewhere between those of
citizens and those of serfs and slaves. Within the city-state itself, *metics* thus
formed a separate extensive class, but the city-state is not always the most

---

[8]I acknowledge the enormous amount of assistance provided by Ste. Croix's *The Class
Struggle in the Ancient Greek World* (1981). I do not follow his Marxist analysis all
the way, but his work combines unusually high levels of scholarship and sociological
sophistication.

appropriate object of our analysis. Obviously, a citizen of Athens resident in a minor city-state would there enjoy somewhat greater power than a *metic* with a more modest homeland. Like women, therefore, *metics* were actually divided by their supposedly common status. They organized themselves only on rare occasions.

So only a minority of the population engaged directly in class struggle – which we shall find has generally been the case in history. But as minorities usually make history, this is no objection to concentrating on class and class struggle now.

Extensive class structure in Greece was fundamentally two-dimensional. On the first dimension, citizens had power over noncitizens, especially over slaves and serfs. On the second dimension, some citizens wielded economic power over other citizens. This reflected the fact that there were two major modes of production, both highly politicized but nonetheless distinct. The first was the extraction of surplus in production from the slave or serf by the free citizen; the second was the less direct extraction of surplus from the small citizen landowner by the great landowner. The second was not a relationship of production in the narrow sense but arose from wider circuits of economic power entwined also with military and political power. In such a stable, long-enduring society as classical Greece, these two modes of production were articulated into a single overall economy. Additionally, at the top, the highest class on both dimensions was itself often integrated. But at the lower levels this was not so, and thus we must analyze two separate dimensions of extensive class structure.

Between citizen and slave or serf was a qualitative class divide. Slaves were owned, were denied rights to land or organization, and were normally non-Greek (though Greeks could become debt-bondage slaves). Citizens exclusively owned land and possessed exclusive rights to political organization; and they were Greek, almost invariably the sons of citizens themselves. Although there were also differences within both slave and citizen groups, the divide between the two was normally unbridgeable. The significance of this divide was always great. Slaves probably never outnumbered citizens, nor did their production level exceed that of citizens working their own land. But as de Ste. Croix points out, these are not the decisive statistics. Slaves contributed a large part of the *surplus,* that is, of the production over and above that necessary for subsistence. Free wage labor was almost unknown; Greek citizen could not work for citizen; and neither leasing nor *metics* could be fully exploited in a noncontractual way. Slave labor contributed most of the surplus *directly* extracted from the immediate producers. Of course, direct extraction is not the whole story. Another substantial part of the citizens' surplus came more indirectly, from the commanding position of the Greek cities in trading relations, which their military, and especially their naval strength, was able to reinforce. Such trade was, as in the normal way of things, partly "free" (and so Greece benefited from its strategic marchland position and its possession of vines, olives, and [Athenian] silver) and partly militarily tilted. Both aspects were significantly regulated by the polis, and so by the citizens. Nevertheless Greek civilization did also depend heavily upon slavery and its surplus.

The citizens were fully conscious of this. Our sources accept slavery without question as a necessary part of civilized life. So, in relation to slaves, citizens were a political, extensive class, fully conscious of their common position and of their need to defend its political conditions.

But they were rarely required to do this, because the slaves did not reciprocate class consciousness. Slaves were imported from diverse areas and spoke diverse languages. Most were spread around individual households, workshops, and small to medium-sized estates (with the exception of the silver mines). They lacked the capacity for extensive organization. They may be considered abstractly, that is, in Marxian terms "objectively," as an extensive class but not *organizationally* – which is what matters sociologically – or politically as a class. Hence the citizen-slave dimension of class was not symmetrical. Citizens were organized, slaves were not. Struggle was presumably continuous but covert. It does not enter the historical record, despite its significance for Greek life.

There is an exception to this: the territorial imperialism of the Spartans, who enslaved the adjacent population of Messenia and Laconia. These "helot" serfs, capable of unity and local organization, were a perpetual source of rebellion. This seems to have been true also of another serf people, the Penestai, who were enslaved by the Thessalians. The lessons – to recruit slaves from diverse peoples and to prevent organization among them – were widely reported by Greek and Roman sources alike.

The slaves' lack of organization also divided them from the second dimension of class, and especially from the lower classes of citizenry. These were organized at the level of the polis. Indeed, their basic interests against the more powerful citizen classes led them to intensify political efforts. Yet their freedom and the strength of the polis actually depended upon slavery. Freedom and slavery had advanced hand in hand, as Finley observes (1960: 72). Thus there was little chance of an alliance of the two largest "lower classes," slaves and the lower free citizenry. Indeed there was not much chance of any significant direct relationship between the two. Most of the lower citizens did not own slaves. Their relationship to slavery was more indirect, a sign of the existence of two separate dimensions of class at the lower end of Greek society.

Slaves were not an active force in history, indispensable as their labor was to those who were. Their praxis did not count. By contrast, even the lowest citizenry possessed class praxis.

In dealing with the second dimension of class, divisions within the citizen body, we do not encounter a simple qualitative divide. Nevertheless this dimension is not difficult for us to understand. Our own liberal, capitalist democracies are not dissimilar to the polis. Both combine formal citizen equality with continuous class gradations. And just as capital ownership gives a partial approximation to any qualitative divide in our society, so did slave ownership in the Greek polis. In Greece other inequalities were generated by such factors as size and profitability of landholding, opportunities for trade, aristocratic birth, birth order, marriage fortunes, and military and political opportunities. The polis in mainland Greece restrained these inequalities rather more successfully than did the Asia Minor polis, and both restrained inequalities much more successfully than did the other states of the Near East (or than did the successor states of Macedon or Rome).

Class inequalities also produced identifiable political factions: on one side, the *demos,* the "common" citizens, usually without slaves (or perhaps with one or two) and including those feeling potentially threatened by debt or interest laws; in the middle, first the hoplites, then later the middling groups identified by Aristotle as the backbone of the polis; on the other side, the aristocrats and large estate holders, able by their use of slaves and indirect exploitation of citizens to avoid labor (and be truly "free") and to mobilize their dependent clients. All were struggling over the interest and debt laws, attempts at the redistribution of land or of the city's collective wealth, the taxation and military-service obligations, access to profitable trade, colonial ventures, offices, and slaves. As so much labor and surplus alike were channeled through the state, and because it was a democracy (or, at other times, democracy was at least an attainable ideal for the lower and middling classes), there was a highly politicized class struggle – like that of our own society. But because there was a *far* more active and militarist form of citizenship than our own, it was also consistently a more violent and visible struggle. *Stasis* was the Greek term for the ferocious faction fighting, violent yet with institutions allowing for regulated "all-or-nothing" endings – like ostracism and oscillation between basic constitutional forms (see Finley 1983).

We can trace its ebb and flow and its contribution to Greek civilization. With the advance of the hoplite/middling farmer came the generally victorious struggle of, first, tyranny and, then, democracy over monarchy and aristocracy. Growing prosperity, commercialization, slavery, naval expansion, and literacy broadened the strength and the confidence of the Athenian-style democracy. But they also widened economic-class differences within and between the poleis. By the fourth century B.C. prosperity was increasingly monopolized by the large landholders. Perhaps, as we might expect from earlier cases, the upgrading of Greece's marchlands from Italy to South Russia, ended Greek monopolies, developed marcher power, and led to economic decline in the cities (as Rostovtzeff 1941 and Mossé 1962 argue) in which the more powerful better survived. In either case, democracy was under strain before the Macedonian attack – and the upper classes may have assisted the Macedonian coup de grace in order to suppress revolution at home.

In the Greek (and especially Athenian) rise, extensive, symmetrical, political class struggle was an essential part of Greek civilization itself. At all three levels of Greek achievement I will summarize in the next section, we can see played out a class dialectic. The polis was established after aristocracies and tyrannies were overcome. The second more diffuse sense of identity, being Greek, civilized, and rational, probably also depended on this democratic outcome. And the third, broadest identity, the notion of human reason itself, is visibly uncertain and contested by classes throughout the period. Relevant here is the contrast between the conception of reason demonstrated by Plato, the "upper-class" representative; Aristotle, the "midling" spokesman; and the spokesmen of the *demos,* about whom we only hear from their opponents. Plato argued that manual work (from which only the upper class was free) degraded the mind. Aristotle argued that the crux of citizen qualification was the possession of moral wisdom, which mechanics and laborers generally lacked but which the middle class possessed. Also relevant, if rather more abstrusely, is the debate about the political significance of arithmetic versus geometry! Antidemocrats argued that arithmetic was inferior because it counted all numbers equally. Geometric proportion, however, recognized qualitative differences between numbers. As the ratio between numbers remains the same in a geometric scale (e.g., 2, 4, 8, 16), quality is rewarded fairly (Harvey 1965 gives the details of the debate). In citing this example, Ste. Croix (1981: 414) truly proves his contention that class struggle enters everywhere in classical Greece! Class might in the last resort have weakened the polis, but for centuries before that it was essential to Greek civilization. And as we shall see in later chapters, it left a legacy – split, it is true, between the kind of upper-class solidarity represented by "Hellenism" and a more popular sense of reasoned inquiry, emerging to influence salvationist religions.

From this section so far it might seem that, in the middle of a discussion of classical Greece, I have converted to Marxism. I did not emphasize class struggle in previous societies. But I stick by the statement made in the conclusion to Chapter 5. Although we must temper certainty because of lack of evidence, it does not seem that extensive, symmetrical class struggle (whether politicized or not) was an important part of the dialectic of early empires of domination. The Iron Age revolution had in certain circumstances encouraged the powers of the peasant farmers, thereby *inventing* extensive subordinate class identity and therefore class struggle in this particular historical period. The "circuits of praxis," that is, class relations, attained a role of "historical track layer." I have been able to describe this period, but *not* preceding ones, in Marxian terminology because this became appropriate to this historical setting.

But there is a second problem with Marxism as applied to ancient history.

It is one thing to describe classes and to trace their subsequent development. It is another to explain their causes. To do this we must step outside the normal apparatus of Marxian concepts, into, especially, the realms of military and political power, as well as economic power.

Empirically, Marx and Engels were willing to do this. They stressed the importance of warfare and militarism to slavery, to the distribution of public lands, to citizenship, and to class struggle in the ancient world. Marx said in the *Grundrisse* that "direct forced labour is the foundation of the ancient world" (1973: 245). He was aware of the frequency with which this was accomplished by enslaving or enserfing conquered peoples. His two alternative conceptions of what he called the "ancient mode of production," that is, appropriation by slavery and appropriation through citizenship, appreciate the militarism and political regulation involved. Yet, as I will argue at greater length in Volume III, his general theory insisted on regarding militarism and warfare as parasitic, nonproductive. I hope I showed in Chapter 5 that this was not the case in the early empires of domination. I have also shown this here, with regard to Greece: Without hoplite military organization, no *eunomic* or *isonomic* polis and probably no class struggle in the fullest, extensive, and political sense. Without the polis and naval supremacy, no commercial monopoly and no major slave-owning economy. Without this whole complex, no Greek civilization worth more than a passing mention. And without this, who knows what world history might have been? Would we be the descendants of a Persian satrapy?

It is worth noting here that Ste. Croix (1982: 96–7) defends materialism in terms different from those of Marx. After effective passages attacking Weber's and Finley's use of *status* (that most vacuous of sociological terms; I shall attack it more roundly in Volume III) in place of class, he switches to attack military/political theories. He does so on two grounds. First, he argues that political power is largely a means by which class differences are institutionalized. They add little life of their own. In Greece, he argues, political democracy (which he accepts was, to a degree, a manifestation of an independent political life) gave way "before the basic economic situation [which] asserted itself in the long run, as it always does." He then explains that democracy was destroyed by the propertied classes "with the assistance first of their Macedonian overlords and later of their Roman masters." This puts too much emphasis on the economic motives of the propertied classes, for the decline of the polis was a military as well as an economic process (as we shall see later), occurring even before the Macedonian and Roman conquests. His second ground is to equate military power with conquest, to equate conquest relations with the distribution of conquered land and wealth, and then to claim that this was exceptional in history. The nonsequiturs are glaring; the argument, false. Military and political power organizations unconnected to conquest have been necessary to our explanation of Greece's rise, maturity, and fall.

It is not my intention, to paraphrase Weber, to replace a one-sided materialism with an equally one-sided military/political theory. Obviously, military/political forms have economic preconditions. But if militarism and states can be productive, their resulting forms may themselves causally determine further economic development, and so economic forms will also have military and political preconditions. We must study their interactions, develop concepts that take them all equally seriously, apply them to empirical cases, and see what (if any) broad patterns of interaction emerge. Such is my methodology in this work. I shall generalize about patterns in my conclusion to Volume I and in Volume III. For the moment, in the specific case of Greece, it seems that military and economic power relations were conjoined from the first. As we cannot fully separate them, we can conclude only that both, in interaction, were necessary – perhaps even nearly sufficient – preconditions of the rise of Greek civilization. Their interaction was then institutionalized in a specific form of political power organization, the small polis situated in a multistate system, which then also became a major autonomous causal organizing force in the maturity of Greece. Finally, aided by the infrastructure of literacy, ideological power also became important in the ways I described above. All four ideal-typical sources of social power seem necessary to a causal explanation of the full flowering of Greek civilization – which seems to vindicate my use of these ideal types in the first place.

The Greek triple power network and its dialectic

Greek social organization included three distinct, overlapping power networks. The strongest and most intense was the democratic polis, the unique product of peasant proprietors with iron plows and weapons, combining in a marketplace and a hoplite phalanx, then developing a commercial integration of agricultural production and trade, and eventually generating a naval power based on the citizen oarsman. Nothing like this had been seen before: It required the historical conjunction of Iron Age innovations plus a unique ecological and geopolitical location astride maritime trading routes between semibarbarian plowing land and civilized empires of domination.

The polis proved the most intensive and democratic organization of collective power over a small space seen before the capitalist Industrial Revolution. It had to be small. Many political theorists believe that tiny size is still essential for truly democratic participation. But ancient democracy doubly required it, given contemporary logistical problems of communication and control.

Athens was easily the biggest. At its height its own territory comprised a little more than 2,500 square kilometers – that is, the equivalent of a circle of radius just over 50 kilometers. Its maximum population, in about 360 B.C., was 250,000, of which about 30,000 were adult male citizens (and about 80,000–100,000 were slaves). We know that the average attendance at its Assembly generally exceeded 6,000 (the quorum), a formidable record of mass democracy and intensive social organization. Sparta was territorially larger (about 8,500 sq. km.) because of its domination over Laconia and Messenia. Its population also totaled about 250,000 at about the same time, with a smaller citizen body – up to 3,000 full citizens plus up to 2,000 with partial citizen rights. The intensity of this core organization of Sparta was even greater than that of the Athenians. Most states were smaller. Plataea had less than 2,000 citizens. It is one of the smallest city-states whose deeds entered the historical record, but it may be typical of the majority whose deeds remain unrecorded. Some of them showed a tendency to band together (for these federal states, see Larsen 1968). The most important was Boetia, which, although it comprised 22 poleis, totaled only about 2,500 square kilometers and had about 150,000 people (figures in Ehrenburg 1969: 27–38).

The size of Athenian territory was about the same as that of modern Luxembourg, although its population was only two-thirds the latter's. Sparta's territory equaled Puerto Rico's today, though its population was only a tenth the latter's. In population, these two major powers were a little smaller than Nottingham, England, or Akron, Ohio; but their citizens interacted like the residents of a much smaller country town. The achievements of the polis were those of organizational *intensity*, not extensiveness. They represented a formidable phase of decentralization in human power relations, not only because they were such small political units in relation to the sprawling Middle Eastern empires of domination that preceded them but also because their internal structure presupposed more extensive, decentralized social networks.

True to its name, the polis was a *political* power unit, centralizing and coordinating the acitivites of this small territorial space. As we have seen, it was largely the product of a combination of economic and military power relations. It is not possible to assign relative weights to these two necessary and closely interrelated forces. The polis produced virtually the whole range of concepts with which we still discuss politics in the world today – democracy, aristocracy, oligarchy, tyranny, monarchy, and so forth. All three stages of the polis's development – the hoplite marketplace, literate commercial, naval expansionist – had immense repercussions on the contemporary Middle East and Mediterranean.

The second power network was that of Greek cultural identity and multistate system as a whole, much larger than any single political unit, covering an enormous territorial space (including seas) and comprising perhaps 3 million people. It was a geopolitical, diplomatic, cultural, and linguistic unit with its own infrastructure of power. Its continued significance derived from the unity given by trading and colonizing connections between essentially similar and democratic poleis or egalitarian-federal *ethne*. Thus literacy, diplomacy, trade, and population exchanges could stabilize linguistic similarity into an enduring, shared, and extensive community for the first time in history. Part of this community managed sufficient cohesion to stand defensively firm (with some wavering) against an assault launched by what was seen to be the greatest state in the world, the Persian empire of domination. But it seems never to have aspired to a political unity. War between city-states was not regarded as "civil war." Even the broadest federations were pragmatic diplomatic and military exigencies, not stages on the way to a "nation-state." "Nationality" was always far more partial an attachment than in our modern world (Walbank 1951).

This second network was essentially decentralized and "federal," the product of a geopolitical opportunity for sea-trading peoples to operate in the space between the empires of the Middle East and the peasant farmers of the plowed lands. Like the Phoenician, its federal mechanism included the autonomous naval galley, colonization, coinage, and literacy. But unlike the Phoenician, it was built up from the democratic polis and so became a more penetrating and cohesive form of organization. Its infrastructure was mostly one of *diffused* rather than authoritative power: Its elements spread "universally," at least among citizen bodies, without much authoritative organization (except in periods of some Athenian or Spartan hegemony).

The third network was even more extensive. It was ideological in form, though naturally it had social preconditions. I referred in Chapter 5 to the outward-looking, unbounded element of later Mesopotamian ideology, willing to confer basic humanity and dignity on any upper-class male capable of the cultivated reason of civilization. This may have been general to early civilizations. As we are still saddled with the linguistic baggage of the late-nineteenth-century emphasis on "ethnicity" – and as we also operate too frequently with unitary, bounded models of society – it is difficult to be sure. But, whatever the case with earlier peoples, many Greeks proclaimed the unity of humanity at large and extended it further over class barriers than their predecessors. It was a problem for them, given both the intensity of their struggles with other peoples and the normalcy of slavery. But they recognized the problem openly.

Sophocles' *Tereus* is a play (surviving only in fragments) about conflict with foreigners. In it the chorus of citizens is given an egalitarian, unifying ideology: "There is one human race. A single day brought us all forth from our father and mother. No man is born superior to another. But one man's fare is a doom of unhappy days, another's is success; and on others the yoke of slavery's hardship falls" (quoted in Baldry 1965: 37). The contradiction between the ideal vision and the practical exigencies is fully recognized.

Thucydides tells us that there is a single "nature of man," of which the "Greek" and "barbarian" are only transient variations. Greek self-consciousness was extraordinary – it was one of contradiction. On the one hand, it saw the "unity of mankind" (as in the title of Baldry's book), united by reason, pragmatically regulating the most violent interstate and class struggles. On the other hand, it recognized contradictory practices: the imputation of reason only to free civilized men, that is, not to slaves, the supposedly servile dependents of eastern rulers, women, children, or barbarians. Later a partial solution was found: Being a Greek, a Hellene, was a matter of the cultivation of reason through "education in wisdom and speech," as Isocrates expressed it. After Alexander's conquests this definition was implemented as policy. Greeks and upper-class Persians and others became the cultivated rulers of the Hellenistic world, from which non-Greek natives were excluded. The definition worked as a restrictive ruling-class device for a time. But eventually Greek "humanity at large" emerged transformed in the salvation religions of the Near East, now fused with other forces.

Let me refer back to Chapter 2 and to the major conclusion of prehistoric archaeology: Humanity has continued as one species, its local adaptations resulting not in subspeciation but in global diffusion of culture. In prehistory, processes of diffusion were always much more extensive than was the capacity of any authoritative social organization. It is true that in the historical record we have seen the emergence of caged organized powers of various sorts. Nothing could be more caged than the hoplite citizen. Even if the balance of movement is toward more authoritative, cohesive, bounded societies, all of these have also generated forces that have diffused over wider spaces than they themselves could authoritatively organize. The greater potential unity of humanity compared to the unity of any given society was evident to participants in the history described so far. The Greeks, following but adding to the conceptions of others, gave such potential unity clear ideological expression. It played an important role in the development of their own social forms. It was also to have a significant influence over the novel, universal religions that were soon to spring up with a less practically bounded notion of that unity.

These, then, are the three principal power networks of Greek society. Each was riven and yet also driven by an overt class struggle, which I termed an extensive, largely symmetrical, politicized class struggle – the first such that we can find in history. The dialectic of Greece was in large part – as Marx said it was – a class struggle. But it was also a dialectic between the three networks themselves. Each seems to have been dependent on the existence of the others for its continued viability; and the vitality and dynamism of Greece seem to have required their interaction. Without the outward-looking orientation of the second and third networks, the polis would have remained in its hoplite phase of development – democratic but tightly disciplined, militaristic in spirit, and lacking rational philosophy and science – like Sparta. Without the potentiality for Greek unity, the polis would have fallen to Persia. Without the polis, Greek identity and culture could not have transcended class. Without the outward curiosity and belief in reason, the Greeks would not have borrowed so fruitfully in developing polis and national identity, and their civilization would not have withstood the Macedonian and the Roman conquerors. Without the democratic polis and an identity that transcended locality, confidence in reason would not have been unleashed. Thus the interrelations of the three levels of social organization were extremely complex. I have only sketched their histories – and a more adequate account would require an understanding of all the major city-states, not just of my conventional Sparta-and-Athens presentation.

The complexity and multiplicity of power networks surely make the Greek achievement a "historical accident," not a stage in an evolutionary world history. Although it was certainly built on top of the longer-term development of the Mediterranean world described in the preceding chapter, a number of opportunities fused in this one place in a quite extraordinary way. Nevertheless, one generalization can be made, although it must be restricted to this one case (for the moment). The Greek achievement of freedom and dynamism was precisely *because* the boundaries of these three power networks did not coincide. No set of power relations could establish dominance and stabilize itself. No state could institutionalize past achievements and rest content with them. No single power existed to appropriate innovation to its own private ends. No single class or state could dominate the others. A multi-power-actor civilization proved once again capable of seizing the "leading edge" of power.

Final contradictions and demise

The noncoincidence of power boundaries also contained contradictions, which were eventually to prove Greece's undoing. I sketch this briefly. Continued success, spread unevenly across the city-states, led to hierarchical "class-type" relations among them. As economic and military resources grew, they were increasingly monopolized and covertly centralized by the upper citizen class of the major states. There was eventually no avoiding this, for Greek prosperity in the fifth century B.C. required centralized defense on at least a regional basis against Persia in the East and Carthage in the West. Athens would not relinquish a hegemony so obtained, but it was not strong enough to hold it against the Sparta-led revolt in the Peloponnesian War. In turn, Sparta's victory inaugurated its own short-lived hegemony from 413. Thebes and Athens threw this off in the years following 380. Thereafter, no city-state managed hegemony or the coordination of regional defense.

Now the contradiction became glaring. On the one hand, the city-state's political autonomy and its economy flourished. Ostensibly so too did its ideological life, for the period 430–420 is that of the most famous philosophers, of Socrates, Plato, and Aristotle. But we detect in their writings an upper-class culture that reflected and reinforced a weakening of the traditional democratic cohesion of the polis. On the other hand, the potentialities of military power relations were being stifled by the small city-state. This needs a little more detail. It is important because the demise of ancient Greece took a military form.

The discovery by various foreign powers that Greek hoplites fought well as mercenaries eventually sapped the viability of the traditional citizen militia. Most leading Greek city-states were richer in wealth than in citizen manpower. In the fourth century, the city-state began to recruit mercenary hoplites. By the 360s even Sparta was using mercenaries in the Peloponnese itself. Mercenaries and their commanders were not citizens and had little commitment to the polis. The growth of larger armies in the Persian Wars had also led to the development of more varied forces and fighting methods – hoplites, archers, cavalry, light infantry, siege warfare requiring greater centralized coordination – which again weakened the internal democracy of the polis. The rules of war – originally essential to the polis system – vanished. In the fourth century there were also tactical developments as light infantry was more extensively drilled and equipped with longer swords and spears. These *peltasts* of the northern marches were on occasion ominously capable of cutting even Spartan hoplites to pieces. Naval forces were comparatively unchanged. With the belated emergence of a Spartan navy, there was a fourth-century tripartite naval balance of power among Athens, Sparta, and Persia, which used Phoenician vessels.

But decisive potential change was now on land. The costs of warfare escalated. Small city-states, and even Athens, could not afford it. Nor could they easily manage central coordination of large, varied forces without destroying their own political and class structures. But more extensively organized and authoritarian states could. Increasingly, two types of commander sensed their power – the mercenary general/tyrant and the king of the northern marches able to mobilize "national tribal" forces. The Sicilian general Dionysios was the first prototype, Iason of Thessaly the second. Some members of the upper classes of the city-states began to betray democracy and enter into negotiations. When Philip, king of Macedon, learned how to combine three roles – to coordinate and discipline mercenaries and Macedonians, to turn them into mules but to reward them with booty, and to enter into a pan-Hellenic upper-class alliance – his forward drive fed on its own successes (for a full account, see Ellis 1976). His kingdom began to look more like an empire of domination than a Greek *ethnos*. Pressure on the city-states ended in total victory at Chaeronea in 338. Philip incorporated them into his tame League of Corinth and then marched into Asia. His sudden death, in 336, brought only a brief halt to Macedonian imperialism, for his son was Alexander. The Greek cities were never again wholly autonomous states. For more than a thousand years they were municipalities and clients of empires of domination.

Bibliography

Albright, W. 1946. *From Stone Age to Christianity*. Baltimore: Johns Hopkins University Press.

Anderson, J. K. 1970. *Military Theory and Practice in the Age of Xenophon*. Berkeley: University of California Press.

Aristotle. 1926. *The "Art" of Rhetoric*, ed. J. H. Freese. London: Heinemann.

1948. *Politics*, ed. E. Barker. Oxford: Clarendon Press.

Austin, M. M., and P. Vidal-Naquet. 1977. *Economic and Social History of Ancient Greece: An Introduction*. London: Batsford.

Baldry, H. C. 1965. *The Unity of Mankind in Greek Thought*. Cambridge: Cambridge University Press.

Barker, P. 1979. *Alexander the Great's Campaigns*. Cambridge: Patrick Stephens.

Braudel, F. 1975. *The Mediterranean and the Mediterranean World in the Age of Philip II*. 2 vols. London: Fontana.

Cartledge, P. A. 1977. Hoplites and heroes: Sparta's contribution to the techniques of ancient warfare. *Journal of Hellenic Studies*, 97.

Davies, J. K. 1978. *Democracy and Classical Greece*. London: Fontana.

Dodds, E. R. 1951. *The Greeks and the Irrational*. Berkeley: University of California Press.

Ehrenburg, V. 1969. *The Greek State*. London: Methuen.

Ellis, J. R. 1976. *Philip II and Macedonian Imperialism*. London: Thames & Hudson.

Finley, M. 1960. *Slavery in Classical Antiquity: Views and Controversies*. Cambridge: Heffer.

1978. The fifth-century Athenian empire: a balance sheet. In *Imperialism in the Ancient World*, ed. P. D. A. Garnsey and C. R. Whittaker. Cambridge: Cambridge University Press.

1983. *Politics in the Ancient World*. Cambridge: Cambridge University Press.

Frankenstein, S. 1979. The Phoenicians in the Far West: a function of Neo-Assyrian imperialism. In *Power and Propaganda: A Symposium on Ancient Empires*. ed. M. T. Larsen. Copenhagen: Akademisk Forlag.

Goody, J. 1968. Introduction. In his *Literacy in Traditional Societies*. Cambridge: Cambridge University Press.

Goody, J., and I. Watt. 1968. The Consequences of literacy. In ibid.

Gray, J. 1964. *The Canaanites*. London: Thames & Hudson.

Grierson, P. 1977. *The Origins of Money*. London: Athlone Press.

Hammond, N. G. L. 1975. *The Classical Age of Greece*. London: Weidenfeld & Nicolson.

Harden, D. 1971. *The Phoenicians*. Harmondsworth, England: Penguin Books.

Harvey, F. D. 1965. Two kinds of equality. In *Classica et Mediaevalia*, 26 and 27.

1966. Literacy in the Athenian democracy. *Revue des Etudes Grecques*, 79.

Heichelheim, F. M. 1958. *An Ancient Economic History*. Leiden: Sijthoff.

Herodotus. 1972. *The Histories*, ed. A. R. Burn. Harmondsworth, England: Penguin Books.

Hopper, R. J. 1976. *The Early Greeks*. London: Weidenfeld & Nicolson.

Larsen, J. A. O. 1968. *Greek Federal States*. Oxford: Clarendon Press.

McNeill, W. 1963. *The Rise of the West*. Chicago: University of Chicago Press.

Marx, K. 1973. *The Grundrisse*, ed. M. Nicolaus. Harmondsworth, England: Penguin Books.

Meiggs, R. 1972. *The Athenian Empire*. Oxford: Oxford University Press.

Momigliano, A. 1975. *Alien Wisdom: The Limits of Hellenization*. Cambridge: Cambridge University Press.

Mossé, C. 1962. *La fin de la démocratie athenienne*. Paris: Publications de la Faculté des lettres et Sciences Humaines de Clermont-Ferrand.

Murray, O. 1980. *Early Greece*. London: Fontana.

Pritchett, W. K. 1971. *Ancient Greek Military Practices*. pt. 1. Berkeley: University of California Classical Studies, 7.

Rostovtzeff, M. 1941. *Social and Economic History of the Hellenistic World*. 3 vols. Oxford: Clarendon Press.

Runciman, W. G. 1982. Origins of states: the case of Archaic Greece. *Comparative Studies in Society and History*, 24.

Ste. Croix, G. E. M. de. 1981. *The Class Struggle in the Ancient Greek World*. London: Duckworth.

Salmon, J. 1977. Political hoplites. *Journal of Hellenic Studies*, 97.

Snodgrass, A. M. 1965. The hoplite reform and history. *Journal of Hellenic Studies*, 85.

    1967. *Arms and Armour of the Greeks*. London: Thames & Hudson.

    1971. *The Dark Age of Greece*. Edinburgh: Edinburgh University Press.

Stratton, J. 1980. Writing and the concept of law in ancient Greece. *Visible Language*, 14.

Thucydides. 1910. *The History of the Peloponnesian War*. London: Dent.

Vernant, J.-P., and P. Vidal-Naquet. 1981. *Tragedy and Myth in Ancient Greece*. Brighton: Harvester Press.

Walbank, F. W. 1951. The problem of Greek nationality. *Phoenix*, 5.

    1981. *The Hellenistic World*. London: Fontana.

Warmington, B. H. 1969. *Carthage*. Harmondsworth, England: Penguin Books.

West, M. L. 1971. *Early Greek Philosophy and the Orient*. Oxford: Oxford University Press.

Whittaker, C. R. 1978. Carthaginian imperialism in the 5th and 4th centuries. In *Imperialism in the Ancient World*, ed. P. D. A. Garnsey and C. R. Whittaker. Cambridge: Cambridge University Press.

8   Revitalized empires of domination: Assyria and Persia

Greece was one polar type of reaction to the northern challenges discussed in Chapter 6. The other pole was the revitalized empire of domination. The main empires contemporaneous with the Phoenician and Greek history just covered were Assyria and Persia. My treatment is brief and sometimes uncertain because sources are not nearly as good as they are for Greece. Indeed, much of our knowledge of Persia is gleaned from Greeks' accounts of their great struggle – an obviously biased source.

In Chapter 5, I set out the four main strategies of rule for the ancient empire: to rule through conquered elites; to rule through the army; or to move toward a higher level of power, through a mixture of the "compulsory cooperation" of a militarized economy and the beginnings of a diffused upper-class culture. On the one hand, the coming of the iron plow and the expansion of local trade, coinage, and literacy tended to decentralize the direction of economic development, making compulsory cooperation somewhat less productive and less attractive as a strategy. On the other hand, the growing cosmopolitan character of these processes facilitated the diffusion of broader class-cultural identities that could also be used as an instrument of rule.

The ruling strategies of the two empires differed within these broad bounds and possibilities. By and large, the Assyrians combined ruling through the army and a degree of compulsory cooperation with a diffused upper-class "nationalism" of their own core. The Persians, coming later into a more cosmopolitan arena, combined ruling through conquered elites with a broader, more universalized upper-class culture. The difference is another sign that, whatever their broad similarities, empires of domination nonetheless differed considerably according to both local and world-historical circumstances. Power resources, especially ideological ones, were developing considerably in the first millennium B.C. First Assyria, then Persia, and finally Alexander the Great and his Hellenistic successors were able to extend the infrastructure of imperial and class rule.

Assyria

The Assyrians[1] derived their name from Assur, a city north of Mesopotamia on the Tigris. They spoke a dialect of Akkadian and were strategically placed

---

[1]Main sources: on Old Assyria, Larsen 1976; on the Middle Empire, Goetze 1975, Munn-Rankin 1975, and Wiseman 1975; and mainly on the New Empire, Olmstead

231

on a major trade route between Akkad and Sumer to the south and Anatolia and Syria to the north. It is as traders that we first see them, sending out trading colonies from Assur and establishing in "Old Assyria" the weak, pluralistic, oligarchical form of rule that was probably typical of ancient trading peoples.

The Assyrians owe their fame to a remarkable transformation in their social structure. In the fourteenth century B.C. they embarked on a policy of imperial expansion, and in the Middle Empire (1375–1047) and New Empire (883–608) they became synonymous with militarism. We know little about this transformation, but it involved resistance to Mitannian and Kassite overlords. Later the Assyrians gained control over both extensive rain-watered cornlands and iron-ore deposits. The Assyrian kings found it easy and cheap to equip their troops with iron weapons and to assist the diffusion of iron agricultural tools among their peasantry on the northern Mesopotamian plains. The geopolitical effect of the Iron Age on the Assyrian Empire was very marked. For though the heartland of the empire sat astride the river trade routes, (as had all its predecessors), it derived most of its surplus from lands under rain-watered cultivation and pasturage. The role of the peasant-farmer and peasant-soldier was quite similar to those in Rome later. The core of the Assyrian Empire – and later the Persian Empire in the same area – were corn-growing plains.

Given our own biblical traditions, it hardly needs saying that the Assyrian Empire was militaristic. Assyrian records and sculptures, and the cries of horror and despair recorded by their enemies, testify to that. However, we must distinguish reality from propaganda in their militarism, even though the two were closely connected. Their connection was the logical outcome of attempting to rule largely through the army. I have argued that in empires of domination, the army option consisted in so terrifying enemies by the flourishing, and occasional use, of maximum repression that they would "voluntarily" submit.

But we should believe only a small fraction of Assyrian boasts. This is clear in one area where scholars have sometimes shown credulity – the question of the size of the Assyrian army of the New Empire. Scholars like Manitius and Saggs (1963) have argued as follows: The army was composed of two elements, the levies of provincial governors and a central standing army. A typical single provincial levy consisted of 1,500 cavalry men and 20,000 archers and infantrymen, and there were many such levies (at least 20 in the full empire). The central standing army was sufficiently large to coerce an overambitious provincial governor – therefore, at least twice the size of any of their levies. Thus the total Assyrian army was several hundred thousand,

1923, Driel 1970, Postgate 1974a and b and 1979, and Reade 1972. It is possible in England to get a striking visual sense of Assyrian power and militarism from the magnificent bas-reliefs and inscriptions in the Assyrian galleries of the British Museum.

probably over half a million. This would agree with the Assyrian claims of often inflicting losses of 200,000 slain on their enemies and also taking hundreds of thousands of prisoners.

What this actually agrees with is Assyrian propaganda, not any grasp of logistical realities. How could an army of "hundreds of thousands" even be assembled in one place, let alone pointed at the enemy, in ancient times? How could they be equipped and supplied? How could they be moved together? The answers are: They could not be assembled, pointed, equipped, supplied, or moved. The predecessors of the Assyrians in the area, the Hittites, were well organized for war. At their peak they put into the field 30,000 men, although they sent them to a meeting place in many separate detachments under separate lords. Their successors, the Persians, managed larger numbers (as we shall see) – perhaps concentrations of about 40,000–80,000. In the especially easy supply situation of the invasion of Greece, Persian forces could reach a little higher plus similar naval forces. Even so, only a small part of these forces could engage in a single battle. The later Romans could also field up to about 70,000, though they normally managed less than half this. The Persian and Roman figures are complicated by systems of peasant conscription. Notionally, every Roman citizen could be put under arms, and perhaps also most Persian peasants. This appears to be the only explanation of supposed Assyrian numbers that would have any grounding in reality. Peasant conscription made the theoretical total enormous, and the Assyrian leaders kept up an ideological pretense that universal conscription could be employed.

Why did the claims apparently achieve plausibility? First, no one did actually count such armies, for the simple reason that they assembled only briefly, being normally dispersed in many detachments. Probably the Assyrian king himself had little idea of the total. Second, the enemy mistook mobility for weight of numbers (as happened later with the victims of the Mongols). Two military feats were accomplished by the Assyrians. They introduced heavier, yet faster breeds of horse, which were plundered from the north and east and reared on the rich grazing lands of the plain. Theirs was perhaps the first organized cavalry, as opposed to chariot, force in Near Eastern history. And they introduced a clearer regimental structure, allowing better coordination of infantry, cavalry, and archers (later imitated by the Persians). Their battle line was itself quite loose and mobile: It combined pairs of infantrymen – consisting of an archer protected by an armored, spear-carrying shield bearer – with horsemen, chariots, and slingers. Significantly, Assyrian military propaganda mixed up the notions of speed and mass – and after all, it is their combination, velocity, that matters in battle. The enemy feared surprise attacks by the Assyrians. The inscriptions of Sargon II (722–705 B.C.) also suggest that a new standing army was ready for action all year round. Both would indicate that there must have also been an excellent Assyrian commissariat.

In short, what was logistically possible for the Assyrians was an improvement in organizational detail and cavalry horses, perhaps dependent on the cumulative improvements in agricultural production introduced by the Iron Age. But the overall constraints of empire were still formidable.

If they always behaved as they liked to boast, and as they obviously sometimes did behave, they would not have lasted long. Here is a typical excerpt from the Assyrian royal annals, boasting of what happened to one defeated city-state:

I felled 3,000 of their fighting men with the sword. I carried off prisoners, possessions, oxen [and] cattle from them. I burnt many captives from them. I captured many troops alive: I cut off of some their arms [and] hands; I cut off of others their noses, ears [and] extremities. I gouged out the eyes of many troops. I made one pile of the living [and] one of heads. I hung their heads on trees around the city. I burnt their adolescent boys [and] girls. I razed, destroyed, burnt [and] consumed the city.

On the other hand, the annals say that on some occasions the Assyrians were positively ingratiating toward the Babylonians. They gave them ''food and wine, clothed them in brightly coloured garments and presented them with gifts.'' (Excerpts from the annals are from Grayson 1972, 1976.) They also varied their choice of vassals – sometimes Assyrian governors, sometimes client kings ruling under their suzerainty. If you paid your tribute and acknowledged Assyrian overlordship, leniency would be shown! Under these conditions, Assyrian order and protection were often welcomed by Mesopotamian city dwellers. But if you resisted or rebelled:

As for those men . . . who plotted evil against me, I tore out their tongues and defeated them completely. The others, alive, I smashed with the same statues of protective deities with which they had smashed my own grandfather Sennacherib – now finally as a belated burial sacrifice for his soul. I fed their corpses, cut into small pieces, to the dogs, pigs, zibu-birds, vultures, the birds of the sky and to the fish of the ocean. [quoted in Oates 1979, 123]

So declared King Assurbanipal (668–626 B.C.).

This is the ''army option'' pursued to its most ferocious known limits in our historical traditions. A militarily inventive group was capable of large conquests, of holding down a terrorized population by the threat and occasional use of ruthless militarism. This also extended to a policy that, if not novel (the Hittite state contained numbers of ''deportees''), was considerably extended: the forcible deportation of whole peoples, including, as we know from the Bible, the Ten Tribes of Israel.

Such policies were largely exploitative. But we can also detect compulsory cooperation in Assyrian militarism. When the royal annals finish their boasts of violence, they turn to its claimed benefits. The imposition of military strength, they claim, leads to agricultural prosperity in four ways: (1) the building of ''palaces,'' administrative and military centers (which provide security and ''military Keynesianism''); (2) the provision of plows for the peasantry (apparently state-funded investment); (3) the acquisition of draught horses (useful in both cavalry and agriculture); and (4) the storing of grain reserves. Postgate (1974a, 1980) considers this to have been fact as well as boast: As the Assyrians advanced, they increased the density of population and extended the area of cultivation into hitherto "desert" lands – even the policy of forcible deportation was probably a part of this strategy of colonization. Militaristic order was still useful for the (expanding) surviving population.

But the Assyrians were also inventive in other ways. As I pointed out in Chapter 5, the principal danger in using the army option may not be the obvious one of incurring only hatred from the conquered. It may rather be the difficulty of holding the army together in peaceful political conditions. The Assyrians used the time-honored mechanism, which we loosely call "feudal," of granting conquered lands, people, and offices to their lieutenants and soldiers in return for military service. And they later kept a mobile field army to watch over all. But this surely would be insufficient to prevent the conquerors from "disappearing" into "civil society." Yet the Assyrian conquerors seemingly did not, or at least there were fewer periods of civil war, disputed succession, and internal anarchy than would be customary in an empire of such size and duration.

The reason seems to be a form of "nationalism." Admittedly, the word may be inappropriate. It suggests a cohesive ideology that spreads vertically through all classes of the "nation." We have not the slightest evidence of whether this was so in Assyria. It seems rather unlikely in such a hierarchical society. Greek "nationalism" was dependent on rough equality and a measure of political democracy, which the Assyrians lacked. It seems safer to assert that the Assyrian upper classes – nobility, landowners, merchants, officers – did conceive of themselves as belonging to the same nation. As early as the fourteenth and thirteenth centuries B.C. came an apparent shift toward national consciousness. The standard reference to the "city of Assur" changed to the "land of Assur." I noted already, in Chapter 4, Liverani's (1979) characterization of Assyrian religion in the New Empire as nationalistic because the very word "Assyrian" came to mean "holy." What we mean by Assyrian religion is, of course, the state propaganda that largely survives to us through sculptural inscriptions and the fortunately preserved library of Assurbanipal. Nevertheless, propaganda is aimed to persuade and appeal, in this case to the most important props of rule, the Assyrian upper class and army. *They* seem to have participated in a common ideology, a normative community that diffused universally among the upper classes. Like the Roman elite, they were predominantly absentee landowners, residing in the capital cities, and presumably also like the Romans sharing a close social and cultural life. Their community seems to have ended abruptly at the boundaries of what was called the Assyrian nation, consigning the outer provinces to a clearly subordinate, peripheral status. This was probably the most novel technique of rule, adding to the cohesion of the empire's core. Ideological power as immanent *ruling-*

class morale seems to make its clearest historical entry so far in this narrative.

Nor was a quasi-nationalism unique at this time to the Assyrians. In Chapter 5, I referred to Jacobsen's view of religions of the first millennium B.C. (in the Near East) as being nationalistic. Judaism is an obvious example. Jacobsen argued that this was a response to the dangerous, uncertain, and violent conditions of the time. But the reverse could be argued: Violence might be due to nationalist sentiments. Cutting people's tongues out before beating them to death with their own idols is not an obvious response to conditions of danger! There is something novel to be explained about the spread of nationalism.

But we cannot really explain it with scholarly detail, for there is precious little available. Here is my own speculation. As literacy, local and regional trade, and rudimentary forms of coinage developed, and as agricultural surpluses grew in the heartlands of states, more diffuse, universal sources of social identity grew at the expense of particularistic, local ones. It is not just large empires that can embody such universalism, as Eisenstadt argues (and whose ideas I discussed in Chapter 5). In other conditions, more decentralized forms of universalism may spread. This probably began to occur at the beginning of the first millennium B.C. Wiseman (1975) detects a growing cosmopolitanism in Assyria and Babylon in the period 1200–1000 B.C., a merging of Assyrian, Babylonian, and Hurrian practices. I cannot explain why broader, more diffuse senses of identity should form two distinct levels, that of the syncretic cosmopolitan culture and that of the proto-nation like the Assyrians or the Jews. But both were moves toward more extensive, diffused identities. Once formed, the Assyrians' growing sense of identity is not difficult to explain: It fed off their type of successful militarism, more or less as it did later, and more visibly, among the Romans of the early and mature republic. But they did not go as far as the Romans or the Persians in extending Assyrian "citizenship/national identity" to the ruling classes of conquered peoples.

The Assyrians were extraordinarily successful conquerors, probably by virtue of their exclusive nationalism. But this also proved their undoing. Their resources became stretched by the responsibilities of militaristic rule. The empire collapsed to its Assyrian core in response to the pressure of Semitic peoples from Arabia whom we call the Arameans.

Eventually the New Empire rose up again, at twice the extent of its predecessors. By the time that the New Empire had become institutionalized, around 745 B.C., a significant change had occurred. The simplified script of the Aramaic language (from which Arabic and Hebrew scripts derived) had begun to penetrate the whole empire, suggesting that beneath the military and ideological nationalism of the Assyrians, an interstitial, regional cosmopolitanism was developing rapidly. A great diversity of conquered peoples were sharing some degree of ideological and economic exchange. The policy of mass deportations had encouraged this. The Assyrians had developed a fairly narrow military/political form of power. Their own social structure supported militarism and was transformed in accordance with its needs, so that, for example, military feudalism emerged as a way of rewarding the troops but keeping them as an active reserve force. But for other sources of power they were relatively ill equipped. Their trading interest seems to have declined, for much external trade was left to the Phoenicians and some internal trade was appropriated by Arameans. Literacy could integrate a larger area, but not under their own exclusive control. Their ruthless policies smashed the military/political pretensions of rivals in the area but left several of them with particular and specialized contributions to make to the empire. An emerging cosmopolitanism was the product, though it lurked beneath the Assyrian spears.

Even this ferocious-seeming empire was not unitary. It possessed two distinct levels of interaction that fed each other creatively during Assyria's rise but that turned into opposition or mutual subversion in its decline. It may well be the same type of process as we can observe much more clearly in the later case of Rome, discussed in Chapters 9 and 10. If so, the Assyrians, like the Romans, lost control of the ''civil-society'' forces that they had themselves encouraged. And their initial response would be to tighten their grip rather than to loosen it through further cultural syncretism.

When challenged militarily, Assyria could not absorb and merge. It could fight to the death. Eventually that came, rapidly and apparently unexpectedly. After dealing, supposedly successfully, with Scythian incursions from the north and with internal unrest, Assyria fell to the combined forces of the Medes and the Babylonians between 614 and 608 B.C. Its cities were destroyed in an upsurge of the hatred of the oppressed. Assyria and its people disappear from our records. Uniquely among the major ancient empires, Assyria has been looked back on fondly by no one, even though we detect Assyrian influence over later imperial administrations.

The Persian Empire

For a short time a balance of geopolitical power existed in the Middle East between the two conquering states, Media and Babylon, and Egypt. The Medes were probably similar to the Persians,[2] over whom they at first exercised lordship. Both states were established in the Iranian plateau and adapted the battle techniques of the mounted bowmen of the steppes to the organization of the Assyrians. Herodotus tells us that the king of Media was the first to organize Asiatic armies into separate units of spearmen, archers, and cavalry – a clear imitation of Assyrian organization.

But then a Persian vassal king, Cyrus II, revolted, exploited divisions within

[2]Main sources were Olmstead 1948; Burn 1962; Ghirshman 1964; Frye 1976; Nylander 1979; and Cook 1983.

the Medes, and conquered their kingdom in 550–549. In 547 Cyrus marched westward and conquered King Croesus of Lydia, thus securing the mainland of Asia Minor. Then his generals took one by one the Greek city-states of Asia Minor. In 539 Babylon submitted. The Persian Empire was established, even greater in extent than the New Assyrian Empire and the largest yet seen in the world. At its height it contained both an Indian and an Egyptian satrapy, as well as the whole of the Middle East and Asia Minor. Its east–west breadth exceeded 3,000 kilometers; its north–south breadth, 1,500. It seems to have covered more than 5 million square kilometers, with an estimated population of about 35 million (of whom 6 million to 7 million were contained in the densely populated Egyptian province). It endured generally in peace for 200 years under the Achaemenid dynasty, until overcome by Alexander.

The enormous size and ecological diversity of this empire need stressing. No other ancient empire held on to such ecologically diverse provinces. Plateaus, mountain ranges, jungles, deserts, and irrigation complexes from south Russia to Mesopotamia, and the coasts of the Indian, Arabian, Red, Mediterranean, and Black seas – a remarkable, but also obviously ramshackle, imperial structure. It could not be held together by relatively tight Assyrian, Roman, even Akkadian, methods of rule. Indeed parts were only held very loosely under Persian rule. Many mountainous regions were uncontrollable and even at the points of greatest Persian strength only acknowledged the most general type of suzerainty. Parts of central Asia, south Russia, India, and Arabia were mostly semiautonomous client states rather than imperial provinces. The logistics of any highly centralized form of regime was absolutely insuperable.

Even here, however, the Persians demanded one specific form of submission. There was only one king, the Great King. Unlike the Assyrians, they did not tolerate client kings, only client vassals and dependent governors. In religious terms the Great King was not divine, but he was the Lord's anointed governor on Earth. In Persian tradition this meant the anointed of Ahuramazda, and it seems to have been a condition of religious toleration that other religions anoint him as well. So Persian claims at the top were unequivocal and formally accepted as such.

Lower down in the political structure, we can also see a claim to a universal imperium, even if the infrastructure could not always support it. The satrap system reminds me of the Inca decimal system, a clear statement that this empire is intended as one, centered on its ruler. The whole empire was divided by Cyrus's son-in-law Darius (521–486 B.C.) into twenty satraps, each a microcosm of the king's administration. Each combined civil with military authority, raised tribute and military levies, and was responsible for justice and security. Each had a chancery, staffed by Aramaic, Elamite, and Babylonian scribes under Persian direction. Treasuries and manufacturing departments existed alongside. The chancery maintained correspondence upward with the king's court and downward with the province's local authorities.

Moreover, a quite consistent attempt was made to provide an imperial infra-structure by adapting whatever lay around within the cosmopolitan empire.

Like the Assyrians, the Persians had established an initial military suprem-acy. Their own cultural and political traditions seem to have been weak. Even their military structures were fluid and their victories, though spectacular, seem to have been based less on overwhelming force or military technique than an opportunism and an unusually developed ability to divide their ene-mies. Their lack of tradition and their opportunism was in this context their strength. Their subsequent achievement was to sit loosely on top of the grow-ing cosmopolitanism of the Middle East, respecting the traditions of their conquered peoples and taking from them whatever seemed useful. Their own art shows foreigners within the empire as free dignified men, able to bear arms in the presence of the Great King.

The foreigners themselves confirm the impression. Thankfulness toward their conquerors for the leniency of rule is unmistakable. I have already quoted Herodotus in Chapter 7. The Babylonian chronicle tells us, "In the month of Arahshamnu, the third day, Cyrus entered Babylon, green twigs were spread in front of him – the state of Peace was imposed upon the city. Cyrus sent greetings to all Babylon" (quoted in Pritchard 1955: 306). The Jews were favored as a counterweight to Babylon and restored to their home in Israel. The form of Cyrus's edict, preserved by Ezra, is of special significance:

Thus saith Cyrus king of Persia, The Lord God of heaven hath given me all the king-doms of the earth; and he hath charged me to build him an house at Jerusalem, which is in Judah. Who is there among you of all his people? his God be with him, and let him go to Jerusalem, which is in Judah and build the house of the Lord God of Israel, (he is the God) which is in Jerusalem. [Ezra 1:2–4]

Cyrus was willing to defer to the God of the Jews for political reasons, as he was all gods. In return the Jews would regard him as "the Lord's anointed" (Isaiah 45:1).

Toleration and opportunism are both apparent in a basic infrastructure of communications, literacy. Persian official inscriptions generally conveyed power claims to the various elite classes of the empire. They were written in three different cuneiform scripts, Elamite (the language centered on Susa), Akka-dian (the language and official script of Babylon and some Assyrians), and a simplified Old Persian invented in Darius's reign. They also added Egyptian, Aramaic, and probably Greek where appropriate. But for official correspon-dence greater flexibility was required, and this was generally provided by Aramaic. This language became the lingua franca of the empire and of the Near East in general right down to the preachings of Jesus. It was used, but not controlled, by the Persians. It was not *their* universalism.

Borrowing was evident everywhere in the infrastructure. The coinage, the gold daric, depicting a crowned, running archer (Darius himself), linked the state to the trading networks of Asia Minor and Greece and was probably borrowed from their models. Royal roads were built on the Assyrian pattern and dotted with an improved staging-post system (which went back to Akkadian times), supplying communications, a means of surveillance, and an influx of strangers as well. Persian cavalry and infantry with spear and bow was coordinated with Greek mercenary hoplites; the Phoenician navy was added to the army.

The Persians' tolerance was not limitless. They had a definite preference for local power structures that had the same form as their own. Thus they were uneasy with the Greek polis and encouraged rule there by client tyrants. The staffing of the satraps was itself a compromise. In some areas Persian nobles were appointed as satraps; in others the local rulers simply acquired a new title. Once in place they were their own masters – if they provided tribute, military levies, order, and respect for imperial forms. This meant that in provinces with well-entrenched administrations, like Egypt or Mesopotamia, the satrap, even if Persian, would rule more or less as the local elites had previously ruled. And in backward areas he would negotiate with his inferiors – sheikhs, tribal lords, village headmen – in a highly particularistic way.

In all these ways the Persian Empire conforms to comparative sociology's ideal type of the imperial or patrimonial regime discussed in Chapter 5. Its center was despotic, with strong universal pretensions; but its infrastructural power was feeble. The contrast comes out clearly through the Greek sources. They dilate at length, appalled yet fascinated, at the rituals of prostration before the king, at the splendor of his costume and surroundings, at the distance he kept from his subjects. At the same time their accounts show that what happened at court was usually far removed from what happened at the provincial roadside. Xenophon's account of the march of the ten thousand Greek mercenaries from Asia back home mentions areas where the local inhabitants are only dimly aware of the existence of a Persian Empire.

On the other hand, this is not the whole story. The empire did endure, even after the Great King was humiliated militarily, as Darius was by the Scythians, and as Xerxes was by the Greeks. Like the Assyrians, the Persians added to the power resources of Empire. Like them the crucial innovation appears to have been in the sphere of ideological power as a form of ruling-class morale. But they developed more of an "international" upper-class ideology than a nationally bounded one. The Persians extended greatly Assyrian forms of education for the children of conquered and allied elites as well as their own noble class. The Persian tradition was that boys (we know little of girls) were taken from the harem at the age of five. Until the age of twenty they were brought up at the royal court or at a satrap's court. They were schooled in Persian history, religion, and traditions, though entirely orally. Even Darius could not read or write, so he proclaimed. Older boys attended court and listened to judicial cases. They learned music and other arts. And great emphasis was placed on physical and military training. Education tended to universalize this class, made it genuinely extensive, and politicized it over the whole empire. The encouragement of intermarriage among the formerly disparate nobilities and the granting of fiefs to people well away from their homelands also reinforced extensive class identity against local particularism. The empire was Persian-led in its highest offices and in its culture, and it always depended on its Persian core; and there were obviously many localities whose traditions were too resilient for incorporation. But what kept the empire one through dynastic intrigues, disputed successions, foreign disasters, and immense regional diversity seems to have been primarily the syncretic, ideological solidarity of its noble ruling class. Universalism had a double center, the Great King and his nobles. Though they squabbled and fought one another, they remained loyal against any potential threat from below or outside, until someone else appeared who could provide more support to their class rule. That was Alexander. Again the process is a dialectical one. Each of these (relatively successful) empires possessed *more* power resources than its predecessors; and it generally acquired them out of the causes of its predecessor's collapse.

There is one other important aspect of Persian ideology. Unfortunately, this is an area of uncertainty for us. It is the religion of Zoroaster. We would dearly like to date the origins and development of Zoroaster, but we cannot. He had a royal patron, perhaps the Persian Teipses (ca. 675–640 B.C.), perhaps an earlier ruler. Probably in a predominantly pastoral setting (the name Zoroaster means "the man of the old camels," as his father's name means "the man of the grey horses"), he began preaching and writing about his religious experiences. They centered on divine revelation, conversations with "the lord who knows," Ahuramazda, who instructed Zoroaster to carry his truth to the world. Among these truths were the following:

The two primal Spirits who revealed themselves in vision as Twins are the Better and the Bad in thought and word and action. And between these two the wise once chose aright, the foolish not so. [and] I will speak of that which the Holiest declared to me as the word that is best for mortals to obey. . . . They who at my bidding render him [i.e., Zoroaster] obedience shall all attain unto Welfare and Immortality by the actions of the Good Spirit. [from the Gathas, Yasna 30 and 45: text quoted in full in Moulton 1913]

In these simple doctrines we have the core of the salvation religions, and of the contradiction they express, over the next 2,000 years. One God, ruler of the universe, embodies rationality, which all human beings have the capacity to discover. They have the power to choose light or darkness. If they choose light they achieve immortality and relief from suffering. We may interpret it as, potentially, a universal, ethical, radically egalitarian doctrine. It seems to cut across all horizontal and vertical divisions; it seems available to all political states and classes. It does not depend on skilled performance of ritual. On the other hand, it embodies authority, that of the prophet Zoroaster, to whom the truth has been first revealed and whose rationality is elevated above that of the common run of mortals.

Such a dual doctrine was not unique in the first millennium B.C. The religion of the Israelite tribes had been undergoing a slow transformation along monotheistic lines. Jehovah became the sole God, and being opposed to competing fertility cults, he became a relatively abstract universal God, the God of truth. Though the Israelites were a favored people, he was God of all peoples without particular relevance to their specifically agrarian way of life. And directly accessible to all people, he nevertheless communicated especially through prophets. The similarity of doctrine with Zoroastrianism goes into specifics (e.g., belief in angels), and it is probable that the Persian religion influenced the development of Judaism. After all, the Persians had restored the Jews to Jerusalem and Israel long continued as a client state. Perhaps there were other monotheist, potentially universal and salvation religions spreading throughout the immense ordered space of the Persian Empire. But doctrine is easier to perceive than either practice or influence. The religion of Zoroaster is especially puzzling. Was it actually transmitted by a mediating (a pun is intended) priesthood, the mysterious Magi? The Magi existed, may have been of Median origin, and seem to have been ritual experts. But they do not seem to have possessed a religious monopoly, and still less were they a caste, unlike their Indian counterparts, the Brahmins. Their distinct status, whether as priests or tribe, may have been in decline during the period of Persian greatness. Was it a popular religion, or, more probably, a religion of the nobility? Was there a growth, or alternatively a decline, in monotheism? How much did Darius and his successors use it as a prop to their rule? Its usefulness to the king is obvious. Both Darius and Xerxes defined their principal enemy as the Lie, also the enemy of Ahuramazda. It seems most plausible that Zoroastrianism represented possibilities for a truly universal religion of salvation, but that it was appropriated in practice by the Great King and diffused among his nobility as an ideological justification, and also as a genuine intellectual and moral explanation, of their joint rule. But it was not the only type of such ideology. And the doctrines it contained were capable of further diffusion across class and state boundaries.

The acid test of Persian power, and the area of greatest documentation, came in the two major confrontations with the Greeks. We can begin with the Greek evaluation of the Persians' military strength in the first confrontation, Xerxes' invasion of Greece in 480 B.C. Of course the Greeks liked to exaggerate wildly the numbers of their main enemies. It has been suggested (e.g., by Hignett 1963) that this was partly based on their misunderstanding the size of the basic Persian unit in calculating their forces. If we reduce by a factor of ten, it is said, we get close to the truth. How do we establish the truth, however, if we have to reject the sources?

One way is to examine the logistical constraints of distance and water supplies. For example, General Sir Frederick Maurice went over a large part of the route of Xerxes' invasion and calculated the extent of water supplies available in the rivers and springs of the region. He concluded that the maximum figure supportable would be 200,000 men plus 75,000 beasts (Maurice 1930). Staggering ingenuity, of course, but still only a theoretical maximum! Actually, other supply constraints would not necessarily reduce this figure greatly because of the ease of supply by sea along the whole invasion route. Herodotus gives an account of four years of preparation and collection of stores along the route in ports held by local client rulers. There seems no reason to disbelieve him, and so the supplies, and therefore the forces, must have been "very large." Some authorities therefore suggest that the Persians crossed between 100,000 and 200,000 personnel over the Hellespont – though only some of these would be combatants. We should add Persian naval forces. There is less controversy over their size, up to 600 ships and up to 100,000 shipboard personnel. Because it was a combined land and sea operation in the easiest possible supply conditions, it could have been larger than any seen hitherto or any that the Persians could have mobilized for action in their territorial heartland.

However, the number who could be put into battle at one time was less. Later Hellenistic armies recruited from the same domains did not exceed 80,000 actual combatants. Thus a majority of analyses today end up with an army in battle of 50,000–80,000 combatants and similar naval forces (see Burn 1962: 326–32; Hignett 1963; and Robertson 1976). From a Greek point of view this still means "enormous," for they could muster only a 26,000-man army plus a fleet rather smaller than the Persian. The power of Persia and the odds against the Greeks were still immense.

But the Persians lost, both against the Greek city-states and later against Alexander. The first defeat was unexpected; and the conflict, closely fought. It might have easily gone the other way and so changed the course of (our) history. But there were deep-seated Persian weaknesses. The defeats reveal much about the current state of social organization. There seem to have been three main reasons, of which two appeared directly on the battlefield, while the third lay rather deeper in Persian social organization.

The first and main reason for defeat was the Persian inability to concentrate fighting power as much as the Greeks. Concentration is, of course, the core means of military power. At Thermopylae they outnumbered the Greeks several times over. At Platae and Marathon they outnumbered them by about 2 to 1. Later, Alexander could put at most about 40,000 men into a battle and was also outnumbered by almost 2 to 1. But the Persians were never able to deploy all their troops at once. Even if they had, they could not have equaled the concentration of fighting power of the charging hoplite phalanx. The Greeks were aware of their superiority, and they tried to deploy it in relatively enclosed terrain – the pass at Thermopylae being perfect in this respect. They attributed it partly to their heavier armor and weaponry and partly to the source of their discipline and obedience, the commitment of free men to their city-state. The famous inscribed epitaph at Thermopylae sums up their sense of the contrast with Persians, driven into battle (so the Greeks claim) with whips. The 300 Lacedaemonians (i.e., the Spartans) had been ordered to hold the pass. They did until they were all dead:

> Tell them in Lacedaemon, passer-by,
> Obedient to their orders, here we lie.

A second Persian weakness was naval. They used the fleets of confederate allies, the Phoenicians and the Greek city-states of Asia Minor, which fought with varying degrees of commitment to their cause. The naval forces seem to have been of roughly equal strength – Persian superiority in numbers offset by having to operate far from their home bases. The core of the empire was virtually landlocked. As the Persians themselves did not take to the sea, they were not exploiting to the full the westward expansion of the ancient economy.

Both land and sea weakness in battle indicate the third and decisive weakness of Persia. The empire was appropriate to the Near Eastern landmass: It was a sprawling confederation of client rulers and states, held under the hegomonic domination of the Persian and Median core and some aristocratic offshoots. The noble class was sufficiently cohesive to rule this extensive empire. But to fight in as tight a military and moral formation as the Greeks did was an unexpected demand, which proved just beyond them. Of the allies, the Phoenicians were loyal because their own survival as a power depended on defeating Greece. But some of the others preferred to side with whoever looked like winning. Nor was the Persian core as tightly integrated as the Greek. The satraps were partly independent rulers, in command of troops, capable of imperial ambitions and revolt. Cyrus himself had come to power in this manner; his successor Cambyses killed his brother in ascending to the throne, and when he died was facing a serious revolt instigated by a rival pretending to be his brother; Darius put down the revolt and suppressed another revolt from the Greek city-states of Asia Minor; Xerxes put down uprisings in Babylonia and Egypt, and on his expulsion from Greece, faced numerous revolts. Thereafter, as Persian power contracted, the civil wars grew more frequent (with Greeks as the key soldiers on both sides).

These problems had military repercussions on campaigns fought against the Greeks. We know that the Great King preferred to keep down the number of his satraps' troops. He possessed 10,000 Persian infantry, the Immortals, and 10,000 Persian cavalry. He did not generally allow a satrap more than 1,000 native Persian troops. Thus the large army had a relatively small professional core, the rest being made up of levies of all the peoples of the empire. The Greeks were aware of this, at least afterward. They realized that their defense had involved two stages. They had first checked the enemy so severely that the Persian confederates had begun to doubt the invincibility of their leader.

This weakening of their commitment forced the king to employ his Persian core troops, who seem to have done virtually all the hard fighting at the major battles. Although the Persians fought bravely and persistently, they were not quite a match in a confined space and at close quarters for an equal number of hoplites (though hoplites were later to need cavalry and archer support in the open terrain of the Persian homelands).

In fact the Great King's army seems to have had a *political* purpose quite as much as a military one. It was an astonishingly varied force, containing detachments from the whole empire and so fairly unmanageable as a single array. But assembling it was an impressive way of mobilizing his own domination over his satraps and allies. When he reviewed his army, the numbers and the sheer spectacle impressed the whole contemporary consciousness. Herodotus tells the story of how the army was counted by herding detachments into a space known to be capable of holding 10,000 men. We can choose to believe this or not (even if we decimate the figure). But the purpose of the story is to express amazement that a ruler should have even more power than he himself had known or than anyone could count. As I indicated in the case of Assyria, this was commoner than the Greeks knew. The logistical tentacles of this array must have spread through every town and village of the empire. Few could be unaware of the Great King's power. The mobilization gave him more power over his satraps, allies, and peoples than peacetime could give. Unfortunately for him, he came to use it against the Greeks in their homeland, an enemy of unsuspected, concentrated resources. The demonstration of power backfired and fueled revolts.

The problem for the Great King was that much of the infrastructure of satrapy could easily *de*centralize rule. Literacy was now out of the control of the state. Coinage implied a dual power structure, shared by the state and local wealth holders. Indeed in Persia, this duality had peculiar characteristics. Coinage seems to have been introduced basically as a means of organizing provisions for the troops. As this organization was partly the responsibility of the king and his direct lieutenants and partly that of the satraps, there was a problem. Who was to issue coins? In fact silver and copper coins were issued by them both, but the gold daric was the king's monopoly. When occasionally satraps issued gold coin, this was treated as a declaration of rebellion (Frye 1976: 123). Coinage could also decentralize power still further, when used for general trade. In Persia internal and external trade were largely under the control of three foreign peoples. Two of these peoples, the Arameans and the Phoenicians, were under the formal control of the empire, but both retained a large degree of autonomy – as we have seen, the Persians merely used the existing structure of the Aramean language and the Phoenician navy. The homeland of the third trading people, the Greeks, was politically autonomous. They also provided the core of later Persian armies. As I noted earlier, the hoplite phalanx did not necessarily reinforce the authority of a very great power – its optimum size being below 10,000 men. Even Zoroastrianism may have been double-edged. Though it was used to bolster the authority of the Great King, it also bolstered the rational self-confidence of the individual believers whose core seem to have been the Persian upper class as a whole. Roads, the "eyes of the king" (the king's spies), and even the cultural solidarity of the aristocracy could not produce the concentrated integration necessary against the Greeks. The *virtue* of Persian rule was that it was looser, that it could take advantage of decentralizing, cosmopolitan forces beginning to operate in the Middle East. Even before Alexander arrived, Persia was succumbing to these forces. But now political disorder at the center did not necessarily lead to the collapse of social order as a whole. Sargon and compulsory cooperation were no longer needed.

Neither the Greeks, nor the Romans, nor their Western successors appreciated this. The Greeks could not understand what they took to be the abjectness, servility, love of despotism, and fear of freedom of the eastern peoples. That caricature is grounded in one empirical fact: the respect shown by many Middle Eastern peoples toward despotic monarchy. But as we have seen with respect to Persia, despotism was constitutional rather than real. The infrastructural power of such despotisms was considerably less than that of a Greek polis. Their capacity to mobilize and coordinate commitments from their subjects were low. Though vastly larger in extensive power, they were notably inferior in intensive power. The Persian subject could hide much more effectively from his/her state than could the Greek citizen from his state. In some senses the Persian was "freer."

Freedom is not indivisible. In our own era there have been two main conceptions of freedom, the liberal and the socialist-conservative. The liberal ideal is of freedom *from* the state, privacy from its gaze and powers. The joint ideal of conservatives and socialists holds that freedom is only attainable *through* the state, through participation in its life. Both conceptions contain obvious merit. If, for effect, we stretch these categories back into ancient history, we find that the Greek polis typified well the conservative-socialist ideal, and that, surprisingly, Persia corresponded to some degree to the liberal ideal. The latter analogy is only partial, for whereas modern liberal freedoms are (paradoxically) guaranteed constitutionally by the state, Persian freedoms were unconstitutional and surreptitious. They were also longer-lived. Greece succumbed to successive conquerors, to the Macedonians and the Romans. Persia succumbed only nominally to Alexander.

Its conqueror was the violent, drunken, emotionally unstable Alexander, whom we also, justly, call The Great. With a mixed force of Macedonian and Greek soldiers, perhaps 48,000 strong, he crossed the Hellespont in 334 B.C. In eight years he conquered the whole of the Persian Empire and a little bit of India too. Behaving like a Persian king, he suppressed Greek and Macedonian protests at his assumption of eastern titles; gave Persians, Macedonians, and

Greeks equal rights; and reestablished the satrap system. By these means he secured the loyalty of the Persian nobility. But he added tighter Macedonian organization to this: the smaller, more disciplined, and methodical army; a unified fiscal system and monetary economy based on the Attican silver coin; and the Greek language. The union of Greece and Persia was symbolized by the mass wedding ceremony when Alexander and 10,000 of his troops took Persian wives.

Alexander died after a drinking bout in 323 at Babylon. His death soon revealed that Persian currents were still running. His conquering thrust had not been toward greater imperial centralization but toward cosmopolitan decentralization. No imperial succession had been arranged, and his lieutenants converted their satraps into numerous independent eastern-style monarchies. In 281, after many wars, three monarchies were secured: in Macedonia under the Antigonid dynasty, in Asia Minor under the Seleucids, and in Egypt under the Ptolemies. They were loose Persian-style states, though the Greek rulers steadily extruded Persian and other elites from positions of independent power within the state (see Walbank 1981). True, they were Hellenistic states, Greek-speaking and Greek in education and culture. But Hellas had changed. Outside Greece itself – and even to a degree within it – cultivated reason, the essential part of being fully "human," was now officially confined to the ruling class. If anything, Greek conquest meant intensifying the traditionally Persian basis of rule, the ideological morale of the ruling class. Persia without Persians, Greeks without Greece – but their fusion created a more cohesive, diffused ruling-class basis for rule than the Near East (or indeed anywhere outside China, where similar processes were occurring) had yet experienced.

Nevertheless, the limited powers of these states meant that other, more subterranean, currents were running. The states existed in a larger, partly pacified economic and cultural space. Their internal powers of intensive mobilization were also limited in fact if not in theory. Except for the still uniquely concentrated case of Egypt, they were federal, containing numerous hiding places and opportunities for unofficial cosmopolitan linkages in which more "democratic" Greek traditions played an important role. From them, and from their successor provinces of the Roman Empire, came many of those decentralized forces to be described in Chapters 10 and 11, and the salvation religions.

The fact that Near Eastern empires were now Greek shifted westward the center of geopolitical power. But on its own western fringes the Greek world encountered different forces. What I described as traditional Greek "conservative-socialist" notions of freedom could spread more easily among peasant cultivators and traders with iron tools and weapons. Greek developments and contradictions were replayed in different forms and with a different outcome on the Italian peninsula. The result was the Roman Empire – the most developed example of Spencer's compulsory cooperation ever seen under preindustrial conditions, the conqueror and yet also the absorber of Hellenism, and the first to become a territorial empire rather than an empire of domination.

Bibliography

Burn, A. R. 1962. *Persia and the Greeks*. London: Arnold.

Cook, J. M. 1983. *The Persian Empire*. London: Dent.

Driel, G. van. 1970. Land and people in Assyria. *Bibliotecha Orientalis*, 27.

Frye, R. N. 1976. *The Heritage of Persia*. London: Weidenfeld & Nicolson.

Ghirshman, R. 1964. *Persia from the Origins to Alexander the Great*. London: Thames & Hudson.

Goetze, A. 1975. Anatolia from Shuppiluliumash to the Egyptian War of Murvatallish; and The Hittites and Syria (1300–1200 B.C.). Chap. 21 and 24 in *The Cambridge Ancient History*, ed. I. E S. Edwards et al. 3d ed. Vol. II, pt. 2. Cambridge: Cambridge University Press.

Grayson, A. K. 1972 1976. *Assyrian Royal Inscriptions*. 2 vols. Wiesbaden: Harrassowitz.

Hignett, C. 1963. *Xerxes' Invasion of Greece*. Oxford: Clarendon Press.

Larsen, M. T. 1976. *The Old Assyrian City-State and Its Colonies*. Copenhagen: Akademisk Forlag.

Liverani, M. 1979. The ideology of the Assyrian Empire. In *Power and Propaganda: A Symposium on Ancient Empires*, ed. M. T. Larsen. Copenhagen: Akademisk Forlag.

Maurice, F. 1930. The size of the army of Xerxes. *Journal of Hellenic Studies*, 50.

Moulton, J. H. 1913. *Early Zoroastrianism*. London: Williams and Norgate.

Munn-Rankin, J. M. 1975. Assyrian Military Power 1300–1200 B.C. Chap. 25 in *The Cambridge Ancient History*, ed. I. E. S. Edwards et al. 3d ed. Vol. II, pt. 2. Cambridge: Cambridge University Press.

Nylander, C. 1979. Achaemenid Imperial Art. In Larsen, *Power and Propaganda: A Symposium on Ancient Empires*, ed. M. T. Larsen. Copenhagen: Akademisk Forlag.

Oates, J. 1979. *Babylon*. London: Thames & Hudson.

Olmstead, A. T. 1923. *A History of Assyria*. New York: Scribner.

  1948. *A History of the Persian Empire*. Chicago: University of Chicago Press.

Postgate, J. N. 1974a. Some remarks on conditions in the Assyrian countryside. *Journal of the Economic and Social History of the Orient*, 17.

  1974b. *Taxation and Conscription in the Assyrian Empire*. Rome: Biblical Institute Press.

  1979. The economic structure of the Assyrian Empire. In *Power and Propaganda: A Symposium on Ancient Empires*, ed. M. T. Larsen. Copenhagen: Akademisk Forlag.

  1980. The Assyrian Empire. In *The Cambridge Encyclopedia of Archaeology*, ed. A. Sherratt. Cambridge: Cambridge University Press.

Pritchard, J. B. 1955. *Ancient Near Eastern Texts Relating to the Old Testament*. Princeton, N.J.: Princeton University Press.

Reade, J. E. 1972. The Neo-Assyrian court and army: evidence from the sculptures. *Iraq*, 34.

Robertson, N. 1976. The Thessalian expedition of 480 B.C. *Journal of Hellenic Studies*, 96.

Saggs, H. W. 1963. Assyrian warfare in the Sargonic Period. *Iraq, 25.*

Walbank, F. W. 1981. *The Hellenistic World.* London: Fontana.

Wiseman, D. J. 1975. Assyria and Babylonia – 1200–1000 B.C. Chap. 31 in *The Cambridge Ancient History,* ed. I. E. S. Edwards et al. 3d ed. Vol. II, pt. 2. Cambridge: Cambridge University Press.

Zaehner, R. C. 1961. *The Dawn and Twilight of Zoroastrianism.* London: Weidenfeld & Nicolson.

9 The Roman territorial empire

The history of Rome is the most fascinating historical laboratory available to sociologists. It provides a 700-year stretch of written records and archaeological remains. They show a society with recognizably the same core identity over that period of time, yet adapting continuously to the forces created by its own, and its neighbors', actions. Many of the processes observed in the course of this chapter were probably also present in several earlier societies. Now, for the first time, we can clearly trace their development.

The interest of Rome lies in its imperialism. It was one of the most successful conquering states in all history, but it was *the* most successful *retainer* of conquests. Rome institutionalized the rule of its legions more stably and over a longer period than any other society before or since. I will argue that this empire of domination eventually became a true *territorial* empire, or at least had about as high a level and intensity of territorial control as could be attained within the logistical constraints imposed on all agrarian societies. Its power had a fundamentally twofold base, refining and extending the two principal thrusts of power development of earlier empires. First it developed a form of the *organized power* of compulsory cooperation, to which I will apply the label of the *legionary economy*. Second it developed the *authoritative power* of class culture to the point where all conquered elites could be absorbed into the Roman ruling class. The first was the major hierarchical, distributive form of Roman power; the second, the major horizontal, collective form. Through their conjunction, what Rome acquired, Rome kept. So the principal task of this chapter is to explain the rise and fall of this novel form of social power.

The origins of Roman power

The Greeks, Phoenicians, and Carthaginians had helped move westward the marcher regions between Iron Age plowers and the civilizations of the eastern Mediterranean.[1] The cross-fertilization occurred anew in the central and northern Mediterranean. On the western coast of Italy the principal carriers were the Etruscans, probably maritime immigrants from the Balkans and Asia Minor fused with local natives. By about 600 B.C. their cultural influence on their

---

[1]General sources used were Scullard 1961; Gelzer 1969; Brunt 1971a and b; Bruen 1974; Gabba 1976; Ogilvie 1976; Crawford 1978; and the documents assembled by Jones 1970: vol. 1.

neighbors was changing hill villages into small city-states. One of these was Rome. Thus two differences separated Greece from Italy: The latter benefited early from the diffused innovations of the civilized trading peoples – literacy, coinage, the hoplite, the city-state. And Italy felt the actual and dominating pressure of these peoples, controlling the seas. Italic peoples were largely denied access to naval power, major sea trade, and migration by sea. The first extant document from Rome, reproduced by Polybius, is a treaty of 508–507 B.C. with Carthage. This confirmed Carthaginian trading monopoly in the western Mediterranean in return for a guarantee of Roman territorial hegemony in its area. Land and sea were kept apart. Eastern influences on Rome, or on any other Latin people, would be applied to a different project, the development of power on land.

We have no real idea why Rome rather than some other city-state of Italy achieved hegemony – or why the Etruscans failed to maintain their regional dominance. All that is discernible is the suitability of certain Roman arrangements after regional hegemony was largely complete. What was useful for the military part of Rome's rise was a looser type of hoplite army with cavalry support in relatively open terrain. The Etruscans were copying hoplite forms from 650 B.C., and the Romans copied them. The reforms of King Servius Tullius (probably around 550 B.C.) integrated heavy infantry and cavalry. His infantry legion, perhaps 3,000–4,000 strong, organized into independent centuries with shield and long spear, was accompanied by 200 or 300 cavalry plus auxiliary detachments.

The legion emerged among peasant farmers, who were less politically concentrated and less egalitarian than in the Greek polis. Rome probably mixed stronger tribal organization with that of the city-state. Three "dualisms" survived in later Roman society. First, the "private" patriarchal household continued to play a strong role alongside the sphere of the public polity: the distinction between the *res publica* (the state) and the *res privata* (private matters). Each sphere later developed its own law, civil and private law. Private law applied to legal relations between families. Second, alongside official relations of citizenship and its division into orders and "classes," there survived strong clientelism, political factions, and cliques. It is plausible to trace these back to clan and quasi-tribal alliances. Third, there was a duality in the official political structure between the senate, probably originating in the role of clan and tribal elders, and the people – summarized by the famous motto of Rome, SPQR, *Senatus Populusque Romanus* (The Senate and the people of Rome). These distinctively Roman dualisms of tribe and city-state suggest the modification of a Greek federation of intense poleis according to the exigencies of expansion on land.

Official political structure had two main elements. The first was the dualism of the Senate versus the popular assemblies. This was the origin of the "orders," senatorial and equestrian, as well as of the political factions, the Popular and the Best (i.e., oligarchical), which were important in the late republic. This coexisted with a second hierarchy, of *class* in its Latin sense.

Our word "class" is derived from the Roman *classis,* a gradation of obligation for military service according to wealth. The later Romans ascribed it to Servius Tullius. At that time the measure of wealth would have been in cattle and sheep. The oldest form transmitted to us by Livy and Cicero is fourth-century. It measured wealth by a weight of bronze. The richest class (eventually the equestrian order) provided 18 centuries (each century comprised 100 men) of cavalry; the next class, 80 centuries of hoplites; the next, 20 centuries of infantry without coats of mail or shields; the next, 20 centuries without greaves; the next, 20 centuries equipped only with spear and javelin; the next, 30 centuries carrying slings. These were called the *assidui,* because they provided financial assistance to the state. Below them were the *proletarii,* able to provide only children *(proles)* to the state and forming one nominal century without military-service obligation. Each century had equal voting rights in the principal popular assembly, the *comitia centuriata.* The system gave property weighting to citizenship but deprived no males, not even proletarians, of the vote. From the beginning, collective organization mixed together both economic and military relations.

It was also a true "class" system in the sociological sense (discussed in Chapter 7). The classes were *extensively* organized over the state as a whole, and they were *symmetrical* in this respect, although clientelism introduced "horizontal" organizations that weakened vertical class struggle. But, as in Greece, the substantial input of military/political forces made it different from modern class systems. Roman success was based on fusing military and economic organization into the state, linking stratification and citizenship to the necessities of land warfare.

Roman militarism combined two elements that (until the Greek hoplites) had been antagonistic in ancient societies: a shared sense of "ethnic community" and social stratification. The fusion was also full of creative tension. It encouraged two contradictory social trends. Contrary to the Greek case, where cavalry were superseded by heavy infantry, in Rome there was simultaneous development of heavy cavalry and heavy infantry. The lower classes' light-infantry role was given to auxiliaries from allied peoples. They themselves became heavily armored hoplites, but with their equipment provided by the state rather than themselves. But class struggle preserved some of the social base of both heavy infantry and cavalry. The patricians were forced to admit wealthy plebs (commoners), thus revitalizing themselves. Meanwhile, the peasant proprietors in 494 went on the first of perhaps five military strikes, refusing to do military service until they were allowed to elect their own tribunes of the people, to intercede between them and the patrician magistrates. The first major strike of recorded history was a success. Class struggles contributed much to the military effectiveness of the Roman Republic.

The combination of tribal and city-state forms, and citizen equality and stratification, also enabled the Romans to deal flexibly and constructively with conquered and client peoples in Italy. Some were given citizenship except for voting rights (which, however, they could enjoy if they migrated to Rome); others were treated as autonomous allies. The main aim was to dismantle potentially hostile leagues of states. Each state preserved its own class system which detracted from its desire to organize against Rome on a popular "national" basis. The federated allies were important right through the Punic Wars, contributing large numbers of auxiliary troops instead of tax or tribute. Rome was still a (small) empire of domination, not a territorial empire, dominating through allies and client states and lacking direct territorial penetration.

These tactics, military and political, enabled Rome, over several centuries, to dominate southern Italy. By 272 B.C., Rome was a loosely federated state with a core of about 300,000 citizens, all theoretically capable of bearing arms, dominating about 100,000 square kilometers, with a literate administration, a regular census, a developed constitution, and laws. Around 290 B.C. the first coin mints appeared. But Rome was still a provincial offshoot of the eastern Mediterranean.

The first transformation came during the long conflict with the Carthaginians, who blocked southern and seaward expansion. In the Punic Wars, which lasted intermittently from 264 to 146, Rome developed a navy and eventually destroyed Carthage, appropriating its entire land and sea empire. The Second Punic War (218–201) was epic and decisive. The turning point came after Hannibal's brilliant thrust with a small army into Italy, culminating in his shattering victory at Cannae in 216. At that moment the Carthaginians failed to supply him for a final attack on Rome. Roman ability to sacrifice revealed the militarism of social structure. For a period of about 200 years, about 13 percent of citizens were under arms at any one time, and about half served for at least one period of seven years (Hopkins 1978: 30–3). Against Carthage they fought a war of attrition, consistently putting greater numbers into the field, replacing their dead and wounded more rapidly than did the Carthaginians. Slowly they pushed the Carthaginians out of Italy and across Spain. On the way they settled scores with Celtic peoples, allies of Hannibal as they had generally been enemies of Rome. The North and the West were now open to imperial conquest. Then they crossed into Africa, destroying Hannibal's army at the battle of Zama in 202. Humiliating peace terms were imposed, including the exile of Hannibal. The western Mediterranean was now open. Eventually Carthage was provoked to revolt and destroyed in 146 B.C., its capital razed to the ground, its library symbolically donated to the barbarian king of Numidia.

We know nothing of the Carthaginian version of events. It is conventional to ascribe the Roman victory to the greater cohesion and commitment of citizen farmer-soldiers over the oligarchical traders and mercenaries of Carthage – a kind of partial replay of Greece versus Persia and Phoenicia. We can only guess at why the Carthaginians could not replace their troop losses as quickly. It may be curiously indicative of the difference that when our main source, Polybius, gives relative troop strengths in the Italian campaign he gives the numbers of the Carthaginian field army (about 20,000) but the number of all Romans and allies able to bear arms (770,000 men)! Polybius was a Greek taken hostage to Rome in 167 B.C. and then brought up there. Sympathetic to Rome, yet with growing concern at its treatment of Carthage (he had been present at its destruction), he articulated the Romans' own militaristic view of their society (Momigliano 1975: 22–49). The size of the Roman field armies, though usually larger than Hannibal's, were nothing special – perhaps the 45,000 defeated at Cannae was the largest, and this was only two-thirds those mustered by the Hellenistic monarchies of the East. But the *centrality* of those armies to Roman society was unparalleled. Thus there was a certain sense in Polybius's distorted figures – all Roman citizens were relevant to the battlefield in a way that all Carthaginians were not.

It is also worth commenting upon the ease with which the Romans acquired sea power. Polybius ascribes it to the courage of their marines, which made up for the Carthaginian superiority in seamanship. Naval warfare had not developed much over quite a long period of time. We are told by Polybius that the Romans captured a Carthaginian galley and copied it. The balance of power had shifted back to the land. A land power like Rome could take to the sea. The Carthaginians had attempted the reverse move, from sea power to territory, and failed – in military terms because of the inferiority and light armor of their main infantry forces. In economic terms they allegedly held together their land empire by the institution of slavery, in mines and extensive plantations. This would not have led to effective morale for collective defense of the territories.

But the decisive edge may have been political. The Romans gradually stumbled on the invention of extensive territorial citizenship. Citizenship was granted to loyal allies and added to the intensive, Greek-style citizenship of Rome itself to produce what was probably the widest extent of collective commitment yet mobilized.

Indeed, the invention was turned against Greece itself. Exploiting conflicts between the city-states and the Macedonian kingdom, Rome subjugated them both. The process has evoked controversy among scholars, many of whom are puzzled by the fact that the Romans did not at first make Macedonia into a province after defeating it in 168 B.C. Were there doubts in Rome about imperialism, it is asked (Badian 1968; Whittaker 1978; Harris 1979)?

But this is to impose later, and firmly *territorial*, conceptions of imperialism onto an earlier phase of Roman history. As we have seen in earlier chapters, previous empires ruled by dominating and supplementing local elites. This is what the Romans had hitherto done, though they were now half-pragmatically, half-stumblingly moving forward toward a different structure.

Their almost total destruction of Carthaginian rule in Spain, Sardinia, Sicily, and finally North Africa was motivated by ferocious revenge for the humiliations imposed by Hannibal and his predecessors. But this policy necessarily resulted, not as hitherto in dominated allies, but in *provinces,* annexed territories. They were ruled directly by designated magistrates, backed by legionary garrisons. This created new imperial opportunities, but it also created internal political difficulties at Rome and among the allies. It also cost money until provincial machinery could be created to extract taxes to support the legions. It took the Romans some time to create the machinery because they had to first solve the political difficulties. For the conquests had undermined the whole structure of the traditional state.

First, the wars had undermined the volunteer citizen army. The legions had become virtually full-time and were paid (see Gabba 1976: 1–20). Military-service obligations plus the actual fighting in Italy had undermined many peasant farms, plunging them into debt. Their land was acquired by large landowners, and the peasants migrated to Rome. There they were forced down into the next class of military-service obligation, the proletariat. The shortage of peasant proprietors meant that the proletariat contributed soldiers, as it had not earlier. Within the army itself, hierarchy increased as the soldiery lost their politically autonomous base. Either the conqueror of Spain and North Africa, Scipio "Africanus," or a slightly later general created the ominous honors and triumph granted to the *imperator,* the "general," but later, of course, the "emperor."

Second, stratification widened for the next century and a half. Later Roman writers customarily exaggerated the degree of equality in early Rome. Pliny tells us that when the last king was driven out in 510, all the people were given a land plot of seven *iugera* (the Roman measure of area – about 1.75 hectares, the area circumscribed by two oxen in a day). This would not be enough for subsistence for a family and must be an understatement. Nevertheless, the image of equality was probably based on reality. But then, as a result of successful imperialism, the wealth of private persons and army pay scales widened inequalities. In the first century B.C., Crassus, reputedly the richest man of his day, had a fortune of 192 million sesterces (HS), roughly enough to feed 400,000 families for a year. Another contemporary notable reckoned that one needed 100,000 HS a year to live comfortably and 600,000 HS to live well. These incomes are 200 and 1,200 times the subsistence level of a family. In the army differentials widened. About 200 B.C. centurions got twice as much booty as ordinary soldiers; but in the first century under Pompey they got 20 times as much, and the senior officers got 500 times as much. Regular pay disparities widened, centurions receiving 5 times as much as soldiers by the end of the republic and 16–60 times as much during Augustus's reign (Hopkins 1978, chap. 1).

The explanation for this widening of stratification is that the profits of empire were available to the few, not the many. In Spain the former Carthaginian dominions contained rich silver mines and large agricultural plantations worked by slaves. Whoever controlled the Roman state could acquire the fruits of conquest, the new administrative offices and their pickings. The popular elements of the Roman constitution served to defend the people from arbitrary injustices. However, *initiating* powers and military and civic office abroad were concentrated among the upper two orders, senators and knights. Taxes, for example, were farmed out to publicans, mostly members of the equestrian order. The profits of empire were vast, and they were unequally distributed.

Third, the intensification of slavery through conquest produced political difficulties. Indeed, this provoked the conflicts that resulted in a solution. Rome had created vast numbers of slaves in large concentrations. Such slaves were capable of collective organization.

In 135, the first major slave revolt broke out in Sicily. Perhaps as many as 200,000 slaves were implicated. After four years of fighting, the revolt was crushed mercilessly, without quarter. Such cruelty was essentially Roman, not to be questioned. But slavery was having a disastrous impact upon poorer Roman citizens. Their spokesman became Tiberius Gracchus, a prominent senator. After lengthy service abroad, he had returned to Italy in 133 and been horrified by the extent of slavery and the decline of the free peasantry. He proposed reviving an old law to distribute public land acquired through conquest to the proletariat. This would ease their distress and increase the number of property owners liable for military service. He argued that nobody should be able to possess more than 500 *iugera* of public land. This was against the interests of the rich, who had been acquiring public land in larger quantities.

Tiberius Gracchus was a ruthless politician and a powerful speaker. He used the recent slave revolt in a speech paraphrased by Appian in *Civil Wars:*

He weighed against the multitude of slaves as useless in war and never faithful to their masters, and adduced the recent calamity brought upon the masters by their slaves in Sicily; where the demands of agriculture had greatly increased the number of the latter; recalling also the war waged against them by the Romans, which was neither easy nor short, but long-protracted and full of vicissitudes and dangers. [1913: I.9]

Slaves did not matter, but citizens did. Their plight aroused his finest rhetoric, reported by Plutarch in his *Life of Tiberius Gracchus:*

"The wild beasts that roam over Italy," he would say, "have every one of them a cave or lair to lurk in; but the men who fight and die for Italy enjoy the common air and light, indeed but nothing else. Houseless and homeless they wander about with their wives and children. And it is with lying lips that their generals exhort the soldiers in their battles to defend sepulchres and shrines from the enemy, for not a man of them has a hereditary altar; not one of those many Romans, but they fight and die to support others in wealth and luxury, and though they are styled masters of the world, they do not have a single clod of earth that is their own." [1921: 10]

Amid mounting tension, with Rome covered with graffiti (indicating widespread literacy), Tiberius Gracchus was elected tribune of the people for that year. Overriding traditional procedures, he set aside the veto of his conservative fellow tribune, passed the land law, and attempted to distribute the royal treasure of Pergamum (see later in this chapter) to the new farmers. The next year he again flouted tradition, trying to get himself reelected to office. Obviously more was at stake than the public-land issue itself – the issue was, Were the people to share in the profits of empire?

The answer was a violent one. On the day of the election, a band of senators led by the chief priest (himself occupying large tracts of state land!) murdered Tiberius Gracchus and his unarmed supporters. The struggle was taken over by his younger brother Gaius, who managed to maintain the land-distribution scheme until his death, also in civil disorder, in 121. It was abandoned in 119, as conservatives within the senatorial order regained political control.

Participatory citizenship had failed. Political conflict within Rome itself had been settled in two bursts of violence – perhaps the first organized violence in the streets of Rome in the history of the republic. The dominance of the upper orders was confirmed and accentuated. The poor were bought off by wheat subsidies, later by ample free wheat distribution, and by the establishment of peasant military colonies, first in Italy and then all over the conquered territories. This involved a further commitment to imperial expansion. In fact, it led to a kind of "welfare-state imperialism," comparable to the twentieth-century phenomenon in two ways, being a response to demands induced by imperial expansionism and mass-mobilization war, and managing to shunt those demands aside from the fundamental structures of power. The ordinary citizen was no longer important in the central political institutions. Rome was ruled less and less by an "ethnic community," more and more by an exploiting "class."

Imperialism rolled on. The professional army was seen as indispensable. Defeats in Gaul led to panic in Rome and to the army reforms of the consul Marius in 108 B.C. Marius sealed the policy of recruiting an army of volunteers from the proletarian class, paying them wages and promising them land pensions after sixteen years' service. The allies would supply almost all the cavalry as well as the auxiliaries. The link between the army and the class gradation of Roman citizenship was broken. The higher command would still be filled by individuals from the higher classes and orders, but the command structure itself was no longer also the hierarchy of citizen gradation. The army was becoming autonomous.

But Marius's reforms accentuated a second, equally important problem. What to do about the allies? By the time we can calculate the actual size of the allied auxiliaries in the armies, they outnumbered the legions themselves. Brunt (1971a: 424) gives figures of 44,000 legionaries and 83,500 allies for 200 B.C. Though this is the highest known disproportion for any year, Brunt shows that allies continuously outnumbered legionaries. Accordingly, the allies began to demand full citizen rights. During the Social Wars (though the Latin should be really translated as "Wars between the Allies") between Rome and some of its Italian allies in 91–89 B.C., this was effectively granted to save further trouble. It was consistent with Roman traditions of ruling in cooperation with local elites. Granting rights to Italian elites was not dangerous now that stratification within the citizen body was increasing.

Italy now began to look more uniform in its structure as Roman rights and duties were extended to other cities, *municipia,* and soldier *coloniae.* Under Caesar, this became true of the empire as a whole. Once it became clear that others could be treated more like allies than Carthage, antipathy to Roman rule among elites became less. Greek cities adapted to Roman domination. Northwest Asia Minor was bequeathed to Rome in 133 by the childless Attalos III, king of Pergamum, because the Pergamene elite were afraid of revolution and looked to Rome for protection. The Romans were gradually developing political unity among the upper classes throughout their republic-empire.

Now that the profits of empire were vast, now that the Italian upper strata as a whole were admitted to the factions, now that the lower strata were no longer to be feared, political faction struggles among the upper class intensified. They could, doubtless, have been contained within traditional political structures but for the changed nature of the army. The principal instrument of control over the republic/empire as a whole was the army. As the army lost its connection to the republican participatory citizenship, it threatened to become an autonomous factor in the situation. More than this: Its own internal unity became problematic.

Marius had slightly increased the legion's establishment to 6,200 plus a cohort of 600 cavalry. He had also reduced the size of the baggage train, thus loading his soldiers ("Marius's mules") with supplies, equipment, and road-building equipment. The individual legion became an effective unit of political consolidation, improving communications systems as it conquered (more of this later). But interlegion integration was a problem. Legions were stationed individually or in armies of up to about six, separated by hundreds of miles. The army could hardly operate as a unified command structure, given contemporary communications. Traditional control by the senate and citizen body was weakening, so the army could not be held together by the state. It tended to fragment into separate armies led by generals divided by a mixture of personal ambition, upper-class factionalism, and genuine political disagreements. All were senators, but some favored the Senate and others the popular assemblies (the Best and the Popular parties); still others allied themselves with no single political or class faction. But none operated or sought to operate without political legitimacy. All were granted specific if vast consular powers to deal with problems of disorder and rebellion in conquered provinces, as well as to conquer new provinces.

The political structure that had to contain them was described by Polybius as a ''mixed constitution.'' He claimed:

It was impossible even for a native to pronounce with certainty whether the whole system was aristocratic, democratic or monarchical. This was indeed only natural. For if one fixed one's eyes on the powers of the consuls, the constitution seemed completely monarchical and royal; if on that of the senate it seemed again to be aristocratic; and when one looked at the power of the masses it seemed clearly to be a democracy. [1922–7: VI, 11]

But the power and the necessity lay with the consular generals, and so the drift was toward monarchy. The general *had* to intervene politically. The loyalty of his troops depended on his ability to secure legislation for pensions, later in the form of land grants. And as we have seen, agrarian legislation was controversial. The consul, holding office for only a year, had to build up a political faction, using violence, bribery, and the threat of violence to achieve the necessary legislation. The contradiction between military and political power was solved by the general.

For the next hundred years, the general with his dependent legions was the arbiter of Roman power, sometimes singly as dictator, sometimes in uneasy alliance as equal consul with rival generals, sometimes in open civil war with them. The history of this period is genuinely, at one level, the history of Marius and Sulla, Pompey, Crassus and Caesar, and Anthony and Octavian. There were two probable alternative outcomes: The empire could fragment (as Alexander's had done) into different kingdoms; or one general could become supreme commander, the *imperator*. When Octavian received the title of Augustus in 27 B.C., he became effectively an emperor, and his successors were eventually designated as such. The republic/empire became finally an empire.

The Roman Empire – with or without an emperor

Most histories of Rome periodize by the official constitution. The republic lasted until the various upgradings of Augustus's powers between about 31 and 23 B.C. Then the principate (first among equals) gave way to the dominate with the accession of Diocletian in A.D. 284. However, the essential structure of Rome remained the same through these constitutional changes, from around 100 B.C. to the beginnings of decline, after A.D. 200, or perhaps even to about A.D. 350. During that period, Rome was an *empire,* with or without an ''emperor'' – ruling vast territories with a would-be centralized army and bureaucracy, embodying enormous inequalities of wealth and power, and having effectively deprived its ordinary citizens of power.

It was an empire of domination; yet it had also incorporated the Iron Age characteristics that elsewhere had tended to subvert structures of compulsory cooperation. It was a monetary economy and a literate society. It contained private property holders. It was cosmopolitan, and in many respects it sat loosely atop a large number of decentralized, provincial power relations. Yet it did not take the Persian path. It incorporated into its own ruling class all the native elites of the empire, and imposed the most intensive and extensive form of compulsory cooperation in the ancient world, which I shall term the *legionary economy*. These two forms of power made of Rome the first territorial empire of history, from around 100 B.C. onward.

I approach this unique Roman power configuration by examining in turn the principal power (or powerless) actors involved in the empire. There were initially four: slaves, free citizens, the upper class of landholders largely composed of men from the senatorial and equestrian orders of Rome and native elites, and the state elite.[2] With time, however, the first two coalesced into one group, "the masses." I shall consider these first.

The masses of the Roman Empire: slaves and freemen

The origins of Roman slavery closely parallel those of Greek slavery. Both Rome and Greece had long had small pockets of slaves, usually from conquered peoples. Neither had any tradition of free citizen working regularly for free citizen. Both experienced labor shortages because of the demands made by political citizenship and military service. Both suddenly acquired large quantities of slaves, although Rome, unlike Greece, acquired its slaves through conquest.

The Carthaginian slave plantations demonstrated that more intensive agriculture generating a larger surplus was possible than the small peasant plot could provide. Roman agricultural treatises began to recommend small labor gangs working on an estate of several hundred *iugera*. Citizens could not be used in this way; slaves could. While the conquests lasted, slaves were cheap to acquire. The economic advantages of slavery were gratefully seized. Because slaves normally came as individuals, not as families (as free labor did), they were cheap to maintain and they did not generate rural underemployment.

We do not know quite how widespread slaves were. Estimates for Roman Italy at the height of slavery in the late first century B.C. vary between 30 and 40 percent of the total population (e.g., Westermann 1955; Brunt 1971a: 124; Hopkins 1978: 102). Our knowledge of the provinces is sketchy, but the slave proportion was almost certainly much less. Good census data in Egypt show only about 10 percent slaves outside Alexandria (where it would have been higher). The famous doctor Galen tells us that slaves contributed about 22 percent of the population in the territory of Pergamum. Slaves remained at

---

[2]This division is only a rough approximation. The position of women will be discussed in Chapter 10, for Christianity revealed their problematic status.

about this level for 100, perhaps 150, years from about 50 B.C. to A.D. 50 or 100 and then their numbers declined as conquest ceased. The Romans did not go in for buying slaves on the Greek scale; nor did they breed slaves in large numbers (as happened in the Americas in our own era). Either could have maintained slavery in such numbers, and commercial slavery was already demonstrably viable. So it becomes a relevant question to ask why slavery was allowed to die out.

The answer does not lie in humanitarian reasons or in fear of slave revolts. Spartacus's great revolt erupted in 70 B.C., and we learn from our records a great deal about how Crassus's suppression of it affected his political career, but little about Spartacus or his followers. We are told that Crassus crucified 6,000 of the rebels. No serious slave revolts occurred thereafter.

Agricultural slaves, said Varro, were "articulate tools"; oxen were "semi-articulate tools"; and carts were "dumb tools." The form of words was necessary because slaves were *owned* as private property. Roman traditions, lacking permanent free labor, could more easily legitimate ownership of land and tools. Agricultural (and mining) slaves were denied membership in the human race. On the other hand, not all slaves could be so treated. Special difficulties were created by the conquest of Greece. Many of those now enslaved possessed a higher level of civilization than their conquerors. Slave professors, doctors, and state bureaucrats were now found in the West. Some of them effectively ran the central administration during the principate and early empire. Varro's theory could hardly apply to such people without great inconvenience, nor did it. Such slaves were able to enter into contracts, receive wages, and buy their freedom, under conditions that were sometimes de jure, sometimes de facto, and often ad hoc. Slavery blurred over into freedom and into free wage labor.

Similar blurring was also under way on the "free" side of the fence, and in the more important agricultural sphere. Slavery was part of the process by which peasant proprietors were pushed down. Some, indebted, lost their land, and migrated to Rome or to colonies of peasant-soldiers in the provinces. Others kept their land but as tenants of landlords, giving labor services to them. Others kept their ownership rights but increasingly worked for landlords as casual laborers at harvest time and other seasonal periods. Tenancy and casual wage labor were creating alternative forms of exploitation of labor to slavery, and among citizens. As slavery grew, so, with a short time lag, did these two statuses, which attained clear-cut legal reinforcement even while slavery was at its height (the process is well described by Jones 1964: II, 773–802; Finley 1973: 85–7; and Ste. Croix 1981: 205–59).

This was extremely important. In ancient peasant economies, to increase the surplus usually meant making the peasant work harder. All further economic development required this. The merging of slavery and freedom provided this on a general scale. Control over the labor of others, either in the form of free wage labor or tenant dependency, was considered compatible with common membership in the same community of power. Even if citizenship became nominal, free laborers and tenants had legal rights and obligations. Members of the same group could now be fully exploited, probably more fully than had been the case in earlier empires. Slavery was no longer essential; other intense exploitative labor forms had evolved.

One of the two alternative statuses, dependent tenancy, gradually became dominant, probably because economic pressure on the free peasantry continued. We have little direct evidence, but it is usually argued that under the principate the *colonus,* a peasant tenant bound by a five-year lease to a landlord, began to predominate. Later dependency became permanent and hereditary. Free peasants sank to serfdom as slaves rose to be serfs. After about A.D. 200, large bands of barbarian prisoners were distributed not as slaves but *coloni.* Slaves were no longer required for intensive exploitation of labor. Over much of the empire the two initially separate statuses of free citizen and slave eventually merged. Perhaps the greatest symbolic expression of the merger was the famous edict of the Emperor Caracalla A.D. 212–213: "I grant the Roman citizenship to all foreigners throughout the world, all kinds of municipal rights remaining unchanged. . . . For the multitude ought not only to share all our toils, but now also be included in our victory" (quoted in Jones 1970: II, 292). All except remaining slaves were now citizens. But the numbers involved and the inequalities among them were too vast for genuine participation. This meant equality under the law, under the state, and under the upper class – sharing more the toils than the victories promised by Caracalla! Participatory, active citizenship was at an end.

Thus, with the important though declining exception of slavery, it makes increasing sense to talk of the people within the Roman imperial domains as *massified,* sharing a common experience and destiny. Gradations of nationality, citizenship, and tenure types became to a degree eroded.

But the masses were not an *active* force in the Roman power structure. They were not even an "extensive class," let alone a political one. By the end of the republic even the populace of Rome itself had been excluded from almost all the political institutions of the state. As to unofficial action, scholars usually point out a "surprising" absence of peasant revolts in imperial Rome (e.g., Jones 1964: II, 811; MacMullen 1974: 123–4). Actually we cannot be really sure whether it is revolts or records that are absent. The literate classes did not seem keen on noticing and chronicling the discontent of their subordinates. Where they did, however, the accounts rarely treat them as phenomena in their own right: They are related especially to the struggles among the powerful. This is reasonable given the apparent nature of most revolts.

Severe social conflict was endemic to the Roman Empire, as it was to all ancient empires. In a barely pacified society, away from the main communication routes those who could afford to fortify their houses did so. Bandits were never eliminated. In a sense, banditry was perverted class warfare. Its recruits were generally runaway slaves, peasants, and soldiers on whom the burden of exploitation had become intolerable. But they did not resist the rent or tax gatherer; they either ran away from or cooperated with him. In fact, as Shaw (1984) points out, bandits were on occasion "semi-official" allies of local lords or even officials, an alternative source of repression in a society that lacked a civil police force.

More organized conflict involving class-type issues and transformational goals is not hard to find either. We can identify four main types. First and most common are the urban riots, not usually a revolt but an appeal to the state for help and justice, generally against local elites and officials (Cameron 1976; de Ste. Croix 1981: 318–21). In addition to this semiinstitutionalized process, we can identify three more threatening types of disturbance. Most striking are the slave revolts, normally by recently enslaved groups and therefore much less frequent in the empire than in the republic. These revolts aimed to kill (or perhaps enslave) the estate owners and to reestablish free cultivation; unfortunately, we know nothing more of the form of production they established. These conflicts were aimed at ending economic exploitation, but they were local and rarely spread. (Thompson 1952; MacMullen 1966: 194–9, 211–16; MacMullen 1974.)

Two further forms of conflict achieved wider organizational form, however, One concerns those dynastic civil wars that did have an element of class grievance (a minority of such cases). Rostovtzeff (1957) argued that the civil wars of the third century A.D. were the revenge of peasant soldiers on their class enemies in the cities. Though this is nowadays an unfashionable view, we can accept two elements of truth in it: The army was a main route of upward social mobility, and for a peasant, booty from the cities was a way of substantially bettering himself. However, in order to accomplish this he had to submit to the authority of his commander, almost certainly a rich landowner. The second form of conflict occurred mainly in the later empire: religious schism. Several of these movements, especially the Donatists of Numidia in the early fourth century, had social and redistributional goals, although these coexisted with regional and religious separatist tendencies, which I discuss in the next chapter.

The class elements of these disorders were undercut by the tendency of local peasants to place themselves under the locally powerful, against the authority of the taxation of the state, in patron-client organizations in "horizontal" struggles. They also depended on noneconomic forms of organization, a preexisting army or a church/sect. And they tended either to be disintegrative (to seek regional autonomy) or to reconstitute the state unaltered (as in the case of a successful dynastic faction). They did not transform the state or the economy – unless in a regressive direction. When the people were politically active, this was generally in clientelist factions, not class organizations. Class struggle was predominantly "latent," its grievances rechanneled into horizontal struggles. Class analysis of the modern sociological type is applicable (with qualifications) to the struggles of the early republic, but its relevance then diminishes.

None of this is surprising if we consider the extent and nature of the peasant economy. As in virtually all preindustrial economies, about 80–90 percent of the people worked on the land. It took 90 percent in agricultural production to release the remaining urban and elite groups. Their own level of consumption was close to subsistence, and they mostly consumed what they produced. Thus, most of the economy was localized. From the point of view of the peasant household head, the economy was largely *cellular*– that is, his exchange relations were bounded by an area of a few miles within which he could reasonably carry his goods for sale or exchange. The technology and costs of transport (to which I shall return shortly) contributed fundamentally to this. This cellular structure was modified by a proximity to a sea or navigable river. In such locations, greater contact with the world was probable. Nevertheless, even the cities, usually on a river or the Mediterranean coastline, depended overwhelmingly on their immediate hinterlands (Jones 1964: II, 714). Even counting such local markets, the volume of trade was low: According to one (perhaps dubious) estimate, in the fourth century A.D. Constantine's new tax on city trade would have produced only 5 percent of the land tax (Jones 1964: I, 466; for an account placing slightly more emphasis on trade, see Hopkins 1977).

Thus the economic-interaction networks of the mass of the population were narrowly confined to their own locality, which sufficed for most of their economic needs. What kind of class action can we expect from this in an extensive empire? "Extensive classes" can exist only if interaction exists. Thus to the extent that Rome was built up of a number of virtually self-sufficient production units, it could contain *many* local, small, similar "classes" of direct producers, but not a societal-wide producing class capable of enforcing its interests. The masses were trapped within the more extensive "organization charts" of their rulers, organizationally *outflanked*. In the peasant economies we have examined so far, only in small, concentrated communities reinforced by citizen military organization (especially in Greece and early Rome) was collective action possible. As the empire expanded and the people were excluded from its political structures, their capacity for extensive organization declined. Roman class structure became less "symmetrical," and class struggle, other than of a latent kind, became less important to its social development. I call the people the "masses" rather than give them the more active-sounding designation of "class."

But the margin above subsistence and self-sufficiency, narrow as it was, is of equal interest to us. After all, the only interest we have in Rome is that it was *not* a primitive community of subsistence farmers, that peasants *were* connected, however tenuously, to a larger, more prosperous, and "civilized" world. The benefits of empire, described in Chapter 5, were present here too, and to a degree we can again attempt quantification.

The economic benefits of empire for the masses

The yield ratio of crops is one of five clues indicating that living standards rose with the achievement of empire and declined when it declined. In almost all agrarian economies, the staple diet was provided by a cereal crop. Part of the gain had to be replanted as seed for the following year's crop. The ratio of total harvest yield to seed replanted gives us an index of the level of development of the forces of production, for it incorporates all improvements in techniques. Rather than discuss at length different plowing techniques, systems of crop rotation, and so forth, I can present the harvest-to-seed ratio. Available data are sporadic and doubtful, but some comparisons can be made right across European history. The Roman figures pertain to the period from the first century B.C. to the second century A.D. – the peak of Rome's power. They vary.

Cicero tells us that titled lands in Sicily yielded between 8:1 and 10:1, on what was obviously good volcanic land. Varro tells us that Etruria yielded between 10:1 and 15:1. This was presumably also a fertile region, for Colomella reports that Italy as a whole yielded 4:1. Most scholars rely on this estimate. Whatever the precision achieved by these Roman figures, there was a substantial drop in yield ratio with the collapse of the empire in the West. We should expect this on other grounds, of course, but the yield figures support it. In the eighth and ninth centuries A.D., figures are available for two French and one Italian manor, which according to Duby (1974: 37–9) show yields of not more than 2.2:1 – and some rather less than this. This would mean that half the harvest was replanted, a proportion dangerously close to starvation level. Slicher van Bath, however, (1963: 17) believes that Duby has miscalculated and that the true ninth-century figure is about 2.8:1 – still substantially lower than Roman yields. Numerous figures over the next two hundred years then show that a slow but steady increase occurred. Thirteenth-century (largely English) yields varied, generally in the range from 2.9:1 to 4.2:1; fourteenth-century yields (adding France and Italy) varied between 3.9 and 6.5 (Slicher van Bath 1963; Titow 1972; see also Table 12.1). For the sixteenth and seventeenth centuries we can use Italian data broadly comparable to those for the Roman period. We find them only slightly higher – varying between 1:1 for very poor areas and 10:1 for fertile areas, with the mean figure around 6:1 (Cipolla 1976: 118–23). The figures suggest the considerable economic achievements of the Roman Empire, agriculturally unmatched in its own heartland for a thousand years.

A second clue about comparative living standards derives from the conventional assumption that payment in cash indicates higher living standards than payment in kind, because the former implies a greater variety of goods being exchanged as commodities. The Price Edict of the Roman emperor Diocletian in A.D. 301 implies a wage distribution to urban laborers of 1 part in kind to 1½–3 parts in cash. A similar government order in sixteenth-century England envisaged that maintenance would absorb at least half the wages of laborers. This may indicate higher living standards in Rome itself and in other urban areas of the empire than in England (Duncan-Jones 1974: 11–12, 39–59). Rent or tax exactions in cash also had the economic merit of encouraging trade, with goods traded to acquire the coinage, whereas rent or taxes paid in kind were simple one-way extractions leading to no further exchange. Rome's taxation involved considerably more cash than any previous state's, except perhaps those of Greece.

A third clue is archaeological. Hopkins concludes that "Roman levels in excavation reveal more artifacts than pre-Roman levels: more coins, pots, lamps, tools, carved stones and ornaments – in sum, a higher standard of living" (1980: 104). In the case of the provinces acquired quite late, such as Britain, we can also discern an increase in agricultural activity, with extensive areas coming into cultivation for the first time.

A fourth clue is for improvement in agricultural techniques. We can see throughout the late republic and early principate the gradual diffusion of a greater variety of crops – vegetables, fruit, and livestock – and of fertilizers (White 1970). There are, however, indications of a later technological stagnation, to which I shall return later in the chapter.

A fifth clue is population size and density. The evidence on Italy, centered on the censuses of the later republic, is quite good, although the rest of the empire's population is conjectural. The classic researches of Beloch (summarized in English by Russell 1958) have been supplemented by recent work (especially by that of Brunt 1971). We estimate Italian population in 225 B.C. at 5 million to 5.5 million, living at a density of 22 persons per square kilometer. By A.D. 14, this had risen to at least 7 million, at 28 persons per square kilometer. According to Russell this dropped with the decline and fall of the western empire, to about 4 million by A.D. 500. It then rose slowly up from about A.D. 600, but only in the thirteenth century did it reach the ancient peak. The population of the empire as a whole is less clear. Beloch estimated it at 54 million in A.D. 14, but this is now considered an underestimate, particularly as regards the western empire (especially Spain). Around 70 million would be the midpoint of recent estimates, a population density of around 21 persons per square kilometer. Chronicling the subsequent decline and then resurgence of the population of the whole empire is not possible, but it probably followed the Italian pattern.

There are two points of interest. First, the population rose with republican/imperial success and declined with its collapse. The Romans successfully supported a larger population than had been possible earlier, or than was reached for more than five hundred years after their political demise. Second, their success was essentially *extensive,* spread over an enormous territorial area of more than 3 million square kilometers. There was one province of extraordinary high density (Egypt, as always, with 180 persons per sq. km.) and two provinces of extraordinary low density – the Danube and Gaul (though the latter is contested by French historians). Cities contributed disproportionately to density figures, but they were spread throughout the empire. Settlement was mostly continuous over a gigantic landmass.

In view of these considerable benefits, it is not appropriate to describe the empire as simply "exploitative," whether the exploitation is by class of class or by city of countryside, as some classicists do (e.g., de Ste. Croix 1981: 13). Exploitation there was, but from it also flowed benefits in the pattern, familiar by now, of compulsory cooperation. What were the tenuous links of exploitation and benefits between the peasant producers and the larger world, which kept so many of them, so densely concentrated, yet also extensively populated, above subsistence? There were two such links – horizontal, "voluntary" links in the form of exchange and trade of goods, and vertical, compulsory links in the form of the extraction of rent and tax. What were their relative weights? It is necessary to consider the nature of the second major power actor, the ruling class, to answer this question.

The extension of the Roman ruling class

That there was a clear ruling class in imperial Rome is not in dispute, but the nature of its power was complex, changing, and even contradictory. The conundrum is not its relationship to the masses, which was institutionalized early in the republic and then became ever clearer, but its relation to the state. For the central contradiction was this: The "upper strata" became very like a class in our modern sense – that is, with a power resting in "civil society" on private-property ownership and de facto autonomy from the state – yet their position largely originated through the state and was continuously dependent on the state for its maintenance. Let us see how this developed.

"Private property" developed in early Rome, but it seems to have "taken off" as a result of the state's rake-off from its conquests. Conquest allowed wealth and control over labor to destroy the main original collective institution, participatory citizenship. It did so through military and civil officeholding. All generals were at first drawn from those members of the senatorial order who held magistracies. As they were drawn by lot, we can see the close connection between high military office and the upper class *as a whole.* Such men controlled the distribution of booty and slaves. The administration of conquered provinces generated even more liquid wealth. The governors, quaestors, and other magistrates were drawn from the senatorial order; and the tax farmers and army contractors, usually from the equestrian order.

Concerning their activities, we have abundant cynical sources. For example, in the second half of the second century B.C., we have this lament: "As for me, I need a quaestor or supplier, who will supply me with gold from the state money-bags." In the first century B.C. came the oft repeated saying that a provincial governor needed to make three fortunes: one to recoup his election expenses, another to bribe the jury at his expected trial for misgovernment, and a third to live off thereafter. Cicero summed it all up: "One realizes finally that everything is for sale" (all quoted in Crawford 1978: 78, 172).

The state *was* such people. Not until the principate was there a separate central bureaucracy, and even then, as we shall see, its capacity to control its upper-class administrators was extremely limited. Wealth was looted and taxed by the state from the conquered peoples, but it was then acquired by a decentralized class. Their rights over this surplus were institutionalized in "absolute" private-property rights, guaranteed by the state but administered by a quasi-autonomous group of aristocratic jurists. A delicate reciprocity existed between state and ruling class.

What kept a degree of integration among this class? Why did Rome not disintegrate into a multi-city-state system or a collection of satrapies? The question points to the main Roman power achievement, the institutionalization of empire over more than 3 million square kilometers and perhaps 70 million persons. A glance at a map shows that its core was the Mediterranean, although it extended considerable distances from the Mediterranean, especially to the north. The overall communications and control limitations of the ancient world, described in earlier chapters, were still in force. Hitherto they had led only to hierarchically and territorially federal regimes, which disintegrated and were reconstituted, often through conquest by marcher lords. Yet Rome remained far more unified and stable through all its vicissitudes. Why?

The answer returns us to the two most effective strategies of imperial rule discussed in Chapter 5. The first concerns primarily the hierarchical relations of the empire. I shall argue that domination became territorialized by the "legionary economy," a heightened form of Spencer's compulsory cooperation. The second strategy concerns horizontal relations, the upper class's growing ideological integration. This second form of power is discussed in more detail in the next chapter, but I now sketch it.

Like most empires before it, Rome generally ruled through local native elites backed by its own governors, garrisons, and legionary camps. In terms of the contrast made in the previous chapter, it adopted the Persian, not the Assyrian, option. Yet the policy soon developed novel forms. Local rulers could stay in their place (with the conspicuous exception of the Carthaginians). Livy puts these words into the mouth of a tyrant of Sparta addressing a

Roman general: "Your wish is that a few should excel in wealth, and that the common people should be subject to them" (quoted in Ste. Croix 1981: 307). In return, the local rulers became Romanized in their culture, at least in the western parts of the empire. This conscious policy involved teaching language and literacy, building theaters and amphitheaters, and loosely integrating local cults into Roman ones. After about a century of Roman dominance, it generally became impossible to detect local cultural survivals among elites of the western provinces. All spoke Latin (and until the third century A.D. many also spoke Greek). In the East the situation was complicated by the status of Greece and by the partial absorption of its language and culture by the Romans. There were two official languages in the East. Though Greek was the main unifying language of the political rulers, Latin was also spoken, mainly in the law courts and army. This complication apart, the East was similar to the West: Both had a high degree of cultural integration among elites. The process has been described by Millar et al. (1967) through the period A.D. 14–284. Membership in the Senate was diffused across the empire, as was the imperial succession. The purple passed from Roman aristocrats to Italian "bourgeois," then to Italian settlers in Spain and Southern Gaul, then to Africans and Syrians, and then to men from the Danubian and Balkan areas. Despite the violence of the actual succession process, this diffusion was a remarkable, historically unprecedented process: For amid it all, the empire held together. No contender seems to have been a provincial "national" leader, attempting either provincial secession or conquest that would have involved establishing the hegemony of a province over the whole empire. Rome's hegemony was uncontested. This was also novel: Hegemony in previous empires had shifted between provinces and capital cities as a result of such civil and dynastic strife.

Literacy had become crucial. Ideological integration was not possible for previous empires because the infrastructure had not emerged. Until messages could be passed and stabilized over extensive territories by means of literacy, similarity of thought and everyday customs was slow to develop in large empires. Elite culture had already developed through literacy among Greeks and Persians. Details of Roman literacy are given in the next chapter, but it had two main characteristics. First, it was *full* upper-class literacy, certainly of males, perhaps of females as well, officially taught to that class and extending also to other classes. Second, it was used within the predominantly oral, informal context of face-to-face relations among the upper class. So the cultural solidarity it transmitted was largely confined to the upper class. The masses were excluded. Writing did not develop much outside of informal upper-class institutions. The development of records and accounts was rudimentary: Neither the state nor private individuals developed single- or double-entry bookkeeping (Ste. Croix 1956). The state possessed few power resources that were independent of upper-class personnel. In previous periods we have glimpsed literacy playing two "immanent" ideological roles – as an instrument of state power and as the cement of class solidarity. These were more closely fused in Rome than ever before.

Thus there emerged a universal *ruling class* – extensive, monopolizing land and the labor of others, politically organized, and culturally conscious of itself. The fully developed republic/empire was not ruled by congeries of particularistic local rulers, or by a Roman conquering core over or through native elites, but by a *class*.

Class structure was what I called in Chapter 7 "asymmetrical": An extensive and political ruling class existed, but without such a subordinate class. It is difficult for modern writers to accept this description. We are used to the symmetry of contemporary class structures, where dominant and subordinate class, organized over the same social space, struggle and compromise. Because we do not find this in Rome, except in its early years, many writers conclude that classes did not exist at all (e.g., Finley 1973: chap. 3; Runciman 1983). But the Roman landholding elite was about as "classlike" as any group in any known society, past *or* present. The conclusion is rather that class structures are highly variable, only a few being symmetrical and therefore being riven by the kind of class struggle described by Marx.

One qualification must be made: Roman upper-class literate culture contained a major fault line, the division into Latin and Greek cultures. This eventually broke the empire in two. Reinforced by geopolitical differences, it proved an enduring division between the civilization of Europe and its eastern neighbors.

Though historically unique, Rome was not unique in its own time. Its near contemporary, the Han dynasty in China, also developed ruling-class cultural homogeneity – indeed, probably greater than Rome's. Again this centered on the transmission of a predominantly secular culture (Confucianism) through literacy. The development of literacy was continuing to play a major role in the shape and durability of power relations. It was the logistical infrastructure of ideological power, able to cement an extensive ruling class. It soon developed further into other classes, to destabilize the very Roman regime it had first bolstered. This story of ideological *transcendence* awaits the next chapter.

The other main power form involved in Roman integration was the territorialization of what in earlier chapters I termed compulsory cooperation. This took the form of a "legionary economy," the logistical infrastructure of which was provided by a militarized economy that began to approach true territoriality. It was historically prior to the ideological class integration, for the latter only applied to territories already conquered by force. The Romans did not encourage assimilatory strategies across their frontiers.

The best analyses of the Roman imperial economy are those of Keith Hopkins. I start with his analysis of trade (1980). Using Parker's (1980) work on shipwrecks in the Mediterranean, he deduces a steep rise (more than three-fold) in seaborne trade after 200 B.C. Trade then leveled off until sometime around A.D. 200, when it began to drop. Similarly, using Crawford's (1974) work on the dies used in minting coins, he deduces that the stock of coinage remained quite stable for the hundred years period prior to 157 B.C. and then rose more or less steadily until it peaked at more than ten times the 157 B.C. level in about 80 B.C. It remained at around that level until around A.D. 200, when debasements began to render useless any inferences about the volume of trade. He is also able to compare hoards of coins found in seven different provinces in the period A.D. 40–260, and thereby to make deductions about the uniformity of the money supply across the empire as a whole. Considering the probable errors in the methods of relying on the accident of finding coin hoards, it is striking that he finds similar trends for all provinces until just after A.D. 200. The empire was a single monetary economy during that period. This is not to deny that it was linked to economic activity outside the empire as well, but to draw attention to the systematic nature of economic interaction *within* the boundaries of empire. This had not occurred in previous empires to anything like the same degree. We are approaching closer to a "unitary society" than hitherto.

Coinage is merely a medium of exchange; trade is merely its form. What actually *generated* this economy, with its coinage and trade? "Conquest" is an initial answer, but how was this translated into economic integration? There are three possible forms of integration: *taxes,* implying vertical integration between citizen and state; *rent,* implying vertical integration between landlord and peasant; and *trade* itself, implying horizontal integration that could be the product of the first two or independent of them.

First, let us consider the spontaneous development of trade. The Roman conquests had removed political boundaries from across the Mediterranean, and opened up the northwest to the long-established wealth and autonomous trading networks of the south and east. This was particularly marked in the exchange of luxury goods and slaves, with which the state was but little involved after the initial conquest. The Roman elite at home and in the provinces used the booty of empire to purchase luxuries and slaves, and this boosted the exchange relations of "civil society." Second, let us consider rents: The use of slaves, serfs, and free labor by landlords also increased the surplus, cash flow, and trade of the empire. We do not know much about this. But, third, we can be reasonably sure that these two forms of integration located within civil society were less important than integration provided by state taxation. This can be seen from overall trade flows. I quote Hopkins's conclusion from an earlier article:

The prime cause of this monetary unification of the whole empire was the complementary flow of taxes and trade. The richest provinces of the empire (Spain, north Africa, Egypt, southern Gaul and Asia Minor) paid taxes in money, most of which were exported and spent, either in Italy or in the frontier provinces of the empire, where the armies were stationed. The rich core-provinces then had to gain their tax-money back, by selling food or goods to the tax-importing regions. . . . Thus the prime stimulus to long-distance trade in the Roman empire was the tax-demands of the central government and the distance between where most producers (tax-payers) worked and where most of the government's dependants (soldiers and officials) were stationed. [1977: 5]

Rome developed a state-led economic system. In this respect, therefore, it is inappropriate to term Rome a "capitalist economy," as Runciman (1983) does, although it had private property and monetary institutions.

But this state-led economy did not have a banking infrastructure to release its coins into the economy on demand (as modern states do). Its only mechanism of disbursement was its own expenditure. Like most ancient states, it did not see currency as a medium of exchange between its subjects, but as a means of collecting revenue, paying expenses, and storing reserves. It guarded this role jealously. When the Emperor Valens heard that private persons were minting their own gold, he confiscated it: The imperial mints existed to supply government needs, not for the convenience of the public (Jones 1964: I, 441). The role of coinage in trade and urban life in general was a *by-product* of the state's own administrative needs (Crawford 1970: 47–84; 1974: 633).

Thus, despite their enormous accumulations of private property and their de facto political autonomy, the upper class depended on the state for the maintenance of the economic system that benefited them. They had sequestered the assets of a conquest state, but the state was still necessary to the existence of those assets.

We have also solved the problem of the economic well-being of the masses, posed in the previous section. For their consumption of specialized goods (like cloth, knives, salt, or wine) also depended on the state-led monetary economy. We cannot fully distinguish either major group of "civil society" from "the state." After a period in which the fragmentation of the Roman conquest state threatened to disintegrate the whole social order, Rome reconsolidated itself into a central-despotic, imperial state. This was a more evolved form of the compulsory cooperation found in the earlier empires of domination described in Chapter 5. So let us turn to the last, and key, power actor: the state itself.

The imperial state and the legionary economy

The constitutional form of the Roman domains – republic, principate, or empire – matters less in the period from about 100 B.C. to A.D. 200 than their underlying unity and continuity. To describe the "real" Roman constitution, the true locus of political power, is necessarily a difficult and laborious enterprise, for it must deal with informal as well as formal arrangements, and these are often unwritten. I short-circuit that enterprise, however, and use a simple measure of the state's power, its *fiscal account:* The expenditure side gives a measure of the functions of the state; the revenues side chronicles the state's relative autonomy from, and dependence on, the groups located in civil society. Obviously the surviving records are limited. This methodology will be extended in later chapters when we encounter states who left more systematic records, and I will discuss its basis and limitations in more detail then. For the moment, I quote Schumpeter's general justification of the method:

The public finances are one of the best starting points for an investigation of society. . . . The spirit of a people, its cultural level, its social structure, the deeds its policy may prepare – all this and more is written in its fiscal history, stripped of all phrases. He who knows how to listen to the message here discerns the thunder of world history more clearly than anywhere else. [1954: 7]

Or, as Jean Bodin more succinctly expressed it, monies are the sinews of the state.

We possess details of imperial finances at only one point in time. This is due to the survival of the emperor Augustus's testament, the *Res Augustae* (reproduced in Frank 1940: 4–17; commented on by Millar et al. 1977: 154–5, 189–201). We have to assume that the two accounts mentioned there, of the *aerarium* (public treasury) and of Augustus's personal household, were in reality separate. Frank believes this to be so.

The expenses of the *aerarium* totaled around 400 million *sesterces* (the basic Roman coin) annually. About 70 percent was spent on the armed forces (60% on the legions and navy, 10% on praetorian and urban cohorts around Rome); about 15 percent on corn distribution to the Roman populace (the *dole* whose name lives on); about 13 percent on the civil service list; and the small residue on public building, roads, and public games. Augustus's personal annual expenses totaled somewhere over 100 million *sesterces,* of which 62 percent went for donations of pay, land, and pensions to his soldiers; 20 percent was distributed to the Roman populace in cash or corn; 12 percent purchased land for himself; and the remainder was spent on temple building and public games. The similarity of the two budgets, despite our expectations that their titles should give different patterns, reveals no real division between Augustus's "public" and "private" functions. As most was spent on the army and other ways of pacifying the Roman populace, Augustus made sure of securing a degree of allegiance to him personally as well as to the state. This was not a very institutionalized state.

The size of the army remained fairly stable at just over 300,000 men for the next three centuries. We have no evidence concerning any increase in civil bureaucracy or functions during this time. Thus military costs remained dominant. Of the other expenditures, the pacification of the people of Rome, literally through bread and circuses (as well as through the praetorian and urban cohorts), was the most important, with more positive civil functions bringing up the rear. Such expenditures reveal the militarism of the Roman state. As we see in later chapters, they differ from those of the medieval and early modern state by the relentless *stability* of their militarism – unlike its successors, the Roman state never experienced enormous rises and falls in its financial size because it was *always* at war. And they are distinguishable from those of the contemporary state by the insignificance of civil functions and functionaries.

The actual bureaucracy was tiny – perhaps 150 civil servants in Rome, and 150 senatorial and equestrian administrators, plus their small staffs of public slaves in the provinces. The state was largely an army. The state-led economy was an army-led economy.

So we must look closely at the all-important army. What were *its* functions? I now combine the economic analysis of the last section with strategic military considerations derived from Luttwak's *The Grand Strategy of the Roman Empire* (1976). The diagrams that follow are based on his.

In the period from 100 B.C. to A.D. 200 there were two strategic phases. The first Luttwak terms the "hegemonic empire" (similar to my "empire of domination"), lasting to around A.D. 100. In this phase (Figure 9.1) there were no clear outer limits to the empire, and no border fortifications. The striking power of the legions was greater than the consolidating powers of the state (as we would expect from Lattimore). It was more cost-effective to use client states to influence, and exact booty from, the outer regions. This was easier in the eastern parts of the empire where civilized states partially controlled their own territories; it was more difficult in stateless Europe where peace tended to require the presence of Roman legions.

In the first phase most legions were not stationed on the frontiers. Their function was internal pacification. The conquest of the zone of direct control was by legions carving out a route of penetration through hostile territories to capture major population centers and political capitals. The next step was to spread out that penetration without losing the military advantage of the legion: the concentrated, disciplined fighting power of 5,000 men plus auxiliaries. Small scattered garrisons would have dissipated this advantage. The solution was the *marching camp*. The legion kept on the move, but at a slow, methodical pace, building its own fortifications and constructing its own communications routes. Marius's reforms had sealed this strategy, converting the heavy infantry into a dual fighting and civil-engineering unit.

This is shown clearly in pictures and descriptions of the legionary troops. The Jewish historian Josephus gives an admiring eyewitness description of the organization of Roman troops, extolling their cohesion, discipline, daily exercises, methods of camp building, and even collective habits at mealtimes. He then describes their marching orders and equipment. Notice what they carry: "The foot soldiers have a spear, and a long buckler, besides a saw, and a basket, a pickaxe, and an axe, a thong of leather, and a hook, with provisions for three days so that a footman has no great need of a mule to carry his

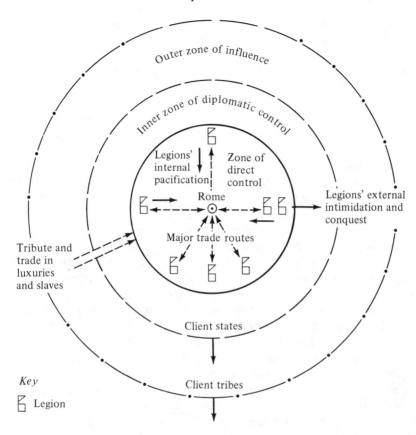

Figure 9.1. *Phase 1 of the Roman Empire: the empire of domination (after Luttwak 1976)*

burdens'' (1854: book III, chap. V, 5). This odd assortment was tied around a long pole, carried like a lance, which Marius's commissariat devised. Only the spear and buckler were battlefield equipment. They are unremarkable, as are the three days' rations. All the rest of the equipment is ''logistical weapons,'' designed to extend the infrastructure of Roman rule. Most were to build fortifications and communications routes: The basket was for earthmoving; the leather strap was for moving turves; the pickax with two different blades was for cutting down trees and digging ditches. Others were primarily for adding to the supplies: the sickle for cutting corn, the saw for wooden equipment and firewood (for discussion of this equipment see Watson 1969: 63 and Webster 1979: 130–1). Contrast this to the equipment of most troops of other empires or city-states – which had carried merely battlefield equipment. The Romans were the first to rule consistently through the army not only with terror, but also with civil-engineering projects. The troops were not reliant on enormous baggage trains, nor did they require local corvée labor to build their roads. The necessity to enter into elaborate negotiations with whoever controlled local food supplies was reduced. It depended on a monetary economy, available to only a few earlier empires. Given this, the legion could move slowly as an independent unit, over all terrain that possessed an agricultural surplus – which, as we have seen, was almost all the territory of the empire – consolidating its rule and its rear as it moved.

The equipment tied around Marius's pole was the final contribution of the Iron Age to the possibilities for *extensive* rule. The legions constructed roads, canals, and walls as they marched, and, once built, the communications routes added to their speed of movement and penetrative powers. Once a province was crisscrossed, taxes and military conscription of auxiliaries, and later of legionaries, were routinized. This often precipitated the first major postconquest native revolt, which would be crushed with maximum force. Thereafter military pressures would ease and Roman political rule would be institutionalized. The new communications routes and the state-led economy could generate economic growth. This was not really a state-led economy in our modern sense, but a military-led economy – a *legionary economy*.

As pacification increased, more of the legions were released for outward expansion. However, expansionist options were not unlimited. The Roman legions were effective in high-intensity warfare against settled and concentrated peoples. Once they encountered nomadic peoples in sparsely settled territories, their advantage and their ability and desire to conquer lessened. There was little point in penetrating southward through the Sahara. Northward the German forests were not impenetrable, but they made military organization difficult. Roman ambitions never recovered after the melée in the Teutoburger Forest in A.D. 9, when Varus led three legions to confusion and utter destruction at the hands of Germans led by the former auxiliary commander Hermann. Henceforth, dangerous semibarbarians would always exist along the northern frontiers.

Eastward lay a different obstacle: the only major civilized state left on Rome's frontiers, Parthia (the conqueror of the Hellenistic Seleucid dynasty of Persia around 240 B.C.). Because of the use of client states in the East, Roman troops there were of low quality, and like all Roman armies, they were rather short of cavalry, useful in eastern deserts. Crassus was ill-prepared for the Parthians in his campaign of 53 B.C., and he and seven legions were annihilated at Carrhae in northern Syria. The Parthians combined heavy cavalry with mounted bowmen: The cavalry forced the Romans to keep in close formation, and the bowmen shot them to pieces. The Romans could reverse this defeat when properly protected by cavalrymen and archers. But

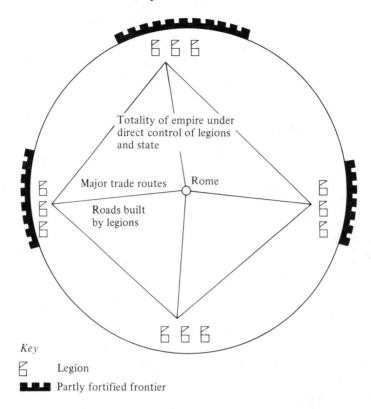

Totality of empire under
direct control of legions
and state

Major trade routes   Rome

Roads built
by legions

Key

Legion

Partly fortified frontier

Figure 9.2. *Phase 2 of the Roman Empire: the territorial empire (after Luttwak 1976)*

the Parthians were not thereafter expansionist, and so not a threat. To conquer them would have required a major effort. This was not forthcoming.

With increasing internal pacification, the legions were now required around the frontiers of the empire. Rome was moving toward the second phase, represented in Figure 9.2, of territorial empire. In this phase the major threat was outsiders raiding the pacified provinces. They could not be eliminated because of their own lack of settlement, so containment was the only strategy. Unfortunately, this required troops all around the perimeter. Frontier fortifications could help to reduce troop costs. They were not intended to keep the barbarians out entirely but to improve communications and to force the raiders to concentrate at their point of entry and exit, making them easier to intercept on their way back (hence perhaps the apparent oddity of building great ditches *inside* rather than outside Hadrian's Wall). The preservation of the legionary

economy required major and unrelenting expenditure of money and manpower. There could be no end to Rome's militarism, even though its strategies
might change.

The compulsory cooperation in the early empires of domination described
in Chapter 5 had been composed of five elements: pacification, the military
multiplier, the assigning of economic value, intensification of the labor process, and coerced diffusion and innovation. The legionary economy contained
all five, intensified and given firm external boundaries.

1. *Pacification.* Internal pacification dominated during the hegemonic/
domination phase, external during the territorial phase. Both provided the
stable, secure environment for rational economic activity; both took an
increasingly territorial character.

2. *The military multiplier.* Coercion intervened in the form of the economy, providing communications and trade infrastructure and a consumption
market in the legions and in Rome that boosted coinage, trade, and economic
development. This was the heart of the legionary economy, a "military
Keynesianism."

3. *The assigning of economic value.* This had changed considerably since
the first empires of domination. As we have seen in intervening chapters, the
growth of the economic power of the peasant farmer and of the trader, and
the development of coinage, had destroyed the central-place economy. Now
value was assigned through a balance of power between state and "civil society," through a mixture of state authority and privately organized supply and
demand. The Roman state provided the coinage, which it distributed through
its own consumption needs. As the state was the principal consumer in the
monetary sector of the economy, its needs had a large impact upon the relative
scarcity and value of commodities. But the producers and the middlemen
traders and contractors constituted private power holders, their rights enshrined
in law and in the value of a monetary economy. The state and private sectors,
entwined, generated a gigantic common market, penetrating every corner of
the empire, its boundaries contributing a degree of cleavage in trade networks. The monetary economy contributed substantially to the development
of a territorial empire.

4. *Intensification of the labor process.* This occurred through the medium
of first slavery, then serfdom and wage labor. The product of the state's military conquest, it had been decentralized under the control of the upper class
as a whole. As Finley remarks, the freer the peasant, the more precarious his
economic position. Agricultural treatises offering advice showed "the viewpoint of the policeman not the entrepreneur" (1973: 106–13).

5. *Coerced diffusion and innovation.* This element was prominent in the
earlier hegemonic/domination phase and then declined markedly in the territorial phase. Diffusion was something of a one-way process from east to west,

as the Romans learned from the civilization of the Greeks and the Middle East. But they coercively carried it to the Atlantic coast. Within the Pax Romana a common culture began to develop. However, erecting frontier fortifications symbolized the onset of a defensive orientation to the world outside and was part of the empire's stagnation, to be discussed later.

These five amounted to a legionary economy, pervading the empire through interdependent flows of labor, economic exchange, coinage, law, literacy, and the other appurtenances of a Roman state that was little more than a committee for managing the common affairs of the rulers of the legions.

Now let us return more systematically to the logistics of communications and to the limitations they had traditionally placed upon the possibility for territorial control. Although the transport constraints remained in general the same, the Romans made three notable advances within them.

The first advance was that by generating such a high level of surplus and in securing part of it for themselves, the Roman elite – part state, part land-owners – could now afford a far higher level of expenditure for control infra-structure than any previous state. Land transport, say of supplies for the legions, might be extremely expensive, but if it was regarded as essential it could be afforded.

Diocletian's Price Edict is relevant here. The edict gives us figures that enable us to calculate the costs of different forms of transport (full text in Frank 1940: 310–421; Duncan-Jones [1974: 366–9] gives a good guide to it). There is one ambiguity: Interpretations of the *kastrensis modius* (a weight measure) can vary by a factor of 2. If the cost of sea transport is set at 1, then the cost of inland waterway transport is 4.9 times as great, and that of road wagon is either 28 or 56 times as great (and transport by camel would be 20% less than by road wagon). Given the choice the state would supply by water. But if this were not possible (e.g., in winter) land transport, however costly, would be used if it were physically possible. Diocletian's edict reveals that the transport costs of moving a wagon of grain 100 miles would be either 37 percent or 74 percent of the wheat cost, which is a considerable increase but on the first estimate still apparently practicable. Larger distances are not given, suggesting that they were not usually covered by land. It is important when dealing with the Romans to separate profit from practicability. Transport was organized primarily to pacify, not to make profits. If movement of supplies was necessary for pacification, and if it were practicable, it would be attempted, almost regardless of costs. The organization was there to do it – at a higher logistical level than any previous society had possessed. Despite its cost it was the perfect instrument for dealing with emergencies. But as *routine* it would eat up the profits of empire – and eventually did so.

The second advance was in extending the space of surplus acquisition. Diocletian's figures assume that the mules or oxen will themselves be fed along the route. If they were not, then they would have eaten up the grain themselves. In an empire in which every nondesert area was extensively cultivated, some surplus food was available everywhere. In a fully organized, monetary economy, the oxen and mules could be fed on less costly, low-quality fodder, thereby keeping the increase in transport costs well below the 100 percent level. Because of the overall constraints (which still operated), the system was capable only of efficient transport over medium distances – say 80–200 kilometers. Sea or river routes would be necessary for larger distances. Combined, they extended over the *whole* empire. There would be virtually no regions that did not produce enough surplus to support staging posts arranged in continuous networks. This was unlike former empires, whose areas of low fertility had always produced large logistical gaps in their supply systems.

The third advance was to organize the acquisition of this surplus. This was done through the logistical structure of the legionary economy. Each *municipium* throughout the empire was required to supply the local troops. Provincial governors and legionary commanders could requisition both land and sea transport to concentrate these supplies, so that a legion, a force of about 5,000 men, was maneuverable as a single unit even during winter. Larger forces could be concentrated and moved only with some preparation; but the movement of armies of about 20,000 men seems to have been an almost routine logistical operation during this period. The organization of the legions penetrated the whole territory of the empire.

The weakness of the legionary economy: a power standoff

But the legionary economy also contained a contradiction. On the one hand both the people and the upper class depended for their well-being, and indeed in many cases their very survival, on the legionary economy provided by the imperial state. Their own activity, their own praxis, could not produce unaided their subsistence needs. And yet, at the same time, the state had partly decentralized many of its functions to the upper class. The effectiveness of the overall structure depended on successfully institutionalizing these contradictory tendencies. But from the revenue accounts, we can see that success was only partial.

I return to the will of Augustus. The annual income of the *aerarium* under Augustus totaled around 440 million *sesterces*. His own annual personal income probably totaled about 100 million to 120 million sesterces.[3] The "public"

---

[3]This estimate is based on the assumption (made by Frank) that personal expenses and income were in rough balance. This total is the sum of all expenses listed by Augustus, divided by the 20 years covered by the list.

income came mainly from taxes and tributes from the provinces (Roman citizens in Italy being exempt from 167 B.C. to the end of the third century A.D.). The "private" income came from two main sources: booty from civil and foreign wars, and cash and land inheritances from the wills of the wealthy (a form of bribery to secure office and favor for their sons), plus a more minor source of Augustus's own estates. At this stage, therefore, the Roman state was mainly financed by conquest. The two stages of the profits of war – booty followed by tribute, then taxation of the conquered and bribes for officeholding – dominate the figures.

This pattern was not subsequently maintained – indeed in the absence of continued expansion it is difficult to see how it could be. We do not have exact figures for any subsequent period, but we know of three changes over the next two centuries. First, it became increasingly difficult for contemporaries to distinguish in any sense between the emperor's and the public funds. Second, taxation was steadily institutionalized, reimposed on Italy, and then maintained without significant public negotiations (and apparently also without increase) at a level that cannot have amounted to more than 10 percent of the annual value of produce. This was the largest source of revenue. Third, the emperor's estates grew enormously – by A.D. 300 Jones (1964: 416) estimates them at 15 percent of all land. This would have been the second main revenue source. The new combined funds were administered in the middle of the third century in one imperial *fiscus* controlled only by the emperor.

Both phases contained unresolved tension. In Augustus's time, the dominant imperial role was that of supreme commander of a great military power. His power was limited by the loyalty of his military confederates and subordinates, not by powers institutionalized in "civil society." On the other hand, revenues deriving from his own estates and from inheritances – which also derived mainly from the estates of great families – lodged power in the property relations of civil society. The first gave autonomous power, the second entailed dependence on civil society.

Tension was also felt in the tax-gathering system from the time of Augustus. The assessment of taxes was nominally shared between the emperor and the Senate, but the Senate's real powers were now declining, and Augustus and his successors had what amounted to arbitrary powers. Yet their capacity to gather taxes was feeble. Tax farmers (and later local landowners and town councillors) were set a total amount of tax to be paid by their area, and they themselves arranged the detailed assessment and collection. As long as they delivered the asked-for total, their methods were their own affair, subject only to ex post facto appeal to the emperor on the grounds of corruption. Although taxation increased, its methods remained unchanged. In the later phase the emperor's arbitrary powers increased as he gained total control over the *fiscus* and its expenditures: But he gained no further control over the *source* of

revenue. It was unresolved tension, a *power standoff* between the emperor
and the upper stratum. The system worked well in delivering a relatively fixed
sum year after year at negligible cost to the budget. But by failing to institutionalize *either* arbitrary or consultative relations between central and local
levels, it could not easily adjust to change. After A.D. 200 it began to disintegrate under external pressures.

At its height, therefore, the Roman Empire was not a particularly cohesive
structure. Its three main constituent elements, people, upper class, and state,
had a degree of autonomy. The Roman people, leveled down to a semifree
status and deprived of participation in the state, were largely made provincial
and were controlled by the local upper class. The poorer young men among
them, however, could also be mobilized in armies by cliques of the upper
class or by the official leadership of the state; neither brought them into stable
power institutions. This was in marked contrast to Roman traditions, the loss
of which was often mourned but which were not entirely dead: citizenship,
rights under the law, possession of coinage, and a degree of literacy. All these
traditions gave the people a certain power and confidence not now harnessed
to the Roman emperor. We see this power exercised in the service of another
god in the next chapter. The members of the upper class had obtained secure
control of their own localities, including the people therein, but were deprived
of collective, institutionalized power at the center. Stable influence at the
center depended on membership in the right informal faction, that is, on
becoming the *amici* (friends) of the emperor. Greater power could be obtained
through the violence of civil war. This could lead to military victory but not
to secure, institutionalized power. The state elite in the person of the emperor
and his armies was indispensable to the goals of the people and the upper
class and in undisputed control of the center. Its penetrative powers within
"civil society" were far greater than those of the elite of Persia but were still
feeble by modern standards. The armies themselves could and did disintegrate
under the pressure of faction fighting among the upper class and provincialism
among the people.

None of these relationships were fully institutionalized. Rights and duties
above those normally extracted were unclear. No framework existed for dealing with prolonged abnormal situations. This was the exact opposite of the
republic of about 200 B.C., whose success was based on digging deep into
reserves of common sacrifice in the face of danger over a very long period.
That very success had destroyed the institutions of common sacrifice and instead
led to the institutionalization of a power standoff between state, upper class,
and people. Thus the legionary economy, though it combined the highest
combination of intensive and extensive social organization yet seen, was
inherently inflexible for it contained no single locus of legitimacy for ultimate
decision making.

The decline and fall of the western empire

The collapse of Rome is the greatest tragic and moral story of Western culture.[4] The most famous storytellers have been those who have combined an appreciation of the tragedy itself with a clear and resounding moral for their own times. Gibbon, in attributing the fall to the triumph of barbarism and religion, was sounding a clarion call for the eighteenth-century Enlightenment: Trust in reason, not superstition allied to savagery! The various phases and factions of the subsequent democratic age have tended to focus their morals on the decline of political and economic democracy, preferring without any doubts the early republic to the imperial form. The Marxist version, from Marx himself to Perry Anderson and Ste. Croix, has blamed slavery and the undermining of the free peasantry (the base of citizenship). The "bourgeois-democratic" version represented by Rostovtzeff has blamed the state for preventing the emergence of the "middle class" *decurions* of the provincial administration. The "bourgeois-industrial" version has stressed the absence of technical inventiveness in the empire. This has been almost universally endorsed by twentieth-century writers (even if its extreme form, attributing collapse to the weakness of Roman manufacturing industry, has been less common).

There are two errors contained within these stories. The first is that the reality being described and moralized over often belongs to the eighteenth to twentieth centuries A.D. and not to Roman times. This is most glaring to us in its earlier manifestations, of course. Gibbon's purposes and errors are transparent. Our own are not. But there is a second error, from which Gibbon was actually freest. By seeing continuity between their own times and Roman times, the storytellers overemphasized the continuity of Roman times themselves. Virtually all nineteenth- and twentieth-century writers have thought the most effective and progressive from of complex society to be some kind of democracy. The democratic era of Rome lay back in the republican age. Therefore, the reasons for the loss of effectiveness and progress in the later empire must be traceable to the decline of republican institutions. Gibbon alone deviated. He wished to attribute the collapse to new forces, Christianity (especially) and later barbarian pressures, and so he saw a sharp break around A.D. 200 with decline beginning thereafter. Gibbon was right in this, even if his reasons were not always correct.

Rome's cohesion depended upon ruling-class integration and upon the twin functions of the legionary economy – to defeat Rome's enemies on the battlefield and then to institutionalize a degree of economic development and secu-

---

[4]Main sources used were Jones 1964; Millar 1967, 1977; Vogt 1967; and Goffart 1974.

rity. Little rocked this cohesion between about 100 B.C. and A.D. 200. This is the period of the development of one ruling-class culture. Trade and the circulation of coinage remained steady during the whole of this period. So did defense of the territories of Rome, which were themselves stabilized around A.D. 117. Endemic civil wars dominate our political record of these centuries, but they were no worse than the civil wars of the late republic. None threatened the survival of Rome at its existing level of economic development and territorial integrity. None of the indicators of later decline can be traced back earlier than the reign of Marcus Aurelius (A.D. 161–180), during which debasement of the coinage first took a serious turn, a major plague struck, depopulation in some localities caused imperial concern, and German tribes raided across the borders.[5] But these now became occasional, not persistent, threats. Most indicators of decline stabilized from the mid-third century.

But a second unflattering label, often applied to the period 100 B.C. – A.D. 200, has some force. There was a *static* quality to much of the Roman Empire once it had repressed the Gracchi and Spartacus and admitted the allies to citizenship. Debate has focused on technological stagnation. The argument is sometimes applied to the classical world as a whole, but it has greatest force in the Roman case. The Romans did not appreciate technical ingenuity as we do, nor did they hasten to apply in a practical manner the fruits of scientific discovery as we do. The record is somewhat uneven. As we might expect, they were inventive in the military sphere. For example, the development of siege engines was quite rapid throughout the empire. But in the sphere that was vital for their economy, agriculture, they lagged. The celebrated cases are the water mill, known in Palestine in the first century A.D., and the reaping machine, known in Gaul at the same time, neither of which spread widely or rapidly. But the historians of technology can produce many other instances, of screws, levers, pulleys, and so forth, whose development and diffusion failed to occur (see the review by Plekert 1973: 303–34). Why?

One traditional answer has been slavery. This is still favored by some Marxists (e.g., Anderson 1974a: 76–82), but it will not stand up. As Kieckle (1973: 335–46) notes, the period when slavery flourished, 500 B.C. – A.D. 100, was more fertile in technical invention and application than was the period of slavery's decline, and in turn that was more fertile than the period after it had declined. A more plausible argument, advanced by Finley (1965: 29–25), incorporates slavery into a wider explanation. Dependent labor was abundant in the ancient world. Thus inventions, almost all of which substitute machin-

[5]Trajan's grants to landowners for the upkeep of orphanages in Italy are sometimes interpreted as indicating a population shortage. There is no other evidence for this, and it is more probable that they indicate either a specific shortage of army volunteers or a decline in the viability of the extended family, consequent upon the growth of cities. Duncan-Jones (1974: 288–319) believes the policy dates from the earlier reign of Nerva (A.D. 96–8) but notes that the scale was small. Perhaps it was what it claimed to be, an act of charity.

ery for human muscle, had less appeal because human muscle was not scarce either in numbers or in motivation (which was coerced). This is more convincing. One of its strengths is that it can deal with Kieckle's objection to slavery. As we have seen, the labor problem was solved less by slavery than by its successor labor statuses – *coloni,* semifree wage laborers working for their subsistence, and so forth. There was more need for inventiveness during the period of slavery's height because of the uneven spread of slavery and its harmful effects on the independent peasantry in its core regions. But it is still an incomplete explanation, because machinery was not substituted for animal muscle either, yet animals were costly and in short supply. Why not?

"Inventiveness" as we usually conceive of it is only a particular and limited form of inventiveness. It is *intensive,* aimed at extracting more outputs in the form of energy and resources from fewer inputs, in particular from fewer labor inputs. By contrast, the major Roman inventions were *extensive,* extracting more outputs from more coordinated, organized inputs. They excelled at extensive social organization. This is not a simple dichotomy between modern and ancient history. The Iron Age revolution (described in Chapter 6) was intensive in its pioneering techniques – they physically penetrated the soil to a greater depth while reducing the extent of authoritative social organization. The Romans capitalized on that base by extending outward, pacifying space and organizing it, as we have seen repeatedly. Remember what hung on Marius's pole! The individual pieces of legionary equipment were not remarkable as inventions (though one general attributed his victories to the *dolabrum,* the pickax). What was remarkable was their combination in a complex, extensive social organization. The brains of Marius's commissariat were not thinking intensively, but extensively. Small wonder that the result was a "first" in human ingenuity, the territorial empire.

Roman concern with extensive organization left them with a relative blind spot for the kind of inventions we value – just as modern writers argue. They were uninterested in substituting machine or animal muscle for human muscle (unless the savings were obvious and no capital outlay was involved). On occasion they would move (as we *never* do) in the opposite direction, moving army supplies from mules to men if there were resulting gains in extensive organization. They were ill-equipped for what we call technological development because all their major achievements were built, not on reducing inputs but on *extending* and *organizing* them.

This model now begs a question that I cannot answer. Were the Romans *also* slowing down in their rate of extensive innovative powers? The answer is perhaps yes, because by A.D. 100 they had reached boundaries they felt to be natural ones, they were exploiting most of the land that could support agriculture, and their political and fiscal organization had also penetrated the whole empire. A full answer would involve asking new questions of the original source material, concentrating on the logistics of organization.

But, ultimately, identifying a slowdown in the empire around A.D. 200 may not be decisive to answering the "decline and fall" question. Roman indigenous developments were not now left undisturbed. By the end of the second century A.D. we can see, as the Romans could, new external threats to their stability. From the patterns of fort building, we know they lacked confidence in the defensibility of any single line over the gap between the upper reaches of the Rhine and the Danube. Between 167 and 180, Rome twice had to fight hard to defend the Danube against the incursions of a Germanic tribal confederacy, the Marcomanni. The Romans were unable to hold the frontier provinces without a mass transfer of troops from the east, where a war against the Parthians had just been concluded successfully. This was doubly ominous. It revealed how dangerous could be a simultaneous war in east and west. And it showed that the Marcomanni were symptomatic of the increasing organizational capacity of the northern "barbarians."

The Roman Empire was upgrading the level of its marcher lords just as empires before it had done. This was occurring in several ways (Todd 1975). First, the agricultural innovations of Rome that did not depend on large-scale social organization – a greater variety of plants, simple machinery, and fertilizer – spread throughout Eurasia and Africa. After about A.D. 200, the agricultural produce of these areas began to offer serious competition to Roman agriculture. Second, military techniques were diffused. As former auxiliary commanders, several barbarian leaders used Roman techniques. They were aware of the enduring Roman weakness in cavalry, and they consciously exploited their own superior mobility. But third (as a response to the success of raiding), their own social structure became more centralized. By comparing the accounts by Caesar, written in the middle of the first century B.C., and Tacitus, written in the second century A.D., Thompson (1965) has chronicled the development of private-property rights as well as tendencies toward kingship. Both were based on authority in war. Both were consciously encouraged by the Romans for diplomatic security. And both were boosted by trade with the Romans, which encouraged more organized slaving raids among the Germans to pay for Roman imports. German social organization advanced considerably. Fortified towns covering 10–35 hectares have been uncovered, their populations not much smaller than Roman provincial towns'. Rome's interaction networks had spilled over its fortified boundaries. Even this was not a unitary society.

Roman reorganization is visible in the twenty-year period after the accession of Septimius Severus in 193. Severus began withdrawing crack legions from the frontiers to mobile reserve positions, replacing them at the frontier with a settler militia. This was a more defensive, less confident posture. It also cost more, and so he attempted financial reform, abolishing tax farming and the tax exemption for Rome and Italy. Did this raise enough? Presumably not, for he debased the silver coinage (as Marcus Aurelius had done before him) and introduced more of it. His son, Caracalla, showed similar concerns. His extension of the citizenship had a financial motive, as well as attempting to mobilize political commitment from the people. He also debased the coinage and increased its supply. Hopkins calculates that between the 180s and the 210s, the silver content of *denarii* minted in Rome fell by 43 percent (1980b: 115).

It would be nice to know more about this crucial period and its mixture of sensitive and crass policy changes. The Severi attempted an intelligent, two-pronged fiscal and military strategy: reviving a peasant-citizen army on the frontier and combining it with a professional reserve army supported by a more equitable tax system. The abolition of tax farming even suggests an attempt at the crucial problem of exaction. But presumably short-term exigencies – sometimes their own survival against rival claimants, sometimes a flurry of incursions over the Rhine, over the Danube, and in the East – led them into debasement, as disastrous a policy as could be imagined in such an economy. A state that issued its coinage through its expenditure demands, yet left the supply side to private producers and middlemen, could not do worse than destroy confidence in its coinage. If debasement was noticed, hoarding and inflation would ensue. Issuing more silver coinage might not have had this effect (I would not presume to arbitrate the Keynesian-monetarist dispute of our own time), but debasing its silver content was debasing one of the main functions of the state in the eyes of its citizens. It is sometimes argued that the emperors did not realize the consequences of their actions. They may not have made the technical connection of debasement with inflation. But as they believed that the value of a coin depended only on its metallic content, debasement could only be a conscious attempt to deceive their subjects. They must have realized that eventual discovery and discontent were inevitable. Debasement could only be a rational strategy to secure a breathing space.

But this was unavailable. The Germans, now capable of large-scale incursion, were emboldened by the deficiencies in the Roman defensive system. But even worse, and more extraneous to Rome, were developments in the Middle East. In 224–6 the Parthian state was overthrown by Persian invaders led by the Sassanid dynasty, whose rule was to last for four hundred years. Rather more centralized than the Parthian state, and capable of more sustained campaigning and siege warfare, the Sassanids were also expansionist. Eventually, the Romans (and their other neighbors) learned to exploit their weakness: unresolved tension between the state and the feudal nobility. But for over a century, Rome had to mount prolonged defense of its eastern provinces and at the same time of its Rhine-Danube frontier. The cost of defense had risen enormously in these fifty years from about 175. To meet it with an unchanged social structure required greater collective sacrifice. The standoff between state, upper stratum, and people would have to be overcome. The policies of the Severi were attempts in this direction. But there was insufficient time. The emperors took money where they could find it, from debasement, from confiscation, but not from a general increase in tax rates, for which the necessary political machinery was not yet constructed. The end of the Severi was fitting. An inconclusive war with the Persians in 231 was followed the next year by more Marcomanni incursions. The army of the Rhine did not get its pay and mutinied in 235, murdering Alexander Severus and replacing him with its general Maximinus, the first of a series of soldier-emperors.

Between 235 and 284, the Roman fiscal-military system broke down, with disastrous effects on the economy in general. The silver content of coins plunged from 40 percent in 250 to less than 4 percent in 270. On occasion we hear of locals refusing to accept current imperial coinage. Prices rose, though it is difficult to be precise about when or by how much. Evidence of urban decline can be found in a drop in inscribed stones commemorating such things as new buildings, charities, gifts, and manumission of slaves. The number of shipwrecks declined (indicating, we assume, a drop in trade, not better weather). Complaints of deserted fields and villages began in midcentury. On marginal land there may have been a substantial population loss, on more typical land much less – which is a roundabout way of saying that we cannot be precise about the extent of the *agri deserti*. The worst aspect of the decline was that it was a self-reinforcing downward spiral. As it became more difficult to supply the troops, they mutinied. Of the next twenty emperors, eighteen died violently, one died in a Persian prison, and one died of the plague. So the invaders found easy pickings, causing more economic dislocation. The 260s were the nadir, seeing a simultaneous attack by Goths in the North and Persians in the East. The Romans claimed there were 320,000 Goth warriors in 2,000 ships. The figures are exaggerated, but reveal how seriously they took the threat. The Goths got as far as Athens, which they sacked, before they were defeated; while the Persians defeated and captured the Emperor Valerian and sacked Antioch.

The empire could have collapsed at this point, either totally or into several Latin and Greek kingdoms (in the way that Alexander the Great's Empire had). Overall population and economic activity would have declined still further, and feudal-type fiscal-military relations might have emerged. But the soldier-emperors managed a series of victories in the 270s and 280s which seem to have given a breathing space of about fifty years. Diocletian (284–305) and his successors, principally Constantine (324–37), took full advantage.

Diocletian's great reforms are fascinating, for they reveal a profound understanding (whose? Diocletian's own?) of Roman social structure and its declining capacity to withstand external threat. They broke radically with the past, accepting the downward spiral of the last century, accepting that a structure of common sacrifice could not be re-created. Indeed, Diocletian attempted to break the autonomous power of the traditional upper class, dividing the senatorial from the equestrian order and depriving the former of both military and civil office.

Obviously the success of this strategy depended on the state's ability to penetrate "civil society" itself, which it had done only feebly in the past. The *attempt* was systematic. In the military sphere, conscription was reintroduced on a permanent basis, and the size of the army virtually doubled. But although both frontier and reserve armies were strengthened, the increase did not denote improvement in the organizational capacity of the army. There were more independent armies of about the same size as before. Julian's force of about 65,000 assembled against the Persians in 363 was probably the largest of this period, but no greater than the largest armies of the late republic. Moreover, the bulk of the new recruits were stationed in relatively small units along the empire's main communications routes. They were used to patrol and pacify all core areas, and specifically to help in the extraction of taxes. Similarly, the civil bureaucracy was increased (probably doubled). Provinces were subdivided into smaller administrative units, perhaps more manageable but certainly less capable of autonomous action (including rebellion). The tax system was rationalized, combining a land tax and a poll tax. The census was revived and regularly carried out. The tax rate was assessed annually according to an estimate of budgetary needs. This annual indiction, announced in advance, was probably the first actual *budget* in the history of any state.

All this might sound like sensible rationalization, but in the conditions of the ancient world it required an enormous degree of coercion. When most wealth, certainly nearly all the wealth of the peasantry, never realized its value in any visible way, how was it to be assessed and then extracted? On the assessment we have a contemporary account of one of Diocletian's censuses by Lactantius:

The greatest public calamity and general sorrow was the census imposed on the provinces and cities. Census officers were posted everywhere and under their activity everything was like a hostile invasion or grim captivity. The fields were measured sod by sod, vines and trees were numbered, animals of every kind were written down, the heads of men were counted, the urban and rural poor were contained in the cities, all the squares were filled with crowds of families, everyone was there with his children and slaves. Torture and blows reverberated, sons were hanged in their parents' presence, the most faithful slaves were tortured to inform against their masters, wives against their husbands. If they reported everything they were tortured to incriminate themselves, and when fear had won the day, things which they did not possess were entered in their names. . . . What the ancients did to the conquered by right of war, he dared to do to Romans. . . . But he did not trust the same census officials, but others were sent to succeed them, as though they could find more, and the returns were always being doubled, not that they found anything, but that they added what they wished, to justify their appointment. Meanwhile, animals were perishing and men were dying, but tribute was paid for the dead nonetheless, so that no-one could either live or die gratis. [quoted in Jones 1970: II, 266–7]

This was exaggerated, of course, but revealing nonetheless. Diocletian, like every pre-nineteenth-century tax collector, had only three strategies. The first two – to tax through the local knowledge and power of the major landlords, or to tax in genuine local consultation with the people – did not extract sufficient monies to meet rising budgetary needs. The landlords took their cut, and the people understated their wealth. The landlord strategy was precisely the one being abandoned; whereas no institution for genuine popular consultation had existed since the early republic. All that remained was the third strategy – to extract with force the maximum assessment and collection consonant with keeping the population alive and productive. An essential part of this strategy, as Lactantius pointed out, was to move on state officials – before they could strike compromises with the locals involving a personal rake-off. This was a heightened form of compulsory cooperation. The compulsion was heightened, the cooperation became more passive. It seems from the absence of revolt that the necessity for a larger army, bureaucracy, and taxation was generally accepted, but the participation of both the people and the upper stratum in their organization lessened.

The increase in coercion implied more than just military force. It implied also social and territorial fixity. As we saw in chapters dealing with much earlier societies, the power of the state depended to a large degree on *trapping* its subjects into particular spaces and roles. Diocletian's reforms involved the same process, not as a conscious act of policy but as a by-product of the new system. The tax system worked better, more predictably, with less need for assessment and policing, if peasants were attached to one particular center for census purposes. Peasants were allocated to villages or towns and forced both to pay their taxes and to assemble for the census there. This was traditional (as we know from the birth of Christ), but now that censuses were more regular and tax exaction annual, it tied peasants (and their children) to their home village. Similar conditions were applied to the urban and crafts sector, where people were tied to particular occupations.

This was interfering with supply and demand (forces that were not recognized at the time). Indeed the tendency of coercive regulation was away from a decentralized, market, coinage economy toward a central-place, authoritative allocation of values. Inflation was considered the product, not of the economy as a whole, but of the avarice of those who took advantage of uneven harvest conditions. It was remediable by force alone, "since" – in the language of Diocletian's edict setting out the maximum prices of hundreds of commodities – "as a guide, fear is always found the most influential teacher in the performance of duty, it is our pleasure that anyone who shall have resisted this statute shall, for his daring, be subject to the capital penalty" (quoted in Jones 1970: II, 311). Raising prices would result in death, provided the state had the resources to stand behind every monetary transaction in the empire! The central-place economy had an alternative to force if that failed to reduce inflation (as it was bound to). It was to move the purchasing power of the state away from the price mechanism altogether, to demand supplies in kind. Some such moves were made, though the exact extent is unclear. It was certainly implied by the decentralized stationing of troops and by the small administrative units – each could obtain its supplies direct from its locality.

Judged by its own pretensions, Diocletian's system could not work because the state did not have sufficient supervisory and coercive powers to enforce it. The economy was sufficiently decentralized for buyers to pay higher prices rather than to report the seller to the nearest official with troops. In practice, the assessment of taxes had to rely on local notables. This is the most interesting aspect of the system. For we can trace the impetus that it exerted on the development of the peasant *colonus,* tied to a piece of land and a landlord. How was the rural taxpayer to be tied to a city or village in practice? This was especially tricky in relatively unurbanized provinces, like much of North Africa. But the answer was clear: by putting him under the control of an estate. Successive edicts chronicle the evolution of this solution. An edict of Constantine in 332 rather neatly demonstrates the consequences of administrative convenience as well as the notion that coercion was necessary for the preservation of freedom:

Any person in whose possession a tenant that belongs to another is found not only shall restore the aforesaid tenant to his place of origin but also assume the capitation tax for this man for the time that he was with him. Tenants also who meditate flight may be bound with chains and reduced to a servile condition, so that by virtue of a servile condemnation they shall be compelled to fulfil the duties that befit free men. [quoted in Jones 1970: II, 312]

The peasant was finally handed over to the landlord by the state.[6]

The standoff had been modified but not ended. The military and political roles of the upper class of civil society had been broken, but the local economy had been handed back to it. The first was an act of policy, the latter an unintended consequence of the military-fiscal needs of the state. A more popular democratic, consultative policy was never seriously considered, for it would have meant reversing the state's greater coercive tendencies.

To the extent that it failed, Diocletian's system probably clamped down on the possibilities for further economic development. The conventional wisdom of our own capitalist age is that even if Diocletian had succeeded in his aims, this would have been the result. This shows the bias among classicists against the innovative possibilities of centralized states. It seems to me that the Roman administration, given its desperate fiscal needs, had as much incentive to improve agricultural techniques as any private landlord, capitalist or otherwise. It was precisely because it did *not* control agricultural production that development in this sphere was stifled. After all, as is often pointed out (e.g.,

[6]In townless areas of North Africa, Shaw (1979) has shown a variant pattern, where the local periodic markets were handed over to landlord control.

by Jones 1964: II, 1048–53), considerable innovation was found in the spheres it did control – the diffusion of the water mill was primarily to saw marble for monuments and only secondarily to grind corn, whereas no agricultural machines could compete with siege engines in their sophistication. Agricultural development was now along surreptitious lines, to be hidden from the state, and therefore slow of diffusion.

By the more modest standards of survival, Diocletian's system was a success. There was apparently something of a "fourth-century revival" (the details of which are uncertain). But any revival has to be considered rather remarkable, given that the state was continuously raising its levels of exaction on the same basic economy. The army continued to grow to over 650,000 men – nearly four times the size of Augustus's forces. The budget indictions doubled between 324 and 364.

The marcher lords and the Persians would not go away, however. Germanic groups were used increasingly as allies and allowed to settle within the frontier regions. Again, an extraneous threat worsened the situation. About 375 the Ostrogothic kingdom of southern Russia was destroyed by Huns from central Asia, pressing the Germanic peoples against the empire. Settlement, not raiding, was the Germanic peoples' intention. Rather than fight them, Valens allowed in the Visigoths. In 378 they rebelled. Valens allowed his cavalry to be pinned against the walls of Adrianople, and he and his army were destroyed. Further settlement of Visigoths, Ostrogoths, and others could not be prevented, and they were now relied on to defend directly the northern frontiers. An armed force that did not require taxation saved money, but in political terms this was a retreat to "feudalism." By 400, units called legions still existed, but they were really regional forces, garrisoning strong defensive positions and usually lacking the engineering capacity to consolidate army victories. The only remaining central field army protected the emperor. The legionary economy existed no more.

Internally, the process of decline hastened from about 370 on. Urban depopulation began. In the countryside land went out of cultivation, and we can be virtually sure that many people died of malnutrition and disease. Probably as a reaction to the pressure, two major social changes occurred. First, hitherto free men placed themselves as *coloni* under the patronage of local landowners' protection from the imperial tax collector. Whole villages were passing into the hands of a patron from about 400 on. Now the growth of *coloni* went against the state's interests. Second, there was a decentralization of the economy, as local landowners attempted to increase their independence from imperial power through the self-sufficiency of an estate economy (the *oikos*). The decline of interprovincial trade was hastened by the invasions themselves as communications routes became insecure. Local landowners and *coloni* together viewed the imperial authorities as more and more exploitative, and together they created a social structure that anticipated the feudal manor worked by dependent serfs. Diocletian's coercive policies had left open the possibility of retreat into a local economy controlled by quasi-feudal lords. Accordingly, in the last century of its existence the Roman state reversed its policy toward the upper class; unable to muster local coercion against it, the imperial authorities were willing to hand it back the civil administration. They sought to encourage landowners and *decurions* to fulfill civic responsibilities rather than evade them. But they no longer had incentives to offer, for the legionary economy had collapsed, finally. In some areas the masses and, to a lesser extent, the local elites appear to have welcomed barbarian rule.

The main area of controversy in this description is whether the collapse had quite such drastic effects on the peasantry. Bernardi (1970: 78–80) argues that the peasants did not die; rather, in alliance with their lords, they evaded the harsh taxes. Thus, "the political organization broke down, but not the framework of rural life, the forms of property and the methods of exploitation." Finley (1973: 152) also doubts whether the Roman peasantry could have been any more harshly oppressed or hungry than present-day Third World peasants, who nevertheless breed satisfactorily. Finley's explanation is that the empire's economy rested "almost entirely on the muscles of men" who – at subsistence – had nothing left to contribute to an "austerity programme" that had lasted through two hundred years of barbarian attack. Thus the increased consumption needs of army and bureaucracy (and also the parasitic Christian Church – reenter Gibbon!) led to a labor shortage. The argument concerns only the precise timetable of the collapse. The political and military collapse is precisely datable: In A.D. 476 the last emperor in the west, the ironically named Romulus Augustulus, was deposed. His conqueror, Odoacer, the leader of a mixed Germanic group, was proclaimed not emperor, but king according to German traditions. The economic collapse presumably both predated and postdated this event.

In this account of the decline and fall, I have given the precipitating role in events to the military pressure of the barbarians. This was considerably and, to the Romans, unexpectedly increased around A.D. 200, and it therefore eased only for one period, around 280–330. Without this shift in geopolitics, all talk of Rome's internal "failures" – to establish democracy, free labor, industry, a middle class, or whatever – would not have arisen. Before A.D. 200, the imperial structure dealt adequately with its internal, as well as external, difficulties, and in so doing it produced the highest level of ideological, economic, political, and military collective power yet seen in the world, with the possible exception of Han China.

Moreover, as Jones has argued (1964: II, 1025–68), different levels of outside pressure probably account for the continued survival of the eastern empire, with its capital at Constantinople, for another thousand years. After the administrative division of the empire, the western empire had to defend all but the last 500 kilometers of the vulnerable Rhine-Danube frontier. Strong eastern defenses along this short distance tended to deflect northern raiders westward. The East had to defend against the Persians, but this could be done by an orderly succession of war, peace treaties, and diplomacy. The Persians suffered from the same organizational and numbers problems as the Romans. The Germanic peoples could not be regulated in this way. There were too many of them, in terms of numbers of political organizations with which the Romans had to deal. We cannot be *certain* of this argument, for the East also differed in its social structure (as Jones admits; see also Anderson 1974a: 97–103). Nevertheless, it is plausible to conclude in the words of Piganiol's famous conclusion: "Roman civilization did not die a natural death: it was assassinated" (1947: 422).

Of course, we cannot leave the matter there. As I have repeatedly emphasized, external pressures are rarely truly extraneous. Two events in the sustained external pressure do appear relatively extraneous to the history of Rome, it is true: the overthrow of Parthia by the Sassanids, and the Hunnish pressure on the Goths. If Roman influences were felt even here, they were presumably rather indirect ones. But the rest of the pressure, especially the Germanic pressure, was not extraneous in any real sense, for Roman influences were strong and causal. Rome gave to its northern enemies the military organization that assassinated it. Rome gave much of the economic technique that sustained the assassination. And Rome's level of development gave also the motive. The Germans adapted these influences to produce a social structure capable of conquest. They were not fully barbarian, except in Roman propaganda: They were marcher peoples, semicivilized.

Thus, to the extent that we can talk of Roman "failure," it was a failure to respond to what Rome itself had created on its frontiers. The causes of the failure were internal, but they must be linked to Roman foreign policy. Two power strategies were open, predominantly military and ideological.

The military strategy was to subdue the barbarians in the traditional way, by extending conquests to the whole of Europe, halting only at the Russian steppes. Rome's frontier problems would then have been similar to those of China, manageable because confronted by relatively small numbers of pastoral nomads. But this strategy presupposed what Rome had not possessed since the Punic Wars, the capacity for collective military sacrifice provided by a relatively egalitarian citizenry. It was not possible in A.D. 200 and would have required profound, secular changes in social structure to make it possible.

The ideological strategy would have been to accept the frontiers, but to civilize the attackers, so that eventual defeat would not have meant total destruction. This could have taken either an elitist or a democratic form – either a Germanic dynasty could have run the empire (or several civilized Roman states) or the peoples could have merged. The elitist variant was the successful Chinese way of incorporating its conquerors; the democratic variant was presented as a possibility, not exploited, by the spread of Christianity. But Rome had never seriously taken its culture outside the area already pacified by its legions. Again it would have required a revolution in political thinking. Not surprisingly, neither the elitist nor the democratic variant was pressed. Stilicho and his Vandal people were the real defenders of Rome around A.D. 400: It was inconceivable that Stilicho could assume the imperial purple, but disastrous for Rome that he could not. It was similarly disastrous that virtually none of the Germans were converted to Christianity before their conquests (as argued in Brown 1967). Again the reasons are basically internal: that Rome had not developed either strategy among its *own* elite or people. The three-way standoff I have described meant that the integration of state and elite into one civilized ruling class had limits, while the people were largely irrelevant to imperial structures. In China, elite homogeneity was symbolized by Confucianism; in Rome the possibilities for popular homogeneity were presented by Christianity. Obviously this issue should involve us in a more detailed analysis of the world salvation religions, those important bearers of ideological power. The next chapters undertake this.

For the moment we can conclude that Rome's failure after A.D. 200 to cope with a higher level of external pressure lay in the three-way power standoff between state elite, upper class, and people. To cope with the semibarbarians in either a warlike or a peaceful way would have required the closing of its power gaps. The gaps were not closed, even though three attempts were made. The Severi made one flawed foray, Diocletian a second, Constantine and the Christian emperors a third. But their failure does not appear to have been inevitable: They were overwhelmed by events. So we are left uncertain as to the full potentialities of this first territorial empire, with its ideologically cohesive elite and its legionary-economy version of compulsory cooperation. Such power forms did not surface again in the area covered or influenced by the Roman Empire. Instead, as in the case of the Persian empire of domination, social development lay with interstitial aspects of social structure, most notably with the forces that generated Christianity.

Conclusion: the Roman achievement

The core Roman institution was always the legion. Yet the legion was never a purely military organization. Its ability to mobilize economic, political, and, for a time, ideological commitments was the main reason for its unparalleled success. Yet as it proved successful, its social mobilization changed in the ways we have observed in this chapter. Those changes are the key to the entire process of Roman social development.

The first phase of conquest saw the Romans as an expanding city-state. They possessed a degree of collective commitment among Iron Age peasant farmers, comparable to the Greeks before them, whose roots lay in a combination of relatively intensive economic and military power. But they adopted more extensive Macedonian military techniques (we may guess) by also possessing tribal elements in their early social structure. The citizen-legion resulted, integrating Rome's class structure (in its Latin sense) to an effective instrument of military conquest. It seems that the citizen-legion was the most effective military machine on land in the Mediterranean area (and probably anywhere in the world at that time) right up to the defeat of Carthage and the appropriation of its empire.

But military success fed back into Roman social structure. Continuous warfare over two centuries generated a professional army, detached from the classes of the citizenry. An enormous influx of booty, slaves, and expropriated estates exacerbated inequalities and enhanced the private property of the senatorial and equestrian elites. Indeed in the second and first centuries B.C. occurred all the developments normal to conquest states: widening inequality; a decrease in popular participation in government; a dialectic between centralized, militaristic control and the subsequent fragmentation of the state as the generals, governors, and tax farmers "disappeared" into provincial "civil society" carrying with them the fruits of the state's conquests as "private" property. As always, this empire of domination seemed rather less powerful in infrastructural reality than in its pretensions – and its weaknesses generated the usual conflicts with allies, its own populus, and its own generals.

Nevertheless Rome was not a "normal" empire of domination, as was proved by its ability to stabilize its rule and to solve at least the first two of the conflicts just mentioned. There were really two main achievements. (I do not count as a major achievement the repression of the original popular-citizen base of Rome, for conquering states are normally able to "organizationally outflank" their lower classes in the way I describe in this chapter. In extensive societies, ruling groups normally have a wider organizational base than do subordinate groups. The masses are trapped within the "organization chart" of the rulers.)

The first major achievement was Rome's treatment of its allies, the *socii*. Taking the Persian rather than the Assyrian route, Rome was prepared to rule through conquered elites (with the notable exception of the vengeance wreaked on the Carthaginians). But then something additional occurred: Most native elites became Romanized, such that it became almost impossible to detect their native origins after a century of Roman rule. Thus, for example, when the republic became an empire in constitution as well as reality, the imperial succession moved around most of the provinces in turn. Thus the *socius*, meaning originally a federation of allies, became more of a "society" in our modern quasi-unitary sense. Or to be more precise, it became a "ruling-class society," for only the elites were admitted into real membership.

True, there was a specific area of weakness in this ruling-class society. It concerned a certain degree of power standoff between the state bureaucracy and the landowning, officeholding provincial ruling class. Rome never quite stably institutionalized these relations, and tensions and civil wars frequently resulted. Only after A.D. 200, however, did this constitute a serious weakness. The degree of ruling-class unity was formidable by the standards of other empires of domination.

Ideological power resources, particularly literacy and Hellenistic rationalism, now provided a degree of infrastructure for cultural solidarity among elites. I discuss these resources in the next chapter, in connection with the rise of Christianity. But the existence of a second set of infrastructural resources has been clearly demonstrated in this chapter. I refer to what I called the legionary economy, Rome's version of compulsory cooperation. This was the second Roman achievement.

I singled out one key symbol of the legionary economy: the pole devised by the commissariat of the general Marius around 109 B.C. Around this pole, carried by most infantrymen, were tied a variety of civil-engineering tools that outweighed the battlefield weapons carried. With these tools the legions systematically pacified the territories they conquered, building communications routes, fortresses, and supply depots. As space was pacified, agricultural surplus and population rose. The legions were *productive,* and so their consumption stimulated a kind of "military Keynesianism." More specifically, the state's military expenditures boosted a monetary economy. As more and more contiguous inhabited space was brought into this economy, Roman rule became territorially continuous and resources, economic and other, diffused evenly across its enormous extent. The existence of a uniform economy between 100 B.C. and A.D. 200 is of enormous significance, even if it was operating within a quite narrow band above subsistence. It was the first extensive civil society, in our modern sense of the term.[7] After the collapse of Rome, such a society reappeared only toward the end of the Middle Ages in Europe (see Chapter 14). Rome was thus the first *territorial* empire, the first predominantly nonsegmental extensive society, at least in its higher reaches.

As a result of this analysis, in this chapter I was able to attack conventional notions concerning the supposed technological stagnation of Rome. True, Rome was relatively uninterested in what I termed intensive technology: increasing output without correspondingly increasing inputs. But Rome made enormous contributions to extensive technology: increasing output by extensively organizing a greater number of inputs. Marius's pole was an excellent example of such ingenuity. I produce more evidence on this point in Chapter 12 when contrasting Roman and medieval architectural technology.

[7]Not even Han dynasty China approached this degree of economic unity. For example, its tax system was a complex system involving requisitions in cash and in various goods in kind, like lengths of cloth, silks, and hemp, and strings of beads. The exchange value of these items against each other required authoritative decisions from power brokers – it did not diffuse throughout society.

Roman extensive powers were unprecedented. They account for the longevity of the empire. But – without repeating in detail the complex conclusion regarding the "decline and fall" question – they also help account for the violence of its eventual demise. Federal empires of domination traditionally had great trouble with their border regions. However, in principle any neighbor could be given marcher (i.e., "semimember) status. But Rome's extensive *territorial* control emphasized the gulf between civilization and barbarism. It was more clearly *bounded* than other empires. The boundaries were also hardened by its ideological power achievement. As we see in the next chapter, its elite culture was exclusive and eventually inward-looking. Barbarians could not be fully civilized unless the legions had first cleared the way with force. But as with all civilizations, the more successful was Rome, the more it attracted the cupidity of its neighbors. Rome found it difficult to institutionalize this cupidity and could only fight it. Eventually the economy began to falter under the strain, and compulsion began to predominate over cooperation. As real citizenship no longer existed, the masses could not be organized to greater sacrifices (as they had been to overcome Carthage centuries earlier). Similarly, the power standoff between state and ruling class frustrated greater attempts at elite mobilization. The legionary economy was not a flexible instrument. Once its routine was broken, Rome descended to the level of other empires of domination, and in that field of comparison its opportunistic abilities were not remarkable. If its legacy to the world was greater than almost any other empire's, that was because its achievements in ideological power were transmitted in a novel fashion: through a world religion.

Bibliography

Anderson, P. 1974a. *Passages from Antiquity to Feudalism*. London: New Left Books.
Appian. 1913. *The Civil Wars*. Vol. 3 of his *Roman History*. Loeb edition. London: Heinemann.
Badian, E. 1968. *Roman Imperialism*. Oxford: Blackwell.
Bernardi, A. 1970. The economic problems of the Roman Empire at the time of its decline. In *The Economic Decline of Empires*. C. M. Cipolla. ed. London: Methuen.
Brown, P. 1967. Review of A. H. M. Jones, *The Later Roman Empire*. *Economic History Review*, 20.
Brunt, P. A. 1971a. *Italian Manpower, 225 B.C. – A.D. 14*. Oxford: Clarendon Press.
    1971b. *Social Conflicts in the Roman Republic*. London: Chatto & Windus.
Cameron, A. 1976. *Bread and Circuses: The Roman Emperor and his People*. Inaugural Lecture, Kings College. London: Kings College.
Cipolla, C. M. 1976. *Before the Industrial Revolution*. London: Methuen.
Crawford, M. 1970. Money and exchange in the Roman world. *Journal of Roman Studies*, 60.
    1974. *Roman Republican Coinage*. Cambridge: Cambridge University Press.
    1978. *The Roman Republic*. London: Fontana.
Duby, G. 1974. *The Early Growth of the European Economy: Warriors and Peasants from the Seventh to the Twelfth Centuries*. London: Weidenfeld & Nicolson.

Duncan-Jones, R. 1974. *The Economy of the Roman Empire: Quantitative Studies.* Cambridge: Cambridge University Press.

Finley, M. I. 1965. Technical innovation and economic progress in the ancient world. *Economic History Review,* 18.

1973. *The Ancient Economy.* London: Chatto & Windus.

Frank, T. 1940. *An Economic Survey of Ancient Rome.* Vol. V, *Rome and Italy of the Empire.* Baltimore: Johns Hopkins University Press.

Gabba, E. 1976. *Republican Rome, the Army and the Allies.* Oxford: Blackwell.

Garnsey, P. D. A., and C. R. Whittaker. 1978. *Imperialism in the Ancient World.* Cambridge: Cambridge University Press.

Gelzer, M. 1969. *The Roman Nobility.* Oxford: Blackwell.

Goffart, W. 1974. *Caput and Colonate: Towards a History of Late Roman Taxation.* Toronto: University of Toronto Press.

Gruen, E. S. 1974. *The Last Generation of the Roman Republic.* Berkeley: University of California Press.

Harris, W. V. 1979. *War and Imperialism in Republican Rome.* Oxford: Clarendon Press.

Hopkins, K. 1977. Economic growth and towns in classical antiquity. In *Towns in Societies: Essays in Economic History and Historical Sociology,* P. Abrams and E. A. Wrigley eds. Cambridge: Cambridge University Press.

1978. *Conquerors and Slaves: Sociological Studies in Roman History.* Cambridge: Cambridge University Press.

1980. Taxes and trade in the Roman Empire (200 B.C. – A.D. 400). *Journal of Roman Studies,* 70.

Jones, A. H. M. 1964. *The Later Roman Empire 284–602.* Oxford: Blackwell.

1970. *A History of Rome through the Fifth Century, Selected Documents.* London: Macmillan.

Josephus, Flavius. 1854. *Works.* Trans. W. Whiston. London: Bohn.

Kieckle, F. K. 1973. Technical progress in the main period of ancient slavery. In *Fourth International Conference of Economic History.* Bloomington, Ind., 1968. Paris: Mouton.

Luttwak, E. N. 1976. *The Grand Strategy of the Roman Empire.* Baltimore: Johns Hopkins University Press.

MacMullen, R. 1966. *Enemies of the Roman Order.* Cambridge, Mass.: Harvard University Press.

1974. *Roman Social Relations.* New Haven, Conn.: Yale University Press.

Millar, F., et al. 1967. *The Roman Empire and its Neighbours.* London: Weidenfeld & Nicolson.

1977. *The Emperor in the Roman World.* London: Duckworth.

Momigliano, A. 1975. *Alien Wisdom: The Limits of Hellenization.* Cambridge: Cambridge University Press.

Ogilvie, R. M. 1976. *Early Rome and the Etruscans.* London: Fontana.

Parker, A. J. 1980. Ancient shipwrecks in the Mediterranean and the Roman Provinces. *British Archaeological Reports, Supplementary Series.*

Piganiol, A. 1947. *L'Empire Chretien 325–395.* Paris: Presses Universitaires de France.

Plutarch. 1921. *Life of Tiberius Gracchus.* Vol. 10 of his *Lives.* Loeb edition. London: Heinemann.

Polybius. 1922–7. *The Histories.* Loeb edition. London: Heinemann.

Plekert, H. W. 1973. Technology in the Greco-Roman World. In *Fourth International Conference of Economic History,* Bloomington, Ind., 1968. Paris: Mouton.

Rostovtzeff, M. 1957. *The Social and Economic History of the Roman Empire.* Oxford: Clarendon Press.

Runciman, W. G. 1983. Capitalism without classes: the case of classical Rome. *British Journal of Sociology*, 24.

Russell, J. C. 1958. Late ancient and medieval population. *Transactions of the American Philosophical Society*, vol. 48, part 3.

Ste. Croix, G. E. M. de. 1956. Greek and Roman accounting. In *Studies in the History of Accounting*. ed. A. C. Littleton and B. S. Yamey. London: Sweet and Maxwell.

1981. *The Class Struggle in the Ancient Greek World*. London: Duckworth.

Schumpeter, J. 1954. The crisis of the tax state. In *International Economic Papers: Translations Prepared for the International Economic Association*, ed. A. Peacock et al. New York: Macmillan.

Scullard, H. H. 1961. *A History of the Roman World, 753 to 146 B.C.* London: Methuen.

Shaw, B. D. 1979. Rural periodic markets in Roman North Africa as mechanisms of social integration and control. *Research in Economic Anthropology*, 2.

1984. Bandits in the Roman Empire. *Past and Present*, 105.

Slicher van Bath, B. H. 1963. Yield ratios, 810–1820. *A. A. G. Bijdragen*, 10.

Thompson, E. A. 1952. Peasant revolts in Late Roman Gaul and Spain. *Past and Present*, 7.

1965. *The Early Germans*. Oxford: Clarendon Press.

Titow, J. Z. 1972. *Winchester Yields: A Study in Medieval Agricultural Productivity*. Cambridge: Cambridge University Press.

Todd, M. 1975. *The Northern Barbarians 100 B.C.–A.D. 300*. London: Hutchinson.

Vogt, J. 1967. *The Decline of Rome*. London: Weidenfeld & Nicolson.

Watson, G. R. 1969. *The Roman Soldier*. London: Thames & Hudson.

Webster, G. 1979. *The Roman Imperial Army of the First and Second Centuries A.D.* London: Black.

Westermann, W. L. 1955. *The Slave Systems of Greek and Roman Antiquity*. Philadelphia: American Philosophical Society.

White, K. D. 1970. *Roman Farming*. London: Thames & Hudson.

Whittaker, C. 1978. Carthaginian imperialism in the fifth and fourth centuries. In *Imperialism in the Ancient World*, ed P. Garnsey and C. Whittaker. Cambridge: Cambridge University Press.

10 Ideology transcendent: the Christian *ecumene*

Introduction

In previous chapters we glimpsed both ideological power configurations identified in Chapter 1. In the examples of the Assyrian and Persian empires we saw ideology as *immanence* and as morale, that is, as the solidification of states and ruling classes through the infrastructures of ideological power – communications, education, and life-style. This was predominantly an oral rather than a literate infrastructure. Earlier, in the first emergence of civilization, we saw ideology as *transcendent power,* that is, as power that cut right across existing economic, military, and political power networks, legitimating itself with divine authority but nonetheless answering real social needs. However, in these cases the surviving evidence was somewhat fragmentary. In later history, with better evidence, we can observe such processes fairly clearly.

This chapter presents evidence of a "competition" between the two configurations of ideological power in the later Roman Empire. On the one hand, ideology solidified the immanent morale of the Roman ruling class. But, on the other, it appeared as the transcendent power of Christianity – what I shall call the Christian *ecumene.* This was innovative, combining extensive and intensive power, largely of a diffuse rather than an authoritative kind, which spread throughout all the major classes of an extensive society. Such transcendence of class, partial though it was, was world-historical in its influence. Both configurations of ideological power answered real social needs, both depended critically on their own infrastructures of power. After a period of conflict, they effected a partial compromise that endured (just) through the Dark Ages to provide an essential part of that later European dynamism described in Chapter 12.

But the dramatic emergence of a far more powerful transcendent religion was not a unique event. In about one thousand years from the birth of Buddha to the death of Muhammad, there arose four great "religions of the book" that have remained dominant over the entire globe: Christianity, Hinduism, Buddhism, and Islam. We can further compress this dating to about seven hundred years if we regard Buddhism and Hinduism as attaining their final forms around 100 B.C. From that time they, like the other two, became critically concerned with individual, universal *salvation* – the goal of relief from earthly sufferings through some kind of systematic moral life plan available to all, regardless of class or particularistic identity.[1]

This chapter deals only with one salvation religion, Christianity. In the next chapter, I discuss Islam and Confucianism briefly. I will follow this with a fuller analysis of Hunduism and Buddhism, concentrating on the former of these two coupled faiths. I will argue that Hinduism represents the pinnacle of the powers of ideology in human experience to date. I take all these religions to be major embodiments of an autonomous, transcendent ideological power in human history. The nature of this power is the theme of this chapter and the next.

Christianity was a form of ideological power. It did not spread through force of arms; it was not for several centuries institutionalized and buttressed by the power of the state; it offered few economic inducements or sanctions. It claimed a monopoly of, and divine authority for, knowledge of the ultimate "meaning" and "purpose" of life, and it spread when people believed this to be true. Only by becoming a Christian could one live a truly meaningful life. Thus its power resided originally in the fit between the Christian message and the motivations and needs of the converted. It is that equation that we need to reconstruct if we are to explain the power of Christianity.

Christianity itself helps us reconstruct one side of the equation. It is, as Muhammad first observed, one of "the religions of the book." Almost from the beginning, its believers wrote down its message and commentaries on that message. Also, the doctrines are concerned with actual (or what are claimed to be actual) historical processes. Christianity legitimates itself with historical documents, the most important of which form the New Testament. With a little historical and linguistic sophistication, scholars have used these documents to follow the development of Christian doctrines.

But the other side of the equation, the needs and motivations of the converts, is murkier. It has been neglected by scholars because of other aspects of Christianity's history. It has been a history of great, almost incredible, success. It spread so rapidly and widely that the process seems almost "natural." The hold of Christianity over our culture has weakened in the last few centuries, but paradoxically this has only reinforced the inclination of scholars to view Christianity's rise as "natural." For most skeptics over the last centuries have not taken up Gibbon's mantle. They have ignored ecclesiastical history, leaving it to the clerics. Clerics characteristically write one of two types of books about Christianity. The first is the inspirational book about the message of Christ, the bravery and faith of his followers, and the relevance

[1]For a brief tour of the world religions and philosophies, see McNeill (1963: 336–53, 420–41). I acknowledge the great influence of Weber on this chapter and the next – less in direct borrowing of his particular explanations than in a general acceptance of his stress on the role of salvation religion in historical development. I reserve direct discussion of his ideas for Volume III.

of these for today. "Relevance" means identifying a basic similarity between human needs then and now, such that the Christian message finds (or should find) a ready response from "human nature." The second type is the theological book about doctrinal issues, which gives little space to motivations and needs except insofar as these can be inferred from the popularity of certain doctrines. At the root of this lack of interest in the recipient is the ultimate and simple conviction that Christianity spread because it was true.

The consequence is an uneven literature on the power of Christianity. A typical product is the well-known introductory book on early Christianity by Chadwick (1968), useful on doctrinal influences and development but perfunctory in analysis of the causes of growth. This field contains little sociological sophistication, so my analysis has to start farther back than I would ideally wish.

A second difficulty is the dual nature of the early Christian appeal. The message spread through a number of particular milieus, starting with rural, Aramaic-speaking Palestine; then to urban Jewish, Greek-speaking communities; then to Greek urban communities; then to Roman towns in general; then to the imperial court and the countryside. It spread first in the east and south, then in the west and north, and finally among the barbarians. As the message traveled, it subtly changed. Even an analysis of doctrine alone allows the conclusion that needs must have differed too. Yet the message, despite such a complicated journey, remained recognizably the same and never lost any of its constituencies (save, to a degree, the first two); this indicates a second, universal level of appeal, which reinforces the conviction that the appeal of Christianity was simple and "natural." But this "universal" appeal is almost entirely confined within the bounds or the influence of the Roman Empire. So, to deal with particularisms and universalism alike, we must turn to that empire.

The universal appeal of Christianity within the Roman Empire

There are three main pieces of doctrinal evidence for the relatively universal appeal of Christianity. The first piece of evidence predates Christ: the growth of monotheist, salvationist, and syncretic currents in Middle Eastern thought over several centuries from the time of Zoroaster. It was not a steady growth – as we saw in Chapter 8 when Zoroaster's monotheistic salvationism weakened in the face of resistance from traditional Iranian religion. But it was gathering apace in the century preceding Christ. The earliest Greek philosophers had advanced the notion of a single prime mover. In later classical times, this became more "religious" in character; for example, a spiritual transcendental force was implied in Plato's conception of "pure form." In the Hellenistic age speculative philosophy often fused with popular mystery cults, some Greek (like those of Orpheus, Dionysus, and the city of Eleusis), some Persian (like Mithras, god of light) to produce cults, participation in which could lead to resurrection after death and salvation. These spread, as did Greek philosophy itself, throughout the Roman Empire. The fusion was only partial, for salvation resulted from participation in ritual, and sometimes also from ecstatic experience, not from a systematic, rational understanding of the world or from its ethical derivative, a moral code of conduct. The other principal element in the syncretic growth was the rigorous monotheism of Judaism. This had probably developed fairly indigenously (after initial Persian influences). Only late in the second century B.C. were the Jews faced with the challenge of Greek culture. They split into two, one group becoming relatively Hellenized (the Sadducees), the other emphasizing a distinctive Jewishness (the Pharisees). The Pharisees were popular-democratic, so as to offset the collaborating, aristocratic Sadducees, and they laid intense ethical requirements on individual family relations as opposed to the Sadducees' stress on wider civilization. But common to both groups was an increasing reliance on the written word, on sacred texts and commentaries. Therefore, literacy and schooling were encouraged.

These movements contained many peculiarities relating to the needs of particular peoples, places, and times. This is especially true of the Jews, subordinated by the Romans while still unreconciled to Hellenism, and thus experiencing national as well as religious and philosophic stirrings. Nevertheless, we can also perceive throughout the Mediterranean world a growing flowing together of currents running toward monotheism, ethical morality, and salvation, increasingly using the means of the written word.[2]

The second piece of evidence postdates Christ. After the establishment of a Christian fellowship but before the emergence of a "Catholic" orthodoxy, Christians were often difficult to distinguish from adherents of some of these other philosophies, religions, and cults. Indeed, between about A.D. 80 and 150, at least a dozen sects split off from the Christian fellowship. We know most of them as "Gnostics," *gnosis* being the Greek word for knowledge of an experiential, even intuitive, rather than rational kind. Most combined philosophic and cultic currents (perhaps receiving influences from as far away as the Brahmins and Buddha). Although they varied, most resembled earlier cults more than Christianity itself did. Initiation rites and mystic experiences were important. Some practiced magic as the antidote to the world's evils, some ascetism and mortification of the flesh, and some became orgiastic (though evidence generally came from their enemies). The rivals used salvation as the solution to earthly evil and suffering more than orthodox Christianity did. Thus there is a sense of overlapping needs, rather wider than any single ortho-

---

[2]On these doctrinal antecedents of Christianity, see especially Bultmann 1956; Cumont 1956; Cochrane 1957; and Nock 1964.

doxy could probably tolerate, enduring even after the establishment of the church.[3]

The third piece of evidence is Christ himself. I follow current orthodoxy among scholars that there was such a man, a prophet, even if the claims to divinity were probably added later.[4] His message as relayed by his early followers (and that is as close as we can get to him) was simple and direct, and it channeled various currents toward a large number of people. He preached the coming of the kingdom of God, as all prophets did. But he added that *anyone* could enter the kingdom, provided only that they purified their hearts and believed in a single, transcendent God. No social qualifications, no esoteric knowledge, no rituals or extraordinary experiences were required. The purification did not presuppose *prior* ethical conduct – conversion (provided it was genuine) itself purified. Nothing could be simpler, more radical, and more egalitarian than this. Though probably Christ never thought directly about the wider world beyond Palestine, by implication his message could have universal appeal.

According to the Gospels, Christ was careful to mention explicitly most types of people whom his followers might have assumed were not included – children (even babies), women, pagan soldiers, tax collectors and toll collectors (considered, we are told, as sinners), sinners and criminals (both male and female), and outcast lepers. "God so loved the world," we are told, "that he gave his only begotten Son, that whosoever believeth in him should not perish, but have everlasting life" (John 3:16).

Our age has been accustomed to contrast faith and reason. But this was not so of Christ's age. Greek philosophy was moving toward combining the two. Indeed, by rejecting mysteries, ritual, and magic, Christ (or his gospel writers) was appealing to rational forms of faith. The connection between faith and ethical conduct was also popular and rational. If faith presupposed morality, then keeping people faithful meant keeping them moral. If a Christian repeatedly sinned, he or she was no longer capable of seeing God. Therefore, the weight of the community would be used to reinforce faith and morality. The community was more interested in keeping people in than in kicking them out – expulsion was rare (Forkman 1972). Similarly, under social pressures, most Christians could be expected to behave well – a point to which I will return.

For these three reasons, if Christ's reported teaching were brought into contact with most groups of people of this time, they would encounter a degree

[3]For the Gnostics, see Jonas 1963 and Pagels 1980; for early heresies in general, see the dispute between Turner 1954 and Bauer 1971.
[4]See Vermes 1976; Schillebeeckx 1979; and Wilson 1984 for reviews of the controversies – remembering, however, that contemporary religious identification (Jew, Catholic, Protestant) and church censorship are often evident, sometimes dominant, in the literature.

of sympathetic response within the empire. The early Christians recognized that their appeal was to the inhabitants of the empire and that they depended on its peace, on Roman order and communications. The universal appeal must therefore have corresponded to the particular needs of Romans. The Roman world was in some way failing to satisfy its inhabitants. In what did its failure reside? Such is the question with which many studies begin.

But in a way it is the wrong question. As indicated in the previous chapter, the empire was a quite striking success around the time of Christ. Like other near-contemporary empires (Persia and Han dynasty China), it had notably contributed social and economic development. Rather, the very *successes* of these empires led to difficulties that required solution. All felt the impact of salvation religions, though they dealt with them in different ways. The religions offered a solution to imperial contradictions, severest in the case of Rome, precisely because Rome's imperial achievements were the greatest.

Christianity as the solution to the contradictions of empire

The Roman and other near-contemporary empires had five main contradictions:

1. *Universalism versus particularism.* The more centralized and territorial an empire became, the more it fostered universalist ties of membership and attachment to itself. In Rome universalism was in the form of an active member, the citizen; in Persia and China, membership was passive, the subject. Both were relatively independent of particularist ties to kin, class, tribe, village, and the like. Yet universalism undermined state rule through the particularist kin solidarity of an hereditary aristocracy, which itself denied the notion of universal membership. The problem could be solved at the highest level by converting this aristocracy into a universal ruling class. But the issue was more difficult for middling groups within the empire.

2. *Equality versus hierarchy.* The active universalism of citizenship generated notions of political participation and equality. As we saw in Chapter 9, this had been frustrated by the hierarchical Roman state, yet citizenship supposedly remained central to Roman rule. The genuine citizenship of Greece and the early Roman Republic also remained important in Mediterranean cultural traditions (though not in China or Persia).

3. *Decentralization versus centralization.* As we saw, the formal constitution of empires *looked* highly centralized and despotic; yet real infrastructural power was far feebler. The resources that flowed into the state flowed out again into the control of decentralized "civil society" groups. As the centralizing achievements of the Roman state – the homogeneous ruling-class culture, the legionary economy, the territorial empire – had been far greater than those of Persia, this meant that far more formidable powers were then decen-

tralized. Among the more important were near-absolute private-property rights, coinage, and literacy, which gave considerable powers to private citizens. Greatest power was decentralized to the provincial aristocracy, but power also flowed to city dwellers, traders, artisans, and ethnic groups like Greeks or Jews strategically located in the cities. Such people could develop both an individual self-confidence and a network of social interaction that could cut across the official network of the centralized state.

4. *Cosmopolitanism versus uniformity.* The increased territorial size of these empires heightened their cosmopolitan character as a more varied mix of languages, cultures, and religions was absorbed. Their success tended to break down preexisting ethnic and other, similar attachments. Yet, as the first three contradictions reveal, these identities could not be simply replaced by a new "official" uniformity that was universalistic, egalitarian or hierarchical, and centralized. Empires excluded the masses from their official cultural communities. The possibility existed for the emergence of a rival, more cosmopolitan sense of normative attachment, a *community*.

5. *Civilization versus militarism.* This was more specifically located – what to do about frontier barbarians and foreigners? The empires had expanded through military domination. Yet the empires also provided civilization, which outsiders would always want. If imperial military power faded, its citizens and subjects might be conquered by the outsiders, unless civilization could be separated from militarism and offered peacefully to outsiders. Some within all these empires were willing to make this switch away from militarism to a pacific civilizing role, although (in Rome and China, but not Persia) this contradicted state militarism.

My explanation of the universal aspect of Christianity's appeal will be that it provided a solution to these contradictions, an imperfect solution but one that over a long period of struggle proved to be better than that offered by the Roman Empire. The other two imperial cases differed in their outcomes, and I will leave them until the next chapter. But the contradictions should not be considered separately, for Christianity found a solution in their combination: a universalistic, egalitarian, decentralized, civilizing community – an *ecumene*.

There is a second, later phase of the story, however. Having found a solution enabling it to seize official power, Christianity then incorporated the contradictions within its own body. In the West it did not face up to these contradictions and ultimately helped preside over the catastrophic, near-total collapse of ancient civilization in the western Mediterranean.

Models of "contradictions" are quite common among scholars – for example, Harnack has a similar point of departure in his classic study of the spread of Christianity (1908: 19–23). The details of the contradictions enable us to locate rather precisely the needs of the converts – especially the nature of the

308 A history of power to A.D. 1760

"sufferings" from which these Romans turned to the release of salvation. Here, however, we reach the nadir of conventional scholarship on early Christianity – the notion of "earthly suffering." It is obviously crucial to Christian doctrine that salvation is a release from earthly suffering, and we can assume that many of the converts were drawn by the promise of this release – but release from what? Unfortunately, our own age conceives of this as "material suffering." Actually there are two versions of this.

The first relates the rise of Christianity to economic crisis and consequent political repression. This is persistent among Marxist writers, emanating from Marx's general desire to explain the rise of all religions as "the cry of an oppressed people." Kautsky (1925) gave the fullest explanation of the rise of Christianity in these terms.

It is simple to refute this. If economic crisis and consequent political repression had played a major part in the rise of Christianity, it would have spread largely after A.D. 200. There was no crisis before that date, indeed probably no major crisis until about A.D. 250. Yet the evidence points to a continuous spread of Christianity from soon after the crucifixion itself. The most that could be argued for the role of economic and political crisis would concern the final phase of the spread, from the town into the countryside, from about 250. We will see that even this was more complex than the "economic-crisis" model would indicate.

This point would not be disputed by any serious scholar today. But economic-crisis theory lives on in another guise. It is generally argued that Christianity spread disproportionately among the poorest classes, "the poor and the oppressed." I deal with this in detail later in this chapter and show that it is untrue. But the popularity of the notion indicates the difficulty our age has in dealing with noneconomic suffering.

The religious part of our age, however, does have a specific way of dealing with this: to argue that materialism itself is a form of suffering from which people wish to escape. This is the famous explanation of Troeltsch. He first disposes of the above economic argument by noting that the early Christian communities, located in the towns, "shared in the gradual improvement in social conditions which took place in urban life." On the other hand, he finds it "undeniable" that Christianity appealed most to the economically and politically "oppressed" (I deny this later in this chapter). So he prefers to talk of the "vast social crisis" of the late ancient world in spiritual terms: "a movement away from materialism and . . . a longing for the purely mystical and religious values of live" (1931: 39–48). The world itself is rejected here. And this is a common argument. Neill (1965: 28, 33, 40), for example, writes, "The second century was an anxious and troubled age" in "the decaying Roman Empire," especially among "the poorer classes," from which the Church at first "drew its members." The anxiety resulted from "the transitoriness of all things and by the desire for immortality." Both authors have it both ways: If there is crisis or "decay" in a material sense, people naturally wish to escape it; but if there is not, they wish to escape from materialism. Such analysis gets us nowhere in explaining why a particular religion arose in a particular time and place.

Nor can it until we dispose of the materialism-idealism dualism underlying these arguments. In this they follow Jesus' reported claim to found his church upon the latter and not the former. But no social movement can be founded on such a separation. Just as no set of people can live "materially" without requiring a "spiritual" infrastructure, a religious, "spiritual" movement cannot reject all "material" infrastructure. Thus the true achievement of the early Christian religion was not the constitution of a separate "spiritual" realm but a novel fusion of the two realms into a transcendent, normative community, an *ecumene*.

Christianity was not a response to material crisis, nor was it a spiritual alternative to the material world. The crisis was one of social identity: What society do I belong to? This was generated by the very successes of the Roman Empire and of Hellenistic civilization, which produced transcendent principles of social organization interstitially from within their own social structures.

Thus there was no "deep crisis" of ancient society. Indeed, to write of contradictions may mislead. The contradictions are merely opposed principles. Empires could choose to repress one or the other, compromise between them, or simply muddle through. There was *no* general crisis, either objective or subjectively experienced, in Rome around the time of Christ. Thus, no such crisis could have played any significant part in the early spread of Christianity. Indeed, the early Christians were relatively happy and prosperous people, conscious of newfound wealth, powers, and vitality, seeking to articulate their emergent, interstitial social and personal identity in philosophy, ethics, and ritual. Their "suffering" was confined to the normative sphere, or deciding what *community* they belonged to. This is – as sociological sophisticates will note – a very Durkheimian model, a point to which I return at the end of the next chapter.

But no conception of "suffering" can explain the rise of a social movement. Whether the Romans were suffering or happy, prosperous or poor tells us little. Neither suffering nor happiness, nor economic nor political nor spiritual crisis, nor even repression, has any necessary causal effect on the emergence of new social movements. Sometimes economic crises and political repression may produce a united movement of reaction among the people; sometimes they divide them. Sometimes they generate political revolution, reaction, or reform; sometimes, religious revolution, reaction, or reform. Mostly they have no result other than an upsurge in despair at the general harshness of life. The outcome is dependent not on the depth of the crisis but on the *organizational forms* of the people being affected. Who precisely is affected by the crisis? With whom are they in communication? With whom do they share normative commitment and a stock of knowledge about the world? What contacts and social knowledge are likely to lead them to blame their rulers for the crisis and to conceive of practical alternatives? What power resources can they mobilize, against whom? These are the decisive questions about responses to crises and to other dramatic social changes, whether they are political, spiritual, or whatever. The organization of power resources – the main theme of this book – is the crucial determinant of the rise of a religious movement, as it is that of any movement. The contradictions of Rome were essentially organizational, the failure to find a solution to a number of organizational alternatives.

Thus the analysis of Christian power must be essentially the same as that of all other powers. We must start with the infrastructure on which it was able to draw. We must make central the *infrastructure of ideological power*. Christianity was not at first a military conquest or an expansion of production and trade, but a conversion process. It was also – not immediately, but fairly shortly – a religion of the book, the Bible. Therefore the communication of ideas and cultural practices, and the specific networks of *literacy* were of great importance.

The infrastructure of ideological power in the Roman Empire

The transmission of ideas and cultural practices was subject to the same overall constraints imposed by communications technology, constraints that should be familiar by now. Sea and river communications routes were the swiftest and longest but were subject to winter interruption. Road routes were slower and provided only relatively local communications. There were no other means of communication. Within these constraints we can identify four main possibilities. I call them *channels* of ideological power.

The first channel was made from the mosaic of villages, cities, tribes, and peoples on whom the Romans imposed their rule. Most smaller entities with a history of shared experience, intermarriage, language, ritual, and beliefs were integrated into single cultures. Given a solidaristic history, such an entity could attain the size of an "ethnic community," of whom the Jews were the outstanding example. Most were much smaller. The religious experience of their localized intensity was a multiplicity of local, tribal, familial, and city-state cults, strongly rooted but with a low capacity for converting the people of any other locality. New messages that emerged into the locality, however, could be speedily spread around it if they seemed true and useful to local experience. As the Romans had interfered little with the internal composition of their localities, they were still largely available as transmitters of messages within their narrow bounds. Nevertheless, transmission through the layer of these units – say, through a whole people like the Jews, or a distinct region like that of the North African province – would be partially dependent on the other three logistical channels to be explored. "Cultural traditions" could communicate unaided only over small spaces. The connections *between* these spaces and cultures, often extremely varied in character, was the main problem for ancient communications in general.

The second channel was the authoritative, official, political-communications channel of the empire. This linked horizontally the rulers of all those localities just mentioned, and it organized them into cities and their territories. It presupposed, though largely left alone, the hierarchical control system of the city-territory itself. The political channel was enormously strengthened by the ruling-class cultural homogeneity referred to in the last chapter. A century after conquest, local ruling elites were almost indistinguishable from each other in their languages, beliefs, and customs. I will explore further in this chapter the infrastructural universalizing and diffusing role contributed by literacy to the solidification of the ruling class.

These first two channels were the "official" ones of the empire, providing two-step ideological reinforcement for its rule. As long as the provincial ruling classes considered themselves as Roman or Roman-Greek *and* remained in control of their localities, the empire would be reinforced. The provincial elites were likely to lose ideological control as they were Romanized unless the masses were also Romanized. This was particularly likely in the rural areas, for the village (and its cults) had no recognized status within the city-dominated official structure of Rome. In this eventuality local elites could fall back upon control by direct repression, for each people was "locked into" its own locality and culture, without a basis for translocal ideology or organization. It could be organizationally outflanked by the use of authoritative power.

But the third and especially the fourth channel were potentially dislocating. They both involved alternative connections among the people. The third channel was the army. In the preceding chapter I stressed the role of the legions in contributing to the communications infrastructure of the empire. Additionally, the army was the main means by which ordinary people, usually peasants, were removed from the cultural prison of their locality and brought into contact with the wider world. This did not generate revolutionary ideologies among the soldiers. They were, after all, the core of the Roman state. A mixture of strict military hierarchy and discipline, regular pay, and local recruiting and billeting practices, generally kept the army as a kind of microcosm of the two-step structure already described – an officer class sharing a homogeneous culture, exercising strong controls over a series of local detachments.

Where troops did mix in large numbers across localities, however, new – and, to the ruling class, slightly worrying – soldier cults developed among them. The cult of Mithras, the ancient Iranian god of light, was the most widespread. This demonstrated that a relatively egalitarian extension of communications networks through the medium of the army would lead to cultural innovation. The soldiers, mixing their stocks of knowledge, values, and norms, did not remain content with their separate provincialism, nor were they satisfied with the official cults of the state. The empire would have to cope with cultural innovation even in its army core.

The fourth and most important channel from the point of view of Christianity was provided by the trading networks of the empire. Agricultural production was either fragmented into smallholdings and villages or was controlled by large landowners who were also the local political rulers. Hence agricultural production relations were mostly part of the official two-step communications system. But trading and artisanal relations were somewhat interstitial to this flow of messages, even though they used the same officially generated and officially protected communications routes. Merchants and artisans tended to have their own social organizations: guilds. And although they lived in cities, they were not as powerful in urban politics as were great landowners. Thus the cities, the core of the official communications and control system, also contained a kind of "alternative infrastructure" of trading and artisanal relationships that also extended over the entire empire and even beyond it. Disproportionately represented within it were traditional trading peoples like the Greeks and the Jews. Their ideas were overrepresented in any communications flow throughout this infrastructure.

This trading and artisan sector initially depended on the authoritative power of the legionary economy of the Roman state. But the more this economy became institutionalized, the more its resources tended to diffuse into civil society. By the time of Christ, the economy of the Mediterranean basin had become thoroughly institutionalized. Artisans and traders had private-property rights, backed up by the civil law (or, if they were foreigners, by its extension, the *ius gentium* – law of the peoples). They had movable assets like tools, ships, and mules, which (as I noted in Chapter 2 when dealing with prehistory) are inherently "private." They had workshops and stalls, which are, like houses, usually considered as private property even in relatively communal societies. They had liquid assets in the form of coins, which could be exchanged for raw materials or finished products or which could be hoarded, privately. In all this the state merely acted as a backdrop to essentially "private" activities – private in the Latin sense of hidden from public gaze. The law guaranteed property rights, the state set out the parameters within which the guild operated, but only the emperor's eyes on the coins watched the interaction process itself. Transactions were essentially nonauthoritative, between autonomous, free individuals, or families, or small "firms" – thus differing from the internal, authoritative, hierarchical structure of the other channels. If this sector generated its own ideology, it would seek to make meaningful and valuable two things that "official" ideology neglected: what constituted individual experience (or perhaps family or "small firm" experience); and how normative, ethical relations could endure between such individuals. The "elective affinity" (to use Weber's term) between such individual and interpersonal needs and Christianity is obvious (so obvious that I hope I do not argue from hindsight!).

Furthermore, this channel of communication contained a second, lower level, parallel to that of officialdom. For the trading and artisan sector interacted with lower social strata, especially the urban proletariat but even with the peasantry. The links with the peasantry were not especially close or frequent. The peasant was more open to the scrutiny of rural elites than to that of the trader or artisan. But the connection was nonetheless there, through monetarized exchange networks penetrating the entire empire. In short, this constituted an entire alternative infrastructure through which ideology could be communicated diffusely – generated by the very success of the empire, not by its failings. The more economically and politically successful it became, the more pronounced became the "fifth column."

Along these four channels, messages and controls passed. One particular medium of communication was of considerable importance in all channels. This was *writing,* widely diffused because the materials, pens and papyrus parchments, were generally available and because much of the population was literate. It is difficult to say exactly who was literate and to what standard, but an attempt at precision is essential for understanding the infrastructure available to a "religion of the book."[5]

I start with the second channel, communications among the ruling class. They were almost all literate, and to quite a high standard – and this probably included women almost as much as men. Political practices in every city required a degree of reading skill, as did active participation in property and matrimonial legal affairs. Literature was itself of great importance, and from about 100 B.C. the famous authors, especially historians and historical poets – men like Horace, Virgil, Caesar, Livy, and Tacitus – were writing and reading aloud for a large audience diffused throughout the republic/empire.

The infrastructure was a universal system of education, modeled on the Hellenistic tripartite system: elementary school, teaching the "three Rs" from the age of 7 until 11 or 12; grammar school, teaching mainly grammar and classical literature, until perhaps 16; and (usually after a break for military service) higher schools, focusing mainly on rhetoric, between about 17 and 20. The schools were usually privately financed by associations of parents within each city, though there was increasing state regulation in the period of the empire. The universality of schooling among the ruling class was weakened at the very top, where the wealthy often chose to use private tutors,

---

[5] I have relied on Marrou 1956: 229–313; Jones 1964: II, chap. 24; and Bowen 1972: 167–216.

especially for daughters. It is also unclear how many of this class's children passed into the higher schools (and then to the universities), especially the girls.

Thus described, there are similarities with our own education system. There are also two differences: The content of the education was astonishingly literary, and it was tied to an oral mode of the transmission of knowledge. Literature, grammar, and rhetoric taught the verbal skills used in public debate, in legal advocacy, and in reading aloud in company. Stratton (1978: 60–102) has convincingly argued that Roman literature was little more than a vast mnemonic system, a technical means of storing cultural meanings and understandings and of recovering them through communal activities of reading and speechifying.

I emphasized in the preceding chapter the *extensiveness* of Roman civilization. Holding together the enormous empire required a large investment in communications technology. Literacy was an important part of this. Hence, the Romans were obsessed with their language, its grammar, and its style, and with the connections of these to literacy and to historical texts dealing with the growth of Roman power. Hence also their concern with rhetoric, the art of communication and debate. This also had a practical connection to the legal system and to the aristocratic profession of jurist. But we must still ask why this professional training was in rhetoric, not statute or case law (like our own). The answer lies in the importance of literate but mnemonic communication in giving *morale* to the ruling class of the empire, giving them common access to the stock of cultural knowledge and reinforcing their cultural solidarity through communal reading and debating activities.

From this the masses were excluded. Participation in most of these communal activities was generally ascriptive, confined to the senatorial and equestrian orders, to the *decurions,* and to the other higher-status ranks of imperial society. This aspect of literary culture was exclusive, useful in preserving the extensive rule of the upper class. Absentee landowners met each other face to face in civic settings, ruled locally through debate, and wrote to – and especially traveled between – other cities. It was a "private" ruling class, fairly closed to outsiders through its cultural practices, as well as through deliberate policy.

Yet the masses were not excluded from all literate activity. As with the Greeks, literate culture was concerned not with preserving sacred dogma but with reflecting and commenting on real life experience. Knowledge itself was not restricted, nor was education. Elementary education was widely diffused, even into some villages. Schoolmasters were of low status. According to Diocletian's invaluable edict, the wage and fees fixed for an elementary schoolmaster suggest a class of thirty pupils if he was to earn as much as a mason or carpenter. This suggests fairly large classes. There were also many literate males from quite ordinary backgrounds who attained a high standard of literacy, either at these schools or from their fathers. These often entered the army, hoping to use their skill to obtain advancement. For example, an Egyptian naval recruit in Augustus's reign, writes to his father because he wishes "to make obeisance before your handwriting, because you educated me well and I hope thereby to have quick advancement" (letter quoted in full in Jones 1970: II, 151). This indicates domestic education among some ordinary folk but not the majority, since he is hoping for advancement from his literacy. From Petronius we also doubt the average level of the school, for he indicates that the boy who can read fluently is the wonder of his class. Many, he indicates, "had not studied geometry or literature or any other daft things like that, but were quite satisfied with being able to read something in big letters and understand fractions and weights and measures" (1930: 59, 7).

Education required wealth, usually coinage, to pay the teacher. The mason or carpenter might be able to afford one-thirtieth of his earnings to pay for the elementary education of a single child, but the ordinary peasant would not be able to afford perhaps one-twentieth of his lower earnings, and certainly not in coinage. The capacities of either to provide for two or more children must also be doubted. Elementary education would also have generally led to what Petronius indicates: greater fluency, but not cultural accomplishments. For these, secondary education would have been required, but children became useful family labor at about this age. Genuine wealth was needed to support idle youths.

Thus there is no point in making a single estimate of literacy among the Romans – except to say that it was much higher than in any society discussed so far, except Greece – because it varied so much. We can identify three distinct levels. At the top, a highly literate, numerate, and culturally cohesive class extended thinly over the whole empire. Their literacy was an important part of their ruling-class morale. The second level consisted of functionally literate and numerate persons who were not full members of the literary culture and who were excluded from rule. They could become clerks to the bureaucracy, landlords, the army, and merchants; they could become elementary teachers; they could help draw up wills, petitions, and contracts; they probably could understand some of the concepts that underlay the products of Roman and Greek classical literature, but they probably could not read them, and perhaps they did not ordinarily come into contact with them. The location and extent of this second level are guesswork, but they must have been uneven. They depended on literate traditions among subject peoples (which is presumably how domestic education could be transmitted). Greeks, Aramean-descended peoples (especially Jews), and some Egyptians were disproportionately literate at this second level. This level also depended on towns, in which the function of literacy was valued and in which cash flowed. In towns, literacy was concentrated among merchants and artisans for the same reasons. Those on the third level were either illiterate or partly literate to the level mentioned by Petronius – the mass of the rural population and the urban proletariat, and the younger sons and daughters of those somewhat above them on the social scale. They were totally excluded from the literate culture of the republic/empire.

The levels were distinct in their social location, and a large cultural gap existed between the ruling class and the rest. Some overlap can be discerned, however. Overlap at the upper levels largely occurred among the more literate peoples who possessed more democratic, less exclusionary institutions. Greeks and Jews of different literary attainments exchanged more diffuse cultural messages than most other provincial populations. Overlap between the second and third levels was more widespread, especially among these peoples and in the cities. Furthermore, however culturally exclusive was the top level, the patterns of literacy beneath it could only result in a desire for greater access to the literate, cultured world. For literate culture conveyed *power:* The more access one had to it, the more control could be exercised over life. This was not just belief but objective reality, since power in the empire was predicated upon literate, cultured communication. If participation in the official culture was precluded, unofficial perhaps radical countercultures might appear. In modern times a large extension of literacy has generally proved dislocating. Stone (1969) has noted that three great modern revolutions, the English Civil War and the French and Russian revolutions, all occurred when about half the male population became literate. It is unlikely that Roman literacy levels were quite this high. But the masses could participate in oral transmission of "radical" written information, provided counter-elites could help.

In studies of communications networks among highly literate peoples in the twentieth century, a "two-step" flow of communication has been noticed. Decatur, Illinois, in A.D. 1945 is 8,000 kilometers and 2,000 years from our present subject matter. But there Katz and Lazarsfeld (1955) discovered that modern mass media had little direct impact on a large sample of American women. Instead, media influence was largely indirect, mediated by community "opinion leaders" who reinterpreted media messages before channeling them downward to their acquaintances. Despite qualifications and criticism, the two-step flow theory has stood up well in subsequent research (Katz 1957; and, for a review, McQuail 1969: esp. 52–7). But how much more pertinent still is the two-step model to the Roman context, of partially literate communities. When valuable information entered such a community in written form, it could be read out aloud to the others by the few literates. Later in the chapter we will see that this was indeed the norm among Christian communities once they were established, and it remained so right through the Middle Ages.

But the ruling class of the empire was not likely to play this role of information leader, having an insular cultural life and a contempt for the intellects of those beneath them. On the other hand, the literates on the second level had more egalitarian exchange relations with those less prosperous than themselves, and their greater literacy was not qualitatively divided by culture. They were the potential oral transmitters.

The medium of literacy reinforced the nature of the communications channels. I have outlined the existence in the Roman Empire of an alternative, interstitial communication system, one used primarily for economic interactions, but one that could transmit ideology in a two-step flow, the first step passing messages among townspeople, the second step eventually reaching most of the people of the empire. It was buttressed by the medium of literacy, which (unlike the cultural aspects of the official communications system) it had no desire to confine or restrict. We can now trace the activation of this system as Christianity began its movement through the particularities of the Roman Empire. As an anticipation of the argument, I offer Figure 10.1, which represents diagrammatically the two information channels and asserts that the second, the unofficial channel, became the Christian one.

The early spread of Christianity

The successive contours of the rise of Christianity are well known. With two exceptions, its class basis and its later penetration of the countryside, they pose no particular problems of analysis. The evidence for the spread is found in Harnack's classic 1908 study, still unrivaled, and in other early studies (e.g., Glover 1909: 141–166; Latourette 1938: I, 114–70).

Christ was thought by some to be the Messiah of the Jews. He was by no means the first to claim to be the Messiah, which was a recognizable prophetic (not divine) role in rural Aramaic-speaking Palestine, where he began. He was presumably a remarkable man, and what he is reported to have said made a great deal of sense. He held out the promise of a rational, moral order to a politically troubled area whose disturbances may have also led to a local economic crisis. This probably was "suffering" along the lines conventionally described. Christ also offered a compromise to the Hellenization/nationalism dilemma of the Jews, deliberately avoiding, it seems, the potential role of national leader against Rome.

Nevertheless, his followers probably surprised themselves when they found a response to Christ's message among the Hellenized Jews of the towns of Palestine, Caesarea, Joppa, Damascus, and even Antioch, the third city of the empire. This may have encouraged their sense that Christ had been divine. Miracles, the story of the Resurrection, and other divine elements were probably now added to the legend. Proselytizing in cities meant a greater commitment to written texts, and to the Greek language, the language of most urban Jews. At this point, about A.D. 45, Paul, a leading Sadducee, was converted. His organizing abilities were thrust outward to the synagogues of the Hellenistic cities of the Middle East. As the earliest debates within the fellowship

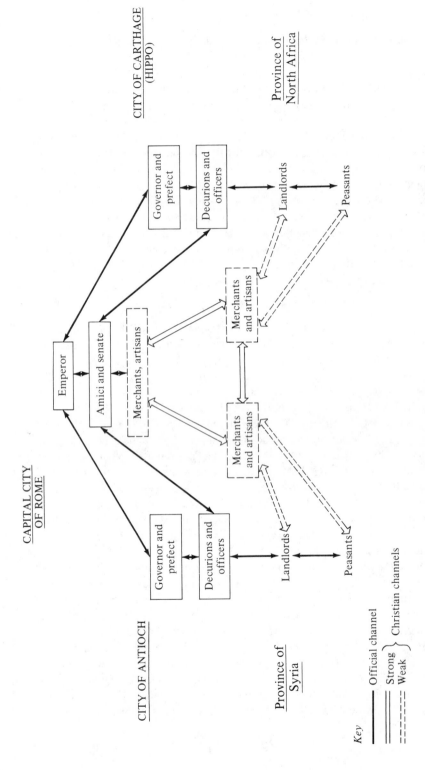

CAPITAL CITY
OF ROME

CITY OF CARTHAGE
(HIPPO)

Province of
North Africa

CITY OF ANTIOCH

Province of
Syria

Emperor

Amici and senate

Merchants, artisans

Governor and
prefect

Decurions and
officers

Landlords

Peasants

Merchants
and artisans

Merchants
and artisans

Governor and
prefect

Decurions and
officers

Landlords

Peasants

Key

——— Official channel

Strong ⎱ Christian channels
Weak ⎰

Figure 10.1. *The Roman Empire: official and Christian channels of communication and control (example of two provinces)*

generally referred to the Greek version of the Old Testament (the Septuagint), the original Aramaic-speaking rural base in Palestine had been left behind. These Greek-speaking Jews, engaged in trade and crafts in a time of prosperity, were not affected by poverty, oppression, or suffering. Christ's teaching, probably modified, combined Greek philosophy and Jewish ethics into a better, freer, more liberating explanation of their way of life than was traditional Judaism. It also appealed to Gentiles, largely Greek, in the same environment. "Love your enemies, and pray for those who persecute you" (Matthew 5:44) was a dramatically outward-looking message.

Thus as soon as the urban missionary activity started, Jewish versus Greek controversies arose concerning, especially, whether Christians needed to be circumcised. According to the Acts of the Apostles (Chap. 15), Paul and his fellow missionary Barnabas of Cyrus had not required this and had created a mixed Jewish-Gentile fellowship in Antioch and elsewhere. The "men from Judaea" (probably including relatives of Jesus') objected, and a council was held in Jerusalem at which Paul and his faction supposedly triumphed. Emissaries bearing letters were sent to the new communities, confirming their legitimacy. The mixed Antioch community assembled, the letter was read out, and they rejoiced – so say our Pauline sources. The victory of the world-religion faction was ultimately decisive. The "bishops of the circumcision," entrenched in Jerusalem, were probably destroyed in the crushing of the Jewish revolts of A.D. 70 and 133. Now written texts passed messages between communities; within the community they were read aloud and debated. The two-step means of communication became predominant. As the epistles traveled between Greek communities, their content became more Greek. The Gnostic challenge forced more syncretic philosophizing onto Christianity. However, the philosophy was "a plain man and woman's," not esoteric.

The oldest datable Christian document after the time of the apostles is a long letter sent by Clement of Rome to the Christians of Corinth in the 90s. The Corinthians had split over doctrinal and organizational issues. Clement used the rhetorical devices of classical literature to persuade them to unite. The message is simple: Disciplined coordination is necessary to the unity of the body of Christ, just as it is to the polis, to the Roman legion, and to the human body itself. The true ethical community is based not on formal theological doctrine but on common "breathing," common spirit. This involves humility before authority, which he claims to be the main part of Christ's message.

Clement's letter made a great impact upon the Corinthians and was frequently read out at their services over the next century.[6] Implicit in the style, the allusions, and the substantive argument was a tremendous claim: The true

---

[6]For Greek influence and a commentary on Clement's epistle, see Jaeger 1962: esp. 12–26. The epistle is in Lake 1912.

inheritors of Athenian and Spartan civic virtue, and of Roman military *virtu,* were the Christians. It was an appeal to Greeks, but to their widest conception of themselves: not as bounded by ethnicity or language but as the bearers of civilization itself to rational human beings at large. This third level of the classical Greek achievement referred to in Chapter 7 could now be renewed because of the strategic location of the Greeks throughout the empire.

By the mid-second century, Christian communities were established in every city in the eastern provinces, many in the central provinces, and a few in the western. These communities were dominated by the Greek language. There was as yet little rural organization. Each community was a largely autonomous *ecclesia* ("assembly"), although they all had broadly similar organizational structures, exchanged epistles, and were beginning to reach a consensus about a common set of gospels and common doctrines. Each *ecclesia*'s sense of commonality was heightened by fierce if intermittent persecution. Eyewitness accounts of martyrdom were promptly written down and circulated throughout the communities. The communications system was activated and the Christian "people" mobilized.

Why were the Christians persecuted?: the mobilization of the popular *ecumene*

The Christians were attracting the attentions of the authorities. The history of the persecutions is complex and controversial.[7] Part of the difficulty was created by two conjunctural factors. First, the Christian religion was long tainted in the eyes of the emperors with the endemic disorders of Palestine. Second, idiosyncratically, Nero persecuted Christians in A.D. 64 on the specious grounds that they (and not he himself, as was suspected at the time) had started the great fire of Rome. These factors apart, there was still fairly systematic persecution. Being a Christian was an offense at the time of Trajan, although the authorities were not interested in persecuting them wholeheartedly. But every fifty years or so, full-scale and ferocious persecution would be initiated by the authorities, and this lasted until the conversion of Constantine in A.D. 312. Why?

There seem to be three main strands in the persecution. First, the Christians were accused of all kinds of "abominations." They were labeled criminals in the moral sense of *mali homines* (bad people) and dealt with by the criminal law. In their defense, the Christians explained that the Eucharist was not cannibalism; that they were not atheists despite their refusal to worship pagan gods; and that incest was not implied by their preference for marriage within their fellowship, nor sexual orgies by their doctrine of universal love. Until

[7]A good introduction to the large literature can be found in three argumentative essays by Ste. Croix (1974), Sherwin-White (1974), and Frend (1974) in a single book. See also Case 1933: 145–99.

early in the third century these charges were sufficiently popularly believed to continue Nero's scapegoating policy. As Tertullian remarked: "If the Tiber rises too high or the Nile too low, the cry is 'The Christians to the lion.' "

The other strands both arose from the monotheism of Christianity. The refusal to acknowledge the divinity of the emperor seems to have been a large factor in Domitian's persecution (81–96), for Domitian was one of the few emperors to take his own divinity seriously. But the third strand was more significant, for monotheism forced Christians to refuse to worship all pagan gods. This was decisive, a break with official Roman ideology. Not that the Roman ruling class seemed fanatic about their gods. Their religion was less a belief system than a series of civic rituals and pageants, reaffirming the solidarity of the citizenry in full view of the gods. With imperial conquests religion had developed two-level rituals of social control: Local religions could be tolerated and even used, by tying their gods and ritual occasions to those of the state as a whole. The integration of the empire depended ideologically on *pax deorum,* the peace of the gods: respect for other gods, not just toleration of them. But when Christ confronted the problem of loyalty to the empire he reportedly said, "Render therefore unto Caesar the things which are Caesar's; and unto God the things that are God's" (Matthew 22:21). Only in spiritual matters was "the Lord thy God a jealous God." Secular respect was due Caesar. But Rome did not separate spiritual and worldly authority. Nor, as we shall see, could it be fully separated by Christianity. Hence refusal to respect the gods of the community was a political challenge to Rome and an impious act in itself. These were the main charges against the Christians that the authorities themselves believed true and serious (see the cross-examinations recorded in *The Acts of the Christian Martyrs* [Mursurillo 1972]).

But this cannot be a sufficient explanation of persecution as long as we remain at the level of doctrine. An emphasis on the autonomy of belief was Christian, not Roman. Because belief did not matter all that much to the Roman authorities, they could have found a way around the difficulties of monotheism. After all, the Persian kings had managed to use the monotheism of Zoroaster to bolster their own rule and the later Roman emperors also did just this. Pliny had written in some puzzlement to Trajan for guidance. He had discovered that the Christians did not practice abominations, that they did not lack respect for the emperor, that they had obediently stopped sharing a common meal after he had forbidden secret society meetings. He also did not like having to deal with a flood of informers and pamphlets resulting from publicized persecution. Trajan did not either, and he counseled inaction. On pragmatic grounds, Rome could have sought to compromise, just as Christ had.

If compromise did not happen (until much later) the most probable explanation is that the idea of monotheism was being transmitted through channels that were a rival to the empire's own. The alternative communications and control network, referred to earlier, was activated to produce a competing set of interconnected, interstitial *communities*. This was the threat to the empire.

Everything fits this explanation. The religion was communicated through interstitial trading networks, and interstitial people, especially the Greeks. These activities were largely invisible to the state. The Christian communities suddenly appeared – hence the alarm at "secret societies" and the rumors of abominations. They were small, tightly knit communities owing more allegiance to each other than was conventional among subgroups located at the urban heart of the empire. The pagan writer Celsius, writing about 180, found their internal coherence remarkable (though he attributed it to persecution). As its title of *ecclesia* (originally the name for the assembly of the Greek polis) reveals, this private community was political, which provided barriers to official state penetration and control.

Moreover, the internal organization of each *ecclesia* was disturbing, because it dispensed with normal vertical and horizontal divisions. God transcended social structure – he did not express it, as earlier religions had done. Salvation was open to anyone, after individual effort. It was up to the individual to work out his or her own salvation through a direct relationship to the divine. The gospels were repeatedly specific on this point, and thus contained a profoundly universalistic and radical element. It struck contemporaries quite forcibly that the church was particularly active in its recruitment of women, slaves, and free common people. This was pronounced as an accusation by critics. But it was proclaimed proudly by some Christian apologists.

This has led to the belief that the church recruited "the poor and the oppressed" in disproportionate numbers (e.g., Harnack, 1908: II, 33–84; and many others). But skepticism is called for. First, after the death of Christ and before about A.D. 250, Christianity was almost exclusively urban. Townspeople were the main part of the 5–10 percent of the population released from unremitting, heavy, agricultural labor at subsistence level. They were privileged in an economic sense, particularly in towns receiving the state's free corn dole.

Second, contemporary statements about recruiting practices are ambiguous. The pagan accusers convey less statistics than surprise that the Christians should be active at all among the common people. The Christian apologists make it clear that popular appeal is the essence of their message, but they also usually add that they recruit higher up the social scale too.

Third, occupational data support a different conclusion. Even in its first rural Palestinian phase the Christian activists tended to be rural artisans rather than peasants or laborers. This artisan base survived the move into the cities. The striking finding of a survey of early Christian tomb inscriptions is the variety of specialized occupations mentioned – a great list of artisans, skilled at anything from making bas-reliefs to mule doctoring; dealers in anything from incense to ivory; clerical and sales workers like bill collectors or copyists; artistes like chorus masters, trumpeters, or gymnasts. They coexist alongside practitioners of humbler personal-service occupations like chambermaids or hostlers and laboring occupations like grave diggers or gardeners. There are also higher occupations like those of magistrates and physicians (Case 1933: 69–70). This seems less like the poor and oppressed than a cross section of urban life. These are the kinds of occupations that predominate in the middle reaches of our contemporary census-classification schemes (and that are often difficult to assign to one middling "social class" rather than another).

Grant's conclusion (1978: 88) is that most Christians belonged to the "middle class." But it is possible that the Christians were also well represented among urban folk who could not afford tomb inscriptions. In any case the appellation "middle class" is one of our own age, rather than the Roman. The Christians and their opponents spoke mainly of "the people," *populus,* and this is the key. The Christians recruited from the people, as opposed to the ruling class. Hence in economic and occupational terms, they were an extremely varied collection. And if we remember that the urban "people" included perhaps 20–30 percent of slaves or freedmen across almost exactly the same spread of occupations (saving only the magistrate), we can see that these categories do not indicate poverty and oppression either. Nor, of course, does the category "woman"! Furthermore, these Christian communities acquired a reasonable economic surplus, because they supported a considerable number of full-time officials as well as charitable works (which does indicate some poverty among them). As Case notes in her discussion of social dogma, the move to the cities involved abandoning the original fellowship's indifference to worldly wealth as well as its ideological identification with the humble, the weak, and the poor.

A few scholars still attached to a material notion of "suffering" turn to "relative deprivation." Gager (1975: 27, 95) argues not that the Christians were absolutely impoverished but, rather, that they were poor and oppressed in relation to their expectations or their aspirations. As Gager has moved away from a purely economic conception of deprivation, it is pertinent to ask, Of what were they deprived? No answer is forthcoming from him.

But having established more precisely who the early Christians were, we can perhaps come to a more precise answer regarding their deprivation. It was not economic: Their occupational base, their communal wealth, and their doctrine all support the conclusion that they were comfortably off by the standards of the day. If they wanted more wealth and were prevented from attaining it (relative economic deprivation), they never expressed this in writing. Indeed, their doctrinal shift toward justifying a modicum of wealth, not luxury, suggest otherwise. But all these urban folk, precisely because they were the people, did share one characteristic of possible deprivation: exclusion from official power. They were not a part of the government of the empire or of their own cities. Among these middling urban groups at precisely the time of the empire's greatest prosperity in the reigns of Trajan and Hadrian, we read of protest and riots against political exclusion in eastern cities. Dio Chrysostom tells us that the artisans "stand aloof in sentiment from the common interest, reviled as they are and viewed as outsiders" (quoted by Lee 1972: 130). However, Lee comments that such people "wanting in" were hardly likely to make themselves even more excluded from civic participation by becoming Christians. This is a serious objection, but only to a narrow conception of political exclusion.

Let us remember that the empire kept a tight hold on communal associations. The exchange of letters on the subject of fire brigades between Pliny and Trajan is famous (reproduced in Jones 1970: II, 244–5). Pliny, governor of the province of Bithynia in Asia Minor, reports that a terrible fire has recently devastated the important town of Nicomedia. No fire brigade exists, and Pliny asks if he can form one. It is rather strange to our eyes that he should have to ask permission at all, and we are also surprised by his assurance that all care will be taken to regulate the fire brigade and to make sure that it only deals with fires. But Trajan's reply seems bizarre. He says that, where established, "this sort of society has greatly disturbed the peace. . . . Whatever name we give them, and for whatever purposes they may be founded, they will not fail to form themselves into dangerous assemblies." Therefore he refuses permission and advises providing fire machines that can be used by the owners of burning houses themselves. Exclusion was applied to all forms of communal association. The urban masses were deprived of all public collective life, all officially sanctioned normative community. The empire was not *their* society.

Yet the economy of urban life, to a much greater extent than rural life, involved collective activities in workplaces and in the marketplace. And these activities required someone to be literate and to read and write for the other less literate participants. Ideas and writings circulated among these small collectivities and discussion groups arose. However, the government sought to prevent it. Add to this that the core of the Christian groups were highly mobile Greeks, that Greek was the lingua franca of almost all eastern towns and many western towns too, that the Greeks had a history of polis collective associations, and that the "political" riots just mentioned occurred in the Greek towns of the eastern empire. We can deduce that the Christians were seeking not political participation, but participation in meaningful, collective life in general. And they found it in a church that claimed to be apolitical, transcendent. It is unlikely that they regarded this as a political challenge to the empire. Even though some may have participated in the odd riot, they were dualists concerned with spiritual salvation, leaving Caesar's concerns to Caesar. But spiritual salvation involved them willy-nilly in communal associations. Against their own doctrine they were drawn into politics in the broadest sense.

At the level of doctrine, the fusion of the spiritual with the associational has often been remarked. Nock concludes his analysis of the Hellenistic content of Christianity with a paraphrase of earlier writers: "Men wanted not to seek truth but to be made at home in the universe" (1964: 102). The phrase "made at home in the universe" is perfect. The "home" was a social home, a community, but one that had universal significance in relation to ultimate meaning and morality. It fused the sacred and the secular, the spiritual and the material, to produce a transcendent *society*. The early Christians always referred to themselves as a "fellowship," a "brotherhood," "brothers and sisters in Christ." They were a rival social organization to the empire.

The threat was clear when the authorities *stopped* believing in the rumors of "abominations." They were convinced instead of precisely the opposite: The Christians were virtuous. Tertullian reported a pagan exclaiming, "See how these Christians love one another," and though he was not perhaps an unbiased commentator, Christian charitable work drew much envious attention. The last major opponent of the Christians, the Emperor Julian, who always referred to them as "atheists," confessed openly, "Why do we not observe that it is their benevolence to strangers, the care of the graves of the dead, and the pretended holiness of their lives that have done most to increase atheism?" (quoted in Frend 1974: 285). Christ's dualism could not be rigorously maintained. At the very least, even without disturbing social hierarchies, Christianity posed an ethical threat. It was apparently superior to the empire in its carryover into the social ethics necessary for interpersonal and familial relations. Even if it concentrated on these areas, it represented an alternative focus of normative attachments.

The empire was confronted by an alternative power organization, extensive in covering capacity, intensive in mobilizing capacity, ethical, and (by its standards) democratic. It relied on diffuse more than authoritative power, so executing its leaders might not stop its organizational drive. In many ways, Christianity represented how Rome liked to idealize its republican past. This attracted ordinary citizens and brought back leveling political tendencies that supposedly had been settled around 100 B.C. The Christians' populist leadership was also likely to generate a more radical, egalitarian opposition faction within the church – like the Gnostics or the Donatists (to be discussed in this chapter later). Christianity was based spiritually and socially on the people. It was subversive as long as it mobilized the people for its own purposes, whatever they were.

What Christ, as related by his followers, realized is that knowledge – in this case spiritual knowledge – is really a very simple affair. Once simplified scripts and numerical systems emerged, eventually permitting an extensive flow of information through mixed written and oral channels, then most of the knowledge relevant to social life is available to the ordinary individual. The "spiritual" questions are particularly simple: The contradictions between life and death, material finitude and ultimate significance, order and chaos, good and evil, are as stark and as recognizable by us all as through all history; sophisticated philosophers and theologians add only technical detail. The genetic constitution of human beings gives a fundamental equality of most mental attributes relevant to the acquisition of general knowledge of the world. Once societies enable large groups of people to ask similar questions about existence and its meaning, a powerful egalitarian force is released. The enabling factors were developed in late archaic societies and the consequences were revolutionary.

Thus Christianity carried a radical, profound, but simple and true message to the world, at least in ideal terms. Once the human being is universalized, there arises a notion of the collective existence of humanity at large, in a universal organization, the Church Universal, the *ecumene*. As its Greek title implies, it presupposed Greek philosophical universalism. But the Greeks had only participatory society covering a tiny area. The *ecumene* presupposed the extensive culture and literacy of the Roman Empire. But as the Romans extended, they became less participatory. It was left to an ideological power movement, a religion, to carry a message of fundamental, even if nominally "spiritual," equality and participation across a social space of millions of people. Christianity implied that human society itself need not be bounded by existing states, by existing class or ethnic divides, that integration could be brought by something other than force, by transcendent ideological power itself. Persecution was ferocious as long as the matter rested there.

The spiritual and the secular *ecumene:* toward a compromise?

Compromise between emerging church and imperial state was clearly possible, however. Christianity could hardly remain unaffected by the hostility of the state. Perhaps faith, communal loyalty, and courage could withstand persecution – though much wavering was evident. Some believe that Christianity would not have survived much more persecution (e.g., Frend 1974). Dualism had led the Christians into their difficulties. But dualism had its ambiguities, and these could be clarified in the interests of the Christian and secular authorities alike. The message of Christ, as related in the Gospels, was clear: The equality of all men and women, of all freemen and slaves, was spiritual rather than secular. So, what were the bounds of the spiritual? Christianity began to accommodate itself to the Roman Empire by defining these bounds more narrowly.

Consider first the specific cases of women and slaves. Women were apparently well represented in early Christianity (e.g., Luke, 8:1–3). As Cameron observes (1908), this was not particularly "revolutionary." Women, more marginal to official Roman culture, were also attracted to other religions, like the cult of Isis. Christianity recruited heavily among middling people in trade, and in this sector women were often active agents in their family business. Nevertheless, when the Christian sects became more important, the participation of women in positions of authority began to seem quite radical. Elaine Pagels has compared the early role of women in the church and in the rival Gnostic sects. Many of the sects allowed women as full participants, prophets, priests, and even bishops. Their texts contained many references to feminine or androgynous characteristics of God (some made the Holy Ghost female so that the Trinity became marriage partners plus a single son). All this was suppressed by Paul, by later writers passing themselves off as Paul (especially the First Epistle to Timothy: "Let the woman learn in silence with all subjection"), and by the majority of the early bishops. Women could be full members, but not officiate. God and Christ were definitely male (Pagels 1980: 48–69).

In this development there is one main uncertainty. There is evidence, reproduced by Ste. Croix (1981: 103–11), that official Roman institutions were becoming less patriarchal, in particular working toward a more egalitarian notion of marriage. But the most sustained historical account of a single province, that of Hopkins (1980) on Egypt, comes to the opposite conclusion – that there had been a steady decline in women's powers within the marriage contract, begun by the Greek conquest and furthered by the Roman. Both share the view, however, that Christianity intensified patriarchy. Its links to patriarchal Judaism eventually reduced the freedom of women, giving secular subordination a sacred authority. The newness of Christianity and its distinctive appeal to women first made gender relations more of a live social issue, and then the church's emergent authority structure suppressed it.

A similar toning down occurred with respect to slavery. This was a delicate matter for Paul, and for the community as a whole. Paul's Epistle to Philemon, which is about the returning of Philemon's runaway slave, contains a subtle hint that perhaps "the bonds of the gospel" should take precedence over the bonds of slavery within the Christian community, but nothing more. The orthodox church doctrine would have been recognizable to Aristotle: Slavery was regrettable but inevitable, given original sin. Slaves could be ordinary members of the church, Christian masters should be encouraged to free faithful slaves, and freedmen could rise high in the church. It was a mildly liberal, but not a subversive, attitude. In this perhaps it paralleled the treatment of women.

These revisions were part of a general move toward hierarchy, authority, and orthodoxy that produced a recognizable "Catholic" church by about A.D. 250. But they were not a principled ideological solution to the problem of social organization. Christ had provided no guidance, and so the church became parasitic upon the empire in these matters.

The Roman Empire (like most ancient societies) had failed to penetrate the everyday life of the mass of the people, urban or rural. It had failed to mobilize their commitment or praxis, or to give meaning and dignity to their lives. Yet it provided the essential parameters of order within which life could continue. Primitive Christian communities could not defend the empire; raise taxes; protect shipping from pirates, or mule trains and camel trains from bandits; organize the commissary for the army and bureaucracy; maintain literacy required by a religion of the book; or meet many other essential preconditions of Christian life. Christ said little about these matters, and the early fellowship did not produce a social cosmology. Although they said important and socially true things about the universal condition of humanity, and reinforced them with a small community structure containing simple, satisfying rituals, they said little about macrosocial organization and social differentiation. The first followers of Christ had to produce solutions from their *own* resources, the stock of beliefs and practices that came from Roman citizenship, gender, stratification position, and ethnic community.

In one respect their answer was distinctively Christian. Their faith continued to provide a general populism. This could take quite radical forms in the countryside (as we shall see), but it was normally paternalist. Christian communities were stratified, but the more privileged looked after the less privileged. Charitable works were a sign of this, but so was the form of the transmission of the religion. Only the Christian elite could read fluently in Latin or Greek, but they were downwardly oriented, willing to transmit the message of texts to the illiterate. The core ceremonies were the participatory Eucharist and the reading aloud of sacred texts, of epistles circulating between the communities, and of sermons prepared from such sources. Momigliano (1971) has noted the almost complete absence within Christianity of a gap between elite and mass culture, in striking contrast to Roman traditions. Indeed by the late fourth century, he argues, pagan writers had been forced to respond in kind so that the elite-mass cultural divide did not exist at all. Hence even when authority began to emerge within the fellowship, it was still somewhat disconcerting to the Roman authorities. For the bishops, deacons, and priests were emerging in core urban areas with more intensive mobilizing power over their people than the secular authorities had over theirs. Brown (1981: 48) notes that we are now in a world where the Christian great are seldom presented to us without an admiring crowd. He calls the capacity of Christian notables to strike chords deep in the people "democratization from on top." The ability to mobilize downward, to *intensify* power relations, was distinctively Christian in this area of the world – and distinctive to the other world religions in other areas. It was a product of this era of historical development, and so far we have never subsequently lost it.

But hierarchy did increase. Christ had left no organization that we can discern. Even the disciples appear to have attained collective power only after an argument with a faction led by Christ's brother James. How were the Twelve drawn from the many who had "witnessed" Christ? Truth needs organizing: how to teach it, how to keep it pure, how to maintain its infra-structure, how to decide what it is. All required power. And although the influences on church organization were diverse, the imperial Roman influence grew. The church developed a municipal structure; each city-community was ruled by a bishop (a governor-equivalent) whose authority ran within the surrounding province. The bishop of Rome derived his growing prestige from the secular preeminence of that city. The church's tithes were taxes. Its heresies had strong provincial bases. Its eventual schism into eastern and western churches followed the political division of the empire. The two extreme tests of its universalism, women and slaves, disappeared from full participation. Pope Leo viewed the earlier practice of admitting slaves to the priesthood:

> Persons whom the merit neither of their birth nor of their character recommends are being freely admitted to holy orders, and those who have not been able to obtain their freedom from their owners are raised to the dignity of the priesthood, as if servile vileness could lawfully receive this honour. . . . There is a double wrong in this matter, that the sacred ministry is polluted by such vile company, and the rights of owners are violated, in so far as an audacious and illicit ascription is involved. [quoted in Jones 1964: II, 921]

Most important, the ecumene was Romanized. Christianity was limited. Most missionary activity outside the empire was among "civilized" eastern rival states. The German "barbarians" were largely ignored. Only one (minor) northern barbarian people, the Rugi, were converted to Christianity while still living outside the Roman frontier. One hundred years after the collapse of the western empire, probably only one further major barbarian people, the Lombards, were converted while inhabiting a territory that had not been formally Roman (E.A. Thompson 1963; but Vogt 1967: 218–23 is not quite so sure). The western *ecumene* was manned by Roman frontier guards.

As Romanization proceeded, relations with the secular authorities became more double-edged. Church and state authorities became greater rivals, but their similarity meant they could fuse. Diocletian's reforms, vastly extending the state bureaucracy, gave upward-mobility opportunities to literate, middling, urban males at the end of the third century. This "nobility of service" contained many Christians, unlike its senatorial and equestrian predecessors, giving unofficial state patronage to the religion (Jones 1963). Then came Constantine's conversion (A.D. 312) and his state patronage of Christianity (324). Constantine's motives are a matter for hot debate – probably sincerity and opportunism were so closely entwined that he himself could not have distinguished them. He seems to have been a superstitious, basically monotheistic man, willing to give thanks for battlefield success to one god who was sometimes the God of the Christians, sometimes the sun god. He appreciated the sacerdotal support of the church's authority structure for his own position atop the Roman public-law system (see Ullman 1976). But support was two-way. If Christianity could not be suppressed, it must discipline its own members in the interests of social order. Constantine himself presided at the decisive Council of Nicaea in 325. The Nicaean Creed ratified Christ as God and Christianity as a state-assisted orthodoxy. The assistance was needed because Christianity was still generating a great deal of heresy and social unrest.

Christianity was a religion of the book. The book contained dogma. By accepting the dogma one became a Christian. All can join; it is an act of free will. But what if one's sense of truth is different, and one prefers, say, a more elaborate Greek philosophy, or the republican virtues of the pagan gods, or the ecstasy of the mystic cult? Christianity, like Zoroastrianism and Islam, defined the essence of humanity as rational acceptance of *its* truth. Therefore rejection of the faith renders one nonhuman. This characteristic of religions of the book detracts from their universalism. Earlier religions had tended to either exclude the masses from participation in higher truth or accept that different ascriptive groups had their own truths. If another group was thought to lack humanity, this had nonreligious sources. Now religion defined and restricted humanity.

Intolerance was also shown to other Christians. Doctrine without a clear social cosmology led to difficulties in determining what was the true doctrine and who should guard it. Differences were evident between the Gospels themselves. In the second century arose sects – Gnostics, Marcionites, Montanists, Manichaeans, Arians, Donatists – with large followings that were mostly suppressed with considerable fury. The disputes that led to the sects turned upon doctrine: on whether Christ was divine, human, or both; whether he was born of woman; whether priests should partake more of the divine than of the human; and what authority should pronounce on all these matters. The core of the disputes was the attempt to mediate Christ's dualism of God and Caesar and to generate organization capable of pronouncing on spiritual matters and generating a community organization of the faithful. The state had a strong interest in resolving doctrinal disputes, for it wanted established a power congenial to its own structure.

By about A.D. 250 church-state relations had taken a new turn in some areas. The power structures of both were urban, yet conversion of some rural areas had begun. By 250 the provinces of Egypt and North Africa, and most of the Asia Manor provinces, were heavily Christianized. Penetration of the original homeland and adjacent rural areas, in Palestine and around Antioch, seems sparse until after Constantine. This was also true in Greece and Italy, while the rural Celtic West was almost completely untouched. Apart from the oddities of the Antioch region (see Liebeschutz 1979) and inland Greece, penetration followed trade and Hellenistic cultural routes. The most Christian provinces supplied mass agricultural produce for the Roman heartland either in, or adjacent to, Hellenistic spheres of influence. They were not the poorest regions; quite the reverse.

Much is obscure about rural penetration (see Frend 1967, 1974, 1979). One province, North Africa, is well documented. North Africa generated the most important heretical sect of the fourth century, the Donatists, and one of their Catholic opponents, Augustine, bishop of Hippo (Carthage), was also the main theorist of the church. Their conflict reveals much about the organizational dilemmas confronting the church as it gradually took over the mantle of empire.

The Donatist heresy and Augustine: the failure to compromise

The Donatists arose in protest against local bishops who had compromised with the imperial authorities during the last of the anti-Christian persecutions after A.D. 250. They argued that Christianity should remain pure, unsullied by worldly affairs. By setting up their own bishops (of whom the principal was Donatus), they challenged the Catholic church. The vagaries of the imperial succession – Constantine's conversion and support of the Catholic faction; the accession of the pagan Julian, who was hostile to the Catholics; then further Catholic emperors – found them in and out of imperial favor. But mixed up in their movement were social-revolutionary tendencies. Some flirted with the rebellion of a Numidian chieftain, Gildo, ensuring unremitting persecution at the joint hands of the Catholic and imperial authorities.

There is an important scholarly dispute about Donatism: the relative contribution of "national/social" and "religious" grievances. The main work is that of Frend (1962), who uncovered many of the "national/social" issues. He argued that the Donatists were concentrated overwhelmingly in the countryside, as opposed to the towns, and among Berber- rather than Latin- or Punic-speaking areas. He emphasized the connection between the Donatists and social revolutionaries, the Circumcellions, landless laborers or small peasant proprietors who rose up against the great landowners of the province. And he argued that the connection with Gildo emerged straight out of provincial, rural, and tribal anti-Roman sentiment. Frend has been interpreted by Brown (1961, 1963, 1967) and MacMullen (1966) as reducing the Donatist heresy to "national/social" factors. They assert that despite the contribution of all these background factors, the decisive issues were religious. They argue that the Donatists were led from the towns and drew support from these, whatever the rural concentration; that in the south of the province they were so dominant as to represent all social groups; that the Circumcellions were used as shock troops in upper-class faction fighting by Donatist men of property; and that there was no "revolutionary plan" or political reconstruction in Donatist-controlled areas. Religious belief was principally at stake, although Brown (1961: 101) explains that this means "nothing less than the place of religion in society."

Any wide-ranging historian or comparative sociologist will recognize the flavor of this dispute and predict its further development along materialist and idealist lines. But such controversy confuses the essential issues. Actually both sides agree on essentials. Frend rejected the notion that doctrine itself was at issue. As he argued, Donatus also wrote a text ("On the Trinity") that was doctrinally heretical, following the Arian line. But this was not part of the controversy in Africa, unlike the East. Both sides in Africa stressed their unity of doctrine on most points. They differed on church organization: "It was the nature of the Church as a society and its relationship to the world rather than its distinctive beliefs that formed the heart of the controversy" (Frend 1962: 315). Brown agrees. The Donatists, he notes, claimed that the church should be "pure," the sole preserver of the holy law: "I care for nothing but the law of God, which I have learnt. This I guard, for this I die; in this I shall be burnt up. There is nothing in life other than this law." This is a typical sectarian claim of a direct relationship to divine law in a hostile, chaotic world. It really did represent, as its adherents claimed, part of the true spirit of the early church. But it was a defensive, defeatist spirit, argued Augustine. The Donatists did not realize that history was on the side of Christianity. "The clouds roll with thunder, that the House of the Lord shall be built throughout the earth: and these frogs sit in their marsh and croak – We are the only Christians."

Behind the intolerance and killings of both sides lay not just a combination of material-social unrest and "doctrine" but, more important and linking the two, different notions of *social organization and identity*. The Donatists were fortified by a truly transcendent separatism – a chosen, pure people in direct relation to God ignoring all alternative bases of social power. Augustine and the Catholic authorities possessed a more worldly, less transcendent Christian-imperial identity. They could organize the civilized world as a whole, enjoying divine grace but also with an obligation to impose a secular discipline upon the world (Brown 1967: 212–43). Thus the dispute turned on more than church organization. The issue, given that Christianity was taking over both local and extensive Roman social order, was, To which *society* do I belong: to an extensive if pragmatic church society or to a local, pure church-society – to an *ecumene* or a sect?

The Donatist answer was clear but wrongheaded. A true Christian society included only the pure. If the rest of the church compromised, then it could go to hell. Localism is its important characteristic, rather than either the rural versus urban, or quasi-class, or ethnic identities. But separatism was not viable at existing levels of agricultural production, population density, or social organization. The Donatists were, as they knew themselves to be, in retreat from the world. Their purist position repeated Christ's own tendency to ignore Rome. They did not accept that Christianity was parasitic upon Rome, that their ethical community could only exist in its present form on top of a territorially extensive framework of pacification and order. Compromise with this framework would be necessary to avoid social regress.

When arguing with the Donatists, Augustine appreciated this. But ultimately he did not. His failure is revealing. In his most important work, *The City of God,* there are sections where he says that Christianity should not ignore Rome but take up its mantle. These purvey a history of Rome from the viewpoint of Christian teleology. Its virtues are praised as anticipations of the Christian era; its men of courage and generosity of spirit, though admirable, were doomed to be a minority in a pagan world. Also its worldly successes, its state, its laws, and its property relations are accepted as necessary to social existence, given original sin. If Roman practices had only been infused with the justice and morality of Christianity, "the Roman commonwealth would now enrich all this present world with its own happiness, and would ascend to the heights of eternal life to reign in felicity." Unfortunately, that did not happen. Augustine's response was not to try to make it happen. Apart from a few casual remarks on the necessity of justice and paternal authority to the harmony of family and state, he said virtually nothing about the earthly side of the desired "city of God." The message instead concerned inner, spiritual peace and redemption in the afterlife. Christians, he said, were bidden "to endure the wickedness of an utterly corrupt state, and by that endurance to win for themselves a place of glory in that holy and majestic assembly . . . of the angels, in the Heavenly Commonwealth, whose law is the will of God" (book II, chap. 19). The conclusion was virtually the same as that of the Donatists. It was only a highly specialized *ecumene,* taking the spiritual side of existence, and leaving the secular world to a Caesar, who – unlike the Caesar confronting Christ – was unfortunately fast decaying.

Augustine's attitude, like that of many of his western contemporaries, differed from voices heard in the east. One Syrian Christian leader said that the Roman Empire "will never be conquered. Never fear, for the heir whose name is Jesus will come with power, and His might will sustain the army of the empire" (quoted by Frend 1979: 41, who also gives other eastern examples). This is what did happen, and helped save the eastern empire for a thousand years. The increasingly hieratic eastern church propped up the rule of the eastern emperors – but not the western.

What is quite striking about Augustine's thousand-page book, written between 413 and 427, is that one could not guess from it that Christian emperors had ruled (with only the exception of Julian's four years) for a whole century, and that the state had, since 391, officially banned the practice of pagan cults. *The City of God* was written to rebut pagan charges that Alaric's sack of Rome in 410 had resulted from the city's adoption of the Christian religion. Augustine's main line of defense was that as Rome was still really pagan, the Christians could not be blamed for this. For Augustine, Rome was still the main enemy. It seems fitting that he should die during the final siege of Hippo, just before the Vandals broke through the defenses and massacred the citizens, Christians and pagans alike. The message of Christ, it was reiterated, was not a worldly one. Augustine had failed to answer the Donatists. He had refused to accept the fusion of power offered by Constantine.

The Donatists and the western Catholic church alike underestimated their dependence on Rome. Their own activities presupposed it, yet they could accept this only in a pragmatic fashion, not doctrinally, if they accepted it at all. This is clear in the sphere of literacy. I argued that the spread of Christianity was heavily dependent on Roman routes and forms of communication, especially upon literacy. Reading the scriptures, commentaries upon them, and texts like Augustine's, presupposed an educational system. The Christians were not happy with the pagan schools. They were still claiming that pagan poison dominated education at the time of the collapse of the empire. Yet they did not rival or penetrate them. The main Christian educational establishments were monastic. They were necessary to people who were retreating from society if they were to retain literacy at all. But for those who stayed in society, pagan education was grudgingly, pragmatically accepted. Only in the final collapse of the western empire did a few episcopal schools emerge alongside the monastic schools to transmit literacy in society independently of Rome.

So Gibbon was partially correct. In concluding that the collapse of the empire was due to the "triumph of barbarism and religion," he had exaggerated. The empire fell because it failed to respond to barbarian pressure, as I argued in the last chapter. Christianity missed its chance to produce its own highly civilized *ecumene* on the base provided by Rome. Every time Christians asserted the supremacy of the spiritual realm, they were backing away from a solution to the contradictions of Roman society that I identified at the beginning of this chapter. They were saying "these are not *our* problems," and they were wrong. For the fabric of Christian life depended on a solution. As we shall see in a moment, most of this fabric was lost. It may have been mere accident that all was not lost.

There were two ideal-typical solutions – and, therefore, also many levels of compromise solution between them. The first was the hieratic solution found in the eastern empire. This would have exaggerated all those characteristics of the early western church we call Catholic. But it might not have worked in the west, threatened by more powerful barbarians, for it was relatively weak in its powers of popular mobilization. The eastern empire itself was later swept aside, except in its heartland around Constantinople, by a religion of greater mobilizing power, Islam. The second ideal-typical solution was the popular one, which would have been more radical and innovative, for there was no historical precedent and it would have antagonized the Roman state. It would have involved the establishment of extensive, relatively dem-

ocratic church institutions, mobilizing the people for the defense of civilization. Rome itself had failed to develop such institutions, and Christianity
repeated the failure. There was still no long-term combination of intensive
and extensive social power because Christianity could not squarely face social
power itself.

Beyond Rome, into Christendom: the specialized *ecumene*

Nevertheless, if one accepted that the empire was doomed, it paid to keep at
arm's length from it and to make a separate peace with the barbarian conquerors. The conquerors were keen to appropriate the diverse fruits of civilization; but they were unable to provide extensive forms of organization. Their
total numbers were small. Politically they could generate small kingdoms;
military, loose federations of warrior aristocracies; economically, small-scale
agriculture and herding; ideologically, oral transmission of "tribal" cultures.[8]
They destroyed rather than supplanted the extensive power networks of the
Roman state, even if unintentionally. Yet they could appreciate and appropriate those virtues of the empire that could take a decentralized, small-scale
form suitable for adoption into their way of life. There seem to have been two
main spheres of continuity and adaptation between Rome and the barbarians:
in religion and in economic life.

In religion, once the barbarians were settling inside the empire, the Christians were far more interested in proselytizing among them than were the
pagan Romans. For the Christians it was to continue the missionary practices
of the last four centuries. Such activity had never been centralized and so was
not dependent on the vitality of the Roman state or even of the bishop of
Rome. Indeed many of the barbarians were converted to the Arian heresy
because the principal missionaries among them, notably Ulfila, were Arians
from the eastern parts of the empire. For their part the barbarians probably
converted to Christianity as a symbol of civilization in general. It was also
the main offer of literate assistance to their more ambitious rulers (even if it
derived ultimately from Roman pagan schools, these were not being opened
to them). Their motives were probably similar to those of many converts to
Christianity in the Third World in recent colonial history.

The barbarians were fairly rapidly converted. None of the major Germanic
peoples who entered the Roman provinces in the fourth and fifth centuries
remained pagan for more than a generation after they crossed the frontier (E.
A. Thompson 1963: 77–88; Vogt 1967: 204:23). They were accepting Roman
civilization without the Roman state. After the final end of the western empire
in 476, Christianity was the monopoly supplier of that civilization's legacy,

---

[8]See especially Wallace-Hadrill 1962; E. A. Thompson 1966, 1969.

especially of literacy. "What the Roman Imperium lost, the Catholic Church recovered," says Vogt (1967: 277).

The second sphere of continuity was economic. It is more difficult to discern, but it concerns the similarity of the late Roman villa to the emergent manor of the early Middle Ages. Both involved small-scale, decentralized units of production, controlled by a lord using the labor of dependent peasants. We can only guess at the history of the transition from villa to manor, but it must have involved compromise between the barbarian leaders and the surviving provincial aristocracy of the empire. The "Gallo-Roman," "Roman-British," and so forth, aristocracies were now at arm's length from the Roman state. The Roman senatorial and equestrian orders had resisted Christianity while their own extensive organization endured. But when cut off from the center, they pooled their resources with the local Christians. They were literate, and so were accepted as valued members of the provincial church. Many became bishops, like Sidonius Appolinaris in Gaul. The descendent of Roman praetorian prefects, he never gave up hope of the restoration of Roman rule. His loathing for the barbarians' illiteracy, culture, manner of dress, and smell was traditional to his class. But by the late fifth century it had also made him a sincere Christian. Christianity was now the most salient part of civilization (see Hanson 1970 for a short account of Sidonius; and Stevens 1933 for a long one).

From the fifth century onward, Christian institutions were the main bulwark of civilization against barbarian social regress. It is a story that has often been told (e.g., Wolff 1968; Brown 1971). The account normally centers on literacy, the transmission of which was now almost entirely through church schools. In the late fourth and early fifth centuries, the church responded to the collapse of the Roman schooling system in the west. Every monk and nun should be taught reading and writing within the monastery, so that sacred texts and commentaries could be read and copied. There was less interest in this period of decline in writing new works, far more in preserving what existed. To long-established, now invigorated, monastic schools were added episcopal schools supervised by each bishop. The two school systems cannot be said to have flourished. Most collapsed, a few just survived. The shortage of literate teachers became chronic. Libraries survived – but in the eighth century, only barely (see J. W. Thompson 1957). But curiously, the way the Christians practiced literacy actually threatened its survival. As Stratton (1978: 179–212) argues, the Christian notion of the *lectio divina,* the private use of literacy as a communication between oneself and God, threatened the wider social, functional base of literacy. It took literacy back away from Graeco-Roman traditions toward Middle Eastern restricted, sacred knowledge.

So the continuity of the literate tradition, and with it of Christianity itself, was a close-run thing. It does not have the look of inevitability. It was helped by the unevenness of barbarian penetration. While Gaul was collapsing in the sixth century, Roman Italy and Britain were holding out. When Italy collapsed in the face of the Lombard invasion of 568, the Franks in Gaul and the Saxons in England were being converted by missionaries from elsewhere. Strong, ambitious rulers like Charlemagne or Alfred the Great recognized that the Christian church's mission was the same as their own. They encouraged literacy, missionary work, and the promulgation of canon as well as secular law. In so doing they preserved more public, functional aspects of literacy as well as restricted, sacred ones and paved the way for the restoration of a diffuse literate culture in the Middle Ages. There was always somewhere a flourishing church and reviving states, and the collaboration and struggle between them were important parts of the later medieval dialectic.

The church was the leading agent of translocal extensive social organization. The invaders' organizational forms were confined within the intense local relationships of the village or tribe, plus a loose and unstable confederation beyond. The church possessed three extensive gifts to such peoples (discussed at length in Chapter 12). First, its literacy represented a stable means of communication beyond face-to-face relations and the oral traditions of a single people. Second, its law and morality represented long-distance regulation. This was particularly important for trade, if that were to recover. If Christians treated other Christians as such, with respect, humility, and generosity, trade would not be casually pillaged. And third, in its retreat from the Roman world, it had created a monastic microcosm of Roman extensivity – a network of monasteries, each with its own economy, but not self-sufficient, trading with other monasteries, with the estates of bishops, and with secular estates and manors. This monastic-episcopal economy was underpinned by Christian norms, even if casual pillage had prevailed elsewhere in society. The *ecumene* survived in material, economic form, an example of social progress and civilization to secular rulers. The Charlemagnes and the Alfreds were sincerely converted to it and encouraged it.

In surviving, however, the *ecumene* had become transformed. For the first time it was existing without a state, no longer parasitic on its form. States came and went, in many forms. Although the church was assisted by Charlemagne, it could provide regulation for the Frankish domains even after the collapse of Carolingian political unity in the late ninth century. Ullmann summarizes the Carolingian "renaissance" as a religious one: "The individual renaissance of the Christians, the *nova creatura* effected by an infusion of divine grace, became the pattern for a collective renaissance, a transformation or renaissance of contemporary society" (1969: 6–7; cf. McKitterick 1977). For "divine grace," read transcendent power. The church provided normative regulation over an area wider than the lord's sword could defend, than his law could order, than market and production relations could spontaneously cover. Within that extensive sphere of regulation, these forms of power could in time recover. But when recovery was complete, when in material terms population and economic production equaled and then surpassed Roman levels, the *ecumene* did not wither away. A territorial empire was never resurrected in Europe. If Europe was a "society," it was a society defined by the boundaries of ideological power, Christendom.

The solution Christianity found to the contradictions of empire was the specialized *ecumene*. It was not concerned only with the "spiritual realm" as Christ had claimed, for its popes, prince-bishops, and abbots also controlled large nonspiritual power resources and many dependent clerks, peasants, and traders. Nor did it possess a monopoly over the "spiritual" realm – including in that realm ethical and normative matters. The secular sphere generated morality too – for example, the courtly love literature, or the concern with honor and chivalry. It was rather a specialized sphere of ideological power, deriving originally from a claim to knowledge about the spiritual realm but institutionalized into a more secular mix of power resources.

Even within that sphere, it had not solved all contradictions. It had internalized one, equality versus hierarchy, in a new doctrinal form. Empires had unconsciously encouraged individual human rationality but consciously suppressed it. The Christian church did both, consciously. Both main levels of its consciousness, popular religious sentiments and theology, have embodied the authority versus individual or democratic-community contradiction ever since (so too has Islam, though in different form). Stratification was now enveloped in moral and normative elements, but these were not consensual. For the next thousand years revolt and repression alike were cloaked in the fervor of Christian justification. Eventually the church could not maintain the balancing act; first Protestantism, then secularization weakened it. The weakness was there from the outset: Christianity lacked its own social cosmology. But this made it an extremely dynamic force. I will draw out the full implications of this for the achievements of ideological power in the conclusion to the next chapter. First, however, let us consider the other world religions.

Bibliography

Augustine. 1972. *The City of God*, ed. D. Knowles. Harmondsworth, England: Penguin Books.

Bauer, W. 1971. *Orthodoxy and Heresy in Earliest Christianity*. Philadelphia: Fortress Press.

Bowen, J. 1972. *A History of Western Education, Vol. I: 2000 B.C.–A.D. 1054*. London: Methuen.

Brown, P. 1961. Religious dissent in the later Roman Empire: the case of North Africa. *History*, 46.

   1963. Religious coercion in the later Roman Empire: the case of North Africa. *History*, 48.

   1967. *Augustine of Hippo*. London: Faber.

   1971. *The World of Late Antiquity*. London: Thames & Hudson.

   1981. *The Cult of the Saints*. London: SCM Press.

Bultmann, R. 1956. *Primitive Christianity in its Contemporary Setting*. London: Thames & Hudson.

Cameron, A. 1980. Neither male nor female. *Greece and Rome*, 27.

Case, S. J. 1933. *The Social Triumphs of the Ancient Church*. Freeport, N.Y.: Books for Libraries.

Chadwick, H. 1968. *The Early Church*. London: Hodder & Stoughton.

Cochrane, C. N. 1957. *Christianity and Classical Culture*. New York: Oxford University Press (Galaxy Books).

Cumont, F. 1956. *Oriental Religions in Roman Paganism*. New York: Dover Books.

Forkman, G. 1972. *The Limits of the Religious Community*. Lund, Sweden: Gleerup.

Frend, W. H. C. 1962. *The Donatist Church*. Oxford: Clarendon Press.

1965. *Martyrdom and Persecution in the Early Church*. Oxford: Blackwell.

1967. The winning of the countryside. *Journal of Ecclesiastical History*, 18.

1974. The failure of persecutions in the Roman Empire. In *Studies in Ancient Society*, ed. M. I. Finley. London: Routledge & Kegan Paul.

1979. Town and countryside in early Christianity. *Studies in Church History*, 16.

Gager, J. G. 1975. *Kingdom and Community: The Social World of Early Christianity*. Englewood Cliffs, N.J.: Prentice-Hall.

Glover, T. R. 1909. *The Conflict of Religions in the Early Roman Empire*. London: Methuen.

Grant, R. M. 1978. *Early Christianity and Society*. London: Collins.

Hanson, R. P. C. 1970. The Church in 5th century Gaul: evidence from Sidonius Apollinaris. *Journal of Ecclesiastical History*, 21.

Harnack, A. von 1908. *The Mission and Expansion of Christianity*. London: Williams & Norgate.

Hopkins, K. 1980. Brother–sister marriage in Roman Egypt. *Comparative Studies in Society and History*, 22.

Jaeger, W. 1962. *Early Christianity and Greek Paideia*. London: Oxford University Press.

Jonas, H. 1963. The social background of the struggle between paganism and Christianity. In *The Conflict between Paganism and Christianity in the Fourth Century*, ed. A. Momigliano. Oxford: Clarendon Press.

1964. *The Later Roman Empire 284–602*. Oxford: Blackwell.

1970. *A History of Rome through the Fifth Century, Selected Documents*. London: Macmillan.

Katz, E. 1957. The two-step flow of communications. *Public Opinion Quarterly*, 21.

Katz, E., and P. Lazarsfeld. 1955. *Personal Influence*. Glencoe, Ill.: Free Press.

Kautsky, K. 1925. *Foundations of Christianity*. London: Orbach and Chambers.

Lake, K. 1912. *The Apostolic Fathers*, vol. I. Trans. K. Lake. London: Heinemann.

Latourette, K. S. 1938. *A History of the Expansion of Christianity*, Vol. I, *The First Five Centuries*. London: Eyre & Spottiswoode.

Lee, C. L. 1972. Social unrest and primitive Christianity. In *Early Church History: The Roman Empire as the Setting of Primitive Christianity*, ed. S. Benko and J. J. O'Rourke. London: Oliphants.

Liebeschutz, W. 1979. Problems arising from the conversion of Syria. *Studies in Church History*, 16.

McKitterick, R. 1977. *The Frankish Church and the Carolingian Reforms*. London: Royal Historical Society.

MacMullen, R. 1966. *Enemies of the Roman Order*. Cambridge, Mass.: Harvard University Press.

NcNeill, W. 1963. *The Rise of the West*. Chicago: University of Chicago Press.

McQuail, D. 1969. *Towards a Sociology of Mass Communications.* London: Collier-Macmillan.

Marrou, H. 1956. *A History of Education in Antiquity.* London: Sheed & Ward.

Momigliano, A. 1971. Popular religious beliefs and the late Roman historians. *Studies in Church History,* vol. 8.

Mursurillo, H. 1972. (ed.). *The Acts of the Christian Martyrs: Texts and Translations.* London: Oxford University Press.

Neill, S. 1965. *Christian Missions,* Harmondsworth, England: Penguin Books.

Nock, A. D. 1964. *Early Gentile Christianity and its Hellenistic Background.* New York: Harper & Row.

Pagels, E. 1980. *The Gnostic Gospels.* London: Weidenfeld & Nicolson.

Petronius. 1930. *Satyricon.* Loeb edition. London: Heinemann.

Ste. Croix, G. de. 1974. Why were the early Christians persecuted? In *Studies in Ancient Society,* ed. M. I. Finley. London: Routledge & Kegan Paul.

1981. *The Class Struggle in the Ancient Greek World.* London: Duckworth.

Schillebeeckx, E. 1979. *Jesus: An Experiment in Christology.* New York: Crossroads.

Sherwin-White, A. N. 1974. Why were the early Christians persecuted? An amendment. In *Studies in Ancient Society,* ed. M. I. Finley. London: Routledge & Kegan Paul.

Stevens, C. E. 1933. *Sidonius Appollinaris and his Age.* Oxford: Clarendon Press.

Stone, L. 1969. Literacy and education in England, 1640–1900. *Past and Present,* 42.

Stratton, J. G. 1978. The problem of the interaction of literacy, culture and the social structure, with special reference to the late Roman and early medieval periods. Ph.D. thesis, University of Essex.

Thompson, E. A. 1963. Christianity and the Northern Barbarians. In *The Conflict between Paganism and Christianity in the Fourth Century,* ed. A. Momigliano. Oxford: Clarendon Press.

1966. *The Visigoths in the Time of Ulfila.* Oxford: Clarendon Press.

1969. *The Goths in Spain.* Oxford: Clarendon Press.

Thompson, J. W. 1957. *The Medieval Library.* New York: Harper.

Troeltsch, E. 1931. *The Social Teaching of the Christian Churches.* London: Allen & Unwin.

Turner, H. E. W. 1954. *The Pattern of Christian Truth.* London: Mowbray.

Ullmann, W. 1969. *The Carolingian Renaissance and the Idea of Kingship.* London: Fontana.

1976. The constitutional significance of Constantine the Great's settlement. *Journal of Ecclesiastical History,* 27.

Vermes, G. 1976. *Jesus the Jew.* London: Fontana.

Vogt, J. 1967. *The Decline of Rome.* London: Weidenfeld & Nicolson.

Wallace-Hadrill, J. M. 1962. *The Long-Haired Kings.* London: Methuen.

Wilson, I. 1984. *Jesus, the Evidence.* London: Weidenfeld & Nicolson.

Wolff, P. 1968. *The Awakening of Europe.* Harmondsworth: England: Penguin Books.

11   A comparative excursus into the world religions: Confucianism, Islam, and (especially) Hindu caste

No laws are possible in sociology. We may begin to search for general formulas of the form "if x, then y," where y is the rise of ideological power; but we realize fairly quickly that ideological power on the scale of early Christianity is rare. Indeed, so far, in well-recorded history it has been confined to one particular historical epoch, between about 600 B.C. and A.D. 700 (and principally only in the latter two-thirds of that period). Furthermore, each of the four world religions or philosophies that rose to power in that period was unique in various ways. On that empirical basis we cannot build social-science laws, for the number of cases is far smaller than the number of variables affecting the outcome. A tentative description of the rise of the religions and philosophies is all we can aim for.

Yet we should not avoid the comparative and theoretical issues raised by the rise of the world religions. This is not only because of their intrinsic importance. For they seem to have accompanied, indeed to have reorganized – in the role of "tracklayers" I described in Chapter 1 – a major turning point in world history. Until this period was complete, the histories of the various major civilizations of Eurasia, different as they were, had belonged to the same family of societies and social developments. For example, though I have not discussed developments in China and India, they would have been recognizably similar to those described so far in the Middle East and the Mediterranean. From the broad alluvial base described in Chapter 4, they too developed empires of domination, adopting the same four strategies of rule, trading centers, city-states, literacy and coinage, variant forms of the Roman legionary economy, and so forth. We could apply to Asia the models of earlier chapters, though we would add regional modifications. I do not exaggerate the similarities. But there is a sense in which the world-religion phase saw a branching of the ways, the emergence of at least four different paths of future development. The branching occurred, at least partially, as a response to the challenge of a major religion or philosophy, which we can see therefore as a tracklayer of history. The four were in the regions covered by Christianity, by Islam, by Hinduism, and by Confucianism. By A.D. 1000 four recognizably different types of society existed, each with its own dynamism and development. Their differences remained for more than five hundred years until one of them, Christianity, proved so far superior to the others that all had to adapt to its encroachments, thus becoming a family of societies once more.

Now it may be thought that the presence in these regions of different religions or philosophies was epiphenomenal. This was not so. But even if it were, the problem of religion and philosophy would still be a crucial index of the reasons for the parting of the ways. It is a problem worth studying in some depth.

But the fact that the developmental paths were all different makes the task of comparative analysis immense. It would be a major scholarly undertaking to analyze all cases, greater even than Weber undertook in his unfinished series of studies of the world religions. In this chapter I aim lower. In the preceding chapter I summarized the power achievements of Christianity. Of the others, the power achievement of Hinduism appears even greater. It forms the main substance of this chapter, preceded by short notes on Confucianism and Islam. Buddhism will figure here only as a moderately successful challenger of Hinduism in India itself.

China and Confucius: a comment

China was the sole major empire to absorb the full impetus of salvation religions and emerge intact, even strengthened.[1] China solved the contradictions of empire by splitting salvationist currents into several distinct philosophies or religions and using the most important one, Confucianism, to legitimate its own power structure.

Confucius, who lived in the late sixth and early fifth centuries B.C. (at the same time as Buddha and as the fermentation period of Greek philosophy; rather later than Zoroaster), gave a predominantly secular answer to the problem also raised by the Greek notion of *paideia,* the cultivation of human reason. There were no ultimate, discoverable standards of reason, ethics, or meaning beyond society. The highest knowable morality was social duty; the only order in the cosmos in which we could participate was social order. It is a doctrine that still appeals to agnostics.[2] Virtuous conduct involved qualities like uprightness or inner integrity, righteousness, conscientiousness, loyalty to others, altruism or reciprocity, and above all love for other human beings. But such qualities are not really "substantive." That is, they are not individual or social goals; rather, they are means or *norms.* They tell us how we should relate to others while pursuing our goals. They presuppose a society with given social goals. Hence the fundamental conservatism of Confucius's philosophy. Being a denial of transcendent salvation, it is equally a denial of

[1] As a general source on Confucianism and its relation to the Chinese Empire, Weber's *The Religion of China* (1951) cannot be bettered. For a biography of Confucius, see Creel (1949). Confucius's *Analects* have been edited by Waley (1938).

[2] See, for example, Gore Vidal's sympathetic treatment of Confucius in his novel *Creation* (1981), a magnificent imaginative reconstruction of the religious and philosophical currents flowing between Asia, the Middle East, and the eastern Mediterranean in the late sixth and early fifth centuries.

radical politics and of what we call "religion." But for this reason it is the true Durkheimian "religion": Society, as it is, is the sacred. Confucianism's role is thus largely one of morale boosting; it introduces no principles of ideological transcendence.

But there was also a novel side to Confucius's teaching. How were these character qualities distributed among humans, and how could they be encouraged? Here Confucius gave a humanist answer, recognizably the same as Buddha's, the same as the Greek *paideia:* Ethical conduct could be cultivated by education. In the eastern Mediterranean such a notion was politically radical, as we saw, for all human beings were thought to possess cultivable reason, and the infrastructure of the Greek polis and of mass literacy made this potentially practicable. Confucius's notion was somewhat less radical. The word for his key ideal, *chun-tzu,* underwent a change of meaning at his hands. From being the word for a "ruler's son" or "aristocrat," *chun-tzu* came to mean a "man of ability" meaning nobility of character. Most languages, including our own, have the same double entendre: "Nobility" and "gentleman" denote both ethical conduct and birth, an aspect of ruling-class morale. For Confucius nobility of character was not private but social. Expressed by culture, etiquette, and ritual, it could be learned and taught. Thus a hereditary nobility was insufficient.

Confucius's message became a major social force well after his death. After 200 B.C. the Han dynasty was allied with a wider social group than the hereditary nobility, generally called in translation the "gentry," indicating landholders without particularistic, dynastic connections to the imperial family. The gentry participated in government as landholders and as educated officials, *literati,* who had passed through a lengthy, state-regulated education system, that was recognizably Confucian. It lasted an incredible two thousand years, until modern times. It was in practice a highly restricted meritocracy. For obvious reasons (plus the inherent difficulty of Chinese script) only the wealthy could put their children through the lengthy education process.

Confucianism was a marvelous instrument of imperial/class rule. It appropriated the rationalistic side of salvationist currents, leaving more spiritual, mystical, and turbulent currents to be expressed in quietist, private cults like Taoism. What might have been a transcendent religious challenge was splintered. It also solved several of the contradictions of empire enumerated in the preceding chapter, which the dynasties of the Chinese Empire (including the Han) were also experiencing. It added universal values and legitimation to a modified particularism of aristocracy and dynasty; it confined egalitarian values to an enlarged ruling class; it provided unified culture to a ruling class otherwise prone to decentralization; and by allowing new entrants into the gentleman category, it could admit educated barbarians into its ruling elite and thus into civilization. These were solutions to four of the five contradictions that destroyed Rome.

How was this possible? The answer is too complex to discuss here, but it includes the absence of the remaining contradiction (number 4 in my Roman list): the relative uniformity of China. Other major Eurasian empires, kingdoms, and city-states were part of a cosmopolitan milieu, more in touch with one another, and the larger ones were ecologically, culturally, and linguistically mixed. This made problematic the question that we have seen Christians raise: "What moral community, what normative society do I belong to?" The main problem of social identity for the Chinese was more hierarchical – "Am I a part of the ruling class?" – rather than horizontal – "Am I Chinese?" – to which the answer for most was probably "Yes." There was less reference to foreign modes of thought, or indeed to anything "ultimate" or "spiritual" that might be thought to transcend the society of China. Hence China produced a secular philosophy rather than a transcendent religion as its dominant ideology.

Islam: a comment

The origins of Islam could not lie in a solution to the contradictions of empire, for the nomadic and trading tribal Arabs of Mecca and Medina lay just outside any such society.[3] Muhammad offered a solution to different social contradictions. The growing wealth of the trading entrepôt of Mecca was monopolized by the elders of merchant princely clans, leading to discontent among younger men of other clans that was fueled by the egalitarianism of the tribes. The desert oasis of Medina had a different contradiction. Tribal feuding had led to the emergence of two roughly equal confederations whose bloody struggles made social order itself precarious. We can thus offer a plausible explanation of why a discontented band of younger sons drawn from a variety of clans in Mecca arose, and of why they espoused a quasi-egalitarian and universal doctrine. Such groups often formed around a vigorous man like Muhammad. It is also possible to appreciate the rationality of the Medinans in inviting the outsider Muhammad and his band to arbitrate their differences and, in a loose way, to rule over them.

But why should this man, band, and ruling group espouse a new religion? Perhaps the Arabs were impressed by the power and civilization of the two empires, the Byzantine and the Sassanid Persian, adjacent to them. The culture of empire was carried to them by Orthodox and Monophysite Christianity and, in the Persian case, by a mixture of Judaism, Nestorian Christianity, and (to a lesser extent) Zoroastrianism. All were monotheist, salvationist, ethical, and (with the exception of Judaism) universalist. Arabs just before Muhammad were apparently attracted by these ideas. Even Muhammad saw himself

---

[3] I have used Watt's studies *Muhammad at Mecca* (1953), *Muhammad at Medina* (1956), and *Islam and the Integration of Society* (1961), supplemented by Levy (1957), Cahen (1970), Rodinson (1971), Holt et al. (1977), Engineer (1980), and Gellner (1981).

in the tradition of Abraham and Christ. In responding to Muhammad, Arabs may have endorsed civilization, as the Germans around the Roman Empire had done. The solution to the contradictions of empire was also the way forward for their neighbors. What is problematic, though, is why the Arabs did not adopt one of those religions but developed their own. I do not know why; nor, I think, do the scholars. But one relevant cause was the immediate military success of Muhammad in Medina. Let me explain this.

Islam is doctrinally simple. It contains the shortest credo of any known religion: "There is no god but God and Muhammad is his Prophet (or Messenger)." Repeating this makes one a Muslim, although it should be supported by four other Pillars of Islam: giving the alms tax, five daily prayers, a month of fasting, and the annual pilgrimage. During the lifetime of Muhammad the credo and Pillars had not crystallized. The earliest passages of the Koran contained five beliefs: the notion of a good, omniscient God; a final Last Day of Judgment, with judgment based on men's ethical conduct; the requirement to worship God; the requirement to act ethically, especially to practice generosity; and the recognition that Muhammad had been sent by God to warn of the Last Day. Within Muhammad's lifetime there were two further developments: Monotheism became explicit, and it came to be believed that God would vindicate his prophets and their followers against their enemies.

This simple message involved the notion of a community, the *umma,* based partly on belief per se, rather than on kinship. Any human being could thus join this universal community, as one could join Christianity. Within two years, this concept of community proved itself superior to the community concept of fragmented tribes in an extremely important activity: hand-to-hand fighting between hundreds of men. Muhammad enjoined a "norm of reciprocity": "None of you truly believes until he wishes for his brother what he wishes for himself." Normative consensus was deliberately engineered. The military morale of the believers was just sufficient to win the crucial first battles necessitated by their bandit activities.

From the very first year, Islam was and remained a warrior religion. This probably helps explain the subordination of women, despite other aspects of egalitarian universalism in Islamic doctrine. Patriarchy did not falter in early Islam as it did in early Christianity – it was probably reinforced by the religion.

The main military asset of Islam was the morale of its cavalry – professional warriors sustained materially by the alms tax, in whom zeal for booty was also a sacred zeal, and in whom a disciplined life entailed military drill. Mecca fell in 630, Syria in 636, Iraq in 637, Mesopotamia in 641, Egypt in 642, Iran in 651, Carthage in 698, the Indus region of India in 711, and Spain in 711. In many cases the Islamic forces defeated better-equipped armies by means of superior coordination and mobility, rather than undisciplined fanatical charges (as has been the Christian image of them). The conquests came astonishingly quickly, and on an unparalleled scale. Probably Islam became a major world force only because it tilted the balance of military power relations. It conquered those areas whose rulers' armies were not sustained by a comparable morale. Persia's armies were multireligious, the largest religion (Zoroastrianism) being the feeblest by this time; Byzantium yielded areas of Christianity least integrated into its own emerging Orthodoxy – the lands of the Syriac, Armenian, and Coptic churches; North Africa was disputed territory between the Christian churches.

The two final military checks – the failure to take Constantinople in 718 and defeats at the hands of Charles Martel at Tours and Poitiers in 732 – ram the point home. In both cases the Islamic attackers met their defensive alter egos: the fortress morale of the hieratic Eastern Orthodox church, and the aristocratic honor and faith of the heavily armored mounted knight. The two military and religious stalemates lasted, respectively, for seven hundred and fifty years and almost a thousand years. Within these limits God *was* on the side of Islam. Islam seemed to sweep the Middle East and North Africa because it was true: Muhammad may have created social order, a meaningful cosmos, through an ethical community whose military morale conquered extensive territories.

After the two checks by Byzantium and the Franks, the empire split apart, never to be politically reunited. Much of that superb military morale was now spent on fighting one another (although expansion was possible in the East against weaker enemies) – a condition that still prevails today. The parallel with Christianity is evident.

Religious splits have also paralleled Christianity's: The question has been how to draw the dividing line between the spiritual and the wordly, and whether there is one ultimate source of hierarchical authority within the faith. The latter debate has taken distinctive forms because the bureaucratization of religious authority was always weaker. Islam has never possessed an organization comparable to that of either the Roman or the Byzantine church. Its more "authoritarian" wing, the Shi-ites, has advocated rule by charismatic imams, carrying on the tradition of Muhammad. And the "Libertarian" wing, the Sunnites, emphasizes less the individual (as in Protestantism) than the consensus of the community of believers. But as in Christianity's schisms there has been no question of any major group seceding from the parent religion. The similarity of all the world religions in this respect is remarkable. Whatever the power and the fury of later Islamic, Christian, Buddhist, Jainist, or Hindu sects, they are of less significance than the activities of the founders and their first disciplines. The world religions remained true *ecumenes*.

Why did Islam appeal not just to the Arabs but to almost all the peoples they conquered? Part of the answer lies in the weakness of its rivals, part in its own strengths. Christianity had failed in the southeast to integrate its doctrine and organization to the needs of the area, hence the separate organization and doctrine of the Armenian, Syriac, and Coptic churches, which were dependent on political boundaries that had limited viability once the Middle East was no longer a series of Roman-type provinces or petty kingdoms. It supported neither local-tribal identities nor a much wider sense of order and society. Islam at first provided a link between the two levels, having a sort of "federal" structure. Its origins and constituent units were tribes, and thus it was a true inheritor of the religion of Abraham; yet it was also a universal salvation religion in whose community anyone might participate. In the early years a Christian or Jew who joined the community was attached to a particular Arab tribe as a "client." But the tribal element weakened as the religion spread. Islam could offer the bureaucrats and merchants of the Persian Empire participation in a society that had actually achieved the wider social order to which the Sassanian Persian dynasty had aspired. Such a federal structure was flexible and loose.

The survival and vitality of the Islamic community, the *umma*, was not due primarily to secular organization once the conquests were complete. Rulers bolstered their control with taxes and armies, but Islam cut right across their domains. Those with an interest in trade wished to participate in the religion that provided such an enormous free-trade area, but traders did not rule Islam. The control, as in the other world religions, was partly ideological. Its mechanisms are rather more complex than Christianity's, however, for its federal structure has not included an authoritative church organization. Nevertheless, the infrastructures of control were in other respects similar. Arabic became the lingua franca and the sole medium of literacy by the end of the eighth century. Islamic control of Arabic, and more widely of education in general, has remained monopolistic until the twentieth century in most countries. Translation of the Koran from the Arabic has remained forbidden because the Arabic text is considered the speech of God. As in Christianity there has been something of a divide between sacred and secular law, but the area controlled by sacred law, the Shariah, has been wider. In general family life, marriage and inheritance have been regulated by the Shariah, administered by scholar-priests (the *ulema*) who have generally been more responsive to a conception of community consensus than to the dictates of secular rulers. Ritual has probably also provided more integration than Christianity – there is rather more of it (five daily prayers plus the collective fasting and pilgrimage), and each Muslim knows that at the precise moment he or she is praying millions of others are doing so in the same way and in the same direction.

Thus the wider sense of community has possessed a technical infrastructure of language, literacy, education, law, and ritual in which the primary transmitters have been culture and the family. A diffuse and extensive sense of cultural community, a precise infrastructure centered on a monopoly of literacy, a fairly high level of intensive penetration of everyday life, and a relatively weak social cosmology – the mixture is not dissimilar to Christianity's.

Hinduism and caste

India is the home of the third of the world religions, Hinduism, and the heartland of the fourth, Buddhism. I will deal with the latter only peripherally, as an offshoot of Hinduism that failed to triumph over its adversary in India. For Hinduism has spawned *caste* (or vice versa), that extraordinary form of social stratification. Many who have studied the Indian caste system regard it as a pinnacle of the power of "ideology." What is the nature of that power?

Materialists sense the obduracy of caste in the face of their theories. A few portray caste as an extreme version of class (an economic concept), others as a form of estate (a political and economic concept). Still others concentrate on caste's role as an extraordinarily effective form of legitimation of material inequalities (also the main drift of Weber 1958). These arguments miss essential features of caste, as we shall see.

The defects of traditional materialism lead others to lean on traditional idealism and to assert that "ideas" have ruled India. So said the French disciple of Durkheim, Celestin Bouglé: "In Indian civilization it is religious beliefs above all, rather than economic tendencies, that fix the rank of each group." And again, the power of the Brahmins (the highest caste) is "entirely spiritual" (1971: 39, 54). Dumont follows this tradition. He argues that caste hierarchy is the principle of Indian unity, "not their material, but their conceptual or symbolic unity . . . hierarchy integrates the society by reference to its values"; caste is "first and foremost . . . a system of ideas and values." Thus it is not surprising that Dumont also quotes Parsons approvingly on the integrating role of core values (1972: 54, 73, 301). Innumerable others put their fingers on various characteristics of Indian thought – its concern with purity, with classification, with divine harmony – as ultimately decisive in the development of caste (for a brief review see Sharma 1966: 15–16). Where conclusions are more cautious, "ideas" are still listed alongside "social/material factors" like tribal and racial factors, as determinants of caste – as, for example, in the influential studies of Hutton (1946) and Hocart (1950). Even Karve (1968: 102–3), intent on uncovering the specific mechanisms and infrastructure of caste interaction, nevertheless lists these as "factors" alongside "the religious and philosophical system of Hinduism." She believes that this was an independent source of legitimation to lower and higher groups alike as well as a cosmology. In fact she devotes separate chapters to the philosophy and to the mechanisms. The dualism of idealism versus materialism is difficult to break down. Nevertheless, the way in which I am breaking it down should be already emerging from previous cases. I argue that caste is, indeed, a form of ideological power, with significant autonomy from economic, military, and political power. But it rests, not on "ideas" as an independent "factor" in social life, but rather on specific organizational techniques that are sociospatially *transcendent*.

Let me admit first, however, that it is difficult to reconstruct even an outline history of Hindu caste, for it is ideologically ahistorical. Its sacred texts view time as a single process whereby the world is gradually running down. "Historical events" figure in the texts only to illustrate this prior conceptual scheme. This separates Hinduism from both Christianity and Islam, both of which centrally legitimate themselves with respect to particular historical events that have an autonomous status. Through their story of cosmic degeneration our sources exaggerate the power and the stability of Hindu religion. It is not easy to work out what actually did happen, still less why it did. In this chapter I describe the organizational techniques of ideological power and trace their general emergence. But I will generally fail to prove why they emerged.[4]

Caste defined

The term caste derives from the Portuguese word *casta,* meaning something not mixed, pure. It was used by the Portuguese, and then by other foreigners in India, to denote a form of stratification in which each caste is a hereditary, occupationally specialized, maritally endogamous community in a hierarchical system that distributes not only power in a general sense but also honor and rights to social interaction centering on notions of "purity." Each caste is purer than the one beneath it, and each can be polluted by improper contact with the one beneath.

To categorize so generally, however, is also to simplify in two main ways. First, the category of caste combines two Indian categories, termed *varna* and *jati*. The *varna* are the four ancient ranks, in descending order of purity, of Brahmins (priests), Kshatriyas (lords and warriors), Vaishyas (variously farmers and merchants), and Shudras (servants). A fifth *varna,* the Untouchables, was added at the bottom much later. These *varna* are found across all of India, though with regional variations. The *jati* is at its core a local-lineage group, and more generally any community of interaction reproducing most of the castelike characteristics. Individual *jati* can be generally fitted into the *varna* ranking, but the linkage is mediated by a third level, a chaotic, regionally

---

[4] I have used extensively the multivolume history edited by Majumdar (1951–), supplemented by Ghurye (1979), on Vedic India; two works by Sharma (1965, 1966) on the late Vedic classical and feudal periods; Bannerjee's (1973), Chattopadhyaya's (1976), and Saraswati's (1977) analyses of the development of Brahminical doctrine; and Wagle's (1966) study of society at the time of Buddha. Thapar (1966) is a useful short introduction to Indian history. The studies of caste referred to elsewhere in the chapter have been my main sources on contemporary caste.

varied proliferation of "subcastes," which comprise more than two thousand conglomerations of *jatis* across India.

Second, however, such a description would suggest too orderly and interlocking a set of social structures. It would be a "substantivist" view of caste. Caste is what anthropologists call a segmentary as well as a hierarchical system: It relates together groups and activities that are merely different from (i.e., not superior to) one another, and this has the consequence that the same person may actually view himself or herself as belonging to units of different orders in different contexts. What is castelike about these different contexts is that they all embody binary hierarchies: those one can eat with or approach or touch versus those one cannot, wife givers versus wife takers, junior agnates versus senior agnates – even the subordination of tenant to landlord or political subject to ruler is expressed in similar symbolic language. Thus caste is not only a set of specific structures but also a more general and pervasive ideology. It imparts to all aspects of social stratification an emphasis on *hierarchy, specialization,* and *purity.* It also exaggerates the normal contradiction of social stratification whereby each social stratum is itself a community yet in its interdependence with other strata creates a second community at the level of the overall society.[5]

Only a broad outline of the initial origins is discernible. Between 1800 and 1200 B.C. Aryan groups entered India from the northwest. Perhaps they conquered and destroyed the ancient Indus Valley civilization, although this may have already decayed (see Chapter 4). After 800 B.C. they penetrated the south of India and gradually became dominant over the whole subcontinent and its indigenous peoples. Of those, only the Dravidians of the South are clearly identifiable to us. It is not certain whether the indigenous peoples possessed a social structure with castelike elements.

From the subsequent literature of the Aryans, the *Vedas* (literally meaning "knowledge"), we learn that the Aryans of the early Vedic age (to about 1000 B.C.) were a tribal confederation led by a chariot-borne warrior class that ruled small-scale, loosely knit "feudal" societies. They introduced deep plowing with oxen into India. Their religion was similar to other heroic-age religions of the Indo-Europeans, and to the myths and sagas of Scandinavia or Homeric Greece. Priests, already called Brahmins, had an important role in social rituals, but as a profession not a hereditary group. They did not control exclusively the central ritual of sacrifice, for lords and householders could also initiate and preside over a sacrifice. Most warriors were not professionals either: The upper stratum of peasant householders would plow and fight. Neither heredity of occupations nor prohibition of intermarriage and interdining are even hinted at in the earliest passages of the *Rigveda,* the earliest text.

[5]This paragraph draws heavily on Béteille (1969: esp. introduction; chaps. 1, 5) and Parry (1979).

But continuous fighting with the Dravidians and others probably had three consequences. The first two are more straightforward: the consolidation of rule over the Dravidians and the emergence of larger-scale states ruled by lords with professional warriors. The Dravidians were exploited in a normal postconquest way – regarded as servile, if not as slaves, their status eventually crystallized as the fourth *varna,* the Shudras. They had darker complexions than the Aryans, which is the one clear indication of racial phenotype taken by some authorities as important to the whole caste system. The Shudras were not considered "twice-born"; that is, they did not originally participate in the cycle of rebirth. Thus the stratification gap above them was the widest in the early *varna* system.

But apparently before this, differentiation was also occurring among the Aryan *varna* themselves. That the lords/warriors crystallized as a professional, hereditary Kshatriya rank is not unusual in such cases. Conquest led to better-organized states and better-coordinated warfare, assisted by the development of iron weapons from about 1050 B.C. The chariot was replaced by more varied and coordinated armies of infantry and cavalry requiring professional training and administration. Increasing differentiation between these warrior lords and the Aryan peasant householders, the Vaishyas (the "multitude"), is to be expected in such a situation. For example, it is of the same general order as the distinction made by the later German barbarians between free warrior nobles and servile peasants.

The third change is more complicated: the rise of the Brahmin *varna.* Part of this rise is easy to understand. The growth of larger, more hierarchical kingdoms required a more hieratic form of legitimation. As in archaic religions in general, the cosmology was at this time less concerned with vitalistic gods than with relations between human beings, especially relations of obedience. It is even part of this general transition to develop private priestcraft, mysteries in which only priests may participate. The second group of texts, known as the *Brahmanas* (composed perhaps in the tenth or ninth century, perhaps much later), shifted from the *Rigveda* concern with practical problems of physical survival to a more esoteric discussion of the effects of magical rituals in regulating social relationships and in preserving *dharma,* the divine order. Sacrifice became more important, as did Brahmin control of it. Now only Brahmins could preside over sacrifices, although Kshatriyas and Vaishyas could ask for them. This control became important, for sacrifices were frequent – on routine occasions such as conceptions, births, puberty, marriages, deaths, and contracts, and even at morning, midday, evening, and irregular decision-making points. Sacrifices brought the community together in ritual (for no avoidance of personal contact was yet evident), and they were feasts and redistributive events. The Brahmins were thus implanted early in the rituals of courts, towns, and even everyday village life. Whatever esoteric theological beliefs developed later, this intensive control, ritualistic rather than theological, remained the core of Hindu control. We lack the evidence to explain this, but, once established, we can see its effects.

The sacrificial role of the Brahmins led to assertions that they were superior to the gods themselves, for they were the actual reaffirmers of the eternal cycle of death and rebirth. This may be a later Brahminical interpolation; but if it is not, it is a distinctively Indian twist to the tendency found throughout much of the archaic world toward theocracy. Kingship was not divine. The king should be firm and should be obeyed as part of obedience toward the sacred law of the cosmos, *dharma*. The majority view of the *Brahmanas* was that dharma was to be interpreted by sages and priests. But this was not uncontested, and some texts asserted the supremacy of the Kshatriyas. Whatever their common interests, these two orders were not merging into a single ruling theocratic class as in Sumer or Egypt. Differentiating tendencies were reinforced by the first emergence of subcastes in the form of occupational guilds. Intermarriage was as yet not prohibited, but it was an object of concern, and stigma attached to a Brahmin or Kshatriya female marrying lower down. Interdining restrictions existed, but not on the basis of *varna* – rather, the basis of a more diffuse concern with kinship and blood relations. Impurity of touch was still unknown.

So two important Indian tendencies were evident but not dominant at this early date: first, a belief that divine order did not rest with secular authority; second, a tendency to proliferate social differentiations, especially within the ruling class itself, leading to elevated claims for the authority of the Brahmin *varna*. These tendencies might be explained by the development of a common transcendent regional culture, such as we found in most early civilizations in Chapters 3 and 4, and by the Brahmins' ability to appropriate the ideological power this represented. Given the paucity of evidence, however, this can only be a hypothesis for this period.

The Aryans appear to have penetrated evenly across almost all of India. We find basically the same way of life – the same economic, political and military forms, and religious rituals and beliefs – right across India, except in the extreme south. The aborigines were also spread right across most of the subcontinent as serfs, adding to the similarity of social practices and problems. This cultural similarity was wider than the interaction networks of the economy, polity, or military organization. Thus social order of a minimal variety was wider than secular authority could reinforce, a common occurrence in the ancient world, as we have seen. It was "transcendent power." Concepts like dharma thus play the same kind of ideological role as the Sumerian diplomatic pantheon of gods, or the culture of Hellas, linking together local authoritative power organizations like village, tribe, or city-state into a broader, diffuse power organization centered on culture, religion, and diplomatic-cum-trading regulation. Obviously Hindu caste structure and dogma eventually became quite peculiar to India. Yet in its origins it appears part of a recognizably common pattern of transcendent ideological power in historic civilizations.

However, elsewhere we generally find one of two historical outcomes to this dual linkage: Either the overall culture fragments, and individual tribe and locality triumph over the broader culture, or (more commonly recorded for posterity) political and military consolidation creates larger secular authorities who appropriate the cultural legacy – as we saw in the case of the Akkadian appropriation of Mesopotamia in Chapter 5. In India the former seems not to have occurred (though it is difficult to be sure), the latter progressed only fitfully (as we shall see), and a third outcome resulted: The Brahmins appropriated the cultural legacy, without relying as much on states, military force, or economic power as any other known power movement in history. This is the Indian uniqueness, I suggest.

Unfortunately, guesswork must take over in the explanation, partly because of inadequate source materials and partly because of the lack of help from scholars. The western scholarly dominance of India has been such that even many Indian scholars insist that Hinduism had no social organization. Because it has never possessed one church hierarchy, they proclaim that there has been little Brahminical organization. This is generally the source of their emphasis on "ideas" as social forces. Yet by the age of the *Brahmanas,* there had emerged a coherent India-wide form of organization, controlled exclusively by the Brahmins, in the sphere of education. Vedic schools run by Brahminical sects existed all over the country. The education united meaning and science – instruction was in religious hymns and rituals, language, grammar, and arithmetic. It was administered to all young Brahmins and some Kshatriyas and Vaisya, who were generally taken away from their homes to learn at the home of a Brahmin teacher or in organized schools. Educational progress was marked by initiations. We possess no accurate dates, but we can guess that literacy became established under exclusive Brahmin control by this time or a little later. A Sanskrit language derived from the Vedic texts became rather later the only medium of literacy (apart from some penetration by Aramaic in the far northwest). Technical knowledge was associated closely with science, meaning, and ritual.

Thus it was not merely that the Brahmins sat astride cultural traditions: They also possessed infrastructural backup to useful knowledge and progress. The combination of the two offered normative regulation, peace, and legitimacy to anyone concerned with an extension of secular social interaction, most notably political rulers and merchants. In this respect it would probably be wrong to emphasize conflicts between the upper *varna* at this time. They ruled together and they progressed together. Political consolidation, economic expansion, and cultural knowledge proceeded hand in hand during the late Vedic age, up to about 500 B.C. Politically we can perceive a consolidation of kingly power, buttressed by Brahminical advisers. Socially and economically the gap between these two *varna* and the lower two widened; they also jointly regulated the occupational proliferation of guilds and merchant groups into subcastes. Between them they monopolized law, into which *varna* now intruded: Interest rates and punishments varied according to *varna*. (Brahmins paid least for their debts and crimes.) Within such ruling-class unity, the division of function between sacred and secular was maintained. True Brahmins were themselves sometimes rulers, but more usually the distinctiveness of an *ideological* Brahminical role, as scholar, priest, and adviser to the ruler, was strengthened. In the sphere of education their monopoly was recognized and widened. The subjects taught included ethics, astronomy, military science, the science of snakes, and others. Initiation rites occurred at age eight, eleven, or twelve according to caste. The title of the *Upanishads* (written 1000 – 300 B.C.) means "secret knowledge." Their most repeated phrase was "he who knows this," the conclusion being that such knowledge brought worldly power. This claim and appeal was directed by lay rulers – two differentiated groups were confronting each other as allies and to some degree as enemies. They were not yet welded into one caste system. Though the power and collective consciousness of the priest *varna* was already probably greater than in most comparable cases, subsequent developments need not have been in the direction of caste.

Over the course of the next three centuries, from about 500 to 200 B.C., we can perceive a struggle between alternative courses of social development. Only at the end of this period was Brahminical power, and caste, secured.

Two threats arose to the Brahmins. The first came from a contradiction within their own tradition. The *Upanishads* had elevated asceticism and an esoteric search for personal knowledge over correct performance of social ritual as the key to salvation. Renunciation of the world is the ultimate goal in these tents. Yet Brahminical social power came from rituals involving "polluting" contact with laymen. The contradiction is still there today (Keesterman 1971; Parry 1980). So it would need little to push this theological search away from priestly control and sacrifice altogether. Such steps were made by both Mahavira, the founder of the Jain sect, and Gautama Buddha around 500 B.C. Both made personal salvation paramount. Salvation resulted from a search for enlightenment and ethical conduct. Both challenged caste particularism, arguing that salvation was equally open to all and that one became a Brahmin by conduct not birth. Concerned with salvation attained by ethical conduct rather than ritual, Buddhism had special appeal to urban trading groups seeking a moral rather than a communal framework for their lives. As both Buddhism and Jainism advocated retreat from the world during the search, they tended to favor leaving earthly superiority to the Kshatriyas. Thus they were useful to the secular authorities, from whom the second threat arose.

Economic and military developments created larger, territorial states, especially under the Nanda rulers of 354–324 B.C., who managed to put larger armies into the field than hitherto. It was under the Mauryan dynasty of 321– 185 B.C. that a full-scale imperial power arose. Aśoka (ca. 272–231 B.C.) succeeded in conquering virtually the whole of India, the only indigenous ruler ever to do so. Mauryan rule was spread by large armies (Greek and Roman sources give figures of 400,000–600,000 men, which are incredible for logistical reasons given in earlier chapters). Centralized irrigation works and state development of virgin land were undertaken, as well as the normal panoply of imperial economic powers described in previous chapters – weights and measures, customs and excise taxes, control of mining and metallurgy, state monopolies over essentials such as salt, and so forth. On the ideological front, the divine origin and right of kingship were asserted and an attempt was made to free kingship from the fetters of the Kshatriya caste. The *Arthashastra*, probably written at this time, reputedly by Kautilya, prime minister of the first Mauryan emperor, also upgraded royal decree and rational law in relation to sacred law. The Mauryans did not use Sanskrit. Emperors, lords, and townspeople gravitated toward Buddhism and Jainism, whose universal theologies fitted better into the formal rationality required by both imperial rule and the city market. The way was open for development either along Christian-type lines – a religion of individual salvation in a symbiotic relationship with imperial rule – or along Chinese lines – a rationalistic belief system propping up imperial and class rule.

The orthodox Vedic tradition responded vigorously. Its theology tended toward monotheism yet accommodated the various Buddhas into a vast pantheon of subordinate gods. It also returned to earlier practices of accommodating diverse popular and tribal gods. The syncretic label of "Hinduism" conventionally dates from this period of assimilation. But its real organizational thrusts remained in local ritual and in education. The Greek traveler Megasthenes gives us the first detailed account of a Brahmin's life in the Mauryan era (its outlines are confirmed by later Chinese travelers). For the first thirty-seven years the Brahmin was a student ascetic, at first living with teachers, then alone, but sitting in public places, philosophizing and advising all who came by. Then he retired to his family home, took wives, and lived luxuriously as a householder, officiating at village rituals. From other sources we know that literacy was now widespread among Brahmins, Sanskrit being finally standardized by Panini in the fourth century B.C. At the age of five the pupil began learning his alphabet, writing and arithmetic. The educational curriculum was now at its peak, and it included "graduate studies" at hermitages that possessed specialized departments in such subjects as Vedic studies, botany, transport, and military science. These organizations were copied by Buddhism and Jainism.

Battle was joined. By 200 B.C. the Brahmins were triumphing, and by A.D. 200 the victory was complete. There seem to have been two main reasons.

First, imperial India collapsed with the death of Aśoka. No subsequent Hindu ruler directly controlled more than a region of the subcontinent. We can partly ascribe this collapse to geography pure and simple. The preponderance of landmass, plus mountains and jungles, over coastline and navigable rivers offered enormous logistical obstacles to authoritative control from one political center. But, as we will see in a moment, it was possible to preserve *diffusely* some of the Mauryan power without an authoritative state. The empire had outlived its usefulness. Second, the Brahmins retained control at the local level with their ritual concerns, while their religious rivals' more sophisticated theologies had minority intellectual and urban appeal once their secular patrons declined in power. Buddhism survived strongest around the fringes of India where regional monarchies endured.

The form of their triumph emphasized its completeness, for the states "voluntarily" handed over much of their powers to the Brahmins. This process is generally termed "feudalization." Indeed, it is similar to events consequent upon imperial decay all over the world. As the imperial state lost its power to control its outlying territories, it handed over effective control to provincial notables or to imperial officials, who then "disappeared" into the provinces, reemerging as independent provincial notables. The process has been described already for various empires of domination (especially in Chapters 5 and 9). It began to appear in immediate post-Mauryan India, gathered pace in the first five centuries A.D., and remained intermittent practice until the Muslim conquests.

But there was a difference in India – control was handed over as much to local Brahmins as to local lords. Sharma (1965) shows that it started as grants of virgin land to groups of Brahmins (and occasionally to Buddhists), often attaching neighboring villages to the gift in order to have the land worked. This was still a policy of social and economic development, now decentralized to local elites. The Brahmins taught local and transferred peasants the use of the plow and manure and instructed them in the seasons and climate; these techniques were eventually recorded in a text called the *Krsi-Paresa*. But from the second century A.D. inscriptions survive indicating that cultivated lands were given away together with administrative rights. The inscriptions generally detail these rights: that royal troops and officials shall not enter the land, and that certain revenue rights are given away, for as long as the existence of the sun and the moon. By the late Gupta age (the fifth and early sixth centuries A.D.), all revenue, all labor dues, and all coercive powers, even the trying of thieves, were being given away. Temples were the recipients as well as Brahmins. By the first half of the seventh century under the relatively powerful ruler of the north, Harsa, the scale of religious feudalism was vast. The Buddhist monastery of Nalanda enjoyed the revenue of 200 villages, as probably did the center of education at Valabhi. On one occasion, Harsa gave away 100 villages, equal to 2,500 hectares, on the eve of setting out on a military expedition. Later rulers gave away as many as 1,400 villages at one go. We also find grants to secular officials. In the period after A.D. 1000, central power was collapsing so fast that vassalage, subinfeudation, and the other characteristics of European feudalism became common. But before then the vast majority of benefices were given to religious groups.

There is also a second difference from European feudalism: The Brahmins were not required to undertake military service or supply land tax. What did they undertake, then? What did the rulers get for their gifts?

The answer is normative pacification. The Brahmins and the Buddhists and other sects were powerful and maintained law and order in the donated areas, using authoritative force backed by a more diffuse ritual organization. Actually there were two subtypes. In primitive areas, the Brahmins integrated tribal peoples into Hindu social structure. They introduced agricultural learning and literacy; and they introduced tribes into the caste system by proliferating sub-castes and mixed castes. In the process they themselves spread out all over India. In relatively civilized, settled areas they also carried forward useful learning. Their language became that of the Gupta emperors. Probably in the late third century A.D. they pioneered the simplified numerical system that later conquered the sciences and the marketplaces of the world as "Arabic" numerals. They emphasized *varna* obligations, and the full notion of caste developed.

Between about 200 B.C. and A.D. 200, *The Book of Manu* attained its final, holy form. It gave the instructions of the creator of the universe to the first man and king, Manu. It explained caste status as the consequence of *karma* accumulated in earlier incarnations. Essential duty was to fulfill the dharma, "the duties, the path to be followed," of whatever position one is born into. To die without longing or desires realizes Brahman, eternal truth. Whatever is, is holy. Reinforced by the subsequent law books, the *Dharma Shastras, The Book of Manu* suggested that caste society was a conceptually connected structure. Actually, if examined as doctrine, it is full of inconsistencies and contradictions. But it emphasizes correct performances of ritual under Brahminical supervision as the key to dharma. Brahminical infrastructural power over the village and over broader normative pacification could put this into practice. Local councils, *panchayats,* became less representative of village or town, more of caste and subcaste. Secular law was devalued in theory and practice. Manu described the king as the upholder of caste, not as an independent law giver. Brahminical laws now penetrated intensively the whole of social life and extensively the whole of India, enveloping family, occupation, guild trade, and capital-labor relations, and joining together law with injunctions about purity and pollution. The secular role of Sanskrit declined as regional languages became intertranslatable, under Brahminical supervision; but its sacred status as the actual speech of the gods was enhanced.

Caste now came in a package that could not be easily unpacked. Its sacred texts also offered the only major source of scientific, technical, legal, and social knowledge; it provided order without which social life would regress; it explained the origin of society; it gave ritual meaning to the everyday and the life cycle; and it provided a cosmology. One could not pick and choose from among these elements, because viable alternatives eventually perished.

Let me concentrate on social order. Chinese travelers to India from Gupta times onward were astonished at its peace and order, which they thought did not depend on police control, criminal justice, taxation, or forced labor. "Every man keeps to his hereditary occupation and attends to his patrimony," said Hiuen Tsang in the seventh century. In fact it was not done without coercion, but the sanctions were local. Deviation from obedience brought impurity, evil, and ostracism. The ultimate penalty was exclusion from social life. The organization that maintained it was without a center, but it covered India.

Thus we must reject the notion of the self-sufficient village community that has often dominated accounts of Indian caste. It emphasizes the self-sufficiency of the village; it argues that translocal relations are only possible given relatively powerful political states, forming "little kingdoms" of social relations; and it argues that the proliferation of subcastes, and the predominance of *jati* over *varna,* is the result of the fragmentation of political power (Jackson 1907; Srinivas 1957: 529; Cohn 1959; Dumont 1972: 196–211). Yet this cannot explain the cultural and ritual uniformity of India, the preservation of peace and order in the absence of powerful states, the regulation by caste of ethnicity and the division of labor. As Dumont and Pocock polemically proclaimed in "For a Sociology of India," India is one, constituted by its "traditional higher, Sanskritic civilization" (1957: 9).

There is evidence for this at various levels. In the locality it has been demonstrated by Miller's (1954) seminal study of the Kerala coast in recent history. Lower castes had social relations outside their caste only within their village, and inside their caste only within villages grouped into a local chiefdom. Chieftain castes had wider social relationships but were still confined by the territory of the suzerain chief they recognized – and there generally existed three of these in Kerala. Only Brahmins traveled freely and interacted throughout Kerala. The Brahmins could thus outflank organizationally any threats to their power.

At the "national" level we can perceive greater cultural similarity among Brahmins than among other groups. Saraswati endorses the traditional division of many cultural traits into northern and southern zones, but he then argues that in most cultural activity there is an essential unity between the zones. He concludes:

The Brahmans are culturally much more homogeneous than what they appear to be physically, linguistically and even socially. What the Brahmans share in common are the traditions of the *Vedas,* the philosophy of the *Upanishads,* the myths and legends, pilgrimage and the practice of the samcharas (rituals) which influence the total way of their life; these are the essentials of their traditions which make them culturally united and distinctive. [1977: 214]

Ghurye (1961: 180) makes a similar point: "The hereditary and prescriptive right of the Brahmins to act as priests to all castes of the Hindus, with only a few exceptions, has been the one uniform and general principle inhering in caste-society through all its vicissitudes." As Saraswati comments, naturally this has to be *organized*. Sacred texts are not endlessly recited and garbled by largely illiterate local priests, musicians do not compose essentially the same themes and cadences, architects do not erect similar temples, family inter-marriage practices are not patterned, because of "spontaneous cultural simi-larity" over at least a thousand years. We can also trace from the time of Manu the gradual organization of *jati* into *varna;* the gradual closing off of alternative marriage opportunities in the Brahminical texts and law books; the standardization of rituals of sacrifice and gift bestowing; the use of mantras that only the Brahmin priest may chant; and the development of the caste *panchayat*. I am not arguing that integration extended to identity of belief, either across India among the Brahmins or across the castes, as perhaps Dumont and Pocock (1957) suggest. Such an idealist position has been refuted by writers showing the intellectual incoherence of the sacred texts, and the lim-ited understanding and interest in doctrine shown by villagers and priests alike (e.g., Parry 1984). Hinduism is a religion less of doctrinal mobilization than of ritual penetration. Ritual is the core of Brahminical organization and so, in turn, of Indian social integration.

Integration of this form seems also to have contributed to overall social stagnation. Literacy was highly restricted in functions and diffusion. Caste also probably aided economic stagnation (though this is controversial and can be easily exaggerated). Being decentralized, caste could not replace imperial infrastructures – thus irrigation systems became localized, coinage dimin-ished sharply over many centuries, long-distance trade decayed. The Brah-mins presided over something of a retreat toward a local-village economy (mitigated partially by the later development of larger temple economies). But being hierarchical, they did not liberate individual rationality and enterprise. In an economic sense, perhaps India got the worst of both worlds – neither the universal rationality of the imperial state nor the individual rationality of a salvation religion.

Politically and militarily, a decentralized India was also ill-equipped to deal with foreign threats, and it succumbed to successive waves of Islamic and Christian conquerors. Locally, however, caste was resilient because it pos-sessed no center that could be captured either by foreigners or by peasant revolts. Its weakness was its strength, as Karve indicates (1968: 125). Passive endurance and resistance was its forte. Gandhi was the last to exploit this politically.

More generally there is a certain inefficiency about a system that dealt with social interdependence by reducing direct reciprocity. As Dumont observes, caste does not observe the norm of complementarity – I bury your dead; you bury mine. Instead, it has devised a specialist function of burying the dead, which only the least "clean" may undertake (1972: 86). This extremist elaboration and ossification of the division of labor was worsened by avoiding physically the presence of those whose services one relied upon. All these drawbacks came in the same package as the advantages of caste. The power of caste permitted a degree of order, but less social development.

The caste package remained dominant in India until the twentieth century. Then it began to change and probably weaken under the impact of British imperialism, industrial development, political nationalism, and secular education. Until then the Brahmins managed to regulate social differentiation loosely. Apart from the Europeans, economic functions, differences between conquerors and conquered, and interethnic and intertribal relations have all been covered by a fantastic elaboration of caste and subcaste. But the Brahmins, apparently only just remained in control. In dealing with subsequent economic, political, and military relations, they were both flexible and opportunist. The Untouchable caste was invented as a way for subordinate outsiders to enter the system, while conquerors or those who somehow managed to acquire land or other economic resources in practice entered at higher levels. And the proliferation of subcastes meant that central and authoritative management of the system was impossible (as all the politicking opened up by the British censuses revealed).

That there are limits to caste hierarchy means that there are limits to Brahminical power in relation to other groups. The Brahmins succeeded in elevating themselves above the lords and the economically powerful in terms of purity, moral worth. Only foreign invaders, Islamic and Christian, succeeded in imposing themselves over them. It appears to be unique to India that the ethically superior should so consistently be those who are thought to possess holiness and purity rather than economic, military, or political power. The "rather than" is appropriate here, for the Brahmins, though they have tended as a whole caste to be both rich and well armed, have kept secular power at an arm's length from themselves. Within the caste, higher status is given to the world renouncer, then the scholar, then the priest (partly polluted by service to other castes), then the officeholder and landholder. Externally, those who can mobilize most popular support have often been holy, ascetic men like Gandhi. But this is a restricted dominance. Caste has not overruled other sources of power by incorporating them. Rather it has shown a degree of indifference to them. Brahminical religion has elevated the spiritual, the eternal, changeless, pure truth, dharma. As long as this is respected, secular society may more or less do as it pleases.

From a cynical, materialist viewpoint this might seem like a conspiracy to share power between sacred and secular elites. In certain respects it is. But it also devalues the ultimate meaning of the secular and diverts potential resources, both of material and of human commitment, to the sacred. It is important to realize that no theocratic tendencies have been observable in India since Vedic times – powerful religious leaders have not sought to conquer the state or the landed classes, but to withdraw a certain distance from it. This has paradoxical consequences, for although the Brahmins have been securely located in everyday social, "secular" life, they have been conservative and, from the point of view of material and social development, regressive. They redistributed and consumed a large part of the surplus, they sought less to direct its reinvestment. They helped distribute political tribute to the states, but they did not struggle hard to influence state goals. The society of India has been profoundly *dual* and contradictory, the sacred opposed to and undermining the achievements of the secular.

Hinduism may reflect the pinnacle of social power that can be attained by a salvationist religion. After all, wholehearted rejection of the world in favor of salvation would lead to the speedy collapse of social life. Thus real conquest and incorporation of economic, military, and political power by a salvationist religion would destroy society. The apparent conquests, by Christianity and Islam, were in reality retreats by ideological power, for their institutions took on a profoundly secular character. Hinduism had a much greater long-term influence on Indian society by refraining from a strategy of total conquest.

After all this, it hardly needs saying that caste cannot be reduced to economic factors or to class. It did not merely or essentially legitimate the interests of dominant economic, political, and military groups, because it reduced their power vis-à-vis the Brahmins, it reduced their freedom of action, and it reduced the power resources available to them. This is true as a historical statement, and it is also true in comparative perspective if India is contrasted to other preindustrial civilizations. Caste did reorganize the course of Indian economic, political, and military developments. It helped structure Indian social stratification. It did, indeed, represent the dominance of ideological power relations in India. But it was no more a system of ideas than a class system or a political state. Like all forms of social organization, it required the interpenetration of ideas and practices. It needed infrastructure of a transcendent type.

We have seen that Hinduism developed a form of pacification, eventually becoming a kind of religious feudalism – preserving order without a central state as did military feudalism, but also with far less assistance from a warrior class. Its power rested on the following infrastructural factors, which we saw emerging over a long stretch of Indian history:

1. Intense ritual penetration of everyday life, greater than any of the other world religions

2. Near monopoly of socially useful knowledge, especially literacy and educational organization
3. Provision of law, at first competitively with states, then as near-monopoly supplier
4. India-wide extensive organization of its priestly caste, the Brahmins, as contrasted to the more local relationships of other groups, including even political rulers
5. The ability, through all the above factors, to regulate interethnic relations and the division of labor through caste organization

The power of Hinduism resembled that of Christianity and Islam in its ability to generate a transcendent social identity independent of military, political, or economic relations. But more than the other religions it was able to buttress this with a more developed transcendent organization. Caste gave character to the *ecumene* and detracted from the power of secular authority. In this way the *ecumene* found a more complete and enduring link between the individual and ultimate social reality. Thus, possibly, had we ventured forth with questionnaire and tape recorders in precolonial India, we would have found a degree of value consensus in that substantive area that has proved most intractable in other cases, social stratification. The moral acceptance of hierarchy is, as Dumont argues, an integral part of caste. Naturally, the acceptance (as everywhere) is partial, contradictory, and contested. But in India contradiction and contest revolve not only around the tendency of lower groups to regard themselves as factually inferior. Here, unlike elsewhere, it also involves their tendency to admit that they are to some degree impure and even evil. This is remarkable, and not only to "the westerner" (as is often remarked). We find few approximations anywhere else on the globe.

So the Hindu *ecumene* had a paradoxical form: It united through differentiation, at both the material and the moral level. But perhaps we should not call Hinduism an *ecumene,* for it seems to deny brotherhood and sisterhood in this life (which has generated an anguished Hindu literature denying this). Caste is inversion of the *ecumene* and the *umma,* recognizably the same order of phenomenon, yet almost their opposite.

Caste provided a clearer connection between the two types of power, collective and distributive. Not only could it mobilize a collectivity, it could clearly and authoritatively stratify it as well. Caste is a form of stratification, not economic (class) stratification, not political (estate) stratification, based on a distinctive form of transcendent organization. This is what Hinduism attained over and above the common ecumenical achievement of the world religions.

Thus the cosmology used to give meaning to all this "made sense." It was a plausible belief system because it led to results. Its correctness seemed vindicated by the existence of order and a degree of general social progress. Hindu caste does not presuppose an innate Indian obsession with classification, with purity, or with other conceptual schemes or values. Rather, its distinctive power organizations provided for the stratification of real human needs in an unusual social situation – unusual but amenable to the conceptual tools of sociology. And it satisfied those wants until it met what we must suspect will eventually be seen as greater power resources, those of the industrial capitalist mode of production and the nation-state.

The achievements of ideological power: a conclusion to Chapters 10 and 11

Over several chapters, I have discussed a number of belief systems that all became prominent in the period from about 600 B.C. to about A.D. 700.: Zoroastrianism, Greek humanistic philosophy, Hinduism, Buddhism, Confucianism, Judaism, Christianity, and Islam. They became prominent because of one crucial shared characteristic: a translocal sense of personal and social identity that permitted extensive and intensive mobilization on a scale sufficient to enter the historical record. In this respect they were all "tracklayers" of history. And they were all novel. Even those that compromised most with locality (Hinduism with its localized *jati* element of caste, Islam with its tribalism) and even those that were most restricted in terms of class or ethnicity (Zoroastrianism, Confucianism, and perhaps Judaism) nevertheless offered a more extensive and universal membership than had any prior social power organization. This was the first great reorganizing achievement of ideological power movements in this period.

Such an achievement had two preconditions and causes. First, it was built on the previous extensive achievements of economic, political, and military power relations. Specifically, it depended on communications and control systems forged out of the trading networks of ancient modes of production, the communicated ideologies of dominant classes, military pacification structures, and state institutions. Belief systems are messages – without communications infrastructures they cannot become extensive. These infrastructures became most developed in late archaic empires of domination. But the more successful the empires were at developing such an infrastructure, the more certain social contradictions intensified. I specified five principal contradictions in some detail in Chapter 10. They were between universalism and particularism, between equality and hierarchy, between decentralization and centralization, between cosmopolitanism and uniformity, and between civilization and barbarism at the frontiers. The empires "unconsciously" encouraged the development of all the former of these coupled qualities of social relationships, yet official imperial structures were institutionally committed to the latter (in the last case, committed to keeping the outside barbarians in that role rather than civilizing them). Thus unofficial groups emerged as the principal bearers of universal, egalitarian, decentralized, cosmopolitan and civilizing practices and values. They developed *interstitial networks* of social interaction, communicating in the interstices of the empires and (to a lesser extent) across their frontiers. These networks centered on *trade,* which we have seen encouraged by the success of the empires yet increasingly out of official control.

Second, these interstitial groups relied upon, and in their turn fostered, something that tended to become a specifically ideological infrastructure, *literary.* An extensive, discursive message will change its form and meaning by the time it travels considerable distances if its original form cannot be preserved. Before the simplification of scripts and of writing materials by the beginning of the first millennium B.C., discursive messages could not be easily stabilized. Nonliterate religions (as noted in Goody 1968: 2–3) tend to be unstable and eclectic. But gradually literacy developed to the point where a single, orthodox belief system could rely on the kind of two-step transmission process found in the Roman Empire (described in detail in Chapter 10). Written messages could be carried between key individuals in each locality, and thence transmitted downward by oral means. This was the *two-step infrastructure of literacy* that supported the extension of ideological power that now occurred.

This communications system may not seem particularly impressive to modern eyes. In particular, literacy was still a minority phenomenon. But then it was not asked to undertake very complex tasks. The transmitted messages upon which these philosophies and religions were built were simple. They touched on three main areas of experience. First came the "fundamental questions of existence": the meaning of life, the creation and nature of the cosmos, the problem of birth and death. Philosophy and theology tended to produce more and more complicated ways of phrasing these questions. But the questions themselves remained, and still remain, simple, and meaningful to all human beings. The second area of experience was interpersonal ethics – norms and morality. "How can I be a good person?" is also a perennial, simple, yet probably unanswerable question of human beings in social relationships. The third area concerned the associated spheres of the family and the life cycle – the focusing of the first two sets of problems on the most intimate social group in which birth, marriage, three-generational relations, and death all occur. Virtually all humans face all three types of problem in more or less the same way – they are universal aspects of the human condition. They had, indeed, been universal since the beginning of society. But *this* was the first historical period in which similar experience could be extensively, stably, and diffusely communicated. Wherever their communications techniques had been built up, ideologies flourished, representing an extraordinary burst of humans' consciousness of their collective powers. Personal and social identity became far more extensive and diffuse, becoming potentially *universal* – the second great "tracklaying" achievement of ideological power. Most of the belief systems carried this communication of universal truths across the genders, classes, and either across state boundaries or in their interstices, their unofficial communications structures. They were *transcendent* across other power organization.

At this point, however, we must begin the eliminations, first removing Zoroastrianism and Confucianism from the discussion. Both predominantly expanded the consciousness and collective powers of males of the Persian nobility and of the Chinese gentry but did not significantly help other groups. This was a considerable compromise with social particularism. It was an example of *immanent* ideology, predominantly boosting the morale and solidarity of an existing ruling class or ethnic community.

In all the remaining cases the belief systems gave a considerable impetus to the transcendent exchange of messages, and therefore of controls, across hierarchical levels, genders, ethnic divisions, and state boundaries. The most common effects were on different classes and "peoples" brought into a common sense of identity. This was also a profound change, for it led potentially to the mobilization of the masses. Hitherto, as I argued in earlier chapters, societies had been strongly federal. Power had been divided among various hierarchical and regional coordinating levels. The masses had not usually been within direct reach of the highest, most centralized levels of power. The beliefs of the masses had not been relevant to the exercise of macrosocial power. Now the masses and the centers of power were ideologically connectible. The connection could take a variety of forms from democracy to authoritarianism, but from now on the beliefs of the masses were far more relevant to the exercise of power. This was the third great "tracklaying" achievement of ideological power.

Let us continue the elimination process. In one further case, Greek humanism, the flowering of this popular belief system also reinforced and legitimated the existing power structure, a relatively democratic and federal multistate civilization of poleis. But in the remaining cases, the popular belief system was indirectly subversive; for it located ultimate knowledge, meaning, and significance outside the traditional sources of economic, political, and military power – in a realm it considered transcendent. In other words, these cases were "religious," concerned ostensibly and primarily with the "spiritual," "sacred" realm, devolving "material," "secular" powers onto secular, nonreligious authorities. All were philosophically dual. Religions that went on to subvert secular authority did so in a specialized "spiritual" way. They intensified institutions of a *specifically ideological* power. This was the fourth great "tracklaying" achievement of ideological power.

Let us pause here, for the achievements mentioned so far add up to a revolution in social-power organization. Belief systems, and more specifically religions, have not played the same general role throughout the historical process. In earlier chapters both the extent and the form of ideological power autonomy have varied considerably. Obviously I could not justify such switches in terms of the supposedly innate qualities of human beings or of societies that have figured largely in debates between materialism and idealism – that is, the general relationship between "ideas" and "material reality" or "material action." In Volume III, I shall argue on general grounds that such debates are not helpful to social theory. But here we can note that careful examination of the historical record reveals a superior explanation.

In any historical period there are many points of contact between human beings that existing power structures do not effectively organize. If these points of contact become of greater significance for social life, they throw up general social problems requiring new organizational solutions. One particular solution has great plausibility when existing power structures remain unable to control the emergent forces. This is a conception of "transcendent" power, divine authority invoked by emergent counter-elites. In the case of the first civilizations, discussed in Chapters 3 and 4, this emerged as the main integrating force in a regional civilization. But its force must have been relatively weak, given the infrastructures of the time, which was confined to a basic level of shared, diffuse civilizational identity and norms just sufficient to trust trading strangers and to underpin multistate diplomacy. The *intensive* penetrative powers of these first great ideologies were restricted.

In the first two millennia of human history, little infrastructure existed for communicating ideas through extensive social space. Until about the time of Assyria and Persia, not even ruling classes could exchange and stabilize the ideas and customs of their members over large spaces. The main infrastructural bases for combining extensive and intensive power were military and economic structures of "compulsory cooperation" and political federations of city-states and tribal and regional elites, sometimes existing within looser, predominantly oral, regional civilizations. Gradually, however, the two preconditions of far more extensive and intensive autonomous ideological power developed: (1) Extensive networks of social interaction developed that were interstitial to official power networks. (2) These networks specifically carried a two-step structure of literate local communication. Gradually larger and more diffused masses of people became part of these interstitial networks. They were placed in a novel but common social situation whose meaning was not given by the traditional beliefs and rituals of existing local or extensive official structures. Articulate persons could generate new explanations and meanings for their situation in the cosmos. As this meaning could not be encapsulated by either local or official traditions, it was interstitial to them, that is, socially transcendent. Belief in transcendent divinity with a direct relation to themselves was the imaginative expression of their interstitial social situation. As both the official structure of empire and their interstitial trading networks encouraged individual rationality, there was a persistent strain in their religion toward rational monotheism. Thus an interstitial social situation was expressed as a salvation religion and communicated through partial literacy into a religious movement of the book.

This is a recognizably "materialist" explanation (provided it is not restricted to economic factors). That is, a social situation generated a belief system that largely "reflected" its characteristics in imaginative form. But because such groups and their breeding grounds were interstitial, their resulting powers of social reorganization were novel and autonomous. Their capacity to lay new historical tracks was heightened by normative commitment, that is, by ideology as *morale,* now acquired by religious conversion. Christians could withstand persecution; Islamic warriors could overcome their supposedly formidable enemies. They created new "societies" to rival those already constituted by traditional mixtures of power relations. In some cases they overcame or outlived those traditional networks. Ideological power was, in this sense and this period, transcendent.

But by being in the world they also had to come to terms with traditional power organizations in three main ways. First, the so-called spiritual realm was centered on a particular social sphere, the life of the individual, his or her life-cycle progression, and his or her interpersonal and familial relations. As a form of power it was extremely *intensive,* centering on the direct life experience of intimate groups. It may have been the most intensive form of power replicated over relatively large social networks to date. This spiritual realm, however, and any popular mobilization consequent upon it, might be merely an aggregation of localities, similar but without organic connections. Such a sphere could not alone easily maintain a high and extensive level of social mobilization. For this it would depend largely on other power organizations. To refer back to an argument I made in Chapter 1: In extensive societies, family structure is not a critical part of macrosocial power arrangements. This dependence on the family restricted the extensive reach and autonomy of ideological power.

Second, this sphere of life was in reality not purely "spiritual." Like all social life it was a mixed spiritual/material, sacred/secular realm. For example, decisions must be taken about correct ethical conduct, about the correct ritual for birth or marriage, or about the nature of death and the hereafter. These involve power, the setting up of decision-making bodies for agreeing on and implementing decisions and sanctions against the disobedient. Extensive power could thus be stabilized. In this sense religions did not so much transcend existing power organization as parallel them, institutionalizing the sacred, routinizing the charismatic (as Weber put it), – a second restriction on the autonomy of ideological power.

Third, the social sphere with which the religions were primarily concerned actually presupposed the existence of other power structures, particularly their communications infrastructures. The religions had to come to terms with, and use the facilities of, previous macropower structures.

The way in which the exact power balance worked out, between the achievements and the restrictions I have identified, varied considerably among the different religions. At one extreme, all managed to obtain near-monopoly powers over the regulation of their core social sphere, especially of the family and the life cycle. They have, indeed, retained many of these powers even to the present day. This was the fifth great achievement of ideological power.

At the other extreme, they all made compromises with existing macro-power structures, accepting the legitimacy of the structures and using them to control their own religious communities. Thus, despite early universal religious pressures, the dominance of men over women and the overall fact of class dominance have not been challenged by the rise of the world religions. These were a fourth and a fifth restriction on the autonomy of ideological power.

In between these extremes lay considerable variety. One rather particular, yet important, power was exercised through religious impact upon military power. In two of the cases there was a connection between a strong interpersonal ethic and military morale. In the case of Islam the religious solidarity of Arab cavalry conquered enormous territories, securing at a stroke the power achievements of Islam over most of this area. In Christian Byzantium and western Europe, religious-military morale was confined within, and considerably reinforced, social hierarchies, increasing authority at the expense of universalism. Christianity was not merely compromising with worldly authorities, but also influencing their form. There proved indeed to be an enduring connection between these two religions and warfare, particularly between faith and the solidarity, fervor, and ferocity of the troops. It was usually to take rather nasty forms – the infidel enemy was likely to be treated as less than fully human and butchered accordingly. This sixth achievement of ideological power reduced the universalism of the second achievement, indicating the contradictory nature of the achievements.

Another problem, and opportunity, was posed for the world religions by the general faltering of the extensive states that had witnessed their rise. The two processes were obviously connected. Even if the states like the Roman were also beset by other major problems, it did not help their chances of survival to have a competing community of identity and attachment operating within and across their boundaries. The Chinese and the Persian states had seized the opportunity to attach this community to themselves, and they had thus helped prevent the emergence of a world religion within their domains. In the remaining cases the states collapsed, repeatedly.

In this context all the world religions achieved one common strategy: to secure near-monopoly control of the infrastructure of literacy, sometimes extending it to all written documents, including laws. Hinduism achieved most in this respect, followed by Buddhism and Islam, with Christianity generally sharing control with the stronger states within its domain. This was the seventh great achievement of ideological power.

In other respects the power struggle varied. Only Hinduism actually took over the structure of extensive controls, instituting caste as the distinctive mechanism through which extensive power could be exercised. Substantial parts of *all* major power relations, economic, political, and military, were developed by its own authority structure, weakening them and making India vulnerable to conquest, foreign political rule, and economic stagnation. But it was nevertheless the pinnacle of the achievements of ideological power. Hinduism alone moved to an eighth achievement: the establishment of a ritual cosmology and a religious society. However, in doing this it completely subverted the second achievement, the popular, universal community. For caste carefully graded humanity into degrees of ultimate worth.

Neither Buddhism nor Islam nor Christianity achieved this much. Buddhism tended to remain more subordinate, operating in the interstices of Hinduism in India and dependent on secular power elsewhere. Islam and Christianity often assumed economic, political, and military powers, but usually in a mold set by traditional secular forms, not by their own religious structure. They felt the force of the third restriction noted above. But in compromising, they kept alive and kicking a deep contradiction between their universal and their authoritarian natures, leaving them much more dynamic than was Hinduism. In Chapter 12 I explore the world-historical consequences of this dynamism.

It is obvious that the diverse achievements of the world religions were not simply cumulative. A part of their achievement, a result of their struggles with secular authorities, was that humanity was led along several different tracks of development. Nevertheless, there was a core to what they did: the mobilization of a popular community, differing considerably from anything hitherto seen in relatively extensive societies. They introduced a *hierarchical intensity* to extensive power relations. The people were mobilized into a normative community.

I have emphasized the normative level, arguing that it enables us to cut through the sterile dualism of "ideas" or "the spiritual" versus "the material." This is an issue I will discuss in more theoretical terms in Volume III. But it is incumbent on me to add a word here about Durkheim, for that great sociologist underpins my argument. Durkheim argued that stable social relationships require prior normative understandings among the participants. Neither force nor mutual self-interest offered a sufficient basis for stability. Thus society depended on a normative, and ritual level, somewhat removed from the "secular" world of force, interests, exchanges, and calculations. Society in the sense of social cooperation was sacred. Durkheim then proceeded to interpret religion, concerned with the sacred, as merely the reflection of society's normative needs.

It is a profound argument, but it is too limiting. For over the last chapters we have seen religion not merely as a reflection of society but also as actually *creating* the normative, ritual community that actually *is* a society. The Christian *ecumene,* the Islamic *umma,* the Hindu caste system were all societies. The religions created a social order, a *nomos,* in situations in which the traditional regulators of society – existing economic, ideological, political, and military power relations – were faltering. Thus their cosmologies were, socially speaking, *true*. The world *was* ordered, and by their own conceptions of the sacred, their transcendent normative and ritual communities. I have extended, not rejected, Durkheim.

But let me back away from any suggestion that I can yet imitate Durkheim by producing a *general* theory of the role of religion in society. So far, the most characteristic feature of religion has been its extraordinary *unevenness*. First it probably had a major, if somewhat murky, role in the federal, segmented power networks of the earliest regional civilizations. Then during more than a millennium of larger empires of domination, its role was largely confined to the immanent strengthening of ruling classes. Then in the next millennium it exploded transcendently in the shape of world-salvationist religions.

I explained the explosion less in terms of the fundamental and stable needs of individuals or societies for meaning, norms, cosmology, and so forth – they may have such needs but they had precious little social significance for the previous millennium – than in terms of the world-historical development of power techniques. Only now could ideological messages be stabilized over extensive social spaces. Only now emerged a series of fundamental contradictions between official and interstitial power networks of ancient empires. Only now were the latter generating socially transcendent organizations in which a cosmology of a universal divinity and rational, individual salvation appeared plausible. This was, therefore, a single world-historical opportunity.

Even to say this is seemingly to overgeneralize. Salvationist religion did not explode universally over this particular historical terrain. The Chinese Empire redirected religion to its own immanent ends. So did Persia. The last of the Hellenistic empires kept it damped down until they were overcome from outside. Only Christianity, Islam, and Hinduism developed transcendent power to overcome existing power structures. Of these, Christianity and Islam adopted one peculiarly dynamic and contradictory power form, whereas Hinduism and its offshoot Buddhism adopted another, more monolithic form. Thereafter, the developmental patterns of all the regions where these religions predominated differed extraordinarily. As I remarked at the beginning of the chapter, what had been up until now a broad "family" of societies across Eurasia was splintered apart in this era.

Of course, the subsequent paths of these diverging societies were not unconnected to their prior characteristics and history: China lacked cosmopolitanism, India lacked imperial strength, Europe had already witnessed more class struggle, and so forth. But one generalization can be made about the impact of salvationism in this period: It *amplified* such deviations. Such was its enhancement of power techniques, of social solidarity, of the possibilities for diffuse communication both vertically and horzontally, that whoever seized its organizations could change their social structure more radically than had probably ever been the case in prior history. A series of true revolutions rolled across Eurasia, led by ideological power techniques and organizations. From then on, China, India, Islam, and Europe went very different ways. Global comparative sociology – always in my view a difficult enterprise – now becomes too difficult. From now on I chronicle only one case, Christian Europe and its offshoots.

The chances of constructing a general theory directly from the social role of religion are therefore slim. It has had no general role of any significance, only world-historical moments. There may have been such moments amid the earliest civilizations, and there certainly were in the era of Christ and Saint Paul, Muhammad, and the Brahmins and Buddha. Upon these men and their followers are built my notion of transcendent religious power. Then I slightly secularize it to include the more worldly flavor of the early civilizational cultures – plus the possibility of analyzing modern ideologies (like liberalism or Marxism) in similar terms. The result is my notion of ideological power – based less on general properties of societies than on a few opportunities presented by the world-historical development of power. It is not much of a general theory of ideology, but it may reflect the real historical role of ideologies.

Bibliography

Bannerjee, P. 1973. *Early Indian Religions*. Delhi: Vikas.

Béteille, A. 1969. *Castes: Old and New*, London: Asia Publishing House.

Bouglé, C. 1971. *Essays on the Caste System*. Cambridge: Cambridge University Press.

Cahen, C. 1970. *L'Islam: des origines au debut de l'Empire Ottoman*. Paris: Bordas.

Chattopadhyaya, D. 1976. Sources of Indian idealism. In *History and Society: Essays in Honour of Professor Nohananjan Ray*. Calcutta: Bagchi.

Cohn, B. S. 1959. Law and change (some notes on) in North India. *Economic Development and Cultural Change*, 8.

Creel, H. G. 1949. *Confucius: The Man and the Myth*. New York: John Day.

Dumont, L. 1972. *Homo Hierarchicus*. London: Paladin.

Dumont, L., and D. F. Pocock. 1957. For a sociology of India. *Contributions to Indian Sociology*, I.

Engineer, A. A. 1980. *The Islamic State*. Delhi: Vikas.

Gellner, E. 1981. *Muslim Society*. Cambridge: Cambridge University Press.

Ghurye, G. S. 1961. *Class, caste and occupation*. Bombay: Popular Book Depot.
    1979. *Vedic India*. Bombay: Popular Prakeshan.

Goody, J. (ed.). 1968. *Literacy in Traditional Societies*. Cambridge: Cambridge University Press.

Heesterman, J. C. 1971. Priesthood and the Brahmin. *Contributions to Indian Sociology*, new series, 5.

Hocart, A. M. 1950. *Caste: a Comparative Study*. London: Methuen.

Holt, P. M. et al. (eds.). 1977. *The Cambridge History of Islam*, esp. Vol. 1A, *The Central Islamic Land, from Pre-Islamic Times to the First World War*, parts I and II. Cambridge: Cambridge University Press.

Hutton, J. H. 1946. *Caste in India: Its Nature, Function and Origins*. Cambridge: Cambridge University Press.

Jackson, A. 1907. Note on the history of the caste system. *Journal of the Asiatic Society of Bengal*, new series, 3.

Karve, I. 1968. *Hindu Society: an Interpretation*. Poona, India: Deshmukh.

Levy, R. 1957. *Social Structure of Islam: The Sociology of Islam*. Cambridge: Cambridge University Press.

Majumdar, E. C. (ed.). 1951– . *The History and Culture of the Indian People*, vol. I, *The Vedic Age*. London: Allen & Unwin 1951. Vol. II, *The Age of Imperial Unity*. Bombay: Bhavan, 1954. Vol. V, *The Struggle for Empire*. Bombay: Bhavan, 1957.

Miller, E. J. 1954. Caste and territory in Malabar. *American Anthropologist*, 56.

Parry, J. H. 1979. *Caste and Kinship in Kangra*. London: Routledge & Kegan Paul.

 1980. Ghosts, greed and sin. *Man*, new series, 15.

 1984. The text in context. Unpublished paper.

Rodinson, M. 1971. *Mohammed*. London: Allen Lane.

Saraswati, B. 1977. *Brahmanic Ritual Traditions in the Crucible of Time*. Simla: Indian Institute of Advanced Study.

Sharma, R. S. 1965. *Indian Feudalism: c. 300–1200*. Calcutta: Calcutta University Press.

 1966. *Light on Early Indian Society and Economy*. Bombay: Manaktalas.

Srinivas, M. N. 1957. Caste in modern India. *Journal of Asian Studies*, 16.

Thapar, R. 1966. *A History of India*, vol. I, Harmondsworth, England. Penguin Books.

Vidal, G. 1981. *Creation*. London: Heinemann.

Wagle, N. 1966. *Society at the Time of the Buddha*. Bombay: Popular Prakashan.

Waley, A. 1938. *The Analects of Confucius*. London: Allen & Unwin.

Watt, M. W. 1953. *Muhammad at Mecca*. Oxford: Clarendon Press.

 1956. *Muhammad at Medina*. Oxford: Clarendon Press.

 1961. *Islam and the Integration of Society*. London: Routledge.

Weber, M. 1951. *The Religion of China*. Glencoe, Ill.: Free Press.

 1958. *The Religion of India*. New York: Free Press.

12 The European dynamic: I.
The intensive phase, A.D. 800–1155

It is impossible for the historical sociologist to contemplate medieval European history "on its own term" without being influenced by premonitions of the Leviathan that was to loom up behind it – industrial capitalism. Little defense is needed for this teleological bias. It is justified by four factors.

First, the capitalist revolution in agriculture and industry of the eighteenth and nineteenth centuries was the single most important boost to human collective power in history. Industrial societies no longer depended almost entirely on the expenditure of human and animal muscle. They could add the exploitation of nature's own energy sources. In all the infrastructural measures of collective power used in these volumes – in yield ratios, population densities, extent of interaction networks, destructive powers, and so forth – an unparalleled quantum leap occurred in this short time.

Second, we can discern movement toward this leap forward gathering force through the whole medieval and early modern period. Setbacks occurred, but the checks did not last long before the forward movement resumed.

Third, all the sources of social power – economic, political, military, and ideological relations – tended to move in a single general direction of development. It is conventional to describe this movement as the "transition from feudalism to capitalism." I shall argue that this is an insufficient description (as does Holton 1984 in concluding his valuable review of debates about the transition), but it nevertheless conveys the sense of an overall movement.

Fourth, this occurred over a single broad sociogeographical area, that fusion of the western Roman Empire and the lands of the German barbarians we know as "Europe." This had not hitherto possessed a social unity, but now did so until the twentieth century.

Thus Europe contained a single set of interrelated dynamics, a transition, breaking through all the more specific periodizations, geographical subdivisions, and historical eccentricities and conjunctures that more detailed history always requires. I will therefore put conjunctures on one side – especially those impinging on Europe from outside – until Chapter 15. The subject matter of this chapter is that dynamism and its origins, the motor of development that medieval Europe possessed and that helped it move toward industrial capitalism.

Let us try to focus a little more closely on that end state to see what we need to explain. First, we cannot fail to be impressed by the upsurge in economic powers, the ability to appropriate the fruits of nature, that had occurred by the mid-nineteenth century. This economic power had accelerated both *intensively* and *extensively*. Intensively, the yield from any particular plot of land or group of people had risen enormously. Humans were penetrating deeper into the earth and rearranging its physical and chemical properties so as to extract its resources. But socially too, their coordinated activities, using greater congealed labor (i.e., capital) in machines, were also far more intensely organized. The praxis of ordinary people intensified its power. These activities were also more extensive, systematically over most of Europe, and then covering narrower routes of penetration over the globe. These took several forms, but the main ones were widening circuits of the production and exchange of commodities. No empire, no society of any kind, had penetrated so intensively or extensively. The principal mechanism in this reorganization of history was economic power – "circuits of praxis" as I termed it. If these economic developments were not mere accident, the preceding medieval social structure must have possessed enormous dynamism of both an intensive and an extensive type. Our explanation should be able to deal with both.

My argument is that the transition included two phases before and after about A.D. 1150. The first saw acceleration largely of intensive powers of economic praxis, the second accompanied it with growth of the extensive power of commodity circuits, slow at first and accelerating by about 1500. The first was a precondition of the second and was the original ground of the transition. It is the subject matter of this chapter, with the growth in extensive power reserved for the next two.

But the end state had changed qualitatively as well as quantitatively. We call it a *capitalist* or an *industrial* revolution (or we hedge our bets and combine the two), each term indicating the viewpoint of a major social theory. For the moment I confine discussion of the two to their chronology.

Capitalism – to be defined in a moment – preceded the Industrial Revolution. Its techniques of organization gradually developed during the early modern period. Most immediately, some of the main organizational techniques used in industry had been applied a century earlier in the agricultural revolution of the eighteenth century. Thus we have to explain first the transition to capitalism. In Volume II we shall find that industrialism subsequently also exerted strong, uniform social influences regardless of whether it occurred in a capitalist society. But that is a problem for the next volume.

Let me define the capitalist mode of production. Most definitions presuppose two components that combine to produce a third. The three are:

1. *Commodity production.* Every factor of production is treated as a means, not as an end in itself, and is exchangeable with every other factor. This includes labor.
2. *Private monopolistic ownership of the means of production.* The factors of production, including labor power, belong formally and entirely to a private class of capitalists (and are not shared with the state, the mass of laborers, the community, God, or anyone else).
3. *Labor is free and separated from the means of production.* Laborers are free

to sell their labor and withdraw it as they see fit; they receive a wage but have no direct claims over the surplus produced.

The development of the commodity form had been long and tortuous. Some periods had contained pockets of capitalism in the sense that merchants, bankers, landlords, and manufacturers might be investing money to make more money, paying wage labor, and calculating the costs of labor against other factors of production. But in no society before the modern era were these *dominant* activities. The freedom of these people to organize their enterprises according to the value of commodities was restricted by the state, by the community, by foreign powers, or by the technical limitations of the time (e.g., lack of coinage for exchange value). The main restrictions were that private ownership was never absolute (not even in Rome) and that indigenous labor could not be treated fully as a commodity.

In these respects early European social structure was traditional. I start with its "feudal" economy (although ultimately I will reject "feudalism" as a comprehensive label for the European context). Definitions of the feudal mode of production vary. The simplest is: *the extraction of surplus labor through ground rent by a class of landlords from a dependent peasantry* (e.g., Dobb 1946). Two elements in this definition require explanation. "Dependency" means that the peasant was legally bound to a particular piece of land or a particular lord so that free movement out of the feudal relationship was not possible. Serfdom was the most usual form of such dependency. "Ground rent" implies that a class of landlords collectively owned the land (e.g., not as private, individual owners) and that a peasantry had to pay a rent normally in labor-services, in order to work it and therefore to live at all. Thus the individual lord did not possess absolute ownership. And as labor was tied to land and to lord, it could not be easily treated as a commodity, exchangeable against other factors of production.

Thus we can add two further issues for our explanation of the transition: *How did ownership become individual and absolute? How did labor become a commodity?* The present chapter only begins to address these issues, because in the first intensive phase of the transition the changes in property relations only occurred in embryo. The discussion will continue in the next chapters.

So far I have discussed the transition as if it were merely economic. Yet we cannot equate this specific economic transition with the entire movement of European history. The capitalist mode of production, like all modes of production, is an ideal type, an abstraction. If capita*lism* came to dominate in actual social life, it was not likely to be as pure as the definition might imply. Like all modes of production, it required force, political institutionalization, and ideology, and its requirements were likely to result in compromise forms of social organization. To explain the rise of capitalism – indeed, of feudalism – we must trace the interrelations of all four principal organizations of power: economic, military, political, and ideological. Thus neither feudalism nor capitalism, if they are used as general periodizations of European history, would be merely economic labels. In view of this it seems unwise to use them as general designations of either medieval or modern Europe. The process of European dynamism is *not* the transition from feudalism to capitalism. To demonstrate this will take me through this chapter and the next two.

In the next two chapters I show that the end state of European society, as well as being capitalism and industrialism, has also been a segmentary series of national networks of social interaction, that is, an international multistate geopolitical, diplomatic network. We cannot explain European structure or dynamism without an analysis of the rise of competitive, roughly equal, national states. In turn, we shall find that they were partly, perhaps even largely, products of reorganizations induced by the development of military power relations.

In this chapter I argue similarly with respect to medieval society. The dynamic that it contained was not a purely economic one, located within the feudal mode of production, as I have defined it, or as anyone else might define it. Most historians agree, arguing that an explanation of "the transition" must encompass a great many factors, some economic, some noneconomic. But their arguments tend to be detailed and, at crucial points, ad hoc. I believe that we can be more systematic than this – by examining the organizational forms of the four power sources. Previous systematic theories of "the transition" have tended to be materialist – neoclassical or Marxian. The transition is only explicable in terms of a combination of economic, military, political, and ideological power organizations.

Summary of the argument

The social structure that stabilized in Europe after the ending of the barbarian migrations and invasions (i.e., by A.D. 1000) was a multiple acephalous federation. Europe had no head, no center, yet it was an entity composed of a number of small, crosscutting interaction networks. In previous chapters I described earlier types of acephelous federation, in early Sumer and in classical Greece. But their structures had been simpler than this one. In these cases each political unit (city-state or federated league of states or tribes) had coordinated economic, military, and, to a degree, ideological power within its territories. The federations of Sumer and Greece were predominantly geopolitical, composed of a number of monopolistic, territorial units. This was not true of *early* medieval Europe (though it became truer later), where interaction networks based on economic, military, and ideological power differed in their geographical and social space and none was unitary in nature. Consequently no single power agency controlled a clear-cut territory or the people within it. As a result most social relationships were extremely localized, intensely focused on one or more of a number of cell-like communities – the monastery, the village, the manor, the castle, the town, the guild, the brotherhood, and so forth.

But the relationships between these multiple power networks were regulated. Order and not chaos prevailed. The major regulatory agency was Christendom, by far the most extensive of the power networks. We shall see that Christendom combined in a contradictory, indeed in a dialectical way, the two main organizational characteristics of ideological power. It was *transcendent,* yet it reinforced the *immanent* morale of an existing social group, a ruling class of lords. This combination helped ensure a basic level of normative pacification, confirming property and market relations within and between the cells. Second, each local power network was relatively outward-looking, feeling itself to be part of a much larger whole and thus potentially expansionist. Previous civilizations had provided infrastructure of extensive power only at great cost, often through what I termed in earlier chapters compulsory cooperation. Now enough of this was provided by ideological means, by Christianity without a state, that expansion and innovation could burst out from the local intensive cell. The early feudal economically centered dynamic was primarily intensive because extensive power was already provided for by Christendom. The economic infrastructure, the village-manor economy, which introduced such crucial innovations as the heavy plow and the three-field system, and the urban-centered trading economy themselves depended on the "infrastructure" of Christianity. The metaphor is perverse, deliberately so, for I wish to attack again infrastructure/superstructure and material/ideal models.

This makes clear one relative unorthodoxy of my argument: Christianity as a *normative* system has been neglected as a causal factor in the emergence of capitalism. It was not only the psychological impact of its doctrines (as in Weberian approaches to the problem) that boosted capitalism, but also that it provided normative pacification, in a Durkheimian sense. This contrast will be discussed in theoretical terms in Volume III.

A second partial unorthodoxy is also implied by this approach: I locate the dynamism far earlier than has been conventional. After all, the factors just mentioned were already in place by about A.D. 800. Once the last marauders – Viking, Muslim, and Hun – were repulsed, say, by A.D. 1000, the dynamism ought to have been evident. I shall argue that this was indeed the case. Thus most factors that play a part in most explanations of the feudal dynamic – the emergence of towns, peasant and lord reactions to the fourteenth-century crisis, the revival of Roman law, the rise of the bureaucratic state and of accountancy, the navigational revolution, the fifteenth-century Renaissance, Protestantism – were the later phases of a dynamic already well established. Accordingly they will not loom large in this chapter.

I do not claim originality in locating the dynamic so early. Duby (1974), Bridbury (1975), and Postan (1975), have located the economic revival well before A.D. 1000. Many historians have emphasized the political, military, and cultural achievements of the Frankish and Norman ruling elites, arguing that a genuine Renaissance occurred in their domains between about 1050 and 1250. Trevor-Roper (1965) argues that its achievements were greater than the better-publicized Renaissance of the fifteenth century.

Many other historians have undervalued the achievements of medieval Europe through an incautious use of comparative sociology. It has become commonplace to compare Europe with its contemporaries in Asia and the Middle East, and to contrast the barbarism of the former with the civilization of the latter, particularly of China. It follows that the point at which Europe "overtook" Asia must have been late. The year 1450 or 1500 is generally chosen as the moment of overtaking, generally because that is the period of the naval expansion of Europe and the Galilean revolution in science. A typical writer is Joseph Needham (1963), who in contrasting Europe and China emphasizes Galileo: With "the discovery of the basic technique of scientific discovery itself, then the curve of science and technology in Europe begins to rise in a violent, almost exponential manner, overtaking the level of the Asian societies." If this is the chronology of the overtaking, then the dynamic of the transition is also likely to be found in late causes.

But this is superficial comparative sociology. Only a few societies can be simply placed above or below each other on a single developmental scale measuring their collective powers. More frequently, societies *differ* in their achievements. This was so in the case of medieval Europe and China. The European self-denigration is misplaced. It comes from obsession with "extensive power." Measured by this standard Europe lagged until after 1500. Just before then Marco Polo could rightly boggle at the splendor and the military and political power of Kublai Khan: No European monarch could appropriate such riches, pacify such spaces, mobilize such a number of troops. The Christian rulers of the northern Mediterranean also fought a long, inconclusive, and often retreating struggle against Islamic states over many medieval centuries. Furthermore most innovations that proved to have great implications for extensive power (notably gunpowder, the mariner's compass, and printing) came from the East. Europe was often inferior, and never superior, in extensive powers until after 1500. But as we shall see, in another range of power achievements, *intensive* ones, especially in agriculture, Europe was leaping ahead by A.D. 1000. Viewed in this light the Galilean revolution was a development of these achievements. Indeed the major achievements of our scientific, industrial, capitalist era can be traced back to around that date.

I begin with an extended description of the multiple power networks up till A.D. 1155. This date has an English significance, marking the beginning of the reign of Henry II, a notable state builder. In European terms the date is arbitrary, but the general periodization it indicates is significant in three respects. First, all the power networks had been brought into play in the general form in which I describe them. Second, Europe's essential dynamism was already evident. Third, any significantly later date would begin to distort the power networks, particularly those that resulted from the military-fiscal-political changes discussed in the next chapter. These tended to favor more unitary, territorial-centralized networks of interaction, in the direction of "national states," to foster more extensive methods of social control, and to weaken the integrating role of Christendom. From around that date, therefore, the model I have just outlined becomes less applicable and the second phase of the transition begins. But if the dynamism was already evident, we must first purge these developments from our explanation.

The dating also makes evident an empirical limitation of my analysis throughout the next chapters. I center discussion on the case of England, though comparisons with other regions of Europe will be made from time to time.

Feudalism as multiple interaction networks: ideological, military/political, and economic power

Ideological power

The most extensive interaction network centered on the Catholic church.[1] Catholic Christendom extended over an area of something like a million square kilometers, about the same area as the most extensive empires of prior history, the Roman and the Persian. It spread by conversion, generally organized after about A.D. 500 under the authority of the bishop of Rome. From about that time also date the claims of this bishop to supremacy over the church, given administrative infrastructure under Pope Gregory I the Great (590–640). The claim owed much of its strength to the appeal of imperial Rome. This can be seen in the wide circulation in the eighth century of the Donation of Constantine, a letter supposedly from the great Christian emperor donating the city of Rome and the western empire to the pope, but in reality a papal forgery.

The infrastructure of papal power over such an enormous terrain was severely limited. But by the late eleventh century, this ideological-power network was firmly established throughout Europe in two parallel authoritative hierarchies of bishoprics and monastic communities, each responsible to the pope. Its communications infrastructure was provided by literacy in a common language, Latin, over which it enjoyed a near monopoly until the thirteenth century. Its economic subsistence was provided for by tithes from all the faithful and by revenues from its own extensive estates. The Domesday Book reveals that in 1086 the church received 26 percent of all agricultural land revenues in England, roughly typical of the Middle Ages in most of Europe (see Goody 1983: 125–7). Ideologically, it was sustained by a monarchical conception of

---

[1] Good general sources for this section are Trevor-Roper 1965 and Southern 1970.

religious authority, asserted to be superior in an ultimate sense to secular authority. In real terms there was a continuous, fluctuating power struggle between secular rulers and the church. But the latter always possessed its own power base. Internally it was governed by canon law. Clerics, for example, were tried in their own courts, over which secular rulers had no powers. The tentacles of this institution reached into the life of every court, every manor, every village, every town of Europe. Its powers enabled it to transform marriage rules and family life, for example (see Goody 1983). Indeed this was the only authoritative interaction network that spread so extensively while also penetrating intensively into everyday life.

There were three achievements and one limitation and contradiction of such extensiveness. First, the Catholic *ecumene* survived and strengthened as a form of diffuse social identity larger than that provided by any other power source. This is so even if we compare the ecumenical identity to that conferred by a relatively large, homogeneous, state-centered country like England after the Norman Conquest. With such a recent mixing of populations and languages it was difficult for a local territorial identity to arise – although it did in time, given population stability. The identity of Christendom was transnational, based not on territory or locality as anyone could actually experience them but on something wider, something more abstract and transcendent.

Let us try a little hypothetical reconstruction of the case of England. If we were able to travel back to England around 1150 armed with questionnaires, tape recorders, and the necessary linguistic skills to ask a sample of the population with all due circumspection to what social group they belonged, we would get rather complex answers. The majority would not be able to give one sole identity. The lords, whom we would interview in Norman French (though we could try Latin), might indicate that they were gentlefolk; Christians, of course; they might elaborate a genealogy indicating also that they were of Norman descent but linked closely to the Angevin king of England and to the English baronage. They would think that, on balance, their interests lay with the lords of the kingdom of England (perhaps including its French possessions, perhaps not) rather than with, say, the lords of the kingdom of France. I am not sure where they would place "the people" – Christians but barbarous, unlettered rustics – on their normative map. The merchants, whom we would interview in a diversity of languages, might say that they were English, or from the Hansa towns of the Baltic Coast, or from Lombardy; if they were English they would probably show more antiforeigner "nationalism" than anyone else, out of sectional interest; they were Christians, of course; and their interests lay in a combination of guild autonomy and alliance with the English crown. The higher clergy, whom we would interview in Latin, would say Christians first and foremost. But we would then usually find both a clear, kin-based, class solidarity with the lords, and an overlapping identity with some lords and merchants, but definitely excluding the people, centered on the possession of literacy. The parish priest, with whom we could try Latin, (and, failing that, Middle English), might say Christian and English. Some would claim, perhaps dubiously, to be *literati*. The peasants, the vast majority of our sample, we would interview in the various Middle English dialects and amalgams of Saxon, Danish, Celtic, and Norman French (of which we only have the vaguest outlines). They would be, but would not call themselves, *illiterati,* an abusive term denoting exclusion, not membership of a community. They would say Christian, and then they might say English or they might say they were Essex or Northumbrian or Cornish folk. Their allegiances would be mixed: to their local lord (temporal or spiritual); to their local village or other kin network; and (if they were freemen) to their king, to whom they swore annual allegiance. The last was rare in Europe, denoting again the exceptional strength of the English crown. We would love to know if the various strata of peasantry had any real sense of being "English." Immediately after the Norman Conquest they probably did – in oppposition to their new rulers. But did they later, when Normans became Anglo-Normans? We do not know.

The main conclusion is unmistakable. The most powerful and extensive sense of social identity was Christian, although this was both a unifying transcendent identity and an identity divided by the overlapping barriers of class and literacy. Crosscutting all these divisions were commitments to England, but these were variable and, in any case, included less extensive dynastic connections and obligations. Thus Christian identity provided both a common humanity and a framework for common divisions among Europeans.

Let us first consider the transcendent, common identity. Its most interesting aspect was the way it built in *extensivity.* Apart from trading activities, the most frequent type of movement around Europe was probably religious in nature. Clerics traveled greatly, but so too did lay people on pilgrimage. Pilgrimage has been called the "therapy of distance." Most people able to afford it would at some point in their lives expiate their sins by traveling across region or even across continent to receive the blessing conferred by holy relics. Cynics said there were enough splinters of the True Cross scattered in all the shrines to build a battle fleet to retake the Holy Land. But Europe was integrated by the scattering, the constant journeying to them, and the cultivated, culminating experience of *praesentia,* the supposed physical presence of Christ or saint at the shrine (Brown 1981).

On the ethical level, the church preached consideration, decency, and charity toward all Christians: basic normative pacification, a substitute for coercive pacification normally required in previous extensive societies. The main sanction the church could provide was not physical force but exclusion from the community – in the last resort, excommunication. *Extra ecclesiam nulla salus* (no salvation outside the church) was accepted almost universally. Even the worst bandit was wary of excommunication, wished to die absolved, and was willing to pay the church (if not always to modify his behavior) to receive it. The darker side of normative pacification was the savage treatment meted out to those outside the *ecumene,* to schismatics, heretics, Jews, Islamics, and pagans. But its great achievement was the creation of a minimal normative society across state, ethnic, class, and gender boundaries. It did not in any significant sense include the Byzantine church. But it integrated the two major geographical areas of "Europe," the Mediterranean lands with their cultural heritage, their predominantly *extensive* power techniques (literacy, coinage, agricultural estates, and trading networks), and northwestern Europe, with its more *intensive* power techniques (deep plowing, village and kin solidarities, and locally organized warfare). If the two could be kept in a single community, then European development was a possible consequence of their creative interchange. Let us not look at this religious community in modern, pious terms. It was also bawdy folklore, satirizing the common religion, carried by traveling players and mendicants whose plays and sermons would strike modern church congregations as blasphemous, as in parodies of all the major religious rituals. Preachers drawing audiences of thousands were conscious of their tricks of the trade. One, Olivier Maillard, wrote marginal notes to himself like "sit down – stand up – mop yourself – ahem! ahem! – now shriek like a devil" (quoted by Burke 1979: 101; cf. 122–3).

The second achievement of the church's extensive identity was that it became the main guardian of civilization, of greater extent than the single political, military, or economic units of the early medieval period. The transcendent nature of the identity was obvious at four levels. First, at the regional level, bishops and priests coordinated campaigns to rid a neighborhood of bandits and predatory lords. One such movement, the Pax Dei, proclaimed in France in 1040, gave protection to priests, peasants, travelers, and women. Bizarrely to our eyes, it also declared an armistice to last from Wednesday evenings to Monday mornings. Although the success of these movements was limited, both lay rulers and the papacy were later able to build on top of them (Cowdrey 1970). They gave rise to medieval distinctions between "just" and "unjust" wars and to the rules governing treatment of noncombatants and the vanquished. None of these norms and rules was universally accepted. The violations were so frequent as to produce cynical and moralizing literature throughout the Middle Ages. Erasmus was inheriting from a long tradition when he wrote of those "who found out the way how a man may draw his sword and sheathe it in his brother's bowels, and yet not offend against the duty of the second table where we are obliged to love our neighbors as ourselves" (quoted in Shennan 1974: 36). But the moralizing and the admonitions were felt to have some potential force, and they emanated not from within the state but from Europe as a whole.

Second, at the political level, the bishops and abbots assisted the ruler to control his domains, providing both sacral authority and literate clerics for his chancellery, backing his judicial authority with legitimacy and efficiency. Later we see this authority proved the source of a great deal more.

Third, at the continental level, the papacy was the main arbiter of interstate politics, preserving a balance of power, restraining overweening monarchs in their conflicts with lesser rulers. Excommunication could release vassals of a monarch from their oath of fealty. Anyone was then entitled to grab his land. The church guaranteed continental order but could unleash chaos. This threat led to the humbling of both Henry II and John, king of England. More spectacular was the treatment of the great German emperor Henry IV, forced in 1077 to wait for three midwinter days in the outer courtyard at Canossa for the pope's absolution.

And fourth, in intercontinental politics, the papacy coordinated the defense of Christendom and the first counterattacks, the Crusades in the Holy Land, which, although they were transitory, indicated that western Christendom would not fall to Islam (although, by revealing the split between the eastern and western churches, they probably contributed to the fall of the Balkans and the isolation of Constantinople). The greatness of Latin Christendom and its papacy was not merely spiritual. In a secular, diplomatic sense the church was superior – without directly commanding a single army.

The third extensive achievement of the church was economic. Its normative pacification enabled more produce to be traded over longer distances than could usually occur between the domains of such a large number of small, often highly predatory, states and rulers. As we see later, the survival of long-distance trade boosted the production of goods for market exchange in the medieval period.

But the economic effects were also qualitative. Just as the church politically outflanked rulers, so too did it economically. To the degree that pacification was provided by Christendom, it was not provided by states. Naturally states did supplement this level of pacification, and after about 1200, as we shall see in the next chapter, they began to replace it. But at first the control they could exercise over production and trade by virtue of functions provided by them was limited. This was especially marked in the sphere of production, logistically more difficult for a state to control than long-distance trade (which moved visibly along a few communication routes). Production relations, including property relations, were largely hidden from state interference. Normative pacification would ensure that property was respected.

Moreover, the Christian *ecumene* affected the form of property relations. When all classes and ethnicities, and both genders, shared (perhaps only just!) a common humanity, with equality in the sight of God, property forms giving monopolistic power to one class, ethnicity, or gender were in theory unlikely to emerge. At the extreme, slavery was in decline among European Christians. But monopolistic property pretensions of the dominant landlord class might be as subject to Christian outflanking as were those of political rulers.

To the degree that Christianity in its original form had powers over the economy, it would disperse property rights, not concentrate them. So, was it still the universal, salvationist religion of Christ?

The question raises again the fundamental limitation and contradiction of Christianity, evident in Chapter 10. Christendom claimed only a specialized *ecumene*, sacred and supposedly not secular. The papacy did not aspire to monopolistic worldly power. If the secular authorities would support its spiritual power and concede borderline issues – its powers to concentrate its own bishops and anoint lay rulers, to discipline clerics in ecclesiastical courts, to monopolize educational institutions – then, said the papacy, they could rule in their own sphere with its blessing. But in practice the two spheres were inseparable. In particular the secular had entered into the heart of the sacred. In Chapter 10 I described how, before the collapse of the western Roman Empire, the church had dithered, unable quite to abandon its communal, relatively egalitarian, and anti-pagan-Roman origins, yet quietly and pragmatically accommodating itself to Roman imperial structures. After the Roman collapse it inherited the imperial mantle. Popes like Gregory I, Leo II (who crowned Charlemagne), and Gregory VII welcomed this. Such a hierarchical vision of the Christian mission was reproduced at the church's lower levels by bishops and priests. It reinforced hierarchical tendencies in secular power structures (to be analyzed in a moment).

The church was contradicting its own humbler origins. It was legitimating a highly unequal distribution of economic resources. More importantly for our story, it was legitimizing a qualitative difference between lords and peasants. There was a secular theory, and a secular reality too, that these groups performed qualitatively different roles in society: The lords defended; the peasants produced. The church tagged on a sacred role. If the new orthodoxy of the church could be expressed in a single phrase it would be the oft repeated adage "The priest prays, the knight defends, the peasant works." There is in this a qualitative separation between property and labor: Only peasants labor!

Thus the church enhanced the class morale of lords, clothing their exploitation with sacred qualities. It is not easy for us to comprehend this. Dominant classes in our own era have long abandoned sacred justifications for pragmatic ones ("capitalism works"). It is easier for us to grasp the element that survived longest – which, indeed, was enhanced throughout the late medieval period: the sacred rights and duties of monarchy. Yet this was not the main thrust of early medieval ideology. While the claims of the English and French kings over their lords generally grew throughout the twelfth century, those of the German emperor weakened. In any case, more attention was focused in all countries on the qualities and bonds shared by lord and vassal. The cult of nobility and knighthood was shared by the prince and the bachelor knight with one manor. Knighthood was defined, as were its duties: loyalty, declining plunder, defending the faith, fighting for the common good, and protecting the poor, widows, and orphans. These were fitted into a broader pattern of morality enjoining the cardinal virtues of chivalry, bravery, justice, prudence, and continence, and a special development, the homage of the knight to his lady. Rituals of tournament, court ceremonials, and the quest arose.

All this was celebrated within the great European literature of the twelfth and early thirteenth centuries, the courtly romances and lyric poetry carried by the poets, troubadors, and *Minnesänger* of the lesser nobility. The limits of the spiritual and the secular are at the heart of some of the most enduring literature and especially of the Arthurian romances. The purity of Galahad, who finds and secures the Holy Grail, is not for this world. The minor blemishes of Percival and Gawain, who can only glimpse the Holy Grail, represent the best that real humans can attain. The grand frailties of Lancelot, Guinevere, and Arthur himself represent both the greatest achievements and the tragic moral compromises of the real world. Almost all of this common European literature is quite inward-looking in class terms. As Abercrombie, Hill, and Turner (1980) shrewdly point out, relatively little literary ideology was concerned with the people or with justifying rule over them. It is less an ideology of class exploitation than an ideology concerned with moral behavior within a class whose exploitation is already firmly institutionalized. This is why so many of the medieval romances can appeal so strongly to us. The quest for honor, decency, and purity takes for granted the particular, and often brutal, social framework of the age and appears "timeless." Yet this quality emerges, paradoxically, from its class-bound assumptions. By combining a search for meaning, for norms, and for ritual and aesthetic expression so powerfully, the literature is an extraordinarily vivid example of ideology as immanent class morale.

Kinship and genealogy provided a kind of infrastructure through which those class messages traveled. Genealogy was actively created and manipulated. As Tuchman puts it:

Marriages were the fabric of international as well as inter-noble relations, the primary source of territory, sovereignty and alliance and the major business of medieval diplomacy. The relations of countries and rulers depended not at all on common borders or natural interest but on dynastic connections and fantastic cousinships which could make a prince of Hungary heir to the throne of Naples and an English prince claimant to Castile. . . . Valois of France, Plantagenets of England, Luxemburgs of Bohemia, Wittelsbachs of Bavaria, Hapsburgs of Austria, Visconti of Milan, the houses of Navarre, Castile and Aragon, Dukes of Brittany, Counts of Flanders, Hainault and Savoy were all entwined in a crisscrossing network, in the making of which two things were never considered: the sentiments of the parties to the marriage, and the interest of the populations involved. [1979: 47]

These connections led almost as often to war as to peace, but both were ritualized to a high degree. The aesthetic spectacles of diplomatic courtship –

the stage-managed procession of the suitor or his representatives, the feasts, the tournaments, even the battlefield encounters of genealogical rivals – solidified the noble class as a whole.

Tuchman gives a neat vignette that summarizes the conflicts but also the ultimate solidarity of the nobility (1979: 178–80). It is drawn from slightly later than this period, but it can be taken as typical of several centuries of noble life. Two great nobles from southern France, the Captal de Buch, a Gascon lord, and Gaston Phoebus, count of Foix (whose names and titles exemplify the ethnic diversity of noble origins), were throughout their lives on opposite sides of the great struggle over France. The Captal was the principal Gascon ally of the English kings, whereas the count owed fealty to the French kings. They were in the opposing armies at the great English victory at Poitiers in 1356. But being cousins and being unoccupied in the peace that followed, they went on crusade together to Prussia. There they enjoyed one of the great and glorious pleasures of the Christian nobility, hunting down and killing pagan Lithuanian peasants. Returning together with their retinues in 1358, they chanced upon one of the principal events of a peasant uprising in northern France, the siege of Meaux. ''At the head of twenty-five knights in bright armour with pennants of argent and azure displaying stars and lilies and couchant lions'' (symbols of France and England), the two charged straight into the peasant ''army'' on a confined bridge. The force of their charge and of their superior lances and axes inflicted terrible carnage on the peasant front ranks. The rest fled, to be butchered in small groups by knights over the next days. To experience a second such glorious episode in so short a period was chivalry indeed, and the deeds were much retold. Whatever the conflicts of the nobility, they could unite against pagans and peasants – those two words being, of course, linguistically cognate!

Just as they had chanced upon a peasant *jacquerie* (''revolt'') so must we. The great aesthetic rituals of nobility alternately awed and infuriated those who had to pay for them, the townsfolk and the peasants. The contrast between reality and what was often felt to be authentic Christianity could hardly be greater.

The two main forms of ideological power, transcendence and ruling-class immanence, normally kept apart in previous history in the Near East and Europe, were now both firmly embedded within the same institutions. Contradictions obviously resulted. As William Langland wrote in *Piers the Plowman* (shortly after 1362), ''For when Constantine endowed the Church so generously, and gave it lands and vassals, estates and incomes, an angel was heard to cry in the air over the city of Rome, saying: 'This day the wealth of the Church is poisoned, and those who have Peter's power have drunk venom' '' (1966: 194).

The primitive church could not be entirely suppressed. Moves toward a hierarchical, class church provoked two persistent responses. The first was a series of revivals and reforms of monasticism, usually denouncing worldly compromises by turning one's back on the world but sometimes also attempting to reform the world as well. The Benedictine reform of 816–17, the Cluniac movement of the tenth and eleventh centuries, most of the new orders of the eleventh to thirteenth centuries – Carthusians, Cistercians, Franciscans, the Mendicants, and the first orders of nuns were all part of this first reaction. As most began locally, they aimed at the worldliness of local bishops and priests and at their kinship with local rulers rather than at the papacy. Popes interested in reform used them as counterweights to the power of both episcopate and secular rulers.

The second reaction was more serious, a series of heresies that denied papal and episcopal authority. To combat these, between 1215 and 1231 the Inquisition and the Dominican Order were founded. This may have been bad news for the heretics, but it is good news for the historian. From the records of the Inquisition have emerged some of the most fascinating and vivid documentation of medieval life and of the role of the church within it. I shall draw on two recent studies that demonstrate vividly the church's internal difficulties.

Le Roy Ladurie has drawn on the Inquisition records on the Cathar or Albigensian heresy in the Pyrenean mountain village of Montaillou. The inquisitor, the local bishop, "pedantic as a schoolman," was driven by a desire to know and to persuade others of the church's truth that exceeded all the practical exigencies of the local situation. "He spent a fortnight of his precious time convincing the Jew Baruch of the mystery of the Trinity, a week making him accept the dual nature of Christ and no less than three weeks of commentary explaining the coming of the Messiah" (1980: xv). The farmers and shepherds were also interested in doctrinal matters, not as disembodied theology but as an explanation of their own world. The church was an important part of that world – it provided the main link with the outside world and its civilization, it was the principal tax gatherer, enforcer of morals, and educator. The obvious contradictions in the church's role seem to have been the main fuel for the spread of the Cathar heresy in Montaillou. The principal village heretic, Belibaste, said:

The Pope devours the blood and sweat of the poor. And the bishops and the priests, who are rich and honoured and self-indulgent, behave in the same manner . . . whereas Saint Peter abandoned his wife, his children, his fields, his vineyards and his possessions to follow Christ. [p. 333]

He drew the most extreme of conclusions:

There are four great devils ruling over the world: the Lord Pope, the major devil whom I call Satan; the Lord King of France is the second devil; the Bishop of Pamiers the third; and the Lord Inquisitor of Carcassonne the fourth. [p. 13]

Apocalyptic visions were an accepted part of medieval cultural communication. Although most mystic visionaries retreated from the world, Christianity (like Islam) generated many political visionaries like – in his own small way

– Belibaste. The political apocalypse was found in almost all social unrest, a part of what Weber called the "rational restlessness" of Christianity – a tremendous commitment to improving the world.

Almost all the villagers were more cautious than Belibaste. But their resentment of the church's power did not stem merely from resentment of peasants against tithes and intervention in their morals. It was encouraged by knowledge of the Bible and of the supposed simplicity of the early church. Such knowledge was initiated by clerics and books, transmitted orally by literate laymen, and occasioned lively and often heretical discussion within the household and outside. The downward transmission of heresy was encouraged by various levels of respect shown within medieval social structure: deference toward the authority of the Bible, toward literacy, toward village social status, toward household heads, and toward age.

Here is an example of this at the literate level. A literate man says:

I was sunning myself beside the house I then owned in Ax . . . and four or five spans away, Guillaume Andorran was reading aloud from a book to his mother, Gaillarde. I asked: "What are you reading?"

"Do you want to see?" said Guillaume.

"All right," I said.

Guillaume brought me the book, and I read: "In the beginning was the Word . . ."

It was the "Gospel" in a mixture of Latin and Romance, which contained many things I had heard the heretic Pierre Authie say. Guillaume Andorran told me that he had bought it from a certain merchant. [p. 237]

(Pierre Authie, a literate law clerk, was a leading Cathar in Ax and was burned at the stake.)

At the nonliterate level, a man tells how he had arranged to meet one Pierre Rauzi to cut hay:

And as he whetted his sickle, he said: "Do you believe that God or the blessed Mary are something – really?"

And I answered: "Yes, of course I believe it."

Then Pierre said: "God and the Blessed Virgin Mary are nothing but the visible world around us; nothing but what we see and hear."

As Pierre Rauzi was older than I, I considered that he had told me the truth! And I remained in this belief for seven or ten years, sincerely convinced that God and the Virgin Mary were nothing but this visible world around us. [p. 242]

Such examples help show that heresy was not a spontaneous, popular uprising against the authority of the church. The church itself possessed a shadow "alternative communications channel," based on the inculcation of literacy, on the simplicity of monastic rules (not always of monastic practices), on itinerant preachers and mendicants, even on the pulpit itself, all of which drew popular attention to the doctrinal and practical contradictions built right into the heart of Christianity: Although its officialdom encouraged submission to hierarchy, its shadow authority encouraged both confidence in human rationality and the judgment of all hierarchy by the apocalypse. The alternative communications channel recalls that of the Roman Empire, through which Christianity had spread (described in Chapter 10).

Such conclusions are reinforced by a second equally fascinating though somewhat later set of trial transcripts relating to the heresy of one Menocchio, an Italian miller, who was brought to trial in 1584 and again in 1599. These have been presented by Ginzburg, who says heresy derived from "a peasant religion intolerant of dogma and ritual, tied to the cycles of nature, and fundamentally pre-Christian" (1980: 112). Unfortunately, this argument is refuted by the evidence Ginzburg himself accumulates. Menocchio was literate and widely read, his position as miller set him astride the center of a translocal economic-communications system, he defended himself in terms of the characteristics of the primitive church and the ethical quality of Christ's own teaching, and even after the first heresy verdict he was appointed administrator of the local church's funds. This is not church orthodoxy versus peasant culture; it is the inevitability of a church generating heresy from its inherent contradictions. And it did so throughout the Middle Ages, culminating in the great Protestant schism of the sixteenth century.

These were expressed as religious protest movements. Yet the dividing line between religious and secular subversion was blurred. The influence of Christianity meant that virtually all peasant and urban revolts had a substantial religious element. The Peasants' Revolt in England in 1381 was primarily political and economic in its aims. But one of its leaders, John Ball, was a priest. His famous inflammatory sermon was based on a primitive Christian myth, widely circulated through Langland's *Piers the Plowman:*

> When Adam delved and Eve span
> Who was then a gentleman?

And one of the major acts of the rebels was to disembowel the archbishop of Canterbury, thought to be the main architect of the hated Poll Tax of 1377. Within every village of Christendom the church played its contradictory roles: legitimating the power of pope, king, and lord but simultaneously subverting them.

It is not merely that an existing amount of class struggle was expressed in the language of Christianity; rather, Christianity extended and reorganized class struggle itself. Let us recall the various "phases" of class struggle enumerated in Chapter 7. The first was *latent* class struggle. This is inevitable and ubiquitous (given any division between producers and expropriators), but it is "everyday," locally confined, surreptitious, and usually invisible to the historian's gaze. There are always classes and class struggles in this sense, but their capacity to structure societies is limited. More extensive forms of power organization in this phase are normally horizontal and clientelist, led by members of dominant classes mobilizing their dependents. The second phase was *extensive* class struggle, in which extensive, vertically divided class organizations predominated over horizontal clientelism. And the third phase was *political* class struggle, aimed at transforming class structure by capturing the state.

With the exception of classical Greece and early republican Rome, class struggle has not yet moved to phases two and three. Now, however, we find Christianity intensifying latent struggle and partially developing extensive struggle. The importance of local economic institutions and the local interdependence of village, manor, and market in any case added to the intensity of latent struggle. But the diffuse, transcendent, apocalyptic egalitarianism of Christianity and its frustration by a highly unequal society and by the ideological class morale of the lords, greatly fueled this. Local struggle is visible throughout the Middle Ages, and most historians attribute a great deal of the European dynamic to it. Christianity's "shadow authority structure" also added extensive organization to peasant revolts, as we have just seen. But in a society where peasants were economically confined to local "cells," this could hardly match the extensive organizational capacity of the lords. Hence extensiveness was not what I termed symmetrical. The lords could outflank the peasants. Peasant movements depended on ruling-class divisions and on the leadership of disaffected lords and ecclesiastics for extensive success (as they had in the later Roman Empire, discussed in Chapter 9).

Transcendent aspects of Christian ideology thrust forward such leadership. Lords' particularist and regional disaffections could be voiced in universal moral terms. This was so in the Albigensian heresy in southern France in the thirteenth century, and even as late as in the northern revolt known as the Pilgrimage of Grace in England in 1536. In other words, social struggles of this kind were not "pure" class struggles. They were reorganized by religious institutions into a distinctive blend of part-class, part-clientelist extensive struggles. The terrain involved might be local or regional, but in the early Middle Ages it rarely concerned the territory of the state. Its *organizer* was predominantly ideological rather than political power. Thus ideological power both encouraged and then rechanneled class struggle.

But perhaps to focus on heresy and revolt is to mislead. These were not the normal, in the sense of the most frequent, outcomes, even if they were the most publicized. Normally contradictions were papered over by institutionalized means, according to the strengths of the contending parties in these institutions. Custom, law, satire, and the market were all forms of institutionalization. In all of them the compromising role of Christianity can be glimpsed, tending to legitimize the possession of autonomous power resources by both lords and peasants.

Military/political power

There were many European states. From the beginning this was a multistate region. The Roman Empire was eventually succeeded by an astonishing variety of geographical units, some of which had clearly defined political centers ("states") and some of which did not. Some corresponded to natural economic or geographic areas, some had a clearer relationship to militarily defensible space, and some covered a terrain whose only logic was dynastic accident and accretion. They were mostly rather small units. For several centuries states of more than, say, 10,000 square kilometers had an unpredictable though short history.

The small size was generally the result of two stages of warfare. In the first stage, the Germanic war bands, organized into tribal confederations under kings, tended to fragment once they had conquered Roman provinces. In the second stage, larger consolidated units again fragmented under the pressure of further barbarian invasions as resistance retreated into the individual fortress and, in the field, into the small group of heavily armed horsemen. These small pockets of "concentrated coercion" (as I defined military power) were efficient in defense against more dispersed invaders. This military logic, given its importance to the maintenance of life and property in the Dark Ages, had important reorganizing consequences for social life as a whole. We shall see that it weakened states, deepened social stratification, heightened nobles' class morale, and added to the dynamic contradictions of Christianity.

From the fortress and the knight emerged the main form of the early medieval polity, the weak feudal state. This had four main elements.

First, supreme power usually rested with a single ruler, a lord, who might have a variety of titles – king, emperor, prince, prince-bishop, count, bishop, plus many local variants of the lesser titles.

Second, the formal power of the lord rested in one of the variant forms of a military contract: The subordinate vassal swore homage and gave service, primarily military assistance, in return for protection and/or the grant of land from the lord. This contract is generally regarded as the core element of military/political definitions of feudalism as a whole (as contrasted to economic ones).

Third, the lord did not possess clear rights of access to the population as a whole. Most functions he fulfilled for the society were exercised through other autonomous power actors, the vassals. In one of the larger states, England after the Norman Conquest, the Domesday Book of 1086 indicates between 700 and 1,300 tenants-in-chief, holding their lands of the king. All other tenants held their land and/or contributed their labor as a result of a contract with one of these vassals (except for those dependent on the king's own estates). Even this number of tenants-in-chief was too large for political organization. Most of the minor tenants-in-chief were clients of the major ones. Painter has put the number of magnates – that is, large landholders with an effective political presence regionally or nationally – at about 160 in the period 1160–1220 (1943: 170–8). The feudal state was an agglomeration of largely autonomous households.

This indirect rule was even weaker in cases, frequent in France and Germany, where the vassal owed allegiance to more than one superior – usually for different parts of his estates. In a conflict the vassal chose which superior to follow. In this situation there was not even a single hierarchical pyramid of military/political power, but a series of overlapping interaction networks. Complexity and competition were heightened in all urban areas. Urban authorities – communes, oligarchies, prince-bishops – generally enjoyed a degree of autonomy from adjacent territorial princes. This was not an English problem, because the Normans had extended their conquest evenly over town and country. It prevailed in a central belt of Europe stretching from northwest to southeast, from Flanders through eastern France, western Germany, and Switzerland to Italy. The instability plus prosperity of this zone involved intense diplomatic activities from both lay and ecclesiastical authorities.

Even without such complexities, where indeed the pyramid of authority existed, the powers of the ruler were feeble and indirect. His ritual functions and the infrastructure of literacy for his bureaucracy were controlled by a transnational church; his judicial authority was shared with church and local manorial courts; his military leadership was exercised only at times of crisis and over retainers of other lords; and he had virtually no fiscal or economically redistributive powers. This weakness of the early feudal state sets it apart from both ancient and modern states. Indeed, in some ways it is misleading to call any of them "states," so decentralized were political functions, and so lacking in territoriality were they.

Fourth, the military nature of the feudal state widened considerably the distance in stratification between lords and people. The overwhelming superiority of the armored mounted knight and the fortress over the peasant and urban infantryman until the fourteenth century, and the functional necessity of knights and fortresses in areas threatened by invasion, increased the yield of "protection rent" exacted by the knights. Only a relatively wealthy man could keep a horse and equip himself with body armor. Eighth-century Frankish laws give the cost of equipment as equivalent to fifteen mares or twenty-three oxen – an enormous sum (Verbruggen 1977: 26). The knight's military effectiveness enabled him to increase his wealth through exploitation of the peasantry. As Hintze (1968) expressed it, the knight–non-knight distinction replaced free-unfree as the main criterion of rank.

Although we cannot quantify stratification, it increased in this early medieval period. One sign of this was the increase in the political dependence of the peasant household on its lord, typified by serfdom. Thus, even if political powers had fragmented from the center they had not dispersed completely. They had rested at the level of the vassal lord, and especially in the powers of his manorial court. The peasant's economic and political subjection jeopardized the egalitarian message of Christ and worsened the church's internal contradictions.

Larger, more centralized states did begin to emerge, mostly where military organization required this. The expulsion of barbarians, organized for example by Charlemagne or Alfred, created monarchies with more extensive, territorial powers centered on large numbers of armed, personal retainers who formed what was in practice, if not in theory, a professional army. Territorial conquest like the Norman conquests of England and Sicily also required such an army. But in a fairly primitive economy, no lord could generate the liquid wealth to pay a large number of mercenaries. The only solution was land grants, which gave the vassal soldier a potentially autonomous power base.

Nevertheless, if an extensive state endured, mere stability enhanced its powers. The networks of local customs and privileges possessed by lords, towns, villages, and even individual peasants tended to settle down into an orderly structure with the prince's courts a final arbiter. Most ordinary and middling persons had a vested interest in the survival of the prince, if only out of fear of uncertainties resulting from his fall. The prince was judicial arbiter between persons and communal institutions, holding the ring between them. His infrastructural power was insufficient to coerce them collectively, but then it was intended only to humble any single person or association that attempted arbitrary usurpation. Where stabilized, such powers were worth supporting. They could also be supported by church anointment. This was the advantage possessed by the prince whose genealogical claim to inheritance was unquestioned.

From about A.D. 1000 we can detect both sustained economic growth and the beginning of a growth in the powers of the state, which gave a more precise judicial bite to the normative pacification of Christendom. After 1200 the more powerful states were entering into direct relations with their people. I discuss this in the next chapter. But the changes were late, slow, and uneven. The growth of royal power had occurred earlier in England and was more complete there than in other countries. By 1150 the English state was probably the most centralized in Europe. Only clerics and those vassals with estates outside as well as inside the Anglo-Norman domains owed allegiance to any competing source of authority; over all other people the king of England's sovereignty was universal. The king had established his legal sovereignty over all lay freemen, but not yet over dependent *villeins* (still subject to the manorial court) or over the clergy (though Henry II remedied this in their secular affairs). The other two main areas of subsequent state growth, the economic and the military, were only slightly more advanced than in other countries. No general power of taxation, no extensively levied customs dues, and no professional army existed. In battle each lord's levy could act independently – it was free to leave the field at any time, a persistent Achilles heel of medieval kings. By both ancient and modern standards even this state was puny. Much remained hidden from the state, excluded from the public realm, *private*. Political-power networks were not unitary but dual, part public, part privately controlled by a class of local magnates.

Economic power

The early medieval economy was complex. It was a backward, near-subsistence economy dominated by two penetrating, intensive, local cellular institutions, the village and the manor. But at another level it generated exchange of commodities through extensive trading networks in which developed two institutions, towns and merchant guilds, which were organizationally somewhat separate from the local agricultural economy. The coexistence of these apparently contradictory tendencies highlights one central feature of the medieval economy: Economic power relations were not unitary but multiple.

I start with the cellular economies of village and manor. It is not difficult to trace their general origins and development – the manor being a merging of the Roman villa and Germanic lordship, the village being primarily the outgrowth of freer, communal aspects of Germanic life; the first contained the key vertical relationship of the early medieval economy, the second its key horizontal relationship.

Hierarchical relations in the early medieval period usually involved personal dependence and un-freedom. The peasants were tied legally/customarily to a particular lord and/or a particular plot of land so that free movement out of this relationship was not permitted. The most general form of dependence was serfdom. The most characteristic economy in which serfdom was embedded was the manor. The manor spread fast wherever Roman rule had existed and rather slower over more northerly Europe. The Danish settlements slowed its progress in eastern and northern England. But by the time of the Domesday Book it was dominant over the rest of England and widespread even there.

On the ideal-typical English manor, the villein held his own plot of land, a yardland or virgate of about twelve hectares, usually distributed in scattered strips intermingled with the lord's own *demesne* strips (although these often became concentrated as a home farm surrounded by peasant strips). Each villein household owed "week-work" labor services – usually one laborer three days a week on the demesne. In addition it owed various feudal dues, usually paid in kind, to the lord. The village also contained freemen and others with more idiosyncratic tenures, who paid forms of rent (again, usually in kind), which implied a free contract between them and the lord. But in practice they could no more break away from the relationship, say by selling their land, than could the villein. Interwoven with this local economy was an administrative system and a manorial court, both controlled by the lord, but in which villeins and freemen might participate as subordinate officers, such as a reeve.[2] This was a dense, tightly integrated economy in which labor

---

[2] Discussion of manor and village can be found in Postan 1975: 81–173. The English manor differed in details from practices dominant elsewhere in Europe; see Bloch 1961: 241–79.

services formed the core relationship, an extremely intensive, but not apparently extensive, form of power relationship.

But around the use and organization of the peasant strips formed a second dense, intensive, local economy, that of the village. We know less of this organization because it did not generally rely on written records. The peasant households formed a village community that adjudicated property and tenure disputes, laid down common rules of husbandry (sharing of plows and manure, rotation of fields, reclamation of woods and marshes, etc.) raised feudal dues and taxes, and enforced order. Relations between the two economic and administrative units of manor and village varied from area to area. Where more than one manor existed within, or crosscutting, a village, then the village community seems to have been of considerable importance. But even where the rule of "one manor, one vill" operated, the two were not identical (principally because not all locals were tenants of the lord).

This meant that no monopolistic power organization existed in the local economy. Formidable as were the powers of the lord, they were restrained by the fact that even the serf could find support from the village community and from customary law. The two power networks were also interpenetrating – peasant and lord were part independent of one another and part implicated in each other's organization, as the distribution of their strips of land reveals. Interpenetration was most pronounced along the old Roman frontier provinces where the German free village and the Roman estate mixed – in England, the Low Countries, northern and central France, and western Germany.

This dual local organization was also implicated in more extensive trade, even in the Dark Ages (Brutzkus 1943; Postan 1975: 205–8). As might be expected from my discussions of previous barbarians, these invaders were not quite so backward or so preoccupied with pillaging and killing to the exclusion of trading as the Christians liked to claim. In fact, the Vikings were the major traders of northern Europe between the ninth and the twelfth centuries, taking furs, iron weapons, and especially slaves to the east and bringing luxury items in return. This type of trade (and its corollary in the south with the Arab world) had been traditional throughout three millennia of trade in goods that were high in value-to-weight ratio or were "self-propelled" (like slaves). Between this type of trade and commodity production of agricultural produce lay a large developmental divide. The great buoyancy of later medieval trade did not arise upon this Viking base, with the exception of the one Viking bulk commodity, timber, transported long distances by sea and along rivers. In this one respect the Vikings contributed to the economic integration of Europe, ensuring continuity to the role of trade between the Baltic and central and southern Europe.

If luxury trade, whether carried by Vikings or anyone else, now had a dynamic effect on medieval Europe this was due to the additional impetuses of states and church institutions. Either kings or monks, abbots, and bishops could pacify localities and guarantee contracts sufficient for trading emporia and fairs to spring up at their gates (Hodges 1982; and various essays in Barley 1977). But they were not alternatives. The Christianity of the kings was relevant to their economic role. Missionaries often accompanied traders, and the expeditions were usually rewarded in both goods and souls. There had been sufficient continuity from Rome, carried largely by the church, for knowledge of former Roman trade routes and techniques to be known. The earliest surge in trade in England probably occurred in the seventh and early eighth centuries. Vast numbers of local coins dating from this period have been discovered. Significantly, none bears a king's name. Only later, with King Offa of Mercia (757–96), do the local kings seem to have gotten in on the act. Viking traders were receptive to Christianity, and a dual process of trade and conversion furthered the integration of northern and sourthern Europe. The normative pacification of Christendom was a precondition of the revival of markets.

More precise mechanisms were added by the local manorial economy. The heightening of stratification and the militaristic forms that it took increased the demand for certain luxuries, and for the artisan traders associated with-them. Lords and knights required armor, weapons, horses, harnesses, clothing and furnishings of distinction, and food and drink of refinement. Their demands rose as a response to military exigencies. In the eleventh century, stone-castle building generated trade in building supplies. The church added specialized demand for greater craftsmanship in building, for parchment and writing materials, and for art. The deepening and militarization of stratification meant that more surplus could be extracted to pay for all this. A few lords, fortunately controlling mines, ports, or crossroads, could extract this from nonagricultural activities; rather more in animal husbandry areas could extract it from the fabrication of leather, wool, or cloth; but most had to extract it from arable farming. We know that the extraction process was not sufficient to satisfy the lords' demand for luxuries until the thirteenth century, because there was a net loss of gold and silver bullion from Europe to the East until this date. Europe's trade deficit was made up by the export of such precious metal coins as it could muster. However, the stimulus to the commodity production and exchange of agricultural produce was considerable. When systematic customs records began in England, in the late twelfth century, both wool and grain exports were already considerable. A letter from Charlemagne to Offa complains of the low quality of the cloth being sent for Carolingian army uniforms. On another occasion, Offa threatened to cut off English exports if Charlemagne failed to agree to a marriage alliance. Around the turn of the ninth century, an expansion of trade appears associated with the emergence of the production of staple commodities on the manors. Local bonds were already tightening. The independent productive spheres of the peasant was also influenced by the market, for the manor itself was largely "an agglomeration of small, dependent farms" (as put by Bloch 1966: 246).

Lord and peasant felt the force of the market. As the manor developed, so did its production of commodity goods alongside subsistence goods. Eventually towns emerged, in the period from about 1050 to 1250. By the time trade was really buoyant, it was accompanied by merchant and artisan institutions with an autonomy unparalleled in other civilizations (which observation is at the core of the more "materialist" parts of Weber's comparative analysis of East and West). Autonomy took several forms: the predominance of foreigners in a country's trade (e.g., in England the process was begun by the Frisians in the seventh century and continued by Vikings, Flemings, Hansa, Lombards and other Italians, and Jews until the fourteenth century), the self-regulating powers of artisan and merchant guilds and banking houses, the political autonomy of urban communes against territorial princes, and the power of the merchant republics (Venice, Genoa, the Hanse). Town influence penetrated the countryside. Although the market entered the manor and village through the production of commodities principally controlled by the lord, urban influence brought notions of freedom summed up by the famous medieval aphorism "Town air makes you free." At the very least, physical flight from serfdom to freedom was possible.

Conclusion: multiple networks and private property
One obvious and one rather subtle conclusion flow from all this: No single group could monopolize power; conversely, all power actors had autonomous spheres. In the political realm the lord, vassal, town, church, and even peasant village had their own resources to contribute to a delicate balance of power. In the ideological realm the traditional contradictions of Christianity remained, spilling over into general political and economic conflict. In the economy, lords, peasants (free and unfree), and towns were all part-autonomous actors capable of action supported by custom in pursuit of economic goals.

Whatever this extraordinarily multiple, acephalous federation would achieve, it was unlikely to be organized stagnation. Historians over and over again use the word "restless" to characterize the essence of medieval culture. As McNeill puts it, "It is not any particular set of institutions, ideas or technologies that mark out the West but its inability to come to a rest. No other civilized society has ever approached such restless instability. . . . In this . . . lies the true uniqueness of Western civilization" (1963: 539). But such a spirit need not induce social development. Might it not induce other forms of stagnation: anarchy, the Hobbesian war of all against all; or *anomie,* where the absence of social control and direction leads to aimlessness and despair? We can marry the insights of two great sociologists to show why social development, not anarchy or anomie, resulted.

The first is Weber, who in noting the peculiar restlessness of Europe always added another word, "rational." "Rational restlessness" was the psychological makeup of Europe, the opposite of what he found in the main religions of Asia: rational acceptance of social order by Confucianism, its irrational antithesis in Taoism, mystical acceptance of social order by Hinduism, otherworldly retreat in Buddhism. Weber located rational restlessness especially in Puritanism. But Puritanism emphasized strands of the Christian psyche that had been traditionally present. Salvation for all in return for individual ethical conduct and judgment of all worldly authority in the fierce, egalitarian vision of the apocalypse – Christianity encouraged a drive for moral and social improvement even against worldly authority. Although much medieval Christianity was put in the service of pious masking of brutal repression, its currents of dissatisfaction always ran strong. We can read an enormous literature of social criticism. Visionary, moralistic, satirical, cynical, this literature can be labored and repetitious, but its peak includes some of the greatest works of the age – in English, Langland and Chaucer. It is pervaded by the psychological quality identified by Weber.

But to put this rational restlessness in the service of social improvement probably also required a mechanism identified by the second great sociologist, Durkheim. Not anarchy or anomie but normative regulation was provided by Christendom. Political and class struggles, economic life and even wars were, to a degree, regulated by an unseen hand, not Adam Smith's but Jesus Christ's. By joining the two men's theories in this metaphor we can observe that Christian hands were piously clasped in the prayers of a whole normative community and were actively employed in rational improvement of an imperfect world. In the next section I explore the economic dynamism stimulated by this invisibly regulated multiplicity of power networks.

The subtler conclusion concerns the impact of these autonomies on an institution that was to assume an important later role: *private property*. As it is conventionally understood today, private property confers *exclusive* ownership of economic resources by *law*. In these two respects, early feudal Europe lacked private property. Bloch remarks that feudalism, unlike both Roman conceptions and ours, had no conception of "purely" economic relationships in land. It was rare for anyone to speak of ownership. Lawsuits turned not on ownership, still less on written documents of "law," but on custom and *seisin* – possession made venerable by the passage of time. Ownership could not exist where land was burdened with particularistic obligations to superiors and community (1962: I, 115). Those who start from such a contrast create for themselves a formidable problem in explaining the transition from feudalism to capitalism. Most have found it necessary to invoke a deus ex machina: the revival of Roman law primarily by the European state, but also by property possessors in general, which became influential about 1200 (e.g., see Anderson 1974b: 24–9).

Yet, although the Roman-law revival was not without significance, the break was less decisive than this would imply. Law is not a necessary part of effective private property – otherwise preliterate societies could barely possess such property. But a concern with law as a criterion of private property conceals what is actually the normal relationship between the state and private property. Conventional modern understandings assume that effective private possession occurs first and that then the state is brought in to legitimate it. To a degree this actually happened from the twelfth century onward in the enclosure movement, part of the transition to capitalism. But as we saw in earlier chapters, effective private possession had been hitherto normally created through the state. Normally, the disintegration of an expansive state had enabled its provincial agents and allies to sieze and keep its public, communal resources for themselves. The essential precondition of this was literally "privacy" – the ability to hide resources from the public domain.

In the early Middle Ages this had happened again as vassals obtained effective possession of lands supposedly held from their lord. In medieval Europe, peasants were able to do likewise from their lords. Indeed, the fact that no community or class organization (state or otherwise) possessed monopoly powers meant that almost everyone had his or her own economic resources, which were "private" in the Latin sense of *hidden* from the control of the state or others. In this sense, European feudalism conferred an extraordinary degree of "private" property. Property was not in the form of land exclusively controlled by a single person or household. But "private," that is, hidden, economic activity was more widespread than it is in our own mature capitalist era (in which around 10% of persons effectively possess 80% of private wealth, and where infrastructurally powerful states and corporations restrict real privacy even further). As early as A.D. 800, European feudalism was dominated by private property, in the sense of hidden and effective possession.

Thus the emergence of capitalist private property presents a somewhat different explanatory problem from those found in most conventional explanations. First, it is not a matter of how people acquired their own private resources from more communal "feudal" institutions, but rather a matter of how a few *preserved* them through changing circumstances – to appear eventually as "capitalists" – and of how the mass of the population *lost* their property rights to appear eventually as landless laborers. Second, the rise of the state was not antithetical to the rise of capitalism, but a necessary element in the elimination of multiple, particularistic obligations by unitary, exclusive ownership. I return to the first problem later in this chapter and to the second in the next chapters.

The feudal dynamic

Economic growth

Formidable obstacles confront attempts to chart the chronology of the European economy. Around 1200, records improve as states and manors began to keep more detailed accounts, but this makes it hazardous to compare pre-1200

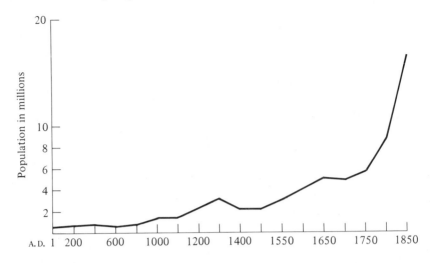

Figure 12.1. *Approximate population of England,* A.D. *1–1850 (sources: Russell 1948; McEvedy and Jones 1978; 43; Wrigley and Schofield 1981; 208–9, 566–9)*

with post-1200 periods. Nonetheless, I believe we can just discern an essential continuity, perhaps from about 800 to the agricultural revolution of the eighteenth century. Continuity has three main aspects: economic growth; a shift in economic power within Europe from the Mediterranean to the northwest; and, therefore, a shift toward forms of power organization prevalent there.

We can start with population trends. We must combine information from the occasional, incomplete census of land tenants (Domesday Book of 1086) or taxpayers (1377 Poll Tax returns) with estimates of average family size and with archaeological excavations of numbers of hectares reclaimed or abandoned. Even the most carefully compiled figures for England (those of Russell 1948 for 1086 and 1377) are disputed (by Postan 1972: 30–5). It is best to round the figures and to even out figures available for different years by graphing them. Figure 12.1 is one such graph. Although the figures for the earlier years are guesses, they correspond to most historians' assessment that by about A.D. 800 the population had recovered to its highest levels under the Roman occupation and that by the time of the Domesday Book it had doubled. It doubled again by the early fourteenth century but then faltered before plunging by perhaps a third, or perhaps by 40 percent, during the Black Death and subsequent plagues. Statistically, however, the fourteenth-century crisis was only a small setback. By 1450 population was rising, never to fall back again. From about 800 to 1750, with the exception of the fourteenth century, growth was probably continuous. Other areas of Europe reveal similar growth, although its rhythms differed (see Figure 12.2).

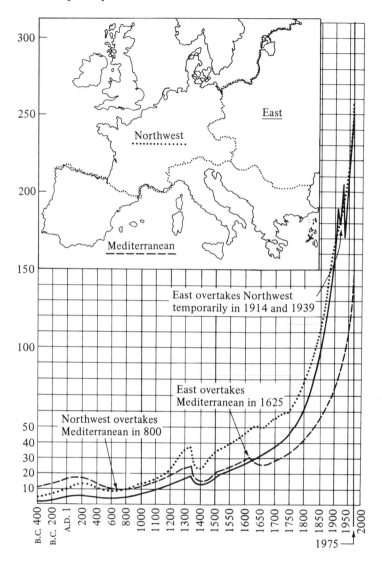

300

250

200

150

100

50
40
30
20
10

East

Northwest
• • • • • • • • • • • •

Mediterranean
– – – – – – – – –

East overtakes Northwest
temporarily in 1914 and 1939

East overtakes
Mediterranean in 1625

Northwest overtakes
Mediterranean in 800

B.C. 400   B.C. 200   A.D. 1   200   400   600   800   1000   1100   1200   1300   1400   1500   1550   1600   1650   1700   1750   1800   1850   1900   1950   2000

1975 —

Figure 12.2. *Europe: subdivision into regions (source: McEvedy and Jones 1978: fig. 1.10)*

So England's rapid and early growth was characteristic of northwestern Europe as a whole. Although the Mediterranean region also grew, it did not recover to its former Roman levels until about three or four hundred years later, around 1200. By 1300, moreover, Italy's population density had been equaled by that of Flanders, while Spain's and Greece's were now lower than those of virtually every region of the North and the West.

Therefore, at a date that varied from about 800 to 1200 according to area, the European countries were supporting larger populations than ever before. With a hiccup or two, they continued their upward movement right through the medieval and early modern periods. This is our first indication of the persistence of the European dynamic, especially in the northwestern part of the continent.

A larger agricultural population can be supported only in two ways: either extensively, by bringing more land into cultivation; or intensively, by increasing the yield ratios of existing cultivated land. Both occurred in Europe, though in varying combinations in different times and regions. Until populations reached their former levels, the extension could be into fields formerly tilled by the Romans. In the South, Roman cultivation had often been so complete that little further extension was then possible. In the North, large areas of marsh and forest land never before cultivated could be reclaimed. This process dominates the records of countries like England and Germany up to around 1200. From about that date, however, the quality of new marginal land was not high. Soil exhaustion and a shortage of animal manure probably brought on a fourteenth-century crisis, leaving the population too unhealthy to withstand the Black Death, a plague that struck between 1347 and 1353 in its first and main wave. If extensive cultivation had been the sole European solution, the continent would now have experienced a similar Malthusian cycle every century or so – and would not have generated capitalism.

But greater intensity of cultivation was also occurring. Here we can use yield ratios. The period before 1200 is poorly documented and controversial. I discussed the figures in Chapter 9. If we accept Slicher van Bath's estimates rather than Duby's, we can discern a modest rise in yield ratios between the ninth and the early twelfth centuries – in England the wheat yield rose from a ratio of about 2.7 to either 2.9 or 3.1 of the planted seed. In most regions the incentive for improvement was lessened by the availability of good virgin land, but after 1200 this alternative was less attractive. Slicher van Bath (1963: 16–17) has summarized the data (see Table 12.1). He divides Europe into four groups of modern countries according to their yields, but they also turn out to be regional groupings. They are:

> Group I: England, Ireland, Belgium, the Netherlands
> Group II: France, Spain, Italy
> Group III: Germany, Switzerland, Denmark, Sweden, Norway
> Group IV: Czechoslovakia, Poland, Lithuania, Latvia, Estonia, Russia

The figures relate to wheat, rye, barley, and oats alike, for the trends for each crop are uniform.

By 1250 Group I countries were substantially increasing their yields. Although there were slumps in the fourteenth (early), fifteenth, and seventeenth centu-

Table 12.1. *European crop yield ratios, 1200–1820*

Phase	Group	Country data sources	Years	Yield
A	I	England	1200–49	3.7
	II	France	ca. 1190	3.0
B	I	England	1250–1499	4.7
	II	France	1300–1499	4.3
	III	Germany, Scandinavia	1500–1699	4.2
	IV	Eastern Europe	1550–1820	4.1
C	I	England, Netherlands	1500–1699	7.0
	II	France, Spain, Italy	1500–1820	6.3
	III	Germany, Scandinavia	1700–1820	6.4
D	I	England, Ireland, Belgium,		
		Netherlands	1750–1820	10.6

ries, the increase continued. By 1500 they exceeded the best large-area figures in ancient Europe. In the later eighteenth century they jumped to a point at which a substantial part of the population could be released for nonagricultural employment – for the first time. [3] And again we see disproportionate and earlier growth in the Northwest, increasing the region's agricultural lead from the thirteenth century onward.

These yield ratios are crucial. They were the sole means of avoiding Malthusian cycles after about 1200: the only way a larger population could be supported on a given territory, the only way population could be released into secondary and tertiary employment. The figures indicate that this potentiality was built into European social structure from a very early date, especially in the Northwest. They are only an indicator of the feudal dynamic, not its cause. But they indicate how early the dynamic began. We can get a little closer to causes by examining the technical changes that were the immediate precipitators of higher yields.

Technique and invention in the Middle Ages
Some historians characterize the Middle Ages as a period "in which technological innovations succeeded each other at an accelerated rate" (Cipolla 1976: 159), as possessing a "technological dynamism," a "technological creativity" (White 1972: 144, 170). Others, in contrast, have argued that "the inertia of medieval agricultural technology is unmistakable" (Postan 1972: 49). Many argue that creativity in general accelerated only later in the Renaissance of the fifteenth century. Before then most of the major inventions diffused to Europe from elsewhere. But it is pointless to talk about "inventiveness" at

---

[3]Eighteenth-century yield figures understate the agricultural improvements of that time, many of which increased the use of fields and variety of crops rather than cereal yields. See Chapter 14.

this general level, as I argued this in Chapter 9 with respect to the Roman period, which is often characterized as "stagnant." The Romans pioneered a series of inventions appropriate to their own power organizations but less so to those of our own times. I labeled these inventions *extensive,* for they facilitated the conquest and minimal exploitation of large land spaces. Similarly, we cannot label the European Middle Ages as simply "creative" or "stagnant." Again we find a particular type of invention predominating, the opposite of the Roman, *intensive* invention.

Let me pursue further the contrast with Rome. One of the major Roman inventions had been the arch, a method of bridging space that does not load the center span more than the columns that flank it. The loads that the arch could support were far greater than the universal earlier building method, crossbeams laid flat across the top of the columns. Roman loads were mostly traffic: people walking around amphitheaters; soldiers and carts traversing bridges; and the heaviest load of all, water flowing down aqueducts to supply the cities. The arch was thus an important part of the Roman conquest of horizontal land space. It was such an advance that it was adopted by all Rome's successors in their more modest building endeavors. But around A.D. 1000 in Islam, then in more sustained fashion in the Christian lands, came important changes to the arch. The circle, the Roman form of the arch, gave way to an oval or a vertical axis, and then to the pointed Gothic arch. The increased upward thrust took weight off the column walls as a whole. The length of the walls could be lessened and pierced with glass and light. But a problem remained, for the higher the upward thrust, the more stress flowed to the outside of the column wall. The problem was solved in the twelfth century with the flying buttress, which was added to the outside of the column wall to absorb its stress (Bronowski 1973: 104–13). This was a tremendous, sustained burst of architectural invention, which produced some of the largest, sturdiest, and most beautiful buildings ever seen. We know because we can still see them: the European cathedrals. This specialized use of such techniques – for they were not applied to other types of building for several centuries – tells us a great deal about medieval society. The conquest was of *height.* The techniques allowed arches to carry greater weights than had the Roman arch, but not so as to carry traffic, not to transport goods or people over distances. The weight was that of a vertical structure: the 38 meters of the vault at Reims (the Beauvais arch of 46 m. collapsed), that of the tower of Ulm. All were reaching up to God above.

It seems peculiarly appropriate that the medieval cathedral builders should convert the Roman conquest of horizontal space into a conquest of vertical space. For they were worshiping Jesus Christ, who had actually conquered horizontal space by alternative means, through conversion of souls!

It also indicates a wider neglect by medieval society of extensive innovation. Jesus and Saint Paul, helped by the infrastructural legacy of the ancient world, had made Christendom one. Extensiveness looked after itself. No major innovations were made in the medieval period in the communication of messages or, with one major exception, in transport technology (see Leighton 1972 for a detailed discussion). That exception concerns the use of horses, developed primarily to improve not communications systems but plowing. Medieval Europe did not innovate along extensive Roman lines.

The metaphor so far is that medieval Europe was interested not in extent but in height. We may continue it: For the most significant economic innovations were in *depth*. The metaphor should evoke what are generally agreed to be the core technological inventions: in plowing, changes in field rotation and in shoeing and harnessing draught animals. To this we should add the water mill (which perhaps unduly stretches the depth metaphor).

All these innovations were widespread by about A.D. 1000, and they all disproportionately increased the yield from heavier soils, that is, from northern and western Europe. Cipolla summarizes the main technological developments of the West:

a. from the sixth century: diffusion of the water mill.
b. from the seventh century: diffusion, in northern Europe, of the heavy plough.
c. from the eighth century: diffusion of the three-field system.
d. from the ninth century: diffusion of the horseshoe: diffusion of a new method of harnessing draught animals. [1976: 159–60]

White summarizes their effect:

Between the first half of the 6th century and the end of the 9th century Northern Europe created or received a series of inventions which quickly coalesced into an entirely novel system of agriculture. In terms of a peasant's labor, this was by far the most productive the world has seen. [1963: 277]

Bridbury (1975) has argued strongly that these innovations were rooted firmly in the ''Dark Ages'' and were not a result of urban and maritime revivals occurring (especially in Italy) from the eleventh century on.

Let us consider the character of these innovations. The heavy plow had an iron coulter knife to incise a furrow, an iron share to cut it deeper, and an angled mold board to tear loose and overturn the sliced earth toward the right-hand side. It could turn over deeper, heavier soils, raise them up, and provide them with drainage furrows. The waterlogged plains of northern Europe could be drained and exploited. But the plow needed more energy for pulling. This was provided by improved shoeing and harnessing of bigger teams of oxen or horses. Field rotation is more complex. But the very complexity and unevenness of the diffusion of ''two-field'' versus ''three-field'' systems indicate that farmers were aware both of the richer potentialities of heavier soils for grain and some vegetable yields and of specific fertilizing problems raised by such soils. The interdependence of arable farming and animal husbandry tightened, and this too shifted power to the northwest, to areas like southeastern England or Flanders where zones of good pasturelands and cornfields interpenetrated. In global terms, moreover, it probably gave western Europe a decisive agricultural edge over Asia and particularly over Chinese intensive rice-cultivation techniques. Energy and manure from animals gave the European a "motor more or less five times as powerful as that possessed by Chinese man," according to Chaunu (1969:366). None of these was merely a technical innovation. They also involved intensive social organization. An economic unit about the size of the village or the manor was useful for equipping an oxen or horse team, arranging its cooperative use (which encouraged the characteristic long strips of early medieval agriculture), and organizing field rotation and manuring. Such organization could increase the yield of heavy soil grains. The water mill could efficiently grind them.

Nothing indicates more clearly the character of early medieval agricultural dynamism than the water mill, invented during the Roman period but not widely diffused until now. Here we have a statistic. The Domesday Book records 6,000 mills in England by 1086 (Hodgen 1939), a figure Lennard (1959: 278) considers an understatement by at least 10 percent, but that averages out at 2 per village and about 1 per 10–30 plows. Some of these water mills were under the control of the local lord, others were independent. But all showed that economic power and innovation had passed to the locality, thoroughly decentralized.

The technology of the increase in yield ratios, and therefore in population, was intensive, not extensive, the product of that local autonomy discussed earlier. The causal mechanisms are beginning to clarify. They were generated by effective local possession of autonomous economic resources, possession that was institutionalized and legitimized by the extensive powers of Christendom. Let us examine the mechanisms of economic extensiveness a little more closely. How was trade regulated, and why was there, relatively, so much of it?

One factor is plain ecology, usually given an important place in neoclassical economic theory. As Jones (1981) argues, part of the "European miracle," when Europe is compared to Asia, resides in Europe's ecological contrasts, which produced a "dispersed portfolio of resources" whereby bulk, utilitarian goods – like grains, meat, fruit, olives, wine, salt, metals, wood, animal skins, and furs – were exchanged across the continent. The high proportion of coastlines and navigable rivers kept transport costs low. Then, Jones continues, consequences flow from economic rationality: States had no interest in pillaging bulk subsistence goods traded as commodities, only in taxing them; in return, states would provide basic social order. Europe avoided the state "plunder machine"; hence, economic development. As a neoclassical economist who believes that markets are "natural," Jones quotes his mentor, Adam Smith: If you have peace, easy taxes, and a tolerable administration of justice, then the rest is brought about by "the natural course of things" (1981: 90–6, 232–7).

But this approach misses several essential preconditions. First, why is Europe to be regarded as a continent in the first place? This is not an ecological but a social fact. It had not been a continent hitherto: It was now created by the fusion of the Germanic barbarians with the northwestern parts of the Roman Empire, and it was bounded by the blocking presence of Islam to the south and east. Its continental identity was primarily Christian. It was known as Christendom rather than Europe. Second, for production to reach levels sufficient for extensive trade required those social preconditions of technical innovation described above. Third, for goods to be "commodities" required that particular, unusual, social form known as private property, also discussed above. Fourth, the main social actors identified by Jones, capitalist merchants and states, are actually drawn from later periods of capitalism and not from this one. This point will take us to the root of Christendom's extensive powers, and I will expand it.

Let us go to the heart of the early medieval trading network. It was a corridor, or rather two parallel diagonal lines, running from northwest to southeast. One line gathered the produce of Scandinavia and the North to the mouth of the Rhine, moving it up the Rhine to Switzerland and thence to northern, especially northeastern, Italy, receiving Mediterranean and eastern produce in return. The other line began in Flanders, gathering North Sea produce, then moving mostly by land transport through northern and eastern France to the Loire and thence to the Mediterranean and northwestern Italy. This second route was more important, and it sent out an offshoot line to the middle Rhine. What is striking about these routes is that they either missed or were somewhat peripheral to those states providing most centralized order – to England, and to the core, crown-domain lands of France and of the German emperor. The equation between states and trade is not totally false; rather, the most involved states were of a different type than the "modern" state.

In the first place we can note a large number of ecclesiastical "states" along much of the route. From Flanders to the Rhône and on the Rhine we find large agglomerations of church estates, ruled from bishoprics and archbishoprics like Noyon, Laon, Reims, Chalons, Dijon, Besançon, Lyon, Vienne, Cologne, Trier, and Mainz, as well as powerful monasteries like Clairvaux and Cluny. We also find that the secular rulers tended to be princelings ruling loosely over a conglomeration of lords. Both princelings and their vassals also kept their eyes open for signs of advantage and movement from the more powerful states of France, Germany, and England to the sides. Thus the duchies of Upper and Lower Lorraine, the duchy and county of Burgundy, the county of Flanders and of Champagne and of Provence, came in and out of alliance and/or vassalage, sometimes through marriage, sometimes through free contract, to France, England, and Germany. Though the great states would dearly have liked to secure more permanent control, because of the richness of these lands, they could not.

So there is a correlation of economic wealth and dynamism with weak states. This encourages many to regard early medieval trade as somewhat "insterstitial" to the world of great landed lords and states. Although this was true of Italy at the lower end of the corridor, it is misleading to apply it anywhere else. It was not a *trading* corridor, separate from agricultural production. The corridor did have initial natural advantages for trade, for it linked the North Sea and the Mediterranean (remember that Islam had closed the Strait of Gibraltar) by way of some of the most fertile land in Europe. But once established, surrounding agricultural activity changed. Flanders developed cash crops, cattle breeding, and horticulture; later it possessed English wool. Northern France's rich soil provided wheat. The Rhône concentrated on salt mining and on what is the major surviving meaning of the word "Burgundy." The lords of these areas, lay and ecclesiastical, benefited enormously. They did not simply provide local order in return for taxes on trade; their own estates became more like capitalist agriculture, producing commodities for exchange. And their purely local order did not degenerate into regional anarchy, because they shared allegiance not to a common state but to a common class. They traveled around each other's courts; listened to the same romances, epics, and sermons; discussed the same moral dilemmas; intermarried; sent their younger sons on Crusades; and kept a wary eye on the great powers. Their economic rationality had a normative base: the *class morale* provided by Christendom.

As we see in the next chapter, this particular area maintained a long association between weak state and economic dynamism, with the rise of the duchy of Burgundy in the fourteenth and fifteenth centuries. The relations between strong states and protocapitalist development may have been established in other European areas by those dates, but not so in the earlier centuries discussed here. The normative solidarity of lords, lay and ecclesiastical, (and to a lesser degree of peasants) as expressed by weak and truly "feudal" states was a necessary precondition for providing order to markets and so extensiveness to early European dynamism.

I do not intend a "single-factor" explanation. In the whole process of European development there is also an extremely long-term persistence of a distinctively "European" peasant-plus-iron economy that fits quite well into a neoclassical explanation of the European miracle. As we have seen, after the Iron Age most of Europe was dominated by peasant families using iron tools and draft animals to dig into rich but heavy, wet soils and exchanging subsistence goods as quasi-commodities. A predominantly nuclear family restricted its fertility through a later age of marriage (demonstrated for the sixteenth century by Hajnal 1965). "Individual" forms of ownership existed as early as the twelfth century in England (McFarlane 1978 – although he regards it as distinctively English rather than common to northwest Europe, an assertion for which he offers no evidence). Perhaps they were established much further back and were part of the later emergence of capitalism. But my argument is that without an understanding of more macrostructures of power – beginning with those in the eastern Mediterranean, continuing with those in the Roman Empire, and culminating with those in Christendom – we could not find in place both the intensive and the extensive power preconditions for the European miracle.

The embryonic transition to capitalism

The difficult part of the explanation is over. From here we can proceed with the aid of two well-established materialist theories of the transition. We have arrived at the point where individual families and local village-and-manor communities were participating in a wider network of economic interaction under institutionalized norms governing property possession, production relations, and market exchange. They possessed autonomy and privacy sufficient to keep to themselves the fruits of their own enterprise and thus to calculate likely costs and benefits to themselves of alternative strategies. Thus with supply, demand, and incentives for innovation well established, neoclassical economics can take up the explanation. And as these actors were not only families and local communities but also social classes, lords, and peasants, Marxism can help our analysis of their struggles.

Indeed, despite the polemics flying between these two schools of economic history, they are essentially similar descriptions of the transition. True, they differ in the emphasis placed on the various factors affecting rational calculations, competition, and class struggle. Neoclassicists prefer factors that are treated as extraneous to social structure (or at least to class structure), like population growth and decline, climate changes, or differential soil fertility. Marxists prefer variations in class organization. Obviously a more detailed explanation of the transition than I am attempting here would have to choose between these arguments. But in general the two schools complement each other quite well and offer a good collective description of the later development of the feudal dynamic. What they lack – and what I have hopefully provided – is an explanation of how the world arrived for the first time at a situation in which their models can apply.

Two parallel tendencies toward the emergence of exclusivity in property rights developed over the medieval period. Exclusivity developed from privacy. One vested exclusive property upon lords, the second on a rich section of the peasantry. Both were part of a general drift toward capitalistic relationships in agriculture, though different regions and periods tended to develop one or the other because something of an inverse relationship existed between the two until near the final demise of the feudal mode of production. The best example of both tendencies was the fourteenth-century crisis. So I will run ahead of my chronological divisions of chapters to briefly describe and relate this crisis to the general tendencies of feudalism. The description is drawn largely from two neoclassical accounts (North and Thomas 1973: 46–51, 59–64, 71–80; and Postan 1975) and two Marxian accounts (Anderson 1974a: 197–209; and Brenner 1976). They do not greatly differ.

In the first phase of the fourteenth-century crisis, changes in relative product and factor values favored the lords. During the thirteenth century prolonged population growth had filled in the map of Europe. Marginal lands of lower quality were being worked and overpopulation threatened. Thus labor was abundant but good land was not. The bargaining power of those who controlled the higher-quality land, that is, the lords, was increased relative to the power of those dependent on their labor, that is, the peasants. The lords increased their rate of exploitation and received direct cultivation of their demesne land through labor services. This tended to happen whenever conditions favored the lords in the medieval economy. Their basic strategy was to draw the independent part of the peasant activity into the manor, reducing the peasants' independent holding to a level sufficient to keep the peasant household alive and to reproduce the next generation's labor force. Now the lords could appropriate any surplus directly (Hindess and Hirst 1975: 236; Banaji 1976). They could also use economies of scale and capital investment in their own demesne to further control over the peasantry. Thus in Marx's words the lord became "the manager and master of the process of production and of the entire process of social life" (1972: 860–1). For example, the water mill tended to come under his control and to be exploited as a feudal monopoly. Peasants were forced to take their grain to the lord's mill, as they were to use his ovens, draw his water, burn his wood, and use his winepress. Such compulsions came to be the hated *banalités,* part of the feudal rights of the lord. They had earlier spread widely in the tenth and eleventh centuries as the lords had taken the economic offensive (see Bloch 1967: 136–68). These strategies were all aimed at developing economic coercion and, if successful, tended to transform the social relations of production. Regardless of legal or customary rights, the peasants' effective possession of the land was being expropriated. Each lord pushed toward exclusivity of land possession. This was the first route toward capitalism.

But after the famines and plagues of the first half of the fourteenth century, relative product and factor values were reversed. The peasants were now favored. Land was now abundant and labor scarce. Peasants lengthened their leases, and villeins acquired exclusive rights to their land with greater possibility of capital accumulation. They could acquire a surplus and use part of it to pay off any dues in kind or cash, rather than in labor services. The more favored ones in terms of the extent and quality of their land would eventually acquire capital equipment and hire laborers with poorer lands themselves. These rich "kulak" peasants developed what is often called a "petty mode of production," increasingly using the factors of production, including poorer-peasant labor, as commodities. This is the second rich-peasant route to exclusive private property and to capitalism (emphasized, e.g., by Dobb 1976: 57–97). Most historians accept both that the peasantry played a large role in the growth in medieval productivity and that this growth led to a differentiation among the peasantry that stimulated early capital accumulation (e.g., Bridbury 1975). It is a reminder of the decentralized nature of the feudal dynamic.

Eventually these two tendencies and social groupings (lords and rich peasants) merged, destroying the two-class structure of lords and peasants, and replacing it with two new classes, a minority of exclusive property holders and the mass of landless laborers – capitalist farmers and rural proletariat. The market ceased to be primarily an instrument of the class of lords and became an instrument of property and capital in general. That is a description of the transition from the feudal mode of production to the capitalist mode.

But before that could occur, one other possibility inherent in the feudal mode was played out. For if the feudal mode gave to the lords a monopoly of the means of physical violence, could they not respond with military force at times when relative product and factor values did not favor them? In particular, would a relative labor shortage necessarily enhance the bargaining power of the peasantry? Why did not extraeconomic coercion, monopolized by the lords, decide the issue? This is not an idle question, for in many other times and places the response of lords to labor shortages has been to increase the dependency of their laborers. We saw this occur in Chapter 9 in the later Roman Empire, and the result was economic stagnation. The immediate answer to these questions is that the European lords did try repression and they nominally succeeded, but to no avail. Returning to the example of late-fourteenth-century labor shortages, there was a wave of landlord reaction. The lords attempted with violence and legislation to tie the peasantry to the manor and to keep down wages (just as late Roman landlords had). All across Europe the peasantry rose up in rebellion, and everywhere (except Switzerland) they were repressed. But their lords' victory proved hollow. The lords were compelled not by the peasants but by the transformed capitalist market and by opportunities for profit, and threat of loss, within it. The weak state could not implement legislation without the local cooperation of the lords; it *was* the lords. And individual lords gave in, leased out their demesnes, and converted labor services into money rents. Anderson concludes his survey of this "general crisis of feudalism" with the statement: "The demesne tilled by servile labour was an anachronism in France, England, Western Germany, Northern Italy and most of Spain by 1450" (1974a: 197–209). The feudal mode of production was finally broken by the market.

Now that would be a deeply unsatisfying sentence – if we stopped the explanation there. Neoclassical economists do leave it there, because they assume the existence of a market in the first place. The "market variant" of Marxism (e.g., Sweezy 1976) also leaves it there, because it has emerged only from empirical sensitivity to the medieval world, not from a theoretical awareness of markets as forms of social organization. Orthodox Marxists reply that production precedes exchange and therefore that production relations determine market forces. But this is untrue. The issue is not the mere fact of production relations, but their *form*. Market opportunities can easily influence the form of production relations, and of social relations in general, as we saw in Chapter 7 in the cases of Phoenicia and Greece. In this case market opportunities, originally the creation of a feudal, Christian ruling class, then acted back upon the class, even though it possessed a monopoly of physical force. The market is itself a form of social organization, a mobilization of collective and distributive power. It is not eternal; it requires explanation. The argument of this chapter has provided the beginnings of that explanation – only the beginnings, however, because in reaching to the fourteenth-century crisis I have run ahead of my story. In the next chapter I shall show how towns and states furthered normative pacification and markets in Europe.

Conclusion: an explanation of the European dynamic

As promised, I have fleshed out the multiple, acephalous federation of medieval Europe. Medieval dynamism, which primarily took the form of a drive toward capitalist development, was mainly attributable to two aspects of this structure. Frist, the multiplicity of power networks and the absence of monopolistic control over them conferred a large degree of local autonomy on medieval social groups. Second, these local groups could operate safely within the extensive networks and normative pacification provided by Christendom, even though Christendom was itself split between being an immanent ideology of ruling-class morale and a more transcendent, classless ideology. Thus paradoxically localism did not stifle an outward, expansionist orientation, but took the form of intense, regulated, class-riven competition.

These paradoxes of localism and expansionism and of class conflict, competition, and order are the crux of the dynamism of the inventions of the age. Medieval Europeans were primarily concerned with intensively exploiting their own locality. They penetrated deeper into heavier, wetter, soils than any previous agrarian people. They harnessed more effectively the energy of their animals. They struck a more productive balance between animals and crops. Their economic praxis was enhanced, and this proved one of the decisive power reorganizations of world history. New tracks were being laid not just for Europe but for the world. The image is of small groups of peasants and lords standing looking at their fields, tools, and animals, figuring out how to improve them, with their backs to the world, relatively unconcerned with more extensive techniques and social organization in the secure knowledge that these were already available at a minimally acceptable level. Their praxis found "ready-made" extensive circuits, and their combination implied a revolutionary increase in the organizational capacities of economic power.

Let us note two particular implications of those circuits of praxis. First, they were relatively popular. They involved the mass of the population in autonomous economic activity and innovation and in extensive class struggle. This was the first time such a level of popular participation in power relations had occurred over such an extensive area – as is frequently noted by comparative historians (e.g., McNeill 1963: 558). It was to be the bedrock of the class-riven democracy of the modern era. Second, they offered a conducive intellectual environment for the growth of what we know as the natural sciences – penetrating beneath the phenomenal appearance of nature in the secure expectation that its physical, chemical, and biological properties will be ordered, but by dynamic as well as eternal laws. Medieval agriculture fostered dynamism and the penetration of nature; Christian natural-law theory provided the security of natural order. In both these areas of popular participation and science we find the same fruitful combination of intensive concern and extensive confidence.

The medieval dynamic was strong, sustained, and pervasive. It may have been implanted as early as A.D. 800. The Domesday Book, with its profusion of water mills, documents its presence in England by 1086. The transition that saw Europe leap forward was not primarily the late-medieval transition from feudalism to capitalism. That process was largely the institutionalization of a leap that had occurred much earlier, in the period that only our lack of documentation leads us to label the Dark Ages. By A.D. 1200 that leap, that dynamic, was already taking western Europe to new heights of collective social power. In the next chapter we shall see how it began to take a different shape after that date.

Bibliography

Abercrombie, N., S. Hill, and B. Turner. 1980. *The Dominant Ideology Thesis.* London: Allen & Unwin.
Anderson, P. 1974a. *Passages from Antiquity to Feudalism.* London: New Left Books.
 1974b. *Lineages of the Absolutist State.* London: New Left Books.
Banaji, J. 1976. The peasantry in the feudal mode of production: towards an economic model. *Journal of Peasant Studies,* vol. 3.
Barley, M. W. (ed.). 1977. *European Towns: Their Archaeology and Early History.* London: Academic Press.
Bloch, M. 1962. *Feudal Society.* London: Routledge & Kegan Paul.
 1967. *Land and Work in Medieval Europe.* London: Routledge & Kegan Paul.
Brenner, R. 1976. Agrarian class structures and economic development in pre-industrial Europe. *Past and Present,* 76.
Bridbury, A. R. 1975. *Economic Growth: England in the Later Middle Ages.* London: Harvester Press.

Bronowski, J. 1973. *The Ascent of Man*. Boston: Little, Brown.

Brown, P. 1981. *The Cult of the Saints*. London: SCM Press.

Brutzkus, J. 1943. Trade with Eastern Europe, 800–1200. *Economic History Review*, 13.

Burke, P. 1979. *Popular Culture in Early Modern Europe*. London: Temple Smith.

Chaunu, P. 1969. *L'expansion européenne du XIIIe au XVe siècle*. Paris: Presses Universitaires de France.

Cipolla, C. M. 1976. *Before the Industrial Revolution*. London: Methuen.

Cowdrey, H. 1970. The Peace and the Truce of God in the eleventh century. *Past and Present*, no. 46.

Dobb, M. 1946. *Studies in the Development of Capitalism*. London: Routledge.

    1976. A reply. From feudalism to capitalism. In *The Transition from Feudalism to Capitalism*, ed. R. Hilton. London: New Left Books.

Duby, G. 1974. *The Early Growth of the European Economy: Warriors and Peasants from the Seventh to the Twelfth Centuries*. London: Weidenfeld & Nicolson.

Ginzburg, C. 1980. *The Cheese and the Worms: The Cosmos of a Sixteenth-century Miller*. London: Routledge & Kegan Paul.

Goody, J. 1983. *The Development of the Family and Marriage in Europe*. Cambridge: Cambridge University Press.

Hajnal, J. 1965. European marriage patterns in perspective. In *Population in History*, ed. D. V. Glass and D. E. C. Everley. London: Arnold.

Hilton, R. 1976. *The Transition from Feudalism to Capitalism*. London: New Left Books.

Hindess, B., and P. Q. Hirst. 1975. *Pre-capitalist Modes of Production*. London: Routledge & Kegan Paul.

Hintze, O. 1968. The nature of feudalism. In *Lordship and Community in Medieval Europe*, ed. F. L. Cheyette. New York: Holt, Rinehart & Winston.

Hodgen, M. T. 1939. Domesday water mills. *Antiquity*, vol. 13.

Hodges, R. 1982. *Dark Age Economics*. London: Duckworth.

Holton, R. 1984. *The Transition from Feudalism to Capitalism*. London: Macmillan.

Jones, E. L. 1981. *The European Miracle*. Cambridge: Cambridge University Press.

Langland, W. 1966. *Piers the Ploughman*. Harmondsworth, England: Penguin Books.

Le Roy Ladurie, E. 1980. *Montaillou*. Harmondsworth, England: Penguin Books.

Leighton, A. C. 1972. *Transport and Communication in Early Medieval Europe*. Newton Abbot, England: David & Charles.

Lennard, R. 1959. *Rural England 1086–1135*. London: Oxford University Press.

Lloyd, T. H. 1982. *Alien Merchants in England in the High Middle Ages*. Brighton: Harvester Press.

McEvedy, C., and R. Jones. 1978. *Atlas of World Population History*. Harmondsworth, England: Penguin Books.

McFarlane, A. 1978. *The Origins of English Individualism*. Oxford: Blackwell

McNeill, W. 1963. *The Rise of the West*. Chicago: University of Chicago Press.

Marx, K. 1972. *Capital*, vol. III. London: Lawrence & Wishart.

Needham, J. 1963. Poverties and triumphs of Chinese scientific tradition. In *Scientific Change*, ed. A. C. Crombie. New York: Basic Books.

North, D. C., and R. P. Thomas. 1973. *The Rise of the Western World: A New Economic History*. Cambridge: Cambridge University Press.

Painter, S. 1943. *Studies in the History of the English Feudal Barony*. Baltimore: Johns Hopkins University Press.

Postan, M. 1975. *The Medieval Economy and Society*. Harmondsworth, England: Penguin Books.

Russell, J. C. 1948. *British Medieval Population.* Albuquerque: University of New Mexico Press.

Shennan, J. H. 1974. *The Origins of the Modern European State* 1450–1725. London: Hutchinson.

Slicher van Bath, B. H. 1963. Yield ratios, 810–1820. *A.A.G. Bijdragen,* 10.

Southern, R. W. 1970. *Western Society and the Church in the Middle Ages.* London: Hodder & Stoughton.

Sweezy, P. 1976. A critique. In *The Transition from Feudalism to Capitalism,* ed. R. Hilton. London: New Left Books.

Takahashi, K. 1976. A contribution to the discussion. In *The Transition from Feudalism to Capitalism,* ed. R. Hilton. London: New Left Books.

Trevor-Roper, H. 1965. *The Rise of Christian Europe.* London: Thames & Hudson.

Tuchman, B. W. 1979. *A Distant Mirror: The Calamitous Fourteenth Century.* Harmondsworth, England: Penguin Books.

Vergruggen, J. F. 1977. *The Art of Warfare in Western Europe during the Middle Ages.* Amsterdam: North-Holland.

White, L., Jr. 1963. What accelerated technological progress in the Western Middle Ages. In *Scientific Change,* ed. A. C. Crombie, New York: Basic Books.

1972. The Expansion of Technology 500–1500. In *The Fontana Economic History of Europe: The Middle Ages,* ed. C. M. Cipolla. London: Fontana.

Wrigley, E. A., and R. S. Schofield. 1981. *The Population History of England, 1541– 1871.* London: Arnold.

13 The European dynamic: II. The rise of coordinating states, 1155–1477

In the late twelfth century the multiple, acephalous federation described in the preceding chapter began a long collapse. Eventually, by 1815, western European power networks had taken a different form: a segmentary series of quasi-unitary networks, spreading over the entire globe. The units were the major "national" states and their colonies and spheres of influence. This chapter explains the beginnings of their rise and their interpenetration with the dynamic forces described in the preceding chapter.

I describe two main phases. In the first, discussed in this chapter, a mixture of economic, military, and ideological forces pushed into prominence a set of "co-ordinated," centralized, territorial states. Central states (normally monarchies), pushing outward from their core role as guarantor of rights and privileges, gradually coordinated some of the main activities of their territories. Local and transnational forms of Christian and "feudal" regulation declined in the face of national political regulation. But the degree of local autonomy remained considerable, so the "real" political constitution was still a form of territorial federalism, cemented by particularistic, often dynastic relations between monarch and semiautonomous lords. I take this phase up to 1477, a significant date not for English history but because it saw the collapse of the last great alternative "feudal" state, the duchy of Burgundy. In the second phase, reserved for the next chapter, these territorially centered relationships began to take an "organic" form in which the state was the centralized organizer of a ruling class.

My most general argument can be expressed in terms of the model of Chapter 1. European dynamism, now primarily economic, threw up a number of emergent interstitial networks of interaction for which a form of organization that was *centralized* and *territorial* was distinctly useful. In the competitive structure of Europe, some states lit upon this solution and prospered. There the power of the state, centralized and territorial, was enhanced.

I enter this argument in a simple fashion, however. In the case of England we possess a marvelous data source. From 1155 onward we possess enough of the financial records of the English state to glimpse its expenditure patterns and, more important, to construct a more or less continuous time series of its total revenue account. I discuss the nature of the state during a period of eight centuries with the aid of a series of statistical tables.

We can start our analysis of the rise of the state knowing what the state spent its money on and how it raised that money. Expenditures give us an indicator, though not a perfect one, of the functions of the state, whereas revenue indicates its relationship to the various power groupings who compose its "civil society." In this period we have to use a slightly indirect method for establishing the former. There are two ways of deducing the quantitative significance of each state function from financial accounts. The more direct way would be to break down expenditure accounts into their main components. I shall do this for the period after 1688 in the next chapter. Unfortunately, the earlier expenditure accounts are usually insufficient for this purpose. But from 1155 revenue accounts are sufficient to construct a time series. Thus the second method of assessing state functions is to analyze revenue totals through time, explaining their systematic variations in terms of changing demands made upon the state. This will be my principal method up to 1688.

The method allows us insight into some of the major issues of state theory. These will be discussed in Volume III over a greater time perspective than this chapter covers. For the moment, it suffices to recall that state theory has been split into two camps asserting fundamentally opposed views of state functions. The dominant state theory in the Anglo-Saxon tradition has seen the fundamental role of the state as *economic* and *domestic:* The state regulates, judicially and repressively, the economic relationships between individuals and classes located within its boundaries. Writers as diverse as Hobbes, Locke, Marx, Easton, and Poulantzas have roughly operated with this view. But the dominant state theory of the Germanic world has been quite different, seeing the state's role as fundamentally *military* and *geopolitical:* States mediate the power relations between themselves, and because these are largely normless, they do so by military force. This view, now unfashionable in the liberal and Marxian era of nuclear stalemate, was once dominant, especially through the work of Gumplowicz, Oppenheimer, Hintze, and – to a lesser degree – Weber. Who is correct over this period of history?

It would be absurd to adhere to one of these perspectives to the total exclusion of the other. Obviously states perform both sets of functions and in relation to both the domestic and geopolitical arenas. After establishing the crude historical importance of the two sets of functions, I attempt to relate them in a more theoretically informed way. My overall conclusion is presented in Chapter 15.

Revenue sources and functions of the twelfth-century state

The first receipts have been analyzed by Ramsay (1925). His research has been subjected to considerable criticism.[1] But here I use his figures, supple-

---

[1]For discussion of the data sources, see Mann 1980.

Table 13.1. *The revenues of Henry II, financial years 1171–2 and 1186–7*

	1171–2		1186–7	
Revenue source	£	%	£	%
Rents from crown lands	12,730	60	15,120	62
Rents from vacant bishoprics	4,168	20	2,799	11
Scutage (i.e., war levy)	2,114	10	2,203	9
Tallages (tax on towns and crown tenants)	—	0	1,804	7
Amercements (legal fines and dues)	1,528	7	1,434	6
Fines (gifts to king for favors)	664	3	1,219	5
Total revenue	21,205	100	24,582	100

Source: Ramsay 1925: I, 195.

mented by the work of later writers,[2] for a simple purpose, on which the criticisms have little bearing. I establish the principal sources of revenue of the twelfth-century state, so as to say something about the relationship of the state to its "civil society."

The revenues of Henry II (1154–89) survive in some detail. Table 13.1 contains the figures for two well-documented years. They illustrate the functions and powers of a relatively strong twelfth-century king. Total revenue was tiny – whatever the king's functions, they involved few officials and little money. The size of the "bureaucracy" exceeded only slightly that of the households of the chief barons and clerics. Soon afterward, King John (1199–1216) estimated that his own budget was smaller than that of the archbishop of Canterbury (Painter 1951: 131).

The bulk of revenue came from crown lands, that is, from the king's "private sources." This was to remain so until Edward I developed extensive customs revenues in the 1270s and could still reappear later whenever a king tried to "live of his own," that is, without financial and political consultations with external groups. Henry VII was the last English king to do this with success, at the beginning of the sixteenth century. Other European monarchs were generally more reliant on their own estates, notably the French until the fifteenth century, the Spanish until the bullion of the New World began to flow in the sixteenth century, and the Prussian into the late eighteenth century. This private-revenue domain was paralleled in expenditure, where a large item was always the cost of the king's own household. Thus our first real

[2]Principal works used in this section are Poole 1951; McKisack 1959; Powicke 1962; Wolffe 1971; Miller 1972, 1975; Braun 1975; and Harris 1975.

glimpse into the nature of state activities reveals an absence of public functions and a large private element. The monarch was the greatest magnate
(primus inter pares) and had larger personal income and expenses than others;
and the state, though autonomous from "civil society," had little power over
it.

The second most important source of Henry II's revenue was his right to
enjoy the rents and tithes of vacant bishoprics. This is an example of "feudal
prerogatives," which all European princes possessed. They reveal an internal
protection function, in this case confined to crises affecting the monarch's
own class. When bishoprics were vacated or when heirs to estates were minors
or women, their succession needed royal guarantee. In return the prince received
the whole or part of the rents or tithes of the estates until the heir came of age
or married. A second prerogative related to the prince's own succession: He
was entitled to levy his subjects for the knighting of his eldest son and the
marrying of his eldest daughter. These "feudal" sources of revenue were
common throughout Europe (although the monarch's powers over bishoprics
was controversial everywhere). They were an erratic source of income unless
the prince exploited them (e.g., by refusing to marry off heiresses, as the
Magna Carta asserts that King John did). They derived from the primus inter
pares role of the king – accepted as arbiter and pacifier among his own class
at times of uncertainty.

The third source derived from judicial authority, both the formal profits of
justice ("amercements" in Table 13.1) and the bribes ("fines") for the king's
favor. Favors were varied: to reverse a judicial decision, to grant an office, to
arrange a marriage, to grant a trade or production monopoly, to excuse from
military service, and to do many other things. Favors and fines ware dispersed
through a system of courts with jurisdiction over a territorially defined area,
the realm of England. There were still three areas of doubtful jurisdiction:
over the secular affairs of the clergy, over minor offenses (largely within the
competence of manorial and other autonomous courts), and over the domains
of vassals who also owed allegiance to another prince.

The twelfth century had seen considerable advance in the territoriality of
justice, in England and elsewhere. It constituted the first state-building phase
in Europe. The first stable institutions of state were the high courts of justice
(and the treasuries, of course). The first officials were the reeves and shire
reeves of England, the prévôts of France, and the ministerials of Germany.
Why?

Strayer (1970: 10–32) notes three relevant factors upon which I will
embroider. First, the church supported a judicial role for the state. Christ had
only claimed to institute a specialized *ecumene*. Secular affairs were left to
secular authorities, to whom the church enjoined obedience. After about A.D.
1000 the whole of Europe was Christianized, and papal support for the state
was felt more evenly.

Second, by about the same date, significant population migrations had ceased, allowing a sense of continuity in space and time to develop among local populations. Territorial propinquity and temporal stability have been the historically normal basis of establishing social norms and judicial rules. The ability of Christendom to provide a degree of translocal normative pacification had resulted from a quite unusual situation: the intermingling of diverse peoples in the same local spaces, all of whom yet wanted to acquire the wider civilization that Christendom possessed. If these populations settled down, intermarried, and interacted over, say, a century, they would require more elaborated local, territorially based rules and norms. An important part of settling down was the gradual emergence of the new territorial languages of Europe. I later chart the development of English. Moreover, a second phase of population stabilization (not mentioned by Strayer) was the conquest of Europe's internal frontiers. Shortly after 1150, no significant virgin spaces were left. Settled populations owing allegiance, even if only temporarily, to one state or another covered the western part of the continent. Although the church still possessed normative powers, these were checked at the states' boundaries. The most spectacular check occurred in the fourteenth century with a papal schism. One pope, in Avignon, was supported by the French crown; the other, in Rome, depended on the German emperor and the king of England. All the states concerned were aware of a contradiction between their desire for Christendom to be reunited and their realpolitik interest in weakening the papacy.

Third, Strayer argues that the secular state was the most efficient provider of peace and security, which "in an age of violence most men sought above everything else." This begs two questions. The first is that in some areas it was not clear *which* state would provide peace and security. There was a great deal of contested dynastic terrain – including the whole of western France, contested by the English and French crowns.

The progress of the Hundred Years' War is instructive as to the powers of the state. Once the French realized (after the battle of Poitiers) that they would probably lose major pitched battles, they avoided them. When attacked, they retreated into their castles and walled towns.[3] The war settled into a series of *chevauchées*, "war rides," in which a small English or French army would raid into enemy territory taxing, pillaging, and killing. The *chevauchées* demonstrated to the opposing crown's vassals that their present liege lord could not provide them with peace and security, and hopefully detach them. By the end of the war, much of France would have been better off without either crown, but this option was not available. In the end the French version of "peace and security" won. The logistical barrier of the English Channel prevented the English from supporting their French, Breton, and Gascon vassals

---

[3]Agincourt, 1415, was the exception; but the French had reason to think they could win. Henry V had been trying to avoid battle because of his troops' weakness. On the Hundred Years' War, see Fowler 1971, 1980, and Lewis 1968.

on a routine basis or from mobilizing the large permanent forces needed for sustained sieges. Gradually the French crown's guarantee of the dense network of local customs, rights, and prerogatives crept westward and southward from its Ile-de-France core. English raiding could only briefly, though nastily, interrupt this. Perhaps also there arose the first stirrings of French "nationalism" where core areas of France shared an "ethnic community" with the French king and hostility to the English. But as Lewis (1968: 59–77) concludes, this was really the *result* of a prolonged war that confirmed that the rule of the two crowns was territorial rather than dynastic. In any case, "ethnic community" was built on top of a common interest in the stability of judicial rules and customs. Where territorial states existed, however fragile they seemed, they were difficult to dislodge from their core. Usurpers and invaders generally fared badly in the period following the Norman expansions, because they threatened established customs. It was easier for Christendom and Islam to dislodge each other's states than it was to change the geopolitical order of Christendom itself. But the Hundred Years' War revealed a creeping consolidation of judicial sovereignty into larger, if still weak, territorial states, caused partly by the logistics of warfare.

But territorial states did not exist everywhere. From Flanders through eastern France and western Germany to Italy and such Mediterranean coastline as remained Christian, different political institutions prevailed. Counts, dukes, and even kings shared power here with urban institutions, especially independent communes and bishoprics. And this was also an economically dynamic area. This raises the second question begged by Strayer. Not all economic development had as yet required state pacification, as he suggests. If it now did, then this resulted from new characteristics of the economy. Economic development brought *new* pacification requirements.

These requirements were more elaborate and mainly technical: how to organize markets, how to honor specific but repetitive contracts, how to arrange land sales in a society in which they had been hitherto rare, how to guarantee movable property, how to organize the raising of capital. The church had not dealt extensively with such matters: In the Roman Empire they had been the concern of the state and of private law; in the Dark Ages they had not been problematic. The church had little tradition of service in this field, and indeed some of its doctrine was not particularly helpful (e.g., usury laws). Most of these technical issues were territorially extensive in their scope, and though the state was not the only power agency that could step into the breach (associations of merchants and townsfolk did so, e.g., in Italy and Flanders), where large states already existed, their relative extensiveness was well suited to them. Hence by common consent, without really oppressing anyone, most larger states began to play a greater regulatory role in economic matters, especially property rights, and were intimately concerned with extensive economic growth. But in this they were largely reacting: The initial dynamism of development came from elsewhere, from the decentralized forces identified in the last chapter. If the states *had* provided the initial infrastructure for development, they would have been assuredly more powerful than they actually were, either in this or in later centuries.

The judicial extension of the state had not gone very far. The organization of justice in this century must be viewed somewhat skeptically. In the reign of John we find a rather tragic instance in the Fine Roll that records that "the wife of Hugh de Neville gives the lord king 200 hens that she may lie one night with her husband." The delivery of the hens was actually arranged, in time for Easter, so we may presume that the lady was satisfied.

John's eccentricities offer a corrective to modern views of judicial systems. Henry II had advanced the centralization, reliability, and "formal rationality" of the English judicial system. Yet it was still milked as a source of wealth, and patronage and corruption were inseparable from justice. The justices, sheriffs, and bailiffs who staffed the provincial administrative machinery were only weakly controlled by the king. I deal with these logistics of authoritative power later in the chapter.

Other states had even less control over their local agents and lords than did the relatively unitary conquest state of Norman England. Elsewhere most judicial functions were not exercised by the state but by local lords and clerics. The impetus to greater centralization generally came from conquest, as it did in France after the great expansion of Philip Augustus (1180–1223), and in Spain as each province was wrested from Islam. By 1200, princes like the kings of England, France, and Castile and the emperor of Germany had brought a measure of judicial control over the territories under their suzerainty. But this takes us into the second state-building phase, just beginning in Henry II's time and revealed in his revenue.

The final source of revenue in Table 13.1 is the taxation represented by tallages and scutage. It reveals the second public function of the state: making international war. Apart from the feudal-succession item referred to earlier, the English crown possessed rights of taxation for one purpose only: "urgent necessity," which meant war. This was not to change until the 1530s. Princes were charged with the defense of the realm, and this involved contributions from their subjects. But each contribution tended to be raised in a different and ad hoc manner. And mostly princes requested not monies but service in person – the feudal levy. In a conquered kingdom like England this could be systematically organized: x number of knights and soldiers provided to the levy for every y area or z value of land held in theory from the king.

Throughout the twelfth century several tendencies undermined the military effectiveness of the levy and led to the second phase of growth in state power. Complex inheritance patterns, especially the fragmentation of holdings, made assessment of military obligation increasingly difficult. Some lords lived in peaceful surroundings, and their levies were increasingly militarily useless. In the late twelfth century the character of warfare also changed as the space of Europe became filled with organized states – now campaigns were longer, involving prolonged siegework. In England, the feudal levy served without pay for two months (and only 30 days in peacetime): after that, their cost fell upon the king. Thus at the end of the twelfth century, princes began to need more money for warfare at the same time as some of their subjects were less willing to turn out in person. Expedients such as scutage (a payment in lieu of providing one's *scutum* – shield), and tallage, a tax on the towns (urban groups being less warlike) were the compromise result.

The state loomed rather larger in the urban sector. The absence of absolute private-property rights meant that land transactions involved cumbersome negotiations sealed by an independent authority, in this case the king. As the towns attracted considerable immigration during the economic expansion of these centuries, the king could expect sizable revenue from land transactions there. Second, the king's role of external protector had particular relevance to international "alien" traders. The king received payment from them in return for protection (Lloyd 1982). The two powers combined to exercise considerable state regulation of merchant guilds in the thirteenth and fourteenth centuries. We shall see that the town-state alliance secured by law the normative pacification begun by the church.

Outside the urban sector, the economic activities of states were still restricted. True, the English monarchy did attempt intermittently to regulate the prices and quality of basic foodstuffs, though it did so in collaboration with local lords. Such regulation became tighter, and applied also to wages, in the special circumstances of the late fourteenth century after the Black Death. In general, however, the state provided few of the infrastructural supports to the economy we found in ancient empires. For example, England did not possess a uniform coinage until the 1160s and France until 1262, and no country possessed uniform weights and measures until the nineteenth century. Compulsory cooperation had been swept aside by Christendom's normative pacification, and the European state never recovered it.

Thus the state loomed little larger than the greatest clerics or magnates. These first revenue accounts reveal a small state living off "protection rent" (Lane 1966: 373–428). External defense and aggression, and the preservation of basic public order, were the overwhelming public functions, and even they were partly decentralized. This picture is still consistent with that painted in the last chapter, of a weak, if now territorialized, state lacking monopoly powers. By 1200, however, two things were beginning to threaten this form of rule. The first was the development of a new military rationale that fostered state territoriality. The second was the problem of pacification between territorial states. Groups acting in that space – especially merchants – would turn increasingly toward the state for protection and in so doing enhance its power. We can see both trends by constructing a time series of total revenue from 1155 onward.

Trends in revenue totals, 1155–1452

In this section I present in Table 13.2 the first part of my time series of revenue totals. The first column of figures gives the actual revenue at current prices. I also adjusted the revenue totals for inflation by calculating constant prices based on their 1451–75 level. Inflation-proof figures also have limitations in meaning. If prices are rising, the monarch will need to raise additional monies and his subjects will doubtless squeal even if in real terms the extraction rate is unchanged. Thus both sets of figures have real, if partial, significance.

First, the price index reveals that in about 1200 prices began to rise sharply, perhaps almost doubling during John's reign and only falling back slightly thereafter. Toward 1300 they rose again, this time for almost a century, again falling slightly thereafter. Direct comparison between revenue totals of different periods has its limitations. Let us take separately current and constant price data.

Revenue at current prices rose throughout almost the whole period. Except for the first decade of Henry II's reign (before he had effectively restored central authority after the anarchy of Stephen's reign), the first substantial increase occurred under John. Then it fell back slightly until Edward I's accession. Then a steady upward trend ensued for a century until Richard II, after which decline ensued (interrupted by Henry V), which lasted until the Tudors. Those kings requiring large increases in revenue were John, the first three Edwards (especially I and III), and Henry V. Additionally, Henry III, Richard II, and Henry IV each managed to maintain most of the rise of his immediate predecessor.

Switching to constant prices, the overall increase is not so steady. In real terms John's exaction increased, though not as greatly as his money exactions, and they are unmatched until Edward III, whose long reign saw a continuously high rate of extraction. Its maintenance (and increase) under Richard II is something of an artifact, contributed by falling prices rather than an increase in money revenue. Henry V still emerges as a revenue-increasing king, and the low revenues of the kings of the Wars of the Roses are also still evident. But in real terms the financial size of the English state reached a peak in the fourteenth century. It did not actually grow substantially thereafter until the late seventeenth century, when it rocketed once again (as we see in the next chapter). These are the trends we must now explain.

Table 13.2. *English state finances, 1155–1452: average annual revenue at current and constant (1451–75) prices*

Reign	Years	Annual revenue in £ (000) Current	Constant	Price index
Henry II	1155–66	12.2	—	—
	1166–77	18.0	60.0	30
	1177–88	19.6	55.9	35
Richard I	1188–98	17.1	60.9	28
John	1199–1214	37.9	71.5	53
Henry !II	1218–29	31.1	39.4	79
	1229–40	34.6	54.1	64
	1240–51	30.3	43.2	70
	1251–62	32.0	40.5	79
	1262–72	24.0	26.7	90
Edward I	1273–84	40.0	40.0	100
	1285–95	63.2	67.9	93
	1295–1307	53.4	41.1	130
Edward II	1316–24	83.1	54.3	153
Edward III	1328–40	101.5	95.8	106
	1340–51	114.7	115.9	99
	1351–63	134.9	100.0	135
	1363–75	148.4	103.8	143
Richard II	1377–88	128.1	119.7	107
	1389–99	106.7	99.7	107
Henry IV	1399–1410	95.0	84.8	112
Henry V	1413–22	119.9	110.0	109
Henry VI	1422–32	75.7	67.0	113
	1432–42	74.6	67.2	111
	1442–52	54.4	55.5	98

Sources: Revenue: 1155–1375, Ramsay 1925 with correction factor added; 1377–1452, Steel 1954. *Price index:* 1166–1263, Farmer 1956, 1957; 1264 onward, Phelps-Brown and Hopkins 1956. For further details of all sources and calculations, see Mann 1980. These figures are directly comparable with those given in Table 14.1.

Revenue and expenditure, John to Henry V

The reign (1189–99) of Richard I, the Lion-Hearted, produced little change. Though Richard waged war throughout his reign, he generally did so with the feudal levy and with ad hoc requests for financial aid. During his reign, however, the papacy raised levies on all lay and ecclesiastical revenues (under threat of excommunication) throughout Europe to finance the Crusades in 1166 and 1188.

The precedent was not lost on Richard's more astute half brother and successor, John. By 1202–3 John's estimated total revenue had risen sixfold to about £134,000, of which a national tax of one-seventh the value of all movable property contributed £110,000. In John's reign (1199–1216) average annual revenue more than doubled over the receipts of Henry II. Controlling for inflation makes the increase less dramatic, but it is the larger increase that John actually extracted. He did so principally through taxation, which contributed over half his revenue and which was increasingly levied in a uniform way over most of the population. Why the increase in his reign?

John's conflict with the church (which provided all the chroniclers) ensured that he received the worst press of any English king. Yet two extraneous factors at the beginning of his reign, disastrous harvests and galloping, little-understood inflation, set him laboring under an insupportable burden. John could not weather these storms by muddling through a period of mounting debt and reduced state activity (as did his successor Henry III). His French possessions were under attack from the resurgent French crown, and they were indeed mostly lost. The character of warfare was changing, becoming more professional and more costly. His needs for funds to pay troops precipitated increased revenue, as for all thirteenth-century kings (and those of subsequent centuries, as we shall see). The fluctuations in Ramsay's thirteenth-century data are consistent.In 1224–5, revenue trebled over the previous year; in 1276–7, it doubled; in 1281–2, it trebled; in 1296–7, it doubled – all occasioned by the onset of war.

Such pressures were not unique to England. By the late twelfth century over Europe as a whole the number of knights (and retainers) equipping themselves was equaled by that of mercenary knights requiring payment. Financial strain was felt by the government of thirteenth-century Flemish towns (Verbruggen 1977), by the commune of Siena from 1286 (Bowsky 1970: 43–6), by fourteenth-century Florence (de la Roncière 1968; Waley 1968), and by France in the thirteenth to fifteenth centuries (Strayer and Holt 1939; Rey 1965; Henneman, 1971; Wolfe 1972). From the end of the twelfth century until the sixteenth, European armies combined professional with levy elements, and they were in the field for longer. After that they became fully professional – England included. And during the thirteenth century, their size, and their size relative to the population, increased dramatically.[4] Such warfare necessitated cash. Loans from Jews and foreign bankers and merchants were resorted to by all the princes, but as temporary expedients. By the reign of Edward I taxation was normal, as Table 13.3 reveals.

The most obvious trend is the overall increase in revenue, doubling in a hundred years. But substantial changes have also occurred in sources of income. The first of these categories, "hereditary crown revenue," is heterogeneous,

---

[4]Sorokin estimated the increase in army size relative to total population between 1150 and 1250 at between 48 and 63 percent for four European countries (1962: 340–1).

Table 13.3. *Average annual sources of revenue in three reigns, 1272–1307 and 1327–99 (in percent)*

Revenue source	Edward I (1272–1307)	Edward III (1327–77)	Richard II (1377–99)
Hereditary crown revenues	32	18	28
Customs	25	46	38
Lay taxation and subsidies	24	17	25
Clerical taxation and subsidies	20	18	9
Total percent	100	100	100
Average annual total £ (current prices)[a]	63,442	105,221	126,068

[a]The totals are not consistent with the totals given in Table 13.2, which are the more reliable (see Mann 1980). The relative contribution of each type of revenue is not affected by the unreliability of the totals.
Source: Ramsay 1925: II, 86, 287, 426–7.

its two major components being rents from crown lands and the profits of justice. From the modern point of view the former are "private," the latter "public," although contemporaries did not know the distinction. The hereditary revenues remained stable in volume, and declined in proportion of the total receipts, as customs revenue and taxation increased. In 1275 Edward I first established an export duty on wool, and other customs and excise duties were soon added. This was a substantial step, not only toward adequate state financing but also toward the emergence of the unitary, territorial state. Customs duties were not imposed unilaterally but after considerable debate and conflict. Exports were taxed so that – in line with current economic theory – English resources would not be drained away abroad at a time of war. A second cause was recognition by merchants that their international activities needed military protection. Indeed, the revenue was supposed to be used for naval purposes and could not be counted as part of the king's own hereditary resources. Neither sentiment could have resulted in customs duties if traders had not felt a collective national interest and identity, an identity that probably had not existed two centuries earlier.

Other states shared a close fiscal relationship with merchants. The French crown depended heavily on taxes and loans from the merchants of Paris, as well as on taxes on highly visible objects of trade (like the infamous *gabelle,* salt tax). The Spanish crown had a special relationship with the *mesta* (sheepherders' guild). The weaker German states exploited internal tolls, with a consequent proliferation of internal customs barriers. The state-merchant alliance had a fiscal-military core.

Direct taxation formed a substantial and well-established part of fourteenth-century revenue, as Table 13.3 reveals. If we add it to the indirect customs taxes, more than half the English crown's revenue was now derived from taxation. Indeed McFarlane (1962: 6) estimates that in the whole period from 1336–1453 (i.e., of the Hundred Years' War) the English crown raised £3.25 million in direct taxes and £5 million in indirect taxes, of which the wool customs and excise duty contributed at least £4 million. Such taxes were always voted for military purposes, though we must note that military considerations had widened into the aggressive economic theory just mentioned.

So we see the same two trends: the escalation of total revenue and the growing role of taxation both linked to the costs of war. Table 13.2 revealed the jump in revenue at the beginning of the Hundred Years' War to be a real one. Again, both the sizes of armies and their sizes relative to the population were increasing in the fourteenth century (Sorokin 1962: 340–1). The character of war also changed. The knights of four major powers, Austria, Burgundy, the count of Flanders, and England, were defeated by the largely infantry armies of the Swiss, Flemish, and Scots in a series of battles between 1302 and 1315. This was followed by the massacre of Crecy in 1346, in which more than 1,500 French knights were killed by British (i.e., Welsh) bowmen. These unexpected reverses did not lead to massive changes in the international balance of power (although they preserved the independence of the Swiss, Flemish, and Scots), because the major powers reacted. Armies combined infantry, bowmen, and cavalry in increasingly complex formations. Infantries with a new independent role on the battlefield needed more drilling than the medieval infantry cast merely in a supporting role to knights. A state that sought to survive had to participate in this tactical race, which therefore escalated war costs for all.[5]

Expenditure data, available sporadically from 1224, give a more complete picture, although they are not easy to interpret. Modern uses of these accounts would have been barely comprehensible to the men who drew them up. They did not distinguish between "military" and "civil" functions or between the king's "private" household expenses and more "public" ones. At times we are uncertain which "department" has primary responsibility for expenditure. Remember that the two principal "departments" were originally the *chamber* in which the king slept and the *wardrobe* where he hung his clothes! Nevertheless, throughout the thirteenth century the expenses of the royal household remained in the £5,000–£10,000 bracket, whereas foreign and military expenses might add figures ranging from £5,000 to £100,000 per annum according to

[5]For military developments, see Finer 1975; Howard 1976:1–19; Verbruggen 1977. For vivid accounts of the humiliations of the French nobility, see Tuchman 1979.

Table 13.4. *Annual averages of expenditure accounts in 1335–7, 1344–7, and 1347–9 (current prices)*

	1335–7		1344–7		1347–9	
Expenditure	£	%	£	%	£	%
Household expenses	12,952	6	12,415	19	10,485	40
Foreign and other expenses	147,053	66	50,634	76	14,405	55
Prests (debt repayment)	63,789	29	3,760	6	1,151	54
Total	223,796[a]	100	66,810	100	26,041	100

[a] Figures given in state budgets rarely add up exactly until the mid-nineteenth century.

the situation of war or peace. Inflation was confined largely to military costs.

More accounts survive from the next century. Some of the most complete are contained in Table 13.4. The three kinds of expenditures listed in the table are the ancestors of those modern categories "civil," "military," and "debt repayment," which will figure throughout my analysis of expenditures. What can explain the enormous variations in total volume and type of state expenditure? The answer is simple: war and peace. In 1335–7 Edward III was at war, personally conducting a campaign in the Netherlands for most of the period; for part of the period 1344–7 he was again at war, in France; and in 1347–9 he was at peace in England.

These figures do not allow us to separate military from civil expenditure entirely. Although the bulk of household expenses continue when the king is at peace, his household follows him abroad on campaign and is more costly there (as the figures reveal). Similarly, "foreign and other" expenses are mostly but not entirely warlike – for example, bribes paid to wavering vassals for their allegiance or alms distributed while on campaign are difficult to categorize. Debt repayment, of loans granted usually by merchants and bankers, might also seem to straddle the distinction between civil and military, but actually these loans were invariably incurred to pay for extraordinary military expenses. Finally, if we wish to estimate the total financial size of the state in this period, we should actually add the *profits* of state activities, notably the judiciary, to expenditure. These would add around £5,000–£10,000 to the cost of civil functions.

When due allowance is made for these difficulties, we can estimate that, as in the previous century, the civil activities of the state remained fairly stable in volume, still not greatly exceeding the leading baronial household's, while the state's total outlay was enormously inflated by the onset of war. In peacetime the state's "civil" activities might comprise between a half and two-thirds of all finances, but in war they normally shrank to around 30 percent and could go as low as 10 percent. (Fullest figures are scattered through Tout's [1920–33] volumes: see also Tout and Broome 1924: 404–19, and Harris 1975: 145–9, 197–227, 327–40, 344–5, 470–503.) As perhaps half those peaceful activities were essentially "private," concerning the king's own household, the public functions of the state were largely military. If a king waged war frequently, his functions became overwhelmingly military. Henry V, more or less continuously at war, during the decade 1413–22 spent about two-thirds of his English revenues plus all his French revenues on warfare (Ramsay 1920: I, 317).

But we have still not grasped the total impact of war on state finances. Table 13.4 also reveals the beginnings of a trend that was subsequently to play a major smoothing role in state finances: debt repayment. From the fourteenth to the twentieth century, states that borrowed heavily to finance wars saw fluctuations of expenditure reduce. Debts were normally repaid over a number of years extending beyond the duration of the war. Thus peacetime expenditure did not return to prewar levels. The state was slowly, steadily increasing its real bulk. The receipts and expenses of Edward III and Richard II (1327–99) fluctuated less (except for a trebling in 1368–9). The sheer cost of war meant that debt repayment could hardly be financed out of the monarch's private or hereditary revenue. Taxation in peacetime was almost inevitable. Furthermore all these fiscal methods increased the machinery of finance itself. The costs collection became an important and a near-permanent item. The English crown minimized the political costs of taxation by deciding the rate of assessment through ad hoc consultation with the taxpayers themselves. In an age when wealth was impossible to determine, no other system was ultimately practicable. But in a relatively centralized system, such as that of fifteenth-century France, the costs of collection could add up to 25 percent or more of all revenue (Wolfe 1971:248). These were also largely the effect of war.

Clear answers are emerging from this analysis of the finances of the medieval state: It was predominantly fulfilling external *military* functions; and the growth in the financial size of the state at both current and constant prices was a product of the growing costs of war. The militarist state theorists seem vindicated. But the implications of this military-led state development will lead to a more complex conclusion.

Implication I: the emergence of the national state

Perhaps too much functionalism pervades the preceding paragraphs, implying the assumption that war was functional for the people of England as a whole. The people of England had not been a meaningful sociological entity in the early twelfth century (as we saw in Chapter 12). War advantaged an alliance between a specific "war party" and the monarch. From the beginning of the fourteenth century the superiority of a part-mercenary and mixed infantry-cavalry army over a pure feudal host was demonstrated repeatedly. Where these forces could be raised, anyone with an interest in warfare must now ally with the king, who could authorize the raising of the sums to finance such a host. There were variant forms of this pattern. In geopolitical areas where no prince could exercise such fiscal authority, smaller predominantly mercenary forces could be raised by king and local counts and dukes to preserve the status quo. And in Flanders and Switzerland the "class morale" of free burghers could be converted into a disciplined, effective infantry force to preserve their autonomy. But all variants meant the end of the feudal host.

The war party was mixed, and it varied from country to country. Two main groups can be identified. First, single-son inheritance systems established a continuous demographic pressure through land-hungry younger sons of the nobility, gentry, and yeoman groups. To them we may add other minor nobles periodically impoverished by changing economic trends. Both were nurtured by the ideology and sense of honor of the noble class in general. In England the higher nobility in general, in control of military campaigns, did quite well out of warfare (McFarlane 1973: 19–40).

The second group was composed of those interested in foreign trade – let us call them merchants, even though they might actually be major barons or clerics, or the king himself, engaged in commercial ventures. The autonomy of medieval merchants continued in its traditional heartlands of Italy, Flanders, and the trade routes between them. As Europe prospered, so their opportunities grew. In size and technical efficiency merchant and banking houses steadily developed. Double-entry bookkeeping is one invention that has often been emphasized by commentators (most notably Weber) as enabling far more precise control of far-flung activities. It seems to have been invented in the fourteenth century, although it was not widespread until near the end of the fifteenth. As Weber saw, it was not yet "capitalism." It was too devoted to the needs of the great nobility – their marriages, military expeditions, and ransoms, all requiring the movement of enormous sums of credit and goods. Thus "rational capital accounting" was devoted to particularistic needs, its logic restrained by defaulting, by the occasional inducement of a marriage alliance, or by naked coercion, in all of which the nobility excelled. In areas where territorial states were growing, the merchant and banking networks became more dependent on the single prince and more vulnerable to his defaulting. The whole of the Italian money market was shaken by Edward III's default of 1339. This was not yet a single, universal financial system, for it contained both an autonomous merchant and banking sector and a nobility and state sector embodying different principles. But national integrating mechanisms were beginning to appear.

Where states' territoriality increased, interstate relations were politically regulated. Without state protection, merchants were vulnerable to plunder abroad. It was not clear that a prince had the duty of protecting alien merchants, and they paid either direct bribes or generous "loans" (which they were aware would be periodically revoked) to him for this privilege. As state consolidation proceeded, such groups lost their autonomy as this relationship became a normal fiscal/protection one and as free territorial space disappeared in western and southwestern Europe.

Hence merchants gradually became "naturalized" in some areas in the thirteenth and fourteenth centuries. In England the Company of Staple, a native association, monopolized wool exports – the principal English export – by 1361. In return it provided the state with its most remunerative and stable source of revenue, the wool export tax. Similar fiscal/protection relations between king and merchants were emerging in all states. They were to last until the twentieth century. They had a common interest not only in defensive pacification but also in aggressive, successful warfare. In England during the Hundred Years' War a commercial war party evolved, making alliance with aggressive sections of the nobility, and even defying the efforts of Richard II (1379–99) to make peace when the war was going badly. Their main interests were to become contractors to the army and, more importantly, to bring Flanders within the orbit of the English wool trade. From now on commercial motivations, the conquest of markets as well as land, were to play a part in wars.

Another way of assessing the degree to which trade was becoming naturalized would be to calculate the proportion of total trade contributed by intranational trade. The greater that proportion, the greater the state-boundedness of economic interaction. I employ this methodology for later centuries. We cannot, however, judge the quantitative significance of international versus national trade in this period. Until the sixteenth century we have no estimates as to the total volume of imports and exports. But we have statistics on wool and cloth exports, which were a significant proportion of total exports (statistics given in Carus-Wilson and Coleman 1963). The domestic market is even more of a problem, for the vast majority of local exchanges totally escaped all official notice. Most would have been transactions in kind, not in cash. As far as the total economy was concerned, these must have been quantitatively *far* greater than long-distance trade, whether national or international, for the whole of this period. But international trade, especially wool and cloth exports, also had particular significance. First, they comprised a large proportion of the nongovernmental cash transactions in the economy, with important consequences for inflation and credit patterns. Second, because of this they were extremely visible to a government dominated by fiscal considerations. Third, they required a far higher degree of political regulation. In this way, the cloth and woolen export trades were probably the "leading edge" of a movement toward greater political naturalization of the economy, with a significance greater than their sheer size alone would have warranted.

The group most directly interested in the extension of the state was the king and his household/bureaucracy. The development of permanent fiscal machinery and mercenary armies enhance monarchical power. Whatever the interests of nobles or merchants in war or pacification, they would resist this. From the beginnings of taxation we read complaints from lords, clerics, and merchants that taxes agreed to for temporary war purposes have become permanent. Clause 41 of the Magna Carta claims freedom for merchants "from all evil tolls, except in times of war." Clause 50 undoes John's attempt to buy foreign mercenaries and immortalizes one of them: "We will remove from the bailiwicks the relations of Gerard of Athée and in future they shall hold no offices in England." The same conflicts appeared in other countries. In 1484 the French Estates General denounced the tendency for the *taille* and other taxes "instituted in the first place because of war" to become "immortal." Charles VIII replied vaguely that he needed the money "for the king to be able, as he ought to be, to undertake great things and to defend the kingdom" (quoted in Miller 1972: 350).

Virtually every dispute between a monarch and his subjects from the Magna Carta to the nineteenth century has been occasioned by the monarch's attempt to generate independently the subjects' two critical resources, taxes and military manpower, the need for the latter usually leading to the need for the former (Ardant 1975: 194–7; Braun 1975: 310–7; and Miller 1975:11). Tilly, writing about the period 1400–1800, summarizes a recurrent causal cycle in the development of the state (I have amended his fifth stage):

(1) change or expansion in armies;
(2) new state efforts to extract resources from the subject population;
(3) the development of new state bureaucracies and administrative innovations;
(4) resistance from the subject population;
(5) [renewed state coercion and/or enlargement of representative assemblies;]
(6) durable increases in the extractive bulk of the state.

Tilly concludes: "Preparation for war has been the great state-building activity. The process has been going on more or less continuously for at least five hundred years" (1975: 73–4). This is a conservative estimate as far as the time period is concerned. We shall see that the pattern, begun in England in 1199 with the accession of King John, has continued until the twentieth century. Indeed it continues today, though in association with a second more recent trend inaugurated by the Industrial Revolution.

Nevertheless, two qualifications must be made. First, the increase in the bulk of the state was hardly dramatic, as we can see from the "constant price" column of Table 13.2. State building appears rather less grand and less designed if we control for inflation. The "durable increase in the extractive bulk of the state" referred to by Tilly is a doubling over nearly five centuries – hardly impressive. True, the monarchs who presided over the real increases – John, Edward III, and Henry V so far – did so as a result of military pressures. But most of the increases at current prices, and therefore most of the political struggles of nearly all monarchs, arose from inflationary pressures. The growth of the state was less the result of conscious power aggrandizement than of desperate searches for temporary expedients to stave off fiscal disaster. The sources of the threat were less the deliberate actions of a rival power than the unintended consequences of European economic and military activity as a whole.[6] Nor was there a great shift in power between the state elite and dominant groups in "civil society." The domestic power of the state was still feeble.

The second qualification concerns the importance of taxation struggles. Conflicts between kings and subjects were not the only, or even the major, form of social conflict during this period. Quite apart from interstate conflict, there existed violent conflicts between classes and other "civil society" groups that were not directed systematically at the state or even fought over its terrain. Such conflicts usually took a religious form. Conflicts between kings and emperors and popes, heresies like the Albigensian or the Hussite, and peasant and regional revolts up to the Pilgrimage of Grace of 1534 – all mixed together varieties of grievance and varieties of territorial organization under a religious banner. Disentangling the motives of the participants is difficult, but one point is clear: Late medieval Europe still supported forms of organized struggle, including class struggle, that were not related systematically to the state either as power actor or as territorial unit. Those forms were largely religious, for the Christian church still provided a significant degree of integration (and therefore of disintegration) within Europe. Though we can hardly quantify the salience of various power struggles, the politics occurring at the level of the emerging territorial state was probably still less salient for most of the population than the politics of the locality (centering on custom and the manorial courts) and of the transnational church (and of church versus state). Insofar as we can talk of "class struggles" in the period, they were resolved without much state regulation: The state may have been *a* factor in social cohesion, but it was hardly *the* factor (as in the definition of Poulantzas 1972).

So the revolts of peasants and townsfolk, frequent as they were, could hardly take a revolutionary turn. If the state was not *the* factor in social cohesion, neither was it in social exploitation or in the solution to exploitation. Peasants and townsfolk sometimes identified the church in these roles and so became determined to transform the church by revolutionary means, replacing it (at least in their own area) with a more "primitive," priestless community of the faithful. But they looked to the state, in its medieval role of judicial arbitrator, to redress the wrongs done by others and to restore rightful customs and privileges. Even where the king had been a party to their exploitation, the rebels often attributed this to "evil," often "foreign," counselors who did not know local custom. On many occasions peasants and townsfolk at the

---

[6]In Table 13.2 (and also in Table 14.1) periods of inflation were also periods of growth in state expenditure needs. In an economy of restricted coin circulation, the state's military-fiscal needs in times of war may have *caused* inflation. This hypothesis needs testing for shorter time periods than my tables represent.

moment of victory in rebellion placed themselves in the hands of their prince – and were rewarded with death, mutilation, and further exploitation. Why did they not learn from their mistakes? Because such revolts were experienced in any one area perhaps only once in fifty or a hundred years, and between times little routine activity (other than the redress of grievances or preparation for war) focused popular attention on the state. Neither the modern state nor modern revolutions existed.

Nevertheless, throughout this period changes were occurring. One impetus was provided by economic expansion. Increasingly, the surplus of manor and village was exchanged in return for consumption goods produced in other areas. From the eleventh century onward, some areas came to be dominated by the production of a single commodity – wine, grain, wool, or even finished goods such as cloth. We do not have exact trade figures, but we guess that the expansion first increased long-distance exchange of luxuries more than it did medium-distance exchange of staples. This reinforced the transnational solidarity of the owners and consumers of these goods, the landlords and urban dwellers. At some point, however, the growth shifted toward develop- ing exchange relations within state boundaries, encouraged not only by an increase in general demand but also by the naturalization of merchants. It is much too early to talk of national markets, but in the fourteenth and fifteenth centuries a territorial core can be discerned in some of the major states – London and the Home Counties, around Paris, Old Castile – wherein growing bonds of economic interdependence and a protonationalist culture develop dialectically (Kiernan 1965: 32). It is largely in these regions that movements emerged that embodied a degree of collective class organization and con- sciousness – as did the Peasants' Revolt of 1381. Class and national con- sciousness are far from being opposites; each has been a necessary condition for the existence of the other.

Such changes were paralleled in religion. Up to the seventeenth century, grievances expressed in religious terms were paramount in social struggles; yet they took on an increasingly state-bounded form. The breakup of Europe's religious unity in the sixteenth century was predominantly into politically demarcated units. Religious wars came to be fought either by rival states or by factions who struggled over the constitution of the single, monopolistic state in which they were located. Unlike the Albigensians, the Huguenots sought toleration from a single state, France. The English Civil War molded quasi-classes and court and country parties into two sides who defined them- selves in predominantly religious terms, but they fought over the religious, political, and social destiny of *England* (plus its Celtic dependencies) as a society. As social groups have done this ever since, we can easily forget its novelty. Such "political" conflict had not dominated the medieval period.

Neither economic nor religious phenomena can in themselves explain these developments. Economic expansion tended to generate history-creating classes, but "economic factors" cannot explain why these "classes" came to have their organized power. Overt, organized class struggle depended first on ideological, religious organizations and subsequently on political, nationally bounded, organizations. Churches had schisms and religious wars, but "religious factors" cannot explain why these took an increasingly national form.

In fact the explanation required is rather less grand and depends less on conscious human action than either ideological or class explanations do. The only interest group that consciously willed the development of the national state was the state elite itself, the monarch and his creatures, who were puny and pressured by inflation. The rest – the merchants, younger sons, clerics, and eventually almost all social groups – found themselves embracing national forms of organization as a by-product of their goals and the available means of reaching them. The national state was an example of the unintended consequences of human action, of "interstitial emergence." Every time the social struggles of these groups were occasioned by tax grievances, they were pushed farther into a national mold. The political struggles of the merchants above all, but of the landed nobility and the clergy too, focused more and more at the level of the territorial state.

In this respect, the enormous increases in state revenue at current prices have genuine significance: Every attempt by the monarch to raise more revenue brought him into consultation or conflict with those who might provide the revenue. Inflation and warfare combined to accentuate the concentration of class and religious struggles in the territorial, centralized state. Two possible competing terrains of social relationships, the local and the transnational, declined in significance; the state, religion, and the economy became more intertwined; and the social geography of the modern world emerged.

But this process involved more than geography; it was beginning to generate a shared culture. The clearest indicator is the development of national vernacular languages out of the earlier combination of transnational Latin and a plethora of local tongues. In the last chapter I referred to the linguistic variety found in mid-twelfth-century England. But territorial propinquity, continuity of interaction, and political boundaries began to homogenize. By the end of the fourteenth century the merging of languages into something we know as English was proceeding among the upper classes. The major literature was still diverse. *Sir Gawain and the Green Knight,* written in the dialect of (probably) north Cheshire and south Lancashire, was in general terms Middle English, but it also incorporated Scandinavian and Norman-French words and style. John Gower wrote his three major works in Norman-French, Latin, and English (significantly, his last work was in English). Geoffrey Chaucer wrote almost entirely in English that remains half-understood today. Around 1345, Oxford grammar masters began to instruct on translation from Latin into English, instead of into French. In 1362 the use of English was authorized in the law courts for the first time. And in the 1380s and 1390s the Lollards translated and published the entire Vulgate Bible. The changes were slow – and in the case of the Lollards they were contested – but they endured. After 1450, upper-class children were learning French as an accomplishment of polite society, not as a vernacular language. The final collapse of Latin came later, paradoxically, with the revival of classical learning in the early sixteenth century – for Greek joined Latin as an accomplishment of the humanely educated gentleman, not as a vernacular – with the establishment of the English church. By 1450 the emergence of English showed where power could, and could not, stably extend. It diffused freely and universally across the territory of the national state, but it stopped at the borders (unless one state possessed enough military power over its neighbors to impose its language).

Implication II: the growth of extensive power and of the coordinated state

In the preceding chapter I argued that the dynamism of early feudal Europe, the original base of capitalist development, lay in *intensive,* local power relations. We can now chart a second phase in the development of this dynamic, an increase in extensive power, in which the state was deeply involved.

Economic growth required an extensive infrastructure quite as much as it did an intensive one. As I argued in the preceding chapter, most of this was at first contributed not by economic actors directly but by the normative pacification provided all across Europe by the Christian church – both transcendently across all social boundaries and also in the form of a "transnational" ruling-class morale. By the twelfth century, however, economic growth was generating technical problems involving more complex economic relations between strangers to which the church was more marginal. The closer relationship between markets, trade, and property regulation, on the one hand, and the state, on the other, gave the state new resources that it could use to enhance its own power, especially against the papacy. These were bolstered considerably in the second militaristic phase of its development. Such resources were most obviously money and armies; but more subtly they were also an increase in its logistical control over its relatively extensive territories.

To begin with, however, states were only one among several types of power grouping that were part of the development of extensive powers. Many commercial innovations of the late twelfth and thirteenth centuries – contractual arrangements, partnerships, insurance loans, bills of exchange, maritime law – originated in the Italian towns. From there they spread northward through the two politically interstitial, parallel lines of trade I identified in the preceding chapter. All reduced transaction costs and permitted more efficient extensive-trading networks. Had economic power stayed in the central Mediterranean and its lines of communication northward, perhaps towns plus the loose traditional contracts of vassalage, and not states, would have eventually fostered the development of industrial capitalism. In fact, one prototype of these alternative arrangements survived almost into the sixteenth century. Before continuing to narrate what might otherwise seem the "inevitable" rise of the national state, we should pause to consider the duchy of Burgundy.

The nonterritorial alternative: the rise and fall of the duchy of Burgundy

In the preceding chapter I examined the two principal parallel medieval trading networks, which went from the Mediterranean to the North Sea. The more important was the westerly route, from the mouth of the Rhône up through eastern France to Flanders. This was controlled not by powerful territorial states but by a number of lay and ecclesiastical princelings, among whom existed complex contracts of vassalage cemented by a high level of noble-class morale. Then (as tended to happen somewhere in Europe every century or so) dynastic accidents and acute use of influence (plus the waning of autonomous ecclesiastical power) secured great power for a single prince, this time the duke of Burgundy.[7] The expansion was throughout the reigns of a remarkable series of dukes, Philip the Bold (1363–1404), John the Fearless (1404–19), Philip the Good (1419–67), and Charles the Bold (1467–77). By the end, almost the whole of the present Low Countries and eastern France down to Grenoble recognized the suzerainty of the duke. He was recognized as an equal power by the kings of England and France (going through a bad patch) and the German emperor.

Yet Burgundian power was less territorially centered and, therefore, less "statelike" than its rivals. The duke did not have a single capital or a fixed court or law court. The duke and his household traveled around his domains, exercising domination and settling disputes, sometimes from his own castles, sometimes from those of his vassals, between Ghent and Bruges in the north and Dijon and Besançon in the south. There were two main blocs of territory, in the south the "two Burgundies" (duchy and county), in the north Flanders, Hainault, and Brabant. These blocs were acquired by marriage, intrigue, and occasionally open warfare, and the dukes then struggled to consolidate their administrations. They centered their efforts (significantly) on the two institutions I have emphasized, a supreme law court and a fiscal-military machine. They achieved successes commensurate with their renowned abilities. But the duchy was a patchwork. It spoke three languages, French, German, and Flemish; it combined the hitherto antagonistic forces of towns and territorial magnates; it confronted a gap of foreign territory between its two halves, normally of more than 150 kilometers (which narrowed, promisingly, to 50 km just two years before the final catastrophe). There was no territorial word for the dynastic duchy. When the duke was in the north, he referred to its territories as "our

---

[7]Main sources on the duchy of Burgundy were Cartellieri 1970; Vaughan 1975; and Armstrong 1980 (esp. chap. 9). Vaughan has also written a vivid series of biographies of the individual dukes. Especially fine is the one on Charles the Bold (1973).

lands around here" and to the two Burgundies as "our lands over there." When in the south, he reversed the terminology. Even his dynastic legitimacy was incomplete. He wanted the title of king but, formally, he owed homage for his western lands to the French crown (whose close relation he was) and for his eastern lands to the German emperor. They could have granted him the title but were unlikely to do so.

He was walking a tightrope. He had united the two main groups (the towns and the nobility) of the central European corridor threatened by the pretensions of two territorial states, France and Germany. Neither the internal groups nor the rival states wanted to see Burgundy as a third major state, but all these parties were mutually antagonistic and could be played off against one another. The duke performed his balancing act skillfully, although inevitably he sided with the nobility rather than the towns.

The Burgundian court exercised a fascination over the minds of contemporaries and successors alike. Its "brilliance" was generally admired. Its celebration of knighthood appealed extraordinarily to a European world in which the real infrastructures of knighthood (the feudal levy, the manor, transcendent Christendom) were in decline. Its Order of the Golden Fleece, combining symbols of purity and valor from Old and New testaments and classical sources, was the most prized honor in Europe. Its dukes, as their nicknames reveal, were the most lauded rulers of their time. Subsequently, Burgundian court ritual became the model for the rituals of European absolutism, although in the process it had to be rendered static. For Burgundian ritual represented *movement*, not territorial centralization: the *joyeuses entrées*, ceremonial processions of the dukes into their towns; the tournaments, during which the fields were gloriously, though temporarily, decorated; the quest of Jason for the Golden Fleece. And it depended on a free nobility, presenting themselves voluntarily and with personal dignity to their lord.

By the fifteenth century such a feudal state confronted logistical difficulties. War required permanent fiscal and manpower arrangements, and a disciplined body of aristocrats, gentry, burghers, and mercenaries who would present such resources on a routine basis to their ruler. The Burgundian ruling classes were too free to be wholly relied upon. The wealth of the corridor helped compensate, but the loyalty of the towns was uncertain and it was not enhanced by the dukes' own class consciousness. Philip the Bold liked to walk on a carpet depicting the leaders of a rebellion in the towns of Flanders – stepping on the commoners who had dared defy him. Burgundian strengths and weaknesses were tested on the battlefield. And there the feudal levy, even one hardened by mercenaries and the most advanced cannonry in Europe, no longer possessed advantages over less knight-centered armies. As in all feudal states, but not in centralized territorial states, a great deal depended on personal qualities and accidents of succession.

Difficulties suddenly combined in 1475–7 into swift demise. Duke Charles's boldness became foolhardiness. Attempting to speed up the territorial consolidation of his eastern lands, he took on too many enemies at once. He ventured outnumbered against the formidable pike phalanx of the Swiss towns. His motley duchy was perfectly represented in his forces for the two final battles: a core of heavily armored, mounted Burgundian knights; Flemish infantry of unreliable loyalty (most of whom were still traveling south at the time of battle); and foreign mercenaries, who advised retreat (as sensible mercenaries often did). The final battle of Nancy in 1477 was a rout once the Burgundian knights failed to break up the pike phalanx. Duke Charles fled, perhaps already wounded. He attempted to gallop a stream and was unhorsed. Lumbering in his heavy armor, he was an easy target. His skull was crushed, probably by an ax. Two days later his naked corpse, stripped of fine clothes, armor, and jewels and partly eaten by wolves, was dragged out of a muddy stream. Identified by means of his long fingernails and old wounds, he was a ghastly image of the end of feudalism.

Without a male heir, the duchy was quickly dismembered, in mirror image of its original growth. Charles's daughter was grabbed for marriage by his ''ally'' Maximilian of Habsburg, the German emperor. His lands submitted one by one to either Habsburg or Valois monarchs.

In the next century the Burgundian lands were still a key part of another somewhat dynastic and territorially decentered state, the Habsburg Empire of Charles V and Philip II. Yet even these regimes had developed in each of their cores – Austria, Naples, Spain, and Flanders – many of the appurtenances of the concentrated, territorially centered ''modern'' state. As Braudel observes (1973: 701–3), by the mid-sixteenth century territorial concentration of resources was what mattered. The vaster but more dispersed resources of the Habsburgs could not be deployed in a fiscal-military concentration equal to that of a medium-sized kingdom with a fertile, docile core, like France. From both extremes states converged on this model. As the Habsburg domains disintegrated into Spain, Austria, and the Netherlands, so did the Swiss towns confederate more closely. In Germany and Italy the process took much longer, but the model was evident. Let us see why.

The logistics of territorial centralization

Concentration of resources proved to be the key in geopolitics. The states who benefited were not so much its leading actors as its unconscious beneficiaries. Economic expansion was the motor. Its penetration into the whole economy of a ''home county'' state core (which Burgundy lacked) gave the opportunity to establish routine, relatively universal rights and duties across a territorially defined core area, useful for economy and battlefield alike. The long-term shift of economic power to the north and west also put some of these areas outside the reach of the Italian-Burgundian tentacles. Northern and western states were increasingly involved in commercial developments. To begin with, new accounting systems appeared virtually simultaneously in state, church, and manor. The records of Henry II, used in this chapter, themselves indicate greater logistical capacity by the state. But they were paralleled by manorial accounts – the earliest yet unearthed is that of the estates of the bishop of Winchester of 1208–9. Literacy was diffusing more widely among people of substance, revealed in the growth of royal writs, such as those addressed by Henry II to his provincial agents, and in the simultaneous circulation of treatises on estate management. The period shows a revival of interest in communication though, and central organization of, territory. This interest and organization were predominantly secular, shared by both authoritative states and more diffused "civil society" elements.

An important part of this revival was the recovery of classical learning.[8] The utilitarian wing of the recovery was the rediscovery of Roman law – of obvious use to the state because it codified universal rules of conduct across the state's territories. But classical philosophy and letters in general were also suffused with the importance of extensive communication and organization among rational human beings (as I argued in Chapter 9). This had always been a latent secular alternative to the extensive normative role of Christianity. This classical knowledge was available in preserved Greek and Latin texts on the edge of Christendom, in surviving Greek culture in southern Italy and Sicily, and more importantly, throughout the Arab world. In the twelfth century, in the Norman kingdoms of the central Mediterranean and in the reconquest of Spain, classical writings with added Islamic commentaries were recovered. The papacy was likely to keep them at arm's length! The knowledge was appropriated by teachers already moving outside the traditional cathedral schools. They institutionalized it in the first three European universities, in Bologna, Paris, and Oxford, at the beginning of the thirteenth century, then in fifty-three more by 1400. The universities blended the theology and canon law of the cathedral schools with the Roman law, philosophy, letters, and medicine of classical learning. They were autonomous, though their functional relationship with both church and state was close, for their graduates increasingly staffed the middle, nonnoble levels of ecclesiastical and state bureaucracies. Their graduates were called clerks. The evolution of this word, from denoting a tonsured man in holy orders to anyone of learning, that is, a "scholar," by the late thirteenth century, is testimony to the partial secularization of learning.

So the communication of messages was markedly improving from the twelfth to the fourteenth century, offering greater possibilities of control through space to the increasing number of literate people (Cipolla 1969: 43–61; Clanchy 1981). This was boosted for the first time beyond the capacities of ancient communications systems in the late thirteenth and early fourteenth centuries by a technical revolution: the substitution of paper for parchment. Innis (1950:

[8]Principal sources for this were Paré et al. 1933; Rashdall 1936; and Murray 1978.

140–72) has acutely described this. As he says, parchment is durable but expensive. Therefore, it is appropriate for power organizations that emphasize time, authority, and hierarchy, such as the church. Paper, being light, cheap, and expendable, favors extensive, diffuse, decentralized power. Like most of the later inventions to be discussed in a moment, paper was not original to Europe. Paper had been imported from Islam for several centuries. But when European paper mills were established – the first known being in operation in 1276 – the potential cheapness of paper could be exploited. Scribes, books, and the book trade proliferated. Spectacles were invented in Tuscany in the 1280s and diffused in two decades around Europe. The volume of even papal correspondence in the fourteenth century was three times what it had been in the thirteenth (Murray 1978: 299–300). The use of writs as instructions to English crown agents multiplied: Thus between June 1333 and November 1334 the sheriff of Bedfordshire and Buckinghamshire received 2,000! This developed simultaneously the bureaucracy of the king and of the local sheriffs (Mills and Jenkinson 1928). Copies of books also multiplied. Sir John Mandeville's *Travels,* written in 1356, has survived in more than two hundred copies (one was in the small library of the unfortunate heretic Menocchio, whom we encountered in Chapter 12). Indicative of the transitional linguistic state of Europe, with vernacular territorial languages gradually replacing Latin, is the fact that 73 copies are in German and Dutch, 37 in French, 40 in English, and 50 in Latin (Braudel 1973: 296).

On the other hand, until printing was invented, literacy and book ownership were restricted to the relatively wealthy and urbanized and to the church. Statistical estimates of literacy are available for slightly later periods, though we know that it was growing throughout medieval England. Cressy (1981) has measured literacy by the ability to sign one's name to evidence given in local courts, as recorded in the diocese of Norwich in the 1530s. Whereas all clergy and professionals and almost all gentry could sign in that decade, only a third of yeomen, a quarter of tradesmen and craftsmen, and about 5 percent of husbandmen could sign. Similarly low levels were found by Le Roy Ladurie (1966: 345–7) in rural Languedoc from the 1570s to the 1590s: Only 3 percent of agricultural laborers and 10 percent of richer peasants could sign. The nonspecialist might doubt whether signing one's name is a good measure of "literacy." But historians argue that it can be used as a measure of reading ability plus a modicum of writing ability. Reading, not writing, was the more widely prized and widely diffused accomplishment. There was no advantage to be obtained from learning to sign one's name before one could read and no general incentive to learn to write unless one's particular power position required it. In the late medieval period, reading and writing were still relatively "public" activities. Important documents, such as the Magna Carta, were displayed in public and read aloud to local assemblies. Documents, wills, and accounts were heard; we still have survivals of the culture of "hearing the word," for example, the "audit" of accounts and "I have not heard from him'' (Clanchy 1981). Literacy was still, paradoxically, oral and still largely confined to public-power arenas, notably church, state, and trade.

At the end of the fourteenth century came a test case that strengthened these confines. John Wycliffe was in the long line of radical proponents of individual, universal salvation without priestly mediation: "For each man that shall be damned shall be damned by his own guilt, and each man that is saved shall be saved by his own merit." He began the Lollard movement, which translated the Bible into English and spread vernacular literature through an "alternative communications network" of craftsmen, yeomen, and local schoolmasters. The church hierarchy persuaded the government that this was heresy. Persecution and repressed rebellion followed. Nevertheless, 175 manuscript copies of Wycliffe's vernacular Bible still survive. And Lollardy survived in the historical shadows.

This confirmed the class and gender restrictions (few women could read and even fewer could write) of public literacy. Nonetheless, within these confines literacy spread throughout the late medieval period, diffusing widely among dominant social groups. The national vernacular was integrating them, beginning to enhance a territorially centered class morale that was a viable alternative to the traditional, nonterritorial, class-morale networks typified by the duchy of Burgundy.

If we turn from symbolic communication to the communication of objects, we can see that transport systems developed more patchily. On land, Roman roads and aqueducts were not equaled during the whole period, and so speed of land communications lagged. On the sea, a slow series of improvements to ancient ships had begun early in the Mediterranean and continued throughout the period with a steadily growing northern and Atlantic input. The magnetic compass arrived from China at the end of the twelfth century; the sternpost rudder was discovered (independently of the much earlier Chinese invention) in the North in the thirteenth. These and other developments increased the tonnage of ships, enabled them to sail through some of the winter, and improved coastal navigation. But the really revolutionary development of full rigging and ocean navigation did not occur until later, in the mid-fifteenth century.

Let us stop the clock at the point at which clocks became part of civilized life, in the early fifteenth century, and look at how far the logistics of extensive power had developed. It is not at first an impressive sight. Long-distance control and communications were of the same general order as they had been in Roman times. For example, the logistics of military mobility were more or less as they had been throughout most of ancient history. Armies could still move for three days without any supplies and for about nine if they did not have to carry water. There were specific improvements. More written messages could be passed, and more people could read them (if not write them); more reliable and speedier coastal shipping routes existed; and vertical communication between the classes had been rendered easier by a common Christian identity and by increasingly shared languages across "national" areas. But on the debit side, land transport was probably no better, while genuinely long-distance communications routes were partially blocked by state boundaries, tolls, somewhat ad hoc trading arrangements, and uncertainty about church-state relations. The extensive recoveries and innovations were still shared between several competing, overlapping power agencies.

But this combination of pluses and minuses did tend to facilitate control over one particular terrain: the emerging "national" state. The comparison with Rome is after all inapt if we are considering political control. The fourteenth-century state of England sought control over an area only slightly more than a twentieth the size of the Roman Empire. If its infrastructural techniques were more or less comparable with Roman ones, it could in principle exercise almost twenty times the coordinating powers that Rome could. In particular its provincial reach was far more secure. In the twelfth century, sheriffs and other provincial agents were required to bring their accounts to Westminster twice a year. In the thirteenth and fourteenth centuries, as the Exchequer became more sophisticated, this was reduced to one visit, lasting about two weeks for each county; but the scrutiny was now keener. Such physical coordination had been impossible for the Romans except within the individual province. In 1322 the process was reversed when the Exchequer and all its records moved to York. The fact that its journey took thirteen days to cover 300 kilometers is usually taken as an indication of the feebleness of communications (Jewell 1972: 26). The fact that it occurred at all, and on a regular basis over the next two centuries, indicates the strength of state control. By Roman standards, English sheriffs were deluged with written instructions and requests, besieged by investigating commissions, and locked into a routine of regularly reporting back.[9] The roads, the rivers and coastal navigation, the literacy, the availability of supplies for armies – all were appropriate for routine penetration of such a restricted territorial area.

Of course the formal powers of the state itself were far less in medieval England. No king seriously believed, or fostered the belief, that he was divine or that his word alone was law, as had many emperors. None acted in this period as if all he needed to add was an army to make this reality. *Despotic* power *over* society was not a formal characteristic of medieval Europe, unlike Rome. The relationship between ruler and ruling class was between members of the same diffused class/national identity. In Rome we saw that the *infrastructural* practice differed from the principle, for no emperor could actually penetrate "civil society" without the aid of semiautonomous provincial notables. This was accepted in practice and in principle by the medieval king. In England the principle of sovereignty gradually changed from rule by the king in council to rule by the king in Parliament, with considerable periods of overlap between the two. The former system involved the great magnates,

_____
[9]The English administrative system has been described by Chrimes 1966.

including the higher ecclesiastics; the latter involved the city burgesses and the gentry of the shires too. Some other European states developed a more formal version of this, the *Standestaat*, rule by a monarch together with separate assemblies representing three or four estates of the realm (nobility, clergy, burghers, and sometimes rich peasants). All these political structures had three features in common: First, government was by the consent and through the coordination of the involved power groupings. Second, permanent coordination presupposed a settled, "universal," territorial state more than it did the particularistic feudal relations of vassals to their lord. Third, the estates were separate entities external to each other, not an organic whole, and had limited powers of interpenetration. State rule depended on territorial coordination of autonomous actors; but if this was effective, it could attain a formidable concentration of collective power. Unlike the Roman power groups (after the decline of the senate), they could meet regularly in council/parliament/estates – generally to coordinate policy. Unlike the Romans, the few powerful magnates could be solidified by dynastic ties. As in the Roman situation, coordination had also to occur at the local level. The sheriff could extract taxes only with the consent of the local wealthy; the justice of the peace could get effective witnesses and juries only with the consent of the local powerful.

The weak point of the system was the lack of organic unity. There were always in this period tensions between the king's administration and the families of substance. Discontent smoldered because of the king's use of "new men," outsiders, "evil counselors," and it found expression when the king failed to "live of his own" with these men and was forced to call on his council/parliament/estates for money. But when the system worked, it was strong in historical terms in coordinating its territories and subjects and in concentrating the resources of its core "home counties," even if it was weak in powers *over* them. And we have seen that its coordinating, concentrating powers were growing. By 1450 it was a territorially coordinating, but not a unitary, "organic" state. It still consisted of two distinct territorial levels, the king and the local magnate, and the relations between them amounted to a territorial federalism.

Technical revolution and its social base

Francis Bacon, writing at the end of the sixteenth century, said that three inventions had "changed the whole face and state of things throughout the world" – gunpowder, printing, and the mariner's compass. We cannot argue with the spirit of the remark, even if we would amend its details.[10] Artillery batteries, movable-type printing, and a combination of ocean navigation techniques and "full-rigged" ships did, indeed, change the extensive face of power

[10]For the three inventions, see Cipolla 1965; White 1972: 161–8; and Braudel 1973: 285–308.

throughout the world. All were probably given initial impetus from the East (although printing may have been independently rediscovered in Europe), but it was their wide *diffusion,* not their invention, that was the European contribution to the world history of power.

Artillery was the earliest and slowest to develop any efficiency: In use in 1326, neither batteries nor handguns were a decisive weapon on land until after Charles VIII of France invaded Italy in 1494, and the first heyday of naval cannons was slightly later. The "navigational revolution" that led to ocean rather than coastal sailing took most of the fifteenth century. Movable-type printing was relatively swift. Datable to 1440–50, it had turned out 20 million books by 1500 (for a European population of 70 million).

The chronological coincidence of their takeoff period, 1450–1500, is striking. So too is their link with the two main emergent power structures of European society, capitalism and the national state. The associated impetus given by these two seems to have been decisive here and absent in Asia. Capitalist dynamism was evident in navigational developments, as well as in the bravery in the service of greed that drove the merchantmen into the unknown ocean. Printing, under the patronage of large moneylenders, was a profitable capitalist business oriented to a decentralized mass market. Artillery factories, privately owned, were the first heavy industry of the world. But the dependence of capital on the national state was evident in two of the cases. The navigators found state finance, licensing, and protection first from Portugal and Spain, then from Holland, England, and France. The artillery was almost entirely in the service of states, and its manufacture was also licensed and protected by the states. Navigators, gunners, and other skilled workers were now required to be literate, and schools were set up in which teaching was in the national vernacular (Cipolla 1969: 49). At first, printing served the more traditional God of Christianity. Until the mid-sixteenth century the majority of books were religious and in Latin. Only then did the national vernacular begin to take over so that printing too would reinforce national-state boundaries, ending the public viability of the transnational languages of Latin and French and the dialects of the various regions of each major state.

The effect of all three inventions is reserved for the next chapter. But coming at the end of this one, they summarize its theme: As the original dynamism of feudal Europe became more extensive, capitalism and the national state formed a loose but coordinated and concentrated alliance, which was shortly to intensify and to conquer both heaven and earth.

Bibliography

Ardant, G. 1975. Financial policy and economic infrastructure of modern states and nations. In *The Formation of National States in Western Europe,* ed. C. Tilly. Princeton, N.J.: Princeton University Press.

Armstrong, C. A. J. 1980. *England, France and Burgundy in the Fifteenth Century.* London: Hambledon Press.
Bowsky, W. M. 1970. *The Finances of the Commune of Siena, 1287–1355.* Oxford: Clarendon Press.
Braudel, F. 1973. *Capitalism and Material Life.* London: Weidenfeld & Nicolson.
Braun, R. 1975. Taxation, sociopolitical structure and state-building: Great Britain and Brandenburg-Prussia. In *The Formation of National States in Western Europe,* ed. C. Tilly. Princeton, N.J.: Princeton University Press.
Cartellieri, O. 1970. *The Court of Burgundy.* New York: Haskell House Publishers.
Carus-Wilson, E. M., and O. Coleman. 1963. *England's Export Trade 1275–1547.* Oxford: Clarendon Press.
Chrimes, S. B. 1966. *An Introduction to the Administrative History of Medieval England.* Oxford: Blackwell.
Cipolla, C. 1965. *Guns and Sails in the Early Phase of European Expansion 1400–1700.* London: Collins.
    1969 *Literacy and Development in the West.* Harmondsworth, England: Penguin Books.
Clanchy, M. T. 1981. Literate and illiterate; hearing and seeing: England 1066–1307. In *Literacy and Social Development in the West: a Reader,* ed. H. J. Graff. Cambridge: Cambridge University Press.
Cressy, D. 1981. Levels of illiteracy in England 1530–1730. In *Literacy and Social Development in the West: A Reader,* ed. H. J. Graff, Cambridge: Cambridge University Press.
Farmer, D. L. 1956. Some price fluctuations in Angevin England. *Economic History Review,* 9.
    1957. Some grain prices movements in 13th century England. *Economic History Review,* 10.
Finer, S. E. 1975. State and nationbuilding in Europe: the role of the military. In *The Formation of National States in Western Europe,* ed. C. Tilly. Princeton, N.J.: Princeton University Press.
Fowler, K. (ed.). 1971. *The Hundred Years' War.* London: Macmillan.
    1980. *The Age of Plantagenet and Valois.* London: Ferndale Editions.
Harris, G. L. 1975. *King, Parliament and Public Finance in Medieval England to 1369.* Oxford: Clarendon Press.
Henneman, J. B. 1971. *Royal Taxation in Fourteenth-Century France.* Princeton, N.J.: Princeton University Press.
Hintze, O. 1975. *The Historical Essays of Otto Hintze,* ed. F. Gilbert. New York: Oxford University Press.
Howard, M. 1976. *War in European History.* London: Oxford University Press.
Innis, H. 1950. *Empire and Communications.* Oxford: Clarendon Press.
Jewell, H. M. 1972. *English Local Administration in the Middle Ages.* Newton Abbot, England: David & Charles.
Kiernan, V. G. 1965. State and nation in western Europe. *Past and Present,* 31.
Lane, F. C. 1966. The economic meaning of war and protection. In *Venice and History,* ed. Lane. Baltimore: Johns Hopkins University Press.
Le Roy Ladurie, E. 1966. *Les Paysans de Languedoc.* Paris: SEUPEN.
Lewis, P. S. 1968. *Later Medieval France – the Polity.* London: Macmillan.
Lloyd, T. H. 1982. *Alien Merchants in England in the High Middle Ages.* Brighton: Harvester.
McFarlane, K. B. 1962. England and the Hundred Years' War. *Past and Present,* 22.
    1973. *The Nobility of Later Medieval England.* Oxford: Clarendon Press.

McKisack, M. 1959. *The Fourteenth Century*. Oxford: Clarendon Press.

Mann, M. 1980. State and society, 1130–1815: an analysis of English state finances. In *Political Power and Social Theory*, vol. I, ed. M. Zeitlin. Greenwich, Conn.: JAI Press.

Miller, E. 1972. Government Economic Policies and Public Finance, 1000–1500. In *The Fontana Economic History of Europe: The Middle Ages*, ed. C. M. Cipolla. London: Fontana.

1975. War, taxation and the English economy in the late thirteenth and early fourteenth centuries. In *War and Economic Development*, ed. J. M. Winter. Cambridge: Cambridge University Press.

Mills, M. H., and C. H. Jenkinson. 1928. Rolls from a sheriff's office of the fourteenth century. *English Historical Review*, 43.

Murray, A. 1978. *Reason and Society in the Middle Ages*. Oxford: Clarendon Press.

Painter, S. 1951. *The Rise of the Feudal Monarchies*. Ithaca, N.Y.: Cornell University Press.

Paré, G., et al. 1933. *La renaissance du xiie siècle: les écoles et l'enseignement*. Paris and Ottawa: Urin and Institut des Etudes Mediévales.

Phelps-Brown, E. H., and S. V. Hopkins. 1956. Seven centuries of the price of consumables. *Economica*, 23.

Poole, A. L. 1951. *From Domesday Book to Magna Carta*. Oxford: Clarendon Press.

Poulantzas, N. 1972. *Pouvoir politique et classes sociales*. Paris: Maspéro.

Powicke, M. 1962. *The Thirteenth Century*. Oxford: Clarendon Press.

Ramsay, J. H. 1920. *Lancaster and York*. Oxford: Clarendon Press.

1925. *A History of the Revenues of the Kings of England 1066–1399*. 2 vols. Oxford: Clarendon Press.

Rashdall, H. 1936. *The Universities of Europe in the Middle Ages*. 3 vols. Oxford: Clarendon Press.

Rey, M. 1965. *Les finances royales sous Charles VI*. Paris: SEUPEN.

Roncière, C. M. de la. 1968. Indirect taxes of "Gabelles" at Florence in the fourteenth century. In *Florentine Studies*, ed. N. Rubinstein. Evanston, Ill.: Northwestern University Press.

Sorokin, P. A. 1962. *Social and Cultural Dynamics*, vol. III. New York: Bedminster Press.

Steel, A. 1954. *The Receipt of the Exchequer 1377–1485*. Cambridge: Cambridge University Press.

Strayer, J. R. 1970. *On the Medieval Origins of the Modern State*. Princeton, N.J.: Princeton University Press.

Strayer, J. R., and C. H. Holt 1939. *Studies in Early French Taxation*. Cambridge, Mass.: Harvard University Press.

Tilly, C. (ed.). 1975. *The Formation of National States in Western Europe*. Princeton, N.J.: Princeton University Press.

Tout, T. F. 1920–33. *Chapters in the Administrative History of Medieval England*. 6 vols. Manchester: Manchester University Press.

Tout, T. F., and D. Broome. 1924. A National Balance-Sheet for 1362–3. *English Historical Review*, 39.

Tuchman, B. W. 1979. *A Distant Mirror: The Calamitous Fourteenth Century*. Harmondsworth, England: Penguin Books.

Vaughan, R. 1973. *Charles the Bold*. London: Longman.

1975. *Valois Burgundy*. London: Allen Lane.

Verbruggen, J. F. 1977. *The Art of Warfare in Western Europe during the Middle Ages*. Amsterdam: North-Holland.

Waley, D. P. 1968. The Army of the Florentine Republic from the twelfth to the
     fourteenth centuries. In *Florentine Studies,* ed. N. Rubinstein. Evanston,
     Ill.: Northwestern University Press.
White, L., Jr. 1972. The Expansion of Technology 500–1500. In *The Fontana Eco-
     nomic History of Europe: The Middle Ages,* ed. C. M. Cipolla. London:
     Fontana.
Wolfe, M. 1972. *The Fiscal System of Renaissance France.* New Haven, Conn.: Yale
     University Press.
Wolffe, B. P. 1971. *The Royal Demesne in English History.* London: Allen & Unwin.

14 The European dynamic: III. International capitalism and organic national states, 1477–1760

The last two chapters focused on different aspects of European development. Chapter 12 concentrated on the local, *intensive* feudal dynamic, especially on its econom;ic dynamic. Chapter 13 moved outward (as Europe itself did), focusing on more *extensive* power relations, especially on the role of the state. Overall, European development was a combination of the two. In the present chapter we see the combination emerge up to the Industrial Revolution. The chapter deals more with extensive than intensive aspects of development, and especially with the role of the state. Therefore, it lacks what perhaps it should ideally possess, a sustained explanaton of the various stages of economic growth toward the Industrial Revolution. A genuine explanation would require both economic theory and a comparative methodology, applied across the various regions and countries of Europe that moved in uneven bursts toward industrialization. England, transforming itself into Great Britain, was the first to industrialize, and Great Britain is discussed here. But answers to the question, Why not Italy, or Flanders, or Spain, or France, or Prussia, or Sweden or Holland? would be a necessary part of the explanation, and they are not discussed here.

This might lead to an excessively British account of the whole process. Britain made it first, but perhaps only just. France and parts of the Low Countries were close behind. Once it became clear across the multistate system that Britain had stumbled on enormous new power resources, it was swiftly copied. Industrial capitalism diffused rather rapidly into other social settings where it seemed equally at home. If we took these countries as autonomous cases, we would have not one dynamic – or, if the language is preferred, one "transition from feudalism to capitalism" – but several. This is the conclusion, for example, of Holton (1984), after careful review of the cases of Britain, France, and Prussia. Yet they were not autonomous cases but national actors in a broader geopolitical, multistate civilization. Forces across that entire whole (and also from outside; see Chapter 15) affected Britain, whose social structure and geopolitical position gave it a certain "edge" in the developmental process at a particular period. Its lead, though narrow, was not accidental.

Unfortunately, that is not a statement I can fully support here, because of the absence of sustained comparative methodology and theory. Nevertheless, a theory is implied in this chapter. It continues the argument of the preceding

450

Table 14.1. *English state finances, 1502–1688: average annual revenue at current and constant (1451–75) prices*

Reign	Years	Annual revenue (in thousands of £)		Price index
		Current	Constant	
Henry VII	1502–5	126.5	112.9	112
Elizabeth	1559–70	250.8	89.9	279
	1571–82	223.6	69.0	324
	1583–92	292.8	77.9	376
	1593–1602	493.5	99.5	496
James I	1604–13	593.5	121.9	487
Charles I	1630–40	605.3	99.4	609
Charles II	1660–72	1,582.0	251.1	630
	1672–85	1,634.0	268.7	608
James II	1685–8	2,066.9	353.3	585

Note: These figures are directly comparable to those given in Table 13.2. For details of all sources and calculations, see Mann 1980.
Sources: Revenue: 1502–5, Dietz 1964a, corrected by Wolffe 1971; 1559–1602, Dietz 1923; 1604–40, Dietz 1928; 1660–8, Chandaman 1975. *Price index:* Phelps-Brown and Hopkins 1956.

chapter. That argument is also commonly adopted by contemporary economists: The growth of a mass-consumption market – initially of farming families – that was able to exploit the labor of a rural proletariat provided the main stimulus to economic takeoff that occurred in Britain at the end of the eighteenth century. The market was predominantly domestic, and domestic equals national. This justifies continued concentration on the emergence of the power organization, which gave birth to the national interaction network: the state. So, remembering that the economic dynamism described in Chapter 12 was rumbling away throughout this period, taking increasingly capitalist forms, let us concentrate on the English state. From time to time I shall listen to the rumblings, and I shall discuss them more fully at the end of the chapter.

I return to the English state's finances as an indicator of its functions. In this chapter, however, the inadequacies of this indicator become evident, and I supplement it with other forms of analysis.

State-revenue patterns, 1502–1688

Table 14.1 presents my time series of revenue totals during the period 1502–1688. No reliable figures are available for the period 1452–1501, and none are available for the reigns of Henry VIII, Edward VI, and Mary. All figures given before 1660 are based on a degree of guesswork (as explained in Mann

1980).[1] In contrast, the post-1660 figures are considered good ones. The table reveals that Henry VII restored the level of state finances, at both current and constant prices, to that enjoyed by Henry V before the disruptions of the Wars of the Roses. Then the figures up to the Civil War show two trends: an enormous price inflation that rocketed actual state finances, and a leveling off in revenue if we control for inflation. The latter trend is surprising, for most historians see a great development of the state occurring under Tudor rule.[2] Let us examine these trends in more detail.

Bothered by neither inflation nor long-lasting wars, Henry VII balanced his books and even accumulated a surplus. His revenue came in roughly equal proportions from three main sources: rents from crown lands, customs duties, and parliamentary taxation. The last staved off the short-lived threats to his throne from rivals and foreign powers. Despite financial reorganizations, his state – in overall size and main functions – was traditional. Paying the expenses of his household, buying the political advice of a few counselors, administering supreme justice, regulating trade across territorial boundaries, issuing a coinage, and waging occasional wars with the help of his loyal barons – that was the sum of state functions, which almost certainly involved less than 1 percent of national wealth and were marginal to the lives of most of the state's subjects.

Over the next two centuries, this state was significantly changed by three forces, two of which were traditional and one novel. Both escalation in the costs of warfare and inflation we have repeatedly encountered. But an increase in the role of the state as the coordinator of a ruling class had not reached the "organic" phase.

The first change, the increase in the costs of war, was predictable on medieval experience: the consequences of the accession of a more warlike king, Henry VIII. Table 14.2 contains Dietz's estimate of cash-expenditure totals during the first years of his reign. Look at the fourfold increase in 1512, the year he began his French wars, and the almost threefold increase the following year, as the campaign intensified! The increases are entirely due to military expenses. As in the three previous centuries, war makes the state substantial. Such jumps at the onset of war reach right up to our own times. But the height leaped now begins to diminish. Henry's French Wars have increased expenditures tenfold in the two years 1511–13. His French and Scottish Wars of 1542–6 increase expenditures about fourfold, if Dietz's figures (1918: 74;

---

[1]Since then, G. R. Elton has persuaded me that the figures for Elizabeth's reign understate total revenue. Some revenue apparently received is difficult to trace in the Exchequer accounts, perhaps as much as a third of traced revenue.
[2]Even if we added an additional third under Elizabeth, the overall trend would be unchanged: Elizabeth would then have raised revenue only a quarter higher than Henry VII's level, an increase dwarfed by the rise after 1660. Then revenue at constant prices doubled over the late-medieval level.

Table 14.2. *Cash expenditures, 1511–20 (in pounds)*

Year	Total expenses	Military expenses	Aid to foreign allies
1511	64,157	1,509	—
1512	269,564	181,468	(32,000 gold florins)
1513	699,714	632,322[a]	14,000
1514	155,757	92,000	—
1515	74,006	10,000	—
1516	106,429	16,538	38,500
1517	72,359	60	13,333
1518	50,614	200	—
1519	52,428	—	—
1520	86,020	—	—

[a] Plus 10,040 crowns.
Source: Dietz 1964: I, 90–1.

1964a: I, 137–58) can be relied on. Fourfold increases are the norm through the next century, although after 1688 they diminish further. It is not that the state changed its spots and waged war more moderately; rather, *peacetime military expenditures have risen.* Table 14.2 concealed that this was already being prepared in Henry VIII's early wars, for at least one item was paid out of a separate account: The upkeep of the garrison at Tournai in France cost £40,000 a year between 1514 and 1518 (when it was surrendered). Now, throughout most years of the sixteenth century, garrison expenditures at Berwick, Calais, and Tournai, and in Ireland, absorbed sums almost as great as the whole of the rest of the expenditures in peacetime put together. The "permanent-war state" was arriving.

The Military Revolution and the state system

Garrison costs were the tip of an iceberg of changes in military organization occurring roughly in the period 1540–1660. To these changes many historians, following Roberts (1967), have given the label the Military Revolution. Firearms were a part of the revolution, although their role is often overstated (as argued in Hale 1965). Their introduction in Europe in the fourteenth and fifteenth centuries was slow, and they made little initial impact on armies' tactics. To the battalions of pikemen that had dominated since the early fourteenth century, handguns were merely added. Larger artillery guns had a greater eventual effect, especially on naval warfare, for they involved investment on a scale that was out of reach of the provincial nobility. The king could batter down the castles of the feudal nobility.

But the gun then led to the triumph of a new type of defensive land warfare, the *trace italienne,* elaborate star-shaped low fortifications behind which musketeers could mow down besiegers, even before they reached the main castle walls (see Duffy 1979). Reducing such bastions with heavy artillery, massive counter-earthworks, or starvation took longer, prolonged campaigns, tied down soldiers, and cost more. Associated with this were the mobile tactical innovations of generals like Maurice of Nassau and Gustavus Adolphus, who realized that the reintroduction of battle lines, made obsolete in the fourteenth century by the Swiss and Flemish, could improve the fire power of infantries armed with muskets. But lines needed far more drilling than battalions, and they needed protection with earthworks if attacked. Roman methods of drilling and digging were recalled and revived. Well-paid, disciplined professionals willing to labor as well as fight were needed more than ever. This increased the centralization of military organizations, and drilling ensured the dominance of mercenaries (and also an eventual end to their troublesome autonomy). Additionally, the size of armies relative to the population increased again in the sixteenth century by at least 50 percent (Sorokin 1962: 340). Parker (1972: 5–6) argues that army size went up tenfold in the century in some instances (cf. Bean 1973). Naval size and costs also escalated from the mid-sixteenth century. At first specialized warships were rare, but even converted merchantmen and merchant seamen required refitting and retraining. Cannonry eventually led to investment in men-of-war. All this not only increased the costs of warfare, but ensured that they would stay high. In war *or* peace, military costs were now considerable. When Louis XII asked his Milanese adviser Trivulzio how the success of his invasion of Italy could be assured, he received this reply: "Most generous King, three things are necessary: money, money and still more money" (quoted by Ardant 1975: 164). With each subsequent escalation of costs, advisers might have added ". . . and yet more money."

All these changes led to a greater role for capital-intensive supplies and, therefore, for centralized, orderly administration and capital accounting, which could concentrate the resources of a territory. The changes enhanced territorially centralized power (the state) but also enhanced the diffusion of commodity forms within that territory (i.e., capitalism). The first appearance of capitalistic methods in Elizabeth's navy and Wallenstein's army has often been commented on. The link between capitalism and the state was growing closer.

I have just compressed a period of military history that covers about two centuries – say, from the first regular, paid artillery company formed by Charles VII of France in 1444 to the deaths of Maurice of Nassau and Wallenstein in 1625 and 1634, respectively. It is therefore necessary to emphasize that military developments constituted a revolution not because of their suddenness but because of their prolonged, cumulative effect. The technology of guns, tactics and strategy, and the forms of military and state organization developed over this whole period. Only at the very end was the transformation complete, perhaps symbolically at the deaths of these two great entrepreneurs of death. As Hintze expressed it, "The colonels ceased being private military entrepreneurs, and became servants of the state" (1975: 200; cf. McNeill 1982: chap. 4).

But what kind of state was favored? Very poor states were in trouble. And the "feudal" state was now finished: The free contractual delivery by vassals of their personal levies during the campaigning system was quite obsolete. Nor could they be stiffened by mercenary bands, now insufficiently capital-intensive. Within city-state systems, as in Italy, the small to medium-sized states – up to the size of about Siena – could not find enough money to maintain their independence in siege warfare. Larger, centralized administrations were required. Indeed, the consolidating and centralizing consequence of the gun seems worldwide – its introduction in Europe, Japan, and various parts of Africa has enhanced central state power (Brown 1948; Kiernan 1957: 74; Stone 1965: 199–223; Morton-Williams 1969: 95–6; Goody 1971: 47–56; Smaldane 1972; Bean 1973; and Law 1976: 112–32). These eliminations ensured that Europe moved toward a *state* system, in other words, that the surviving units would be relatively centered and relatively territorial. The looser feudal conferations, the roving military machines, and the small interstitial towns and princelings were the casualties of war.

So Europe also became a more orderly *multi*state system in which the actors were more nearly equal, more similar in their interests, and more formally rational in their diplomacy. The whole of Europe was now repeating the earlier experience of the smaller Italian multistate system, and so much of the early military and diplomatic technique was diffused from Italy. These techniques had secured a long geopolitical stalemate in Italy, preserving it as a multistate system. The defensive diplomacy of states was aimed at preventing anyone from attaining hegemony.

The Military Revolution was not likely to change this geopolitical stalemate by destroying front-rank or large states. The fundamental logistical infrastructure had barely changed. Armies could still march for a maximum of nine days over European terrain (where water was abundant). Then they stopped, plundered local harvests, and sat down to bake bread for a further three days, before resuming their march. In the late seventeenth century a number of generals – Marlborough, Le Tellier, Louvois – began to pay considerable attention to the organization of supplies, but they were still able to generate only something like 10 percent of their needs from their bases. Armies still lived off the countryside. Without a revolution in land transport, the constraint was the yield ratio of the crops grown around the line of march. As we saw in Table 12.1, this was slowly improving up to the eighteenth century (when it leaped ahead). This may have been the overriding determinant of the growth in the size of armies. But it still put upper limits on size, mobility, and deployment patterns such that no one state could overwhelm other front-rank or large states with numbers or velocity of movement.[3] Thus the payoff from war could not be hegemony, only avoidance of utter defeat. Europe would remain a multistate system, playing what on land amounted to an endless zero-sum game. The front-rank states could pick off the weaker ones, but against one another there was stalemate in land warfare – although the sea presented other possibilities. One important contribution to stalemate was a more general characteristic of multistate systems: Whereas the leading power stumbles across new power techniques, the more successful of its rivals react and copy in a more ordered, planned fashion. The advantage of late entry is not a trait of multistate systems that began with industrialization.

But what was likely to be the internal structure of these states? More than one option was still open. One curiosity that performed rather well was Wallenstein's massive "capitalist" enterprise in the Thirty Years' War. Granted large estates confiscated from Protestants in Friedland, he milked their resources to assemble and train an army. The army then moved around north Germany, cowing towns into paying tribute, which enabled him to expand his forces to 140,000. But for his assassination, who knows what "state" such an effective general might have founded? This exception apart, there were two main types of state that were favored to acquire the leading edge of military power. This is because there were two main requirements: the acquisition of great and stable sources of wealth, and the development of a large, centralized military manpower administration. Thus a very rich state could pay for and administer armed forces that were fairly separate from the rest of its civil activities or from the life of its inhabitants. Or a state that had some wealth but that was richer in manpower could generate large, competitive armed forces with a fiscal-manpower extraction system that was more central to its own overall administration and to social life in general. Later in this chapter, we shall see these "fiscal" and "mobilized" alternatives develop into "constitutional" and "absolutist" regimes. Thus great wealth or population size, if reasonably concentrated and able to be mobilized by uniform administrative techniques, were now considerably advantaged. Over the next centuries the major Italian republics (Genoa and Venice), Holland, and England were favored by their wealth, and Austria and Russia by their populations and relatively uniform state machineries. Spain and France enjoyed both advantages and, indeed, they came closest to military-led political hegemony over Europe. They were ultimately undone by the multistate system.

The major monarchs and republics of Europe moved unevenly toward total control of the war machine, with Spain and Sweden in the van and England and Austria bringing up the rear. The financial impact was felt by Spain early. Ladero Quesada (1970) shows that a threefold increase in Castilian royal expenditure in 1481 and a doubling in 1504 were preponderantly results of

[3]I am indebted for the details of this paragraph to Creveld 1977.

war. Throughout the period 1480–92 the conquest of Granada cost at least three-quarters of all expenditure. When it was finished, the machinery was not dismantled but turned to other international ventures. Parker (1970) notes that in the period 1572–6 more than three-quarters of the Spanish budget went to defense and debt service (cf. Davis 1973: 211). The severe sixteenth-century increase in state expenditures in Europe as a whole was due mainly to escalating military costs and to the evolution of more permanent debt-repayment systems (Parker 1974: 560–82).

England brought up the rear because the costs of its main armed force, the navy, did not escalate until well into the seventeenth century. Only when England and Holland supplanted privateering with empire building and encountered each other's naval power did their states take off. The three Anglo-Dutch naval wars date this to the 1650s, 1660s, and 1670s. From the mid-1660s for the next two hundred years, the navy was the largest item in English state expenditures, except in a few years when land forces or repayment of war loans overtook it. Under Elizabeth and the first two Stuarts combined military expenses could go as low as 40 percent of all expenses in years of peace, but under Charles II and James II they never fell below 50 percent and were bolstered by heavier debt repayment (Dietz 1923: 91–104; Dietz 1928: 158–171; Chandaman 1975: 348–66). The permanent war state arrived in England in two stages. Although the Tudor garrisons were its harbingers, Pepys's navy constituted its main thrust.

This was reinforced by the second traditional disrupter of the state: inflation. Table 14.1 shows that only after 1660 did the state's financial size increase substantially in real terms (the jump probably occurred during the undocumented period of the Commonwealth in the 1650s), largely because of military and debt-repayment expenditures. Tudor inflation had an innovating effect on the state, as it had traditionally had, the effect heightened by its sheer extent. Prices rose sixfold in the hundred years following 1520, probably close to the Europe-wide figure.[4] It was then historically unprecedented for European states (although our own century appears likely to exceed it). Real wealth was expanding throughout the period, so that higher prices could be borne. But inflation adversely affected some sources of crown revenue, especially rents from lands. Pressured by inflation and the growing current costs of war, the governments of Henry VIII, Edward VI, and Mary resorted to nonrepeatable maneuvers – expropriation of the church, debasement of the coinage, the selling of crown lands, wholesale borrowing. Under Henry VIII one important and permanent development occurred: peacetime taxation. From around 1530 it cannot be assumed that taxation was occasioned by the onset

[4]The causes of this rise are unclear. Much of the influx of Spanish silver from the New World – a contributing factor – was smuggled, and therefore its movement cannot be traced (Outhwaite 1969).

of war (Elton 1975) although taxation grants were still almost entirely devoted to remedying inflation and bearing military costs.

These years may mark an important shift. In 1534 the preamble to the parliamentary grant of taxation refers for the first time to the general civil benefits of the king's government. This appears to refer largely to pacification needs in Ireland and to fortifications and harbor works. Schofield nonetheless considers it "revolutionary," because rather general references to the king's "greatness and beneficence" begin to dot parliamentary language (1963: 24–30). So what about the "civil functions" of the Tudor and Stuart state? Were they widening? This will raise the third innovator, the increase in the coordinating role of the state to the point at which the national state becomes an organic unit.

If we look merely at finances, an increase in civil functions is not discernible in the sixteenth century. Household expenses rose between Henry VII's reign and Elizabeth's last years about fivefold (Dietz 1932), about the same as the rise in prices. No other nonmilitary expenses rose farther. Yet with James I a change occurred. His civil expenses rose above Elizabeth's level at a time of price *de*flation. In the last five years (1598–1603) of Elizabeth's reign average annual outlay was around £524,000, of which military expenditures contributed 75 percent. James I made peace with all foreign powers and reduced his military expenditures (largely for Irish garrisons) to 30 percent of his budget. During the period 1603–8 his average annual outlay was around £420,000; so civil expenditures had increased by a quarter (Dietz 1964: II, 111–13; with added recalculations, explained in Mann 1980). Dietz (1928) showed three contributing factors. First, unlike Elizabeth, James was married with children, and his household costs were therefore greater. Second, he was extravagant, as his opponents claimed: Spending £15,593 on Queen Anne's child bed showed prodigality! But "extravagance" merged into a third expense factor, which was becoming integral to all states: rewarding noble officeholders. James bought the loyalty and service of his magnates partly because he felt insecure as a Scottish foreigner on the throne. But the "spoils system" became common throughout Europe, even under supposedly stronger kings than James. The cost of spoils was not extraordinary, being dwarfed by military expenditures. But their significance was greater than their cost, for they heralded an extension of state functions.

From coordinated to organic state

Let us first view the "spoils system" from the perspective of the nobility and gentry. The great families of the time were far less great than their predecessors. Several historians have calculated the revenues of late Tudor and early Stuart noble families. The ninth earl of Northumberland's revenues totaled less than £7,000 per annum in the period 1598–1604 and rose to about £13,000 in 1615–33 (Batho 1957: 439). Sir Robert Spencer, reputedly the wealthiest man in the kingdom, received £8,000 at most in the early seventeenth century (Finch 1956: 38, 63). The Cecils, the greatest officeholders at the turn of the century, dwarfed these figures: The first earl of Salisbury's income in the period 1608–12 was about £50,000, although the second earl, dependent more on land than office, was reduced to an income of about £15,000 in 1621–41 (Stone 1973: 59, 143). Nevertheless, all these figures are tiny in relation to crown revenues. This had not been so in the medieval period. The magnates were now great *as a class* rather than as a handful of individual families and their households.

It follows that the medieval conciliar form of government – the king in his council of about twenty great men – was no longer appropriate as a means of consultation. Either an office structure centered on the court or representative assemblies were more appropriate – the relatively "absolutist" and "constitutional" paths discussed later in this chapter. It also follows that the great men could not be involved in a personal lord-vassal relationship. To impress a much larger number, the monarch now became public, displaying quality with ostentatious pomp and pageantry. At its extreme this became bizarre, as we can see from this description of Louis XIV:

The king of France was thoroughly, without residue, a "public" personage. His mother gave birth to him in public, and from that moment his existence, down to its most trivial moments, was acted out before the eyes of attendants who were holders of dignified offices. He ate in public, went to bed in public, woke up and was clothed and groomed in public, urinated and defecated in public. He did not much bathe in public; but then neither did he do so in private. I know of no evidence that he copulated in public; but he came near enough, considering the circumstances under which he was expected to deflower his august bride. When he died (in public), his body was promptly and messily chopped up in public, and its severed parts ceremoniously handed out to the more exalted among the personages who had been attending him throughout his mortal existence. [Poggi 1978: 68–9]

More important than public display was the rise in public legislation. Rules of conduct could now be less easily handed down through the lord-vassal chain. A common first stage in the move from particular to universal rules of government in England, France, and Spain was the "home counties"– centered rule referred to in Chapter 13. In England the Yorkist king Edward IV (1461–83) had recruited lesser men – leading knights and gentry – from the Home Counties into his household. He ruled this rich core area more directly (elsewhere rule was through the great magnates). By the time of Henry VIII men from these counties constituted the majority of the king's Privy Chamber. A map of the counties supplying two or more Gentlemen of his Privy Chamber (Falkus and Gillingham 1981: 84) reveals a bloc of contiguous counties in East Anglia and the Southeast, plus only three counties elsewhere. A last stage in the process can be discerned in eighteenth-century England: a "class-nation" stretching across the whole country comprising gentry, nobility, burghers, and political "placemen" – all of whose wealth was acquired or used capitalistically. In between was a complex transition, greatly affected by the peculiarities of civil and religious strife. Overall, however, it was a secular process of capitalist class development within a nation.

The powerful men as a class were equally useful to the state. Although their autonomous military resources were now less necessary, the monarch required their wealth. They were also in control of local administration and justice in most countries, and they thus had access to the wealth of their neighbors. Their powers of passive resistance against the state, especially against the tax collector, were considerable. No monarch could govern without them. They were drawn increasingly into central state offices, both military and civil. Not the household but the *court* was now the focus of activity, and *offices* the focus of hopes. The number of offices increased, though in different ways in different countries.

We can distinguish two principal variables. First, land-based states drew the nobility more into their armies than naval powers did into their armed forces. In the seventeenth and eighteenth centuries, higher commands and the entire army officer corps except for artillery became dominated by nobles in all countries, in contrast to the more middle-class naval officers (Vagts 1959: 41–73; Dorn 1963: 1–9). Second, some monarchs, unwilling or unable to consult about direct taxation, intensified the historic process of selling royal offices, especially through tax farming. France is the clearest example, although the practice was widespread (Swart 1949). Everywhere, the favor of the monarch, the "extravagance" of James I, the "spoils system," increased in scope and quantity, *centralizing* the historic social solidarity of the monarch with the landed nobility and, therefore, also centralizing and politicizing their solidarity and their conflicts.

Centralizing tendencies made state finances an incomplete guide to state activities. Neither the financial benefits nor the costs of the spoils system were enormous, yet the coordinating role of the monarch had grown considerably. The political implications inaugurated a set of conflicts between "court" and "country" parties that were an important step in the development of "symmetrical" and "political" class struggle, forcing the nobility, and reinforcing the merchants, toward a state-bounded role.

In England court and parliament became the two major arenas of national conflict and coordination. The court was the more particularistic, distributing rights and duties in a network of patron-client relationships. This merely added numbers, a crowd of courtiers, to old conciliar practices. Parliament was more novel, even if it were not yet as powerful. Its legislative activity had increased enormously. In the first seven sessions of Elizabeth's reign, 144 public and 107 private acts were passed, and an additional 514 bills failed to pass (Elton 1979: 260). Note the roughly equal number of public and private acts. The latter related to one particular locality, corporation, or other set of relations.

It indicates the decline of the great baronial and church households that private disputes were now brought frequently to Westminster. Universal *and* particular rules were laid down in one dominant place, though central coordinating power was still shared with the court. This was not yet a unitary state.

The sphere of social legislation is a good example of these trends. The English state, like most major states, had long accepted responsibility for ultimate control of wages, prices, and mobility in crisis conditions. Under the Tudors and Stuarts the legislative scope widened. Economic and population expansion produced social turbulence. Forcible enclosures caused much parliamentary discussion; and a threefold growth in population destablized London between 1558 and 1625. Fear of public disorder and charitable sentiments were combined in the Elizabethan Poor Law. Formally, the scope of the new laws was vast. Local taxes would pay for money and work materials to those who wanted to work and punishment and correction for the idlers. Local justices of the peace would administer the system under the overall control of the Privy Council. The Poor Law was not even the main thrust of the legislation, but a backup to a wide range of statutes intended to regulate wages and conditions of employment, control labor mobility, and provide food to the poor at times of famine. This apparently represents a widening of the functions of the state: no longer merely a war machine and law court of last resort, but an active controller of class relations.

The reality was less revolutionary. We do not know exactly how the Poor Law was enforced, but this indicates that enforcement was uneven and under local control. The justices of the peace were, of course, the local gentry. The taxes levied were small, much less than the amount of private charity given for similar purposes (except during the Interregnum, from about 1650 to 1660). From 1500 to 1650 at least £20,000 per annum was bequeathed by private individuals toward charitable purposes – almshouses, direct relief, hospitals, workhouses, and so forth (Jordan 1969: chap. 5). This sum exceeded the total expenditure of the Tudor state on civil functions, if we exclude household and court expenses.

Tudor *claims* were all-encompassing: to enforce positively the welfare and morality of their citizens and expand industry and trade. But the claims were not put into practice. The reason was finance – inflation, warfare, and the private needs of the household and court dominated expenditure. "Virtually nothing was spent by the state toward the realization of the social ends envisaged by the contemporary publicists," concludes Dietz (1932: 125). Similar pressures were felt by all European monarchs. That is why the arresting title of Dorwart's book *The Prussian Welfare State Before 1740* (1971) is fanciful, outside of the realm of ideology. Dorwart's evidence shows that in practice the Prussian state relied on locally powerful groups quite as much as did the English state (see, e.g., his account of police functions, pp. 305–9).

Nevertheless, the change in state ideology indicates the decline in the transnational power of the church. Although the legislation of the period was filled with charitable exhortation, the state was not so much expressing a sense of its own duties (as the modern welfare state does in its legislation) as giving voice to the common ideology and morale of the dominant classes, previously voiced by the church. The administrative apparatus appears as an aid offered to local charity and control of the poor, and that aid was not, for the most part, needed. The social legislation was an example not of greater despotic state powers *over* society but of greater collective organization, greater *naturalization*, of the dominant groups in society. If they could agree on political issues, they would be capable of considerable national cohesion.

In Elizabethan culture and language, the change was most evident. Aided considerably by the circulation of printed books and surges of literacy (Cressy 1981), the English language became standard and standardized across the realm. That standardization has endured. English-speakers today may have some difficulty in understanding some of the more elaborate poetry and also some everyday speech patterns of the Elizabethans – if we take Shakespeare's plays as embodying both – but there is also an Elizabethan style of writing about human sentiments that appears direct and transparent to us today. Here, for example, is a verse by Sir Walter Raleigh who, as one of the most learned and cultivated courtiers of his day, was about as far removed from the people as anyone of his time:

> But love is a durable fire
> In the mind ever burning.
> Never sick, never old, never dead,
> From itself never turning.

This is poetry written in *our* vernacular. The clearest example of the relative stability of English as a vernacular language through the centuries dates from the next reign: the King James Bible used in all English Protestant churches from 1611 to the 1970s. Both examples point to a single conclusion: As a cultural and linguistic unit, England was virtually complete by about 1600. Whatever new groups, classes, and even countries might subsequently join it, their manners of speech and writing would be absorbed into an existing community.

But not everyone was an active member of this community. Who was? Again we can look at cultural artifacts, as the symbolism of the monarch in Parliament. Late in her reign, in 1601, Elizabeth surrendered to a parliamentary offensive against her control of monopolies. Characteristically, she pretended that no dispute had occurred. In her "golden speech" she said:

Though God hath raised me high, yet this I count the glory of my crown, that I have reigned with your loves. . . . I was never so much enticed with the glorious name of a king or royal authority of a queen, as delighted that God hath made me his instrument to maintain his truth and glory and to defend his kingdom from peril, dishonour, tyranny and oppression. Though you have had and may have many mightier and wiser princes sitting on this seat, yet you never had nor shall have any that will love you better. . . . And I pray you, Mr. Comptroller, Mr. Secretary, and you of my council, that before the gentlemen depart into their counties you bring them all to kiss my hand. [quoted in Elton 1955: 465]

Her protestations were propaganda, not truth. But how significant it is as propaganda! Medieval monarchs did not identify with the commons in this way; nor did they invoke God purely as a symbol of national unity (significantly, Elizabeth's greatest propagandist, Shakespeare, tries to persuade us otherwise in his historical plays). Note also the complete unity of class and national allegiances. It is "the gentlemen of the counties" (together with the lords, bishops, and merchants) who *are* the nation in Parliament. As a collectivity, a *class,* extensive and political, not any longer as a set of family lineages, they control the nation's administration, army, polity, judiciary, and church. At this time, according to the Oxford English Dictionary, the word "nation" lost its medieval sense of a group united by common blood descent and was applied to the general population of the territorial state. Naturally this did not include the masses in any active sense; they were excluded from the political nation. They were not mobilized or organized; they lay passively at the base of the structure. Class relations were still asymmetrical, although now one class was fully, universally, politically organized.

The symbolism became complete as one by one the commons filed past the old queen, kissing her hand. The ideology was universal and organic. The interdependence of crown and propertied classes was now so close that ideology could soon also be reality. But to arrive at this point, we must discuss two further features of the sixteenth century, Protestantism and the European expansion. They turn us toward international space.

The Protestant schism and the end of extensive Christian power

I argued in Chapter 10 that Christianity after the collapse of Rome provided an *ecumene,* a universal fellowship across Europe, within which social relations were stabilized even in the absence of political unity. Southern Euope gradually recovered to its former level of civilization, and this was carried to much of northern Europe. The church was not hostile to economic development, as we saw. But economic growth stirred up four forces with which the church would be distinctly uneasy. These were the rise of modern science, of a capitalist class, of northwestern Europe, and of the modern national state. The first two emerged principally through the development of city life, the last two through geopolitics. Together the four constituted a massive problem for Rome that it was unable to overcome without inducing schism. In the towns, classical city habits and thoughts revived, especially in Italy. Confidence in human activity and energy became exemplified in the Renaissance movement – pride in the human body, confidence that human rationality could probe all matters, hope that government could be ruled by reasoned statecraft. None of this was alien to established Christianity, and several popes were at the heart of the movement. But it secularized the *ecumene* for the literate classes. Humanism revived classical learning, the study of Greek. It traveled across frontiers without the aid of church organization. It emphasized one horn of the dilemma of salvationist religion – individual rationality rather than church authority – in a church that tended, in its compromise with secular power, to emphasize the other horn.

The church was uneasy with the development of scientific rationality. Here it committed a terrible blunder. Its emphasis on authority had elaborated a complete set of cosmological doctrines that were central to its imperial legacy of authority but that were hardly central to original Christian dogma. Unfortunately they could also be refuted. For centuries, church authority was unwittingly undermined by men like Galileo (who showed that the earth was in no particular "hierarchical" position in relation to other heavenly bodies), Buffon (who showed that the earth was considerably older than 4,004 years), and Darwin (who showed that the human species was a branch of sensate life in general). The earlier scientists were often persecuted, usually to their surprise. The legacy was disastrous for the church. Its pretensions to a cosmology were broken in a particularly damaging way by the demonstration that its doctrine was false. By the seventeenth century even loyal intellectuals like Pascal were separating "faith" from "reason." Science was no longer incorporated into religion. For many of its practitioners, modern science has been actively hostile to religion.

It is worth dwelling on the break between religion and science, given its importance to the anticlerical movement of the last centuries. From the Enlightenment through Comte and Marx to modern secular humanism has run a current of thought asserting that religion was merely a reflection of humanity's early history, reflecting powerlessness in the face of nature. Once science and technology can tame nature, religion is obsolete. Now our problems are social, not cosmological, it is asserted. Adherents of religion cannot deny that science has taken over many areas that religion traditionally explained: they merely retort that these are trivial areas (e.g., Greeley 1973: 14). We saw in earlier chapters that they are right. Not since the beginnings of civilization have the religions discussed in this book devoted much attention to the natural world. Their concerns have been overwhelmingly *social,* not natural: How is a society, or a society of believers, to be established, and how is it to be governed? The core of none of these religions would be affected by the growth of science and technology unless the religions showed hostility to these forces. The whole apparatus of modern science and technology would probably not have affected the power of religion one way or the other had not socially based ideological conflicts appeared between them.

Two such conflicts arose. The first was the conflict between authority and reason. Vast numbers of people all over Europe were actively intervening in nature in historically unprecedented ways, and many were speculating on the overall scientific meaning of such technology. It was suicidal for the church to claim authority over the knowledge that was so derived. It could not enforce its claim over such diffuse discoveries. But the second conflict was the more important, for it affected all versions of Christianity alike. Christianity could not easily incorporate two emergent forms of consciousness, class and national ideologies, and so they became secular, competing ideologies. This is the crucial story to be told in this section.

The church's second problem was with merchants and emergent capitalists. This raises the knotty issue of the "Protestant Ethic" thesis – Weber's argument that a mutually reinforcing affinity existed between the "Protestant Ethic" and the "spirit of capitalism." I can briefly only deal with the thesis here. Certain of Weber's points seem generally accepted. First, there was a tension between the centralized authority of the Catholic church and the decentralized decision making required in a market system by those who owned the means of production and exchange. Second, there was a tension between a fixed order of statuses legitimated by the church and the requirements of commodity production, in which nothing apart from property ownership is given a fixed and authoritative status. In particular, labor has no intrinsic value under capitalism: It is a means to an end and is exchangeable against other factors of production. Third, a tension existed between the social duty of the rich Christian to be "luxurious" (i.e., to maintain a large household, provide extensive employment, and give to the poor) and the capitalist's need to claim private ownership rights over the surplus so as to provide a high level of reinvestment.

These tensions meant that entrepreneurs seeking to find ultimate meaning in their activities would find the established church no great help. Many would be more attracted to a "primitive" doctrine of individual salvation, unmediated by a hierarchy of priests or estates, in which hard work and asceticism were moral virtues. Entrepreneurs, artisans, and "protoindustrializers" organized on a wide territorial scale, with their activities stretched into agricultural areas and so linked to rich farmers, would not find very appropriate the Catholic meaning system or the Latin language it was expressed in. They were now largely literate in their national vernaculars and thus were capable of exploring religious texts for themselves. The writings of Erasmus, Luther, Calvin, and other religious explorers would help them toward a more appropriate meaning system, which in turn would increase their normative solidarity. The result was what Weber described: enhanced religious "class solidarity" of burghers and entrepreneurs, whose convictions enabled them better to change the world (see the brilliant interpretation by Poggi 1984).

This class might seek a new modus vivendi within the church or break out in the direction of a more individual form of salvation. Both options were possible. Christianity is a salvationist religion; its medieval hierarchical structure was an opportunistic accretion; its abuses and scandals went in cycles and were periodically corrected; its radicals had always pointed to a simpler, more ascetic, primitive church as the real model of the Christian community; Luther and the other rebels railed against simony, nepotism, the selling of indulgences, and a priestly interpretation of the Eucharist, as had many before. To explain why in some places but not others people broke out of the church and founded Protestantism, we need to consider power organizations neglected by Weber. This brings me to the church's third and fourth problems.

The third threat was the geopolitical product of economic development. Once northern and far-western Europe were brought into the *ecumene*, the uneven development discussed in Chapter 12 affected the regional balance of power. The North and the West became more powerful. After the navigational revolution of the fifteenth century, this became a pronounced tilt, giving a clear advantage to those areas adjacent to the Atlantic and Baltic. But the church's organizational center was in Rome, and its traditional locus of activity was the Mediterranean. Logistics and geopolitics meant that its ability to control emerging power centers in Sweden, north Germany, Holland, and England was low. Its diplomatic traditions were concerned largely with balancing the pretensions of secular powers within its heartland – Italian states, Spain, France, southern Germany, and Austria. The church was geopolitically threatened. This gave the distinctive geographical curve to the Catholic-Protestant divide that makes a mess of simple Weber-inspired (or Marx-inspired) explanations of the emergence of capitalism in terms of Protestantism (or vice versa). Northern and western Europe (and some of northeastern Europe), regardless of penetration by capitalism, gravitated to Protestantism. The sudden increase in political and economic power that accrued to these regions produced a crisis in meaning of which ideologists had to try to make sense.

This regional divide was reinforced by the fourth problem, the rise of the national state. This emerged from outside the church and was not caused by any of its actions. It concerned the development both of military power and of the class-nation. In the long run this favored the relatively territorial, relatively centralized and coordinated state. State-led national mobilization weakened the church's transnational *ecumene*. Rulers now had the military capacity and national support to resist the papacy and its closest territorial allies, should they wish. The major northern and western rulers did so wish. Their wishes and increasing power then reacted back upon some of *their* traditional subregional opponents, who thus became stauncher supporters of Rome. This accounts for most of the regional exceptions, Catholic Ireland and Poland in particular.[5]

[5]It may also account for Hugenot southern France.

These four problems combined complexly during the sixteenth and seventeenth centuries. Only by combining them can we explain the emergence of Protestantism. Christians throughout Europe were aware of the intellectual and moral failings of the church, and of the need for reform. Among entrepreneurial groups in trade, industry, and land a special need arose for a more relevant meaning system expressed in vernacular language. The farther from Rome, the more acutely this need was felt. Any doctrinal innovation that devalued the authority of Rome would also make special sense to ruling political elites. What followed was quick interplay between all four power sources, leading to the end of the united Christian *ecumene*.

In 1517 Luther had barely nailed his theses to the church door in Wittenberg before he was "protected" by Frederick the Wise, elector of Saxony, the major north German opponent of the Austrian emperor, from attendance and possible punishment at the Roman Curia. This immediately prevented a purely religious compromise. It was a political as well as theological dispute from the start. His protest spread quickly among the princes and towns of north and central Germany. Through market and military-recruiting networks, it penetrated the peasantry, already confident of their military prowess through service as mercenary *lansquenets* (pikemen) in German and foreign armies – a curious final outcome of the emergence of the pike phalanx! Encouraged by misunderstanding the title of Luther's essay "The Freedom of a Christian Man," they rose in revolt in the Great Peasant War of 1524–5. Luther corrected them with his tract "Against the Murderous and Thieving Hordes of Peasants," repaying his political debts. The German princes, he said, had a divine right to rule and to organize the emerging faith as "provisional bishops." Thirty years of disputation and armed struggle saw the suppression of radical Protestants (like the Anabaptists, who rejected any kind of political or ecclesiastical authority). The Peace of Augsburg, in 1555, enshrined the principle of *cuius regio, eius religio;* that is, all subjects should follow the religion of their prince (although the imperial cities were granted religious toleration). Revolt in the Netherlands against Catholic Spain and the opportunism of the rulers of England and Scandinavia had produced the geopolitical-religious curve by 1550. The emerging capitalist powers of Holland and England fostered a greater degree of literacy and allowed greater latitude of religious observance, if not actual toleration. After terrible religious-political wars, all these Protestant powers, plus Catholic France resisting Spanish hegemony, forced the southern and central Catholic powers to recognize the political, religious, and economic divide at the Peace of Westphalia, in 1648. *Cuius regio, eius religio* was confirmed, and so it remains. The religious map of Europe drawn up in 1648 remains virtually unaltered today. No dynamic force has arisen from within Christianity to alter it – the clearest sign of Christianity's subsequent decline and of the rise of a secular society.

The religious wars had seemed to threaten Europe's unity, built originally on Christendom. The settlement divided Europe into a Catholic and a Protestant part, a division that has had many subsequent ramifications. In the short term it hastened the speed of change in northern and western Europe and retarded it elsewhere. To pick out one example, Protestant states translated the Bible into their vernacular languages and some (especially Sweden) encouraged literacy based on Bible reading. Catholic states did not. Protestant national identities thus developed faster than Catholic.

Yet Europe maintained an ideological, increasingly secular identity. In this the role of France seems crucial. France was the main country that faced in both geopolitical and geoeconomic directions – with both Mediterranean and Atlantic pretensions, light and heavy soils, and commercial trade and aristocratic land. Its opportunism in the Thirty Years' War – siding with the Protestant states yet suppressing its own Protestants – showed that European unity could be maintained diplomatically within an ordered multistate civilization while religious cement was disintegrating. Although national languages developed, they were intertranslatable, and by many educated men and women of the ruling classes. For the next two or so centuries France played a crucial role of ideological intermediary, especially among nobilities, between what were potentially two Europes. Its language tended to become that of both the nobility and diplomacy, thus providing a nonreligious sense of normative community to rulers throughout Europe.

Within this framework, in several of the Protestant countries and, to a lesser extent, in some Catholic ones, religion became an essential part of the organic unity of the national state. This was especially true of England, with its national Protestant church headed by its monarch. But the Elizabethan settlement, as Hanson (1970) has observed, embodied a contradiction. The organic, civil consciousness that it sought to foster blended two distinct traditional political theories. The first conceived of government as authority descended from on high, from the king alone or from privilege and status in general. The second saw government as embodying liberty ascended from the people. They had been the twin traditional pillars and contradictions of Christendom, class ideology and transcendent ideology, now thoroughly nationalized. A claim that reconciliation was possible would face challenges from both above and below.

From above, Elizabeth's organic claim was contested by Charles I and James II, who stumbled toward the undoing of the organic unity of monarch in Parliament. They emphasized the court at the expense of Parliament and attempted "to live of their own" while developing a standing army. Because they could not reverse all the fiscal and legislative trends I have described, a return to the medieval practice of coordinated rule was impracticable. Absolutism was where this courtly path led, as their opponents realized. From below came murmurs from the excluded classes, especially in the New Model Army of the Civil War. Both challenges were associated with religious faiths – despotism with Catholicism and High Anglicanism, populism with Dissent

– because the Protestant Chruch of England was an essential part of the organic identity they were challenging. The Catholic and Calvinist factions of the opposition were more transnational in their orientations; so their defeat heightened the nationalism of the new community.

The Settlements of 1660 and 1688 more or less confirmed what Elizabeth had claimed – the monarch would rule with the consent of the people in Parliament, their organic unity cemented by Protestantism. Thus the English Civil War does not figure in my narrative as a revolution, nor do the events of 1688. These were not massive social changes but failed royalist coups. True, they stirred up potentially greater social movements, but these were suppressed. In the settlements both major terms, "the people" and "Protestantism," were given clear and restricted definitions.

The people were defined by the Lord Chancellor to Parliament in 1661:

It is the privilege . . . the prerogative of the common people of England to be represented by the greatest and learnedest and wealthiest and wisest persons that can be chosen out of the nation; and the confounding the Commons of England . . . with the common people of England was the first ingredient into that accursed dose . . . a Commonwealth. [quoted in Hill 1980: 12]

The franchise was restricted: In 1740 the Commons was elected by a smaller proportion of the population than in 1640. The property criterion for jury service was ten times higher even than this. The people were now the propertied – probably a slightly larger proportion than the 3 percent to whom Gregory King in the 1690s attributed an income of £100 a year. They now met in one place (though in two Houses) at Westminster. The power of the court was in decline. The nation *was* a class, and its energies could be mobilized.

Protestantism, too, was carefully defined. The High Anglicans, usually substantial families, were brought into a more doctrinally latitudinarian church. Dissenters were tolerated outside the church in the towns (though not in the counties) but were excluded from public office. By the time of George I, the only religion that mattered in English politics was Catholicism, and all that mattered was that it stayed abroad. Throughout much of the eighteenth century, a secular, literate, rational, confident, integrated ruling class of nobility, gentry, and burghers, led by a monarch, *was* the nation of Great Britain.[6] It was the only extensive, organized, politicized class in the nation. Class struggle was not "symmetrical" – although the capitalistic actions of this class (treating all economic resources as commodities, enclosing its lands, and expropriating peasants' rights) were gradually homogenizing subordinates as well. In the 1760s came the first significant challenges from below (reserved for Volume II).

The weakness of Protestantism and Catholicism alike in relation to the national

[6]In these chapters, for reasons of space, I have avoided one great national complication, the incorporation of Wales, Ireland, and Scotland into the English/British state. The defense of my English imperialism is that it mirrors what happened in reality.

state was soon revealed. Transnational Calvinism suffered from the failure of England to intervene significantly in the Thirty Years' War. All transnationalism took a beating when Catholic France suppressed its own Protestant Huguenot minority and then intervened in the war on the Protestant side. "National capitalism" was beginning to reign supreme on the Atlantic after 1652 when the two major Protestant powers, England and Holland, began their forty-year naval battle for international commercial hegemony.

Protestantism was more subordinate to the national state than was Catholicism. Its organizational forms, not already in existence, were usually determined by the state, as in England, Scotland, and the whole of Scandinavia and the Baltic. In the Netherlands and France, Protestant organization took different forms (because of involvement in civil wars), but it was similarly subordinated to powerful lords and burghers. Swiss Calvinists and English Puritans left distinctive marks on both ecclesiastical and general social organization, especially the Puritans. They reinforced trends toward constitutional monarchy in England and established republican colonies in the New World. Elsewhere in the New World, the expansion of Christianity was in forms determined by the official religion of the colonizers' home state.

The full effect of geopolitics on religion can be perceived in Martin's *A General Theory of Secularization* (1978: esp. 15–27). He notes that the principal forms of secularization in Christianity can be predicted on the basis of three variables (the last two of which are geopolitical): (1) the differences between Protestantism and Catholicism; (2) whether either kind of church is in a monopolistic, duopolistic, or pluralistic position within the national state; and (3) whether political revolutions have their origin within the national state or outside it. Variables (2) and (3) demonstrate the importance of the organization of the national state. Like so many sociologists, Martin implicitly accepts the primacy of the national state by referring to it throughout as a "society"; that is, he assumes it to be the basic unit of analysis. Protestantism was not a transcendent, society-creating force. Unlike original Christianity, it tended to reinforce the boundaries and the morale of existing political-power networks, its intensive penetrative powers contributing to their transformation into fuller "societies." That is the common link, for example, in Fulbrook's (1983) account of the twists and turns of church-state relations in three countries: Protestantism might turn revolutionary (England), absolutist-reinforcing (Prussia), or quietist (Württemberg), but everywhere its restructuring was of given, state-defined "societies."

Protestantism's strength lay elsewhere, in intensity of personal faith, in experience of direct communion with God, in the strength of its apocalyptic visions, and in the conviction of personal salvation. Like all salvationist religions, it linked this to the rituals of birth, marriage, and death, and to the routine of local life. It sectarian offshoots created highly committed, small religious communities and doctrinal intensity. Thus its penetration into everyday life and into esoteric intellectual life was sometimes as strong as in the Christian tradition as a whole. But it lacked both secondary social organization and a complete theory of social order. It was less complete as a cosmology than earlier Christianity. Its greatest impact was probably on the development of high science, the last great achievement of the rational restlessness of Christianity. (I do not emphasize this source of dynamism, because I do not see a subsequent continuity between high science and technological innovation until after the Industrial Revolution was well under way.)

Catholicism fared a little better. Its greater concern with social order, with hierarchy, with social duty led it to intervene constantly in secular power processes – through teaching orders, brotherhoods of businessmen, Catholic trade unions, and political parties. They are still with us today, and they generally have greater power than their Protestant counterparts.

But no more than Protestantism can the Catholic church avoid the fundamental secularism of modern European civilization. Modern Europe has been integrated by four interrelated, secular institutions: (1) by the capitalist mode of production, which soon took the form of (2) industrialism, both of which have been regulated normatively and geographically channeled by (3) a national state within (4) a multistate, geopolitical, diplomatic civilization. All four institutions have generated their own ideologies, and in combination these have severely weakened Christianity. Thus the fundamental ''tracklaying'' role of Christianity has been rendered obsolete through its own success. Its *ecumene* established, other forces have taken over, both in more intensive penetration of the *ecumene* and in extensive penetration of much of the rest of the globe. Its own *ecumene* broke down amid terrible religious wars, in which denominations denied each other's basic humanity. When the states and the churches reached their modus vivendi, state diplomacy was the main instrument of peace. The *ecumene* was secularized. The main secular actors within it – princes, nobles, merchants, bankers, protoindustrialists, artists, scientists, intellectuals – had dual identities – both a nationality and a transnational European identity. They exchanged goods, ideas, marriage partners, and so forth, not quite ''freely'' but in ways restricted only by well-regulated international channels of communication.

Note that I am giving a specific meaning to the process of secularization: Religion's *extensive* power declined as it lost much of its capacity for social organization to secular power sources and to a predominantly secular European culture. This does not render Christianity obsolete in general; nor does it involve predicting any further decline. Christianity has retained a near monopoly over problems of meaning that emanate from key human experiences – birth, sexual desire, reproduction, and death. And Christianity manages to provide an organizational and ritual framework that links these experiences into a meaningful family life cycle; in its more successful areas, such as Ireland and the United States, it further integrates the family into local community life and even plays a wider normative role in the state. In these functions it is flourishing. The obituaries that sociologists used to pronounce over its presumed murder by secular society have been retracted. Now sociologists remark on its continued vitality, its membership stability, and in some countries (notably the United States) even its membership increase.

Over *this* area of meaning, ethics, and ritual, it has no serious rival. Neither capitalism, nationalism, nor later forces such as socialism have effective means of linking the family, its life cycle, and death to the macrosocial forces they embody. But over the extensive organization of power, Christianity lost much of its force from the sixteenth to the eighteenth century, broken by mutually reinforcing development, in economic, military, and political power. Consequently it will barely figure again in my narrative.

Inter-national expansion

The trend toward the organic unity of the class-as-nation was reinforced by the most dramatic change in the sixteenth and seventeenth centuries: the breaking of the European boundaries.[7] In some ways, however, European expansion merely continued earlier trends. Geopolitically it reinforced the movement of power toward the West. The Portuguese navigational revolution coincided accidentally with the final Islamic conquest of Constantinople. The Mediterranean became a lake, not a through trade route, and enormous opportunities for expansion were given to the Atlantic powers. They could exploit them because by the time of the navigational revolution the more powerful states of western Europe were already monopoly licensers of international trade, granting rights of trade to groups of merchants (usually their own nationals) in return for revenue. Hence expansion of international trade would not necessarily reduce the economic salience of national states.

I return to trade statistics. At this time foreign trade was probably increasing at a faster rate than total national income, and this may have been a reversal of the trend of the last few centuries. As yet we have no good figures for the ratio of trade to national income such as I present for later periods. Gould, however, (1972: 221) estimates a fivefold real increase (i.e., discounting inflation) in foreign trade between 1500 and 1700, which is probably at least twice the increase in national income as a whole. This was not a truly international economy, for the trade increase was from a very small base,[8] and the national state helped organize it. In the sixteenth century various

[7]Discussion of European expansion is drawn mainly from Hechscher 1955: 326–455; Cipolla 1965; Lane 1966; Davis 1973; Parry 1973, 1974; Wallerstein 1974; and Lang 1975.

[8]Total trade (imports plus exports, at a time when reexports were insignificant) during the early years of Henry VII's reign might have reached about £500,000, i.e., about 3–4 times the financial size of the state and probably under 5% of (an almost entirely national) national income.

states began to collect statistical materials on their total trading patterns – evidence enough of state implication. In England, Elizabeth's reign offers the first statistics. By 1559–61 wool and cloth were maintaining their medieval dominance over exports, though cloth predominated over wool, indicating a substantial domestic textile industry. Cloth constituted 78 percent of exports, and wools and cloths together more than 90 percent. Imports were more diverse, but largely luxury items. Two-thirds of traffic concentrated on Antwerp and almost all the rest on the ports of France and the Iberian peninsula. By 1601– 2 little had changed except that Amsterdam and the German ports had replaced Antwerp (because of disruptions caused by the revolt in the Netherlands). But one important development was the gradual replacing of foreign ships by English ones in overseas trade – sealed eventually by the navigation acts of the 1650s and 1660s. Ships had a nationality (see Stone 1949).

Thus there was little integration of international trade with the mass of the people as a whole: A *sector* was involved in exports, and a *class* in the import of luxuries. This was not a national economy integrated as a whole into an international one. Although England's trade differed from other countries, the pattern of one important staple (cloth, grain, or perhaps timber) plus a range of luxury goods was usual. The significance of trade to economic activity as a whole was slightly greater in the Netherlands, but French trade was less than a quarter per capita of its population (so estimates Brulez 1970).

Trade also depended on state regulation. Expansion onto other continents enhanced the state-boundedness of capitalist development. No prior regulation of international relations among the European powers, and between them and other powers, existed there. Transnational elements of the early medieval economy had depended on Christian normative regulation. As the economy became more extensive, it depended more on alliance with the state. The expansion out of Europe thrust trade and warfare, merchants and the military arm of the state, even closer together.

This can be seen in the economic policies and philosophy of mercantilism. Mercantilist policies had two thrusts: internally to eliminate local feudal privileges and customs, assist enclosures, and regulate the terms of wage labor; and externally to tax and license international trade, prevent the outflow abroad of bullion, and thereby maintain an export surplus. Such policies began to be applied in the fifteenth century, that is, before the European expansion, although they did not dominate state policy until the mid-eighteenth century. Their dominance then lasted for something less than a hundred years.

These policies were underpinned by a mercantilist philosophy of which the central thesis was that the wealth of the world constituted a finite sum and its distribution therefore constituted a zero-sum game. Prosperity flowed from an orderly distribution of internal (i.e., national) resources and external protection against foreign powers. Country A could only grow wealthy at the expense of country B once internal order was attained. The exact influence of the philosphy is controversial,[9] but the rise of policies embodying a close connection between "power and plenty" (to use the contemporary phrase) was obvious.

Mercantilism reinforced two trends that we have noticed from the thirteenth century: naturalization of economic activity and militaristic coordination of state and economy. It was also rational, given the conditions of the time. The idea that wealth was ultimately finite was plausible until the end of the eighteenth century. It was reinforced by the clear relation between the wealth of a country and its state's ability to win wars. The conquest of external markets, dictated by the needs of early manufacture, was largely won at the expense of neighbors. The Dutch grew rich at the expense of Spain and France, inflicting heavy losses on French industry and trade in the late sixteenth century. The English grew rich at the expense of Spain and France; the French at the expense of Spain. When Spain strengthened protectionism in the 1620s, this immediately harmed French merchants and manufacturers. The French responded with protectionism (Lublinskaya 1968).[10] In theory, protectionism could be ended if one power became hegemonic and dictated "free trade" terms (as Britain virtually did in the early nineteenth century), but before then a balance of power prevented hegemony. The alternative was for each country to obtain its markets within a demarcated non-European colonial sphere of influence. This deflected, but could not end, the warlike drift of European history. Short, sharp colonial wars were rational – the victor acquired the disputed colonial area, the vanquished could be mollified by the grant of less desirable colonial areas. There were plenty of spoils still to be divided.

It is impossible to decide precisely who benefited from mercantilism and from successful war. Doubtless substantial sections of the peasantry remained largely unaffected by the expansion of trade. And warfare – provided it did not take place over one's own terrain – was not noticeably harmful to the civilian population, especially if it was organized according to the "fiscal" rather than the "mobilized" principle contrasted above. Then it was fought by professionals and was not costly in terms of social wealth as a whole. Successful warfare was to no one's disadvantage in the victorious state (unless very heavily taxed or mobilized) and was probably to the benefit of the majority. The people of England were the major gainers, for no wars were fought over their terrain and they generally enjoyed the fruits of victory. For them it is not fanciful to talk of the common benefits of warfare. Schofield documents a gradual decline in opposition to taxation in the first half of the sixteenth

[9]Contrast Hechsher 1955 with the essays in Coleman 1969.
[10]Lublinskaya overstates her case. She argues that the unevenness of the "17th century crisis" can be totally explained in this fashion. Other factors contributed, however: e.g., internal state regulation for purely fiscal purposes probably went so far in France and Spain as to stifle economic growth (see North and Thomas 1973: 120–31). But some contemporaries would have agreed with her. As James Beckford, a great London merchant, said of France in Parliament: "Our trade will improve by the total extinction of theirs" (quoted in Dorn 1963: 9).

century. The wealthier classes in general became more willing to grant funds toward an aggressive foreign policy (1963: 31–41, 470–2). But whether common or not, the benefits clearly divided the inhabitants of each state from those of others. The economy was now strongly state-bounded, and satisfaction and dissatisfaction alike were now expressed within the confines of each territorial state.

So far, then, the significance of the development of the state in the sixteenth and early seventeenth centuries lies less in its overall bulk than in its growing role as the locus of the class-nation. It was still tiny in size. Indeed, as a proportion of national wealth at a time of general economic expansion its revenue and expenses must have been declining, though we have no reliable figures on national income until much later.[11] It is worth remarking the apparent painlessness of tax extraction in Tudor England. The sums extracted were lump sums, assessed on local communities' net wealth by themselves, and collected over a very short period of time. Schofield has demonstrated that the sums granted by Parliament were invariably forthcoming. The sums required by the Tudor state must have been a very small proportion of national resources. In terms of its resource-requiring functions, the Tudor and early Stuart state was late medieval. To its main traditional activity of making war, it had merely added a more regular administrative and fiscal machinery, which, nonetheless, still served military ends. Even when the state began to grow formidably in size, under the Commonwealth and then the later Stuarts, it was still almost entirely along these tracks hallowed by the centuries. If we talk of a Tudor revolution in government (to echo the title of Elton's classic work), we are describing a social and administrative reorganization of existing resources, a concentration of social networks at the level of the territorial state.

If this conclusion is valid for England, we might, nonetheless, doubt its application to other countries in which states loomed larger. This raised the problem of "absolutism." Discussion of this will take us beyond the date of 1688.

Absolutist and constitutional regimes

As with all ideal types that have emerged from particular historical cases, the concept of absolutism can lead us in two directions. Are we concerned more with developing absolutism as an ideal type, capable of extension to other cases, or do we wish to describe and distinguish particular European regimes?

---

[11]Bean (1973: 212) asserts that less than 1% of national income was spent on warfare by states in the medieval period, over 2% in the sixteenth century, and 6–12% in the seventeenth century. This is assuredly wrong. For it to be true, national income would have had to have been in decline in the sixteenth and seventeenth centuries, an impossible assumption.

I address the latter issue. Can the components of the ideal type distinguish between two apparently different forms of regime in Europe from the fifteenth to the eighteenth century – on the one hand, the "constitutional" monarchies and republics, principally England and Holland, and, on the other hand, "absolute monarchies" such as Austria, France, Prussia, Russia, Spain, Sweden, and the Kingdom of the Two Sicilies? Let us start with the ideal type. Absolutism had two principal components:

1. *The monarch is the sole human source of law,* although as he is subject to the law of God, some residual right of rebellion exists if he transgresses "natural law." In absolutism there are no representative institutions.

At the close of the medieval period, all European monarchs governed with the concurrence of small, informal but representative assemblies privileged by law. In many countries these were suppressed in the following period. Assemblies met for the last time or the next-to-the-last time in Aragon in 1592, in France in 1614, in the Spanish Netherlands 1632, and in Naples in 1642 (Lousse 1964: 46–7). The regimes that supplanted them are termed absolutist, until representative assemblies reemerged at the close of the eighteenth century. This criterion demarcates "constitutional monarchies" ("the king *in* Parliament") like England and Holland from most continental "absolutist" regimes.

2. *The monarch governs with the aid of a permanent, professional, dependent bureaucracy and army.* The officers, civil and military, have no significant autonomous power or social status except for that conferred by their office.

Traditionally, the king had governed and made war with the aid of magnates who had significant independent resources in land, capital, military power, and church institutions. In 1544 the state officials of the Spanish crown's Milan possession were asked to give a part of their wealth to the crown, as traditionally required by their personal oath of loyalty. But they refused, on the grounds that their earnings from office were necessary reward for services rendered, not a gift from the crown. This, according to Chabod (1964: 37), is a precise example of the emergence of a new "bureaucratic" and absolutist conception of state office. On the military side, a consequence of the change is a "standing army" that – in addition to its necessity for the defense of the realm – can be used to repress internal dissent and to enhance the monarch's power over "civil society."

The theories of absolutism I consider first relate the rise of monarchical power to some determinate state of "civil society," and especially to class relations. There are three competing versions: Absolutism is explained by the survival of the *feudal* mode of production, or it is associated with the rise of the *capitalist* mode, or it is a product of a *transitional* class structure where neither the one nor the other is dominant. Anderson (1974: 17–40) argues that the expansion of production and exchange relations meant that feudal serfdom could no longer be politically supported by parceled manorial authority – dependent class relations now require a centralized authority. The feudal nobility was the main prop of absolutist regimes. Wallerstein (1974) and Lublinskaya (1968) argue that emerging capitalist relations required a "strong" state in the core areas of Europe to legitimize its social revolution and to protect its foreign expansion. Mousnier (1954) argues that absolutism arose in a transitional period when the monarch could play off emerging bourgeoisie and traditional nobility against each other. Each theory has merit, and each is notably better at explaining some states than others (Eastern Europe equals late feudalism; Spain equals emerging capitalism; France equals transition). But they also have weaknesses. First, they have too pronounced a view of the differences between the two forms of regime and the two types of class structure on which they are supposed to be built. Second, they neglect the crucial intervening role of war in linking class to regime form. To begin with, the notion of a "strong" regime is overgeneralized. We must distinguish between the two principal meanings of a strong regime: power over civil society, that is, *despotism;* and the power to coordinate civil society, that is, *infrastructural* strength. Absolutist states were not infrastructurally stronger than constitutional ones. Internationally, England, a constitutional state, eventually emerged as dominant. Domestically the matter is also unclear, for *all* states had acquired a monopoly of law making and increased their coordinating powers, Elizabeth's England quite as much as the Spain of Philip II. All that remains of the difference is despotic power, on which I will comment in a moment.

Second, the essential change in class structure that affected the state was the same everywhere: the decline in the great baron and his household and the rise of more numerous families of substance, requiring new forms of political organization, partly to repress the peasantry, but mainly to help organize the lords themselves to extract taxes, influence the monarch, intermarry, and generally enjoy a sociocultural life. The tendency for magnates to lose economic and military autonomy was general throughout Europe, occurring in the "constitutional" as well as the "absolutist" regimes. Their conversion into "officers" did not necessarily lead to absolutism.

If the differences are not so systematic, and if we remember that the object of our inquiry, the state, was still puny, then we should allow for idiosyncracy in the states' development. The essence of absolutism was that the monarch acquire a measure of financial and manpower autonomy from his more powerful and organized subjects. Yet the numbers involved were not particularly large. If the monarch eschewed foreign wars and could live on his own, he could generate a small surplus, acquire a professional army, repress representative assemblies, and then raise more money by arbitrary means. The difficult part came next, as we shall see. Prussian and Russian absolutism had their origins in the extensive private estates of their rulers. Charles I was proceeding along this path when, unfortunately for him, the army he acquired was Scottish and Puritan and did not prove amenable to his particular type of absolutism. James II also created a professional officer corps, which would not then support his Catholicism. Others were luckier. Spanish absolutism was founded on the gold and silver of the New World; French absolutism, on the delaying, divisive strategy of the sale of offices. Political canniness, windfalls in foreign policy, and financial expediency would steer one state toward absolutism, another toward constitutionalism.

If we seek general causes on top of these, say, class organization, we should seek *their* cause. After all, we have seen that class relations in all countries had become focused at the level of the state partly as a by-product of geopolitical relations, in this context the most important aspect of state activity.

The first relevant geopolitical variable is the difference between land and sea power. The association of a professional army with absolutist regimes is genuine, but perhaps it is more peculiar than has been implied so far. It is really cheating to specify a standing *army*. That effectively excludes England and Holland. But if we included a standing *navy*, that would let both in, especially in the period when they were thoroughly constitutional, after 1660. Armies can be used for internal repression; navies cannot. The English Parliament never feared a professional navy the way it feared a standing army. Therefore, navies and armies tend to be associated, respectively, with constitutional and absolutist regimes. Only Spain could not fit such a generalization (being absolutist yet a mixed land and naval power). When states' main original functions were warlike, it makes more sense to explain their variety in terms of war than in terms of derivative functions like class regulation.

But by the same token the marginality of the state to internal social life reduced the strength of absolutism itself. Ideology claimed the monarch was subject to divine, not human, law. But he was no ancient emperor – he was not the sole source of law; of coinages, weights, and measures; of economic monopolies; and of the rest of the panoply of ancient economic infrastructure. He could not impose compulsory cooperation. He owned only his own estates. "Private," in the sense of "hidden," property was deeply embedded in European social structure. It had been bequeathed to feudalism by transnational forces, and the small and medium-sized successor states could hardly have overturned it even had the thought occurred to them.

What were the projects of a ruler embarked on the absolutist path, having raised a small standing army from his own resources plus expedients? He could build splendid palaces, entertain lavishly, and repress his own internal rivals, but he could not easily raise the sums to take on his fellows abroad in an era of rising military costs and near stalemate in land warfare. Yet this was still the primary function of the state. How was either fiscal or manpower mobilization to be stepped up? Even the standing army could not ensure extraction. In a preindustrial society, as I have stressed, it is not easy even to assess where landed wealth is, let alone extract it. The profits of trade are more visible – they move. Hence the motto of almost all agrarian states: "If it moves, tax it!" But trade was small and usually delicate. Effective taxation for warfare required assessing and extracting landed wealth. Mobilization of one's own population for military service meant taking peasants from the land. Both required the cooperation of major landowners, to release their peasants, give their wealth, and assess and extract the wealth of their neighbors. In practice all regimes depended on major landowners.

In this vital task, the constitutional and absolutist regimes differed fundamentally. At first, because armies had been professional and relatively small, peasant mobilization was not considered. The early differences turned on "fiscal," not "mobilized," means. England and Holland relied on taxation of both the landed and trading rich with their consent. Absolutist regimes relied on taxation of the landed poor and trading rich, with the consent and repressive help of the landed rich. This was almost certainly due to the greater penetration of capitalism into the class structure of the former countries. "Nobility," "gentry," "yeomen," and "merchants" were all becoming in actuality more like "capitalists." They were more uniform in their political orientations, and less amenable to monarchical divide-and-rule strategies than elsewhere.

In most absolutist regimes, unlike the constitutional ones, the landed nobility were generally exempt from taxation, whereas the peasants, merchants, and urban bourgeoisie were not. Exempting powerful groups from taxation meant that representative assemblies could be avoided – because the main issue of representative government, taxation, did not arise. Instead, the court was the sole institution of state, and only the nobility need be included there. The sale of court offices was an added strategy, both as a revenue source and as a means of admitting some wealthy nonnobles into the ruling class (e.g., the *noblesse de la robe* in France). Nevertheless, despotism was considerably less organic than its constitutional counterpart, for it operated through a greater number of divisions and exclusions. There were stronger court and country factions as well as the normal division between included and excluded classes. Whereas constitutionalism reinforced the development of an organic capitalist class, absolutism tended to block it or crosscut it with other political divisions.

Because it was less organic, this absolutism at first proved weaker infrastructurally. This again was a systematic variable because weakness was found out and punished by war. Marlborough's successes showed the great strength of a well-organized fiscal machine supplying a professional army. Spain was the first major power to be found wanting. Unable to tax uniformly, the state devolved fiscal and recruiting powers onto tax farmers and onto local communities and magnates. War decentralized Habsburg Spain and so defeated it. As Thompson comments (1980: 287), "War was . . . less a stimulant than a test of the state." France was next. Under Richelieu and Mazarin, the crown centralized its fiscal-military machine in the mid-seventeenth century, but only through buying the consent of the nobility and rich peasantry with tax exemptions (for details, see Bonney 1978). In the eighteenth century, intensified war found out this weakness.

But as it did so, another strategy was discovered that boosted the strength of absolutism. As armies and their fire power increased, the professional expertise required of ordinary soldiers did not keep pace with their numbers. This was primarily an eighteenth-century development, dependent on improvements in muskets and in agricultural productivity. Agriculture could release more men from labor and could feed larger campaigning armies. Peasants could be forcibly mobilized, trained to a level well below that of a mercenary, and yet give a good account of themselves in battle. Thus the "mobilized" military machine could compete on equal terms with the "fiscal" one, and the lead of Britain and Holland could be cut. Russian armies, long mobilized, became more valuable, and the conscripted element of the Prussian and Austrian armies became larger and more effective.

France wavered, facing both ways geopolitically, geoeconomically, and constitutionally. Most French political theorists began to favor constitutionalism as they succumbed in war after war to the British. Their one victory was in alliance with the American revolutionaries (even more constitutionalist than the British). The pressures contributed to the French Revolution, from which emerged a more lethal, mobilized war machine that could be adapted by a variety of regimes. But before Bonaparte, absolutist forms of rule were weakened by their particularism. The possibility of releasing the collective energies of whole classes now existed but was ignored by absolutism. This mattered less in military organization (at least in land warfare) than it did in economic organization. Absolutist states did not learn to mobilize "late-development" strategies until the late nineteenth century. Until then, the most effective development came through the collective, but diffusely organized, energies of the capitalist class. The paradox of absolutist states of this period was that they were superficially class-conscious, yet they failed to realize the novel, universal significance of classes, acting as if they were merely particularistic dynasties and households writ large.

Their failure was probably due to particular geopolitical and military pressures. They were predominantly struggling within central Europe, many of them landlocked, hoping for territorial gains in a largely zero-sum game. So they attracted the traditional group most interested in landholding: the nobility, especially its younger sons. In contrast, sea powers hoped for trade gains and attracted those with realizable capital, which meant any person of substantial property. They could mobilize the entire fiscal energy of the propertied classes and ultimately unite them as a class-nation. For *they*, and not the state or the dynastic privileges it had traditionally allied with, were providing the dynamism of European society. There is something in the argument that constitutional regimes were conducive to, and responsive to, emerging capitalism, for they fostered the unity of a private property class. And absolutist regimes tended to preserve the social structure of feudalism and keep apart different types of property ownership. But the differences were expressed in state policy through the instrument of war.

Thus constitutional and absolutist regimes were subtypes of a single form of state: a weak state in relation to the powerful groups of civil society, but a state that increasingly coordinated those groups' activities to the point where we may begin to talk of an organic class-nation whose central point was either the court or the court/parliament of the state.

A test of the power and autonomy of the states can be found in the colonial empires. The state's near monopoly over foreign relations allowed it more room for maneuver in colonial than in domestic matters. Let us see how that developed.

Constitutional and property relations in the colonies were initially varied, bearing the stamps of different European constitutions. The Portuguese crown undertook all trading ventures itself until 1577, fitting out its own ships, buying, selling, and taking the profits. The Spanish crown attempted to closely control the trade and government of the Americas through the Council of the Indies and the licensed monopoly of the Seville merchants' Consulado. The French crown also involved itself directly in trade, putting up most of the venture capital. In contrast, the Dutch and British initiatives were usually private, and their empires were at first largely the property of private organizations such as the India companies.

We should note, however, a common element in these arrangements. The companies were confined to nationals. Whether state-administered or privately administered, foreign trade and dominion were generally monopolistic and state-bounded. All constitutional forms implied greater coordination of military and economic organization within each state and its colonial sphere of influence.

As colonialism developed, a common pattern emerged. On the military side, by the late eighteenth century the capital investment needed for military protection of foreign trade and possessions outran the capacity of private companies. All states adopted a common imperial form in which the state coordinated military and economic expansion. On the economic side, a reverse trend developed so that no state eventually owned its colonial economies. To some extent this was due to the military success of England. Critics of the regimes in France and Spain claimed that private ownership was more efficient and led to greater wealth and power. But crown control was also undermined from within by smuggling involving its own colonials and agents associating with rival powers. More precious metals probably flowed illicitly out of the Americas, for example, than were carried by the Spanish Silver Fleet.

Absolutism was never strong enough to overthrow private-property rights. The French and the Spanish did not behave differently in the New World than in their mother countries, and their crowns never showed the will or possessed the resources to force them to change. The logistics of power were only moderately favorable to the crown. The man-of-war or the armed merchantman was a tremendous concentration of firepower, and it could cover vast sea spaces. But it could only coerce those in its vicinity. For most colonies a show of force from the crown in Europe might come once a year. Paperwork was effective at maintaining the broad parameters of colonial rule between times. All administrations had to account on a regular basis, using standardized, mass-printed forms. All officials were fully literate in reading and writing, so errors and omissions were assumed to be deliberate. But for most of the year within these accounting parameters, the colonials were effectively independent. The crown recognized this institutionally by rewarding its officials with the perquisites of office, not with salaries. The state was commercial even in its own body politic.

In any case, the same logistics of internal control could be tied by the larger trading companies to capitalist accounting methods. In 1708, for example, the English East India Company revolutionized its accounting system by establishing proper headings for capital and current accounts and for recording systematically the monthly cash inflow and outflow. The accountant general's office in London could now assess the profitability of each branch of trade, anticipating, so says Chaudhuri (1981: 46) the methods of the multinational corporation. Paper was now a major logistical tool of the authoritative power of both state and capitalist enterprises, which operated in an increasingly close alliance. This alliance provided the infrastructure for what Steensgaard (1981: 254) calls "the unique combination of the time perspectives of power with the time perspectives of profit, in . . . the balance between the forces of the market and the power of government." Such was European colonization.

By the eighteenth century no state intervened in its economy, either domestically or in the colonies, to the extent common among some of the ancient empires. The two groups in "civil society" that could aid the running of the colonies – nobles and merchants – had originated in the decentralized power structure of medieval Europe. Their interest lay in maintaining this structure, not in state control. Thus from the seventeenth century onward, the power of monarchs was continuously undermined from within. As we saw in Chapter 12, economic networks had already been depoliticized centuries before the emergence of capitalism. The state was fundamentally weakened by its infrastructural inability to penetrate civil society. This is as true of absolutist as of constitutional regimes.

The similarities of the two kinds of regime were far greater than their differences. In the next section we see that their finances were essentially similar. They shared two principal characteristics: Their power was limited by their largely military functions and did not include a share in property rights, and they extracted fiscal revenues and coordinated their dominant classes primarily for military purposes. Their differences concerned merely the forms of coordination – one approaching organic unity, the other backing away from it – that were determined by the way in which two emerging power networks, classes and national states, related to each other on the battlefield.

State expenditures and warfare, 1688–1815

A reliable annual set of accounts for the central government of Great Britain for the period after 1688 has been collected and standardized by Mitchell and Deane (1962) and Mitchell and Jones (1971). Conveniently, the 1690s also mark the beginning of a "long century" (until 1815) of a fairly regular succession of periods of peace and major war in Europe. Utilizing expenditure data for this period, we can systematically test the hypotheses suggested for earlier periods.

The chronology is straightforward. After William III's initial Irish campaigns and naval battles, peace lasted from 1697 until 1702. During this period, in 1694, the foundation of the Bank of England placed English borrowing and debt repayment on a regular basis that has lasted until the present day. Then the War of the Spanish Succession, involving repeated campaigns by the duke of Marlborough, lasted from 1702 until 1713, followed by a largely peaceful period until 1739. Then began the War of Jenkin's Ear, which soon became the War of the Austrian Succession and lasted until 1748. A period of uneasy peace was ended by the Seven Years' War, 1756–63. Then there was peace until the American War of Independence merged into prolonged naval wars between 1776 and 1783. Then there was peace again until 1792, from when the French Revolution and Napoleonic Wars lasted more or less continuously until 1815, though with a short lull at the beginning of the century, sealed by the Peace of Amiens 1801. This is a much more regular sequence of war and peace than in the nineteenth or twentieth century. As it also predates the influence of industrialization on state expenditures, it gives us a convenient test for the preindustrial period.

In Figure 14.1, I present the main results in graph form, separating total expenditures and their three components – military, civil, and debt-repayment expenses. The graph is of expenditures in real terms, that is, controlled for inflation by using once again the price index of Phelps-Brown and Hopkins (1956). I have controlled for prices at their level in 1690–9, the beginning of the period.[12] The expenditures at current prices, together with the price index itself, are given in Table 14.3.

---

[12]Thus these figures are not comparable with those of Tables 13.2 and 14.1, which present current prices and constant prices at their level in 1451–75. For technical

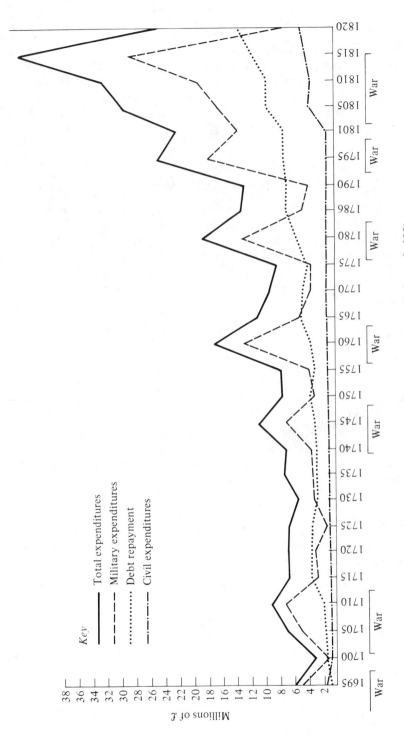

Figure 14.1. *British state expenditure, 1695–1820 (at constant prices: 1690–9 equals 100)*

Table 14.3. *State expenditures for Great Britain, 1695–1820 (in millions of pounds at current and constant 1690–99 prices)*

Year	Price index	Military expenditures		Debt repayment		Civil expenditures		Total expenditures	
		Current	Constant	Current	Constant	Current	Constant	Current	Constant
1695	102	4.9	4.8	0.6	0.6	0.8	0.8	6.2	6.1
1700	114	1.3	1.1	1.3	1.1	0.7	0.6	3.2	2.8
1705	87	4.1	4.7	1.0	1.2	0.7	0.8	5.9	6.8
1710	106	7.2	6.8	1.8	1.7	0.9	0.8	9.8	9.2
1715	97	2.2	2.3	3.3	3.4	0.7	0.8	6.2	6.4
1720	94	2.3	2.4	2.8	3.0	1.0	1.0	6.0	6.4
1725	89	1.5	1.7	2.8	3.1	1.3	1.5	5.5	6.2
1730	99	2.4	2.4	2.3	2.3	0.9	0.9	5.6	5.6
1735	82	2.7	3.3	2.2	2.7	0.9	1.1	5.9	7.1
1740	90	3.2	3.6	2.1	2.3	0.8	0.9	6.2	6.8
1745	84	5.8	6.9	2.3	2.7	0.8	1.0	8.9	10.6
1750	93	3.0	3.2	3.2	3.5	1.0	1.1	7.2	7.7
1755	92	3.4	3.7	2.7	2.9	1.0	1.1	7.1	7.7
1760	105	13.5	12.8	3.4	3.2	1.2	1.1	18.0	17.1
1765	109	6.1	5.6	4.8	4.4	1.1	1.0	12.0	11.0
1770[a]	114	3.9	3.4	4.8	4.2	1.2	1.1	10.5	9.2
1775	130	3.9	3.0	4.7	3.6	1.2	0.9	10.4	8.0
1780	119	14.9	12.5	6.0	5.0	1.3	1.1	22.6	19.0
1786[b]	131	5.5	4.2	9.5	7.2	1.5	1.2	17.0	13.0
1790	134	5.2	3.9	9.4	7.0	1.7	1.3	16.8	12.5
1795	153	26.3	17.2	10.5	6.8	1.8	1.2	39.0	25.5
1801[c]	230	31.7	13.8	16.8	7.3	2.1	0.9	51.0	22.2
1805	211	34.1	16.2	20.7	9.8	7.8	3.7	62.8	30.0
1810	245	48.3	19.7	24.2	9.9	8.8	3.6	81.5	33.3
1815	257	72.4	28.2	30.0	11.7	10.4	4.0	112.9	44.0
1820	225	16.7	7.4	31.1	13.8	9.8	4.4	57.5	25.6

[a] Between 1770 and 1801 the detailed items fall short of the total given by about £500,000. No reason for this is given in the source.
[b] 1785 figures follow an idiosyncratic budgeting system.
[c] 1800 figures are incomplete.
Sources: Mitchell and Deane 1962, Mitchell and Jones 1971.

Note first the upward trend in the financial size of the British state: Between 1700 and 1815 real expenditures rise fifteenfold (and the increase at current prices is thirty-five-fold!). This is easily the fastest rate of increase we have seen for any century. We guess that state expenditures have also increased as a proportion of gross national income. In 1688, using Deane and Cole's (1967)

reasons explained in Mann (1980), I have estimated the price index at the average of the expenditure year and two previous years (previously the price index has been averaged over whole decades).

calculations based on Gregory King's contemporary account of national wealth, we can estimate state expenditures as comprising about 8 percent of gross national income (for the method of calculation, see Deane 1955); by 1811 it had risen to 27 percent. Although these figures are not very reliable, the magnitude of difference is impressive.

But the upward trend is not steady. The total rockets suddenly six times. It will come as no surprise that all but one of these are at the beginning of a war, and all six are due primarily to a large rise in military expenditures. Furthermore debt repayment, used exclusively to finance military needs, rises toward the end of each war and is maintained in the first years of peace. The pattern is beautifully regular: Shortly after the end of all six wars, the rising debt repayment line crosses the military line coming down, exceeding it by an increasing margin each time. This has the effect of flattening the impact of war. Looked at year by year, the largest increase in total expenditures at current prices over the previous year was only just over 50 percent (in both 1710–11 and 1793–4), which is much lower than the 200–1,000 percent increases we saw prevalent at the onset of wars right up to Henry VIII. And in peacetime it is now largely military expenditures (and especially the navy) and debt repayment that keep up the relative level. A "permanent war state" has arrived with a vengeance! Civil expenses are remarkable steady and small. They do not rise above 23 percent in any year (in 1725 after a decade of peace) over the entire period. During the Napoleonic Wars a new trend appears, however. From about 1805 the civil expenses, having remained static over the previous century, now begin to rise. I leave this until the next volume. The permanent war state also means that after each war state expenditures do not fall back to the prewar level, even in real terms. In midcentury the poet Cowper expressed this in a simple couplet:

> War lays a burden on the reeling state,
> And peace does nothing to relieve the weight.

These figures confirm every hypothesis made for previous centuries on the basis of sketchier data. State finances were dominated by foreign wars. As warfare developed more professional and permanent forces, so the state grew both in overall size and (probably) in terms of its size in relation to its "civil society." Each new war led to a larger state in two stages: an initial impact on military expenses and a delayed impact on debt repayment. As yet the functions of this state – a "constitutional" state, let it be remembered – are overwhelmingly military. Other functions largely spin off from its wars.[13]

[13]One exception to this exists. By the end of the eighteenth century, the Poor Law, financed locally (and not appearing in these figures) but arguably a function of the state, was costing large sums, although the sums are tiny in relation to military expenditures. If we add its costs to civil expenditures, their combined total does not exceed 20 percent of the new grand total. If we further add all local-government expenses (available from 1803), it is still below 25 percent until 1820. See Volume II for details.

Table 14.4. *Austrian state expenditures, 1795–1817 (in percent)*

Year	Military	Debt repayment	Civil	Total expenditures at current prices (in millions of guldern)
1795[a]	71	12	17	133.3
1800	67	22	11	143.9
1805	63	25	12	102.7
1810	69	20	11	76.1
1815[b]	75	4[c]	21	121.2
1817	53	8	38	98.8

[a]Beer's figures are somewhat incomplete for the period 1795–1810. In 1795 I have assumed that the missing sums belong to civil expenditures and in 1800–10 to debt repayment. This is the most obvious interpretation. As Beer always provides us with both the military and total expenditures, the military percentages are certainly accurate.
[b]Beer breaks down "ordinary" expenditures for 1815 and 1817, but not total expenditures (which were 132.9 and 122.1 million gulders respectively).
[c]Substantial English subsidies in the period 1814–17 kept down the state debt. Without this, military-related expenditures would be a higher proportion and civil expenditures a lower one.
Source: Beer 1877.

Such trends were not peculiar to Great Britain. Here are some rather sketchy figures for other countries. First, Austria, for which figures are available from 1795 (see Table 14.4). As Austria was a land-based power, its military expenditures were almost entirely devoted to an army (whereas rather more than half Britain's were naval). These figures show a similar dominance of military expenditure, though to a lesser degree than in Britain, especially in peacetime (1817). Austrian military strength was relatively mobilized rather than fiscal, deriving more from large conscripted levies. These were disbanded in times of peace, and thus the fluctuations in percentages were greater than in Britain.

Data available over a similar period for the United States are given in Table 14.5. I deal more systematically with U.S. figures in Volume II. But one word of caution: The United States is a *federal* system. For a more complete picture of the American "state(s)," we should also consider the finances of the component states. But unfortunately the relevant data are not available for this period. Thus these figures understate the real size of the "American state," and they overstate the military component (since the armed forces are predominantly the responsibility of the federal government). The finances of the federal government, however, are similar to those of European states, once we take account of the peculiarities of American foreign policy. The only period of actual declared war was 1812–14, although tension with the British

Table 14.5. *U.S. federal government expenditures, 1790–1820 (in percent)*

Year	Military[a]	Debt repayment	Civil	Total expenditures at current prices (in thousands of dollars)	Number in armed forces
1790[b]	19	55	26	4.3	718[c]
1795	39	42	19	7.5	5,296
1800	56	31	13	10.8	7,108[d]
1805	23	39	38	10.5	6,498
1810	49	35	16	8.2	11,554
1815	72	18	10	32.8	40,885
1820	55	28	16	18.3	15,113

[a] Includes veterans payments (see volume II for an analysis of this important item).
[b] Expenditure figures are an average of the period 1789–91, as given in the source.
[c] 1789 figure.
[d] 1801 figure.

was high during a wider timespan, from about 1809, while the United States established a stance of fairly wary neutrality from 1793. These periods of genuine peace, armed neutrality, open warfare, and then peace again are visible in the columns of Table 14.5. Overall, the degree of military and debt-repayment predominance is lower than in the British case but of the same general order as the Austrian. The same ratchet effect of war upon finances as in Britain appears to be felt.

Sketchier evidence survives for other countries. The Prussians went over much later to deficit financing. Higher revenues from crown estates and greater taxation powers over peasants and merchants enabled the rulers to finance war without borrowing until the late eighteenth century. In 1688 "between one-half and five-sevenths went to service the army" (Finer 1975: 140). In 1740, the last year of peace for Prussia, the three main items in the Prussian budget were the army (73%), the civil service and court (14%), and a reserve fund (13%) (Seeley 1968: I, 143–4). In 1752 Prussia spent 90 percent of its revenues for military purposes in a year of peace (Dorn 1963: 15). By the mid-1770s the army absorbed 60 percent of revenue while civil expenditures took only 14 percent (Duffy 1974: 130–18) – was the balance debt service? This was certainly so by 1786, when the three main items were the army (32%), the court and government (9%), and debt charges (56%) (Braun 1975: 294) – remarkably similar to the British budget for that year.

Virtually every history of Prussia emphasizes the militarism of its regime with a choice aphorism – for example, "It was not Prussia that made the army, but the army that made Prussia" (Dorn 1963: 90). The Prussian state was, indeed, the most militaristic in eighteenth-century Europe. But it was this not by virtue of the character of its state activities (these were identical with those of other states), but rather by virtue of the *size* of its militarism (for Prussia devoted more of its resources to the army). In 1761 the Prussian army represented 4.4 percent of its population, compared to the French figure of 1.2 percent (Dorn 1963: 94). In the late seventeenth century Prussia was taxed twice as heavily as France, which was taxed ten times as much as England (Finer 1975: 128, 140) – though such figures depend on guesswork about national income. We can date the development of the Prussian administrative machinery even if we cannot exactly quantify its finances. The principal constituents of Prussian absolutism established by Frederick the Great – the peacetime standing army itself, the tax system agreed with the Junkers in 1653, the development of the military commissaries – were a response to the Swedish threat in the Thirty Years' War. The next step was the emergence of the *Generalkriegskommisariat* in the 1670s. This enabled the state to reach down to the localities for taxes, supplies, and manpower and entangled military with civilian and police administration. That too was a response to Swedish campaigns (cf. Rosenberg 1958; Anderson 1974; Braun 1975: 268–76; Hintze 1975: 269–301).

The Russian and Austrian states developed, though less far, in response to the same outside threats. Poland failed to respond to Swedish dominance and ceased to exist. As Anderson concludes,

Eastern Absolutism was thus centrally determined by the constraints of the international political system into which the nobilities of the whole region were objectively integrated. It was the price of their survival in a civilization of unremitting territorial warfare; the uneven development of feudalism obliged them to match the state structures of the West before they had reached any comparable stage of economic transition towards capitalism. [1974: 197–217; quote from p. 202]

Small wonder then that he, a Marxist, precedes this with a plea for a Marxist theory of war!

Most of the French royal archives burned in two eighteenth-century fires. For the seventeenth century, Bonney (1981) grapples with the surviving accounts of one chief clerk to the *intendant des finances*. The figures are similar to the British ones. War rockets military expenses, and then "extraordinary expenses" (debt repayment?) rise through the war's end. Military and extraordinary expenses always outweigh civil items in this period (1600–56), by a factor of about 10 in most of the years. For the eighteenth century we have stray remarks like those of Jacques Necker, the finance minister, that in 1784 the army swallowed over two-thirds of the revenue – and France also had a sizable navy (quoted in Dorn 1963: 15). This is rather higher than the proportion of English military expenditures for that year.

In the Netherlands between 1800 and 1805 military expenditures combined with debt repayment exceeded 80 percent of the total (Scharma 1977: 389, 479, 497) – similar to the English figures for those war years. For various

German principalities in the seventeenth and eighteenth centuries, military expenditures absorbed 75 percent of the total budget in most years, rising well over that in the middle of wars (Carsten 1959). In 1724 Peter the Great's military expenses totaled 75 percent of Russian state finances (Anderson 1974: 215–16).

Each state had its peculiarities, but the overall pattern is clear. A state that wished to survive had to increase its extractive capacity over defined territories to obtain conscripted and professional armies or navies. Those that did not were crushed on the battlefield and absorbed into others – the fate of Poland, Saxony, and Bavaria in this century and the next. No European state was continuously at peace. A peaceful state would have ceased to exist even more speedily than the militarily inefficient ones actually did.

So far, I have treated state military functions as synonymous with external functions. But – it might be objected – is not the state's military force used for domestic repression, and is it not then integrally linked to internal class relations? There is force in this objection. In every European country the army was used for internal repression. Standing armies were seen everywhere as an instrument of both naked class exploitation and of despotism. But internal repression did not causally determine the growth of the state. First, as I have shown, the growth of the state's size was occasioned throughout the period by warfare between states and only marginally by internal developments. Second, the need for internal repression organized by the state (rather than by local lords) was usually occasioned in the first place by the state's need to raise money for warfare. Third, variations between different countries in the degree of internal repression can be explained in relation to war-finance needs. I have quoted Anderson to this effect in the case of eastern Europe. If the poorer states of that region were to survive, they would have to tax and mobilize more intensively, which meant they had to use more repression. At the other extreme, a rich trading country like England could maintain great-power status without intense extraction and, therefore, without a standing army. To this we might add the geopolitical consideration: Naval powers have difficulty using their forces for internal, dry-land repression. The overall argument stands: The growth of the modern state, as measured by finances, is explained primarily not in domestic terms but in terms of geopolitical relations of violence.

Inter-national and national capitalism, 1688–1815

In the eighteenth century, British statistics for trade and national-income components flowed in abundance. Deane and Cole (1967) have calculated trade and national-income figures and trends throughout the century. Calculations of foreign trade, improvements of the pioneering scholarship of Schumpeter (1960) on customs records, can be used without further ado. But this is not so for national income. No original official source exists. Figures exist only for the production of various individual commodities, each of which can then be taken as the indicator of a sector of economic activity – for example, beer production for consumer goods, coal for energy consumption, corn production for agriculture. Aggregating these into an overall income figure additionally requires an economic theory: a theory of the relative importance of different types of activity in the overall economy. In the case of the eighteenth century, this means a theory of economic growth and, more specifically, a position on one of economic theory's major controversies, the role of foreign trade in growth (for a general discussion of the controversy, see Gould 1972: 218–94). Unfortunately, that is what we are trying to find out: the relation between foreign trade and the economy as a whole.

Thus Deane and Cole's methodology is partly circular. It starts from an assumption that foreign trade will be important and includes (1) a heavy weighting for export-oriented activity and (2) an associated assumption that agricultural productivity remained low for most of the century. The latter assumption has been challenged in recent years by writers to whom I shall refer in a moment. They conclude that large improvements in agricultural productivity, and in the consumption and nutritional standards of the agricultural population, occurred in the first half of the eighteenth century and were then maintained in the second half. The effect of this on Deane and Cole's figures has been discussed by Crafts (1975). The first assumption also looks less strong if agriculture, not generally export-oriented, was growing in its contribution to national income. This is argued by Eversley (1967): A "warm-up" period from 1700 onward to industrial "takeoff" after 1780 was caused mostly by increasing agricultural surplus available for household consumption, especially by middling social groups, which stimulated the domestic market more than it did exports.

In view of these challenges, I retreat to a simpler, cruder level of measurement of national income, the estimates of two contemporaries, Gregory King and Arthur Young. Using these figures and comparing them with trade figures that have a different base can produce only rough estimates of the trade-to-income ratio. Table 14.6 gives the figures. The table suffices to show general orders of magnitude for the first two dates, with rather greater accuracy for 1801.

According to these figures, foreign trade comprised about a quarter of all trade cash transactions around 1700. This figure is higher than the 15 percent Gregory King and Deane and Cole support. It may be too high. By 1770 the ratio was still of the same general order of magnitude, that is, about 20 percent. But by 1801 the ratio was approaching a third. There seems little doubt that foreign trade was increasing much faster than national income in the last two decades of the eighteenth century – Deane and Cole (1967: 309–11) estimate it at more than three times as fast. The arguments concern only the earlier parts of the century. The secular trend between 1500 and about 1870

Table 14.6. *Estimates of national income, foreign trade, and population,*
1700–1801, England and Wales, and Great Britain

	National income (in millions of £)	Total foreign trade, i.e., imports plus domestic ꝰ exports (in millions of £)	Population (in millions)
England and Wales, 1700[a]	50	12	5.5
England and Wales, 1770[b]	128	26.5	7.0
Great Britain, 1801[c]	232	70	10.0

[a] Income figure is based on Gregory King's estimate for 1688 of £48 million; foreign-trade figure is Deane and Cole's 1967 (p. 319) revision, to include costs of insurance and freight of imports, of Schumpeter 1960; population as assessed by Eversley 1967: 227.
[b] Income figure is Arthur Young's; foreign-trade, Deane and Cole; population, Eversley.
[c] National-income and population figures given by Mitchell and Deane 1971: 6, 366; foreign-trade in Deane and Cole, slightly increased in proportion to the increase in Schumpeter's unrevised figures between 1800 and 1801 (which were not revised by Deane and Cole).

was that foreign trade increased faster than national cash income – but it was either interrupted or slowed in the period 1700–70. Whatever the exact trends, Britain's international economy was smaller than its national one in 1800, but it was beginning to catch up.

This does not indicate a decline in the economic salience of the national state in the face of a transnational economy. Deane and Cole (1967: 86–8) provide figures on the geographical distribution of markets that reveal otherwise. In 1700 more than 80 percent of export trade and more than 60 percent of import trade were with Europe, but by 1797–8 these figures had fallen to just over 20 and 25 percent. The explanation is partly a rise in trade with Ireland, the Isle of Man, and the Channel Islands. These were counted in the overseas-trade statistics, though they were obviously a part of the British domestic sphere of influence. But most of the rise of trade was with British colonies in North America and the West Indies. These markets were largely closed to foreign competitors. Indeed the growth of colonies affected British trade patterns throughout the eighteenth century. In 1699–1701, wool and cloth, though still the major English export (at 47% of exports), had declined relatively in the face of the reexport trade, mainly reexporting sugar, tobacco, and calico cloth from the British colonies to Europe. Navigation acts and the mercantilist climate prevented much direct trade between the two. Now such goods comprised 30 percent of both imports and exports. In return the English exported manufactured goods to their colonies and continued to import luxuries from their chief European rivals (Davis 1969a). These trends grew in the eighteenth century and were joined by a new one: importing raw materials from the northern and southern fringes of Europe, especially the Baltic (Davis 1969b).

Thus we can perceive only limited transnational interdependence. Britain's covered the British Isles, its colonies, and in a more specialized way the European fringes, especially Scandinavia. It did not extend to the other major European powers, with which *inter*-national trade predominated. This was regulated carefully by the states and mainly consisted of the direct import and export of goods involving few of the population in either production or consumption. The American War of Independence gave a substantial jolt to this set of networks, but it proved less damaging than the British feared. By 1800, Americans found that free trade followed similar routes to earlier colonial trade. They remained within the British sphere of influence.

The trading patterns of each of the major states differed. But the general trend was that most of the growth of foreign trade was confined within its own sphere of influence, albeit now crossing the globe. A segmentary series of economic-interaction networks was developing, reinforced as we have seen by political, military, and ideological pressures. Between the segments, trade tended toward bilateralism: Imports and exports tended toward balance, with deficits and surplus settled in bullion or bilateral credit. What is usually called the rise of "international" capitalism should be hyphenated to emphasize that inter-national capitalism was not yet transnational.

So let us look more closely at this national economy. Even before 1700 it was a predominantly cash economy. According to Gregory King, in 1688 25 percent of the employed population lived in the almost wholly cash economy of nonagricultural employment. It is impossible to be exact about the amount of coinage flowing through the remaining 75 percent in agriculture, but virtually no one was still delivering all their rent in kind or receiving most of their wages in kind. The coins being exchanged had the king's (or queen's) head on them and could flow freely throughout the realm, but not so easily outside that realm.

Second, few political or class blockages of free circulation existed: no internal tolls, few proscriptions against economic activity by different ascriptive categories of persons, and no significant status or class barriers. The only significant blockage, the qualification for political or economic activity, was property itself. Anyone with property could enter into any economic transaction, guaranteed by the universal legislation and the coercive power of the national state. Property was now measured quantitatively, by its cash value, and commoditized, as we would expect in a capitalist economy. Thus *everyone* possessed property (though in vastly different quantities). Even if they did not possess enough of it to vote or serve on a jury, they could still participate as a separate actor in the economy.

These two features did not ensure that there actually *was* a national market

– networks of economic interation built up quite slowly, and for the whole of the eighteenth century regions and localities were often poorly integrated. But it did mean that economic growth could flow freely and diffusely right across the nation, both geographically and hierarchically, without authoritative, political action. That was not true for most other countries of the time. Thus in Britain as a national unit, capitalism was diffused widely, evenly, and organically through its social structure *before* the massive economic growth of the later eighteenth century began.

This mattered considerably because growth took the form repeatedly encountered in medieval and early modern Europe. It was agricultural, locally based, decentralized, diffused, and "quasi-democratic." It represented true praxis diffused across the national-capitalist circuits just described.

Agricultural growth spurted around 1700, perhaps a little earlier.[14] In the space of half a century, perhaps a little more, it doubled the average disposable surplus from about 25 to 50 percent of total inputs. This probably enabled a reduction in the age of marriage, a rise in fertility, and a lesser fall in mortality rates, and still left spare capacity. So, although it generated population growth, it outstripped fertility capacity. Thus the Malthusian cycle was broken (although two difficult phases were encountered at the middle and end of the century). It involved improvements in productivity. Perhaps the most important was the gradual elimination of fallow land. Fields could be used every season by rotating more varied crops – by planting a succession of cereals and vegetables, each of which used different chemicals or substrata of the soil, and some of which had a regenerative effect on a soil exhausted by others. It is the technique vegetable gardeners still use today. This is why yield ratios understate eighteenth-century improvements. As fodder crops were part of the rotation system, more animals could be reared, which was a calorific improvement and also provided better manure for the soil. Some of the crops were the result of colonial imports: the turnip, potato, maize, carrot, cabbage, buckwheat, hops, colza, clover, and other fodder plants. Other improvements concerned the greater use of horsepower (made possible by fodder), refinements of the plow and horseshoe and greater use of iron in them, and greater interest in seed selection and animal breeding.

It is difficult to explain why this improvement occurred now and in England. It is easy, however, to see what it did not involve. It did not presuppose complex technological developments – these did not appear until near the end of the century. It did not involve high science, though this was also developing. It did not presuppose large amounts of capital. It was not led by the commercial towns or classes. It was pioneered in the countryside by farmers, some wealthy and others relatively modest in their property holding – the

[14]The next three paragraphs are based especially on the work of Deane and Cole 1967; Eversley 1967; Jones 1967; John 1967, 1969; McKeown 1976; and Wrigley and Schofield 1981.

middling groups in agriculture. (Eversley calls them and their nonagricultural associates "the middle classes," but this conveys too class-bound a flavor.) And it presupposed a landless rural proletariat, driven from their land over several centuries to work as "free labor" for these farmers.

The surplus thus generated was widely diffused in a large number of small amounts. There was a limit to what farming families and their associates could consume in the way of basic foodstuffs (i.e., the elasticity of food consumption in relation to income is slight). Thus a surplus was available to exchange for more varied household-consumption goods. Three candidates, available from small-workshop and putting-out industries, were clothing, iron goods, and goods made from other raw materials like pottery or leather that could make useful household items. The mass production of low-cost goods of all three types boomed. England imported more than twice as much raw cotton per annum in the period 1750–60 than it had in the period 1698–1710. Iron consumption increased by more than 50 percent between 1720 and 1760 at a time when industrial need for iron was rising only very slightly. Bairoch (1973: 491) estimates that horseshoes alone accounted for 15 percent of iron production by 1760.

Here we have the probably proximate causes of the Industrial Revolution itself: the boost to its three main industries, cotton, iron, and pottery; the stimulus to their development, which then turned into technological and scientific complexity; the generation of steam power; capital-intensity; and the factory system. In the course of the eighteenth century, Britain's became a national economy: a network of economic interaction based on the middling agricultural household as producing and consuming unit, generating slowly, and then (after 1780) rapidly, an industrial sector boosted by its demand and worked by its surplus proletarians. I leave the Industrial Revolution for Volume II.

In this chapter I have shown the interpenetration of the capitalist and national bases of industrialism. The capitalist mode of production, as defined earlier, is a purely economic abstraction. Real-life capitalism, the form of economy that actually triumphed for a time over Europe and the whole globe, actually presupposed, and embedded within itself, other forms of power, especially military and political power. Specifically, along with production, capitalism comprised markets and classes, "organic" national states vying within a diplomatically regulated, multistate civilization. Europe was a multi-power-actor civilization in which the major independent actors were individual property owners and what I termed "class-nations." I continue this discussion in a broader historical framework in the next chapter.

Bibliography

Anderson, P. 1974. *Lineages of the Absolutist State*. London: New Left Books.
Ardant, G. 1975. Financial policy and economic infrastructure of modern states and

nations. In *The Formation of National States in Western Europe*, ed. C. Tilly. Princeton, N.J.: Princeton University Press.

Bairoch, P. 1973. Agriculture and the industrial revolution, 1700–1914. In *The Fontana Economic History of Europe, Vol. 3: The Industrial Revolution*, ed. C. Cipolla. London: Fontana.

Batho, G. R. 1957. The finances of an Elizabethan nobleman: Henry Percy, 9th earl of Northumberland (1564–1632). *English Historical Review, 9.*

Bean, R. 1973. War and the birth of the nation-state. *Journal of Economic History, 33.*

Beer, A. de. 1877. *Die Finanzen Ostereiches.* Prague.

Bonney, R. 1978. *Political Change in France under Richelieu and Mazarin.* London: Oxford University Press.

   1981. *The King's Debts: Finance and Politics in France, 1589–1661.* Oxford: Clarendon Press.

Braun, R. 1975. Taxation, sociopolitical structure and state-building: Great Britain and Brandenburg Prussia. In *The Formation of National States in Western Europe*, ed. C. Tilly. Princeton, N.J.: Princeton University Press.

Brown, D. M. 1948. The impact of firearms on Japanese warfare, 1543–98. *Far Eastern Quarterly, 7.*

Brulez, W. 1970. The balance of trade in the Netherlands in the middle of the sixteenth century. *Acta Historiae Neerlandica, 4.*

Carsten, F. L. 1959. *Princes and Parliaments in Germany.* Oxford: Clarendon Press.

Chabod, F. 1964. Was there a Renaissance state? In *The Development of the Modern State*, ed. H. Lubasz. London: Collier-Macmillan.

Chandaman, C. D. 1975. *The English Public Revenue 1660–88.* Oxford: Clarendon Press.

Chaudhuri, K. N. 1981. The English East India Company in the 17th and 18th centuries: a pre-modern multinational organization. In. *Companies and Trade*, ed. L. Blussé and F. Gaastra. London: University of London Press.

Cipolla, C. M. 1965. *Guns and Sails in the Early Phase of European Expansion 1400–1700.* London: Collins.

Coleman, D. C. (ed.). 1969. *Revisions in Mercantilism.* London: Methuen.

Crafts, N. F. R. 1975. English economic growth in the eighteenth century: a re-examination of Deane and Cole's estimates. *Warwick University Economic Research Papers, 63.*

Cressy, D. 1981. Levels of illiteracy in England, 1530–1730. In *Literacy and Social Development in the West: A Reader*, ed. H. J. Graff. Cambridge: Cambridge University Press.

Creveld, M. van. 1977. *Supplying War: Logistics from Wallenstein to Patton.* Cambridge: Cambridge University Press.

Davis, R. 1969a. English foreign trade, 1660–1770. In *The Growth of English Overseas Trade in the Seventeenth and Eighteenth Centuries*, ed. W. E. Minchinton. London: Methuen.

   1969b. English foreign trade, 1700–1779. In *The Growth of English Overseas Trade in the Seventeenth and Eighteenth Centuries*, ed. W. E. Minchinton. London: Methuen.

   1973. *The Rise of the Atlantic Economies.* Ithaca, N.Y.: Cornell University Press.

Deane, P. 1955. The implications of early national income estimates. *Economic Development and Cultural Change, 4.*

Deane, P., and W. A. Cole. 1967. *British Economic Growth 1688–1959: Trends and Structure.* Cambridge: Cambridge University Press.

Dent, J. 1973. *Crisis in France: Crown, Finances and Society in Seventeenth Century France*, Newton Abbot, England: David & Charles.

Dietz, F. C. 1918. Finances of Edward VI and Mary. *Smith College Studies in History*, 3.

1923. The Exchequer in Elizabeth's reign. *Smith College Studies in History*, 8.

1928. The receipts and issues of the Exchequer during the reign of James I and Charles I. *Smith College Studies in History*, 13.

1932. English public finance and the national state in the sixteenth century. In *Facts and Figures in Economic History*, essays in honor of E. F. Gray. Cambridge, Mass.: Harvard University Press.

1964a. *English Government Finance 1485–1558*. London: Cass.

1964b. *English Public Finance 1558–1641*. London: Cass.

Dorn, W. 1963. *Competition for Empire 1740–1763*. New York: Harper & Row.

Dorwart, R. A. 1971. *The Prussian Welfare State Before 1740*. Cambridge, Mass.: Harvard University Press.

Duffy, C. 1974. *The Army of Frederick the Great*. Newton Abbot, England: David & Charles.

1979. *Siege Warfare*. London: Routledge & Kegan Paul.

Elton, G. R. 1955. *England Under the Tudors*. London: Methuen.

1975. Taxation for war and peace in early Tudor England. In *War and Economic Development*, ed. J. M. Winter. Cambridge: Cambridge University Press.

1979. Parliament in the sixteenth century: function and fortunes. *Historical Journal*, 22.

Eversley, D. E. C. 1967. The home market and economic growth in England, 1750–80. In *Land, Labour and Population in the Industrial Revolution*, ed. E. L. Jones and G. E. Mingay. London: Arnold.

Falkus, M., and J. Gillingham. 1981. *Historical Atlas of Britain*. London: Grisewood and Dempsey.

Finch, M. 1956. *The Wealth of Five Northamptonshire Families, 1540–1640*. London: Oxford University Press.

Finer, S. 1975. State and nation-building in Europe: the role of the military. In *The Formation of National States in Western Europe*, ed. C. Tilly. Princeton, N.J.: Princeton University Press.

Fulbrook, M. 1983. *Piety and Politics: Religion and the Rise of Absolutism in England, Württemberg and Prussia*. Cambridge: Cambridge University Press.

Goody, J. 1971. *Technology, Tradition and the State in Africa*. London: Oxford University Press.

Gould, J. D. 1972. *Economic Growth in History*. London: Methuen.

Greeley, A. M. 1973. *The Persistence of Religion*. London: SCM Press.

Hale, J. R. 1965. Gunpowder and the Renaissance. In *From the Renaissance to the Counter-Reformation*, ed. C. H. Carter. New York: Random House.

Hanson, D. W. 1970. *From Kingdom to Commonwealth: the Development of Civic Consciousness in English Political Thought*. Cambridge, Mass.: Harvard University Press.

Hartwell, R. M. 1967. *The Causes of the Industrial Revolution in England*. London: Methuen.

Hechsher, E. F. 1955. *Mercantilism*. 2 vols. London: Allen & Unwin.

Hill, C. 1980. *Some Intellectual Consequences of the English Revolution*. London: Weidenfeld & Nicolson.

Hintze, O. 1975. *The Historical Essays of Otto Hintze*, ed. F. Gilbert. New York: Oxford University Press.

Holton, R. 1984. *The Transition from Feudalism to Capitalism*. London: Macmillan.

Howard, M. 1976. *War in European History*. London: Oxford University Press.

John, A. H. 1967. Agricultural productivity and economic growth in England, 1700–1760. In *Agriculture and Economic Growth in England: 1650–1815*, ed. E. L. Jones. London: Methuen.

1969. Aspects of English economic growth in the first half of the eighteenth century. In *The Growth of English Overseas Trade*, ed. W. E. Minchinton. London: Methuen.

Jones, E. L. 1967. Agriculture and economic growth in England, 1660–1750: agricultural change. In *Agriculture and Economic Growth in England,1660–1815*, ed. E. L. Jones. London: Methuen.

Jordan, W. K. 1969. *Philanthropy in England, 1480–1660*. London: Allen & Unwin.

Kiernan, V. G. 1957. Foreign mercenaries and absolute monarchy. *Past and Present*, 11.

1965. State and nation in western Europe. *Past and Present*, 31.

Ladero Quesada, M. A. 1970. Les finances royales de Castille à la veille des temps modernes. *Annales*, 25.

Lane, F. C. 1966. *Venice and History*. Baltimore: Johns Hopkins University Press.

Lang, J. 1975. *Conquest and Commerce: Spain and England in the Americas*. New York: Academic Press.

Law, R. 1976. Horses, firearms and political power in pre-colonial West Africa. *Past and Present*, 72.

Lousse, E. 1964. Absolutism. In *The Development of the Modern State*, ed. H. Lubasz. London: Collier-Macmillan.

Lublinskaya, A. D. 1968. *French Absolutism: the Crucial Phase, 1620–1629*. Cambridge: Cambridge University Press.

McKeown, T. 1976. *The Modern Rise of Population*. London: Arnold.

McNeill, W. H. 1982. *The Pursuit of Power*. Oxford: Blackwell.

Mann, M. 1980. State and society, 1130–1815: an analysis of English state finances. In *Political Power and Social Theory*, ed. M. Zeitlin, vol. 1. Greenwich, Conn.: JAI Press.

Martin, D. 1978. *A General Theory of Secularisation*. Oxford: Blackwell.

Mitchell, B. R., and P. Deane. 1962. *Abstract of British Historical Statistics*. Cambridge: Cambridge University Press.

Mitchell, B. R., and H. G. Jones. 1971. *Second Abstract of British Historical Statistics*. Cambridge: Cambridge University Press.

Mousnier, R. 1954. *Les XVIe et XVIIe siècles*. Paris: Presses Universitaires de France.

North, D. C. and R. P. Thomas. 1973. *The Rise of the Western World: A New Economic History*. Cambridge: Cambridge University Press.

Outhwaite, R. B. 1969. *Inflation in Tudor and Early Stuart England*. London: Macmillan.

Parker, G. 1970. Spain, her enemies and the revolt of the Netherlands 1559–1648. *Past and Present*, 49.

1972. *The Army of Flanders and the Spanish Road 1567–1659*. Cambridge: Cambridge University Press.

1974. The emergence of modern finance in Europe, 1500–1730. In *The Fontana Economic History of Europe: The Middle Ages*, ed. C. M. Cipolla. London: Fontana.

Parry, J. H. 1973. *The Age of Reconnaissance: Discovery, Exploration and Settlement 1450–1650*. London: Sphere Books.

1974. *Trade and Dominion: European Overseas Empires in the Eighteenth Century*. London: Sphere Books.

Phelps-Brown, E. H., and S. V. Hopkins. 1956. Seven centuries of the price of consumables. *Economica*, 23.

Poggi. G. 1978. *The Development of the Modern State*. London: Hutchinson.

1984. *Calvinism and the Capitalist Spirit*. London: Macmillan.

Roberts, M. 1967. The Military Revolution 1560–1660. In Roberts, *Essays in Swedish History*. London: Weidenfeld & Nicolson.

Rosenberg, H. 1958. *Bureaucracy, Aristocracy and Autocracy: The Prussian Experience 1660–1815*. Cambridge, Mass.: Harvard University Press.

Scharma, S. 1977. *Patriots and Liberators: Revolution in the Netherlands, 1780–1813*. London: Collins.

Schofield, R. S. 1963. Parliamentary lay taxation 1485–1547. Ph.D. thesis, University of Cambridge.

Schumpeter, E. B. 1960. *English Overseas Trade Statistics, 1697–1808*. Oxford: Clarendon Press.

Seeley, J. R. 1968. *Life and Times of Stein*. 2 vols. New York: Greenwood Press.

Smaldane, J. P. 1972. Firearms in the central Sudan: a reevaluation. *Journal of African History*, 13.

Sorokin, P. A. 1962. *Social and Cultural Dynamics*, vol. III. New York: Bedminister Press.

Steensgaard, N. 1981. The companies as a specific institution in the history of European expansion. In *Companies and Trade*, ed. L. Blussé and F. Gaastra. London: London University Press.

Stone, L. 1949. Elizabethan overseas trade. *Economic History Review*, ser. 2, vol. 2.

1965. *The Crisis of the Aristocracy 1558–1641*. London: Oxford University Press.

1973. *Family and Fortune: Studies in Aristocratic Finance in the Sixteenth and Seventeenth Centuries*. Oxford: Clarendon Press.

Swart, K. 1949. *The Sale of Offices in the Seventeenth Century*. The Hague: Nijhoff.

Thompson, I. 1980. *War and Government in Habsburg Spain, 1560–1620*. London: Athlone Press.

U.S. Bureau of the Census. 1975. *Historical Statistics of the United States*. Bicentennial ed. pt. 2. Washington, D.C.: Government Printing Office.

Vagts, A. 1959. *A History of Militarism*. Glencoe, Ill.: Free Press.

Wallerstein, I. 1974. *The Modern World System*. New York: Academic Press.

Wolffe, B. P. 1971. *The Royal Demesne in English History*. London: Allen & Unwin.

Wrigley, E. A., and R. S. Schofield. 1981. *The Population History of England, 1541–1871*. London: Edward Arnold.

15 European conclusions: explaining European dynamism – capitalism, Christendom, and states

In the three preceding chapters, I narrated essentially a single story. It concerned the history of a single "society," Europe. It also had two central themes: First, how do we explain European dynamism? Second, what have been the relationships between political and economic power organizations, between states and capitalism, in this dynamic process? We can now conclude our discussion of both themes.

The European dynamic

In the mid-twelfth century, Europe consisted of a multiple, acephalous federation of villages, manors, and small states, bound loosely together by the normative pacification of Christendom. It was already the most agriculturally inventive civilization seen since the Iron Age had begun. Yet its dynamism was buried within intensive, local power networks. In extensive and in military and geopolitical terms it was not yet powerful, and it was not much noticed by the world outside. By 1815 the dynamism had exploded outward upon the world, and it was obvious that this particular civilization was the most powerful, both intensively and extensively, that the world had seen. The last three chapters described and attempted to explain this prolonged surge to power. They argued that the early agricultural dynamic within a framework of normative pacification became harnessed to three more extensive power networks: (1) capitalism; (2) the modern, organic state; and (3) a competitive, diplomatically regulated multistate civilization in which the state was embedded.

The dynamic, unlike the Industrial Revolution in which it culminated, was not sudden, discontinuous, or qualitative. It was a long-drawn-out, cumulative, and perhaps somewhat unsteady process, but nevertheless a process rather than an event, lasting for six, seven, or even eight centuries. I have attempted to convey above all else in the last three chapters the essential continuity of the dynamic, from a beginning we cannot date (for it is obscured by the Dark Ages of the records), then through a stage clearly recognizable about 1150–1200, and then continuing right up to 1760 and the eve of the Industrial Revolution.

This immediately reveals that some popular factor explanations of the dynamic are extremely limited. It was *not* due fundamentally to the twelfth-century

500

town, or thirteenth- to fourteenth-century struggles between peasants and lords, or fourteenth-century capitalist accounting methods, or the fourteenth- to fifteenth-century Renaissance, or the fifteenth-century navigational revolution, or the scientific revolutions of the fifteenth to the seventeenth century, or sixteenth-century Protestantism, or seventeenth-century Puritanism, or seventeenth- to eighteenth-century English capitalist agriculture – the list could be continued. Each and everyone of these is weak as a general explanation of the European miracle, for one reason: They start *too late* in history.

Indeed, some of the greatest social theorists – Marx, Sombart, Pirenne, Weber – have concentrated a fair proportion of their efforts on relatively minor or late aspects of the whole process, and their followers have often amplified this tendency. In the case of Weber, for example, there has been extraordinary subsequent concentration on the role of Protestantism and Puritanism, although these are minor, late contributions. Yet Weber himself stressed the very general, long-drawn-out nature of what he called the "rationalization process," and he also implied that Puritanism largely restated the original Christian message of rational, radical salvation. In these respects, he was much closer to the mark, seeing a very broad historical process and characterizing its essential unity as "rational restlessness." Indeed, such a quality characterizes all the particular single-factor explanations just given. But if they are all similar, we want to know the underlying cause of their unity.

One thing seems clear: If there was a unity and a cause, they must have existed already by the time the events just listed began. What were they? Perhaps we should first ask by what methodology we could arrive at a solution. There are two competing methods.

The first is the comparative method, practiced extensively by sociologists, political scientists, and economists. Here the attempt is to find systematic similarities and differences between Europe, which did see a miracle, and other civilizations, initially similar in certain respects, which did not. This was the method employed classically by Weber in his comparative studies of religion. As interpreted by Parsons (1968: chap. 25), Weber supposedly demonstrated that whereas in economic and political terms China (and perhaps India) was as favorably placed to develop capitalism, it lagged in religious spirit. Puritanism in particular and Christianity in general were the decisive causes, says Parsons. It is, however, doubtful that Weber really intended such a crude explanation. It is far more likely that he was aware of what I am about to say.

Let us consider more modern explanations of why China did not see a comparable miracle. We should first note that some sinologists reject the very comparison as false. Imperial China, they say, did have at least one period of prolonged social and economic development, in the Northern Sung dynasty, about A.D. 1000–1100. This was a "half miracle," ultimately aborted but perhaps repeatable with a different outcome in some later historical period, had China been left alone to its own devices. Yet most sinologists see China as having institutionalized stagnation and imperial "dynastic cycles" rather than dynamism by about A.D. 1200. Unfortunately, they provide at least four alternative, plausible explanations: (1) The ecology and economy of endlessly repeated cells of rice cultivation held back the division of labor, long-distance exchange of commodities, and the development of autonomous towns. (2) The despotic imperial state repressed social change, especially by prohibiting free exchange and overtaxing the visible flow of goods. (3) The geopolitical hegemony of the imperial state meant no multistate competition, and so no dynamic forces were allowed to enter Chinese territories. (4) The spirit of Chinese culture and religion (following Weber) emphasized from very early times the virtue of order, conformity, and tradition. (For reviews, see Elvin 1973 and Hall 1985.)

These are all plausible accounts. It is likely that the forces they identify were all contributory and interconnected and that the causality was extremely complex. The problem is that four plausible contributing forces have been suggested and that Europe differs in respect to all of them. Europe's ecology was not rice-dominated, and it was extremely varied; its states were weak; it was a multistate civilization; and its religion and culture expressed the spirit of rational restlessness. We have no means of knowing by comparison which of these forces, alone or in combination, made the crucial difference, because we cannot vary them.

So can we amass other cases of civilizations that possess varying mixes of these forces in order to get a good spread on our crucial variable? Unfortunately not. Consider for a moment one obvious additional case, Islamic civilization. Why did the Miracle not occur there? The literature on this question is equally complex and contentious. And naturally it tends to deal with somewhat different configurations of forces. One distinctive feature of Islam has been tribalism; another, that religious fundamentalism recurs powerfully, usually from a desert tribal base. Thus one of the most plausible accounts of Islam's stagnation is that of Ibn El Khaldun and Ernest Gellner: An endless cyclical struggle was played out between townsmen/traders/scholars/states, on the one hand, and rural tribesmen/prophets, on the other. Neither has been able to maintain a consistent direction of social development (see Gellner 1981). But in what other civilizations are we able to vary such a configuration? It is unique to Islam. There are more relevant forces and configurations of forces than there are cases. Europe, China, India, Japan, Islam – are there any other cases to which the overall question might be relevantly addressed? As each differs in many respects from all the others, there is no chance of using the comparative method in the way Parsons attributes to Weber.

Indeed there is another difficulty: None of these cases was autonomous. Islam was in contact with all; and influences flowed mutually across them. Islam and Europe fought long and hard against one another, not only greatly influencing one another but also leaving a certain amount of world history to be decided by the fortunes of war. Let us listen to Gellner's nicely malicious comment on the whole European miracle debate:

I like to imagine what would have happened had the Arabs won at Poitiers and gone on to conquer and Islamise Europe. No doubt we should all be admiring Ibn Weber's *The Kharejite Ethic and the Spirit of Capitalism* which would conclusively demonstrate how the modern rational spirit and its expression in business and bureaucratic organisation could only have arisen in consequence of the sixteenth-century neo-kharejite puritanism in northern Europe. In particular, the work would demonstrate how modern economic and organisational rationality could never have arisen had Europe stayed Christian, given the inveterate proclivity of that faith to a baroque, manipulative, patronage-ridden, quasi-animistic and disorderly vision of the world. [1981: 7]

The comparative method has no solution to these problems, not because of any general logical or epistemological defects it might have but because, in dealing with the problems we simply do not have enough autonomous, analogical cases. Confronted by that empirical reality, we must turn pragmatically to the second method, of careful historical narrative, attempting to establish "what happened next" to see if it has the "feel" of a pattern, a process, or a series of accidents and contingencies. Here we still need explicit but broad concepts and theories about how societies generally work and about how human beings behave, but we employ them in a historical narrative, looking for continuity or conjecture, pattern or accident. Historical, not comparative, sociology has been my principal method. What can it establish, and what has it established?

Throughout this volume we have repeatedly encountered one major objection to conceiving of social change as systemic, as internally generated by the patterned tensions, contradictions, and creative energies of a given society. It is that the sources of change are geographically and socially "promiscuous" – they do not all emanate from within the social and territorial space of the given "society." Many enter through the influence of geopolitical relations between states; even more flow interstitially or transnationally right through states, taking little notice of their boundaries. These sources of change are heightened in the case of social development. For we are concerned here, not with the continuous history of a given territory, but with the history of "leading edges" of powerful societies and civilizations, wherever these most advanced edges of power are found. In Europe, the lead traveled northward and westward across the three preceding chapters, from Italy, up the central trade corridors to the territorial states of the northwest and eventually to Great Britain.

So, if we are to locate a pattern to the dynamic, it must take account of two complications: geographical shifts in the central dynamic, and extraneous and perhaps conjunctural relations with the non-European world.[1] For most of our

[1] In addressing these problems, I acknowledge the influence of a seminal work by McNeill, *The Shape of European History* (1974).

narrative the latter means largely taking account of the international and transnational influences emanating from Islam. Some of these will be assuredly accidental from the point of view of Europe itself, and our conclusion will be a mixed one. I will take account of these two complications in turn. First I discuss the "internal" aspects of the European dynamic, taking account of its travels northwest, but ignoring the presence of Islam. Then I turn to Islam.

Let me start with the clear patterning in Chapter 12 existing, especially in the West, by 1155. It contained several disparate power networks whose interactions encouraged social and economic development. There were small peasant villages crosscutting lords' manors, both penetrating and draining wet soils, increasing agricultural yields beyond anything yet known over such an extensive area. But these groups required also more extensive power conditions: They depended on long-distance exchange of commodities, in which another geographical area, the northern shores of the Mediterranean, was the leader. They depended on general recognition of norms regarding property rights and free exchange. These were guaranteed by a mixture of local customs and privileges, some judicial regulation by weak states, but above all by the common social identity provided by Christian Europe. This was one civilization, but within it no single region, form of economy, state, class, or sect could impose its domination completely over others. It was essentially a *competitive* civilization – competition flourished within state boundaries, between states, and right across state boundaries – but competition was normatively regulated. The combination of social and ecological diversity and competition with normative pacification led to that controlled expansionism and inventiveness that Weber's label of "rational restlessness" conveys quite well. As we shall see in the next chapter, competitive "multi-power-actor civilizations" have been one of the two main sources of social-power development.

European dynamism was systemic. First, it characterized Europe as a whole, indeed integrating its diversities into one civilization. Naturally, the forms emerging in northwestern Europe, on which I concentrated, differed considerably from those of the Mediterranean or central Europe. But the same spirit pervaded the continent. Thus the geographical shifts of dynamism actually presupposed its unity. Second, it was patterned because it long endured, overcoming demographic and economic crises, military defeats at the hands of Islam, religious schism, and internal attempts at imperial geopolitical hegemony. Its ubiquity in the face of so many challenges reveals that it was systemic.

But if we turn to explaining its origins, things no longer look quite so systematic. For when we identify the various components of this twelfth-century structure, we find that their origins lie in a great diversity of times and places. We can simplify some of this. Peasant strip farming and village communities descended primarily from the Germanic barbarians, manors, and major trade routes, mostly from the late Roman world. Many economic, military, and political practices recognizably fused these two traditions. Thus we can get a certain mileage out of seeing this medieval, perhaps this "feudal," pattern as the fusion of two prior patterns, the Germanic and the Roman. Anderson (1974), for example, uses the term *mode of production* so broadly that we can partially concur with him when he says that the "feudal mode of production" fused the "Germanic tribal mode" and the "ancient mode." But even this overpatterns what happened. It is not good at dealing with other types of regional contribution to the eventual pattern: for example, the distinctive Scandinavian inputs of sea trade, navigation techniques, and small, cohesive warrior kingdoms. Also it fits Christianity too easily into this pattern as the transmitter, through Rome, of the "classical legacy." Yet Christianity, though it had come through Rome, was essentially bringing the influence of the eastern Mediterranean and the Near East – of Greece, Persia, Hellenism, and Judaism. It proved to have a distinct appeal to peasant farmers, traders, and minor kings right across Europe, and so its influence later transcended the boundaries of the Roman Empire. Although the power structures of Rome are an essential background for understanding, say, the origins of the manor, and those of Germany for understanding vassalage, Christianity's origins were somewhat interstitial to both. Its reorganizing capacities were not limited to bringing about a Roman-German fusion.

Further, if we look inside these Germanic or Roman "patterns" we find them less than cohesive, themselves composed of influences from different times and places. For example, in earlier historical chapters, I charted over a very long time spectrum the gradual growth of Iron Age peasant agriculture. This steadily enhanced both the economic power of the wet-soil peasant cultivator and the military power of the peasant infantryman. The two went hand in hand. They traveled northward across the Roman border into Germany during the Roman principate, and then they returned together in the form of Germanic invasions. But then they separated. The economic trend continued, and economic power continued slowly shifting northwest to the medium-sized farmer. But the military trend was reversed, as the conditions of defensive warfare against non-Germanic barbarians, and available eastern models of heavy cavalry, enabled noble knights to elevate themselves above the free peasantry. Frankish feudalism, in many ways prototypical of later feudalism, was thus a mixture of the very, very old, deep-rooted drift of "European" peasant society and of the brand new, the opportunistic, the "un-European."

For all these reasons it is difficult to avoid the conclusion that the *origins* of the European miracle were a gigantic series of coincidences. Many causal paths, some long-term and steady, others recent and sudden, others old but with a discontinuous historical growth (like literacy), emanating from all over the European, Near Eastern, and even central Asian civilizations, came together at a particular time and place to create something unusual. And after all, that is also how I earlier treated the origins of civilization itself (in Chapters 3 and 4), and how I treated the dynamism of Greece (in Chapter 7).

True, we can reasonably break into this complex chain of coincidences and generalize with acceptable accuracy. But our generalizations cannot concern "social systems." Medieval or "feudal" society was not the result of the dynamism or the contradictions of a preceding social system, "social formation," "mode of production," or whatever unitary term is preferred. Nor was it the result of the fusion of more than one of these social systems. It has been my constant theme that societies are not unitary. Instead they comprise multiple, overlapping power networks. None of these can fully control or systematize social life as a whole, but each can control and reorganize certain parts of it.

In particular, the European miracle cannot be interpreted as "the transition from feudalism to capitalism," as the Marxist tradition has it. We have seen that feudalism, capitalism, and their modes of production are no more than useful ideal-types. With them, we can organize and explain some of the diverse empirical influences on European development; but we cannot derive a satisfactory explanation of European development from them alone. For this task we need to combine such economic ideal-types with ideal-types derived from the other sources of social power, the ideological, military, and political.

Thus our generalizations in the present instance concern how various power networks, organizing different but overlapping spheres of social life and of the European lands, came together to create particularly fertile soil for social creativity. Let me instance the four main power networks operating in this case.

First, Christendom, fundamentally an ideological power network, broke out from an eastern Mediterranean urban base to convert, reorganize, and even create the continent of "Europe." Its normative pacification minimally regulated the struggles of the other, less extensive networks; and its semirational, semiapocalyptic visions of salvation provided much of the psychological motivation for this-worldly creativity. Without this ecumenical reorganization, neither markets, nor property ownership, nor "rational restlessness" would have flowered so within these territories.

Second, inside the *ecumene,* small states added a little judicial regulation and confirmation of customs and privileges. Their reorganization, more limited in scope and extent, varied across Europe. States generally combined Roman pretensions (either imperial or urban *dignitas*) with Germanic or Scandinavian tribal traditions and with structures that had themselves been recently reorganized by military exigencies (armored mounted retinues, castles, vassalage, greater expropriation of the peasantry, etc.).

Third, military power networks overlapped with, and provided much of the specific dynamic of, the early medieval state. Conditions of local, defensive warfare developed the feudal levy in some parts and the urban militia in others. According to local circumstance, these encouraged feudal monarchies or urban communes, with all kinds of mixed principalities lying in between. This military dynamic contributed greatly to the reorganization of class relations. It intensified social stratification, further subordinated the peasantry, and often enmeshed their strips of land with the lord's manor. Greater surplus extraction from the peasantry enabled the lords to trade more commodities, and this intensified rural-urban relations as well as relations between the North, the West, and the Mediterranean.

Fourth, economic power networks were multiple but closely linked. Local production relations varied according to ecology, tradition, and the impact of all the above-mentioned networks. In the Northwest I identified two main and often interdependent units, the village and the manor. Enough of their surplus was traded as commodities to link village and manor to far more extensive trading networks, especially north–south ones. They encouraged the development of north–south corridors across the central landmass, and much of Italy, as a rather different form of society. Here princelings, bishops, abbots, communes, and merchant oligarchies all provided less territorialized forms of integration of town and countryside, production and exchange. From very early on, from before our records begin, the embryonic forms of these economic power networks were showing extraordinary dynamism, especially with regard to agricultural productivity in the northwest.

These four main power networks reorganized varying spheres and geographical extents of early medieval social life. As can be seen even from this brief review, their interrelations were complex. Applied to this era, they are half ideal types, half actual social specialization. I have singled out one, Christendom, as *necessary* for all that followed. The others also made a significant contribution to the resultant dynamic, but whether they were "necessary" is another matter. Could they have been substituted by other configurations of power networks without destroying the dynamic?

This question is especially difficult to answer because of the historical development of the dynamic. Each power network tended to make a distinctive contribution to its reorganization in different periods. Yet each was being constantly reorganized itself by the others. In Chapter 12 I characterized a relatively intensive phase of the dynamic, in which local power actors, principally lords and peasants, improved their agriculture within the normative pacification of Christendom. In this phase states provided little. Later, however, the logic of battle provided distinct military-fiscal boosts to state powers. This coincided with an expansion of trade. The particular combination of these military/political- and economic-power networks then led to a greater general role for states. This included the secularization of geopolitical spaces into a full-fledged, diplomatically regulated multistate civilization. Regulated competition between these states then became a novel part of the European dynamic, alongside the more traditional forms of competition between economic actors, classes, and religious groups. As the last collapsed in significance after about the seventeenth century, the dynamic, though continuous, had differing components in different periods.

A second complication results from geographical variations in the dynamic. Different parts of Europe made reorganizing contributions at different times. The list of "single factor" theories I gave earlier reveals this well. Some emanate from Italy, some from Germany, France, the Low Countries, England. Indeed, if we lengthen the list to include all the factors that seem to have helped Europe along, then the geographical patterning of the dynamic becomes very complex.

It is at this point that we should widen our focus to discuss Islam. Europe borrowed some things from Islam, though precisely what is still controversial. Whether its borrowings – principally, it seems, the recovery of classical learning through Islamic intermediaries – made a critical contribution to European development is still unclear. But the necessity of military defense is another matter. There would have been no *European* dynamic, and perhaps no sustained dynamic at all, if Islam or the Mongols had conquered all or even half of the continent. Defense can be examined systematically.

At first sight the defense does not look patterned. It first centered on kingdoms like the Franks, then on parties of Normans who traveled right across Europe to fight and found their Mediterranean kingdoms. Then they were aided in the period of the Crusades by some of the great monarchs of the time, French, German, and English. Then, with the decay and collapse of Byzantium, Burgundian and French knights made brief forays, though the main Islamic pressure was now felt by Venice, Genoa, and the Slavic kingdoms. Then Spain and Austria took the strain. The final turning point, outside the gates of Vienna in 1683, was achieved under the leadership of a Polish king. *Everyone* seems to have had a hand in the defense of Europe. Put differently, an enormous variety of social structures found across Europe protected the dynamic through their military-power organizations.

Through this example we can perceive both contingency and pattern in the historical and geographical shifts. Contingent factors were important because Islam's periods of pressure either were primarily the result of factors internal to itself or emanated from the eastern periphery of Europe, which often contributed little directly and positively to the European dynamic. Some contingencies had immense repercussions. When the Turks took Constantinople and closed the eastern Mediterranean, they changed the European balance of power. The trade of the central Mediterranean powers declined at the same time as their military commitments grew. The Atlantic powers seized their opportunity, and the West became dominant. This was, in a sense, a world-historical accident.

But in another sense, the shift of power was part of a long-term drift toward the West and the Northwest. This has been proceeding in virtually the whole of this volume, and so it is more appropriately a subject for the next, concluding chapter. But we should now recall it so that we do not take as a local accident something that may have been part of a pattern. Islamic pressure and its geopolitical consequences were not entirely accidental. In most main historical periods, the "leading edge" of civilization, of collective power, has found eastward expansion difficult. It has fought a defensive, and sometimes losing, battle against aggressive eastern neighbors. Only Alexander the Great reversed this normal flow, expanding Hellenic civilization eastward. Rome consolidated this but was unable to take it farther eastward.

In Europe, two geopolitical processes were consistent with the historical norm. First, Europe was blocked eastward. It never remotely threatened to overpower Islam in its heartlands – nor the Huns, Mongols, or Tartars in the steppes. If Europe were to expand, it would not be eastward – and ecology and climate ensured that it would not be to the north or south either. Second, it was quite likely that if the easterly parts of this civilization, whether or not they were its "leading edge," collectively took the strain successfully, they would, in so doing, drain themselves. After Poitiers and the Lechfeld and certainly after the thirteenth century, central and western Europe were safe. But in the long run the eastern European kingdoms, Byzantium, the Norman adventurers, Venice, Genoa, and Spain would commit so many of their resources to this unproductive struggle that they would be unlikely to make a continuing positive contribution to the European dynamic. Only much later, when the tide turned, could Austria and (most spectacularly) Russia gain from the struggle against Islam and the Tartars.

Now this says nothing about whether the leading edge *would* proceed further westward. For this to occur, a quite separate set of conditions was necessary. Power potentialities were also required in the West, so that those looking westward, or those in the western marches, could exploit them. They would *want* to do so, because all other directions were blocked. But whether they *could* do so was entirely contingent on what lay there capable of exploitation. Note that I have now reversed what was patterned and what was contingent. We have two halves of an overall conjunctural explanation. From the point of view of each, the other was contingent. From the point of view of western Europe, the struggle of the East with Islam was accidental (and lucky). From the point of view of the East, the West's opportunities were accidental (and largely unlucky).

The West's opportunities came in two main forms. First were the agricultural opportunities presented by deeper, wetter, more fertile soils and by a local social structure (described above) capable of exploiting them. These opportunities began in the Dark Ages and continued intermittently until the eighteenth-century "agricultural revolution." Second were navigational opportunities presented by the Atlantic and Baltic coastline, and by appro-

priate local social structures. These opportunities were exploited in two distinct phases: the early Viking-to-Norman expansion, and the fifteenth- to seventeenth-century expansion of cohesive (i.e., "coordinating" and "organic"),
medium-sized seacoast states from Sweden to Portugal. I concentrated on the
latter phase, particularly on the form of state and multistate systems appropriate to exploiting these opportunities (and which I summarize in the next
section).

At the end of all these processes stood one organic, medium-sized, wet-
soil island state, perfectly situated for takeoff: Great Britain. Was it accident
or part of a macrohistorical pattern? The broad answer is now forthcoming.

The European dynamic was the accidental conjunction of two macropatterns, long antedating the medieval experience of Europe, acting on the unique
but internally patterned power networks of Europe. The two macropatterns
were political blockage to the east and agricultural-cum-trading opportunity
to the west. The first pattern was carried forward into the medieval and early
modern period by Islam and, to a lesser extent, by Mongol and Tartar empires
whose structure and power remain outside the scope of this volume. The
second pattern and its impact on medieval Europe were fully discussed in the
three preceding chapters. In the medieval era, agricultural-cum-navigational
opportunities were exploitable by a historically conjunctural, but internally
patterned, set of overlapping power networks. These were (1) the normative
pacification of Christendom, later largely replaced by a diplomatically regulated multistate civilization; (2) small, weak political states, growing in centralized-territorial coordinating and organic powers, but never internally or
geopolitically hegemonic; and (3) a multiplicity of part-autonomous, competitive, local economic-power networks – peasant communities, lordly manors,
towns, and merchant and artisan guilds – whose competition gradually settled
into that single, universal, diffuse set of private-property power relations we
know as capitalism. By 1477 these power networks were developing into their
simpler, modern form: a multistate, capitalist civilization, into whose internal
composition we will delve in a moment. This conjunction of part-patterned
processes and part-historical accidents is as close as we can come to an overall
theory of European dynamism using historical forms of explanation. The lack
of comparable cases makes us unlikely to get much closer using the comparative method.

Capitalism and the states

The second central theme, especially of the last two chapters, has been an
analysis of the interrelations and the relative weights of capitalism and the
state in influencing this momentous process of European development. I have
conducted the argument in a particular way, extending a methodology used
earlier in Chapter 9, a quantitative study of state finances, concentrating on

the case of England/Britain. The surviving fiscal records enable us to perceive clearly the role of the English state during this period, and the states' role in the rise of European capitalism and European civilization more generally. So let us start by summarizing the functions of the English state as revealed merely by the fiscal record.

Simply from an analysis of state finances, the functions of the state appear overwhelmingly military and overwhelmingly geopolitical rather than economic and domestic. For more than seven centuries, somewhere between 70 and 90 percent of its financial resources were almost continuously deployed in the acquisition and use of military force. And although this force might also be used for domestic repression, the chronology of its development has been almost entirely determined by the incidence and character of international war.

For several centuries the state grew only fitfully and in small degrees, though each real growth was the result of war developments. Most of its apparent financial growth before the seventeenth century was actually due to inflation, disappearing when we examined finances at constant prices. But in the seventeenth and eighteenth centuries the state's real financial size grew rapidly. Before then it was tiny in relation to the resources of the economy and marginal in relation to the life experience of most of its inhabitants. By 1815 – a year of major war, of course – it loomed large over civil society. The "modern state" had arrived, the product of the developments often called the Military Revolution – professional and permanent armies and navies. Even as late as 1815 its public civil functions were negligible in financial terms.

This is not to argue for a military determinism. The character of military technology is closely related to the general form of social life and in particular to the mode of economic production. The purposes of warfare also became more economic in a modern sense, as the expansion of the European economy became more entwined with the military conquest and retention of markets as well as land. But nevertheless states and the multistate civilization developed primarily in response to pressures emanating from the geopolitical and military spheres. Thus theories that assign the state's main function as the regulation of its internal "civil society" – whether this is seen in functional or in Marxist class-struggle terms – seem simplistic. All states do possess such functions, but over this particular geographical and historical terrain, they appear from the perspective of financial costs to have been largely derivative of their geopolitical role.

This argument is simplistic, however. It is based only on finances and, therefore, tends to underestimate functions that were relatively costless but may be considered important in other senses. The other major aspect of the modern state's rise was its monopolization of judicial powers, at first confined to adjudicating disputes concerning customs and privileges, later extending to active legislation. This did not cost much because in this role the state was largely *coordinating* the activities of powerful groups in "civil society." In the late medieval period these groups had considerable powers in their own provincial localities (as had always been the case in extensive historical societies) and sometimes they also possessed a national estate-like organization. But, for a mixture of economic and military reasons, coordination became closer. The second phase of the modern state began to appear, the *organic* state. The state and the monarch (or, more rarely, the republic) was the point around which this organism grew. In England the form adopted was constitutional monarchy, securely established after 1688. But the organism also became a capitalist class, which united landed and trading interests (i.e., "nobility," "gentry," "yeomen," "bourgeoisie," etc.) but excluded the mass of the people. Other countries adopted a slightly less organic form of state, absolutism, which usually included the nobility but excluded the bourgeoisie. Absolutism tended to remain to a greater degree at the coordination level, arranging relations between groups – increasingly classes – that were organizationally segregated from each other. It was consequently slightly less effective at infrastructural penetration and social mobilization than the more organic constitutional state (although this was less true in military- than in economic-power organizations).

Organic states, especially constitutional states, were novel in history over such extensive territories. They represented the decline of the territorially federal state, characteristic, as we have seen, of almost all previous extensive societies. Hitherto rule had been a compromise between central and provincial power arenas, each possessing considerable autonomy. Now the compromise was itself centralized, and the near-unitary state was born. Its infrastructural reach and penetration over its territories was greater than any extensive state hitherto.

The precipitating factor of this secular trend was almost always the fiscal pressures on the state emanating from its international military needs. But the underlying cause of the extension of the state's coordinating powers lay more in the extension of class relations over a wider geographical terrain through the transition from broadly "feudal" to capitalist economics. Economic resources, including the local autonomy and privacy from the state discussed in Chapter 12, gradually crystallized into what we call private property. As the production and trade of these local units rose, states were increasingly drawn into the regulation of more precise, technical, yet more universal property rights. The states began to supplant Christendom as the main instruments of normative pacification, a process that became spectacular and irreversible in the Protestant schism and the settling of the wars of religion in the sixteenth and seventeenth centuries.

Note, however, that I write "states," not "the state." For, whatever the normative (and repressive) requirements of capitalism, it did not create its own, singular state. As I shall repeatedly note in the next volume, there is nothing inherent in the capitalist mode of production to lead to the development of class networks, each one of which is largely bounded by the territories of a state. For both the coordinated and the organic states were increasingly *national* in their character. We have been witnessing the emergence of many networks of economic power and many class struggles, and the perpetuance of many states over a single civilization. Once again, as in Sumer and in Greece at the time of their flowering, a dynamic civilization contained both small, unitary, state-centered units and a broader, geopolitical "federal culture."

Thus, by the time of the Industrial Revolution, capitalism was already contained within a civilization of competing geopolitical states. Christianity no longer defined its essential unity; indeed, it is difficult to pin down the nature of this unity other than that it was "European." Diplomatic channels constituted its principal organization, and geopolitical relations consisted of trade, diplomacy, and warfare, which were not seen as being mutually exclusive by the states. More diffuse than that, however, was a sense of common European-cum-Christian (and soon -cum-white) identity that was not carried by any transnational authoritative organization. Nevertheless, economic interaction was largely confined within national boundaries, supported by imperial dominions. Each leading state approximated a self-contained economic network. International economic relations were authoritatively mediated by states. Class regulation and organization thus developed in each of a series of geographical areas shaped by existing geopolitical units.

And so the process and outcome of class struggles became significantly determined by the nature and interrelations of the states. This has been noticed by others. Tilly has wondered, somewhat ingenuously, whether the seventeenth-century French peasantry really was a "class," as the term is conventionally understood. For instead of fighting against their landlords, these peasants usually fought alongside their lords against the state. Why, he asks? Because the state's need for taxes and manpower for international warfare drove it to expropriate peasants and to encourage commercialization of the economy (which also threatened peasants' rights). Tilly concludes that the French peasantry was typical, not exceptional. As he put it, "For our own era, the two master processes (of social development) are . . . the expansion of capitalism and the growth of national states and systems of states." Interconnected, these two processes explain class struggle, he argues (Tilly 1981: 44–52, 109–44).

The story is taken forward from the eighteenth century by Skocpol. She demonstrates that modern class revolutions – her examples are the French, the Russian, and the Chinese revolutions – resulted from interconnections between class and state struggles. The conflicts of peasants, lords, burghers, capitalists, and others became focused on the fiscal extraction process of inefficient ancien régime states, struggling to withstand the military presence of their more advanced rivals. Class was politicized only because this was a competitive multistate system. Her theoretical conclusion is that the state has two autonomous determinants. She quotes Hintze: "These are first, the structure of social classes, and, second, the external ordering of the states." Because the external ordering is autonomous of class structure, so is the state irreducible to social classes (Skocpol 1979: 24–33).

Although I agree with these empirical statements and conclusions, I would like to situate them within a wider historical and theoretical framework. The power autonomy of states is not a constant. As we saw in earlier chapters, medieval states had precious little power, very little determining rule over the development of class struggles, and not much more rule over the outcome of warfare (which was fought mostly between conglomerations of autonomous feudal levies). Gradually, however, the states acquired all these powers, and I have tried to explain *why* they did. States provide *territorially centralized organization* and *geopolitical diplomacy*. The usefulness of such power organizations was marginal in the early Middle Ages. But its functionality for dominant groupings began to grow, especially on the battlefield and in the organization of trade. Despite counterthrusts from territorially decentralized agencies as diverse as the Catholic church, the duchy of Burgundy, and the private India companies, this usefulness continued to grow, as it has done ever since. To understand why, however, we must stand back outside our own era, in which we take such things as strong states for granted. This is the point of doing historical sociology on a broad scale.

In the narrower time scale of this chapter, I have described two separate senses in which economic, military, and political power relations may influence one another and lay down the tracks for social development. The first sense concerned the shaping in space of emergent class relations by existing geopolitical units. This is an aspect of "collective power" (as explained in Chapter 1). In this case, the classes of capitalist society were shaped spatially by their growing dependence on states for the regulation of property rights. Merchant and landlord capitalists entered and reinforced a world of emergent warring yet diplomatically regulating states. Their need for, and vulnerability to, state regulation both internally and geopolitically, and the state's need for finances, pushed classes and states toward a territorially centralized organization. State boundaries were heightened, and culture, religion, and classes were naturalized. Eventually British, French, and Dutch bourgeoisie existed, and economic interaction between these national units and classes was small. Each major geopolitical state was itself a virtual network of production, distribution, exchange, and consumption (what I called a "circuit of praxis") in a wider regulated, interstate space. These national parameters were set centuries before we may legitimately talk of the second major class of the capitalist mode of production, the proletariat. This was the world the proletariat entered, and will enter in the next volume.

Furthermore, these political and geopolitical parameters implied warfare between rivals in a way that the capitalist mode of production, as a pure type, does not. Nothing in the capitalist mode of production (or the feudal mode if that is defined economically) leads of itself to the emergence of many networks of production, divided and at war, and of an overall class structure that is nationally segmental. It is an extraordinary paradox that the puny, marginal state of the late feudal and early modern period – excessively pleased with itself if it had managed to grab as much as 1 percent of gross national product – had such a decisive role in structuring the world in which we live today. This will be pursued into the nineteenth and twentieth centuries in the next volume. But we have already witnessed the power of states within a multistate civilization in historical transformation. In this first sense the reorganization runs clearly from military and political power relations to economic ones.

The second sense is the more traditional one in sociological and historical theory. It concerns the "despotic" power of the state and state elite as against the power of given social classes: an example of Parsons's "distributive power" (as discussed in Chapter 1). In previous chapters I argued that ancient imperial states often exercised substantial power over classes because the states' own "compulsory cooperation" was necessary for economic development. This was not so in medieval states. It was initially, but not eventually, true of European colonial states abroad. Although initial colonial conquest was usually the province of the states and although their armies, navies, and civil adminstration were necessary to maintain pacification, the power of colonial states from the seventeenth century onward was undermined by the development of the depoliticized, decentralized economic relations that had always been stronger than the states in their European homeland. I argued that economic power circuits had been already depoliticized long before the emergence of capitalist commodity production. Absolutism was unable to recapture control over the circuits of economic praxis. After the eclipse of Spain and Portugal, no state ever formally owned the means of production in its colonies, and none ever did so at home.

While the medieval state remained small, it could attain a large measure of *autonomy,* existing off its own financial resources plus extortion from such dependent groups as foreign merchants, Jews, or poorly organized domestic merchants. This involved little power *over* society, however. And after the Military Revolution no state could retain its autonomy and survive on the battlefield. Additional finance, and later manpower, was required, and this involved collaborating with better-organized civil groups, especially with the landed nobility and with commercial oligarchies in trading states. This collaboration was turning gradually into an organic unity between state and dominant classes. States diverged along absolutist and constitutional lines in response, but all were now collaborating closely with their dominant classes. The private interests and sphere of action of the state elite now became more difficult to distinguish. In the seventeenth and eighteenth centuries it begins to make sense to describe the state – paraphrasing Marx – as an executive committee for managing the common affairs of the capitalist class. Thus no significant degree of distributive power over the internal groups of "civil society" was exercised by the state during this long period. In this second sense causal determination flowed primarily from economic power relations to the state.

There is no meaningful way of ranking the strength of these two opposite causal patterns so as to arrive at a conclusion of the form: Economic (or political/military) power predominated "in the last instance." Each reorganized early modern societies in fundamental ways, and the two were jointly necessary for the Industrial Revolution and for other fundamental parameters of the modern world. They were to continue their close, dialectical relationship – as we shall see in Volume II.

Economic power relations – that is, modes of production and classes as actual historical entities and forces – cannot "constitute themselves," without the intervention of ideological military and political organizations. The same obviously applies in reverse to states and political elites. As always in sociology, our analytic constructs are precarious – actual modes of production, classes, and states depend for their existence on broader social experience. Neither economic determinism nor political or military determinism would take us very far in any analysis. However, in the present context, a combination of these three power networks – given the particular decline of ideological power witnessed in Chapter 14 – offers a powerful explanation of the tracks set down for the modern world.

By the mid-eighteenth century, capitalist economic relationships and a series of territorial states possessing a monopoly of military force had jointly inaugurated a novel social form: a *civil society* (henceforth not to be written inside quotation marks, as it has been hitherto) bounded and externally regulated by a *national* (or in some central European cases, multinational) *state*. Each civil society was broadly similar because this was also *a multistate civilization*. Each tended toward an organic whole – not a territorially federal conglomerate, like virtually all hitherto-extensive societies. Through this whole flowed diffuse power forces, abstract, universal, impersonal, not subject to a particularistic and hierarchical series of state, regional, and local authoritative decision takers. These impersonal forces generated the greatest, most sudden revolution in human collective powers: the Industrial Revolution. And it should be added, their power and the mystery of their diffused impersonality also generated the science of society, sociology. In the next volume I use sociology to analyze that revolution.

Bibliography

Anderson, P. 1974. *Passages from Antiquity to Feudalism*. London: New Left Books.
Elvin, M. 1973. *The Pattern of the Chinese Past*. Stanford, Calif.: Stanford University Press.

Gellner, E. 1981. *Muslim Society*. Cambridge: Cambridge University Press.
Hall, J. 1985. *Powers and Liberties*. Oxford: Basil Blackwell.
McNeill, W. 1974. *The Shape of European History*. New York: Oxford University Press.
Parsons, T. 1968. *The Structure of Social Action*. 2nd ed. Glencoe, Ill.: the Free Press.
Skocpol, T. 1979. *States and Social Revolutions: A Comparative Analysis of France, Russia and China*. Cambridge: Cambridge University Press.
Tilly, C. 1981. *As Sociology Meets History*. New York: Academic Press.

16 Patterns of world-historical development in agrarian societies

The role of the four power sources

We have reached the end of this long history of power in agrarian societies. We can now pause to ask the obvious question: Amid all the detail, can we discern general patterns of power and of its development? We shall not be in a position to give a proper answer to the question until we have compared agrarian to industrial societies, these being the subject matter of Volume II. In any case a proper answer is necessarily complex and lengthy, to be attempted in a third volume. But we can discern provisionally some of the general contours of that answer.

The general lineaments of power have been obvious in every chapter since I presented my formal model in Chapter 1. I have narrated a history of power in society – and, therefore, almost a history of society *tout court* – in terms of the interactions of four sources and organizations of power. The interrelations of ideological, economic, military, and political power, treated systematically, have provided, I would argue, an acceptable overall account of social development. Therefore, the history of the societies discussed here have been patterned primarily by these power networks rather than by other phenomena. Of course, such an assertion requires qualification. As I noted in Chapter 1, any account of society pushes some aspects of social life to center stage and others to the wings. One particular aspect in the wings of this volume, gender relations, will move near center stage in Volume II, when they begin to change. Nevertheless, those aspects that generally *are* at center stage in most other accounts of agrarian societies seem adequately explained by my IEMP model of organized power.

Furthermore, the basic reason for this has proved to be as stated in Chapter 1. Power is most fruitfully seen as *means,* as *organization,* as *infrastructure,* as *logistics.* In the pursuit of their myriad, fluctuating goals, human beings set up networks of social cooperation that imply both collective and distributive power. Of these networks, the most powerful in the logistical sense of being able to bring forth cooperation, both *intensively* and *extensively,* over definite social and geographical space, are ideological, economic, military, and political power organizations. Sometimes these organizations appear in societies as relatively specialized and separate, sometimes as relatively merged into each other. Each attains its prominence by virtue of the distinct organizational means it offers to achieve human goals. It is then capable in decisive "world-historical moments" of generally reorganizing social life or, to use a

518

metaphor similar to Weber's "switchman" metaphor, of laying down the tracks of world-historical development. The means are as stated in Chapter 1.

Ideological power offers two distinct means. First it offers a *transcendent* vision of social authority. It unites human beings by claiming that they possess ultimately meaningful, often divinely granted, common qualities. Such qualities are claimed to be the essence of either humanity itself or at least of humans presently divided by "secular" organizations of economic, military, and political power. In the historical periods considered here, the transcendence has usually taken a divine form: The spark that supposedly ignites common humanity is thought to come from God. But this is not necessary, as the more secular case of classical Greece in Chapter 7 showed. More obviously, in our own time Marxism's transcendence, a good example of an ideological power movement, is secular ("Workers of all lands unite"). Whether ideological power becomes significant in any time or place thus depends on whether the existing, dominant power organizations are seen by social actors themselves to block the possibility of achieving desired, attainable social goals through transcendent social cooperation. The appeal of salvation religions to interstitial trading and artisan groups who transcend both state boundaries and the main organizations of agrarian-class exploitation is the obvious, persistent example of this volume, discussed in most detail in Chapters 10 and 11.

The second means of ideological power is what I called *immanence*, the strengthening of the internal morale of some existing social group by giving it a sense of ultimate significance and meaning in the cosmos, by reinforcing its normative solidarity, and by giving it common ritual and aesthetic practices. Thus economic classes, political nations, and military groups that acquire such immanent morale develop a greater self-confidence, which enables them to reorganize history consciously. Weber's discussion of the impact of Puritanism on the morale of early capitalist entrepreneurs and burghers is a classic example. Within this volume the most obvious examples, however, are cases of imperial ruling classes. We saw that the achievements of the rulers of Assyria, Persia, and Rome were heightened by their ability to equate ultimate definitions of "civilization," that is, of meaningful social life, with the collective life of their own class. It is worth adding, however, that we have not found true "nations," as opposed to more restricted "ruling-class nations," in agrarian societies (although we will find them in industrial societies in Volume II). There were good logistical reasons for this. In agrarian societies the passing of messages and symbols downward through the stratification hierarchy was generally restricted, at one extreme, to simple hierarchical commands and, at the other extreme, to the general, diffuse, and somewhat vague transcendent content of religions.

These two means of ideological power are rather different, and they have often been opposed. Where ideological movements combined elements of both, contradictions were set up with immense implications for social development. As we saw in Chapters 12 and 13, the contradiction between transcendent salvation and the immanent class morale of medieval lords, both fueled by Christianity, was a central part of the "rational restlessness," that is, of the dynamism of European civilization.

The means of *economic power* are what I termed *circuits of praxis*. Economic power distinctively integrates two spheres of social activity. First is the active intervention of human beings in nature through labor, what Marx called *praxis*. It is characteristically intensive, involving groups of workers in local, close, dense cooperation and exploitation. Second, goods taken from nature are circulated and exchanged for transformation and ultimately for consumption. These *circuits* are characteristically extensive and elaborated. Economic power thus gives access to both the routines of everyday life and praxis of the mass of the people, and to the ramified communications circuits of societies. It is, therefore, always a formidable and essential part of any stable power structure. It has not, however, been the "motor of history" as Marx liked to argue. In many times and places the forms of economic power have been importantly shaped and reshaped by other power sources. In general the "weakness" of economic power relations – or, if you prefer, of social classes – has been their dependence for further expansion on effective norms of possession and cooperation. In some times and places these norms have been established predominantly by military pacification – what I called in Chapters 5, 8, and 9 *compulsory cooperation* (following Spencer). In others it was established predominantly through *normative pacification,* that is, through the transcendent norms of an ideological power movement. This was seen especially in Chapters 11 and 12, where salvation religions provided normative pacification. In both types of case we find economic power and social classes reorganized principally by the structures of military or ideological power.

Nevertheless, we have also seen important cases in which circuits of praxis were themselves a principal reorganizing, tracklaying force of history. This was especially true of the Iron Age peasant farmer and trader, beginning in Chapter 6 and flourishing in early classical Greece in Chapter 7. Thereafter, though never reorganizing society "unaided," economic-power relations were usually of great significance for social change. Of course, this volume has stopped the story at the moment when the significance of classes and class struggle was to be enormously enhanced, that is, through the agency of the Industrial Revolution. I will say more about the history of class in a moment.

The means of *military power* are *concentrated coercion*. This is obviously so in battle itself (according to Clausewitzian principles of strategy). Through battles the logic of destructive military power may decide which form of society will predominate. This is an obvious reorganizing role of military power throughout much of history. But a role in reorganizing societies also comes from its uses in peacetime. Where forms of social cooperation can be socially and geographically concentrated, there is a potentiality for increasing its yields by intensifying coercion. In several ancient empires as discussed in Chapters 5, 8, and 9, we saw this actualized in "compulsory cooperation," a means of controlling societies and of increasing their collective powers by intensifying the exploitation of concentrated pockets of labor. These were tenuously linked together by extensive, military-led communications infrastructures capable of limited and punitive power exercised over very large areas. Hence the characteristic "dualism" of military-led ancient societies. The relatively novel and controversial aspect of my analysis is not the acknowledgment that such militaristic empires existed (this has long been recognized) but the claim that they fostered social and economic development by such means. Militarism has not always been merely destructive or parasitic, a point I made most forcefully in a critique of dominant theories in comparative and historical sociology near the end of Chapter 5.

The first means of *political power* is *territorial centralization*. States are called forth and intensified when dominant social groups, pursuing their goals, require social regulation over a confined, bounded territory. This is most efficiently achieved by establishing central institutions whose writ radiates outward monopolistically, across the defined territory. A permanent state elite is set up. Even though it may be originally the creature of the groups that instituted or intensified the state, the fact that it is centralized and they are not, gives to it logistical capacities for exercising autonomous power.

These autonomous state powers are precarious, however. The state's central strength is also its weakness: lack of penetrative powers into the decentralized reaches of "civil society." Hence an important part of the reorganizing capacities of political power was not exercised autonomously but as part of a dialectic of development. States' recently acquired centralized powers were lost as its agents "disappeared" into "civil society," then were reacquired more powerfully than before, then were lost again, and so forth. And, in turn, an important part of this process was the development of what we call "private property," resources "hidden" from the state, which – contrary to bourgeois ideology – are not natural and original, but have usually arisen from the fragmentation and disappearance of collective, state-organized resources. I argued these points most forcefully in Chapters 5, 9, and 12.

But the principal manifestation of political power does not concern autonomous "despotic" powers exercised by a centralized political elite. These, as suggested above, are precarious and temporary. The main reorganizing force of political power rather concerns the geographical infrastructure of human societies, especially their boundedness. I have made it a principal argument of this volume that human societies are not unitary systems but varying conglomerations of multiple, overlapping, intersecting networks of power. But where state powers are enhanced, then "societies" become more unitary, more bounded, more separated out from one another, and more structured internally.

Additionally, their interrelations raise a second means of political power, *geopolitical diplomacy*. No known state has yet managed to control all relations traveling across its boundaries, and so much social power has always remained "transnational" – leaving an obvious role for the diffusion of both transnational class relations and transcendent ideologies. But an increase in territorial centralization also increases orderly diplomatic activity, both peaceful and warlike. Where centralization is proceeding in more than one neighboring territorial area, a regulated multistate system will develop. Hence in most cases an increase in state internal powers is also simultaneously an increase in the reorganizing capacities of geopolitical diplomacy within a multistate system.

The outstanding example of this is in early modern Europe. Rather slight increases in the internal powers of hitherto puny states (primarily the result of military-fiscal problems), intensified the social boundedness of most of western Europe. By 1477, when the great (and predominantly nonterritorial and nonnational) duchy of Burgundy collapsed (as recounted in Chapter 13), social life was partially "naturalized." In Chapter 14 we glimpsed already what will be central to the whole of Volume II: National (later, nation-) states had become one of the two most dominant social actors – alongside social classes. The interrelations of nation-states and classes will be the central theme of Volume II. But if the nation-states of today do annihilate human society in a nuclear holocaust, the causal processes could be traced back (if anyone survived to practice sociology!) to the largely unintended reorganizing powers of those puny but plural states. The capacity of state power to reshape the territorial scope of human societies has been sometimes great. It may be final.

One other set of peculiarities should be noted about political power: its relations to the other power sources. As I noted in Chapter 1, most previous theorists argued that political and military power could be treated as identical. Although we have seen cases where this was not so, there has undoubtedly been a generally close connection between the two. Concentration and centralization often overlap, as do physical coercion and the coercion emanating from monopoly regulation over a bounded territory. States generally seek greater control over military force, and the stronger states have generally achieved a near monopoly of military power. I will comment on this overlap further in a moment. Conversely there has existed something of a negative correlation between political and transcendent ideological power, as we saw most clearly in Chapters 10 and 11. Powerful states, ancient and modern, perhaps fear more than any other opponent the "invisible connections" that ideological movements can establish across their official channels and boundaries.

The peculiarities of each power source and their complex interconnections will be discussed at length in Volume III. I have touched on them here to show the difficulties in the way of any general theory of power sources as independent "factors," "dimensions," or "levels" of societies – such as we find, for example, in Marxian or neo-Weberian theory. The power sources are distinctive organization means that are useful to social development, but each presupposes the existence and interconnections of the others to varying degrees. These "ideal types" are in social reality rarely pure. Actual social movements normally mix up elements of most, if not all, power sources in more general power configurations. Even if one is temporarily predominant, as in the examples listed above, it emerges out of social life in general, exercises its track-laying, reorganizing powers, and then becomes progressively more difficult to distinguish from social life in general once again. I will return to these more general configurations later.

Moreover, there is no obvious, formulaic, general patterning of the interrelations of power sources. It will be evident by now, for example, that this volume cannot support a general "historical materialism." Economic power relations do not assert themselves as "finally necessary in the last instance" (to quote Engels); history is not "a discontinuous succession of modes of production" (to quote Balibar 1970: 204); class struggle is not "the motor of history" (to quote Marx and Engels). Economic power relations, modes of production, and social classes come and go in the historical record. In occasional world-historical moments they decisively reorganize social life; usually they are important in conjunction with other power sources; occasionally they are decisively reorganized by them. The same can be said of all the power sources, coming and going, weaving in and out of the historical record. So, most emphatically, I cannot agree with Parsons (1966: 113) when he says, "I am a cultural determinist. . . . I believe that . . . the normative elements are more important for social change than . . . material interests." Normative and other ideological structures have varied in their historical force: We simply do not find an ideological movement of the enormous world-historical reorganizing powers of early Christianity or Islam in many times or places – which is not to deny their powers in these cases. Nor is it true, as Spencer and other military theorists asserted, that military power was the decisive tracklaying agency in extensive preindustrial societies. Chapters 6 and 7 saw many exceptions, most notably Greece and Phoenicia. Political power seems to have attracted fewer enthusiasts. But they would be equally stymied by the comings and goings of political power.

So perhaps we are forced back to the kind of agnosticism Weber once expressed in his inimitable style of convoluted confidence, concerning the relations between economic and other "structures of social action":

Even the assertion that social structures and the economy are "functionally" related is a biased view, which cannot be justified as an historical generalization, if an unambiguous interdependence is assumed. For the forms of social action follow "laws of their own" as we shall see time and time again, and even apart from this fact, they may in a given case always be co-determined by other than economic causes. However, at some point economic conditions tend to become causally important, and often decisive, for almost all social groups, and those which have major cultural significance; conversely, the economy is usually also influenced by the autonomous structure of social action within which it exists. *No significant generalization can be made as to when and how this will occur.* [1968: I, 340; a similar assertion is also found in I, 577; emphasis mine]

Are there no patterns to the comings and the goings? I think there are some partial patterns, which we have discerned. I start with the most general, most world-historical development. Then I consider the patterns involved in this. Along the way I dispose of other potential patternings that often form important parts of social theories.

A world-historical process

Social power has continued to develop, somewhat unsteadily perhaps, but nonetheless cumulatively throughout this volume. Human capacities for collective and distributive power (as defined in Chapter 1) have increased quantitatively throughout the historical periods I have covered. Later I qualify this statement in three ways, by pointing out that it often seems to develop through accidental conjuncture, that the process is internally uneven, and that it has been geographically shifty. But for the moment let us dwell on the fact of development itself.

Seen in the very long run, the infrastructure available to power holders and to societies at large has steadily increased. Many different societies have contributed to this. But, once invented, the major infrastructural techniques seem almost never to have disappeared from human practice. True, often powerful techniques have seemed inappropriate to the problems of a succeeding society and thus have declined. But, unless completely obsolete, their decline has proved temporary and they have been subsequently recovered.

A process of continuous invention, where little is lost, must result in a broadly one-directional, one-dimensional development of power. This is obvious if we examine *either* the logistics of authoritatively commanding the movement of people, materials, or messages, *or* the infrastructures underlying the universal diffusion of similar social practices and messages (i.e., what I defined as authoritative and diffuse power). If we quantify the speed of message carrying, of troop movements, of the movement of luxury or staple commodities, of the kill ratios of armies, or the depth of soil penetration by the plow, of the capacities of dogmas to spread yet remain the same – then on all these dimensions of power (as on many others), we find the same overall process of growth.

Thus the societies, armies, sects, states, and classes considered here have been able to deploy an increasing repertoire of power techniques. We could thus begin to write that kind of enthusiastic, evolutionary history of social organization in which each succeeding invention performed better its core task than preceding techniques. Seen from this perspective, a list of "power jumps" is not difficult to devise. Here are some of the social inventions that have crucially increased power capacities, and whose role I have indeed emphasized in this volume:

1. Animal domestication, agriculture, bronze metallurgy – prehistory
2. Irrigation, cylinder seals, the state – ca. 3000 B.C.
3. Cursive cuneiform, military commissaries, corvée labor – 2500–2000 B.C.
4. Written law codes, the alphabet, the spoked wheel on fixed axle – ca. 2000–1000 B.C.
5. Iron smelting, coinage, the naval galley – ca. 1000–600 B.C.
6. Hoplites and phalanxes, the polis, diffuse literacy, class consciousness and struggle – ca. 700–300 B.C.
7. The legion armed with Marius's pole, salvation religion – ca. 200 B.C. – A.D. 200
8. Wet-soil plowing, heavy cavalries and castles – ca. A.D. 600–1200
9. Coordinating and territorial states, open-sea navigation, printing, a Military Revolution, commodity production – A.D. 1200–1600

There is obvious variety in this list. Some items are economic; others are military, ideological, or political. Some appear as narrow and technical; others, as extremely broad and more obviously social. But they all have in common a capacity to improve the infrastructure of collective and distributive power, and they all have a proved survival capacity. The only reason that any have disappeared totally is that they are simply superseded by more powerful infrastructures – as, for example, in the eventual obsolescence of cuneiform script or Marius's pole. Such, therefore, is the descriptive detail of this first pattern of world-historical development. We can then begin to explain it by focusing on the causes of each jump, as I have done throughout the volume.

But let us pause here to note that this pattern of infrastructural growth precludes the possibility of another type of pattern. There has been such an enormous, cumulative increase in power capacity that we cannot easily embrace societies from different historical epochs in the same comparative categories and generalizations. Indeed, along the way (and especially in Chapter 5), I criticized comparative sociology for attempting this far too readily. Categories like "traditional aristocratic empires," "patrimonial empires," "feudalism," and "militant societies" lose their discriminating power if applied too broadly across the historical spectrum. This is not primarily because history is infinitely varied (though it is), but because history *develops*. What is the sense in calling both the Inca Empire (located at about 2000 B.C. in the world-historical list of inventions given above) and the Spanish Empire (located in the last phase of the list) by the same term of "traditional aristocratic empire," as Kautsky (1982) does? It took only 160 Spaniards and their power infrastructures to destroy the Inca Empire totally. Similarly, the "feudalism" of medieval Europe differed enormously from that of the Hittites in its power resources. Europeans had a salvation religion, stone castles, iron plows with mold boards; they could sail across seas; their war horses were perhaps three times heavier, as was their armor. Categories like "feudalism" or "empires" (of varying adjectival forms) may be of limited help. True, there may be a certain common dynamic quality to lord-vassal relationships in feudal societies, or emperor-noble relationships in empires, across eons of world history. But the terms cannot be used as designations of the *overall* structure or dynamic of societies such as these. More decisive in this respect is a careful location of the society in world-historical time.

Thus most of the labels used in this volume for overall societies and civilizations have been applicable *only* to specific eras in world-historical time. This was not my original theoretical stance. Rather, it has turned out to be empirically the case. Let us consider some examples, which will raise in turn all four sources of power; first, military-led societies.

Empires of "compulsory cooperation" had a certain force and developmental role from about 2300 B.C. until A.D. 200 at the latest. We could not find them earlier because the infrastructure on which they relied (military commissaries, corvée labor in the list of inventions given above) had not yet been invented. And they became obsolete when more advanced techniques of diffused power, centered on salvation religions, appeared. Indeed, even within that broad era, there were great differences between the power available at the beginning to Sargon of Akkad and to the Emperor Augustus near the end. These derived from several sources but perhaps principally from the emerging infrastructure of upper-class cultural solidarity, which gave the Roman Empire powers undreamed of by Sargon. "Compulsory cooperation" was changing into a far broader and greater power configuration within its period of dominance. Not that it was totally dominant within this period: It was competing with other, more diffuse decentralized power structures, exemplified by Phoenicia and Greece. "Compulsory cooperation" is relevant only in some places in a definite era.

Second, the role of extensive ideological movements has also been historically confined. Salvation religions exerted enormous reorganizing powers from about 200 B.C. to perhaps A.D. 1200. This was not possible before this period because it depended on recent infrastructural inventions like diffused literacy and the emergence of trading networks that were interstitial to the structures of contemporary empires. Subsequently, its role of normative pacification was secularized into a multistate European system. So its reorganizing role declined.

Third, let us consider states. Here the violence done to the historical record by concepts that are too general is sometimes extraordinary. Wittfogel's notion of "Oriental Despotism," for example, attributes to ancient states powers of social control that were simply unavailable to *any* of the historical states considered here. As is sometimes observed, he was really describing (and attacking) contemporary Stalinism rather than ancient states. The latter could do virtually nothing to influence social life beyond the ninety-kilometer striking range of their army without going through intermediary, autonomous power groups. It is worth stating again that none of the states considered in this volume could even know the wealth of their subjects (unless it was actually moved along main communications routes), and they could not extract it without having to strike bargains with autonomous, decentralized groups. This will change fundamentally in Volume II, where modern views of the powerful, unitary state will become much more relevant. States in this volume have shared certain common qualities, but they are those of an "unmodern" particularity and marginality to social life. As I have already emphasized, where states have reorganized social life, this has rarely been in terms of power exercised over other internal power groups. It has more usually concerned the territorial structuring of what "societies" are considered to be. But this capacity, generally ignored by sociological and historical theory, has also been historically variable. For territoriality and boundedness also have infrastructural preconditions. What was achieved by the early modern European state depended on the growth of the volume of written communication, accountancy methods, fiscal/military structures, and so forth generally denied to earlier states.

The world-historical development of classes

These points are exemplified in economic-power relations. This volume has contained a history of class and class struggle, using the phase model set out in Chapter 7. This history can now be summarized.

In Chapter 2 we saw that prehistoric societies did not usually contain classes in any form. No group could stably institutionalize effective possession of land and/or the economic surplus so as to deprive others of the means of subsistence. In such societies labor was truly free: Working for someone else was voluntary and unnecessary for subsistence. Then in Chapters 3 and 4 we saw the emergence of classes, social collectivities with institutionalized, differential rights of access to the means of subsistence. More specifically, some slowly acquired effective possession of the best or the only land, as well as rights to use the labor of others. From now on class struggle between landlords and peasants of various statuses (free, servile, slave, etc.) over rights to land, labor, and surplus was a ubiquitous feature of all agrarian societies.

It is possible that in the earliest city-state civilizations, discussed in Chapters 3 and 4, struggle over emerging class differences was an overt and important feature of social and political life. The inadequacy of the source material restrains us from certainty. But in subsequent, more extensive societies, especially in the earlier empires of history, this was not so. Class differences were pronounced, but class struggle remained largely *latent* (i.e., at the first phase), doubtless continuing at a concrete local level but without extensive organization. Conflict was predominantly "horizontally" rather than "vertically" organized – local peasants were more likely to be mobilized by their local superiors in clan, tribal, patron-client, village, and other organizations rather than by other peasants in class organizations. This was also true, to a lesser extent, of lords, whose interconnections tended to be particularistic and genealogical. They generally lacked universal, class sentiments and organizations. In these early empires class struggle was definitely not the motor of history. I argued this most strongly in Chapter 5.

The first sign of change began among lords. In later empires such as the Assyrian and the Persian (Chapter 8) we can trace the emergence among them of an *extensive* (phase 2) and *political* (phase 3) class, extensive because they were uniformly conscious and organized over most of the empire, and political because they helped rule the state as a class. The "immanent class morale" of these lords became pronounced. But this class structure was not *symmetrical*. The peasantry (and other subordinates) were still incapable of extensive organization. Only one class was capable of action for itself. Asymmetrical structures remained characteristic of most Near Eastern societies throughout the agrarian period. Again, therefore, class struggle was not the motor of this history, though the single, ruling class did impose its own character on Near Eastern civilization as a whole.

The Iron Age brought novel class possibilities to other regions. These were discussed in Chapter 6. By conferring greater economic and military power on the peasant plowman and infantryman and on trade and the galley, they enhanced the collective organization of peasant proprietors and traders against aristocratic lords over relatively small social spaces. In classical Greece (in Chapter 7) this flowered into extensive, political, *symmetrical* class structure (phase 4). Class struggle was now *a*, if not *the*, motor of history, within the bounds of the small city-state. Such class structures were probably passed to the Etruscans, and they reemerged with rather more capacity for extensive organization in early Republican Rome. However, class struggle in both Greece and Rome had a particular outcome, the triumph once more of a reinforced asymmetrical class structure, dominated by an extensive, political ruling class. In the Macedonian and Hellenistic empires and in the mature Roman Republic/Empire, lower-class citizen movements were outflanked by the extensive ideological and organizational solidarity of landlord aristocrats. In this phase, extensive political class struggle was not entirely latent, but it became less and less a motor of history. In Rome clientelism and political and military factions took over from classes as the main power actors (Chapter 9).

Nevertheless, the very success of such empires also generated countervailing forces. As trade, literacy, coinage, and other relatively diffuse and universal power resources developed interstitially within the empires, "middling" trader and artisan groups became capable of far more extensive community solidarity. In Rome its principal manifestation was early Christianity (Chapter 10). But as it rose to power, the Christian church began to compromise with the imperial ruling class. After a period of confusion and cataclysm, Christianity emerged into medieval Europe (in Chapter 12) as the core carrier of *both* ancient class traditions, upper-class solidarity and popular-class struggle. Because Christendom was far more extensive than the reach of any state, and because its organization transcended state boundaries, class struggle took religious forms, was often extensive, was sometimes symmetrical, but was rarely political, rarely aimed at the transformation of a state. Yet, with the growing naturalization of European social life (Chapters 13 and 14), class structure became far more political. This strengthened upper class organization within the individual state. Indeed the more advanced states at the end of our period were ruled by what I called a class-nation. But as yet it contributed less to lower-class solidarities, and may indeed have weakened them by weakening egalitarian salvation religion in general. Class structure thus reverted to a more asymmetrical form, at least in Great Britain, the principal case considered here. In other countries, however, the ruling class was less homogeneous, and class struggles and issues were simmering, shortly to explode. Everywhere two major universalizing processes, the commercialization of agriculture and the growth of national identity, were preparing the way for a return to phase 4 classes, extensive, political, symmetrical (at least within the boundaries of the individual state). The emergence of industrial society was shortly to convert them into a motor of history once again.

There are three points about this history of class. First, classes have not played a uniform role in history. Sometimes class struggle has been its motor, though this has never resulted merely from the antecedent forms of class structure (as orthodox Marxists argue). In Greece and Rome military and political organization were also necessary conditions of the emergence of symmetrical classes, as the organization of the national state has been a precondition of the development of modern symmetrical classes (much more of this in Volume II). But a second form of class structure has also played a major historical role: the society characterized by a single, extensive, and political ruling class. When lords became capable of a common sense of community and of collective organization, considerable social change and development resulted, as was suggested tentatively in the case of Assyria and Persia and as was proved in the case of Rome. The emergence of an upper *class* was a decisive phase in world-historical development. These are two very different types of class structure that might be said to contribute in a major way to the motor of history. They must be set alongside periods in which class relations were much less significant power networks. Clearly, therefore, any general theory of class must take account of such massive variations.

The second point is that the history of class is essentially similar to that of the nation. This is important because in modern thought classes and nations are usually regarded as being antithetical. It is not only that the very societies in which classes became unusually developed – Assyria, Persia, Greece, republican Rome, early modern Europe (plus, of course, nineteenth- and twentieth-century Europe) – were also those with a pronounced national consciousness. It is also that this *must* be so, given that class and nation have the same infrastructural preconditions. They are universal communities, dependent on the diffusion of the same social practices, identities, and sentiments across extensive social spaces. Societies integrated by more particularistic, federal, authoritative power networks are incapable of transmitting *either* set of diffuse message. Societies capable of this will develop both classes and nations – or more commonly the various restricted forms of both (e.g., the "ruling class-nation") that I have charted throughout this historical narrative. This similarity of class and nation will become a dominant theme of Volume II, for we will find that the twists and turns of class and national struggles in the nineteenth and twentieth centuries have always been closely entwined. Any particular outcome – let us say a revolution or a welfare state – has been dependent on the history of both. In charting the gradual, interconnected emergence of classes and nations throughout history, I have set the scene for the dominant power struggles of our time.

The third point returns us to world-historical time, and thus indicates what a general theory of class might look like. For classes, like every other type of power actor, have definite infrastructural preconditions that gradually emerged throughout the historical period. Classes cannot exist as social actors unless people similarly positioned in relation to economic-power resources can exchange messages, materials, and personnel with each other. Dominant classes have always found this easier than subordinate ones, but even they could not manage it in extensive societies until infrastructures gradually developed to allow for the diffusion among them of common education, consumption patterns, military discipline, legal and judicial practice, and so forth. With subordinate class organization, in the city-states of Greece and Rome, we are dealing with much smaller social spaces. But even collective citizen organization over areas as tiny as modern Luxembourg, among a population like that of a modern county town, had preconditions that had taken millennia to develop. The Iron Age peasant farm, the hoplite phalanx, the trading galley, alphabet script – these were the infrastructural preconditions for class struggle, all in place around 600 B.C., and most in decline in the face of more extensive, authoritative power infrastructures by 200 B.C. Such examples show that classes have depended for their reorganizing powers on the infrastructures of world-historical development. A theory of class would have to be situated within a theory of this.

In all these respects, therefore, actual power actors and their achievements depended on their location in world-historical time. Ideal types at the level of those distinguished in Chapter 1 may be applicable across its whole spectrum, but actual social structures have been more variable than most orthodoxies have cared to acknowledge. Those variations are, within broad limits, patterned and explicable – but by *historical,* not comparative and abstract, structures and theories. Our theories and concepts must be situated in world-historical time.

Historical accidents

But let me begin to qualify this world-historical pattern. First, it may be world-historical, but it still often feels like accident. It was *one* process, but only just. There were phases, notably at the time of the "Indo-European" movements and in the European Dark Ages, when the whole preceding process seemed to be nosediving into self-destruction. Because the secular trend was cumulative, these and other "turning points" could have led to quite other processes of social change. When amplified by their own cumulative dynamics, these could have had very different eventual outcomes. The "might have beens" and "almost weres" could have led into fundamentally different historical tracks. If the pass at Thermopylae had not been defended to the death, if Alexander had not drunk so heavily that night in Babylon, if Hannibal had been resupplied quickly after Cannae, if Paul had not outorganized the "men from Judaea," if Charles Martel had lost at Poitiers, or if the Hungarians had won at Nicopolis – these are all accidental "almost weres" of one predominant type. They might have reversed the East-to-West power drift that I shall shortly pick out as one of the major world-historical patterns of this volume.

As is customary when instancing the "nearly weres," I have picked out the accidental fortunes of "great men" and battles. That is only because they are easiest to spot as world-historical moments. But even the broadest of social movements encounter watersheds when a whole network of anonymous social interactions reinforce one another to carry the movement over the watershed and then swiftly down the new course of social development. In the face of persecution, the early Christians possessed extraordinary courage, which at some point "proved" that they had been chosen by God. The Spaniards kept on so resolutely westward in search of El Dorado, despite the severest hardships, that they must have seemed gods. Yet the Burgundians collapsed within weeks of the Battle of Nancy. And Henry VIII seems to have attached England permanently to Protestantism as an unintended consequence of selling church lands to the gentry. But we guess at the existence of all these watersheds because we have few direct insights into the motivations of the many men and women involved in all of them.

So world-historical development did occur, but it was not "necessary," the teleological outcome of a "world spirit," the "destiny of Man," the "triumph of the West," "social evolution," "social differentiation," "inevitable contradictions between forces and relations of production," or any other of those Truly Grand Theories of Society that we inherited from the Enlightenment and that still enjoy periodic revivals. If we insist on viewing history "from the outside," as in all these post-Enlightenment visions, the result is theoretical disappointment: History seems just one damned thing after another. If the damned things are patterned, it is only because real men and women *impose* patterns. They attempt to control the world and increase their rewards within it by setting up power organizations of varying but patterned types and strengths. These power struggles are the principal patternings of history, but their outcomes have often been close-run.

The uneven development of collective power

The second qualification is that, although in the long run power development may look cumulative, one-directional, and one-dimensional, the actual mechanisms involved have been various and uneven. Let me give a military example.

By 2000 B.C. armies had organized to the point where they could march ninety kilometers; then win a battle, receive the submission of the enemy, and resupply; and then march on to repeat the process. Various groups subsequently refined these extensive techniques of aggressive conquest warfare. This almost continuous and broadly cumulative path of power development ended with the Roman legionary – an engineer and a "mule" as well as a fighter, able to march, dig, fight, lay siege, and pacify any contemporary enemy. But then such aggressive, extensive techniques became less appropriate to the kind of intensive, local defense required by the later empire. The legion fragmented into local militia. Then mounted knights and their retinues, with stone castles and contingents of foot archers, consolidated this defensive system and held off the most powerful extensive armies of the early Middle Ages (Islam, Huns, Tartars, Mongols). With the growth of states and commodity production and exchange, more extensive aggressive forces then revived. In the seventeenth century the most acute generals turned back consciously to the Roman legionary, turning the infantryman (now wielding a musket) into an engineer and a mule once again.

This was a highly uneven process. In the very long run armies acquired cumulatively greater powers. In the very short run each form of army was superior to its precursor at what it was called on to do. But in between these two levels there lay not development but oscillation between different types of military struggle – which I have simplified into swings between extensive, aggressive war and intensive, defensive war. In the whole process, therefore, the social preconditions and social effects of military power varied considerably according to these different roles. The development of military power was at least two-dimensional.

This argument can be generalized. I have distinguished pairs of power types – intensive and extensive, authoritative and diffuse, collective and distributive – each polar type of which may be more or less appropriate to the situation of a group or a society. Thus, despite my earlier list of "world-historical inventions," societies cannot be simply ranked above or below one another in their overall power. In Chapter 9, for example, I argued that the Roman Empire was especially good at extensive power. When scholars criticize it for lacking "inventiveness," they are looking at it through the perspectives of our kind of inventiveness, which has been largely intensive. Then I divided European development into a relatively intensive phase, lasting until about A.D. 1200, followed by a phase in which extensive techniques of power also developed. If we compared the European and Chinese civilizations, we could conclude that the European was more powerful only at a relatively late date, perhaps around 1600. Before then its powers were just *different:* more intensively adept, but less adept at extensive power.

In the very long run the British Empire was more powerful than the Roman; the Roman, more powerful than the Assyrian; the Assyrian, more powerful than the Akkadian. But I can manage such a generalization only because I have omitted all intervening cases and all nonimperial societies. Was Rome at its height more powerful than classical Greece? Had they met on the battlefield the probable outcome would have been a Roman victory (although a naval battle would have been an even match). The Roman economy was more developed. Far more intangible are the predominantly ideological and political power factors. The Greek polis produced more intense authoritative mobilization; the Romans perfected extensive authoritative techniques. Roman ideology diffused broadly, but only among its ruling class; Greek ideology diffused across class boundaries. The result of these comparisons is not just hypothetical. There was a real historical outcome, but it was not one-dimensional. Rome conquered the Greek successor states but was itself converted by the Greek successor ideology, Christianity. The original question – Which was more powerful? – is not answerable. Power and its development are not one-dimensional.

A dialectic between two types of development

But this negative answer leads us to the possibility of another, more positive one. It raises the question, Is there pattern to the variability of intensive and extensive, authoritative and diffuse, collective and distributive power? More particularly: Have we glimpsed a potentially cyclical, or even a dialectical, pattern to their interactions? There are some indications that this might be so.

In this particular history two main types of power configuration have pioneered jumps in world-historical collective social development.

1. *Empires of domination* combined military concentrated coercion with an attempt at state territorial centralization and geopolitical hegemony. So they also combined intensive authoritative powers along the narrow routes of pen-

etration of which an army was capable, with weaker, but still authoritative and far more extensive, power wielded over the whole empire and neighboring clients by its central state. The principal reorganizing role is here played by a mixture of military and political power, with the former predominating.

2. In *multi-power-actor civilizations,* decentralized power actors competed with one another within an overall framework of normative regulation. Here extensive powers were diffuse, belonging to the overall culture rather than to any authoritative power organization. Intensive powers were possessed by a variety of small, local power actors, sometimes states in a multistate civilization, sometimes military elites, sometimes classes and fractions of classes, usually mixtures of all of these. The predominant reorganizing forces were here economic and ideological, though in varied combinations and often with political and geopolitical help.

The main examples of empires of domination in this volume have been the Akkadian, Assyrian, and Roman empires; the main examples of multi-power-actor civilizations have been Phoenicia and classical Greece, and then medieval and early modern Europe. Each of these cases was notably creative in its use and development of the sources of social power. Each invented power techniques that figure in the world-historical list I gave earlier. Each, therefore, made notable contributions to the single process of world-historical development.

The fact that there are several examples of both types immediately means that "single structure" or single-factor theories of social development are false. Prominent among these has been neoclassical economic theory, which I have criticized in various chapters. This theory sees history as capitalism writ large. Social development supposedly results when societies let rip essentially "natural" forces of competition. Although this might seem to have an obvious affinity with my type 2, it cannot cope with two major features of the typology. First, it cannot even begin to explain – because it denies – the creativity of type 1 empires of domination. Second, it does not see that to understand type 2 an explanation of normative regulation is required. *Regulated* competition is not "natural." If competition is not to degenerate into mutual suspicion and aggression and so result in anarchy, it requires elaborate, delicate social arrangements that respect the essential humanity, the powers, and the property rights of the various decentralized power actors. In the light of world history, neoclassical theory should be seen as bourgeois ideology, a false claim that the present power structure of our own society is legitimate because it is "natural."

But this is not the only influential false theory. I have already criticized the more ambitious varieties of historical materialism that see class struggle as the main motor of development. Class struggle has an obvious place in type 2, for classes are some of the principal decentralized power actors found there. But they are not the only ones, or always the most important ones. And class struggle is of far less creative significance in most examples of type 1, as I argued especially in Chapters 5 and 9. Indeed, given the great difference between the two types, it is difficult to see any single power configuration as playing *the* dynamic role in world history. Neither "ideas as switchmen" nor an overall "rationalization process," as Weber occasionally concluded. Not the division of labor or social differentiation, as a whole host of writers from Comte to Parsons have argued. Nor even is there a single historical transition, from one kind of creativity to another – say, from militant to industrial societies, as Spencer put it. The two types of dynamism seem to have intermingled and succeeded one another throughout much of world history.

This, in turn, raises another, more complex potential pattern. The Akkadian Empire (and its early equivalents elsewhere) arose from the first multi-power-actor civilization of Mesopotamia. Phoenicia and Greece arose on the edges of, and depended on, Near Eastern empires. The Roman Empire was similarly dependent on Greece. European Christendom was erected on Roman and Greek ruins. Was there some kind of dialectic between the two types? Was each capable of certain innovations before reaching the limits of its own power capacities? And was further social development possible only when its polar opposite type arose to exploit precisely what it could not? Positive answers to these questions would certainly entail a general theory of world-historical development.

We should start to answer cautiously. Remember the conjunctural qualities of the process. Even over five millennia I have found only a few clear-cut examples of types 1 and 2. We could add a few examples that are predominantly of one type: Later Mesopotamian empires and the Persian Empire were largely of type 1; city-states of Asia Minor and Palestine at the beginning of the first millennium B.C., and perhaps the Etruscans, were predominantly of type 2. But we do not end up with a large number of cases, and we are nowhere near an ability to use statistical analysis. There is just *not enough* macrohistory to satisfy the comparative sociologist. Nor has the succession of types been invariant; nor have the cases been of equal "purity" of type; nor has the succession process been over similar social and geographical space. If there has been an interaction, perhaps we should not call it a "dialectic," with the suggestion of history as essence and system. Rather we should explore the possibility of repeated creative interplay between examples that approximate the two ideal types of power dynamism.

This more modest level of theory finds more support. Moreover, some of the very objections just mentioned actually provide further support for such a model. No empire was in reality a purely militaristic one; no competitive civilization was entirely decentralized. Some of the least pure cases such as Persia (discussed in Chapter 8) were mixing more nearly equal quantities of the two. Within the relatively pure cases, the internal dynamics often resembled the external process of creative interplay.

I argued in Chapter 5 that the first empires of domination contained a dynamic of development (because it was so persistent, I called it a dialectic). Through compulsory cooperation their states increased collective social powers. But such powers could not be kept under the state's control. Its own agents "disappeared" into "civil society," bearing state resources with them. Thus the very success of the state also enhanced the power and "private property" of decentralized power rivals such as aristocracies and merchants; and resources that had started as authoritative ended up as diffuse power – literacy being the outstanding example.

In this the dialectics of private-property development are especially interesting, for it seems that what happened in empires of domination was merely an extreme example of a more widespread historical development. Our own society regards private property and the state as separate, antithetical forces. Liberalism views property rights as originating in the struggles of individuals to exploit nature, to acquire its surplus, and to transmit it to family and descendents. In this view public power is essentially external to private property rights. The state may be brought in to institutionalize property rights, or it may be viewed as a dangerous threat to them; but the state is not a part of the *creation* of private property. Yet we have seen repeatedly that this is not historical fact. Private property emerged in the first place, and has usually been subsequently enhanced, through the struggles and fragmenting tendencies of public power organizations.

This happened most obviously when centralized collective power units fragmented into smaller local ones. Those who commanded these local collective units could obtain distributive power over them and hide this power from larger units; that is, they could keep it *private*. In time it was institutionalized as private property, recognized in custom or law. We saw this happening in three principal bursts: in prehistory and in the beginnings of civilization and stratification (Chapters 2 and 3); in empires of domination as decentralization and fragmentation proceeded (Chapters 5 and 9); and in medieval Christendom as lord and richer peasant alike managed to hide local power resources under their control from weak states and had their customary rights written into law (Chapter 12). Private property was not in its origin or in most of its historical development something *opposed* to the public domain. It emerged out of conflicts and compromises between competing collective power actors in the public domain. These have usually been of two main types, the local and the would-be centralized, engaged in a confederal relationship with each other. Private property emerged from the public, though not a unitary, communal domain and from the use of collective power within it.

Now let us turn to the dynamics of the other ideal type, multi-power-actor civilizations. Here too the dynamic seems to have led toward its opposite, greater hegemonic centralization, although this was not such a consistent process (and I did not dignify it with the label of a "dialectic"). Thus the multistate civilization of early Mesopotamia moved under the hegemonic control of one city-state, then fell to an empire of domination. The Greek multistate civilization moved toward alternate Athenian and Spartan hegemony, before falling to Macedonian imperialism. European civilization moved from a highly decentralized regulatory structure, in which church institutions, states, military-elite alliances, and trading networks all shared control, to predominant regulation by multistate diplomacy, and then toward the near hegemony within it of one power, Great Britain. (This last process will be further described in Volume II.)

Thus within both types there has been fairly often repeated interplay between forces that roughly resemble in their main characteristics the two ideal types themselves. Again it begins to look like a single world-historical process. It runs like this: In the pursuit of their goals, human beings set up organizations of cooperation that involved both collective and distributive powers. Some of these organizations proved to be of greater logistical efficacy than others. We may at a first level of generality distinguish the four power sources as highly effective in this way. But then, further, we may note that two broader configurations of the sources, empires of domination and multi-power-actor civilizations, have been the most effective of all. Indeed, the two have been so effective that they account for the most sustained bursts of the historical development of human powers. Yet each type eventually reaches limits of its power capacities. It lacks adaptability in the face of new opportunities or threats created by the uncontrolled, interstitial development of a new combination of power networks. Its very success has come from a stable institutionalization of formerly dominant power structures that is now anachronistic. Its very developmental success has set in motion other power networks – which are antithetical to its own institutions. Empires of domination have unintentionally generated more diffuse power relations of two main sorts within their own interstices: (1) decentralized, property-owning landlords, merchants, and artisans, that is, upper and middling classes; and (2) ideological movements, located primarily among these classes, but also embodying more diffuse and universal notions of community. If these diffuse power relations continue to grow interstitially, a decentralized multi-power-actor civilization may result, either from the collapse of the empire or from its gradual metamorphosis. But in turn, this emergent civilization may institutionalize itself, and then it too becomes less adaptable to changed circumstances. It also generates its own antithetical, interstitial forces, in this case tendencies toward state centralization and militaristic coercion, coupled perhaps with the emergence of one hegemonic geopolitical state, which may eventually result in the reemergence of an empire of domination. In Chapter 1, I called this general model of creative interplay that of *institutionalization* and *interstitial surprise*. I have now given it more content.

But I do not wish to push this model into being the "essence of history" – hence the number of "may" statements in the preceding paragraph. In the particular history I have recounted, such a pattern has occurred on several occasions. There has been great variability in the length of time covered by each single phase of creative interplay. The details have varied considerably. So too has the adaptability of dominant institutions. I noted this, for example, when contrasting the Roman and the Chinese Han empires. In my discussion of the "decline and fall" issue, in Chapter 9, I emphasized the alternative options open to the later Roman Empire: Christianization of barbarian elites or further conquests. Yet, of course, the empire did collapse. On the other hand, the Han dynasty coped with a not dissimilar situation. It managed to civilize its barbarians and incorporate diffuse class and ideological power forces into its imperial structure. In this way, there developed the resilient gentry/ scholar, bureaucrat/Confucian power configuration that took China into a quite different historical path of development – of three relatively early bursts of social development (Han, Tang, and Sung), followed by dynastic cycles, stagnation, and eventual decay. Similarly, I would not like to be interpreted as implying that the destiny of the West is to fall to more centralized and coercive forms of society, and certainly not to the "militarized socialism" of the Soviet Union. As Volume II will show, the creative interplay between the two types of power configuration is continuing in our own time, but in more complex ways than this. What I emphasize about the overall process is that its patterned center has been creative interplay between two macroconfigurations of power, and that part of the creativity has consisted in a variety of paths of development and of eventual outcomes.

The migrations of power

The third and final qualification to be made to the model of world-historical development concerns its geographical shiftiness. My repeated claim that I have written a historical account is a sham. I have written a developmental account of an abstraction, power. I have not chronicled one "society," state, or even place. I have picked up societies, states, and places quite promiscuously as they have acquired the "leading edge" of power and have dropped them as soon as they have lost it. I lost interest in Mesopotamia many chapters ago, then in the whole of the Near East, then in Greece and Italy, and most recenlty in much of the continent of Europe. This reveals that the leading edge of power has migrated throughout much of history.

Thus there is one further potential pattern that world-historical development *cannot* assume. It has not been an evolution, in the strict sense of that term. Development cannot be explained in terms of the immanent tendencies of society. A later, higher phase of power development cannot be explained merely in terms of the features of the earlier, lower one. It cannot be, when we are dealing with different geographical and social areas in the two phases. Theories of social evolution rely on a systematic view of social development

– on its "structural differentiation"; its "contradictions" or "dialectics"; its competition among the "fittest" persons, groups, or states; its "rationalization process"; or whatever. There are three objections to this. First, there has never existed a social system in the whole history recounted here. "Societies" have always been overlapping, intersecting power networks, open to external, transboundary, and interstitial, as well as internal, influence. Second, those that have been more systemic, in the sense of being more tightly patterned and bounded, have not played any overall greater role in social development than those that were less systemic. Third, social development has migrated, seemingly quite promiscuously, owing sometimes to relatively "internal" processes of change, sometimes to relatively external ones, and usually to complex interactions between the two.

The question remains, however, Is this process of interactive power migration patterned in some other, nonevolutionary way? The answer is yes. We can find two types of pattern in the migration.

The first pattern makes more precise the pattern presented earlier, of institutionalization/interstitial surprise. It is an extended version of the "marcher lord" theory referred to in Chapter 5. A regionally dominant, institution-building, developing power also upgrades the power capacities of its neighbors, who learn its power techniques but adapt them to their different social and geographical circumstances. Where the dominant power acquires the stable, specialized institutions of either an empire of domination or a multi-power-actor civilization, some of the emergent interstitial forces it generates may flow outward to the marches, where they are less confined by institutionalized, antithetical power structures. Hence the bearers of interstitial surprise have often been marcher lords. The world-historical process acquires their migratory legs.

Again, however, I have retreated to "may" statements. There *has* been such a tendency, but it has not been invariant. Interstitial forces have sometimes exploded in the geographical (though not the "official") core of an existing society, as they did in the later Roman Empire, for example. In any case, the tendency in this particular segment of world history for marcher lords to take over may have been primarily caused by the second type of migratory pattern.

The second pattern concerns the *westward* and *northwestward* drift of the leading edge of power in this volume. I discussed this in the first half of the last chapter and will not repeat its details here. Admittedly, the first part of the process is largely an artifact of my method. The leading edge in this narrative migrated northwestward from Sumer to Akkad, then farther northwestward into southern Asia Minor, the Assyrian heartland. But I ignored counter-tendencies in this period because Asia was not my focus. In the ancient period right up to the Persian Empire expansion eastward toward India and northeastward into central Asia also occurred. Only Islam later combined eastward and westward expansion – by then, however, Islam's western frontier was a real barrier to expansion. But the nonartifactual part of the western drift was that Phoenicia, Greece, Rome, and then European regions in several phases of development moved the leading edge of power steadily westward until it reached the Atlantic coast. In the next volume this migration will diversify, continuing west to America, but also moving eastward out of Europe.

Now obviously there is no *general* advantage accruing to power actors in the West rather than the East or South. As I explained in the last chapter, the drift westward and northwestward has been the product of the accidental conjunction of three particular ecological and social circumstances: (1) geographical barriers of desert southward, (2) the barrier of powerful empires and confederacies with a similar structure to those of the Near East eastward and northeastward, and (3) two interrelating ecological peculiarities westward. The geological combination of successive layers of heavier, wetter, deeper, richer, rain-watered soils and the navigable, varied coastlines of the Mediterranean, Baltic, North, and Atlantic seas "just happened" to create developmental possibilities northwestward at crucial but repeated historical junctures. These northwesterly marcher lords were indeed relatively unfettered, yet encouraged to expand and innovate, by the dominant institutions of their period (as the marcher-lord theory suggests). Their *continued* success, however, was surely not social at all, but a gigantic series of accidents of nature linked to an equally monstrous series of historical coincidences. Iron was discovered just when eastern Mediterranean trade could "take off"; it just happened to exist naturally in conjunction with heavier soils suitable for iron plowing throughout Europe. Just when Rome collapsed but Christendom survived, Scandinavians were opening up the Baltic and North seas and Germans were penetrating deeper into the soil. Just when the western European states were beginning to rival the southern and central ones, Islam closed the Strait of Gibraltar and America was discovered with Atlantic-coast navigational techniques. I have striven hard to find micropatterns in all these events in my narrative chapters, and to find macropatterns in this chapter and the last. But a necessary feature of all these patterns has been the accidental westward drift of world-historical development.

This must restrain any "significant generalizations" we might make in response to Weber's challenge, quoted earlier in the chapter. In this chapter I have generalized about the organization means offered by the four power sources; about the two most powerful configurations of the sources, empires of domination and multi-power-actor civilizations; about the dialectic between them as the core of world-historical development; and about the mechanism of institutionalization/interstitial surprise by which this has proceeded. Yet at the end of the day these are only generalizations about the development of one civilization, that of the Near East and Europe, which has also contained many accidental features. And I have stopped the clock in 1760, even before the apogee of that civilization. In Volume III, I shall move to a higher level of theoretical generality; but I must first delineate the patterns and accidents of industrial societies.

Bibliography

Balibar, E. 1970. The basic concepts of historical materialism. In *Reading Capital,* ed. L. Althusser and E. Balibar. London: New Left Books.
Hall, J. 1985. *Powers and Liberties.* Oxford: Basil Blackwell.
Kautsky, J. 1982. *The Politics of Aristocratic Empires.* Chapel Hill: University of North Carolina Press.
Parsons, T. 1966. *Societies: Evolutionary and Comparative Perspectives.* Englewood Cliffs, N.J.: Prentice-Hall.
Weber, M. 1968. *Economy and Society.* 3 vols. Berkeley: University of California Press.

Index

Absolutism, 459, 475–83, 512
Accident, historical, 121, 227, 503–6,
    508–10, 530–1, 540–1
Agricultural techniques, 45, 48, 51–2,
    185–6, 266, 286, 356, 403–6, 494–5,
    501, 509, 524
Akkadian Empire, 75, 91, 98, 101, 131,
    133–54, 157, 160, 166, 167, 169, 171,
    192–3, 231, 238, 533, 534, 535
Alexander the Great, 138–40, 191, 226, 228,
    231, 238, 243, 246–7, 259, 288, 508,
    531
Alluvial agriculture, 5, 16, 73–5, 77–82,
    102, 105–6, 116, 118–9, 123–7, 130,
    137, 152, 174
    defined, 78
Andean America, 20, 74–5, 121–4, 171,
    173, 175, 198, 525
Arameans, 157, 193, 194, 236, 238, 245,
    317
Archers, *see* Artillery
Aristocracy, *see* Lords, aristocrats, and no-
    bles
Aristotle, 5, 197, 208, 214, 220, 221, 227
Army, rule through, 142, 143, 231–4, 274–8
Artillery, 48, 132–3, 180, 202, 209, 233,
    276, 378, 428, 446, 453, 480, 532
Artisans, 80, 82, 114, 125, 154, 193,
    312–13, 315–17, 322–3, 397, 510
Aryans, 162, 175, 181, 182, 183, 350–3
Assyria, 24, 75, 81, 120, 123, 138–40, 149,
    154, 157, 160, 167, 182, 184–6, 188,
    191, 194, 199, 201, 212, 231–7, 240,
    268, 519, 528, 529, 533, 534
Athens, 197, 203, 205, 207–11, 215, 218,
    221, 223–4, 227, 320, 537
Authoritative power, 8–10, 47, 89, 92, 120,
    122, 125, 131, 143, 148–55, 172, 226,
    250, 290, 311, 530
    defined, 8
Authority, 7, 37, 39, 44, 49, 53, 59, 60,
    63–70, 85, 99–101, 124
Aztecs, *see* Meso-America

Babylon, 75, 134, 138, 144–5, 149, 150,
    154, 156, 157, 166, 167, 182, 184, 187,
    193, 194, 203, 234, 236–9
Barbarians, 85, 164, 182, 213–16, 225, 262,
    276, 286–8, 294–5, 298, 307, 329,

    334–8, 343, 351, 376, 392–3, 395, 407,
    505
Buddhism, 301, 342, 343, 354–7, 363–71,
    398
Bureaucracy, 95, 96, 144, 157, 192, 261,
    268, 273–4, 289, 377, 392, 418, 476
Byzantium, 293–4, 333, 334, 344–6, 368,
    382, 383

Cage and caging (social), 39–40, 42, 47–9,
    67–9, 74, 75, 77, 80, 85, 86, 88, 89,
    93, 100, 102, 105–27, 130, 142, 226,
    290
Capitalism and capitalist mode of production,
    16, 17, 25, 50, 272, 373–7, 398–9,
    408–13, 431, 446, 450–95, 501, 506,
    510–16
    defined, 374–5
Carthage, 191–2, 215, 227, 250–1, 253–6,
    258, 260, 268, 296, 345
Caste, 196–7, 348–63, 368–9
    defined, 349–50
    Jati, 349–50, 358, 359, 363
    Varna, 349, 351–4, 357, 358, 359
Castles, *see* Fortifications
Cavalry, 48, 132–3, 157, 164, 185, 202,
    209, 228, 233–5, 251–2, 276, 286,
    345–6, 391–2, 428, 525, 532
Chariots, 114, 132–3, 157, 162, 179–85,
    197, 202, 350
China, 9, 94–5, 164, 170, 294–5, 342–4,
    377, 501–2, 532–3
    Han dynasty in, 95, 120, 123, 163, 188,
    270, 293, 297, 306, 343, 538
    origins of, 20, 74–5, 80, 105
    Shang dynasty in, 88, 106–8, 118, 120
Christianity, 213, 359, 363–71, 505
    in Dark Ages, 334–8, 529
    in Medieval and early modern Europe, 19,
    377, 379–90, 434–6, 500, 503–7,
    512–13, 529, 535, 536
    in Roman period, 115, 295, 301–33,
    528–9, 531
Cities, *see* Towns, urbanization, and cities
Citizenship, 153, 200, 207–11, 218–23,
    252–9, 262, 264, 267, 282, 298, 306
City-state, 39, 48, 65, 82, 91, 92, 93,
    97–102, 120, 126, 130–3, 140, 146,
    147, 150, 152, 157, 184, 190, 192, 194,
    195, 238, 250–2, 527, 530

Civil society, 50, 51, 144, 159, 165–6, 170,
    235, 237, 271, 278, 281, 289, 296, 297,
    306, 417, 434, 441, 444–5, 476–82,
    493–5, 511, 516, 521
Civilization, 48, 63, 294–5, 298, 307,
    334–8, 366, 519
    defined, 38, 73–4
    origins of, 5, 16, 23, 36–40, 65, 73–102,
    105–27
Clan, see Lineage
Class, and class struggle, 8, 10, 15, 17, 34,
    59, 76, 84, 101, 106, 115, 153, 190,
    200, 207, 213, 216–23, 251–2, 262–4,
    267, 270, 322–3, 363, 365, 380,
    384–90, 409–12, 434, 463, 513–16,
    520, 522, 523, 527–31, 534–5
    defined, 24–5, 216
    extensive, 24–5, 216–23, 241, 252,
    262–4, 270, 389–90, 463, 528–9
    latent, 24, 216, 264, 389–90, 527
    political, 24–5, 195, 212, 217–23, 226,
    241, 262, 270, 389, 463, 528–9
    symmetrical and asymmetrical, 24–5,
    216–21, 252, 264, 270, 463, 528–
    9
Clientelism and vassalage, rule through, 69,
    84, 120–1, 125, 142, 143, 165, 183,
    216, 220, 231, 234, 238, 240, 242,
    251–2, 258–9, 263–4, 296, 380, 386,
    391–3, 399, 420–1, 429, 438–40,
    458–61
Coinage, 10, 23, 89, 150, 165, 192–5, 207,
    225, 231, 239–40, 245, 251, 253, 272,
    284, 286–8, 307, 396
Collective power, 37, 53, 57, 75, 83, 131,
    148, 153–4, 166–7, 195, 230, 364, 373,
    378, 514, 522–3
    defined, 6–7
Colonial empires, 69, 121, 198, 203, 205–6,
    220, 225, 472–5, 481–3, 515
Communal labor, 45–6, 51–2, 60, 63, 80,
    83, 86, 94
Communal property, 51–3, 83, 87
Communications infrastructures, 136–7, 145,
    149, 150, 154, 157, 161, 173, 240, 258,
    274–6, 310–13, 319–20, 322, 363, 379,
    388–9, 404, 441–5
Community, 57, 92, 197–201, 223–4, 305,
    319–20, 322, 324–5, 345–6, 350, 358
Comparative sociology, 30, 105–27, 130,
    167–74, 188–9, 240, 341–2, 370–1,
    378, 501–3, 525–6, 535
Compulsory cooperation, 56, 130, 143,
    145–55, 158, 162, 165–7, 174–6, 198,
    231, 234–5, 247, 250, 259–60, 267,
    268, 270, 272, 278–80, 290, 297, 366,
    423, 515, 520, 521, 526

Comte, A., 13, 464, 535
Confederal societies, see Federal and confed-
    eral societies
Confucianism, 270, 295, 301, 342–4, 363–5,
    398
Conquest, 11, 53–8, 74, 84, 91, 105, 107,
    123, 135, 140–55, 157, 160, 161, 203,
    213, 222, 236, 247, 250, 253–8, 260,
    267, 272, 281, 296, 351, 359, 361,
    391–3, 420–1
Conquistadores, 120–1, 123, 173, 525, 531
Constantine, 320, 329–30, 379, 386
Core-periphery, 76, 81, 82, 84, 85, 93, 98–
    100, 102, 106, 107, 124–5, 144, 147,
    163–4
Courts, 69, 137, 145, 158–60, 239, 282,
    435, 439, 460–1, 468
Crete, see Minoan Crete

Decline and collapse of society, 39, 66–70,
    105, 115, 119–21, 175, 182–3, 186–7,
    191, 227–8, 236–7, 283–94, 298,
    356–7, 368, 439–40, 479–80, 509,
    531
Democracy, 64, 68, 86, 93, 97, 99, 106,
    153, 185–8, 190, 193, 195, 197–211,
    220–1, 224, 283, 291, 294–5, 328, 334,
    365, 413
Despotic power, 26, 68, 93–8, 169–74, 240,
    246, 306, 477–81, 502, 515–16, 521
Development, world-historical, 30–2, 98,
    114, 117, 118, 120–1, 134, 147–55,
    161–7, 169, 172–5, 241, 295–8, 301,
    359, 361, 369, 371, 373, 412–13, 503,
    508–10, 518–41
Dialectic, 36, 130, 161–7, 169, 172–5, 190,
    221, 226, 241, 296, 337, 536–7, 539,
    540
Diffused power, 8–10, 46, 47, 82, 89, 90,
    92, 100, 102, 125, 149, 152–3, 160,
    165, 184, 197, 206, 225, 236, 250,
    278–9, 301, 524
    defined, 8
Diffusion theory, 1, 35, 74, 79, 85, 116–19,
    179–80
Dimensions and levels of society, 1, 11–22,
    77, 175, 523
Diocletian, 136, 266, 279–80, 288–92, 295,
    314, 329
Diplomacy, see Geopolitics and diplomacy
Distributive power, 53, 75, 83, 250, 515
    defined, 6–7
Domination, empires of, see Empires
Durkheim, E., 4, 13, 22–3, 47, 309, 343,
    369–70, 377, 398–9

Ecology, 45–6, 52, 61–2, 74, 78–83, 92–3,
    102, 106, 107, 110–12, 117, 123–4,

137, 157, 174, 195–6, 238, 356, 405–6, 502, 540
Economic power, 11, 28, 44–6, 49–53, 58–62, 64–70, 78–89, 94–8, 124–7, 146–55, 185–9, 196–7, 216–23, 252–7, 260–72, 278–80, 290–1, 308–10, 322–3, 361, 373–4, 394–9, 409–12, 434–6, 490–5, 507, 516, 520
  defined, 24–5
Ecumene, 301, 307, 309, 320–38, 346, 362, 380–4, 463–4, 471, 506
Education, 26, 143, 154, 165, 173, 207, 226, 240–1, 313–15, 334, 336, 343, 347, 353–5, 384, 436–7, 441
Egalitarianism, 36, 37, 49, 50, 53, 67–9, 78, 82, 86, 159, 201, 203, 255, 305, 325–6, 328, 363, 384, 390, 392, 529
Egypt, 48, 74–5, 80, 88, 92, 94–6, 105, 107, 123, 138, 152, 158, 159, 163, 164, 170, 175, 182, 184, 186–7, 191, 193, 194, 211, 212, 237, 238, 267, 327, 345
Empires, 16, 109, 114, 130–76, 178, 182–90, 192, 194, 210, 217, 222, 224–5, 228, 231–48, 250–98, 306–7, 337–8, 343–4, 355–6, 363–4, 370, 533–8
Engels, F., 51, 59, 65, 70, 222, 523
Ethnicity, 43, 53, 90–3, 159, 166, 174, 181, 197, 200, 204, 213, 215–16, 225, 252, 257, 310, 363, 365, 421
Evolution, 1, 34–44, 47–70, 75, 79, 116–17, 127, 130, 179–80, 531, 538
Extensive power, 7–10, 25, 26, 176, 267, 276, 285–6, 298, 314, 337, 374, 378, 381, 437–8, 471, 532–3
  defined, 7

Family and kinship, 14, 42–3, 52, 59, 73, 83–7, 93, 113, 145, 197, 200, 216–17, 251, 312–13, 325, 327, 351, 357, 367–8, 380, 384–5, 408, 471–2
Federal and confederal societies, 14, 16–17, 43, 52, 58, 89–93, 97–8, 106, 120–1, 123, 126–7, 131, 170, 174, 176, 181, 184, 192, 198, 200, 210, 225, 247, 253, 257–8, 268, 347, 350, 365, 370, 376, 512, 516
Feudalism, 15, 18–20, 108, 144, 157, 167, 171–4, 183, 235, 237, 288, 292, 350, 356–7, 361, 373–6, 398–9, 409–13, 450, 476, 505, 506, 512, 525–6
  feudal levy and, 18–20, 101, 393, 422–3, 431, 507
  feudal mode of production and, 19, 375, 409–12, 476, 505, 512
  feudal state and, 11, 19–20, 391–3, 416, 419, 438–40, 455

Fortifications, 26, 41, 48, 84, 99–101, 116, 131, 135, 140, 141, 143, 162–4, 180, 184, 202, 228, 263, 274, 277, 279, 391–2, 396, 453–4, 525
Functionalism, 2, 12, 75, 116
  functionalist theory of state origins and, 49–50, 53, 61, 127

Gatherer-hunters, 34, 36, 37, 42–4, 48, 49, 51, 81, 85, 90, 125
Geopolitics and diplomacy, 26, 28, 91–2, 102, 110–12, 126, 132, 141, 142, 149, 152, 156, 157, 185–9, 192, 195, 198, 202, 205, 210, 224–5, 237, 270, 376, 383, 454, 466, 468, 470, 490, 507–8, 510, 511, 513–14, 522, 537
Gumplowicz, L., 26, 53–4, 60, 71, 417
Greece
  classical, 23, 24, 114, 138, 139, 149, 152, 153, 158, 159, 188, 195–228, 233, 239, 242–8, 250, 253, 254, 260, 261, 314, 342–3, 363–5, 376, 505, 519, 520, 523, 528–9, 533, 534, 535
  Mycenaean, 61, 115, 162, 175, 181, 182, 186–7, 191, 196, 204, 350
  Roman, 279, 307, 312, 319
  see also Athens; Sparta
Gunpowder, see Artillery

Hellenism, 115, 226, 243, 247–8, 303–4, 309, 317–19, 505, 509, 528
Herders, see Pastoralists, herders, and nomads
Herodotus, 114, 214–15, 237
Hinduism, 301–2, 348–63, 368–71, 398
Historical method, 30–2, 40, 169, 173–4, 370–1, 503, 530–2
Hittites, 75, 158, 181, 183, 184, 185, 187, 191, 193, 233, 234, 525
Hobbes, T., 36, 58–9, 417
Hoplites, 199–204, 208, 209, 220, 222, 223, 224, 226, 228, 243, 245, 251–2, 525, 530
Human nature and goals, 3, 4–6, 12, 14–15, 30, 366
Hunter-gatherers, see Gatherer-hunters

Idealism, 5, 20–1, 77, 126, 332, 348–9, 359, 366, 369–71, 377, 523, 535
Ideological power, 11, 28, 46–8, 76–7, 126–7, 155–61, 174, 294–5, 297, 301–38, 341–71, 379–90, 463–72, 506, 519–20, 526
  defined, 22–4
Immanence, ideological, 22, 24, 28, 157–61, 174, 235, 270, 301, 377, 386, 519
Incas, see Andean America

India, 238, 246, 345, 348–63, 501
Indo-European, 14, 179–89, 197, 350, 531
Indus Valley, 20, 74, 80, 88, 105–7, 175,
    182, 350
Industrial Revolution, 373–4, 450, 495, 500,
    513, 516
Industrial society, 30, 31, 56, 363
Infantry, 18–20, 48, 100, 132–3, 159,
    162–3, 180, 185–6, 199–204, 224, 233,
    251–2, 254, 428, 431, 454, 505, 528,
    532
Infrastructural power, 26, 109, 122–3, 125,
    130, 165, 170, 223, 246, 270, 306, 310,
    357, 361, 477–83, 512, 524–7, 530
Institutionalization of power, 7, 14–16, 30,
    59, 68, 101, 123, 125, 144, 151, 160,
    170, 250, 268, 281, 282, 283, 312, 502,
    537–40
Intensive power, 7–10, 25, 26, 159, 185–8,
    224, 285–6, 328, 366–7, 369, 374, 378,
    404–6, 500, 507, 532–3
    defined, 7
Interstitial emergence, 15–19, 23, 30, 188,
    190, 236, 295, 322, 363–4, 366, 416,
    436, 503, 519, 528, 537–40
Iron Age, 46, 63, 67, 112, 162, 179, 184–9,
    194, 196–7, 204, 221, 223, 232, 250,
    259, 276, 285, 295, 505, 520, 528, 530
Irrigation, 41, 46, 74–5, 78–99, 101, 105–
    10, 116, 119, 121, 124–7, 130, 146,
    149, 156, 159, 174, 193, 355
Islam, 11, 58, 301–2, 334, 338, 344–8, 359,
    363–71, 377, 378, 382, 383, 407,
    502–4, 508–10, 540
Israel, *see* Jews and Judaism

Jesus Christ, 305, 309, 317, 321, 326, 345,
    384, 392, 398, 404
Jews and Judaism, 159, 191, 234, 236, 239,
    242, 274, 304, 307, 310, 312, 317–19,
    333, 344–5, 363, 382, 505, 515

Kassites, 134, 157, 162, 165, 166, 167, 181,
    182, 187, 232
Kings, *see* Monarchy
Kinship, *see* Family and kinship

Labor, 40–1, 44–6, 50–1, 54, 59, 113, 278
    corvée, 26, 122, 143, 149, 150–1, 165,
    276
    dependent, 19, 84–6, 98, 125, 151, 214,
    262, 284–5, 291, 336, 375, 410–12
    free, 151–2, 194, 214, 218, 260–2, 278,
    374–5, 410–12, 495, 527
    see also Communal labor; Peasantry; Serf-
    dom; Slavery; Surplus labor
Lattimore, O., 9–10, 26, 33, 45, 142–3,
    145–6, 274

Law, 109, 145, 156, 160, 206–7, 253, 282,
    312, 320, 354, 357, 368, 377, 380, 395,
    398–9, 419–22, 441, 460–1, 477,
    511–12, 524
Legionary economy, 250, 260, 268, 272–83,
    292, 296, 306
Legions, 251, 257–9, 274–8, 280, 286–9,
    292, 295–6, 311–12, 319, 532
Liberalism, 20, 21, 146, 246, 371
    liberal theory of state origins and, 49–53,
    58–60, 83, 127
Lineage, 42, 44, 51, 60–2, 64, 68–9, 113,
    166, 169–70, 196–7, 349, 385–6
Literacy, 10, 23, 73–74, 88–90, 93, 96, 105,
    107, 112, 114, 115, 117, 118, 125, 152,
    159–60, 173, 184, 192–3, 198, 204,
    206–7, 223–5, 231, 239, 245, 251, 253,
    256, 269–70, 307, 313–17, 334, 336,
    347, 353–5, 364, 368, 379–81, 388,
    392, 441–3, 462, 465, 524
Locke, J., 36, 50–1, 58–9, 417
Logistics, 9–10, 26, 82, 98, 109, 122–3,
    134–42, 161, 164, 174, 182, 204–5,
    233–4, 238, 242–5, 250, 270, 275,
    279–80, 355, 440–5, 455–6, 482, 519,
    524
Lords, aristocrats, and nobles, 16, 19, 101,
    109, 111, 159, 170, 196, 200, 203,
    240–2, 263, 289–91, 343, 350–4, 360,
    365, 375, 380, 384–6, 391–3, 410–12,
    459–60, 468, 501

Macedonia, 75, 114, 138–9, 151, 188, 202,
    220, 223, 227–8, 254, 528, 537
Malthusian cycles, 46, 52, 65, 115, 154
Manors, 19, 154, 336, 394–7, 406, 434,
    441, 504, 507, 510
Marcher lords and marches, 82, 101, 110,
    120, 130–3, 142–5, 149, 156–7,
    162–4, 166, 174–6, 181–2, 190, 196,
    209, 210, 220, 228, 286–8, 292,
    539–40
Marius and Marius's Pole, 139, 257–8,
    274–6, 285, 297, 524
Markets, 8, 9, 10, 23–5, 46, 125, 146, 149,
    157, 192, 200, 224, 355, 397, 411–12
Marx, K., 4, 5, 11, 13, 15, 24, 25, 36, 51,
    59, 222, 270, 283, 417, 464, 501, 520
Marxian theories, 10–13, 17–18, 23, 30,
    221–2, 283–4, 308, 371, 376,
    409–12, 506, 519, 529
    of state origins, 49–51, 58–60, 65, 83,
    127
Materialism, 5, 12–13, 20–1, 77, 222–3,
    308–9, 332, 348–9, 360–1, 366, 367,
    369–71, 376, 377, 409, 523, 534–5
Maya, *see* Meso-America

Megalithic societies, 61–6, 109, 123
Mercantilism, 473–5
Mercenaries, 101, 114, 142, 163, 186, 194–5,
   202–3, 206, 207, 228, 240, 253, 393,
   426
Merchants, 90, 112, 114, 132, 154, 192–3,
   198, 312–13, 315–17, 380, 397, 427–8,
   431–2, 510, 515
Meso-America, 20, 74–6, 118–21, 175
Mesopotamia, 17, 23, 30, 48, 66, 138, 211,
   376, 535, 537
   origins of civilization in, 20, 41, 50, 73–
   102, 105, 106, 107, 120, 121, 124–5
Migration, 46, 116, 151, 180–4, 187, 205,
   250–1, 420, 538–40
Militarist theory, 26, 75, 511, 523
   of state origins, 49–50, 53–8, 84, 99–101,
   116, 123
Military Keynesianism, 150, 234, 278, 297
Military power, 6, 8–11, 18–20, 28, 48–9,
   53–8, 68–9, 98–101, 108, 109, 112,
   120, 125–7, 135–42, 157, 162–4,
   174–6, 179–84, 196–204, 218–20,
   222–3, 232–7, 239, 242–5, 251–9,
   263, 264, 273–8, 294, 307, 345–7, 368,
   390–3, 428, 453–7, 479–80, 506–9,
   511–14, 516, 520–1
   defined, 11, 25–6
Minoan Crete, 61, 74–5, 88, 105, 115–17,
   175, 182
Mode of production, 1, 5, 12, 24–5, 65, 153,
   218, 222, 505–6, 511, 516, 523
Monarchy, 50, 69, 93, 98–101, 107–10,
   131, 135, 140, 151, 158, 159, 169–74,
   196, 200, 220, 221, 224, 238, 240, 259,
   286, 293, 352, 353, 355, 380, 384, 476
Muhammad, 301, 302, 344–5
Multi-power-actor civilizations, 73–101,
   105–27, 130, 189, 190–228, 379–99,
   504, 516, 533–8
Mycenae, see Greece, Mycenaean

Nation, 4, 8, 10, 92, 235–6, 459–60, 462–3,
   469, 519, 529–33
Nation-state or national state, 17, 91, 225,
   363, 379, 416, 430–7, 444–5, 466, 468,
   490–4, 513, 522, 528–9
Nationalism, 16, 155, 157, 160, 225, 231,
   235–6, 240, 262, 269, 331–2, 380
Navies and naval power, 114, 191–2, 198,
   204–5, 208–11, 224, 228, 243–4, 251,
   253–4, 377, 445–6, 457, 478, 501, 505,
   509–10, 524, 528
Neoclassical economic theory, 376, 406,
   409–12, 534
Neolithic Revolution, 38–44
Nile, 74, 75, 80, 92, 95–6, 108, 110–13

Nobilities and notables, see Lords, aristocrats, and nobles
Nomads, see Pastoralists, herders, and nomads
Norms, normative solidarity, and normative
   pacification, 22, 45, 48–9, 86, 163,
   200–3, 253–4, 282, 309, 325–6,
   337–8, 342, 344–8, 353, 357–9, 367,
   369–70, 377, 381–90, 408, 420, 504,
   507, 510, 512, 520, 527

Officeholding, 144, 171–2, 175, 210, 220,
   235, 238, 256, 267–8, 329, 343,
   458–60, 476–9, 482
Oligarchy, 86, 93, 97, 99, 108, 194, 203,
   224, 232, 253
Oppenheimer, F., 26, 53–4, 71, 123, 417
Organizational outflanking, 7, 8, 264, 296,
   390, 528

Parsons, T., 6, 13, 23, 33, 348, 501, 515,
   523, 535
Particularistic power, 158, 170–1, 240–1,
   270, 306, 343, 365, 528, 530
Pastoralists, herders, and nomads, 45, 48, 52,
   54, 57, 58, 81, 85, 90, 92, 102, 107,
   110, 121, 124–5, 133, 134, 162, 164,
   180, 184, 294
Patriarchy, 31, 34, 217, 251
Patrimonial, 167, 171–4, 240, 525
Peasantry, 185–6, 195–201, 206, 208, 221,
   223, 225, 232–4, 251, 255–7, 261–7,
   290–3, 295, 313, 336, 350–1, 356, 390,
   410–12, 501, 504, 505, 507, 510, 513,
   528
Periphery, see Core-periphery
Persia, 24, 75, 114, 139, 140, 152, 160, 167,
   188, 191, 195, 202, 208, 212, 214–16,
   222, 225, 227, 228, 231, 232, 237–48,
   253, 260, 268, 276, 282, 287–8, 292,
   294, 306, 321, 344, 347, 505, 519, 528,
   529, 535
Phoenicia, 24, 149, 188, 190–5, 198, 204–6,
   208, 211, 214, 225, 228, 237, 244, 245,
   250, 253, 523, 534, 535
Polanyi, K., 24, 60–1, 71, 87, 192
Polis, 195, 197–204, 212, 217–18, 222–8,
   240, 246, 319
   defined, 197
Political power, 28, 77, 85–7, 93, 94, 97–
   100, 102, 106, 112–13, 121–2, 126,
   142–5, 170, 196, 222–3, 237–9, 311,
   322–4, 390–3, 440–5, 506, 510–16,
   521–2
   defined, 11, 26–7
Population size and density, 44, 68, 80, 97,
   98, 106, 108, 118, 119, 122, 196–7,
   224, 235, 238, 266–7, 292–3, 399–402

Population size and density (*cont.*)
  pressure of, 36, 43, 46, 52, 75, 80, 100, 149, 154, 205
Power
  defined, 6
  IEMP model of, 2–3, 6, 27–30, 77, 518–23
  leading edge of, 31, 130, 190, 227, 509, 538
Praxis, circuits of, 25, 28, 126, 153, 158, 185–6, 190, 207, 219, 221, 280, 374, 412–13, 514–15, 520
Prehistory and prehistoric societies, 16, 30, 34–70, 107, 120, 123, 131, 148, 180, 216, 226, 527
Prestige goods, 61–2, 64, 66–7, 82, 125
Primacy, ultimate, 3–6, 12, 30, 516
Private property, 38, 49, 51, 58–60, 65, 82–5, 87, 89, 93, 98, 101, 111, 124, 126, 147, 148, 165, 175, 180–1, 260, 267–8, 272, 286, 296, 307, 374, 398–9, 407, 409–12, 478, 504, 510, 521, 536
Production, *see* Mode of production
Protestantism, 377, 398, 435–6, 463–72, 501, 512, 519, 531
Puritanism, *see* Protestantism

Rank societies, 36, 37, 38, 53, 59–60, 62, 64, 67–70, 83, 84, 86–7, 101, 180
Rationality, 161, 170, 195, 211–16, 221, 226–7, 247, 305, 338, 343, 355, 359, 366, 398, 501, 503, 504, 520
Reason, *see* Rationality
Redistributive chiefdom, 50, 60–2, 68, 85, 150
Redistributive state, 85, 87, 89, 94, 107, 111, 116–17, 121–2, 126, 127, 131, 149, 150, 183, 192, 198
Revolts, 109, 214, 219, 244, 256–7, 261–4, 276, 324, 331–2, 338, 359, 386–90, 411, 435, 469, 513–14
Rome, 91, 94, 113, 123, 138, 139, 143, 147, 152, 153, 160, 161, 163, 167, 188, 197, 199, 202, 205, 208, 220, 223, 227, 233, 235, 238, 250–98, 404, 441, 444, 504, 519
  as empire, 17, 75, 150, 164, 259–98, 303–17, 384, 390, 533, 534, 535
  as Republic, 30, 151, 155, 251–9, 528–30
Rousseau, J.-J., 36, 51, 59
Ruling class, 25, 59, 73, 165, 169, 217, 227–8, 257, 258, 260, 267–72, 283, 294–7, 377, 469, 519, 528–30
  culture and, 108, 143, 145, 159–61, 167, 221, 226, 231, 235–6, 240–2, 247, 250, 268–70, 284, 301, 306, 311, 313–16, 343, 384–6, 408

Salvation, 28, 113, 226, 241–2, 295, 301–4, 308, 322, 324, 341–8, 354–5, 359, 361, 366, 370, 381, 384, 443, 464–6, 501, 519, 520, 526
Sargon of Akkad, 99, 131–50, 152, 154, 156, 157, 161, 162, 164, 166, 174, 246, 526
Science, 73, 90, 114–15, 160, 184–5, 211–13, 221, 284–5, 353–7, 378, 413, 464–5, 501
Serfdom, 151–2, 165, 213–14, 262, 278, 351, 375, 392, 394–5
Slavery, 26, 54, 58, 59, 84, 85, 109, 141, 151–2, 154, 165, 207, 211, 213–14, 218–19, 222, 225, 254, 256, 260–2, 267, 278, 283–5, 322, 326–7, 329, 351, 383, 395
Smith, A., 8, 146, 148, 398, 406
Social formation, *see* Dimensions and levels of society; Society
Socialism, 20, 50, 246
Society
  defined, 13
  theories of, 1–3, 12–14, 16–32, 39, 43, 46, 52, 68, 77, 98, 102, 108, 111, 113–14, 123–4, 126–7, 179, 200–1, 270, 286, 296, 325, 332, 338, 470, 503, 506, 521, 539
Sparta, 196, 201, 203, 206, 207, 208, 216, 224, 226, 227, 228, 242, 268, 320, 537
Spencer, H., 13, 26, 55–6, 71, 146, 247, 520, 523
State, 26–7, 34, 41, 167, 194–5, 246, 272–82, 288–92, 324–30, 332–5, 343, 355–6, 361, 390–3, 416–17, 430, 433–4, 510–16, 526–7
  contemporary, 16, 17
  coordinated, 416, 437–8, 468, 483, 510–12, 525
  defined, 37
  finances of, 208, 210, 238, 272–4, 280–2, 416–30, 451–3, 483–90, 510–11
  organic, 416, 450–95, 510, 512
  origins of, 36, 49–70, 73–102, 105–27
Status, 4, 10, 196, 222
Stonehenge, 63–4, 69, 77, 106
Sumer, *see* Mesopotamia
Surplus, 51, 61, 65, 66, 79, 80, 83, 84, 113, 114, 143, 146, 148, 150, 157, 185, 196, 218, 232, 260–2, 279–80, 494–5, 507
Surplus labor, 59, 113

Taxes, 95, 111, 144, 147, 165, 174, 194, 220, 256, 263–4, 266, 271, 276, 280–2, 287–90, 292, 345, 355, 393, 422, 425–8, 457–8, 475, 479–80, 502
Technological development, 136, 162, 185,

194, 284–5, 291–2, 297, 373, 403–6, 445–6, 524–5

Teleology, 31, 134, 195, 333, 373, 531–2

Temples, 85–7, 89, 96, 99, 106, 107, 109, 114, 116, 119, 126, 356

Territorial empires, 134, 135, 143, 144, 145, 248, 250, 253, 254, 260, 278, 297, 306, 337–8

Territorial federalism, 170, 268, 512

Towns, urbanization, and cities, 19, 41, 73–4, 79, 82, 86–7, 91–2, 98–9, 106, 107, 112, 116, 118, 119, 126, 140, 192, 223–4, 258, 263–4, 312–13, 317–20, 322–3, 377, 392, 397, 423, 437, 438, 461, 465, 501, 502, 507

"Tracklayer" of history, 28, 153, 175, 185, 221, 341–2, 363, 364, 471, 514, 518–20

Trade, 24–5, 41, 43, 45, 60, 64–6, 79, 80, 81, 90, 106, 108, 111–12, 116–19, 121–2, 124, 131–2, 135, 148–9, 163, 165, 183, 185–6, 192–3, 195, 198–9, 205–11, 231–2, 237, 264, 270–2, 312–13, 364, 383, 394–7, 407–8, 432, 435, 472–4, 490–4

Transcendence, ideological, 22, 23, 28, 77, 126–7, 156–7, 161, 270, 301, 326, 344, 349, 352, 361, 362, 365, 377, 381, 386, 390, 519

Transition from feudalism to capitalism, 373–6, 398–9, 409–13, 450, 476, 506, 512

Tribe, 43–4, 61–2, 91, 92, 120, 122–3, 132, 159, 162, 180, 185, 197, 200, 216, 240, 251–2, 344–5, 350, 357, 363, 502

Tyranny, 200, 203, 220, 221, 224, 228, 240

Universal or universalistic power, 10, 23, 89, 170–3, 225, 231, 236, 238, 240–2, 270, 303, 305, 306, 326, 343, 363, 364, 368, 530

Value, economic, 60, 89, 131, 148, 150, 193–4, 278, 289, 375, 409–12, 431

Vassalage, see Clientelism and vassalage, rule through

Vikings, 187, 377, 395–6, 505, 509

Villages, 41, 44, 51, 61, 68–9, 81, 97, 180, 185, 240, 351–2, 357–8, 394–5, 406, 504, 507

War, 18–20, 48, 76, 100–1, 107, 109, 116, 132, 137–8, 140–2, 154, 155, 199–204, 215–16, 222, 225, 227–8, 242–5, 251–5, 257–9, 273–7, 286–8, 292–4, 351, 391, 420–3, 426, 429–31, 438–40, 453–8, 474, 478–81, 487–90, 508–9, 511, 531–3

Weber, M., 4, 11, 22, 28, 32, 33, 144, 153, 171–2, 208, 213, 222, 223, 302, 313, 342, 348, 367, 388, 397–8, 417, 431, 465–6, 501–3, 519, 523–4, 535, 540

Weberian theories, 10–13, 17–18, 24, 30, 173, 377

Wittfogel, K., 10, 79, 93–8, 102, 104, 169, 174, 526

Women, 217, 260, 314, 322, 326–7, 329, 368, 443

Writing, see Literacy

Yield ratios, 265, 373, 402–3, 504

Zoroaster, 212, 241–2, 246, 303, 321, 342, 344, 346, 363–5